The Routledge Companion to Black Women's Cultural Histories

In the social and cultural histories of women and feminism, Black women have long been overlooked or ignored. *The Routledge Companion to Black Women's Cultural Histories* is an impressive and comprehensive reference work for contemporary scholarship on the cultural histories of Black women across the diaspora spanning different eras from ancient times into the twenty-first century. Comprising over 30 chapters by a team of international contributors, the *Companion* is divided into five parts:

- A fragmented past, an inclusive future
- Contested histories, subversive memories
- Gendered lives, racial frameworks
- Cultural shifts, social change
- Black identities, feminist formations

Within these sections, a diverse range of women, places, and issues is explored, including ancient African queens, Black women in early modern European art and culture, enslaved Muslim women in the antebellum United States, Sally Hemings, Phillis Wheatley, Black women writers in early twentieth-century Paris, Black women, civil rights, South African apartheid, and sexual violence and resistance in the United States in recent history.

The Routledge Companion to Black Women's Cultural Histories is essential reading for students and researchers in Gender Studies, History, Africana Studies, and Cultural Studies.

Janell Hobson is Professor and Chair of Women's, Gender and Sexuality Studies at the University at Albany, State University of New York, USA.

"I am humbled by this breathtaking collection of essays from an extraordinary group of scholars. Spanning the diaspora and the millennia, this timely collection explores both familiar and new areas of Black feminist historical analysis and cultural interrogation, highlighting new writings on Black women's intellectual traditions and challenging the silences in the archives that have long denied women of color – both free and enslaved – their roles in making history. From the queens of Ancient Egypt to modern day activists and leaders, there is much here for everyone. This is an essential addition to bookshelves and classrooms everywhere!"

Kate Clifford Larson,
author of *Bound for the Promised Land: Harriet Tubman,
Portrait of an American Hero*

"The collection we need in this global moment, *The Routledge Companion to Black Women's Cultural Histories* reveals how Black women around the world are central to our current conceptualizations of knowledge, politics, art, literature, feminisms, and survival. This set of essays is a must-read for anyone seeking to understand the struggles we all face and how, with Black women as our guides, we can push for a better and vibrant future."

Ashley D. Farmer, University of Texas at Austin, USA,
author of *Remaking Black Power: How Black Women Transformed an Era*

"*The Routledge Companion to Black Women's Cultural Histories* is unprecedented in its scope and ambition. In 35 chapters, scholars from Africa, the Americas, and Europe, at different stages of their careers, document the transformative creativity of Black women across the African diaspora. Collectively these chapters demonstrate the complexity, strength, heterogeneity and communal nature of Black women's cultural history. They also inform our understanding of race and gender today, by questioning white canonical constructions of culture and creativity and finding new ways to narrate histories of those long silenced by archives and professional historians. This bold new collection will shape the field of Black women's cultural history for some time to come."

Kate Dossett, University of Leeds, UK,
author of *Radical Black Theatre in the New Deal*

The Routledge Companion to Black Women's Cultural Histories

Edited by Janell Hobson

LONDON AND NEW YORK

First published 2021
by Routledge
2 Park Square, Milton Park, Abingdon, Oxon OX14 4RN

and by Routledge
52 Vanderbilt Avenue, New York, NY 10017

Routledge is an imprint of the Taylor & Francis Group, an informa business

British Library Cataloguing-in-Publication Data
A catalogue record for this book is available from the British Library

Library of Congress Cataloging-in-Publication Data
Names: Hobson, Janell, 1973- editor.
Title: The Routledge companion to Black women's cultural histories / Janell Hobson.
Description: Milton Park, Abingdon, Oxon; New York, NY: Routledge, 2021. | Includes bibliographical references and index. |
Identifiers: LCCN 2020041185 | ISBN 9780367198374 (hardback) | ISBN 9780429243578 (ebook)
Subjects: LCSH: Women, Black–History. | Women, Black–Social conditions. | Women, Black–Social life and customs.
Classification: LCC HQ1163 .R68 2021 | DDC 305.48/896–dc23
LC record available at https://lccn.loc.gov/2020041185

ISBN: 978-0-367-19837-4 (hbk)
ISBN: 978-0-367-70755-2 (pbk)
ISBN: 978-0-429-24357-8 (ebk)

Typeset in Bembo
by Deanta Global Publishing Services, Chennai, India

In memory of Carmen R. Gillespie

Contents

Contents

Contents

Figures

Contributors

Aje-Ori Agbese is Associate Professor at The University of Texas Rio Grande's Department of Communication. Her research focuses on Nigerian media, media history, journalism, global media and communication, African history and politics, and media and gender. She is the author of two books, various journal and encyclopedia articles, and book chapters. She has also presented her work at national and international conferences. She is the recipient of six teaching awards, including the UT System's Regents Outstanding Teaching Award.

Solange Ashby received her PhD in Egyptology from the University of Chicago with a specialization in ancient Egyptian language and religion. She has conducted doctoral research at the temple of Philae in Egypt and participated in the excavation of a royal tomb in the Kushite cemetery of El-Kurru in Sudan. Her dissertation explores the prayer inscriptions of Nubian groups that traveled to the Egyptian temples of Lower Nubia, including Philae. Dr. Ashby's expertise in sacred ancient languages – including Egyptian hieroglyphs, Demotic, and Coptic, Ethiopic, Biblical Greek, and Biblical Hebrew – underpins her research into the history of religious transformation in Northeast Africa and the Middle East during the period when monotheistic religions (Judaism, Christianity, and Islam) replaced traditional religion in Egypt and Nubia. Dr. Ashby is the author of *Calling Out to Isis: The Enduring Nubian Presence at Philae*. She is currently working on a book about the queens of Kush, which will be the first monograph dedicated to the history, religious symbolism, and political power of these ancient African women. Dr. Ashby holds a fellowship at Catholic University's Institute of Christian Oriental Research.

Gretchen Bauer is Professor of Political Science and International Relations at the University of Delaware, where she teaches African politics and gender and politics. Her research focuses on women's political leadership in Africa. She has been a visiting researcher at the Institute for Public Policy Research in Windhoek, Namibia and the University of Botswana in Gaborone, Botswana. She has been a Fulbright Scholar and a MIASA Senior Fellow at the University of Ghana, Legon in Accra, Ghana and a Democracy and Development Fellow at the Ghana Centre for Democratic Development in Accra, Ghana. She is the co-editor of *Women in African Parliaments* (2006), *Women in Executive Power: A Global Overview* (2011), and *Gender and the Judiciary in Africa: From Obscurity to Parity?* (2016), and author of dozens of journal articles and book chapters. Her current work focuses on women's underrepresentation in parliament and cabinet in Ghana.

Carole Boyce-Davies is Professor of Africana Studies and English at Cornell University and the author of the prize-winning *Left of Karl Marx. The Political Life of Black Communist Claudia Jones* (2008); the classic *Black Women, Writing and Identity: Migrations of the Subject* (1994); *Caribbean*

Spaces: Escape Routes from Twilight Zones (2013) on the internalization of Caribbean culture; and a bi-lingual children's story *Walking/Ann Avan* (2016/2017) in Haitian Kreyol and English. In addition to over 100 journal essays, articles, and encyclopedia entries, Dr. Boyce-Davies has also published 12 critical editions on African, African Diaspora, and Caribbean literature and culture, such as the two-volume collection of critical and creative writing *Moving Beyond Boundaries* (1995): *International Dimensions of Black Women's Writing* (volume 1), *Black Women's Diasporas* (volume 2); the three-volume *Encyclopedia of the African Diaspora* (Oxford: ABC-CLIO, 2008), and *Claudia Jones Beyond Containment: Autobiographical Reflections, Poetry, Essays* (2011). A member of the scientific committee for the United Nations Educational, Scientific and Cultural Organization's updated *General History of Africa*, she edited the epistemological forum on Global Blackness for the African Diaspora volume. Her current research project is for a manuscript on Writing Black Women's Political Leadership in the African Diaspora.

Maya Cunningham is an ethnomusicologist, cultural activist, and vocalist. She is pursuing a PhD in Afro-American Studies and Ethnomusicology at the University of Massachusetts, Amherst. Cunningham also received an MA in ethnomusicology from the University of Maryland, College Park. She holds a BMus. in jazz studies from Howard University and an MA in jazz performance from Aaron Copland School of Music at Queens College. Her research interests are in traditional African American music and cultural identity. In 2017, she received a Fulbright fellowship to study traditional music and national identity in Botswana. Cunningham has also received fellowships to study Black music and culture in the Gullah region, the Mississippi Delta, and culturally responsive music education models in Ghana and India. She has presented her research and writing at conferences nationally and internationally. These include the Society for Ethnomusicology, the Association for the Study of African American Life and Culture, the National Council for Black Studies, the University of Nottingham, the University at Albany, and New York University. In 2017, she launched Ethnomusicology in Action, a project that uses research in Black music to teach African American children about their heritage through traditional music.

Nneka D. Dennie is Assistant Professor of African American history at Washington and Lee University. She is a Black feminist scholar with specializations in nineteenth- and twentieth-century Black women's intellectual thought. Dennie earned her PhD in African American Studies at the University of Massachusetts Amherst and her BA in Political Science at Williams College. Previously, she held appointments at Davidson College and the Massachusetts Institute of Technology. Dennie's work has appeared or is forthcoming in *Palimpsest: A Journal on Women, Gender, and the Black International* and *Atlantic Studies: Global Currents*. Her first monograph, *Re-defining Radicalism: The Rise of Black Feminism and the Politics of Respectability in the Nineteenth Century*, is under contract with the University of Pennsylvania Press. In 2018, she co-founded the Black Women's Studies Association.

Nathan H. Dize is a PhD candidate in the Department of French and Italian at Vanderbilt University, where he specializes in Haitian literature and history. He is the content curator, translator, and co-editor of the digital history project *A Colony in Crisis: The Saint-Domingue Grain Shortage of 1789*. With Siobhan Meï, he coedits the "Haiti in Translation" interview series for *H-Haiti*. He is the translator of Makenzy Orcel's *The Immortals* (SUNY Press, forthcoming), Kettly Mars's *I Am Alive* (University of Virginia Press, forthcoming), and Louis Joseph Janvier's *Haiti for the Haitians* (Liverpool University Press, forthcoming).

Carolyn Fluehr-Lobban received her PhD in Anthropology and African Studies from Northwestern University in 1973. She is a founder of the Sudan Studies Association in 1981 and twice past-president. She is Professor Emerita of Anthropology at Rhode Island College – where she received the faculty awards for both scholarship and teaching – and Adjunct Professor of African Studies at the Naval War College, Newport. Her research subjects cover Islamic law and Islamic society; women's status in Muslim societies; race, ethics, and anthropological research; human rights and cultural relativism; and comparative studies in law and society. She is the author of several books on Islamic law and society in Sudan, two in Arabic translation. She has conducted research in the Sudan and North Africa since 1970. She has authored textbooks on race and gender: *Race and Racism, an Introduction* (2006; 2017 2nd edition) and *Female Well-Being, toward a Global Theory of Social Change* (2003, co-edited). Together with a Haitian translator, Asselin Charles, she brought to a modern audience the work of nineteenth-century writer Antenor Firmin, *The Equality of the Human Races* (2000; 2004). At Rhode Island College, she taught courses on race, gender, African, Middle East, and Islamic studies. She is the board chair and immediate past-president of the World Affairs Council of Rhode Island.

Claire Oberon Garcia is Professor of English and dean of faculty at Colorado College. Her research and teaching interests include women of the Black Atlantic in the early part of the twentieth century. She is co-editor of the collection *From* Uncle Tom's Cabin *to* The Help: *White-Authored Narratives of Black Life* and several book chapters and journal articles, including "Remapping the Metropolis: Theorizing Black Women's Subjectivities in Interwar Paris" in *Black French Women and the Struggle for Equality 1848–2016*, Félix Germain and Silyane Larcher, editors, University of Nebraska Press Series France Overseas: Studies in Empire and Decolonization; "'No one, I am sure, is ever homesick in Paris': Jessie Fauset's French Imaginary," book chapter in *Paris, Capital of the Black Atlantic: Literature, Modernity, and Diaspora*, Jonathan Eburne and Jeremy Braddock, editors, Johns Hopkins University Press; and "Citizens of Babylon: Henry James's Modern Parisian Women." She has a chapter in *Henry James's Europe: Heritage and Transfers*, Dennis Tredy, Annick Duperray and Adrian Harding, editors. She co-authored, with the Jamaican writer Alecia McKenzie, the article "Fighting for the Right to Remember: More Museums and Sites Dedicated to the Memory of Slavery Are Being Created, But They're Igniting Debate," that appeared in *New African Magazine*. She also contributed to the exhibit catalogues for *Beyond Mammy, Jezebel, and Sapphire* and *ReOrientations: Defining and Defying 19th Century French Images of the Arab World*. Her work has also appeared in *Palimpsest: A Journal on Women, Gender, and the Black Atlantic, The Feminist Wire, The Ethnic Studies Review, The Chronicle of Higher Education, The Henry James Review*, and the *International Journal of Francophone Studies*. Her book, *"For They Have Seen the Relativity of All Things": Black Women Writers in Paris, 1900–1960*, is under contract with the University of Georgia Press.

Kyra D. Gaunt is an author, professor, performer, and digital ethnomusicologist who illuminates the prevalence of gender-based, linguistic, and sexual violence against girls on YouTube. She has a PhD from the University of Michigan. Her research critiques how music and technology limit the agency of girls, particularly underage Black and Brown girls, as they develop their political voice beyond their exposure to a pervasive culture of sexist media and entertainment. Her first book, *The Games Black Girls Play: Learning the Ropes from Double Dutch to Hip-Hop* (New York University Press), funded by the National Endowment for the Humanities and the Ford Foundation, won the 2007 Alan Merriam Prize from the Society of Ethnomusicology. The monograph advanced early studies of hip-hop, black girlhood, and hip-hop feminism along with her subsequent publications. In 2018, she was featured in the TED video "How the Jump Rope Got Its Rhythm," which went viral, reaching over seven million views in 26 languages. Her collaboration with the renowned "ideas worth spreading" TED community continued from 2020 to 2022 as one of 10 Senior TED Fellows selected from over 500 fellow world-changers. Gaunt is also a federally certified expert witness on social media, and her original music is available on iTunes, CD Baby, and Spotify.

Carmen R. Gillespie (1965–2019) was Professor of English at Bucknell University, where she also served as founder and director of the Griot Institute for the Study of Black Lives and Cultures. Gillespie authored several scholarly works, including *A Critical Companion to Toni Morrison* (2007) and *A Critical Companion to Alice Walker* (2011), and she edited *Toni Morrison: Forty Years in the Clearing* (2012). She also published a poetry chapbook, *Lining the Rails* (2008), and three full-length poetry collections: *Jonestown: A Vexation*, which won the 2011 Naomi Long Madgett Poetry Prize; *The Blue Black Wet of Wood*, which won the Two Sylvias Press 2016 Wilder Series Book Prize; and *The Ghosts of Monticello*, which won the 2017 Stillhouse Poetry Contest. She also wrote the libretto for the opera *The Ghosts of Monticello*, the music for which was composed by Garrett Fisher. The opera was premiered by the Bucknell Opera Company in February 2015. Gillespie once served as the executive director of the Toni Morrison Society.

Annette Gordon-Reed is the Charles Warren Professor of American Legal History at Harvard Law School and Professor of History in the Faculty of Arts and Sciences at Harvard University. She is the author of, among other books, *Thomas Jefferson and Sally Hemings: An American Controversy*, *The Hemingses of Monticello: An American Family*, and with Peter S. Onuf, *"Most Blessed of the Patriarchs": Thomas Jefferson and the Empire of the Imagination*. She is the editor of *Race on Trial: Law and Justice in American History*. *The Hemingses of Monticello* won 16 book prizes, including the Pulitzer Prize and the National Book Award.

Nicholas Grant is Associate Professor in American Studies at the University of East Anglia in the United Kingdom. He is a historian of the twentieth-century United States. His research focuses on race, internationalism, and transnational activism. Nicholas's first monograph, *Winning Our Freedoms Together: African Americans and Apartheid, 1945–1960*, was published as part of the University of North Carolina Press's *Justice, Power and Politics* series in 2017. To date, his work has also appeared in the *Radical History Review*, the *Journal of American Studies*, and *Palimpsest: A Journal of Women, Gender and the Black International*. Nicholas is currently working on a book project that examines how aviation shaped debates about race and citizenship in the era of decolonization – focusing specifically on the global efforts to restrict the operation of South African Airways in the second half of the twentieth century.

Monica Hanna is an international figure in the world of archaeology. She did her undergraduate studies in Egyptology and Archaeological Chemistry at the American University in Cairo, 2004. Hanna then pursued an MA in Teaching English as a Foreign Language in 2006 at the American University as well. She later joined the University of Pisa, Italy to complete her doctorate, entitled *Problems of Preservation of Mural Paintings in the Theban Necropolis: A Pilot Study on the Theban Tomb 14 using 3D Scanning Techniques*. From July 2011 until November 2012, Monica was a postdoctoral fellow in the Topoi Cluster of Excellence in the Department of Egyptology and North African Studies at Humboldt University. Currently, Hanna is the acting dean of the College of Archaeology and Cultural Heritage, Arab Academy for Science and Technology and Maritime Transport in Aswan, Egypt, where she has founded a program specialized in Archaeology and

Cultural Heritage with eight departments for the BA level: Egyptian Archaeology, African Archaeology, Ancient Near Eastern Archaeology, Islamic Archaeology, Maritime Archaeology, Industrial Archaeology and Contemporary Heritage, Material Culture Conservation, and Architectural Conservation in Aswan. In Alamein, she is also creating the STEAM.LAB in the Arab Academy for Science and Technology and Maritime Transport, which focuses on interdisciplinary graduate research in digital heritage, cultural heritage economics, and cultural property and environmental law.

Janell Hobson is Professor and Chair of Women's, Gender and Sexuality Studies at the University at Albany and is the author of *Venus in the Dark: Blackness and Beauty in Popular Culture* (2005; 2nd ed. 2018) and *Body as Evidence: Mediating Race, Globalizing Gender* (2012). She received her PhD in Women's Studies from Emory University and teaches on the subjects of Black women's histories, transnational feminisms, media, and popular culture. Hobson has edited or co-edited significant volumes and special issues of refereed journals, including "Harriet Tubman: A Legacy of Resistance" for *Meridians: feminism, race, transnationalism* (2014) and *Are All the Women Still White? Rethinking Race, Expanding Feminisms* (2016). She also writes for the popular press and is the author of *Ms. Magazine*'s much lauded cover story, "Beyoncé's Fierce Feminism" (2013). Hobson is presently working on her third book, *When God Lost Her Tongue: Historical Consciousness and the Black Feminist Imagination*, forthcoming with Routledge.

Vanessa M. Holden is Assistant Professor of History and African American and Africana Studies at the University of Kentucky. Dr. Holden's current book project, tentatively titled *Surviving Southampton: Gender, Community, and Resistance During the Southampton Rebellion of 1831* (University of Illinois Press), explores the contributions that African American women and children, free and enslaved, made to the Southampton Rebellion of 1831, also called Nat Turner's Rebellion. Dr. Holden's work and writing has been published in *Slavery and Abolition: A Journal of Slave and Post-Slave Studies, Perspectives on History, Process: A Blog for American History*, and *The Rumpus*. She also blogs for *Black Perspectives* and *The Junto: A Group Blog on Early American History*. In addition to her work on enslaved women and slave rebellion, Dr. Holden co-organizes the Queering Slavery Working Group with Jessica Marie Johnson (Johns Hopkins University). Her second project, *Forming Intimacies: Queer Kinship and Resistance in the Antebellum American Atlantic*, will focus on same gender–loving individuals and American slavery. Dr. Holden also serves as a faculty adviser or consultant on a number of public history and digital humanities projects, including *Freedom on the Move* (a digital archive of runaway slave ads), *Black Horsemen of the Kentucky Turf* (an exhibit chronicling the intersecting histories of African Americans and the horse industry in Kentucky), and a grant project aimed at bringing a driving tour and museum to Southampton County, Virginia, that interprets the Southampton Rebellion. Find her on Twitter @drvholden.

Jenn M. Jackson is an assistant professor at Syracuse University in the Department of Political Science. Jackson's research is in Black Politics, with a focus on group threat, gender and sexuality, political behavior, and social movements. Jackson's first book project investigates the role of group threat in influencing Black Americans' political behavior. Methodologically, she utilizes quantitative analyses of survey data and experiments as well as qualitative analysis of in-depth interviews with young Black Americans, ages 18 to 35, to investigate both intergroup and intragroup differences in responses to and ideas about group threat. She finds that Black women are most likely to express concerns about state-based and intragroup threat. Comparatively, Black men vary drastically in their responses to group threat depending on their sexual orientation, gender expression, and vulnerability to stereotypes. Jackson received her doctoral degree from the Department of Political Science at the University of Chicago, where she also received a graduate certificate in Gender and Sexuality Studies.

Nicholas R. Jones is Assistant Professor of Spanish and Africana Studies (Bucknell University). His research agenda explores the agency, subjectivity, and performance of Black diasporic identities in early modern Iberia and the Ibero-Atlantic world. His work enlists the strategies, methodologies, and insights of Black Studies in the service of Early Modern Studies and vice versa. His scholarly interests reimagine the lives of early modern African diasporic people via the global circulation of material goods, visual culture, and ideological forms represented in archival documents and literature from West-Central Africa, Iberia, and the Americas. He is the author of *Staging* Habla de Negros: *Radical Performances of the African Diaspora in Early Modern Spain* (Penn State University Press, May 2019) and a co-editor of *Early Modern Black Diaspora Studies: A Critical Anthology* (Palgrave, December 2018) with Cassander L. Smith and Miles P. Grier. Jones also is a co-editor of the *Routledge Critical Junctures in Global Early Modernities* book series with Derrick Higginbotham and has published widely in peer-reviewed venues such as *Hispanic Review*, *Journal for Early Modern Cultural Studies*, *postmedieval: a journal of medieval cultural studies*, and *University of Toronto Quarterly*.

Paul H.D. Kaplan is Professor of Art History at Purchase College, State University of New York. He is the author of *The Rise of the Black Magus in Western Art* (1985) and of numerous essays on European images of Black Africans and Jews. He served as Project Scholar for the artist Fred Wilson's "Speak of Me as I Am," an installation in the American Pavilion at the 2003 Venice Biennale. In 2008 and 2012, he was a fellow of the Du Bois Institute for African and African American Research at Harvard University. He is a major contributor to volumes 2, 3, and 4 of Harvard University Press's *The Image of the Black in Western Art* (new ed., 2010–12). His new book, *Contraband Guides: Race, Transatlantic Culture and the Arts in the Civil War Era* (Penn State Press, 2020), extends his research into the nineteenth century and American art and literature.

Lynne Ellsworth Larsen received her MA and PhD in African Art History from the University of Iowa. Her dissertation, entitled "The Royal Palace of Dahomey: Symbol of a Transforming Nation," examines how the pre-colonial royal architecture located in Abomey, Benin has changed in form and function throughout its colonial and post-colonial periods. As a recipient of generous grants from the Project for the Advanced Study of Art and Life in Africa, the Marcus Bach Fellowship, and the U.S. Student Fulbright Fellowship, she was able to spend a total of 12 months in Benin carrying out this research. In addition, she was awarded a Pre-doctoral Fellowship at the University of Rochester's Frederick Douglass Institute for African and African-American Studies. She has been an Assistant Professor of Art History at the University of Arkansas at Little Rock since Fall 2016. Her current book project is entitled *Mud, Blood, and Vodun: The Construction, Subjugation, and Reclamation of Dahomean Architecture*.

Joyce Green MacDonald is Associate Professor of English at the University of Kentucky, where she teaches courses on Renaissance drama. She is the author of *Women and Race in Early Modern Texts* (2002) and other publications on race, performance, and adaptation in Shakespeare. She completed a book on Black women and Shakespearean adaptation in the Americas.

Beverly Mack is Emerita Professor of African and African American Studies at the University of Kansas, where she taught for 24 years. She also has taught at Georgetown, Yale, and George Mason Universities. Professor Mack conducted fieldwork among Muslim women in northern

Nigeria and Morocco, funded by Fulbright-Hays and Carnegie Corporation fellowships. She has received five grants from the National Endowment for the Humanities, many of which funded the writing of her books, which include *Muslim Women Sing: Hausa Popular Song*; three volumes with colleague Jean Boyd (*Educating Muslim Women: The West African Legacy of Nana Asma'u, One Woman's Jihad: Nana Asma'u, Scholar and Scribe*, and *The Collected Works of Nana Asma'u, Daughter of Usman 'dan Fodiyo 1793–1864*); and one volume, *Hausa Women in the Twentieth Century*, with her colleague Catherine Coles. Professor Mack's most recent book, *Beyond Asma'u: Muslim Women's 'Yan Taru Educational Model into the 21st C*, is in production.

Barbara McCaskill is Professor of English at the University of Georgia, where she has served for 28 years. She also serves as associate academic director of the Willson Center for Humanities & Arts. She has written, edited, or co-edited five books: *The Magnificent Reverend Peter Thomas Stanford, Transatlantic Activist and Race Man*, with Sidonia Serafini (UGA Press, 2020); her monograph *Love, Liberation, and Escaping Slavery: William and Ellen Craft in Cultural Memory* (UGA Press, 2015); *Post-Bellum, Pre-Harlem: African American Literature and Culture, 1877–1919*, with Caroline Gebhard (NYU Press, 2006); *Running a Thousand Miles for Freedom: The Escape of William and Ellen Craft from Slavery* (UGA Press, 1999); and *Multicultural Literature and Literacies: Making Space for Difference* (SUNY Press, 1993), with Suzanne Miller. She is co-editor with Caroline Gebhard of the essay collection *African American Literature in Transition, 1880–1900*, for the 18-volume series on the development of this literature published by Cambridge University Press. She has collaborated on award-winning public history projects such as the Civil Rights Digital Library and the Georgia Incarceration Performance Project. Harvard University's Hutchins Institute for African American & African Research selected her to present three consecutive talks for its Alaine Locke Lectures Series.

Amade M'charek is Professor of Anthropology of Science at the Department of Anthropology, University of Amsterdam. She is the principal investigator of the RaceFaceID project, a European Research Council consolidator project on forensic identification and the making of face and race. Although she has also conducted research on medical practices, her focus is mainly on genetic diversity, population genetics, and forensic DNA practices. Her interest is in the ir/relevance of race in such practice and the ways in which race is done in them, and in the relation between the individual and the collective. She has published on these topics, e.g. *The Human Genome Diversity Project: An Ethnography of Scientific Practice* (2005 Cambridge University Press), "Fragile Differences, Relational Effects: Stories about the Materiality of Race and Sex" (2010 *European Journal for Women Studies*), and "Tentacular Faces: Race and the Return of the Phenotype in Forensic Identification" (2020 *American Anthropologist*). More recently, her research includes the forensic identification of drowned migrants; see e.g. "Identifying dead migrants: forensic care work and relational citizenship" (2019 *Citizenship Studies* with Casartelli) and "Harraga: Burning Borders, Navigating Colonialism" (2020 *The Sociological Review*).

Robin Mitchell is an award-winning Assistant Professor of History; she currently teaches at the California State University Channel Islands. She received her doctorate in Late Modern European History from the University of California, Berkeley, with a Designated Emphasis in Women, Gender, and Sexuality. Her research interests include race and gender in nineteenth-century France; the African Diaspora in nineteenth-century Europe and America; and scandals, crime, and spectacles. Her scholarship includes *Vénus Noire: Black Women, Colonial Fantasies, and the Production of Gender & Race in France, 1804–1848* (Athens: University of Georgia Press, 2020); "Ourika Mania: Interrogating Race, Class, Space, and Place in Early 19th-Century France,"

Black Paris: Circulation, and the Mapping of Black Experience, special edited edition of *African and Black Diaspora: An International Journal* (2015 online; 2017 in print); "L'Affaire de la Négresse Henriette Lucille: Race, Gender, and Social Status in Eighteenth-Century France," *Transnational Subjects: History, Society and Culture*, Volume 2, Number 2 (April 2012); and "Another Means of Understanding the Gaze: Sarah Bartmann in the Development of Nineteenth-Century French National Identity," *Black Venus, 2010: They Called Her "Hottentot,"* eds. Deborah Willis and Carla Williams (Philadelphia: Temple University Press, 2010).

Uche Okonkwo holds a PhD in History and Strategic Studies from the University of Lagos, Nigeria. He is of the Department of History and International Studies, University of Nigeria, Nsukka. His research interest is in the area of Social and Economic History. He has researched extensively on women, sexuality, alcohol, commodity marketing, and Church history with a focus on Pentecostalism. His forthcoming book is titled *The Politics of the Slaughter House: Animal Cruelty and the Social History of Dogs in Nigeria* (2020).

Elizabeth Pérez is Associate Professor of Religious Studies at the University of California, Santa Barbara. She is an ethnographer and historian of Afro-Diasporic traditions and LGBTQ religious experience. Her first monograph, *Religion in the Kitchen: Cooking, Talking, and the Making of Black Atlantic Traditions* (New York University Press, 2016) was awarded the 2017 Clifford Geertz Prize in the Anthropology of Religion by the Society for the Anthropology of Religion and received Honorable Mention for the Caribbean Studies Association's 2019 Barbara T. Christian Literary Award. Her research has been published in several edited volumes, including *New West Indian Guide*, *Journal of African-American History*, *Journal of Religion in Africa*, *Religion*, *Nova Religio*, *Culture and Religion*, *Journal of Africana Religions*, *African and Black Diaspora*, and *Material Religion*, among other journals. Her next book project examines the challenges faced by transgender people as religious actors in the contemporary United States.

Allison O. Ramsay is a lecturer in Cultural/Heritage Studies in the Department of History at the University of the West Indies, St. Augustine Campus. She holds a BA in History with First Class Honours from the University of the West Indies, Cave Hill Campus, an MA in History from the University of the South Pacific, and a PhD in Cultural Studies with High Commendation in Cultural Studies from the University of the West Indies Cave Hill Campus. She teaches courses in Caribbean History and Heritage Studies at the University of the West Indies. Her research interests include fraternal organizations, museums, landships in Barbados, Caribbean festivals, Cultural and Heritage Studies, Caribbean heritage, and Caribbean history.

Michele Reid-Vazquez is an associate professor in the Department of Africana Studies at the University of Pittsburgh, where she directs the Afro-Latin American and Afro-Latinx Studies Initiative. She specializes in the history of race and gender relations, migration, identity, and politics in the African Diaspora in the Caribbean and Latin America, and in Afro-Latinx populations in the twentieth- and twenty-first-century United States. In addition to numerous articles and essays, she is the author of *The Year of the Lash: Free People of Color in Cuba and the Nineteenth-Century Atlantic World* (2011). Her second monograph, *Black Mobilities in the Age of Revolution*, is under contract with the University of Pennsylvania Press.

Naaborko Sackeyfio-Lenoch is Associate Professor of African History at Dartmouth College. Her research focuses on twentieth-century Ghana and West African history. She is the author of *The Politics of Chieftaincy: Authority and Property in Colonial Ghana: 1920–1950*. She has written articles on the politics of land and urban space; decolonization and nation building in Ghana; trade unions and international labor alliances; and transnational women's activism in Ghana. She is currently working on a book-length project about Global Ghana. The study examines the history of Ghana's internationalism and the role the country played in the global and cultural politics of the 1960s–1990s.

Daniel F. Silva is Associate Professor of Luso-Hispanic Studies at Middlebury College. His research and teaching interests include postcolonial critical cultural studies in Lusophone and global contexts; critical race and ethnic studies; racialization processes; imperial and colonial discourses; critical approaches to intersections of race, gender, and sexuality; and global studies. He is director of the Center for the Comparative Study of Race and Ethnicity at Middlebury College and a contributing member of the International and Global Studies Program. He is the author of *Anti-Empire: Decolonial Interventions in Lusophone Literatures* (Liverpool University Press, 2018) and *Subjectivity and the Reproduction of Imperial Power: Empire's Individuals* (Routledge, 2015). He is also the co-editor of *Emerging Dialogues on Machado de Assis* (Palgrave, 2016) and *Lima Barreto: New Critical Perspectives* (Lexington Books, 2013). He is co-editor of the book series *Anthem Studies in Race, Power, and Society* with Anthem Press and has published scholarship in *Hispania*, *Chasqui*, and *Transmodernity*.

James Smalls is Professor and Chair of the Department of Visual Arts at the University of Maryland, Baltimore County. His research and publications focus on the intersections of race, gender, and queer sexuality issues in nineteenth-century European art and in the art and culture of the Black diaspora. He is the author of *Homosexuality in Art* (2003) and *The Homoerotic Photography of Carl Van Vechten: Public Face, Private Thoughts* (2006). He is currently completing a book entitled *Féral Benga: African Muse of Modernism* and is conducting research for a book-length study on the racial and colonial politics of nineteenth- and early twentieth-century ethnographic sculpture.

Flávia Alessandra de Souza has a degree in Social Sciences from the Universidade Estadual Paulista Júlio de Mesquita Filho (2001), a master's degree in Social Sciences from the Federal University of São Carlos (2004), and a doctorate in Sociology from the Federal University of São Carlos (2008), with an internship PhD at the University of Pittsburgh (2007). She worked as a guest lecturer at the University of New York City – City University of New York, John Jay College of Criminal Justice, Department of Latin American and Latina / o Studies (2009). She has been Professor of Sociology, based in the Department of Philosophy and Human Sciences at the State University of Santa Cruz, Ilhéus-BA, Brazil, since 2009. She is a member of the International Sociology Association and has interdisciplinary experience in Race Relations, Black Movement and Local Power in the Interior of São Paulo, Afro-Latin America, Black Women, and Expressions from Africa and the African Diaspora.

Denise A. Spellberg is Professor of History and Middle Eastern Studies at the University of Texas at Austin. She is a scholar of early Islamic society with a focus on religion and gender. Her research includes the study of Muslims in Europe and America. She is the author of *Politics, Gender, and the Islamic Past: The Legacy of 'A'isha bint Abi Bakr* (Columbia University Press, 1994) and *Thomas Jefferson's Qur'an: Islam and the Founders* (Knopf, 2013), which has been translated into Indonesian, Turkish, and Arabic. She has won support for her research and teaching from the National Endowment for the Humanities, the Ford Foundation, and the Carnegie Scholars initiative on the study of Islam in the United States.

Valquíria Pereira Tenório is Professor of Sociology at the Federal Institute of São Paulo, Brazil. She has a degree in Social Sciences (2001) and a master's degree in Sociology from the São Paulo State University (2005) and a doctorate in Sociology from the Federal University of São Carlos (2010). She was a research scholar in the Department of History at the University of Pittsburgh (2007–8). She is a member of the Center for Afro-Brazilian and Indigenous Studies at the Federal Institute of São Paulo and coordinates a reading book club called UBUNTU, organizing readings and discussions about Black authors. She is a researcher at the Center for the Study of African Cultures and Languages and the Black Diaspora, the Laboratory for African, Afro-Brazilian and Diversity Studies, and the Unesp Black Center for Research and Extension, Group of Work FCL-ARARAQUARA. She has experience in Ethnic-racial Studies, Education for Ethnic-racial Relations, Oral History, Sociability and Black Identity, and the Brazilian Black Movement. She was a director of the Municipal Matonense Institute of Higher Education from 2010 to 2015. Also, she is a member of the Latin American Studies Association and the Brazilian Studies Association.

Jennifer Thorn is a professor of English and director of the interdisciplinary minor in Gender Studies at Saint Anselm College. She works in the transatlantic eighteenth and nineteenth centuries, with a special focus on the history of childhood, class, and race, and is the author of many book chapters and articles on early American and eighteenth-century British texts. The editor of the collection *Writing British Infanticide: Child-Murder, Gender, and Print, 1722–1859*, she is at work on a book, *Black Children, Slavery, and Piety in Early New England*, which focuses in part on Phillis Wheatley; also related to this book project is the chapter "Lemuel Haynes and 'Little Adults': Race and the Prehistory of Childhood in Early New England," included in *Literature of the Long Eighteenth Century and the Child*, ed. Andrew O'Malley (2019).

Egodi Uchendu is Professor of History at the University of Nigeria. In addition to her teaching job, she has worked as a researcher in several locations in and outside Africa and received several awards and fellowships. Her studies revolve around women in conflict situations, men and masculinities, African historiography, and emerging Muslim communities in Eastern Nigeria. She currently leads the African Humanities Research and Development Circle and directs the Centre for Policy Studies and Research at her university. For more information, visit www .egodiuchendu.com.

Donna E. Young is the founding dean of the Faculty of Law at Ryerson University in Toronto, Canada. Before assuming her deanship, she was the President William McKinley Distinguished Professor of Law and Public Policy at the Albany Law School and a joint faculty member at the University at Albany's Department of Women's, Gender and Sexuality Studies. She has taught courses in Criminal Law, Employment Law, U.S. Federal Civil Procedure, Gender and Work, and Race, Rape Culture, and the Law. Dean Young was a staff member at the American Association of University Professors' Department of Academic Freedom, Tenure, and Governance in Washington, DC and was a member of the American Association of University Professors' Committee A, the preeminent national body setting standards and investigating academic freedom disputes in the United States. She has been a fellow at Cornell Law School's Gender, Sexuality, and Family Project, a visiting scholar at Osgoode Hall Law School's Institute of Feminist Legal Studies, an associate in law at Columbia Law School, a visiting scholar at the Faculty of Law at Roma Tre University in Rome, Italy, and a consultant to the International Development Law Organization, for which she traveled to Uganda to conduct field research on the relationship between gender inequality and law in the context of the HIV/AIDS crisis.

The Routledge Companion to Black Women's Cultural Histories

An Introduction by Janell Hobson

History weighs heavily on my mind as I write this introduction during a global pandemic. What the history books will say about this moment – in the wake of the coronavirus that had spread worldwide in 2020 – remains to be seen, but pandemics have often altered the course of history, and not just in the obvious examples of the bubonic plague in medieval Europe or the pandemics that wiped out indigenous America during the "age of discovery." Looking specifically at the histories of Black women, there are examples of local African women (señoras or *signares*) healing the earliest European traders on the West African coast when the latter suffered from tropical diseases. These intimate liaisons provided traders with a sure footing and a foundation on which to build the centuries-long transatlantic slave trade (ca.1518–ca.1807), not just in restored health but in African women's facilitation of local languages, customs, and economic trading.[1]

There is also the later example of the victory of the Haitian Revolution – begun in 1791 under the presumed leadership of a mambo (Vodou priestess), under the influence of an African-based goddess, Ezili Dantor,[2] and culminating in Haiti's independence in 1804 – enabled not just by the bravery and resistance of formerly enslaved revolutionaries but also by the raging yellow fever pandemic that wiped out Napoleon's army. This eventually led to the sale of the Louisiana Purchase in 1803, which mapped out both a "manifest destiny" agenda for the United States and the eventual "scramble for Africa" that would unfold a century later among European nations. As our current history and earlier histories have taught us, it is often the *response* to the virus, not the virus itself, that steers the course.

Interestingly, during the lockdown of the United States, my social media feed circulated news stories that highlighted certain histories of pandemics. Such stories urged us to take advantage of the social isolation to create our best work. They used as examples white Englishmen from the past, like Shakespeare, who wrote *King Lear*, and Isaac Newton, who discovered gravity, during the London plagues of 1606 and 1665–6, respectively.[3] Curiously, these articles failed to reference Virginia Woolf's *A Room of One's Own* (1929), in which she speculated on the gendered nature of such men who could attend to their creative endeavors, given how they often relied on a woman (mother, wife, sister, housekeeper) to keep their homes clean, cook meals for the table, wash their clothes, and offer relative comfort while they devoted time to invent clever word play or calculus. Building on Woolf, Alice Walker specifically wonders about the "creative geniuses" among our ancestral Black mothers, especially those who were enslaved, who may have been overburdened with work but who may have nonetheless expressed their artistry through song and through the growth of "our mothers' gardens."[4]

This cultural history of Black women is often erased in general historical studies, but this edited collection seeks to remedy this issue by placing such women at the center, for such histories can relate across time and illuminate lessons of survival and resistance. Subsequently, when we ponder the history of "creative genius," let us remember not the intellectual men but the healing women during times of pandemic. Black women like New Orleans Voodoo priestess Marie Laveau (1801–81), who healed many during a yellow fever epidemic in the nineteenth century with her knowledge of medicinal herbs[5] (perhaps learned from her own mother's garden), and Harriet Tubman (ca. 1822–1913), whose many roles – Underground Railroad conductor, spy, and scout during the Civil War – included that of a nurse, who also used her knowledge of medicinal herbs to cure Union soldiers of dysentery.[6]

It was her role as nurse that placed Tubman in South Carolina, where she would eventually become the first woman in U.S. history to lead a military raid on June 2, 1863, at the Combahee River that freed 750 slaves. Tubman, later in life, would establish a home for the sick and elderly among the formerly enslaved, which reinforced her commitment to challenging the prevalent ableism, racism, sexism, and classism of her society. These oppressive systems affected her own life when in her old age, funds had to be raised so that she could pay the admittance fee to the same home she had helped to establish.[7] Tubman's heroic efforts, which were supposed to have been memorialized with her likeness on a new $20 U.S. paper currency that is now delayed, are often forgotten when compared with the heralded individualism of Shakespeare and Newton. Will the same fate befall our current nurses and other "essential workers" keeping so many of us alive and functioning during a time of crisis? What constitutes a history worth remembering, and how do race and gender shape such memories?

A history framed through the lens of Black feminist theory reveals the underpinnings of intersectional inequalities as well as the modes of resistance to them. It is within this framework that a Black women's cultural history can be formulated, which is the focus of this unprecedented collection of 35 chapters in *The Routledge Companion to Black Women's Cultural Histories*. The authors in this volume represent a wide selection of scholars across genders, races, and ethnicities at different stages during their careers – from doctoral candidates to distinguished scholars to emerita professors. They also hail from such diverse countries as the United States, Canada, Trinidad and Tobago, Nigeria, Brazil, the United Kingdom, the Netherlands, and Egypt. Importantly, these authors have integrated intersectional and transnational analyses in their scholarly inquiries into Black women's histories. This includes "queering" certain histories, as Daniel F. Silva does with the history of the seventeenth-century Ndongo ruler Njinga Mbande. Similarly, Vanessa M. Holden examines the archival evidence of trans and same sex–desiring free Black women in nineteenth-century North America, while Jenn M. Jackson inquires how certain Black feminists in the twentieth century are erased from history precisely because of their failures to adhere to respectability politics.

Other approaches to the archive reveal potential Muslim identities among enslaved women in the antebellum United States, as Denise A. Spellberg argues, or transnational praxis in activism, as explored in the chapters by Nneka D. Dennie, Claire Oberon Garcia, Carole Boyce-Davies, and Nicholas Grant. Still others interrogate the methods of *claiming* a history: from the use of genetics to confirm African identity, as Amade M'charek explores, to the tracing of African American women's singing traditions back to the African continent, as Maya Cunningham suggests, to the challenge that such a constructed lineage is even possible – given the plurality and complexities of ethnic identities and "situated knowledge" – as Kyra D. Gaunt posits. Whether the history illuminates the lives of reigning monarchs, enslaved women, poets, singers, dancers, activists, religious leaders in kitchenspaces, or community organizers shifting definitions of beauty, the chapters organized here cover a wide range of complex issues impacting Black women.

Meticulously assembled, this edited volume follows in the intellectual trajectory of other collections highlighting the philosophies and histories of Black women. If, as the late Carmen R. Gillespie (1965–2019) argues in her chapter in this volume, "Black women's feminist literary renaissance of the late twentieth century," that 1970 represents a milestone in the literary output of African American women, then writer Toni Cade Bambara's *The Black Woman: An Anthology*, published that year, is worth mentioning as a precursor to these endeavors. Collecting a wide array of voices speaking from the interconnected oppressions of racism and sexism to create the in-between space for Black women's experiences, Bambara assembled one of the earliest volumes to include language describing the nexus between these dual oppressions, as articulated in Frances Beale's "Double Jeopardy," which would later be expressed as "interlocking oppressions" (in the Combahee River Collective's "Black Feminist Statement"), "the master's tools" by poet and essayist Audre Lorde (1984), the "matrix of domination" by sociologist Patricia Hill Collins (1990), more popularly "intersectionality," as coined by legal scholar Kimberlé Crenshaw (1989), and more recently "misogynoir," as coined by scholar-activist Moya Bailey (2010).

The anthology *All the Women Are White, All the Blacks Are Men, but Some of Us Are Brave: Black Women's Studies* (1982) built on Black feminist writings during the 1970s and spawned two other collections in the twenty-first century: *Still Brave: The Evolution of Black Women's Studies* (2009) and *Are All the Women Still White? Rethinking Race, Expanding Feminisms* (2016). A decade after *Some of Us Are Brave*, Margaret Busby's *Daughters of Africa* (1992) assembled one of the first international anthologies on oral and written literature by women of African descent from ancient times to the late twentieth century. A few years later, Beverly Guy-Sheftall's *Words of Fire: An Anthology of African-American Feminist Thought* (1995) became one of the first collections to provide an historical overview of African American women's feminist writings. Other scholars, like Stanlie M. James and Abena P.A. Busia (1993) and Boyce-Davies (1995), edited volumes that covered the African Diaspora from a Black feminist perspective (including the United States, the Caribbean, Latin America, and the African continent). To that end, the volume *Toward an Intellectual History of Black Women* (2015) provides a diasporic and historic lens through which to explore the intellectual productions and writings of women of African descent, a different focus from Berry and Gross's *A Black Women's History of the United States* (2020), which foregrounds U.S. history from the perspectives of Black women even as it explores the earliest transatlantic histories that have framed this cultural context.

While this Routledge Companion has been shaped by these earlier projects, it has nonetheless expanded, widened, and deepened these subjects across the Diaspora, from ancient times to the present, thus making it the first of its kind in covering Black women's histories in a comprehensive manner, both globally and historically. Given our focus on women of African descent and how cultural history can encompass a wide array of cultural practices, ideas, and beliefs – including literature, art, music, dance, food, religion, intellectual production, activist development, and other cultural expressions – this volume chooses a wide lens and a long reach to interrogate race and gender from an historical and interdisciplinary perspective. The politics of choosing a "start point" – do we begin with the transatlantic slave trade? Ancient Egypt or Kush? Mitochondrial Eve on the African continent? – is just as contentious as an "end point," given how history continues to unfold in the present. And yet, this volume is forced to determine its beginning and end in an effort to be both inclusive and informative about what we might mean when we craft a subject called "Black women's cultural histories."

Consequently, the collection is loosely organized both thematically and chronologically. Part I, "A fragmented past, an inclusive future," charts the earliest periods relating to Black women's cultural histories and includes the latest scholarship that has provided more inclusive approaches to mapping out and reconfiguring Black women's fragmented past. The opening chapter, "Women are from Africa, and men are from Europe," by Egyptologist Monica Hanna, offers critical interventions into the field of Egyptology, which has been shaped by both Western imperialism and male-centered scholarship. Given the importance of Ancient Egypt in Afrocentric ideologies, and the salience of the rhetoric and imagery of this celebrated culture, a chapter on the subject seemed pertinent, though not without problematizing the field's Eurocentric gaze, which has severed Egypt from its African context, as well as the Afrocentric response in reclaiming its significance to the continent. Here, Hanna unpacks the loaded raced and gendered constructions of "Ancient Egypt" as a site for cultural identity while suggesting ways that local Egyptians – through women's leadership – can reclaim this history for themselves and for a wider inter-African network.

Relating to this work is Solange Ashby's subsequent chapter, "Priestess, queen, goddess: the divine feminine in the kingdom of Kush," which seeks to recognize the power and prestige of the ancient queens of Kush, in what is now modern-day Sudan. These queens, however, are often ignored in comparison to Egyptian queens, since "Kush falls into obscurity, because it is not incorporated into studies of the ancient world, nor is it included in Africana Studies, which unfortunately still tends to begin the study of African history with European colonialism and slavery in Africa." Ashby's chapter proposes a different critical intervention by reframing and refocusing on Kushite female rulers, who were often more powerful than the more famous rulers of Egypt.

The next chapter, by Carolyn Fluehr-Lobban, examines representations of the ancient Queen of Sheba, who is referenced across the three monotheistic religions of Judaism, Christianity, and Islam and is associated with both present-day Ethiopia and Yemen, two countries separated by the Red Sea. The artistic representation of the Queen of Sheba is one of numerous examples of Black female subjects in early modern European art and culture, as examined in Paul H.D. Kaplan's following chapter, which recognizes how these artistic subjects can be both stereotypical and complex in character. Similarly, Nicholas R. Jones's chapter explores the status of Black women in early modern Iberia and their symbolic acts of resistance in Spanish literature, which complicates stereotypical renderings of Black womanhood.

The subsequent chapter, by Joyce Green MacDonald, interrogates the "legend of Lucy Negro" in Elizabethan England and the possibility that she may have been the inspiration behind William Shakespeare's "Dark Lady" sonnets. Ten years after the publication of these sonnets, the arrival in 1619 of captive Africans to the English colony of Virginia would mark a milestone date in African Diasporic history; these captives originated from the Ndongo region (present-day Angola), which would be ruled by Njinga Mbande (1563–1663) from 1624 until her death. This fearless leader is the focus of the final chapter in this section, in which Silva utilizes the intersectional lens of race, gender, and sexuality to "reassemble," as it were, representations of Queen Njinga that were distorted by European explorers and colonists before being rehabilitated in postcolonial projects.

Part II, "Contested histories, subversive memories," explores cultural memory and revisionist histories from precolonial Africa to the era of the transatlantic slave trade on both sides of the Atlantic. In the opening chapter, Aje-Ori Agbese examines contemporary Nigerian cultural narratives – including film, animation, and theater – that memorialize precolonial heroic women who lived from the twelfth to the sixteenth century. Such popular narratives, Agbese argues, engage the past to make sense of present-day gender issues as they relate to Nigerian nation-building. In a different context, Beverly Mack presents in the next chapter the history of another Nigerian figure, Nana Asma'u (1793–1864), who serves as a "model for literate women

Muslims," not just during her own era but also within the twenty-first-century context of a Pittsburgh-based Muslim community seeking to recreate Asma'u's *'Yan Taru* program of women's education. This example of African women's literacy, however, seems to have disappeared during the transatlantic slave trade, as Spellberg explores in the chapter "Finding 'Fatima' among enslaved Muslim women in the antebellum United States."

Tracing in slave databases the name "Fatima" – representative of one of the daughters of the Prophet Mohammad and, therefore, a popular name within Muslim communities – Spellberg proposes an alternative methodology that breaks the silence on what Marisa J. Fuentes terms the "violence of the archive" by recovering enslaved women's Muslim identities, which might be revealed through this name. While there are no records to date suggesting any of these women wrote, much less in Arabic, Spellberg does point to scholars who posit that the early childhood writings of Phillis Wheatley (c. 1753–84) might suggest her exposure to Islamic education, given her possible origins among the Fulani, a recognized Muslim group in the Senegambia region. However, Phillis Wheatley's name recalls not an Islamic moniker but the actual slave ship that brought her to America, and in the next chapter, "Phillis Wheatley and New England slavery," Jennifer Thorn interrogates how Wheatley's history of "exceptionalism" – as the first African American and second woman to publish a book of poems – is circumscribed by misrepresentations of New England slavery.

A different "founding mother," given her ties to American founding father and third U.S. president Thomas Jefferson, can be gleaned from the history of Sally Hemings (1773–1835), as examined in the following chapter, "Sally Hemings: writing the life of an enslaved woman" by Annette Gordon-Reed, author of the Pulitzer Prize–winning *The Hemingses of Monticello: An American Family*. Carefully assessing the different responses to Hemings's narrative over time, Gordon-Reed interrogates how her story was first about race and later about gender, while Sally Hemings herself is oftentimes reduced or missing from these historical discussions, thereby arguing that she deserves her own pride of place in a history that often denies the agency of enslaved women.

The subsequent chapter, by Nathan H. Dize, narrates the bravery of 16-year-old Félicité Kina from Martinique, who traveled to France while pregnant to be near her husband and stepson, who were jailed alongside Haitian revolutionary leader Toussaint Louverture. Dize explores how prison archives reveal the specific mode of what historian Stephanie M.H. Camp calls the "everyday resistance" of Black women that proved to be as effective as military resistance in achieving freedom, as Kina enabled this for herself and her family in the world of the Haitian Revolution. Part II closes with James Smalls's chapter, "The then and now of subjugation and empowerment: Marie Benoist's *Portrait d'une négresse*," which analyzes how Benoist's painting dating from 1800, which hangs in Paris's Louvre Museum, depicts both exceptional ideas as well as standard tropes of Black womanhood.

Part III, "Gendered lives, racial frameworks," covers much of the nineteenth century, which intensified concepts of race that correlated with more entrenched gender roles and definitions. Within this era of chattel slavery and expanding colonialism, Black women – enslaved or free – were constantly targeted for social, cultural, and political control, while they in turn enacted different forms of resistance in their quest for freedom, dignity, and full humanity. Robin Mitchell's chapter, "A history of Black women in nineteenth-century France," which opens this section, argues that France's defeat in the war against its former colony of Saint-Domingue (Haiti) led to national trauma, subsequently resulting in further colonial subjugation of the African continent and Black women's bodies by proxy. This is represented in the exhibition of South African Sara (or Sarah) Baartman (ca. 1770–1815), called the "Hottentot Venus," as well as other African-descended women in France.

Black women would experience similar subjugation in North America, but certain women found ways to resist oppression not only as freedom-seekers but also as queer subjects, as provocatively argued in Holden's chapter, "Living free: self-emancipated women and queer formations of freedom." Comparing the lives of trans woman Mary Ann Waters, living as a free Black woman in Maryland in the 1850s, and Minty Caden, a same sex–desiring woman who fled slavery with her partner decades earlier to Nova Scotia, Canada during the war of 1812, Holden does the necessary work of "queering slavery, queering freedom" in order to "critique what consent could mean within the context of the American slave regime." Such narratives have rescued Black women from the silence of the archive, just as Michele Reid-Vazquez proffers in her reframing of enslaved women as leaders of slave uprisings in her chapter "'Blood, fire, and freedom': enslaved women and rebellion in nineteenth-century Cuba."

Likewise, Nneka D. Dennie highlights three modes of Black women's transnational abolitionism – slave revolts, the Black press, and the lecture circuit – in her chapter "Black women and Africana abolitionism." Alternatively, Barbara McCaskill explores how late nineteenth-century African American women writers articulated new iterations of "Africa" alongside their own depictions of a respectable, emancipated Black womanhood in the chapter "Ethiopia's woke women: the nineteenth century re-imagines Africa." Maya Cunningham's chapter, "Singing power/sounding identity: the Black woman's voice from hidden Hush Arbors to the popular," explores the legacy of Black women's singing as a site of liberation, developed from the "Hush Arbors" of enslaved African Americans' worship services, which remained hidden until after emancipation, with public performances from Harriet Tubman before progressive audiences, to the Fisk Jubilee singers who popularized Negro spirituals on their world tour during the late nineteenth century. Finally, Allison O. Ramsay's "Jamettes, mas, and bacchanal" explores alternative forms of embodied performance and resistance among working-class Black women on the Caribbean islands of Trinidad and Tobago. Called Jamettes, these women were instrumental in formulating the earliest cultural expressions of Trinidad's Carnival during the late nineteenth and turn of the twentieth centuries through dance, masquerade, songs (that eventually became calypsos), stick-fighting, and street riots.

Part IV, "Cultural shifts, social change," focuses on how women of African descent resisted the forces of colonialism, legal segregation, apartheid, and heteropatriarchy that unfolded during the late nineteenth and early to mid-twentieth centuries. In her opening chapter, Lynne Ellsworth Larsen provides an historical overview of the royal women of Dahomey, in what is now present-day Benin, some of whom served as warriors and were popularized in the French colonial press and world fairs as "Dahomey Amazons." A different royal woman is investigated in Naaborko Sackeyfio-Lenoch's chapter "Reframing Yaa Asantewaa through the shifting paradigms of African historiography," which examines the histories told about Yaa Asantewaa (1840–1921), who fought against the British colonial forces that eventually occupied Ghana. Such anti-colonial resistance also finds a parallel in the Aba Women's War of 1929 in Eastern Nigeria, as explored in Egodi Uchendu and Uche Okonkwo's chapter on Igbo women's resistance strategies against the British empire.

Beyond the African continent, women of African descent brought their resistance directly to Europe, as Claire Oberon Garcia examines in her chapter "Black women writers in early twentieth-century Paris," which juxtaposes the writings of Antillean Negritude women like the sisters Paulette Nardal (1896–1985) and Jeanne Nardal (1900–93) and Suzanne Roussy Césaire (1915–66) with African American writers like Jessie Redmond Fauset (1882–1961) and Gwendolyn Bennet (1902–81). These women lived as either colonial subjects or expatriates in the city of Paris during the interwar years while they formed Black Diasporic identities. Likewise, Boyce-Davies interrogates such identities through "The transnational Black feminist politics of Claudia Jones," a radical Black communist (1915–64) born in Trinidad, whose activism in Harlem, New York eventually led to her deportation during the McCarthy era. She settled in her later years in London during the Windrush generation, where she continued her pro-Black, feminist, and class-based community organizing.

Similarly, Grant explores the Black internationalism that developed between African American and South African women activists who set the stage for the respective twentieth-century civil rights and anti-apartheid movements. Finally, Jackson's chapter questions why Pauli Murray (1910–85), Shirley Chisholm (1925–2004), and Marsha P. Johnson (1945–92) – who were instrumental, respectively, in such landmark events as the U.S. Supreme Court ruling on *Brown v. Board of Education* (1954), the run for the U.S. presidency (1972), and the Stonewall uprising (1969) – eventually faded from history. She further argues that a Black queer feminist praxis can guard against this.

Part V, "Black identities, feminist formations," is the concluding segment of this collection, which covers much of the late twentieth century into the twenty-first century and addresses the subjects of Black identity and feminist movements. The chapter "Traces of race, roots of gender: a genetic history" by M'charek examines three episodes in the development of genetics and the racial and gender politics of DNA, which link genetic root-seeking among those of African descent to the groundbreaking science that discovered "mitochondrial Eve" DNA, tracing the origins of humanity back to the African continent, and emerging from a sequence from the HeLa cell line, based on the cancer cells extracted from the body of Henrietta Lacks (1920–51), an African American woman from Baltimore, Maryland. This "triptych," as M'charek calls her chapter, positions presumably Black female bodies at the literal "origins" of human history, which has repercussions for the constructions of Black identities and Black bodies. Meanwhile, Gaunt's chapter "Is twerking African?" draws from the same intellectual premise, which seeks to de-essentialize ideas of Africanness, especially when attempting comparisons between different contemporary dance forms associated with Black women and girls, including the popular "twerk." Contesting "biological" or "genetic arguments," Gaunt instead focuses on ethnic diversity within the African Diaspora, how "situated knowledge" informs diverse dance forms, and also how modern technologies perpetuate Black women's sexualization, which prompted cultural arguments for African universality in attempts at respectability. Exploring a different performance of identity is Valquíria Pereira Tenório and Flávia Alessandra de Souza's chapter, "Sites of resistance: Black women and beauty in Black Brazilian communities of São Paulo and Bahia," which looks at events such as the "Baile do Carmo," an elegant ball in São Paulo, and the "Ebony Goddess" beauty pageant, launched by the Ilê Aiyê block of Salvador de Bahia, that promote Black aesthetics among communities in Brazil to counter anti-Black racism. Similar to Ilê Aiyê's embrace of Candomblé, Elizabeth Pérez identifies Afro-Diasporic religion as a significant site for resistance and feminism, as explored in her chapter, "Hail to the chefs: Black women's pedagogy, sacred kitchenspaces, and Afro-Diasporic religions," which looks specifically at cooking and the space of kitchens as "Black Atlantic traditions [that] hold out myriad paths to serving the spirits, gods, and ancestors."

A different legacy is analyzed in Gillespie's chapter on the Black feminist literary renaissance, which offers an historical overview of the vibrant record of Black women's literary productions since the arrival of African women in North America. Specifically, this renaissance experienced a flowering of Black women's poetry, novels, plays, and essays during the 1970s and 1980s. At the heart of this literary explosion is the work of Nobel laureate Toni Morrison (1931–2019) as both writer and editor, who oversaw several cultural works that contributed to this literary renaissance.

Such writings inevitably broke the silence on Black women's experiences with sexual violence, which is the subject of Janell Hobson and Donna E. Young's chapter "Black women, sexual violence, and resistance in the United States." Highlighting the legal and political battles of Mechelle Vinson and Anita Hill against sexual harassment, this chapter examines how African American women have collectively emerged as feminist leaders in the anti-violence movement. Finally, Gretchen Bauer's closing chapter, "African women's political leadership: global lessons for feminism," analyzes the triumphs and challenges that African women face when assuming leadership positions in government and the implications for feminism moving forward, both on the continent and in other parts of the world.

If humanity began its journey on the African continent, it makes sense to end by contemplating the state of Africa's future and how it might be shaped by women's visions for leadership, community, and solidarity. A world that started with Black women must now center their lives if we are to continue as a global community. In the words of Farah Jasmine Griffin: "The world as we know it will end if it does not heed the insights of black feminism. Because black feminism has never only been about black women … It's been about a more just world."[8] The vibrant history of Black women, which crosses continents and time periods, offers invaluable lessons on their concerted efforts at resistance to interlocking oppressions, their agency, and restorations of their humanity at every turn.

Notes

1 George E. Brooks, *EurAfricans in Western Africa: Commerce, Social Status, Gender, and Religious Observance from the Sixteenth to Eighteenth Century* (Athens: Ohio University Press, 2003).
2 Joan Dayan, "Erzilie: A Women's History of Haiti," *Research in African Literatures* vol. 25, no. 2 (1994): 5–31.
3 See Gillian Brockell, "During a Pandemic, Isaac Newton Had to Work from Home, Too. He Used the Time Wisely," *The Washington Post* (March 12, 2020). Available: www.washingtonpost.com/history/2020/03/12/during-pandemic-isaac-newton-had-work-home-too-he-used-time-wisely/ (accessed April 15, 2020). See also Andrew Dickson, "Shakespeare in Lockdown: Did He Write King Lear in Plague Quarantine?" *The Guardian* (March 22, 2020). Available: www.theguardian.com/stage/2020/mar/22/shakespeare-in-lockdown-did-he-write-king-lear-in-plague-quarantine (accessed April 15, 2020).
4 Alice Walker, "In Search of Our Mothers' Gardens: The Creativity of Black Women in the South," *Ms.* (1974).
5 Martha Ward, *Voodoo Queen: The Spirited Lives of Marie Laveau* (Jackson: University of Mississippi Press, 2004).
6 Sarah H. Bradford, *Harriet, the Moses of Her People* (New York: Lockford & Son, 1897).
7 Kate Clifford Larson, *Bound for the Promised Land: Harriet Tubman, Portrait of an American Hero* (New York: Random House, 2004), 288.
8 Janell Hobson, "Farah Jasmine Griffin on the Legacy of Black Feminism – and the Black, Feminist Future," *Ms.* (February 20, 2020). Available: https://msmagazine.com/2020/02/20/farah-jasmine-griffin-on-the-legacy-of-black-feminism-and-the-black-feminist-future/ (accessed April 15, 2020).

References

Bailey, Moya. "They Aren't Talking about Me…" *Crunk Feminist Collective* (March 14, 2010). http://www.crunkfeministcollective.com/2010/03/14/they-arent-talking-about- me/
Bambara, Toni Cade, ed. *The Black Woman: An Anthology*. New York: New American Library, 1970.
Bay Mia, Farah Jasmine Griffin, and Marsha S. Jones, eds. *Toward an Intellectual History of Black Women*. Chapel Hill: The University of North Carolina Press, 2015.
Berry, Daina Ramey, and Kali Nicole Gross. *A Black Women's History of the United States*. Boston: Beacon Press, 2020.
Boyce-Davies, Carole, ed. *Moving beyond Boundaries (vol. 2): Black Women's Diasporas*. New York: New York University Press, 1995.
Bradford, Sarah H. *Harriet, the Moses of Her People*. New York: Lockford & Son, 1897.

Brockell, Gillian. "During a Pandemic, Isaac Newton Had to Work from Home, Too. He Used the Time Wisely." *The Washington Post* (March 12, 2020). https://www.washingtonpost.com/history/2020/03/12/during-pandemic-isaac-newton-had-work-home-too-he-used-time-wisely/ (accessed April 15, 2020).

Brooks, George E. *EurAfricans in Western Africa: Commerce, Social Status, Gender, and Religious Observance from the Sixteenth to Eighteenth Century.* Athens: Ohio University Press, 2003.

Busby, Margaret. *Daughters of African: An International Anthology of Words and Writings by Women of African Descent from Ancient Egyptian to the Present.* New York: Random House, 1992.

Camp, Stephanie M.H. *Closer to Freedom: Enslaved Women & Everyday Resistance on the Plantation South.* Chapel Hill: University of North Carolina Press, 2004.

Collins, Patricia Hill. *Black Feminist Thought.* New York: Routledge, 1990.

Crenshaw, Kimberlé. "Demarginalizing the Intersection of Race and Sex: A Black Feminist Critique of Antidiscrimination Doctrine, Feminist Theory and Antiracist Politics." *University of Chicago Legal Forum* (1989), Article 8. https://chicagounbound.uchicago.edu/uclf/vol1989/iss1/8 (accessed April 15, 2020).

Dayan, Joan. "Erzulie: A Women's History of Haiti." *Research in African Literatures* vol. 25, no. 2 (1994): 5–31.

Dickson, Andrew. "Shakespeare in Lockdown: Did He Write King Lear in Plague Quarantine?" *The Guardian* (March 22, 2020). https://www.theguardian.com/stage/2020/mar/22/shakespeare-in-lockdown-did-he-write-king-lear-in-plague-quarantine (accessed April 15, 2020).

Foster, Frances Smith, Beverly Guy-Sheftall, and Stanlie M. James, eds. *Still Brave: The Evolution of Black Women's Studies.* New York: The Feminist Press, 2009.

Fuentes, Marisa J. *Dispossessed Lives: Enslaved Women, Violence, and the Archive.* Philadelphia: University of Pennsylvania Press, 2016.

Guy-Sheftall, Beverly, ed. *Words of Fire: An Anthology of African-American Feminist Thought.* New York: The New Press, 1995.

Hobson, Janell, ed. *Are All the Women Still White? Rethinking Race, Expanding Feminisms.* Albany: SUNY Press, 2016.

Hobson, Janell. "Farah Jasmine Griffin on the Legacy of Black Feminism – and the Black, Feminist Future." *Ms.* (February 20, 2020). https://msmagazine.com/2020/02/20/farah-jasmine-griffin-on-the-legacy-of-black- feminism-and-the-black-feminist-future/ (accessed April 15, 2020).

Hull, Gloria T., Patricia Bell Scott, and Barbara Smith, eds. *All the Women are White, All the Blacks are Men, but Some of Us are Brave: Black Women's Studies.* New York: The Feminist Press, 1982.

James, Stanlie M., and Abena P.A. Busia, eds. *Theorizing Black Feminisms: The Visionary Pragmatism of Black Women.* New York: Routledge, 1993.

Larson, Kate Clifford. *Bound for the Promised Land: Harriet Tubman, Portrait of an American Hero.* New York: Random House, 2004.

Lorde, Audre. *Sister Outsider: Essays & Speeches.* Freedom: Crossing Press, 1984.

Walker, Alice. "In Search of Our Mothers' Gardens: The Creativity of Black Women in the South." *Ms* (1974).

Ward, Martha. *Voodoo Queen: The Spirited Lives of Marie Laveau.* Jackson: University of Mississippi Press, 2004.

Woolf, Virginia. *A Room of One's Own.* London: Hogarth Press, 1929.

Part I

A fragmented past, an inclusive future

1

Women are from Africa and men are from Europe

Monica Hanna

This chapter is an experiment to analyze colonialism and patriarchy in the field of Egyptian archaeology and how they interact with the interpretation of the past as well as the management of Egyptian heritage today. Given the focus of this companion on Black women's cultural histories, a chapter exploring the Western imperialist and male-dominated origins of a field of study that has severed Egypt from its African context raises crucial issues on the cultural meanings of ancient Egypt. It further invites critical interventions that can bring such studies toward more inclusive, inter-African frameworks.

After the Napoleonic expedition to Egypt at the end of the eighteenth century, the Western obsession with ancient Egypt was revamped. The expedition was composed of soldiers as well as the famous savants, or "scholars." Fascination with ancient Egypt continued throughout the nineteenth and twentieth centuries. Egyptomania inspired the West, which was in a phase of identity creation, to appropriate ancient Egypt into its new selfhood through the physical import of thousands of ancient Egyptian objects for its museums and the usurpation and inclusion of the ancient Egyptian past into its own historical narrative (Breger 2005, 206).

Imperialism and colonialism (Trigger 1984, 365) also went hand in hand with androcentrism (Nelson 2004, 152) in the interpretation of archaeological data and the construction of the ancient Egyptian past, which was in turn used in Western identity formation. Not only did ancient Egypt affect colonialism and imperialism, but as suggested by Michel Foucault, it still holds a strong connection to postcolonial ideology (Foucault and Sheridan 1972, Breger 2005, 136–7). Imperialism, colonialism, postcolonialism, and androcentrism thus worked to create a discontinuity pretext between modern Egyptians and their past. The result of this schism is that the white Western man, as opposed to a modern Egyptian woman from Upper Egypt, was thought to resemble the ancient Egyptian. Gender claims have been at the heart of the cultural discontinuity pretext, on the one hand, and of cultural appropriation, on the other hand. Egyptian objects in museums of North America and Europe help to construct their identities through the "otherness" of cultures (Breger 2005, 137). Ancient Egypt was first completely interpreted by imperialist white men while they willfully ignored the social history of modern Egyptians and how they engaged with their past.

As a trained indigenous Egyptologist, I attempt in this chapter to analyze how colonialism and androcentrism together affected the way we experience ancient Egypt in the twenty-first century in relation to Eurocentrism and Afrocentrism. This I will carry out through an inter-disciplinary approach, relating philosophical and social concepts of embodiment such as those of Merleau-Ponty (Merleau-Ponty 1962) and Foucault (Foucault 2012, Foucault and Sheridan 1972) and the feminist theories of Butler (Butler and Trouble 1990) and Gatens (1991). My analysis of past colonialism is based on the works of Said (Gbazoul 2007, Said 1995, 1989), Trigger (1984), and Reid (2002, 2003, 1985, 1992, 2015). The research design is an integration of action research, constructivism, and critical discourse analysis.

Imperialism, colonialism, postcolonialism, and androcentrism

In 1932, a journalist wrote in the newspaper *al-Balagh*: "It is indeed a matter of deep regret that the monuments should be ours and the history should be ours, but that those who write books on [the] history of ancient Egypt should not be Egyptians" (Reid 2003, 1). During the French expedition to Egypt, military occupation by soldiers was coupled with cultural imperialism by the savants who found the Rosetta Stone. It was later deciphered by Jean-Francois Champollion through the copies that were made by the French; they had lost the war to the British, who had confiscated the stone as a spoil of war. However, most scholars attribute to Champollion the discovery of ancient Egypt and the birth of the field of Egyptology.

That Egyptology was born in Europe has led to a continuous Western hegemony over Egypt's past, which continued as cultural colonialism even after Egypt declared independence in 1922 and even after the regime change in 1952. Egypt was exploited by European imperialism, and at the heart of such exploitation was Egypt's heritage. Mohamed Ali (1805–49), the first de facto independent ruler of Egypt – he himself was not Egyptian – did not really appreciate the value of ancient monuments. Much of Egypt's heritage was ransacked by nineteenth-century European explorers/treasure hunters who joined a race between countries to own the best objects in their museums (Fagan 2009, 65). For example, the Louvre Museum in Paris used dynamite in the temple of Dendera to remove the Zodiac, which is now, ironically, in a dark side-room of the museum (Waxman 2008, 74). Consuls and diplomatic missions in the nineteenth century focused on bringing back home the best objects they could find without any regard for the rights of the Egyptian people or their relations with their past. The relationship between the West and the East has been one of control, dominance, and cultural appropriation (Said 1995, 11).

This cultural appropriation has mostly been male dominated and presented a white male–perceived idea of ancient Egypt. Egyptology evolved to be a "scientific" study of ancient Egypt, whose practice is only for the well-educated; consequently, many Western academics take it as a justification for the "guardianship" of the field as well as the numerous objects sequestrated by imperialism (Sedra 2004, 249). Furthermore, Egyptology was deemed at its conception to be a subdiscipline of the classics; this was best explained in Bernal's *Black Athena* – despite the legitimate criticism it drew in general – on how Western academic circles focused on marginalizing the contributions of ancient Egypt to the Greco-Roman culture, rationalizing that Africans were not capable of producing culture of such sophistication (Bernal 1991, 241–66). Most Western Egyptologists never learned Arabic; in fact, the Egyptological languages are English, French, German, and Italian. Interaction with indigenous communities was considered a nuisance by some, and from several experiences working with archaeological missions, the situation remained like this until the post-2011 political uprising.

This male-driven Western hegemonical attitude can be found, for example, in the writings of Gustave Flaubert, especially when he describes the courtesan Kuchuk Hanem from Esna, a region in the south of Egypt, and plays on the stereotype of the "oriental" woman (Said 1995,

11). Kuchuk Hanem was exploited physically by Flaubert but never had the chance to have her voice written as part of the history (Said 1995, 11). The narrative of their encounter is only from his point of view as the white wealthy man who spoke on her behalf to feed the stereotype of the oriental woman, a recurrent image in the exchange between the Orient and the Occident (Said 1995, 11): erotic and highly sexualized. Similarly, the esteemed Egyptologist Jan Assmann (1996, 68) describes Queen Nefertiti as a "love-poem in stone" and reiterates how her "very refined sensuousness and almost erotic grace and radiance" are embedded in the masterpieces of Egyptian art during the Amarna Period (1350 BCE). Both descriptions of Egyptian women show how the male-dominated ideology of Western stereotypes of the Orient has continuously been propagated uncritically.

The reception of an androcentric Egypt

The Western stereotypes of Egyptian women proliferated through the scholarship of mainly Western male academics as well as some Egyptians until very recently. Despite the fact that archaeology and anthropology, as part of humanities and social sciences, started to evolve based on the feminist critique, Egyptology took years to realize the changes in social theory around it due to its weaker theoretical foundation. Postmodernist archaeology focused more on the reconstruction of historical landscapes and the analysis of technology, industry, and economies, shifting to a new type of inferential archaeology (Hamilakis, Pluciennik, and Tarlow 2012, 4–5). This shift marked in archaeology a more representational analysis of how the body in the past experienced different norms of life and resulted in the publication of several studies by feminist scholars interested in gender analysis of the past through the different experiences of embodiment (Meskell 1998, Joyce 2004, Joyce and Meskell 2014).

The West has created a disembodied meaning of the past through its masculine theory of knowledge, which does not incorporate a female perception that is embodied and multisensory (Edwards, Gosden, and Phillips 2006, 7). Egyptology, like other disciplines of archaeology, cultural anthropology, and history, placed the man in the middle of cultural evolution and production and confined women to a marginal position, so that men's activities represented the whole society (Nelson and Rosen-Ayalon 2001, 30). This awareness of the marginalization of women led in the 1970s to the first discussions of the role of women in archaeology, history, and their related disciplines. Women in ancient Egypt were mostly studied when they were powerful, such as Merneith, Ahhotep, Ahmose-Nefertari, Hatshepsut, Nefertiti, and Cleopatra. More recent is the case of the God's Wives of Amun, such as Shepenwepet and Amenirdis (Ayad 2009), because primarily, in Western ideology, power is gendered male (Nelson and Rosen-Ayalon 2001, 30, Sweely 2012, 187).

Nefertiti, whose famed bust was unethically smuggled to Berlin by Ludwig Borchardt, has also been the object of a political imperialist fantasy through her metonymic appropriation, which helped with the construction of modern Western identity (Breger 2006, 283). Women who were outside the realm of power were probably thought to have taken their stereotypical roles of childbearing and household upkeeping, which was fostered by the imagery of Isis suckling Horus that later filtered into Classical and Christian art (Koloski-Ostrow, Lyons, and Kampen 2003, 562). It was not until recent years that archaeologists started looking at gendered goods in the Predynastic Period as a way to relate and understand women's roles in the formation of the Egyptian state around 3200 BCE (Wrobel 2004, 170–92).

The archaeological discoveries at Deir el-Medina by Ernesto Schiaparelli at the beginning of the twentieth century, shedding light on the lives of common women, prompted gender studies to relate to women in ancient Egypt (Sweeney 2009, 154, Matić 2016, 181). More studies targeted women's gender roles through understanding the architectural design of the houses of Deir el-Medina or their less rich burial equipment (Meskell 1991, 221–6), while others argued that women contributed more to the family income than men because of their weaving activities (Sweeney 2009, 5, 2011, 5). The narrative about Egypt, as with many other colonized countries, has been *feminized* (Baron 2005) as submissive and inferior; on the other hand, colonizing Europe was *masculinized* as assertive and advanced (Ströbeck 2016, 334).

With British imperialism in Egypt, the image of modern Egyptian women was quite negative and unrealistic (Youngkin 2016, 16). Early British female writers did not want to engage with modern Egyptian women and instead wrote about the ancient Egyptian goddesses by assimilation to Greek goddesses. They also saw the effects of Islamic and Arabic culture as a threat (Youngkin 2016, 16–18). This idealization and romanticism of ancient Egypt has skewed the image of ancient Egypt in the Western world and created a schism between modern Egypt and ancient Egypt. The West wanted ancient Egypt to be completely detached in order to keep the modern Egypt under their control. After all, they believed that if it had not been for Champollion, the rest of the world would never have known anything about ancient Egypt, ignoring all the Arabic historians – whom they could generally not read in their original language – who have described ancient Egypt and written about it extensively (El Daly 2005). Imperialism and androcentrism in the nineteenth and twentieth centuries went hand in hand and have affected how Egyptians view their own culture today and the discipline of Egyptology as a whole.

Androcentrism, Afrocentrism, and Eurocentrism

With the advent of the movement in the 1980s of Afrocentrism, particularly the "Nile-Valley Afrocentrism," ideological relations shifted in identification with ancient Egypt. In the construct generated by Eurocentrism, what is "Black" in Africa is the area of sub-Saharan Africa that directly contradicts the European self-image and identity (Mudimbe 1988). In this view, Egypt, while being located geographically in Africa, was more closely related to the Mediterranean and Near Eastern culture that later interacted with the Classical world, which is interpreted as creating Western culture. Africa is important because it helped identify what Europe was not in relation to the level of civil complexity and development (O'Connor and Reid 2003). There are, however, several sociological and anthropological factors involved in understanding the reactions modern Africans have toward ancient Egypt (O'Connor and Reid 2003, 2).

Similar to the appropriation of ancient Egypt by the West in the nineteenth and twentieth centuries, the Afrocentric ideology in the 1980s has also attempted to create direct links with the Nile Valley; there was no material evidence for either appropriation, but rather, a strong ideological foundation. Ideology can be seen in the creation of new meanings, dialogues, and identifications that have a different power structure. It was important for Europeans to place ancient Egypt as more Mediterranean and Near Eastern, as opposed to African, while it was equally important for Afrocentric thought to place Egypt well into the African continent, in both cases to define one's power relationship with the other (O'Connor and Reid 2003, 4–6). The heritage of Africa was ignored by imperialist European ideology and reduced to ancient Egypt, or sometimes other cultures, such as the Axumite or the Zimbabwe, were acknowledged while discrediting many contributions by African people (Rowlands 2003, 39).

Gender has also had an important role in identifying the relation between Afrocentrism and Eurocentrism. It serves as a clear mirror to reflect the attempt to appropriate ancient Egypt through creating a new narrative. Eurocentrism has used the bust of Nefertiti to create new identities and assimilation to ancient Egypt (Breger 2006, Hanna 2020). The bust was renowned in Berlin as a symbol of great success for women and was even received with flowers; the bust in the 1930s in Berlin was a "Star Object" (Breger 2006, 289). Germany at that period, and particularly the Weimar Republic, which had just lost its monarch and royal status, saw in the bust of Nefertiti another royal insignia to identify with its metonymic loss of monarchy (Breger 2006, 291). Nefertiti was "Aryanized" through her presumed Asiatic links and thus, European rather than African, while her husband Akhenaten also found a place through the assumption of his Aten religion as monotheism in the European fascist discourse of that period (Breger 2006, 193, Hornung and Lorton 2001).

By contrast, the late twentieth-century Afrocentrism of famous rapper Queen Latifah draws on allusions to Nefertiti through her name, her image, and the culture of Africa in her fight against sexism and racism (Roberts 1994, 246). She also links sexism with racism (Roberts 1994, 249) through the different images she shows in the music video of her 1990 rap song "Ladies First." Other artists, such as Beyoncé and Rihanna, have also appropriated similar imagery of Nefertiti's bust in their twenty-first-century performances to highlight the beauty of African American women and resistance to patriarchy and racism (Painia 2014).

Such politicized performances of Afrocentrism contrast with performances of "orientalism" by white British singers like Adele, who appropriated a traditional Amazigh African tribe dress worn by women in the Siwa Oasis of Egypt with very little acknowledgment of its origin, while her fashion designer Chloé claimed that it was their own design (Masry 2016). However, when other experimentations are carried out by Europeans, such as the "Little Warsaw" artistic installation with Nefertiti, it is usually regarded as artistically and culturally appropriate (Breger 2005, 2006, Ikram 2011). The dynamics of such cultural interventions and experimentation should be analyzed through the lens of colonization versus decolonization and the accepted Europeanness of Egyptian heritage, while its Africanness is either marginalized or dismissed.

The challenges for women in indigenous Egyptology today

Despite many pioneering women in the field of Egyptology who have left their mark on the discipline, it has mostly remained a male-dominated career. The male archaeologist stereotype has also been further promoted by an "Indiana Jones" mentality (Hanna 2019); the hat, the discovery, the gold, the secrets, and the academic promotion fueled many of the archaeological projects. This model has also permeated Egyptian Egyptology in a postcolonial transfer of ideas. The discoveries have always been more important than conservation projects or site management. More and more sites were left open after discoveries without proper upkeep and preservation, just to satiate the pride and the thrill of the continuous Western-fed ideology of discovering more secrets, more gold, and more kings.

This has also been reflected in how archaeological space is governed, in that communities (particularly of women and children) are not usually welcomed in the archaeological space. The social history of women performing fertility rituals, sometimes associated with archaeological space, has often been written off the academic record, deemed unimportant, and perhaps also looked down upon as superstition (Inhorn 1994, 500–50). Indigenous Egyptology has struggled for years to catch up with imperialist Egyptology, primarily because many Western scholars feared that Egyptians would take over (Reid 1985, Sedra 2004). Indigenous Egyptology was also heavily criticized by Western Egyptologists, from the time of its inception, as having appropriated ancient Egypt for a selfish political agenda (Sedra 2004, 250). Egyptian Egyptology has been resisted since the first school that taught Egyptology (by Henrich Brugsch) (Reid 1985, 235–6). It was not until 1952's regime change that Egyptians took into their own hands the management of Egyptian antiquities.

The first modern Egyptian woman to finish her high school education was Nabawiyya Musa in 1908. She went on to Cairo University – back then known as the "Egyptian University" – where she further lectured on the role of women in modern and ancient Egypt (Reid 2002, 55). Afifa Iskander was allowed to follow classes in Egyptology, but not to take a degree, at the end of the 1930s (Reid 2002, 56). The first female student from the Department of Egyptian Archaeology graduated in 1941, and by 1949, three more had graduated (Fares 2017, 76).

Many more women have studied after 1952 and have had their imprint on the field of Egyptology, such as the late Prof. Soad Maher (1917–96), first female dean of the College of Archaeology in Cairo University, and then Prof. Tohafa Handoussa of Cairo University and Prof. Fayza Haikal, now Professor Emeritus at the American University in Cairo, both born in the 1930s. Today, in Egyptian academia and in the field, many women are deans, department heads, and deputies. However, the fieldwork has always been challenging for women. Women are still trying to catch up due to the lack of dedicated funding that would encourage Egyptian women to take the lead. Many times, women are victims of gender stereotypes in which it is often suggested that they would not fit in desert or "dangerous" environments. Not only are women not available in leading positions in the field, but also, many of the leading positions in the Ministry of Antiquities and Tourism have been reserved for men. Women in the field have multiple times experienced sexual harassment, gender bullying, and patriarchal attitudes. I have personally experienced all three, and many of my colleagues in different sectors have experienced them too. There is still not enough support, academically or institutionally, for women to react to such offenses.

In the post-2011 political events, it was women who took several initiatives to protect cultural heritage when the state had failed. Omniya Abdelbar created "Save Historical Cairo"; Yasmine Dorghamy and Mennatallah al-Dorry created "Soriqa: Stop the Heritage Drain"; May al-Tabbakh, along with other colleagues, created "Save Alexandria"; and Marwa al-Zeiny and I created "The Egypt's Heritage Taskforce." All these initiatives tried to stop heritage crimes, such as looting, illicit thefts, and the demolition of historical buildings, which were happening to the archaeological sites due to a security vacuum (Hanna 2013c, 2015, 2013b, a, Ikram and Hanna 2013). All these different teams of women were quite successful and were even invited into the 50-people committee for writing the constitution of 2013. They managed to draft together a new constitutional article that exerted better protection of Egypt's cultural heritage:

Article 50. Egypt's civilization and cultural heritage, whether physical or moral, including all diversities and principal milestones – namely Ancient Egyptian, Coptic, and Islamic – are a national and human wealth. The State shall preserve and maintain this heritage as well as the contemporary cultural wealth, whether architectural, literary, or artistic, with all diversities. Aggression against any of the foregoing is a crime punished by the law. The State shall pay special attention to protecting components of cultural pluralism in Egypt.

(2014)

Many of these women were accused of dissidence and attacked by radicals or by other men who simply felt threatened by their different initiatives and narratives. However, none of the attacks has managed to stop them, especially because of the public support they have received and the mutual support they have provided to each other. Indigenous Egyptologists are weighing their interest in decolonization and empowerment of communities living around archaeological sites against their situation as women in these societies, especially if they want to create research or joint projects with their neighbors for feminist archaeology (Ströbeck 2016, 339). Through their embodied experience of heritage, these women are the most capable and experienced in carrying out groundbreaking research.

Feminism and ancient Egypt

The Western misconception that women's equal rights can only be attained in non-Islamic nations undermines the feminist movement in Egypt and shows a typical orientalist and colonialist stereotype that only asserts a Western model of democracy. Most women who come from the African continent can relate to a common symptom of oppression due to colonialism, imperialism, racism, sexism, and androcentrism (Collins 2003, 52–4). Too many Westerners still discredit the movements of women in Egypt and elsewhere (Kumawat 2019, 54) that were started at the beginning of the twentieth century by pioneers such as Nabawiyya Musa, mentioned earlier, and Huda Shaarawi (Hoodfar 1992, 11). Qassem Amin, at the turn of the twentieth century, wrote two books discussing women's right to education, the abolition of polygamy, and the place of women in the public sphere (Amin and Peterson 2000). Nabawiyya Musa also expressed her feminist reform ideas in an impressive play called *Nub Hotep*, whose characters are mostly women in leadership roles in the Egyptian society of the time, which was first printed in 1912 and recently reprinted in 2014. Unfortunately, the play has never been translated into any European language.

During the 2011 uprising, many of the images of ancient Egypt resurfaced and were mixed with modern political emblems. There was a famous graphic image of Tutankhamun with the cap of Che Guevara, which was used on stickers, graffiti, and magazines. Then, there were fantastic graffiti by Alaa Awad and Ammar Abou Bakr on Mohamed Mahmoud Street, right next to Tahrir Square, the epicenter of the popular protests in Cairo. However, what was really symbolic was how the defense of women who were sexually harassed and attacked by paid mobs in Tahrir Square (Al-Ali 2014) was expressed through the image of the iconic bust of Nefertiti.

The Nefertiti bust was modified to wear a gas mask to show support for women facing riot police violence. The use of Nefertiti's bust was not a Western imperialistic influence but rather, a call on an ancestral image of power by the indigenous communities of women and feminists (Gerlach 2016). There are numerous parallels in literature and the arts in the twentieth century that use an image of ancient Egypt to strengthen feminism, but unfortunately, these have rarely been part of the narrative of Western descriptions of the reception of ancient Egypt.

Conclusion

The construction of the modern identity of Egyptian women and Egypt as a whole is at the heart of decolonizing cultural heritage through the democratization of past discourse. The imperialist androcentric perspective of Egypt has continued in the postcolonial period, and today, the field of Egyptology is the perfect example. This is starting to shift due to the political changes in Egypt post-2011 and also due to the admission of a younger, more sensitive generation in the fields of Egyptology, Egyptian archaeology, and Egyptian heritage. Indigenous Egyptian women and their role in the past and the present in the wider context of African women are also being considered. Common ground regarding how the past plays in the present were visible in the use of ancient Egypt during the Egyptian 2011 revolution and the imagery of ancient women during the Sudanese 2019 revolution (Hanna 2020, Reily 2019). This important cultural identification gives ancient Egypt its original links to Africa in attempts to decolonize 200 years of Western appropriation. The racism and colonialism of traditional Egyptology must be challenged through inter-African networks.

With the "me too" era, more Egyptian women are also taking historical figures as role models, and not just the queens such as Hatshepsut, the warriors such as Ahhotep, and the goddesses such as Isis; they are also looking at how women in their conventional roles throughout history managed to keep ancient Egyptian society together. Egyptian women Egyptologists such as Fayza Haikal have also looked into how ethnoarchaeology reconciles the discontinuity pretext between ancient and modern Egypt (Haikal 2003). It is through such reconciliation that the imperialistic and androcentric images of ancient Egypt can be truly challenged and remediated.

A new creation of identity through the past that is affective, intellectual, and economic changes individual reactions and their engagement with Egyptian heritage. Egypt's past must be looked upon not as separate compartments of history in the same spatial perspective but rather, through more detailed temporality and sensoriality of the heritage. The only hope for the future sustainability of Egyptian heritage is through creating meaningful identification with the past and casting new networks of relating with this heritage. This will also not be possible if the atrocities of imperialism are not amended.

Contested objects of heritage in Western museums that have been taken under colonial rule must be open to new negotiations. When repatriation occurs in the future, it must be not only a repatriation of the objects but also a repatriation of the knowledge associated with these objects, which was constructed away from their historical contexts. Female Egyptian Egyptologists should also receive more support to conduct their own excavations and fieldwork. Networks with other women working in the field in the Middle East and Africa are also completely lacking. These would strengthen their inter-African ties and create new networks that are non-Western to support them against challenges in the field.

References

2014. "Constitution of the Arab Republic of Egypt." In *Article 50*. Egypt. https://www.constituteproject.org/constitution/Egypt_2014.pdf.

Al-Ali, Nadje. 2014. "Reflections on (Counter) Revolutionary Processes in Egypt." *Feminist Review* 106 (1):122–128.

Amin, Qassem, and Samiha Peterson. 2000. *The Liberation of Women*: American University in Cairo Press.

Assmann, Jan. 1996. "Preservation and Presentation of Self in Ancient Egyptian Portraiture." In Peter Der Manuelian, ed. *Studies in Honor of William Kelly Simpson*, volume 1, 55–81. Boston: Museum of Fine Arts, Boston.

Ayad, M.F. 2009. *God's Wife, God's Servant: The God's Wife of Amun (ca. 740–525 BC)*: Taylor & Francis.

Baron, Beth. 2005. *Egypt as a Woman: Nationalism, Gender, and Politics*: University of California Press.

Bernal, Martin. 1991. *Black Athena: The Afroasiatic Roots of Classical Civilization, Black Athena*: Vintage.

Breger, Claudia. 2005. "Imperialist Fantasy and Displaced Memory: Twentieth-Century German Egyptologies." *New German Critique* 96:135.

Breger, Claudia. 2006. "The 'Berlin' Nefertiti Bust: Imperial Fantasies." In *The Body of the Queen: Gender and Rule in the Courtly World*, 1500–2000, 281. New York: Berghahn Books Ltd.

Butler, Judith, and Gender Trouble. 1990. "Feminism and the Subversion of Identity." *Gender Trouble* 3:1.

Collins, Patricia Hill. 2003. "Toward an Afrocentric Feminist Epistemology." In Yvonna S. Lincoln and Norman K. Denzin, eds. *Turning Points in Qualitative Research: Tying Knots in a Handkerchief* 47–72. Rowman Altamira.

Edwards, Elizabeth, Chris Gosden, and Ruth Phillips. 2006. *Sensible Objects: Colonialism, Museums and Material Culture*: Berg Publishers.

El Daly, Okasha. 2005. *Egyptology: The Missing Millennium*: UCL Press.

Fagan, B. 2009. *The Rape of the Nile: Tomb Robbers, Tourists, and Archaeologists in Egypt, Revised and Updated*: Basic Books.

Fares, Inas. 2017. "Educational Institutions of Egyptology in Egypt the 1865–1928." *The Academic Journal of Tourism and Guidance of Alexandria University* 14 (14-B):105.

Foucault, Michel. 2012. *The History of Sexuality: An Introduction, Vintage*: Knopf Doubleday Publishing Group.

Foucault, Michel, and Alan Sheridan. 1972. *The Archaeology of Knowledge*. New York: Pantheon Books.

Gatens, Moira. 1991. "Feminism and philosophy: Perspectives on difference and equality." *Philosophical Quarterly* 43(173): 513–519.

Gbazoul, F.J. 2007. *Edward Said and Critical Decolonization, Alif (Cairo, Egypt)*. [Special Issue]: Amercain University in Cairo Press.

Gerlach, Julia. 2016. "Frust Junger Männer Entlädt Sich in Sexueller Gewalt." *Deutschlandfuk Kultur*. https:// www.deutschlandfunkkultur.de/aegypten-frust-junger-maenner-entlaedt-sich-in-sexueller.1008. de.html?dram:article_id=342325.

Haikal, Fayza. 2003. "Egypt's Past Regenerated by its Own People." *Consuming Ancient Egypt* 123–138. UCL Press.

Hamilakis, Y., M. Pluciennik, and S. Tarlow. 2012. *Thinking Through the Body: Archaeologies of Corporeality*: Springer US.

Hanna, Monica. 2013a. "Looting in Egypt: The Unfortunate Site of Abusir el-Malek." *Society for the Study of the Egyptian Antiquities Newsletter* 2013:3.

Hanna, Monica. 2013b. "Losing Heritage, Losing Identity." *al-Rawi* 2013:22.

Hanna, Monica. 2013c. "What Has Happened to Egyptian Heritage after the 2011 Unfinished Revolution?" *Journal of Eastern Mediterranean Archaeology & Heritage Studies* 1 (4):371.

Hanna, Monica. 2015. "Documenting Looting Activities in Post-2011 Egypt." In *Countering Illicit Traffic in Cultural Goods: The Global Challenge of Protecting the World's Heritage*, 47. Paris: ICOM.

Hanna, Monica. 2019. "Egypt's Heritage is More Than an Indiana Jones Movie." *The Hill*. https //thehill. com/opinion/international/440035.

Hanna, Monica. 2020. *Contesting the Lonely Queen*. Edited by Fazil Moradi. Duke's University Press.

Hanna, Monica. Forthcoming 2020. "Contesting the Lonely Queen." *Public Culture Restitution and Imperial Knowledge*.

Hoodfar, Homa. 1992. "A Background to the Feminist Movement in Egypt." *Al-Raida Journal Spring* 1992 (57): 11–13.

Hornung, Erik, and David Lorton. 2001. *Akhenaten and the Religion of Light*: Cornell University Press.

Ikram, Salima. 2011. "Collecting and Repatriating Egypt's Past: Toward a New Nationalism." In *Contested Cultural Heritage: Religion, Nationalism, Erasure, and Exclusion in a Global World*, 141–154. New York: Springer.

Ikram, Salima, and Monica Hanna. 2013. "Looting and Land Grabbing: The Current Situation in Egypt." *ARCE Bulletin* 202:34.

Inhorn, Marcia. 1994. "Kabsa (aka Mushāhara) and Threatened Fertility in Egypt." *Social Science & Medicine* 39 (4):487.

Joyce, Rosemary. 2004. "Embodied Subjectivity: Gender, Femininity, Masculinity, Sexuality." In Lynn Meskell and Robert W. Preucel, eds. *A Companion to Social Archaeology* 82–95. John Wiley & Sons.

Joyce, Rosemary, and Lynn Meskell. 2014. *Embodied Lives: Figuring Ancient Maya and Egyptian Experience*: Routledge.

Koloski-Ostrow, A.O., C.L. Lyons, and N.B. Kampen. 2003. *Naked Truths: Women, Sexuality and Gender in Classical Art and Archaeology*: Taylor & Francis.

Kumawat, Deepa. 2019. "Breaking the Stereotypes from Victims to Survivors: Black Feminist Study of Maya Angelou's 'Still I Rise' and 'Phenomenal Woman'." *Glass Ceiling and Ambivalent Sexism (Critical Perspectives of Gender Trouble)* 96.

Masry, Enas El. 2016. "Adele's Egypt-Inspired Dress Sparks Cultural Appropriation Controversy." *Egyptian Streets*. Accessed 04/03/2020. https://egyptianstreets.com/2016/07/01/adeles-egypt-inspired-dress -sparks-cultural-appropriation-controversy/.

Matić, Uroš. 2016. "Gender in Ancient Egypt: Norms, Ambiguities, and Sensualities." *Near Eastern Archaeology* 79 (3):174–183. doi:10.5615/neareastarch.79.3.0174.

Merleau-Ponty, Maurice. 1962. *Phenomenology of Perception Phénoménologie de la Perception*: Routledge & Kegan Paul.

Meskell, Lynn. 1991. *Archaeologies of Social Life: Age, Sex, Class Etcetra in Ancient Egypt*: Wiley.

Meskell, Lynn. 1998. "An Archaeology of Social Relations in an Egyptian Village." *Journal of Archaeological Method and Theory* 5 (3):209.

Mudimbe, Valentin Y. 1988. "The Invention of Africa: Gnosis." *Philosophy, and the Order of Knowledge* 27 (1988): 191–92.

Nelson, Sarah. 2004. *Gender in Archaeology: Analyzing Power and Prestige*: Altamira Press.

Nelson, Sarah, and Myriam Rosen-Ayalon. 2001. *In Pursuit of Gender: Worldwide Archaeological Approaches*: Rowman Altamira.

O'Connor, David, and Andrew Reid. 2003. *Ancient Egypt in Africa*: Taylor & Francis.

Painia, Brianne 2014. *'My Crown Too Heavy Like the Queen Nefertiti': A Black Feminist Analysis of Erykah Badu, Beyoncé Knowles, Nicki Minaj, and Janelle Monae*: The George Washington University.

Reid, Donald. 1985. "Indigenous Egyptology: The Decolonization of a Profession?" *Journal of the American Oriental Society* 105 (2):233.

Reid, Donald. 1992. "Cultural Imperialism and Nationalism: The Struggle to Define and Control the Heritage of Arab Art in Egypt." *International Journal of Middle East Studies* 24 (1):57.

Reid, Donald. 2002. *Cairo University and the Making of Modern Egypt, Cambridge Middle East Library*: Cambridge University Press.

Reid, Donald. 2003. *Whose Pharaohs?: Archaeology, Museums, and Egyptian National Identity from Napoleon to World War I*: University of California Press.

Reid, Donald. 2015. *Contesting Antiquity in Egypt: Archaeologies, Museums, and the Struggle for Identities from World War I to Nasser*: American University in Cairo Press.

Reily, Katie. 2019. "The Iconic Photo of Her Helped Fuel Sudan's Revolution. Now, She and Other Women Are Being Sidelined." *Time*. Accessed 04/03/2020. https://time.com/5712952/alaa-salah-sudan-women-protest/.

Roberts, Robin. 1994. "'Ladies First': Queen Latifah's Afrocentric Feminist Music Video." *African American Review* 28 (2):245–257.

Rowlands, Michael. 2003. *The Unity of Africa*: UCL Press.

Said, Edward. 1989. "Representing the Colonized: Anthropology's Interlocutors." *Critical Inquiry* 15 (2):205.

Said, Edward. 1995. *Orientalism*: Penguin Group.

Sedra, Paul. 2004. "Imagining an Imperial Race: Egyptology in the Service of Empire." *Comparative Studies of South Asia, Africa and the Middle East* 24 (1):249.

Ströbeck, Louise. 2016. "Gender and Sexuality." *Handbook of Postcolonial Archaeology* 3:327.

Sweely, T.L. 2012. *Manifesting Power: Gender and the Interpretation of Power in Archaeology*: Taylor & Francis.

Sweeney, Deborah. 2009. "Gender and Oracular Practice in Deir el-Medîna." *Zeitschrift für Ägyptische Sprache und Altertumskunde* 135 (2). doi:10.1524/zaes.2008.0017.

Sweeney, Deborah. 2011. *Sex and Gender*: UCLA Encyclopedia of Egyptology.

Trigger, Bruce G. 1984. "Alternative Archaeologies: Nationalist, Colonialist, Imperialist." *Man* 355–370.

Waxman, Sharon. 2008. *Loot: The Battle Over the Stolen Treasures of the Ancient World*: Henry Holt and Company.

Wrobel, Gabriel. 2004. "The Benefits of an Archaeology of Gender for Predynastic Egypt." In *Ungendering Civilization*, 170–192. London and New York: Routledge.

Youngkin, M. 2016. *British Women Writers and the Reception of Ancient Egypt, 1840–1910: Imperialist Representations of Egyptian Women*: Palgrave Macmillan US.

2

Priestess, queen, goddess
The divine feminine in the kingdom of Kush

Solange Ashby

The symbol of the *kandaka*[1] – "Nubian Queen" – has been used powerfully in present-day uprisings in Sudan, which toppled the military rule of Omar al-Bashir in 2019 and became a rallying point as the people of Sudan fought for #Sudaxit – a return to African traditions and rule and an ouster of Arab rule and cultural dominance.[2] The figure of the *kandake* continues to reverberate powerfully in the modern Sudanese consciousness. Yet few people outside Sudan or the field of Egyptology are familiar with the figure of the *kandake*, a title held by some of the queens of Meroe, the final Kushite kingdom in ancient Sudan. When translated as "Nubian Queen," this title provides an aspirational and descriptive symbol for African women in the diaspora, connoting a woman who is powerful, regal, African.

This chapter will provide the historical background of the ruling queens of Kush, a land that many know only through the Bible. Africans appear in the Hebrew Bible, where they are frequently referred to by the ethnically generic Hebrew term כּוּשִׁי, which is translated "Ethiopian" or "Cushite." Kush refers to three successive kingdoms located in Nubia, each of which took the name of its capital city: Kerma (2700–1500 BCE), Napata (800–300 BCE), and Meroe (300 BCE–300 CE).

Both terms, "Ethiopian" and "Cushite," were used interchangeably to designate Nubians, Kushites, Ethiopians, or any person from Africa. In Numbers 12:1, Moses' wife Zipporah is called כּוּשִׁי, which is translated as either "Ethiopian" or "Cushite" in modern translations of the Bible.[3] The Kushite king Taharqo (690–664 BCE), who ruled Egypt as part of the Twenty-fifth Dynasty, is mentioned in the Bible as marching against enemies of Israel, the Assyrians (2Kings 19:9, Isa 37:9). Perhaps best known to Christians is the Apostle Philip's teaching and baptism of the "Ethiopian" eunuch, an official of the "Candace of Meroe," which occurred on the desert road from Jerusalem to Gaza (Acts 8:27): "Now there was an Ethiopian (Greek: Αἰθίοψ) eunuch, a court official of the Candace, queen of the Ethiopians, in charge of her entire treasury." This New Testament reference in imprecise Greek describes the powerful treasurer of the Kingdom of Meroe and its *kandake*, the revered "Queen Mother."

The biblical allusion to the Candace of Kush places us squarely in the period to be discussed in this chapter. As the Acts of the Apostles purports to describe the period immediately after the death of Jesus, it must recount events of the first century CE. This is precisely the period when Kushite queens reached the pinnacle of their power, ruling jointly with their husbands and in at least three instances, holding the throne of Kush as sole rulers.

Review of previous scholarship

Frankly, not much has been written on the queens of Kush. Short articles[4] and book chapters[5] describe the status, role, and iconography of the women who ruled one of the great political powers in the ancient world. In contrast, much has been written about the queens of Egypt who infrequently and with great difficulty attained sole rule of their kingdoms. Yet Egyptian queens are acclaimed as the most powerful women of the ancient world. The exhibit *Queens of Egypt*, which was on display at the National Geographic Museum in 2019, presented the queens of Egypt in a slightly patronizing way that undermined the fact of their power, while it also completely ignored the culturally aligned and geographically proximate rule of the queens of Kush. Not surprisingly, the history of sole rule by powerful queens in the Kingdom of Kush is completely overlooked in the book associated with the exhibit, *When Women Ruled the World: Six Queens of Egypt*. In it, author Kara Cooney claims:

> In one place on our planet thousands of years ago, against all the odds of the male-dominated system in which they lived, women ruled repeatedly with formal, unadulterated power. Like Nitocris, most of these women ruled as Egyptian god-king incarnate, not as the mere power behind a man on the throne. Ancient Egypt is an anomaly as the only land that consistently called upon the rule of women to keep its regime in working order, safe from discord, and on the surest possible footing – particularly when a crisis was under way.[6]

The omission of Kushite queens from an analysis of female power in the ancient world could be due to two factors: first, Egyptologists tend not to know much about Kush; second, Egypt has been associated with the Mediterranean world, while Kush is relegated to Africa. For as long as the discipline of Egyptology has been around, there has been a division between those who would see ancient Egypt as part of the Near East, the biblical world, the eastern Mediterranean (mainstream Egyptologists in academia) and those who seek to situate ancient Egypt in its African context (primarily scholars of African descent from other disciplines).[7] This means that Kush languishes in obscurity, because it is not incorporated into studies of the ancient world, nor is it included in Africana Studies, which unfortunately still tends to begin the study of African history with European colonialism and slavery in Africa. In this paradigm, which is a result of the failings of both Egyptology and Africana Studies, Egyptian queens merit historical examination, while Kushite queens are ignored into non-existence. This chapter is one small step toward rectifying that omission; a full-length work on the queens of Kush is long overdue.

Queenship in Kush

Nubia refers to a geographic location in the Middle Nile valley, the area between the First and the Fourth Cataracts of the Nile,[8] which today comprises southern Egypt and northern Sudan. The people who lived there in antiquity are called Nubian, as are the modern people who still call the area home. In modern times, the Nubian people have been displaced by successive dam-building schemes in Egypt and Sudan, which have flooded Nubia[9] (Figure 2.1).

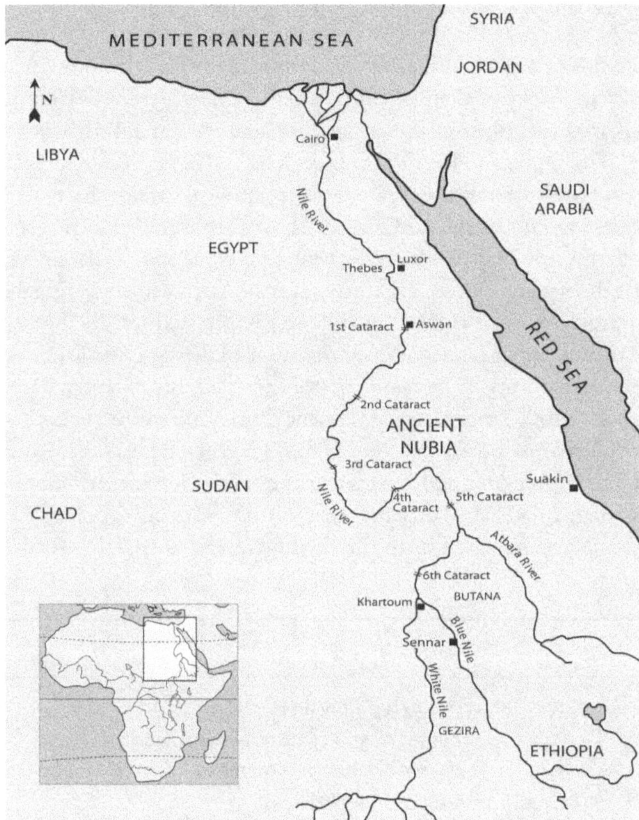

Figure 2.1 Map of ancient Nubia. Reprinted courtesy of American University in Cairo Press.

Kerman queens (2700–1500 BCE)

Due to Kerma's eschewal of writing, we are unable to identify the rulers of Kerma by name. Kings of Kerma were buried in large tumuli, mound burials surrounded by subsidiary interments, sacrificed retainers, and cattle. High-status female burials within the king's burial complex may have belonged to queens.[10] One individual's elite burial goods may be illustrative of the dual role of a Kerman queen: female complement to her royal husband and priestess. The woman buried in K1503, a subsidiary burial in royal tumulus KX, which was the second royal burial of the Kerma Classic period (1750–1550 BCE), was interred with rich grave goods: imported objects from Egypt, a faience scarab seal indicative of economic agency, and items that seem to indicate the ritual status of a priestess. Wearing a silver headdress evocative of the ram's horns of the god Amun, she wore an elaborate costume, which included a leather skirt with a silver beaded drawstring (Minor 2018, 252). Evidence suggests that the beaded, multicolored leather skirt was associated with a select group of Nubian women who may have served as priestesses. Predating the Kerman examples, tattooed females excavated from a C-Group Nubian cemetery at Hierakonpolis in Upper Egypt were buried in similar leather skirts.[11] Even earlier Nubian priestess-queens were buried in the Eleventh Dynasty funerary complex of Mentuhotep II (2055–2004 BCE) at Deir el-Bahari in Egypt (Ashby 2018, 67, 73).

Napatan queens (800–300 BCE)

Because Napatan rulers adopted the use of Egyptian hieroglyphs to decorate their monuments, we can describe more fully the titles and roles of their queens. Napatan queens were buried in the Kushite royal cemeteries at el-Kurru and Nuri in Sudan near the ancient capital of Napata and the sacred mountain of Gebel Barkal at the Fourth Cataract, where the ram-headed god Amun was worshiped. In life, they served to birth the next royal generation, to legitimate the rule of their sons, and as priestesses in the cult of the god Amun. They were installed as singers, sistrum players, and God's Wives of Amun.[12] Napatan queens were revered as kings' daughters, kings' sisters, and kings' mothers. Both Napatan kings, Taharqo and Aspelta, traced their female lineage to the dynasty's founder to proclaim their right to assume the Kushite kingship. In several inscriptions, Taharqo traced his mother Abar's descent from the sister of the dynastic founder Alara. Similarly, Aspelta listed seven generations of female ancestors to trace his ancestry back to the founding of the Napatan dynasty. Both kings claimed descent from Alara's sister, Pebatma (Haynes and Santini-Ritt 2012, 172). Pebatma bore the titles Sistrum Player of Amun-Re, King of the Gods; sister of the king; daughter of the king; and Divine Mother of the Divine Adoratress (Amenirdis I) (*Fontes Historiae Nubiorum I*, 145). In her ritual relationship with the god Amun, Pebatma partnered with Amun to conceive and then birth the divine-human king.

Napatan queens:

King	Queen(s)	Progeny
Alara	Kasqa	→Tabiry, wife of Piahkhy
Kashta	Pebatma	→Khensa, Abar, Peksater, Neferukakashta, wives of Piahkhy→Amenirdis I, God's Wife of Amun→Shabaqo
Piankhy	Khensa, Abar, Tabiry, Peksater, Neferukakashta	→Shepenwepet II, God's Wife of Amun→Taharqo, son of Abar→Arty, wife of Shebitqo
Shabaqo	Qalhata	→Tanwetamani→Isisemkhebit, wife of Shebitqo→Piankharty, wife of Tanwetamani
Shebitqo	Arty, Isisemkhebit	
Taharqo	Naparaye, Tabekenamun, Takhatamani, Atakhebasken, …salka	→Amenirdis II, God's Wife of Amun→Nesishutefnut, son of Takhatamani→Atlanersa, son of … salka
Tanwetamani	Piankharty, Malqaye	

Some scholars have connected the matrilineal succession in Kush to a larger African practice and have noted its continuation in medieval kingdoms of the Sudan right up until the imposition of British colonial rule in 1916 (Fluehr-Lobban 2004, 5). The presence and participation of the king's mother were essential in Napatan coronation rites. Taharqo, Anlamani, Aspelta, and Irike-Amanote all note the presence of their mothers at their coronations (Haynes Santini-Ritt 2012, 172). As part of her ritual role in the coronation, the king's mother delivered a speech to Amun requesting him to grant her son the Kushite kingship (Ibid., 173). In several Kushite coronations, the king's great wife is depicted taking part in the ceremonies along with the king's mother: [Taharqo (690–664 BCE), Tanwetamani (664–655/53 BCE), Harsiotef (early fourth century BCE), and Nastasen (late fourth century BCE)] (Ibid).

> The king is always accompanied by female members of his family – in one scene by his mother and in the other by his wife. It is significant that they assist him on the occasion of

this crucial ceremony by shaking a sistrum and libating, exercising priestly functions at this most important moment inaugurating the king's reign. Their presence is not coincidental but purposeful; they were participants in the ceremony which epitomized Kushite kingship, implying that the feminine counterpart of the king was eminently important. There is no representation of the coronation during Napatan times that excludes the king's wife or his mother.

(Lohwasser 2001, 68)

Hathoric associations were strong in the cultic role of the Kushite queens. Hathor was the goddess of love, music and dance, childbirth, and divine drunkenness. Lana Troy says of Egyptian royal women: "The role of the royal women is not distinct from that of the goddess Hathor but is rather her mortal manifestation and complement" (Troy 1986, 54). Similarly, Kushite queens were mortal manifestations of the goddess Hathor, which was reflected in the titles they held: Great One of the i3mt-scepter/Mistress of the i3mt-scepter,[13] Great One of the ḥts-scepter,[14] Sistrum Player,[15] and Chantress[16] (Troy 1986, 190–2). The titles Mistress of the i3mt-scepter and Great One of the ḥts-scepter both refer to cultic implements carried by priestesses of Hathor. The title wrt ḥts, "great one of the ḥts-scepter," is an archaic title found frequently in the titulary of royal women of the Old and Middle Kingdom in Egypt (Troy 1986, 79). The ḥts-scepter has ritual associations with the carrying chair (Troy 1986, 81), which itself is strongly associated with the Egyptian queen in her ritual roles as early as the predynastic period and in the Pyramid Texts, which adorned the burial chambers of the Old Kingdom Egyptian kings of the late Fifth Dynasty and the Sixth Dynasty (ca. 2350–2100 BCE) (Troy 1986, 80–1).

Similarly, the i3mt-tree is a symbol of the goddess Hathor. While this title appears in Egypt as early as the Thirteenth Dynasty (1773–1650 BCE), its early importance for Kushite royal symbolism is attested in the royal building program of the Kushite king Taharqo (690–664 BCE) in Egypt, where the king, who is depicted performing the ḥts-ceremony, holds an i3mt-tree in his hand (Troy 1986, 80–5).

However, the title held by most of the Kushite queens was that of "Chantress," singer of the prayers and praises of the god. The royal women participated in worship by communicating directly with the god through the vehicle of their voices raised in a singing prayer (think Aretha Franklin, not Gregorian chants) accompanied by the rhythm of the sistrum, a bronze rattle sacred to Hathor.

God's Wives of Amun

A potent avenue to political power for Kushite royal women of the Twenty-fifth Dynasty (747–656 BCE) was to serve as God's Wife of Amun and the Hand of God, both titles held by the Kushite princesses Amenirdis I and Shepenwepet II. Attested in Egypt first in the early Eighteenth Dynasty, the God's Wife of Amun was the powerful complement to the Egyptian king. Created for the first queen of the Eighteenth Dynasty, Ahmose-Nefertari, the position of God's Wife of Amun entailed much more than sacred duties. King Ahmose's Donation Stele confirms that he created and funded the Second Priesthood of Amun for his sister-wife Ahmose-Nefertari. The benefices of that office were granted to the God's Wife of Amun in perpetuity (Bryan 2000, 229).

The position of God's Wife of Amun granted royal women of the Eighteenth Dynasty independent sources of income and, therefore, political power. Kushite kings of the Twenty-fifth Dynasty employed this tradition to place their daughters in the highest seat of power in Thebes. This Upper Egyptian city served as the capital of the Eighteenth Dynasty and was the site of the powerful temple of Karnak dedicated to the god Amun. As Kushites gained control of Egypt, Kashta's daughter, Amenirdis I, was adopted by the previous God's Wife of Amun. In this position, she served as the virtual ruler of Upper Egypt. Amenirdis I, in turn, adopted her niece, Shepenwepet II, daughter of Piankhy. Amenirdis II, daughter of Taharqo, was the third Kushite God's Wife of Amun. While it is said that Kushite rulers adopted the Egyptian practice of assigning royal women the role of God's Wife of Amun in order to assume control of Egypt, placing Kushite royal women in the service of Amun was a tradition practiced in Kush before their conquest of Egypt. Alara dedicated his sisters as sistrum players in the temples of Amun in Kush, and Anlamani repeated the practice with four of his sisters, who were dedicated to Amun temples in Napata, Kawa, Pnubs, and Sanam (Török 1995, 96). Associating royal women with the power and wealth of the temples of Amun in Egypt and Kush served a similar purpose: to create a collateral line of power for the royal women who surrounded and supported the king, perhaps granting legitimacy to his right to rule through their royal lineage. The office of God's Wives of Amun reached its pinnacle of power during Kushite rule.

Most Kushite royalty chose to be buried in their homeland. However, several Napatan queens of the Twenty-fifth Dynasty were buried at Abydos, the site of the sacred burial of the god Osiris and of ritual burials (cenotaphs) of generations of Egyptian kings.[17] Abydos is the only site in Egypt with Kushite royal burials except for those of the God's Wives of Amun at Medinet Habu (Leahy 1994, 175).

Meroitic queens (300 BCE–300 CE)

While the level of power attained by Napatan queens was highly unusual in the ancient world, Meroitic queens consolidated even greater power, resulting in a series of sole-ruling queens during the first century BCE and the first century CE. Because no king list equivalent to those found in Egypt has been discovered thus far in Meroe, our understanding of the chronological succession of Meroitic rulers is still deeply unresolved. Regnal years and even place of burial have yet to be firmly established and agreed upon by most scholars. This section will discuss five independent ruling queens of Meroe based on the following provisional chronological order:

Queen	Burial Beg N (Begrawiyah North cemetery at Meroe) Bar (Gebel Barkal)	Date
Shanadakhete	Beg N. 11?	First century BCE or first century CE[18]
Amanirenas	Bar. 4? Beg. N. 21?	25 BCE
Nawidemak	Bar. 6	Early first century CE
Amanishakheto	Beg. N 6	Early first century CE
Amanitore	Beg. N 1	Mid-first century CE

The Meroitic era was characterized by a strong return to indigenous practices. It was during this period that the Meroitic hieroglyphic and cursive scripts were developed, which allowed inscriptions to be crafted in the native language of the kingdom instead of the Egyptian hieroglyphs that had predominated in the Napatan period. Similarly, we see a prominence given to the worship of indigenous deities: Apedemak (lion-headed creator god), Amesemi (falcon-crowned goddess, consort to Apedemak), Arensnuphis, and Sebiumeker (hunter and guardian gods). These Meroitic gods were worshiped in conjunction with deities shared with the Egyptian pantheon: Hathor, Isis, Osiris, Amun, and Mut.

Figure 2.2 Amanitore bark stand from Wad ban Naqa. Ägyptisches Museum, Berlin. Sandra Steiß © Ägyptisches Museum und Papyrussammlung.

Meroitic queens carried several Meroitic-language titles that indicated their political and ritual roles: *qore* and *kandake*. The former title was used exclusively by the ruler, male or female. Of the five queens listed in the preceding table, three used the title *qore*, which would indicate that they ruled as monarchs: Amanirenas,[19] who ruled with her husband Teriteqas and continued to rule after his demise; Nawidemak[20]; and Amanishakheto, whose dazzling jewelry is on display at the Egyptian Museum in Berlin and Munich.[21] The title *kandake* was held by the "queen mother."[22] In the Meroitic royal ideology, the *kandake* was the king's sister and mother of the legitimate heir to the throne. Of the five Meroitic queens listed, three held the title *kandake*: Amanirenas,[23] Amanishakheto,[24] and Amanitore,[25] who reigned as co-regent with her husband Natakamani. It appears to have been common knowledge among Greek and Roman scholars of the time that "[t]he Ethiopians do not publish the fathers of the kings, but hand them down as sons of the Sun. But the mother of each they call Candace."[26]

The period of successive sole-ruling queens (mid-first century BCE to mid-first century CE) is considered the Golden Age of the kingdom of Meroe. The queen buried in Beg N 11, perhaps Shanadakhete, was the first ruling queen of Meroe. The pylons in front of her burial pyramid show the powerfully built queen in the posture of subduing her enemies, a pose reserved in Egypt solely for kings. Her successor, King Tanyideamani, inaugurated the Meroitic writing system and established an administrative hierarchy to control newly claimed territories in Lower Nubia. Amanirenas may have been the "one-eyed Candace" referred to by Strabo (*Geography* 17 1.54) who engaged Roman troops in battle as they attempted and failed to extend

Figure 2.3 Pyramids at Meroe. © Chester Higgins / All Rights Reserved.

their conquest of Egypt by moving south into Lower Nubia. Both Amanirenas and Nawidemak were buried in the northern royal cemetery at Gebel Barkal, perhaps as a result of their battles to hold those territories and repel the Roman invaders.

The multitude of artifacts that bear the name of Queen Amanishakheto attest to the power and wealth of her reign, as does the cache of jewelry removed from her funerary pyramid by the Italian treasure hunter Giuseppe Ferlini. The Meroitic Golden Age came to fruition during the reign of Natakamani and Amanitore, who are credited with reviving the use of Egyptian-language inscriptions, creating a new iconography for their funerary chapels, and inaugurating a prolific royal building program that included renovation and construction of temples at Amara, Sai Island, Tabo, Napata, Dangeil, Meroe, and Wad ban Naqa.[27] It was during this Golden Age of ruling queens that Nubian priests began arriving at the temples of Lower Nubia (Philae and Dakka) to conduct rites on behalf of their Meroitic royal patrons. Over the course of two centuries, these priests and administrators would make large royal donations of gold, ordain local priests, plant sacred trees at the temple and adjacent burial of Osiris, and perform the uniquely Nubian funerary rite of pouring milk libations for the resurrection of their deceased king or queen.[28] The appearance of religious inscriptions by Meroitic priests, ambassadors, and even rulers (Teriteqas and Amanirenas, co-rulers, left inscriptions at Dakka; Yesbokheamani had his name inscribed in cartouches at Philae) in the Egyptian temples of

Dakka and Philae confirms the power and reach of the kingdom of Meroe during the first three centuries of the Common Era.

Female power in the ancient African world

While Egyptian ruling queens presented themselves as male by wearing the traditional kilt and false beard of a king, ruling queens of Meroe were extravagant in the depiction of their powerful feminine presence. Their voluptuous bodies with full breasts and wide, curvy hips suggested physical power. As the female complement to the king, Kushite queens established Maat, divine right order attained by balance in all things. Both female and male essence was necessary to achieve this balance. The king's potency as the "bull of his mother" was matched by the sacred sexuality of the queen, who served as an earthly manifestation of the goddess Hathor. Female sexuality as the essential enlivening element of creation can be seen throughout the imagery of Nile Valley religion: in the myth of Isis conceiving her son Horus by hovering over the corpse of her deceased husband Osiris; in the appearance of nude women as sacred dancers of Hathor in the rejuvenating rites of the king's Sed-Festival, celebrated after 30 years of his reign; or in the funerary rites performed to resurrect the dead. The Nubian funerary ritual of offering a libation of the breastmilk of Isis at the grave of her brother-husband Osiris demonstrates the Kushite belief in the enlivening powers of sacred female sexuality.

Meroitic queens are often depicted with their breasts bare on temple walls and in their funerary chapels.[29] Displaying evidence of their fecundity, queens alluded to their reproductive abilities and allied their power with that of the goddesses who bestowed divinity on the king by suckling him. Breast milk as the vehicle by which divinity was transmitted from a deity to the monarch is not unique to Kush. In Egypt, the king is suckled by a goddess at his birth, at his coronation, and during his funerary rites as a means to resurrection through the consumption of this magical fluid. In Kush, however, queens too had access to this divine liquid and, perhaps, allude to their ability to produce it themselves by being depicted bare breasted in scenes of power depicted on ritual objects and temple walls.

While the audacity of the queens of Egypt who attained sole rule is striking in the ancient world, where Mesopotamian, Greek, and Roman queens were often simply breeders of the next generation, the power of Egyptian queens pales beside the status and concomitant respect accorded to the queens of Kush. Depicted as the same size as their husbands, accorded independent wealth, and allowed access to divinity through suckling from the goddess, the royal women of Kush should be remembered as shining examples of members of a society that revered its mothers and the power of their sacred sexuality.

Kushite kings showed concern to demonstrate their legitimacy to rule by tracing their female line back to esteemed foremothers. This is the definition of a matrilineal society. While it was neither egalitarian nor matriarchal, the centrality of women to Kushite royal legitimacy and to local Nubian kinship ties demonstrates the importance of women in this African civilization. That the Kushite history of powerful women (*kandakes*) served as a potent symbol in the protests that toppled the Arabized dictator al-Bashir is stunning and testifies to the enduring centrality of women in this culture. Among the demands for an end to corruption, dictatorship, and state-sanctioned violence, some protestors in Sudan have also called for a rejection of Arab identity and a return to indigenous African traditions in Sudan, calling their movement #Sudaxit.[30] This suggests a powerful confrontation of ideologies as the misogyny present in the three major monotheistic religions is rejected and replaced with a native tradition of honoring women as mothers, as bearers of a sacred sexuality, and as complementary, essential participants in a society in balance.

Notes

1 The Meroitic royal title *kandake* is rendered Kandaka in popular culture and in some scholarly writing. I will use *kandake* to be consistent with the writing of the name in Meroitic script.

2 www.bbc.com/news/world-africa-48126363?SThisFB&fbclid=IwAR2IXfIyh8NiVfTGHwPbUFla _SLYaZQTiCCKWqeBpVHhBCcT_5CPAAfJBlk. From the article: "The hashtag #Sudaxit has been popular with the protesters and harks back to Sudan's African, rather than Arab, identity. This graffiti says: 'We demand that Sudan leaves the Arab League. We are black people, the sons of Kushites'" – a reference to the ancient kingdom of Kush.

3 The ethnic term "Cushite" (Strong's 3569) appears 26 times in the Bible: Nu 12:1 (twice), 2Sa 18:21 (twice), 2Sa 18:22, 2Sa 18:23, 2Sa 18:31 (twice), 2Sa 18:32 (twice), 2Ch 12:3, 2Ch 14:9, 2Ch 14:12 (twice), 2Ch 14:13, 2Ch 16: 8, 2Ch 21: 16, Jer 13:23, Jer 38:7, Jer 38:10, Jer 38:12, Jer 39:16, Da 11:43, Am 9:7, Zep 1:1, Zep 2:12. The toponym Kush (Strong's 3568) appears another 30 times: Gen 2:13, Gen 10:6, Gen 10:7, Gen 10:8, 2Kings 19:9, 1Ch 1:8, 1Ch 1:9, 1Ch 1:10, Esth 1:1, Esth 8:9, Job 28:19, Ps 7:1, Ps 68:31, Ps 87:4, Isa 11:11, Isa 18:1, Isa 20:3, Isa 20:4, Isa 20:5, Isa 37:9, Isa 43:3, Isa 45:14, Jer 46:9, Ezek 29:10, Ezek 30:4, Ezek 30:5, Ezek 30:9, Ezek 38:5, Nah 3:9, Zep 3:10.

4 Angelika Lohwasser, "Queenship in Kush: Status, Role, and Ideology of Royal Women" *JARCE* 38 (2001): 61–76; Carolyn Fluehr-Lobban, "Nubian Queens in the Nile Valley and Afro-Asiatic Cultural History" in *Proceedings of the Ninth International Conference for Nubian Studies, Museum of Fine Arts, Boston, August 21–26, 1998*, ed. Timothy Kendall (Boston: Northeastern University Press, 2004), 256–64; Ife Jogunsimi (Carruthers), "The Role of Royal Women in Ancient Egypt" *Kemet and the African Worldview: Research, Rescue, and Restoration. Selected Papers of the Proceedings of First and Second Conferences of ASCAC 24–26 February 1984*, ed. Maulana Karenga and Jacob H. Carruthers (Los Angeles: University of Sankore Press, 1986), 30–41.

5 László Török, *The Birth of an Ancient African Kingdom. Kush and Her Myth of the State in the First Millennium B.C. Cahiers de Recherches de L'Institut de Papyrologie et de Egyptologie de Lille 4* (Lille: Université Charles-de-Gaulle, 1995), 92–114; Joyce Haynes and Mimi Santini-Ritt, "Women in Ancient Nubia," in *Ancient Nubia: African Kingdoms of the Nile*, ed. Marjorie M. Fisher et al. (Cairo: The American University in Cairo Press, 2012), 170–85. A full-length book has been written on the royal women of Kush, but it is in German. See Angelika Lohwasser, *Die königlichen Frauen im antiken Reich von Kusch*, Meroitica 19 (Wiesbaden: Harrassowitz, 2001).

6 Kara Cooney, *When Women Ruled the World: Six Queens of Egypt* (Washington, DC: National Geographic Society, 2018), 10.

7 To date, most universities situate the study of Egyptology in the Department of Near Eastern Studies or some variant on that name. Many Egyptian artifacts are housed in a "Semitic" museum or displayed in galleries of the Ancient Near East. By contrast, scholars of African descent such as Martin Delaney, William Leo Hansberry, W. E. B. DuBois, Cheikh Anta Diop, and many more have stressed the inherent Africanity of Egypt and Nubia. For the history of this scholarly tradition, see Debora Heard, *In the House of the Lion and the Ram* (Ph.D. diss., University of Chicago, 2021), 11–19. This glaring divide has been bridged occasionally by conferences such as Manchester University's 2009 "Egypt in its African Context."

8 A cataract is an area of the river where boat traffic is impeded by rocks, which create rapids. The cataracts of the Nile are numbered from north to south. The First Cataract, just south of the town of Aswan and immediately north of the island temple of Philae, has traditionally served as the border between Egypt and Nubia. The Fourth Cataract at the southern end of Nubia is in the vicinity of the sacred site of Gebel Barkal, where the god Amun was venerated.

9 Nubians have been relocated to Kom Ombo in Egypt and New Halfa in eastern Sudan as a result of the complete flooding of their homeland by successive dams built in Egypt and Sudan. https://timep.org /commentary/analysis/nubians-the-egyptian-state-and-the-right-of-return/. A diasporic community exists in Cairo, Alexandria, and Khartoum as well as in Saudi Arabia and other lands of the Gulf, Europe, and the United States.

10 Elizabeth Minor, "Decolonizing Reisner: A Case Study of a Classic Kerma Female Burial for Reinterpreting Early Nubian Archaeological Collections through Digital Archival Resources," in *Nubian Archaeology in the XXIst Century. Proceedings of the Thirteenth International Conference for Nubian Studies, Neuchâtel 1ˢᵗ–6ᵗʰ September 2014*, ed. Matthieu Honneger (Leuven, Paris, Bristol, CT: Peeters, 2018), 256.

11 Renée Friedman, "The Nubian Cemetery at Hierakonpolis, Egypt. Results of the 2003 Season. Excavations of the C-Group Cemetery at HK27C," *Sudan and Nubia 8* (2004): 47–50; Solange Ashby, "Dancing for Hathor. Nubian Women in Egyptian Cultic Life," *Dotawo 5* (2018): 73–4.

12 *Fontes Historiae Nubiorum*, vol. *1*, ed. Tormod Eide et al. (Bergen: John Grieg AS, 1994), 144–5.

13 Amenirdis I, Shepenwepet II, Khensa, Takhatamani, Naparaye, Shepenwepet II, …salka, Khalese.

14 Amenirdis I, Khensa.

15 Pebmata, Amenirdis I, Shepenwepet II, Khensa, Abar, Takhatamani, Naparaye, …salka, Khalese, Nasalsa.

16 Amenirdis I, Shepenwepet II, Peksater, Khensa, Abar, Tabekenamun, Takhatamani, Naparaye, …salka. Various titles have been subsumed under the heading "Chantress": wr.t ḥsw.t "great of praises"; ḥsy.t šmʿ.t "singer"; sḥtp.t nṯr m ḥrw=s "one who pacifies the god with her voice"; niš.t ḥkn.w "the one who recites prayers"; iny.t nṯr r st=f "the one who brings the god to his place."

17 Kushite queens buried at Abydos include Pebatma, Peksater, Isisemchebit, and Meritamun. Joyce Haynes and Mimi Santini-Ritt, "Women in Ancient Nubia," 179–80; Anthony Leahy, "Kushite Monuments at Abydos" in *The Unbroken Reed. Studies in the Culture and Heritage of Ancient Egypt in Honour of A. F. Shore*, ed. Christopher Eyre, Anthony Leahy, and Lisa Montagno Leahy (London: Egypt Exploration, 1994), 175–88; László Török, *Ancient African Kingdom*, 94.

18 "The new date for Queen Shanadakhete would place her among six (sic) other Meroitic rulers: Teriteqas, Queen Nawidemak, Queen Amanirenas, Queen Amanishakheto, Amanikhabale, Natakamani, and Queen Amanitore who, based to some extent on classical sources, are believed to have reigned from the late first century BC to the end of the first century AD." Janice W. Yellin, "The Chronology and Attribution of Royal Pyramids at Meroe and Gebel Barkal: Beg N 8, Beg N 12, Bar 5 and Bar 2," *Journal of Ancient Egyptian Interconnections* 6:1 (2014): 80.

19 Amanirenas as *qore*: Kawa (REM 0628), Meroe City (REM 1003).

20 Nawidemak as *qore*: gold statue base in the Allen Memorial Art Museum. See M. F. Laming Macadam, "Queen Nawidemak," *Allen Memorial Art Museum Bulletin* 23:2 (1966): 43, 58.

21 Amanishakheto as *qore*: stela found in the Amun-Temple sanctuary at Naqa. Dietrich Wildung, "Götter und Herrscher. Gods and Rulers," in *Königstadt Naga. Naga Royal City*, ed. Karla Kröper, Sylvia Schoske, and Dietrich Wildung (Berlin-Munich: Staatliches Museum Ägyptischer Kunst München, 2011), 32–4, fig. 34, 186, fig. 217.

22 Wenig asserts that six Meroitic queens are attested with the title *kandake*: Bartare, Kanarta, an unnamed queen attested at Kawa, Amanirenas, Amanishakheto, and Amanitore. See Steffen Wenig, *Untersuchungen zur Ikonographie der Darstellungen der meroitischen Königsfamilie und zu Fragen der Chronologie des Reiches von Meroe* (Berlin-London: Golden House Publications, 2015), 99–102. See also *Fontes Historiae Nubiorum*, vol. 2, 549.

23 Amanirenas as *kandake*: Dakka (REM 0092), Meroe City (REM 0412), Stela of Akinidad (REM 1003, where the queen is both *qore* and *kandake*). See *Fontes Historiae Nubiorum*, vol. 2, 715–23.

24 Amanishakheto as *kandake*: Obelisk from Meroe, Stelae from Naqa, see *Königstadt Naga. Naga Royal City*, ed. Karla Kröper, Sylvia Schoske, and Dietrich Wildung (Berlin-Munich: Staatliches Museum Ägyptischer Kunst München, 2011), figs. 34, 217 (Kat. 11), figs. 37, 213, 218 (Kat. 14); Stela from Qasr Ibrim (REM 1151).

25 Amanitore as *kandake*: Naqa Lion Temple inscription (REM 004), Beg. N 1 funerary chapel; RCK vol. 3 Pl. 18F. See also *Fontes Historiae Nubiorum*, vol. 3, 901–2.

26 Bion of Soloi in the first book of the *Aethiopica* as quoted in F. Ll. Griffith, *Meroitic Inscriptions, vol. II: Napata to Philae and Miscellaneous* (London: Egypt Exploration Fund, 1912), 39. See also *Fontes Historiae Nubiorum*, vol. 2, 550–1.

27 Claude Rilly, "Meroitic Texts from Naga," in *Königstadt Naga. Naga Royal City*, ed. Karla Kröper, Sylvia Schoske, and Dietrich Wildung (Berlin-Munich: Staatliches Museum Ägyptischer Kunst München, 2011), 190.

28 Solange Ashby, *Calling Out to Isis: The Enduring Nubian Presence at Philae* (Piscataway, NJ: Gorgias Press, 2020), 117–206.

29 A recent publication claims: "Another less common look of the Meroitic queen shows her bare breasted, wearing only a long, often patterned, skirt" (Haynes and Santini-Ritt 2012, 184). However, I have identified five examples of Meroitic queens depicted with their breasts bared in their funerary chapels. *Royal*

Cemeteries of Kush, vol. 3 (Boston: Museum of Fine Arts, 1952): Kanarta (Pl. 3A), Nawidemak (Pl. 13A), Bar. 4 Amanirenas (?) (Pl. 13C), unknown queen Bar. 3 (Pl. 14A), and Amanishakheto (Pl. 16A). This number does not include the numerous goddesses depicted topless or the bare-breasted mourners who may have been queens or female members of the royal family. Figure 2.2 of this chapter shows Queen Amanitore bare breasted on her bark stand dedicated at Wad ban Naqa. For Bar. 4 as the burial place of Amanirenas, see Yellin 2014, 82–5, esp. 84.

30 See note 2.

Bibliography

Ashby, Solange. "Dancing for Hathor. Nubian Women in Egyptian Cultic Life." *Dotawo 5* (2018): 63–90.

Ashby, Solange. *Calling Out to Isis: The Enduring Nubian Presence at Philae*. Piscataway, NJ: Gorgias Press, 2020.

Bryan, Betsy M. "The Eighteenth Dynasty before the Amarna Period," In *The Oxford History of Ancient Egypt*, edited by Ian Shaw, 218–271. Oxford: Oxford University Press, 2000.

Fluehr-Lobban, Carolyn. "Nubian Queens in the Nile Valley and Afro-Asiatic Cultural History." In *Proceedings of the Ninth International Conference for Nubian Studies, Museum of Fine Arts, Boston, August 21-26, 1998*, edited by Timothy Kendall, 256–264. Boston: Northeastern University Press, 2004.

Haynes, Joyce and Mimi Santini-Ritt. "Women in Ancient Nubia." In *Ancient Nubia: African Kingdoms of the Nile*, edited by Marjorie M. Fisher et al., 170–185. Cairo: The American University in Cairo Press, 2012.

Hoffman, Inge. "Zu den Titeln *ktke* und *pqr*." *ZDMG Suppl. III*, no. 2 (1977): 1400–1404.

Leahy, Anthony. "Kushite Monuments at Abydos." In *The Unbroken Reed. Studies in the Culture and Heritage of Ancient Egypt in Honour of A.F. Shore*, edited by Christopher Eyre, Anthony Leahy, and Lisa Montagno Leahy, 171–192. London: Egypt Exploration, 1994.

Lohwasser, Angelika. *Die königlichen Frauen im antiken Reich von Kusch*. Meroitica 19. Wiesbaden: Harrassowitz, 2001.

Lohwasser, Angelika. "Queenship in Kush: Status, Role, and Ideology of Royal Women." *JARCE 38* (2001): 61–76.

Macadam, M.F. Laming. "Queen Nawidemak." *Allen Memorial Art Museum Bulletin* 23, no. 2 (1966): 42–71.

Minor, Elizabeth. "Decolonizing Reisner: A Case Study of a Classic Kerma Female Burial for Reinterpreting Early Nubian Archaeological Collections through Digital Archival Resources." In *Nubian Archaeology in the XXIst Century. Proceedings of the Thirteenth International Conference for Nubian Studies, Neuchâtel 1st-6th September 2014*, Orientalia Lovaniensia Analecta 273, edited by Matthieu Honneger, 251–262. Leuven: Peeters, 2018.

Sackho-Autissier, Aminata. "Les candaces, des reines régnantes." In *Meroe: un empire sur le Nil*, edited by Michel Baud, 178–179. Paris : Louvre Museum, 2010.

Török, László. *The Birth of an Ancient African Kingdom. Kush and Her Myth of the State in the First Millenium B.C.* Cahiers de Recherches de l'Institut de Papyrologie et de Egyptologie de Lille 4. Lille: Université Charles-de-Gaulle, 1995.

Troy, Lana. *Patterns of Queenship in Ancient Egyptian Myth and History*. Acta Universitatis Upsaliensis. Boreas: Uppsala Studies in Ancient Mediterranean and Near Eastern Civilization 14. Uppsala: Almqvist and Wiksell, 1986.

Wenig, Steffen. "Pabatma-Pekereslo-Pekartror. Ein Beitrag zur Frühgeschichte der Kuschiten." In *Studia in honorum Fritz Hintz*. Meroitica 12, edited by Dietlind Apelt et al., 333–352. Berlin: Akademie Verlag, 1990.

Wenig, Steffen. *Untersuchungen zur Ikonographie der Darstellungen der meroitischen Königsfamilie und zu Fragen der Chronologie des Reiches von Meroe*. Berlin: Golden House Publications, 2015.

Wildung, Dietrich. "Götter und Herrscher. Gods and Rulers." In *Königstadt Naga. Naga Royal City*, edited by Karla Kröper, Sylvia Schoske, and Dietrich Wildung, 22–51. Berlin: Staatliches Museum Ägyptischer Kunst München, 2011.

Yellin, Janice W. "The Chronology and Attribution of Royal Pyramids at Meroe and Gebel Barkal: Beg N 8, Beg N 12, Bar 5 and Bar 2." *Journal of Ancient Egyptian Interconnections 6*, no. 1 (2014): 76–88.

3

Queen Balqis, "Queen of Sheba"

Carolyn Fluehr-Lobban

The Queen of Sheba exists in history more as a legend than a historical figure. It is a major task of this chapter to distinguish myth from history. Her ethnic identity is often described as of Yemeni or Sabean origin, but she may have been both ethnically and politically Ethiopian. As a ruler of Ethiopia-Abyssinia, she can be placed within the Red Sea littoral and thus as a woman of African and Afro-Asiatic importance. Why and how she became sexualized as either seduced or a seductress in her famous encounter with King Solomon of Jerusalem has, perhaps, much to do with the patriarchal cultural environments in which her story has been told—in the West and the East. But her central role in Ethiopia is that of founder of the Ethiopian royal dynasty through her son Menelik, the product of a romantic encounter between Sheba and Solomon of Jerusalem sometime during the reign of King Solomon (970–931 BCE).

A critical review of her multicultural tale will be analyzed here through the cultural lenses of Western Christian, Eastern Muslim, and non-Chalcedonian Christian African religious traditions, making her identity one of an African woman. Her story is mostly a tale related in religious-political terms. Over the millennia of Ethiopian history, there have been 17 named queens from a total of 312 named regents, the overwhelming majority being men. According to the official list of Ethiopian kings from the *Kebra Nagast*[1] recorded by the Ras Tafari Makonnen (Haile Selassie) in 1922, the history of kings began in Biblical times of the "Great Flood," continued through the fabled "Fall of the Tower of Babel" and through the time before the birth of Christ, and continues after the birth of Jesus, distinguishing between those pre-Christian and Christian sovereigns.

According to the *Kebra Nagast*,[2] six queens preceded Sheba, known in Ethiopia as "Makeda," the mother of Menelik I, from whose birth Ethiopian dynastic history was born and firmly fixed with the state. Ten queens followed her over the lengthy course of Ethiopian dynastic history. In some cases, royal mothers ruled partly with their sons, a feature known to be present in Kush-Meroë in ancient Sudan during the millennium BCE. Indeed, there is a strong case to be made that ancient Nubian royalty was absorbed into the Ethiopian list of kings after Ethiopia's conquest of Meroë by King Ezana in the fourth century CE (Kramer, Lobban, and Fluehr-Lobban, 2013:144).

Sheba was a monarch of the ancient kingdom of Saba/Sheba who is referenced in the triple Judeo-Christian-Islamic tradition: in Ethiopian/Habeshan[3] history, the Hebrew Bible, the New

Testament, and the Qur'an. "Saba/Sheba" was an ancient name for a kingdom on the Red Sea in northeast Africa and southwest Asia, or modern Ethiopia and Yemen. In ancient times, Ethiopia was incorrectly known as Abyssinia, Nubia, or Kush/Cush, although this represents a confusion in the original sources between the ancient Sudanese kingdoms of Kush-Meroë (950 BCE–325 CE), with its capital at Napata, and that of neighboring Abyssinia-Ethiopia, with its capital at Axum. This prior Sudanese kingdom of Kush and its capital Meroë along the Nile at the fourth cataract were conquered by the Ethiopian King Ezana in 325 CE, as previously mentioned. It is probable that the Ethiopian list of kings incorporated the previous Kushite regents mentioned in the Bible as hailing from Ethiopia. The most famous of the pharaohs of Kush, Taharqa (Tir-ha-ka), is referred to as the "king of Ethiopia" (2 Kings: 19:8). In the pre-Christian civilization, "the earliest inscriptions of the rulers of the ancient kingdom of D'mt in northern Ethiopia and Eritrea mention queens of very high status, possibly equal to their kings."[4]

This confusion regarding "Ethiopia/ Ethiopians," meaning the "land/peoples of the burnt faces," is traceable to Greek texts describing Nubia, contemporary southern Egypt, and northern Sudan. The well-attested Meroitic/Nubian kings Kashta, Sabaka, and Piankhi are listed in the Bible among the Ethiopian kings (Book of Kings, 1:10–11). The names of Egyptian kings or deities, Amenhotep and Senefrou, also appear in this list of Ethiopian kings, referencing a larger geographical area than that associated with modern Ethiopia. It is tempting to see in the Biblical reference to Cush an historical association with ancient Kush at Meroë, the land of the "Kandakes" who appear in the Ethiopian list of kings or regents.

The Queen of Sheba is also known as "Makeda." The etymology of this Ethiopian name, *Makeda*, is uncertain, but British scholar Edward Ullendorff holds that it is a corruption of "Candace," the Ethiopian (read Nubian) queen mentioned in the New Testament.[5] In Arabia and the Islamic world, the Queen of Sheba is known as Balqis. She is associated with the historic ruins of Mar'ib, where there is a Sabaean temple with eight pillars that Yemenite tradition calls "Mahram Balqis," "Balqis' sanctuary." This reflects a memory of ancient Sabean queendoms with a strong dimension of spiritual leadership.[6]

The tale of Solomon and Sheba across three religious traditions

The story of Solomon and Sheba has recognizable consistencies across the Judeo-Christian-Islamic religious traditions. Solomon is a recognized king famous for building the Temple of the Ark of the Covenant in Jerusalem; for his wisdom and sagacity; and for his great number of wives and concubines. Sheba, known as Makeda in Ethiopian traditions, is most often mentioned as a queen from Saba, an important trading nexus in northeast Africa. Solomon sought to acquire gold, ebony, and sapphires for the building of the Temple and employed the services of an intermediary, Tamrin. Sheba, who heard of the wisdom and wealth of Solomon from this trader, planned and executed a grand journey, bearing numerous gifts of the East, to meet him in Jerusalem. The tale of their mutual attraction, as told in Ethiopian tradition, has Sheba testing his wisdom with riddles and Solomon tricking her into staying the night in his palace – resulting in their eventual sexual union and Sheba's conversion away from "idolatry" to acceptance of Yahweh and monotheism; eventually, she is seen as an early convert to Christianity. The story varies by religious tradition, but the Ethiopian version culminates in the birth of Solomon's son Menelik, the first king in the new Ethiopian Christian dynasty. Sheba returns to Ethiopia and establishes a capital at Axum, where the Ark is secretly brought by Menelik after a visit to meet his father in Jerusalem; Ethiopian Christians believe it resides there to this day and that they are its caretakers.

The oldest account of the Queen of Sheba comes from the Bible, in the Old Testament book of Kings (11:10–14). During the period of the 39-year reign of King Solomon, 970–931 BCE, it is related in the Bible that he had 700 wives and 300 concubines. Solomon is considered one of the 48 prophets in Judaism, and Islam considers him a major prophet. Although a revered person in the Christian Bible, his role is more one of sage and wise ruler. The encounter between the Queen of Sheba and King Solomon, emphasizing either the romantic and/or the political, is treated most seriously in Ethiopian religious texts, especially the *Kebra Nagast*, and in Muslim sources, both textual in the Qur'an and in folkloric renditions. The names of Solomon and Sheba also have notoriety in Western Christianity as a story, but they lack the meaningful ancestral connotations they have in Ethiopian sources or the allegorical power they have in Islamic texts, perhaps because Sheba/Balqis is an eastern woman of Asiatic and African importance.

The Ethiopian narrative is derived from the primary religious document of Ethiopian Christianity,[7] the *Kebra Nagast*:

> When the Queen met Solomon she gave him rich presents (Chap. 25), and he supplied her with food and servants and rich apparel. The Queen was fascinated as much by his wisdom as by his physical perfections …
>
> During her stay in Jerusalem Makeda conversed daily (Chaps. 26, 27) with Solomon, and she learned from him about the God of the Hebrews … She herself worshipped the sun, moon and stars, and trees, and idols … but under the influence of Solomon's eloquent words she renounced Ṣabaism …
>
> At length Makeda sent a message to Solomon that it was time to return to her own country. When Solomon heard this he [was] determined to company with her, for he loved her physical beauty and her shrewd intelligence, and he wished to beget a son by her. Solomon had 400 wives and 600 concubines, and among them were women from Syria, Palestine, the Delta, Upper Egypt and Nubia.
>
> … Nine months and five days after Makeda bade Solomon farewell she brought forth a man child, and in due course she arrived in her own country, where she was received with great joy. She called her son Bayna-Leḥkem, [Menelik] "the son of the wise man," and he grew into a strong and handsome young man. At the age of twelve he questioned his mother as to his parentage, and … he continued to do so until she told him; and ten years later … Makeda sent him to Jerusalem, accompanied by her old chief of caravans, Tâmrîn (Chaps. 32, 33). With him she sent a letter to Solomon, telling him that in future a king should reign over her country … and that her people should adopt the religion of Israel.

In this Ethiopian telling of the tale of Solomon and Sheba, Makeda lays claim to the Solomonic line for the Ethiopian royal dynasty, an African patrilineage descending from the Hebrew king. The *Kebra Nagast* credits her with building her capital Debra Makeda on a mountaintop, the new capital city at Azeba, Aksum. Boavida and Ramos argue that this founding narrative served to establish the legitimacy of the political change to Ethiopian royal rule that was then bolstered by King Solomon and monotheism, and ultimately Christianity, which became the state religion and was entwined with its political structure, which lasted for 20 centuries until the reign of Haile Selassie that ended in 1975.[8]

In the Christian Bible, Sheba appears by inference in the Song of Solomon and also in the Bible's most famous passage from the book of Kings. As the story is related, Sheba, hearing of Solomon's wisdom from a traveling merchant, journeyed to Jerusalem to meet him. After their encounter, which was an intellectual exchange with strong romantic overtones, Sheba is said to declare: "From this moment I will not worship the sun, but will worship the Creator of the sun, the God of Israel." The Ethiopian queen converted to Judaism.

From The Holy Bible, Revised Standard Edition, Kings 10:1–2 (308–9):

> Now when the queen of Sheba heard of the fame of Solomon concerning the name of the Lord, she came to test him with hard questions. She came to Jerusalem with a very great retinue, with camels bearing spices, and very much gold, and precious stones … And Solomon answered all her questions; there was nothing hidden from the king which he could not explain to her. And when the queen of Sheba had seen all the wisdom of Solomon, and … the burnt offerings which he offered at the house of the Lord, there was no more spirit in her.
>
> And she said to the king, "The report was true which I heard in my own land of your affairs and your wisdom, but I did not believe the reports until I came and my own eyes had seen it; and, behold, the half was not told me; your wisdom and propriety surpass the report which I heard. Happy are your wives! Happy are these your servants, who continually stand before you and hear your wisdom! Blessed be the Lord your God, who has delighted in you and set you on the throne of Israel. Because the Lord loved Israel forever, he has made you king that you may execute justice and righteousness." Then she gave the king a hundred and twenty talents of gold and a very great quantity of spices and precious stones, never again came such an abundance of spices as these which the queen of Sheba gave to King Solomon.
>
> And King Solomon gave to the Queen of Sheba all that she desired, whatever she asked besides what was given to her by the bounty of King Solomon. So she turned and went back to her own land, with her servants.

In this account, the Queen is a peer of King Solomon, not a subordinated or inferior figure.

There are various stories of how Sheba became pregnant by King Solomon, thus giving birth to their son Menelik, who became the founding ancestor of royal Ethiopian descent. In some accounts, before Sheba departs, Solomon deceives her into sleeping with him. Staying in his palace, she had asked him to swear that he would not force her into sex. He agreed, on condition that she would not take anything from his house by force. He fed her a lot of spicy food, and in the night, when she reached for water in her thirst, he appeared and said that she had broken her promise, having taken water, the most valuable of all things. So, according to the *Kebra Nagast* and the Bible, Makeda consented to have sex with Solomon. As she departed, he gave her a ring for their future son. Then, Solomon dreamed that the sun [and its worship] were no more in Israel. When Makeda's son Menelik came of age, he traveled to Jerusalem for his father's blessing and was recognized by the ring. Solomon wanted Menelik to succeed him as king, but he insisted on returning to Ethiopia. So, Solomon put together a noble company to go back with him. Angry at being forced to leave their homes and families, these young men secretly took the Ark out of the Temple and away to Africa. Menelik was not implicated in this deceit, but he found out along the way. He was divinely transported back to Ethiopia through the skies, thwarting Solomon's attempt to recover the Ark. Menelik's return to Ethiopia was celebrated with great pomp at Axum, and Makeda gave up her throne to him. Ethiopia became "the second Zion." The Queen of Sheba is also mentioned as the "Queen of the South" in the New Testament (Matthew 12:42): "The Queen of the South will arise at the judgment with this generation and condemn it; for she came from the ends of the earth to hear the wisdom of Solomon, and held, something greater than Solomon is here"; the same wording appears in

Luke 11:31 in the context of Jesus saying that she and the Ninevites will judge the contemporaries of Jesus who rejected him.

In Islamic sources, Sheba is known as Balqis and has an acknowledged south Arabian origin. Yemen and Ethiopia share a heritage across the Red Sea, where rule by women in antiquity was established after the advent of Islam with two acknowledged ruling queens, Asma bint Shihab al-Sulayhiyya (d. 480 AH/1087 AD) and her daughter in law 'Arwa bint Ahmad al-Sulayhiyya. They co-ruled with a husband or son, Queen 'Arwa ruling for nearly half-a century. Both queens bore the same royal title, *al-sayidda al-hurra*, "the noble lady who is free and independent, the woman sovereign who bows to no superior authority." These queens descended from the pre-Islamic regents of the realm of Sheba, the family tracing its roots to the Yam clan of the Hamdan tribe. Shi'a Islam is notable for its emphasis on heredity over meritocracy in leadership succession; thus, the Yemenite sovereigns brought a sense of hereditary rule to Ethiopia and parts of Shi'ite Africa, including the powerful Fatimid dynasty in Egypt. The Yemenis bestowed upon these queens the affectionate title of "Balqis al-sughra" or "little queen of Sheba," or more precisely, "young queen of Sheba".[9]

Balqis is introduced in the Quran as a ruler who worshipped the sun, and as being led by Satan instead of Allah. In her story, Balqis loses her throne when a *jinn* (spirit) working for Solomon steals it. Although stripped of her assets, Sheba gains in spirituality and surrenders first to Allah and then to his prophet Solomon (Mardrus, 142). Thus, in the Muslim telling of Sheba's story, she is a convert to Islam before her encounter with Solomon.

Mernissi asks: did she actually marry Solomon, or was she a consort? Nothing in the Quran tells us that she was a virgin or that they were married. However Muslim theologians and historians have decided that she was a virgin, perhaps for predictable reasons of patriarchal revisionist history. Nonetheless, Mernissi argues that Balqis as a royal woman poses a problem for historians, with al-Mas'udi – a highly regarded Muslim historian – declaring that she was born from a human father and a *jinn* mother, implying magic or intervention of the supernatural. With such a throne and a people at her feet, Balqis could not be completely human, and there are vivid stories of her possessing the cloven feet of a donkey (Ibid., 143).

Despite such assaults on her dignity, Balqis has held her own against these onslaughts to reduce or humiliate her. Balqis remains a powerful figure today in Arab poetry, and many contemporary poets use her name to suggest "a female presence such that she still fascinates and enchants" (Ibid., 140). Mernissi argues that although Shi'ites have been more liberal toward women holding power, ultimately it is Yemeni culture, more than Shi'a Islam, that is the main factor in the persistence of her story. In Yemen, female rulers were needed for political legitimacy (Ibid., 158).

In the Qur'an, the verses telling the story of Solomon and Sheba (Sura 27:22–4) specify that Solomon, hearing "news from Saba" of "a woman ruling over them" and in possession of a great throne (Sura 27:22–3), is said to have uttered these words:

> Indeed, I found a woman ruling them, and she has been given of all things, and she has a great throne. I found her and her people prostrating to the sun instead of Allah, and Satan has made their deeds pleasing to them and averted them from [his] way, so they are not guided, so they do not prostrate to Allah …
>
> *(Holy Qu'ran: Sura 27:24–5)*

After this news of a "great queen from the east," Solomon sent a letter to Sheba through the messenger Tamrin. The last portion of the Qur'anic passage sheds light not only on the peaceful intent of Sheba but also on her understanding of the destructive effects of war on innocent citizens, while her method of pacification is the initiation of a peace process through a display of generous gifts, as described by Madrus from both Christian and Muslim accounts:

> As she approached: "O King of Kings, the Queen of the South and of the Morning stays at four parasangs from the King's tents, with a glittering escort and a mighty army." And so Solomon spread forth his magnificence. Then he rose up on his two feet, and went to meet his destiny.
>
> First he saw a single line of fifty elephants opening the way, blaring with lifted trunks, heavy and unafraid; and their rank was dressed as straight as a brass wall. They were half-hidden by their cloths and towers; and were led by rose-copper-colored Abyssinians, with small gold cords as tresses in their hair. These cornacs held gilded sticks in their left hands and cried in their own tongue terrifyingly. (no page no.)

Solomon related: "An 'ifreet of the jinn[10] said 'I will bring it [Sheba's throne] to you, before you rise from your seat, and I am indeed capable of it and faithful.' He said: 'Disguise her throne for her, so that we might see she be well-guided or will be one of those who are not well-guided.' When she arrived, it was said (to her): 'Is your throne like this one?' She said 'it looks like it.' However, when she worshipped, apart from Allah, … she was indeed one of the unbelieving people."

The Qur'an's Sura 27 portrays a powerful "pagan" woman in a compromised yet mystical light and is the closest that the Qur'an gets to a prophetess as an early convert to Islam, although the historical dates do not match with the story, as Islam is not introduced until the seventh century CE. Also, in the Qur'anic account, she is shown coming not to seek wisdom but to avert a disastrous invasion of her country. Solomonic Israel was likely incapable of mounting such an invasion, least of all against far-away Yemen or Ethiopia. But because the Queen of Sheba appears in the Qur'an, Muslims have spread her story around the world, although it has become heavily mythologized.

Race and representation

Contemporary Ethiopian folk pictorial renditions of the story are enhanced with indigenous details that are missing from the foreign renderings of the tale. The story begins with the river birth of a giant serpent, "Arwe," who becomes the ruler and demands tribute from his subjects. Agabos, Sheba's father, ends this feudal tradition by poisoning a goat, which is fed to the serpent, who then dies. Agabos becomes king, and upon his death, Makeda (Azeb) succeeds him. From this founding genealogical background, the story continues along the same lines as related earlier; however, the "peculiarity of the Ethiopian story must be stressed" (Boavida and Ramos, 2005:86). In one of these folk paintings, specific local cultural details are included, such as portraying the Menelik family member playing an Ethiopian lute, the *gena* (a stringed instrument or lute, known as the *rabab* in Arabic).

Racial mythology has surrounded the legends of Sheba. The Queen of Sheba has been an alluring subject across the ages, continuing into the present era, where she is revered in Ethiopian lore and remains an enigmatic figure across the triple religious tradition in both the West and the East. Her physical representation varies across the many cultures and regions where her story has migrated. This section offers a glimpse of the diverse ways in which Sheba has been portrayed, not only by race (skin color and physical features) and culture (dress and setting) but also by gender, especially how she is portrayed in terms of agency. For example, in a painting by a contemporary Ethiopian artist Bizuhayeu Taddesse,[11] Sheba is portrayed as lighter in skin tone than her Ethiopian attendants and darker than King Solomon, perhaps depicting her Asiatic as well as African roots, as the king bends to kiss her hand in what is, presumably, their encounter in Jerusalem. Although the cultural setting is Orientalist, the cultural-racial diversity of her attendants is evident.[12]

Ethiopian folk portrayals are often produced for the tourist trade but nonetheless keep the legend of Sheba alive into the present moment and reveal a conscious racial and cultural differentiation between Sheba and the other characters essential to her story. In these panels, there is a clear difference in skin colors.[13] The servant is Black, Makeda is red, and Solomon is white. Moreover, in these twentieth-century portrayals, white dress covering the whole body for males and females is typical, along with traditional rural houses made of clay ("adobe") walls and thatched roofs, both consistent with contemporary Ethiopian culture.

In Madrus' Islamic text, Abyssinians are described as "rose-colored" (no page number). In European imagery, Sheba was typically portrayed as white, although she was depicted as a Black woman for the first time in 1181 CE in the monastery of Klosterneuberg, Germany, where she appears as a dark-skinned queen in royal regalia (Figure 3.1). Jan Nederveen Pieterse has analyzed this as part of a stylistic re-evaluation of Black, no longer seen as demonic once Ethiopia was viewed as a Christian land. This may have contributed to an association of Ethiopia with the fabled African Christian kingdom ruled by Prester John, which was both a destination and viewed as a potential Christian ally during the Crusades.

Figure 3.1 Queen of Sheba as Black, 1405 AD. Solomon and Sheba, c.1452 AD.

Unlike the eastern writers, European authors and artists often showed Solomon as the political superior of the Queen of Sheba and also as her spiritual senior and initiator. They also added a racial distortion, whitening her, a feature that can also be seen in Persian manuscripts. While race is still viewed in the eye of the beholder, there is no doubt that Sheba is an African queen, irrespective of her physical attributes. Depictions of the Queen of Sheba and thus, of Ethiopia can be seen as reflecting changing images and the utility of these images of the African – from negative to positive at various historical times: 1) as positive when Europe needed an ally during the Crusades against the eastern Islamic threat; 2) as negative during the eighteenth and nineteenth centuries as colonialism advanced and the continent became "darkest Africa"; and 3) as a twentieth-century postcolonial revival of a majestic African queen redeeming the continent's history and providing a case of an African queen with independence, agency, and healthy sexuality. Happily, in the world of gender scholarship, we are at a moment where women of African descent and their enthusiastic allies can begin to re-envision who the Queen of Sheba may have really been, beyond the scriptural traditions within which her original story has been told.

Notes

1 The *Kebra Nagast* (The Glory of Kings) *The True Ark of the Covenant*. Translated from Ge'ez and edited by Miguel F. Brooks (Lawrenceville, NJ: Red Sea Press, 1995).

2 In the *Kebra Nagast*, there are named queens whose dates reflect the western Christian calendar and the Ethiopian lunar calendar having 13 months [No. IV, Queens Borsa: 1246; 4254; XIII Eylouka: 1769; 3731; VIII Nehassat Nais (after the Fall of the Tower of Babel; 3096; 2904; Kasiyope; 3629; 1890; Mumazes; 3829; 1671; Helena; 4163; 1307; Makeda (78 sovereigns reigned in Ethiopia before the advent of Menelik I); Nicauta Kandae; Hadina; Nikawla Kandat; Akwawsis Kandake III [#34, 36, 39]; Awsena; Wakana (2 days); Ahywa Sofya (last three after Christianity; Sofya a Queen Mother); Adhana I and II; Zaudita and Tafari Makonnen (1916) – Haile Selassie, 1930–74. In October 2018, the Ethiopian government appointed its first woman president, Sahle-Work Zwede (*NY Times*, October 26, 2018). www.newworldencyclopedia.org/entry/Queen_of_Sheba

3 Ethiopia is known in Arabic as *al-Habash*, and Ethiopians as *al-Habashiyeen*.

4 Rodolfo Fattovich, "The 'Pre-Aksumite' State in Northern Ethiopia and Eritrea Reconsidered" in Paul Lunde and Alexandra Porter ed., *Trade and Travel in the Red Sea Region*, in D. Kennet and St J. Simpson ed., Society for Arabian Studies Monographs No. 2. BAR International Series 1269 (Archaeopress, Oxford: 2004, p. 73).

5 Book of Kings (11:10–14) The Holy Bible, Revised Standard Edition, containing the Old and New Testaments (New York: Penguin Books, 1974).

6 J. C. Mardrus, *Muslim Account of the Visit of Queen Sheba to Jerusalem The Queen of Sheba*. Translated into French from his Arabic text as *The English Version* by E. Powys Mathers (New York: Bernard G. Richards Co., Inc., 1925).

7 Coptic Christianity is the eastern, Monophysite branch of Christianity whose theology denies the divinity of Jesus Christ. Its popular bases are in Christian Egypt and Ethiopia, who share a common patriarch, or pope.

8 My husband and I saw Haile Selassie in 1971 during an official visit to Khartoum on the occasion of the opening of the new Sudan National Museum, which featured an entire floor with a collection of frescos removed from Christian churches at Faras, Sudan, during the lengthy period of Christianity from the 5th to the 15th century AD. They bear a close resemblance to Ethiopian religious paintings.

9 Fatima Mernissi, *The Forgotten Queens of Islam*, 140–1. Translated from the French by Mary Jo Lakeland (Minneapolis: University of Minnesota Press, 1993).

10 Jinn are invisible beings, either harmful or helpful; 'ifreet are demons. *A Dictionary of Modern Written Arabic, Arabic-English*, edited by J. Milton Cowan, third printing (Beirut: Libraire du Liban, 1980).

11 Postcard reproduction of a painting from the National Museum of Ethiopia, "The Queen of Sheba," traditional painting, 1.23 × 2.52 cm, by Bizuhayeu Taddesse.

12 Jan Nederveen Pieterse, *White on Black, Images of Africa and Blacks in Popular Western Culture* (New Haven: Yale University Press, 1992), 25.

13 Isabel Boavida and Manuel Ramos, 2005. "Ambiguous Legitimacy: the Legend of the Queen of Sheba in Popular Ethiopian Painting," in *Annales d'Ethiopie/ Annee* 2005/21: 85–92.

References

Anderson, Knud Tage. "The Queen of the Habasha in Ethiopian History, Tradition and Chronology." *Bulletin of the School of Oriental and African Studies* 63:1 (2000): 31–63.

Boavida, Isabel and Manuel Ramos. "Ambiguous Legitimacy: the Legend of the Queen of Sheba in Popular Ethiopian Painting." In *Annales d'Ethiopie/ Annee 2005/21*. 2005.

Fattovich, Rodolfo. "The 'Pre-Aksumite' State in Northern Ethiopia and Eritrea Reconsidered." In Paul Lunde and Alexandra Porter ed., *Trade and Travel in the Red Sea Region*, in D. Kennet & St J. Simpson ed., Society for Arabian Studies Monographs No. 2. BAR International Series 1269. Oxford: Archaeopress, 2004.

The Holy Bible. *Revised Standard Version, Containing the Old and the New Testaments*. New York: Penguin, 1974.

An Interpretation of The Qur'an. English Translation of the Meanings a Bilingual Edition, translated by Majid Fakhry. New York: New York University Press. 2002.

Kramer, Robert, Richard Lobban and Carolyn Fluehr-Lobban. 2013. *Historical Dictionary of the Sudan*. Lanham, MD: Scarecrow Press.

Mardrus, J.C. *Muslim Account of the Visit of Queen Sheba to Jerusalem* [The Queen of Sheba, Translated into French from his own Arabic Text by J.C. Mardrus, The English Version by E. Powys Mathers]. New York: Bernard G. Richards Co., Inc, 1925.

Mernissi, Fatima. *The Forgotten Queens of Islam*. Translated from the French by Mary Jo Lakeland. Minneapolis, MN: University of Minnesota Press, 1993.

Pieterse, Jan Nederveen. *White on Black, Images of Africa and Blacks in Western Popular Culture*. New Haven, CT: Yale University Press, 1992.

4

Black women in early modern European art and culture

Paul H.D. Kaplan

Drawing on much recent scholarship, this chapter aims to highlight the visibility of women of African descent in European art from the end of the Middle Ages through the Renaissance and Baroque eras (1300–1700).[1] While such visual representations are less numerous than those of Black African men, they are nevertheless relatively common, with hundreds of surviving examples. Most (though not all) of the examples I am about to cite are illustrated in the multiple volumes of the *Image of the Black in Western Art* (new edition, Cambridge, Belknap Press of Harvard University Press, since 2010) or in the project's photo-archive, a major research resource.[2] Several important textual references to Black women (from epic, drama, and lyric poetry) will also be incorporated into this discussion. In this chapter, I use "Black" and "African" to denote people (and images of people) associated with Africa south of the Mediterranean rim.

While the European iconography of Black women during this period includes elements that are still all too familiar, contrasting idealized white "beauty" and white dominance with notions of Africans' supposed inherent subordination and physical imperfection, this visual disparagement of the appearance of Black women is far from universal in the European artistic record. Starting in the early 1500s, some European artworks celebrate the beauty of Black women, and especially within mythological and allegorical subjects, Black female bodies came to be eroticized and sometimes idealized. At the same time, Black women saints were venerated in a few regions of European Christendom, and this era also witnessed part of the very early development of Black Madonna imagery, a phenomenon still significant in modern religious practice.

The four centuries between 1300 and 1700 witnessed the growth of a Black European population, largely (though not entirely) fueled by the importation of enslaved African people through both the West African and the North African slave trade.[3] That growth was irregular in both time and space, with the greatest concentrations to be found in Iberia and Italy, but even in the more northerly regions (Scotland, Germany), a Black presence is attested. The proportion of women and men among these enslaved populations varied, but there were always women present. When domestic service was the principal type of labor required of the enslaved, as it frequently was in Europe, women were often preferred.[4] Nevertheless, in European images of dark-skinned Africans, men are distinctly more prevalent. There are two obvious reasons for this: the general preponderance of male figures in Early Modern art and the salience of the African Wise Man (in depictions of the Adoration of the Magi story) as an exemplar of holy Blackness in religious art.[5] In the many European images (from the 1520s on) of African pages attending on adult white European men and women, the gender of the attending figure is not always easy to determine, but it appears that boys were much more often depicted than girls.[6] The Afro-European population was in general a marginalized one, and on the evidence of imagery, Black women were even more marginalized.

Despite this, Black women are hardly invisible in earlier European art, even if their presence has been regularly ignored until quite recently. They appear in a wide range of roles and in many different media. Some of the artists who created the works cited in this chapter are unidentified, but others are famous names (Dürer, Velázquez, Mantegna) in the history of art. The production of images containing representations of Black women was not confined to a single European region, though Italy and Germany loom large (as with images of Black men).

Sacred subjects

Medieval artists and their audiences in northern Europe were well acquainted with the concept of a Black Queen of Sheba (Hall 2000, 360–5). The Queen's story, told in the Old Testament (1 Kings chapter 10), describes her as a powerful and wealthy ruler of a far-off land (usually identified with southwest Arabia or the adjoining northeast coast of Africa) who makes a long journey to visit the Hebrew King Solomon, to whom she presents precious gifts. The biblical tales make no mention of skin color, but as early as 1181, Nicholas of Verdun's Klosterneuburg Altarpiece (*IBWA* 2:1:120–3, fig. 103) (a metal and enamel work for a church near Vienna) depicts her with an emphatically dark complexion. Other such images followed, including an Austrian manuscript illumination from ca. 1330–1 (*IBWA* 2:2:41–3, fig. 11), where she is accompanied by two Black female attendants. However, after 1400, images of the Queen much more often portray her with light skin, and only some of her attendants (variably male and female) retain an African appearance.[7]

It seems likely that the Black Queen was displaced by the growing importance of the Black Wise Man/King in Adoration of the Magi imagery. The Queen herself survives as a Black woman mostly in a rather rare apocryphal scene where she is shown (and condemned) for encouraging Solomon to worship a pagan idol (*IBWA* 2:2:68–70, figs. 43–5). These xenophobic depictions of African womanhood, which suggest that Solomon has been corrupted by the attractions of an exotic Other, can be linked to a range of further images from the later 1400s in northern Europe: a Foolish Virgin (from a biblical parable) shown as Black on Berne Münster (Switzerland) from 1466–80;[8] a demonic dark-skinned woman assisting at a corrupted or "black" version of the mass in the Dutchman Hieronymus Bosch's *Temptation of St. Anthony* (c. 1500);[9] and in an early fifteenth-century French illumination of Christine de Pisan's treatise on Fortune, a figure described and depicted as a crowned female Janus with a lucky face (white) and an unlucky face (black) (*IBWA* 2:2:101–3, fig. 82). Here, the unfavorable side of fortune is not only dark-skinned but also articulates several of the period's stereotypically African physiognomic features: large turned-up nose, emphatic cheekbones, prominent lips. The abstract European fear of darkness as "unfortunate" meets ethnically specific xenophobia. While in the 1300s and 1400s, European rulers and intellectuals had been intrigued by new knowledge of the Black Christian kingdom of Ethiopia, the pejorative imagery just cited might reflect a longstanding European association of blackness with the demographics of the Islamic world and thus with a civilization which Europeans viewed as their bitter religious and geopolitical rival.

Significantly, more admiring images of dark-skinned women in the later 1400s tend to eliminate the secondary physiognomic elements of African identity (lips, nose, cheekbones, tightly curled hair). A Dutch Bible of ca. 1465–70 includes the rare subject of the Black Bride from the

Old Testament's Song of Songs ("I am black but beautiful O ye daughters of Zion") embracing her allegorical spouse (*IBWA* 2:2:157–9, fig. 136). The Bride's brown skin and earring differentiate her from her similarly dressed pale handmaidens. Solomon is the lover with whom she converses, and this biblical passage may have helped generate images of the Black Queen of Sheba, also rumored to be Solomon's lover. The Black Bride – better known in biblical exegesis than in imagery – may also have played a role in the still only partly understood early development of Black Madonna imagery.[10]

Very dark-skinned images (typically sculptures) of Mary holding an equally dark-skinned infant Christ were abundant throughout Europe by the 1700s, but any hint of the reigning stereotype of African facial features or hair is exceedingly rare in these works. Many of these venerated sacred sculptures, which often date back to the twelfth century, had featured white skin before 1700, though at least one example, that of Le Puy in central France, seems to have had dark skin (and perhaps recognizably African features) already in the late fifteenth century.[11] (Many of these works were destroyed during the French Revolution, while others have been profoundly altered over the centuries, complicating the problem.) However, most Europeans did not explicitly connect Black Madonnas with African identity before 1700.

While Renaissance art had no widely distributed, powerful, sacred Black African female protagonist to rival the African Magus/King of the Adoration story, there were some regional cults of Black women saints. In northern Germany (Brandenburg and Saxony), the veneration of a Black African version of the Roman-Egyptian soldier saint Maurice flourished, and just before the collapse of this cult (due to the spread of Lutheranism), a corresponding female figure (St. Fidis, said to be the sister of Maurice) emerged.[12] In sixteenth-century Iberia, and later in the Americas, a little-known early Christian Ethiopian saint, Efigenia, received new emphasis, and Afro-European confraternities (lay religious associations) were devoted to this daughter of an Ethiopian king.[13]

Servitude and the erotic

But these noble or princely women, ideals of holy Black femininity, had little to do with the reality faced by the enslaved African women who began to arrive in Europe in the late Middle Ages. Only intermittently, however, do the visual arts afford us a view of the kind of ordinary domestic labor African women were compelled to perform: a glimpse can be seen in several early sixteenth-century Portuguese and Italian sacred pictures (*IBWA* 2:2, figs. 195, 198 and 3:1:124–6, fig. 54). Much more common, beginning around 1470, are images which record the place of Black women at aristocratic courts and households. Along with Black men and boys (who appear much earlier in these pictorial roles), Black women were, to put it bluntly, fashionable accessories to the wealthy and powerful, suggesting the reach of European hegemony across the globe.[14] Perhaps the first Black maidservant of this type visible in European art looks down from the ceiling of Andrea Mantegna's *camera picta* in the Ducal Palace of Mantua (finished by 1474) (*IBWA* 2:2:213, fig. 190). This work almost certainly records a specific individual, as the rest of the room is crowded with likenesses of the ruling Gonzaga dynasty and their retainers.

Roughly two decades later, Isabella d'Este, daughter of the ruler of nearby Ferrara, married into the Gonzaga family, and she immediately sought to obtain young Black girls for her entourage (Kaplan 2005). An adolescent African girl was regarded as insufficiently dark in complexion, so early in 1491, Isabella asked her agent in Venice to procure a young and especially dark-skinned Black girl between the ages of one-and-a-half and four. After being thwarted in a bidding war for a whole free African family, including a wife and little girl, by her mother Eleonora duchess of Ferrara, Isabella quickly obtained from a Venetian orphanage a two-year-old Black girl; and in 1497, Isabella purchased another enslaved little Black girl for her sister Chiara.

It seems likely that Mantegna's masterful 1492 drawing, *Judith and Her Maidservant with the Head of Holofernes* (see Figure 4.1), alludes to Isabella and her obsession with African girls. A maidservant to the Jewish heroine is mentioned in the biblical Book of Judith, but no text implies that the servant is African; and the prior iconographic tradition contains no trace of a Black serving girl. Mantegna was eager to please Isabella, and the highly finished drawing may have been a gift to her. The maidservant, unlike Judith, is not idealized and may well be based on a life study, but she is clearly a subordinate character – smaller, younger, frumpier, more compositionally marginal, without Judith's confidence and strength. Mantegna went on to produce three other versions of this composition, and it was recorded in a print, which no doubt helped spread the innovation of the Black maidservant – the motif later appears in works by Correggio, Titian, Paolo Veronese, and other artists (Kaplan 2005, 145–7, fig. 31).

While at least one African woman in Italy, the mother of the illegitimate Alessandro de' Medici, first Duke of Florence, became linked in a more intimate way to a ruling dynasty,[15] it is in German art that we see evidence of a more elevated status of Black women at court. Two elaborate sacred paintings, of ca. 1515 and 1530, incorporate handsome and finely dressed Black women in groups of ladies-in-waiting to duchesses (of Calenberg in the north, and Bavaria in

Figure 4.1 Mantegna's 1492 *Judith and Her Maidservant, Florence, Uffizi.*

the south) (Kaplan 2013, figs. 1.2–1.3, 1.5–1.6). These women are as elaborately arrayed as their white counterparts, and they show the same pious and respectful attitudes to the saintly figures who dominate the works. But while many European images of Black women are derived from the actual presence of individuals of color, there are others which are detached from that social reality. *The Masque of Blackness*, a spectacle produced at the English court in 1605, included the queen and her white ladies-in-waiting dancing in blackface in the roles of the daughters of Niger, who make a pilgrimage to worship an allegorical white sovereign denoting James I. The spectacle survives in imagery only through drawings made by the production designer, Inigo Jones; dark skin was clearly essential, but it does not look as if any other physiognomic features associated with Africans were imitated (see Figure 4.2) (*IBWA* 3:1:242–6, fig. 130).

Figure 4.2 Inigo Jones, Daughter of Niger, from "Masque of Blackness" 1605, Derbyshire, Chatsworth House. The Picture Art Collection / Alamy Stock Photo.

James and his queen, Anne, had previously ruled Scotland, where there was a tradition stretching back at least a century of both Black women at court and also blackface pageantry.[16] (Here, as elsewhere in Europe, Black courtiers comprised both enslaved and free people – manumission was common across the continent, especially at the death of slave-owners.) For example, during a tournament held in 1507 and 1508 in Edinburgh, a performer (either an actual Black woman or a local person in blackface) was dressed up as a noble lady to whom the tournament itself was dedicated; at the final banquet, a mechanical cloud transported her into the heavens. But it is likely that this chivalrous veneration was a parody. No extant works of visual art record it, but the court poet William Dunbar reveals his anti-Black misogyny in verses on this "black ladye with the big lips." Though he feigns praise, her lips and nose are made to seem grotesque, and he compares her to beasts such as apes, toads, and cats. At the end of the poem, she becomes a sexual prize: victorious knights will win her embraces, while the losers must humiliate themselves by kissing her behind. Both revulsion and desire are apparent here, and there were in fact several earlier epic poems in which erotically potent Black ladies figure.[17] Some members of the audience for the *Masque of Blackness*, it is relevant to note, were repulsed by the blacked-up queen and her entourage. Especially in the British Isles, developing notions of aristocratic female beauty which prized pallor ("fairness") in women may have had an impact on these reactions.

Nevertheless, already in the early 1500s, eroticized images of Black women begin to proliferate, though it is not always easy to gauge their implications. The numerous Black women (and a few men) distributed among the entirely naked male and female personages of the enigmatic central panel of Bosch's *Garden of Earthly Delights* (c. 1500–10) are just as difficult to interpret as the work as a whole, but it seems likely that they are meant to amplify the sensuality of the work (*IBWA* 2:2:261–8, figs. 248–53). (They might be connected to European reports of unembarrassed exposure of the body among African and Native American populations.) The fully clothed figure of an African woman who holds up the coat of arms of a Swiss family (Basel, stained glass, 1521) shows off her décolletage, and her earrings and turban mark her as an exotic Other (*IBWA* 2:2:28, 30, fig. I.14). [In the 1520s, the wearing of earrings was still dismissed by older Europeans as a "Moorish" fashion (*IBWA* 3:1:109).] Sexually provocative white figures in both religious and mythological paintings are increasingly accompanied by Black women attendants who are either nude or scantily clad. In Marco Bigio's *Three Fates* (Siena, c. 1535) (*IBWA* 3:1:133–4, fig. 60), the Fates themselves are white, but just behind them stands an equally nude Black woman who squeezes milk from one of her breasts. (Medieval science recommended the milk of Black nursemaids as especially nourishing.[18]) Likewise, the Dutch Cornelis van Haarlem's *Bathsheba at Her Bath* (1594) (Spicer 2012, 41, fig. 16) depicts a white beauty attended by a shapely, unclothed Black woman.

A subservient position was not always required, especially in works of art on a smaller scale. The late Renaissance rage for carved cameos encouraged images of Blacks, as the onyx stone used frequently had a dark layer.[19] Heads of Africans are common, both male and female, and one of the loveliest (Milan?, late sixteenth century) depicts a Black woman adorned with a crescent moon, the symbol of Diana herself (see Figure 4.3) (*IBWA* 3:1:151–4, fig. 76). Indeed, ancient art had sometimes represented Diana in dark stone, and a ca. 1520 astrological fresco in Mantua had shown this version of the goddess with dark skin and features of African type (*IBWA* 3:1:103–4, fig. 41). Furthermore, a bronze statuette depicting a standing nude woman, of uncertain authorship (Italy?, France?, Low Countries?, late sixteenth century), used the darkened patina of the material, confirmed by the conventional marks of an African face, to represent a Black woman at her bath (in the mode of Venus) (Spicer 2012, 51, 128, fig. 40).[20] This work must have been popular, as many castings survive today. Its Mannerist attenuation of the body's proportions was then much esteemed and can also be found in an African female nude

Figure 4.3 Black Diana, cameo. Vienna, Kunsthistorisches Museum.

embodying the concept of Night in a 1594 engraving designed by Hendrik Goltzius (*Black Is Beautiful*, 53–6). While the normative canon of female beauty in this era increasingly stressed light skin ("fairness"), the piquancy of dark skin was also appealing to some, as in Giambattista Marino's poem in which the white male author professes himself a "slave" of an alluring (and presumably enslaved) Black woman (*IBWA* 3:1:172; Hall 2000, 346–9).

The nudity of the *Black Woman at Her Bath* statuette is elegant and classicizing, but there were already early signs of a coarser, hypersexualized approach, probably encouraged by the slave trade's burgeoning exploitation of the labor and sexuality of Black women, especially in colonial outposts.[21] A disturbing picture by the Bologna painter Bartolomeo Passarotti (c. 1580) (*IBWA* 3:1:154–7, fig. 79) combines grotesque, lascivious figures from the white underclass with an equally grotesque and lascivious Black couple, whose tongues protrude from their mouths.[22] All are in the grip of drink, and the picture alludes to an ancient bacchanal, but the setting is clearly contemporary and proletarian.[23] Dark skin had long been associated with female lustfulness in European science and medicine (Biller 2005, 483–7). In a troubling Dutch picture of the seventeenth century, by Christian van Couwenbergh, the sexual humiliation and apparent rape of a Black woman by white men is the theme, yet it is treated as a comic event.[24] No doubt, the rapid expansion of the Dutch slave trade in these years affected the dehumanization of the Black woman in this painting. These works bring us closer to the norms of racist iconography as it developed more fully from the eighteenth to the twentieth century.

Anthropology, allegory, and individuality

The increasing European global hegemony of the sixteenth and seventeenth centuries also led to the rise of European images (especially prints) categorizing the peoples of the world in a mixture of triumphalist and proto-anthropological modes. Black women, of course, appeared in this imagery. In a 1509 woodcut (after a design by the German Hans Burgkmair), the inhabitants of "Guinea" (West Africa) include a woman adorned only in jewelry, suckling a child (*IBWA* 2:2:272–5, fig. 257).[25] The man and children in this composition are also naked, the absence of clothing signifying an uncivilized state rather than erotic attraction. The costume books and illustrated travel treatises of the later 1500s, however, usually clothed exemplars of Black African women, especially if they were meant to signify members of the upper echelons of African society (*IBWA* 3:2:49–50, fig. 32).

In allegorical images, nudity returns, as for example in the famous title page to Abraham Ortelius' influential atlas, the *Theatrum Orbis Terrarum* (first ed. Antwerp, 1570) (see Figure 4.4) (*IBWA* 3:2:77–9, fig. 50). This composition illustrates the four continents with female figures: Europe and Asia are lavishly dressed, while America is naked and Africa nearly so. The point was to emphasize the distinction between civilization and barbarism, and as the Atlantic world came more and more to be defined by the enslavement of Africans in the seventeenth century, Black women (and men) are depicted with little or no clothing with ever greater frequency. One of the justifications for the slave trade was that it supposedly redeemed Africans from barbarism (in social and religious terms), and nakedness was a prime symbol of that state.

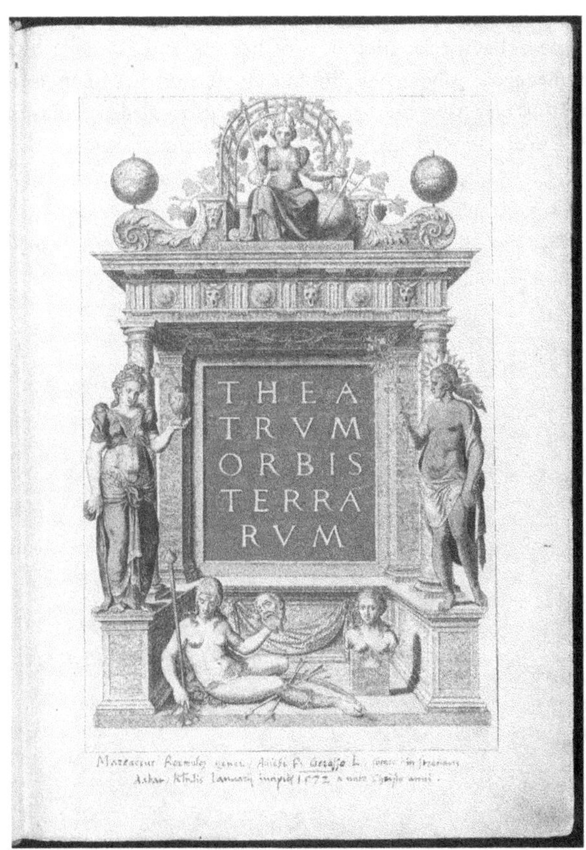

Figure 4.4 Abraham Ortelius title page to Theatrum Orbis Terrarum, 1570. Lilly Library Bloomington.

In the course of the 1600s, a much more explicit visual symbol of white hegemony over Black populations emerged: the slave collar. While Black men were the normative bearers of this device in visual representation, toward the end of the century, it began to be applied to women, as in a 1688 picture by the Swiss Gregor Brandmüller.[26] The enslaved woman, apparently a nursemaid to four little white boys, is naked from the waist up save for the shining silver collar. This brutal painting anticipates the genre of the "mammy" which later developed in the United States.

While in most cases, the enslaved status of Black female figures in a European image can only be fully confirmed by the inclusion of some explicit attribute like the slave collar, there are many works where either the context or the image itself strongly implies enslavement. One of these is Albrecht Dürer's exquisite silverpoint drawing of a Black woman (1521), now in the Uffizi in Florence, inscribed "Katherina, twenty years old" (see Figure 4.5) (*IBWA* 2:2, 3:1). Like Mantegna's 1492 *Judith and Her Maidservant* (see Figure 4.1), this is a finely finished drawing, not a casual sketch. It has many of the features of a commissioned portrait – name and age, bust-length 3/4 pose, a profound seriousness of expression. It cannot be described as a genre study or sketch for future use – Dürer's prints and paintings depict many Black men but no women.

Yet Katherina could not have commissioned the work, since Dürer's diary makes it clear that she was the servant of the Portuguese business consul in Antwerp, and as at this point Portugal was the epicenter of the European slave trade, she was almost certainly enslaved. Her lightly sketched outfit is respectable, as those of the enslaved in wealthy households often were. Her downcast eyes model appropriately humble behavior for members of her sex and class, yet her expression also seems to manifest her own melancholy at her difficult fate. Dürer has been able to see and make a kind of loveliness for this face that both avoids idealization and yet makes Katherina's beauty unmistakable to the European viewer. The inclusion of her name in the

Figure 4.5 Albrecht Dürer, *Katherina*, 1521, Florence, Uffizi. The Picture Art Collection / Alamy Stock Photo.

Figure 4.6 Diego Velázquez, *Kitchen Maid*, ca. 1619. Dublin, National Gallery of Ireland. Album / Alamy Stock Photo.

inscription is precious to us today, as it is one of very few of any Black subject in a European work of this era to have been preserved.

Nearly a century later, Diego Velázquez painted two versions of a composition usually known as the *Kitchen Maid* (see Figure 4.6) (*IBWA* 3:1:202–4, fig. 112).[27] These works are part of Velazquez's production of genre scenes of the urban poor during his early years in Seville, a global commercial center and a major slave entrepôt. In the version now in Dublin, Christ's revelation of his resurrected self to two of his apostles at Emmaus is blurrily visible in the background; in the other, the Black serving-woman is alone. In both, the labor of washing up is balanced by a poignancy of expression. The Dublin picture paradoxically foregrounds a socially marginal individual (in terms of race, class, and gender), with holy male figures consigned to a liminal space behind. The message is clear: Christ's offer of salvation is to all, including those of the lowest status. Like Dürer's *Katherina*, Velázquez's composition endorses the humanity of Black women, but even these generally sympathetic works stress humility as well. The notion of a potent Black femininity is increasingly rare in European art toward the end of the Early Modern period.

Although the Image of the Black in Western Art project has been of inestimable help in bringing to light the iconography of blackness in the European tradition, many more Early Modern individual images of Black women remain to be discovered, and the intensive analysis of these images and their relationship with the social realities of the period is still at a preliminary level. In the next stage of research, among the most vital questions to address are the distinctions between the depiction of Black and white women, and the connections to the representations of Asian and indigenous American women. Through such comparative studies, a more distinct characterization of the European image of Black women is likely to emerge.

Notes

1 One of the few to address this topic directly is the cultural historian Kim F. Hall, in her "Object into Object? Some Thoughts on the Presence of Black Women in Early Modern Culture," in Peter Erickson and Clark Hulse, eds., *Early Modern Visual Culture: Representation, Race and Empire in Renaissance England* (Philadelphia: Penn Press, 2000), 346–79.

2 Edited by David Bindman and Henry Louis Gates, Jr.; see especially vol. 2, parts 1–2, and vol. 3, parts 1–2; cited as *IBWA* in the following. The two versions of the photo-archive are housed at the Hutchins Center at Harvard (also digitally available on Artstor) and the Warburg Institute at the University of London.

3 Charles Verlinden, *L'esclavage dans l'Europe médiévale*, 2 vols. (Bruges: De Tempel and Ghent: Rijksuniversiteit, 1955–77); T.F. Earle and K.J.P. Lowe, eds., *Black Africans in Renaissance Europe* (Cambridge: Cambridge University Press, 2005). While people of color had been present in Europe well before 1300, especially in areas like Spain and Sicily, which had once been controlled by Islamic powers, their numbers expanded after 1300 in many other areas.

4 Sergio Tognetti, "The Trade in Black African Slaves in Fifteenth Century Florence," 213–24, in Earle and Lowe.

5 Paul H.D. Kaplan, *The Rise of the Black Magus in Western Art* (Ann Arbor: UMI Research Press, 1985).

6 See for example the portrait of Laura Dianti by Titian; Paul H.D. Kaplan, "Isabella d'Este and Black African Women," 125–54, in Earle and Lowe.

7 See for example the ca. 1510–20 miniature in the Grimani Breviary; Paul H.D. Kaplan, "The Calenberg Altarpiece: Black African Christians in Renaissance Germany," in Mischa Honeck, Martin Klimke, and Anne Kuhlmann, eds., *Germany and the Black Diaspora: Points of Contact, 1250–1914* (New York: Berghahn Books, 2013), 21–37, 29, fig. 1-4.

8 Hans Werner Debrunner, *Presence and Prestige: Africans in Europe* (Basel: Basler Afrika Bibliographien, 1979), 61, pl. 6.

9 Pilar Silva Maroto, ed., *Bosch: The 5ᵗʰ Centenary Exhibition* (London: Thames & Hudson, 2017), 72–3, 238–45.

10 See also *IBWA* 2:1:202–3 on the Bride. On Black Madonnas: Sophie Cassagnes-Brouquet, *Vierges noires* (Rodez: Editions du Rouerge, 2000); Monique Scheer, "From Majesty to Mystery: Changes in the Meanings of Black Madonnas from the Sixteenth to Nineteenth Centuries," *American Historical Review* 107 (2002): 1412–40.

11 Elisa A. Foster, "Out of Egypt: Inventing the Black Madonna of Le Puy in Image and Text," *Studies in Iconography* 37 (2016): 1–30.

12 *IBWA* 2:1:193, fig. 166.

13 Erin Kathleen Rowe, "Visualizing Black Sanctity in Early Modern Spanish Polychrome Sculpture," in Pamela Patton, ed., *Envisioning Others: Race, Color and the Visual in Iberia and Latin America* (Leiden: Brill, 2016), 51–82, 55, 65–8.

14 Esther Schreuder, "'Blacks' in Court Culture in the Period 1300–1900; Propaganda and Consolation," in *Black Is Beautiful: Rubens to Dumas* (Zwolle: Waanders, 2008), 20–31.

15 John Brackett, "Race and Rulership: Alessandro de' Medici, First Medici Duke of Florence, 1529–1537," in Earle and Lowe, 303–25. Alessandro's daughter Giulia appears in a Renaissance portrait but without a particularly marked African identity; Joaneath Spicer, ed., *Revealing the African Presence in Renaissance Europe* (Baltimore: Walters Art Museum, 2012), 114, fig. 64.

16 Louise Olga Fradenburg, *City, Marriage, Tournament: Arts of Rule in Late Medieval Scotland* (Madison: University of Wisconsin Press, 1991), 244–64.

17 Jeffrey Jerome Cohen, "On Saracen Enjoyment: Some Fantasies of Race in Late Medieval France and England," *Journal of Medieval and Early Modern Studies* 31 (2001): 113–46, 119; Thomas Hahn, "The Difference the Middle Ages Makes: Color and Race before the Modern World," *Journal of Medieval and Early Modern Studies* 31 (2001): 1–37, 17.

18 Peter Biller, "Black Women in Medieval Scientific Thought," in *La Pelle Umana/The Human Skin* (*Micrologus* 13) (Florence: Sismel/Edizioni del Galluzzo, 2005), 477–92, 479–83.

19 Gisela Schäffer, *Schwarze Schoenheit: "Mohrinnen-Kameen"-Preziosen der Spätrenaissance im Kunsthisorischen Museum Wien. Ein Beitrag aus postkolonialer Perspektive* (Marburg: Jonas Verlag, 2009); Kim F. Hall, *Things of Darkness: Economies of Race and Gender in Early Modern England* (Ithaca: Cornell University Press, 1995), 215–27.

20 Maraike Bückling, *Der Negervenus* (Frankfurt: Liebieghaus, 1991).

21 Jennifer L. Morgan, "'Some Could Suckle over Their Shoulder': Male Travelers, Female Bodies, and the Gendering of Racial Ideology, 1500–1770," *William and Mary Quarterly* 54 (1997): 167–92.

22 Paul H.D. Kaplan, "Bartolomeo Passarotti and 'Comic' Images of Black Africans in Early Modern Italian Art," in Angela Rosenthal with Adrian Randolph and David Bindman, eds., *No Laughing Matter: Visual Humor in Ideas of Race, Nationality and Ethnicity* (Hanover, N.H.: UPNE/The Dartmouth College Press, 2015), 23–48.

23 However, half a century later, a Dutch painter illustrated a scene from an ancient novel with a lustful Ethiopian king and queen, whose features and expressions are caricatured; see *IBWA* 3:1:325–6, fig. 188.
24 Diane Wolfthal, *Images of Rape: The '"Heroic" Tradition and Its Alternatives* (Cambridge: Cambridge University Press, 1999), 189–97.
25 Stephanie Leitch, *Mapping Ethnography in Early Modern Germany; New Worlds in Print Culture* (New York: Palgrave Macmillan, 2010), 63–99.
26 Alain Parent, *Une autre Amérique* (La Rochelle: Le Musée, 1982), 34, no. 6.
27 Tanya J. Tiffany, "Light, Darkness, and African Salvation: Velázquez's *Supper at Emmaus*," *Art History* 31 (2008): 33–56.

Bibliography

Biller, Peter. "Black Women in Medieval Scientific Thought." In *La Pelle Umana / The Human Skin (Micrologus 13)*, 477–92. Florence: Sismel/Edizioni del Galluzzo, 2005.
Bindman, David, and Henry Louis Gates, Jr. eds. *Image of the Black in Western Art*. New edition. Vol. 2, parts 1–2, and vol. 3, parts 1-2. Cambridge: Belknap Press of Harvard University Press, 2010–12.
Brackett, John. "Race and Rulership: Alessandro de' Medici, First Medici Duke of Florence, 1529–1537." In *Earle and Lowe*, 303–25.
Bückling, Maraike. *Der Negervenus*. Frankfurt: Liebieghaus, 1991.
Cassagnes-Brouquet, Sophie. *Vierges Noires*. Rodez: Editions du Rouerge, 2000.
Cohen, Jeffrey Jerome. "On Saracen Enjoyment: Some Fantasies of Race in Late Medieval France and England." *Journal of Medieval and Early Modern Studies* 31 (2001): 113–46.
Debrunner, Hans Werner. *Presence and Prestige: Africans in Europe*. Basel: Basler Afrika Bibliographien, 1979.
Earle, T.F., and K.J.P. Lowe, eds. *Black Africans in Renaissance Europe*. Cambridge: Cambridge University Press, 2005.
Foster, Elisa A. "Out of Egypt: Inventing the Black Madonna of Le Puy in Image and Text." *Studies in Iconography* 37 (2016): 1–30.
Fradenburg, Louise Olga. *City, Marriage, Tournament: Arts of Rule in Late Medieval Scotland*. Madison: University of Wisconsin Press, 1991.
Hahn, Thomas. "The Difference the Middle Ages Makes: Color and Race before the Modern World." *Journal of Medieval and Early Modern Studies* 31 (2001): 1–37.
Hall, Kim F. *Things of Darkness: Economies of Race and Gender in Early Modern England*. Ithaca: Cornell University Press, 1995.
Hall, Kim F. "Object into Object? Some Thoughts on the Presence of Black Women in Early Modern Culture." In *Early Modern Visual Culture: Representation, Race and Empire in Renaissance England*, edited by Peter Erickson and Clark Hulse, 356–79. Philadelphia: Penn Press, 2000.
Kaplan, Paul H.D. *The Rise of the Black Magus in Western Art*. Ann Arbor: UMI Research Press, 1985.
Kaplan, Paul H.D. "Isabella d'Este and Black African Women." In *Earle and Lowe*, 125–54, 2005.
Kaplan, Paul H.D. "The Calenberg Altarpiece: Black African Christians in Renaissance Germany." In *Germany and the Black Diaspora: Points of Contact, 1250–1914*, edited by Mischa Honeck, Martin Klimke, and Anne Kuhlmann, 21–37. New York: Berghahn Books, 2013.
Kaplan, Paul H.D. "Bartolomeo Passarotti and 'Comic' Images of Black Africans in Early Modern Italian Art." In *No Laughing Matter: Visual Humor in Ideas of Race, Nationality and Ethnicity*, edited by Angela Rosenthal with Adrian Randolph and David Bindman, 23–48. Hanover, NH: UPNE/The Dartmouth College Press, 2015.
Leitch, Stephanie. *Mapping Ethnography in Early Modern Germany; New Worlds in Print Culture*. New York: Palgrave MacMillan, 2010.
Morgan, Jennifer L. "'Some Could Suckle over Their Shoulder': Male Travelers, Female Bodies, and the Gendering of Racial Ideology, 1500–1770." *William and Mary Quarterly* 54 (1997): 167–92.
Parent, Alain. *Une autre Amérique*. La Rochelle: Le Musée, 1982.
Rowe, Erin Kathleen. "Visualizing Black Sanctity in Early Modern Spanish Polychrome Sculpture." In *Envisioning Others: Race, Color and the Visual in Iberia and Latin America*, edited by Pamela Patton, 51–82. Leiden: Brill, 2016.
Schäffer, Gisela. *Schwarze Schoenheit: "Mohrinnen-Kameen"-Preziosen der Spätrenaissance im Kunsthisorischen Museum Wien. Ein Beitrag aus postkolonialer Perspektive*. Marburg: Jonas Verlag, 2009.

Scheer, Monique. "From Majesty to Mystery: Changes in the Meanings of Black Madonnas from the Sixteenth to Nineteenth Centuries." *American Historical Review* 107 (2002): 1412–40.

Schreuder, Esther. "'Blacks' in Court Culture in the Period 1300-1900; Propaganda and Consolation." In *Black is Beautiful: Rubens to Dumas*, 20–31. Zwolle: Waanders, 2008.

Silva Maroto, Pilar, ed. *Bosch: The 5th Centenary Exhibition*. London: Thames & Hudson, 2017.

Spicer, Joaneath, ed. *Revealing the African Presence in Renaissance Europe*. Baltimore: Walters Art Museum, 2012.

Tiffany, Tanya J. "Light, Darkness, and African Salvation: Velázquez's *Supper at Emmaus*." *Art History* 31 (2008): 33–56.

Tognetti, Sergio. "The Trade in Black African Slaves in Fifteenth Century Florence." In *Earle and Lowe*, 213–24.

Verlinden, Charles. *L'esclavage dans l'Europe médiévale*. 2 vols. Bruges: De Tempel and Ghent: Rijksuniversiteit, 1955–77.

Wolfthal, Diane. *Images of Rape: The 'Heroic' Tradition and Its Alternatives*. Cambridge: Cambridge University Press, 1999.

5

Black women in early modern Spanish literature

Nicholas R. Jones

We must proceed with caution when examining and retelling the lives of Black women in early modern Iberia (Castile, Catalonia, and Portugal). Sub-Saharan African women and their descendants abound in the cultural history, literary production, and visual culture of early modern Iberia. Omnipresent, Black women lived in Renaissance urban centers across Portugal and Spain, such as the cosmopolitan cities Lisbon and Seville. And in these metropolises, Iberian society often celebrated and exalted Black women's beauty, strength, and value. In Lisbon, for instance, it was not uncommon for the locals across all rungs of society to identify the city with Black femininity and Black womanhood via the phrase "Black women are the mothers of Lisbon."[1] Like Lisbon, the city of Seville and the kingdom at large had a voluminous Black population that reached a height of 11 percent. Seville's Black population was ethnically diverse, originating from Angola and the Congo Basin, the Cape Verde Islands, the Kingdom of Dahomey, the Senegambia and the Rivers of Guinea, as well as Mozambique and neighboring Portuguese outposts in East Africa and Goa. The overwhelming presence of Blacks and their descendants in Seville gave way to the city's alias as the *tablero de ajedrez*, or chessboard table. In these cities, the real lives and vitality of Iberian Black women cannot be disassociated from this rich heritage and legacy.

What is more, the lived experience and cultural representation of Black women in Iberian early modernity – spanning roughly the late fifteenth to early eighteenth centuries – shared little to no resemblance to early modern Anglophone and Francophone depictions of and reactions to Black women. During the Renaissance, clergymen and travelers from northern Europe openly expressed their visceral shock and disapproval of Portugal and Spain's large Black populations, most notably the presence of free Blacks who visually displayed their power and wealth, as well as the common sight of interracial unions between Black women and white men.[2] In this chapter, I would like to nuance and underscore for my readers that the lives of early modern Iberian Black women *cannot* and *must not* be flattened to the sole example of Black Venus in France or other so-called "Negress" figures typically imagined in Anglophone and other northern European contexts. To be clear, I do not wish to claim that early modern Iberian society operated as an idyllic, utopic paradise where *misogynoir* did not affect Black women. Many historical records, literary texts, and pictorial images can illustrate this fact. However, my main contention here is that the early modern Iberian archive – in its complexity and vastness of sources – and the literary works that mirror it empower me to tell the stories of Black women who disrupt the scholarly narrative we have thus inherited from Anglophone and Francophone sources – North American and European alike – that assumes and positions Iberia as having lacked and not offered any significant contribution to Black women's lives in the African diaspora. Perhaps we owe this sentiment to the legacy of the propagandistic anti-Spanish Black Legend catapulted by the English, Dutch, and French.

Black women in early modern Iberia

To that effect, what was the status of real Black women in early modern Iberia? Between the fourteenth and eighteenth centuries, sub-Saharan Africans living in the Iberian Peninsula were both enslaved and free. They contributed to early modern Iberian society and global imperial expansion by serving as cartographers and mariners on long-distance transatlantic voyages, laborers who built urban infrastructure, and free migrants who produced crops and material goods. Some worked as apprentices in art studios and ceramic workshops, while others were butchers, cobblers, fisherman, public executioners, scribes, stable workers, and wine makers. Regarding our interests, the lives of Iberian Black women – enslaved and free – also varied. The most common means by which the enslaved could have acquired her freedom was first, by buying it; second, by being voluntarily freed by the owner; or third, by the owner dying. Because a large-scale agrarian plantation society, like those operative in Brazil, the Caribbean, and the United States, did not exist in Spain or Portugal, historical records document enslaved Black women working in a variety of spaces, including bakeries, brothels, convents, churches, orphanages, and royal palaces. Enslaved or not, Iberian Black women were skilled and talented, for they brought with them a repository of knowledge from sub-Saharan Africa. Most notable are the street vendors known as *regateiras*. Brandão in his census reports that on the Lisbon waterfront, early in the morning, "black women sold rice pudding, couscous, and chickpeas from pots which they carried on their heads."[3]

The fascinating lives of free Black women in early modern Iberia dispel common misconceptions for present-day readers. In rural areas, for example, Black women cultivated and tilled the land of their own farms in the countryside, whereas others performed as actresses in theater troupes. Early modern Iberian society created and maintained institutional networks whereby free Black women owned taverns and inns. On both sides of the Atlantic, in Lisbon and port cities across Spain and the Spanish Caribbean, these African and African-descended women were known as either *negras horras* or *morenas horras* (in Portugal, *negras forras*).[4] These women used their assets and monies earned to free other enslaved Black women and men, pay local taxes, and build community spaces – both religious and secular – for Blacks living in their immediate communities.

To further demonstrate the complexity and richness of free Black women's lives in Spain, let us consider the embroideress Catalina de Soto, known as the "Queen of Black Women," or "*Reina de negras*" in Spanish. The jurist and historian Francisco Bermúdez de Pedraza describes Catalina as follows: "I met her as a young man and used to tag along behind her because I was so amazed by the great novelty of seeing a clean and well-dressed black woman with two white women servants walking behind her."[5] She was famous for her embroidery and needlework; Bermúdez de Pedraza records that de Soto also appraised trousseaux for wealthy white women during their engagements.

The meticulous record keeping of the Spanish Inquisition serves as another site that has preserved the agency, power, and savvy of Iberian Black women. The life story of Catalina Muñoz from sixteenth-century Valencia offers us another glimpse into the ways in which real Black women channeled the Divine through healing, conjure work, and divination. Catalina obtained her power and position by capitalizing on the fame – often referred to in her trial record as "*escándolo*" ["scandal"] – she acquired as a spiritual advisor and healer to the Valencian religious community of Sanct Martín Church. Muñoz established a personal and public relationship with God and the saints.

Before her trial in 1588, Saints Francis, Domingus, Sebastian, Vicente Ferrer, Michael the Archangel, and Lady Magdalene appeared to Catalina in visions. Walking through the streets of Valencia, she displayed the wounds and crown of thorns of the Passion of Our Lord. As a healer, she healed the infirm and returned straying lovers to their partners from concubines by breaking illicit relationships with her prayers. Muñoz's trial record states that she "amassed a large clientele who ran after her, begging her to reveal occult and secret things that they desired to know."[6] While inquisitorial authorities and historians alike have attempted to reduce Catalina to misogynist clichés, she, as a free Black woman living in sixteenth-century Valencia, sustained her social standing and power through capitalizing on the fame of her visions to become the spiritual counselor of not only her clients and acquaintances but also the city's religious elite. I reject the notion that Muñoz's and de Soto's lives are, were, and therefore must be treated as "exceptional." To do so only empowers and reinforces a reductively pejorative stance on Black women's agency, personhood, and worth, as if they could never escape, resist, or supersede the clutches of European colonialism and anti-Black racism.

Black women abound in the literary production of early modern Iberia. Omnipresent, these women bear the names Antonia, Boruga, Catalina, Dominga, Eva, Francisca, Guiomar, Ines, Margarita, Maria, Lucrecia, and Sofia, to name only a handful, which also mirror real Black women documented in numerous archival documents ranging from baptismal records, bills of sale, marriage licenses, Inquisition dossiers and testimonies, royal inventories, and wills. In the pages that follow, this chapter analyzes a short-skit scene from the playwright Lope de Rueda's play *Los engañados*. In doing so, I argue for highlighting Iberian Black women's agency, authority, and power – each codified in forms of Africanized Spanish (*habla de negros*) and material culture – in order to destabilize and revise present-day critics' and readers' misguided and misunderstood perceptions of early modern Iberian Black women as obscenely hypersexual and brutishly weak.[7]

A literary case study: Lope de Rueda's Guiomar in *Comedia de los Engañados*

In the third act of *Los engañados* (1538/1558), Lope de Rueda showcases the domestic house servant Guiomar, who argues with the aggressive white house servant Julieta and reasons with the "open-minded" *dama* Clavela.[8] In this *paso*, or short skit, Rueda plots a two-pronged ideological viewpoint about race relations in Renaissance Spain: (1) anti-Black sentiments against Black Africans (as demonstrated by Julieta) and (2) an awareness of Black humanity and personhood (as demonstrated by Clavela). Throughout the skit, Julieta violently attacks Guiomar because she talks back and refuses to renounce her noble sub-Saharan African lineage. In particular, this scene showcases Guiomar speaking in *habla de negros*. Scholarly readings of *habla de negros* provided by Hispanists and linguists since the 1960s have traditionally emphasized the burlesque, comical, and picturesque aspects of the speech form. Spanish philologist Frida Weber de Kurlat, for example, describes the *habla de negros* according to its "posibilidades estéticas y dramáticas puramente cómico-burlescas" [aesthetic and dramatic possibilities that are purely comical and burlesque] [1962, Weber de Kurlat, 139]. Even recent scholarship has repeatedly insisted that "black Spanish must be understood as a linguistic fabrication used as a comic device [that] is a purely literary language" (Lipski, "Perspectivas," 301–5).[9]

59

I propose an alternative reading of *habla de negros* that, while acknowledging that this comical and burlesque speech employs racist appropriations of Africanized Spanish, also highlights its inherent subversive power within a particular historical context. As I maintain throughout *Staging* Habla de Negros: *Radical Performances of the African Diaspora in Early Modern Spain,*

> [j]ust as much as the critique and deconstruction of "white" literary constructions of *habla de negros* are undoubtedly valid, my scholarly endeavor is not centered around nor fixated on repeating a scholarly narrative that has tendentiously emphasized the way in which white Spanish poets and playwrights have excoriated Blackness through their putative anti-Black stereotyping via habla de negros speech forms.

Via the literary case study of Guiomar, and other Black women who spoke in *habla de negros*, real or otherwise, I channel Black speech through the Bakhtinian paradigms of the carnivalesque and heteroglossia. I turn to these concepts in order to demonstrate how *habla de negros* texts empower the unwritten speech of their Black African speakers. While this is not always evident in every single *habla de negros* work, I aim to highlight the way in which practitioners of Africanized Spanish utilize their Black characters to simultaneously reify and contest prevailing stereotypes while also speaking with an inherent expressive power, or heteroglossia, that situates them as subversive, thinking Black subjects.[10]

To demonstrate Julieta's and Guiomar's point of contention in the text, I cite the crux of the three women's conflicted exchange as follows:

GUIOMAR: Jesus, Jesus! Doesn't your Grace think to ask who I am? God knows, and the entire world knows, that I'm the niece of Queen Berbasina; in-laws of the Marquis of Cucurucú, across the seas and lands.

CLAVELA: Your aunt was a Queen, Guiomar?

GUIOMAR: Oh, my Lady! Your Grace thinks that I'm a daughter of some black wretch in these parts? It has been a century since Madam Bialaga has been dead.

CLAVELA: What a respectable name she had to last her for a century!

GUIOMAR: Yes, my Lady. Madam Bialaga was my mother's name, and my father's name was Eliomor. But he prefers the name Don Diego.

JULIETA: Look how you just run your mouth. What respectable names for a dog!

GUIOMAR: That's why my first son, who was born in Portugal, is called Dieguito; like his grandfather.

CLAVELA: His grandfather you mean to say.

GUIOMAR: Yes, my Lady, his grandfather.

CLAVELA: Do you have any children, Guiomar?

GUIOMAR: Oh my Lady! Don't bring that up, for it makes me cry. I have a son who's in the Indies of San Juan, Puerto Rico. This August he wrote me a letter. He's as fresh as a countryside flower over there! Oh, how I miss my son so much!

JULIETA: How foolish and drunk!

GUIOMAR: Who's drunk, you fresh bitch? Oh get me a hammer! I swear to God I hope bad whoring falls on you, such that you never see the sight of meat or get laid!

CLAVELA: Oh how bitter. You mean to say, "carnestoliendas"; you're a horrible speaker!

JULIETA: I hope you get syphilis! How about that!

GUIOMAR: Go on, you cowardly crud; I'm not salvaging my honor on you.

JULIETA: Oh what a fantasy! Hush then, Queen Black Bitch, since your Highness has now sent all of her blacks to make gunpowder.

GUIOMAR: Diarrhea mouth! You and your shit-filled mouth! Take this stick here and go fuck
yourself.
CLAVELA: Enough, let her be Guiomar. If not, then tell me: what is it that your son wrote in
the letter?
GUIOMAR: I've memorized what my son said:
    "My most Illustrious mother, Guiomar:
    The letter I'm writing to you isn't a farewell, but rather a polite gesture of saying that
I'm fine and all is well. Blessed be God. Praise be to God. Amen."
    Oh! May God give him life. My son is my heart; he came from this belly here!
CLAVELA: Don't cry, Guiomar, don't cry.
GUIOMAR: I have no other choice, because we've gone through it all; as deep as pockets run.[11]

This passage rehearses a critical moment where Guiomar articulates her authority, which is
inextricably linked to her sub-Saharan African agency in the following two ways: (1) her noble
lineage and familial bonds traceable to West Africa and (2) the larger history of Luso-African
diplomacy and letter writing. For skeptics of Guiomar's humanity, intelligence, and power in
this scene, I underscore her embodiment as a savvy Black woman who puts on notice the racist
ideology and logic that deems enslaved Black women as illiterate and inept.

The names of women Guiomar shares in the abovecited quote – her aunt Reina Berbasina
[Queen Berbasina] and her mother Doña Bialaga [Lady Bialaga] – signal her affiliation with
and genealogical connection to real West African aristocracy. What I observe here in Rueda's
portrayal of historically rooted references to Spanish sociocultural exchanges with West-Central
Africa is not far-fetched. In fifteenth-century Iberia, for instance, the first Black Africans arriving in major urban centers such as Lisbon and Seville were free emissaries and royal sovereigns. Although a traditional reading may dismiss words such as "Berbasina," "Bialaga," and
"Cucurucú" [cock-a-doodle-doo] as the immediate comic-induced effects of *habla de negros*
language, I historicize the etymology of "Berbasina" – as it relates to Guiomar's reference to her
aunt as Queen Berbasina – in late-sixteenth-century Iberian terms as "an ethnonym derived
from the Wolof political title *Bur ba Siin*, meaning the 'ruler of Siin.' Like its neighbor Saloum,
Siin was a Serer homeland that had been incorporated into the former Jolof empire. Serers
from both Siin and Saloum were known to Iberians as 'Berbersí,' 'Berbecín,' or 'Berbacins.'"[12]
Borrowing from David Wheat's brilliant *Atlantic Africa and the Spanish Caribbean, 1570–1640*,
I frame Guiomar's connection to Berbasina historically in order to center these proper nouns
as real sites that once existed and facilitated sub-Saharan African and Iberian trade. Even more,
the word "Bialaga" gestures a relationship to the Bight of Biafra. While Guiomar's aunt (Queen
Berbasina) and mother (Lady Bialaga) could have been hypothetical royal sovereigns, the fact
that she positions them as "cuñados de la marqués de Cucurucú, por an mar y por a tierras"[13]
[the sisters-in-law (or coinage; money), bound by sea and land, of the Marquis of Cucurucú] is
highly erudite and suggestive on Rueda's part.

The playwright's *cuñados* wordplay aligns Guiomar's maternal elders with African nobility, the
minting of coins and other metal objects, *and* the monetization of Black bodies (especially the
offspring of royal African sovereigns sent to the Iberian Peninsula, and in this case, Guiomar). In
the context of *cuñados*, Rueda foregrounds – as mediated by Guiomar's *habla de negros* language –
a familial bond and genealogical logic that are then overlaid with the economic subtext of slave
trading. Guiomar's agentive voice, as Rueda designs it in the text, highlights the (re)production
of people like that of a *cuño* [stamp; seal] that also (re)produces the proto-capitalist modernity of
an effigy minted by the stamp itself. Guiomar's insightful commentary positions her as a thinking subject who in one sense, inverts racial relations and in another sense, subverts the power

invested in Julieta's anti-Black racism. The rhetorical value of Guiomar's autobiographical mode in the skit, as she relates it back to her royal African lineage and the sinister legacy of African slave trading, both animates and captivates Clavela's protection and sympathy. Once Guiomar finishes recounting her story, Clavela abruptly silences Julieta with the quip: "Calla rapaza. ¿Y reina era tu tía, Guiomar?" [Hush, you thievish raptor! And so, Guiomar, your aunt was a queen?]

If Guiomar's assertive *habla-de-negros* speech acts underscore her royal sub-Saharan African lineage, which many Iberian African women (re)claimed, then let us acquire another ideation of how Rueda's *Los engañados* anchors her authority, savvy, and intellect via the letter she reads from her son Dieguito: "Lutríssima madre mía Guiomar, la carta que yo te cribo no e para besamano, sino que sa bono. Bendito sea Rios, loado sea Rios, amén."[14] [Most Illustrious mother of mine, Guiomar! The letter I write to you here is not intended as a farewell, but rather a polite gesture of saying I'm fine and all is well. Blessed be God. Praised be God. Amen.] Via the correspondence, Guiomar reveals the letter's origins when she shares Dieguito's post in "la India le San Joan de Punto Rico" [the Spanish Indies in San Juan, Puerto Rico].[15] While the letter does not reveal any (auto)biographical information about Dieguito – although we are told he was born in Portugal and named after Guiomar's father Eliomar, or Don Diego(z) – it does inform us, however, that enslaved and free Black Africans were literate, thinking subjects who received authorization to travel from Seville to the Spanish Americas.[16] Further, I also treat Rueda's repetitive instantiation of global Spanish imperialism as a concerted technique for cohering the geographic circulation of commodities, knowledge, and merchandise in imperial Spain. Through the performative act and textual insertion of Dieguito's letter, again read aloud by his mother Guiomar, Rueda then imbues *Los engañados* with an intertextual quality. To advocate for Black women's agency, I reiterate Guiomar's personhood as a literate subject, for she enacts the ceremonious gesture of reading her son's letter. As a performance, the letter she reads aloud to Clavela, Julieta, *and* the audience at large has an affective appeal: the audience can identify with the nostalgia Guiomar expresses for her son sent off to the Americas.

Rueda's theatrical representation of the remittance of letters, letter writing, and the event of African mariners and migrants settling in the Spanish Caribbean does much more than parody the historical imagination of imperial Spain's participation in the trans-Atlantic and trans-Pacific colonial enterprises. Instead, it inculcates in the most profound way the verisimilitude of Black Africans' roles as *de facto* and *de jure* agents in early-colonial Spanish territories across the globe. What I am signaling here is that Rueda's geographical reference to San Juan, Puerto Rico dialogues with a larger sixteenth-century transatlantic imperial Spanish discourse. And for Rueda's audience, I would insist that Black Africans of Dieguito's ilk are not a foreign concept. "The Spanish empire's reliance on Africans to populate and sustain its Caribbean colonies," explains Wheat, "stands in stark contrast to other European powers' use of voluntary or indentured European migrants for these purposes."[17] He further states,

> Although western European expansion in the Americas might be imagined as a series of interactions between native Americans, white settlers, and Black slaves, these ostensibly primordial categories cannot adequately explain the development of Spanish Caribbean sites in which racial descriptors often failed to correspond to fixed legal, social, or economic status.[18]

David Wheat's population estimates confirm and render plausible Rueda's literary account of Dieguito's life overseas in early-colonial Puerto Rico:

> [n]early forty thousand African and Africa-descended workers inhabited Spanish Caribbean seaports and rural areas by the first decade of the seventeenth century, revealing that in the

early modern Iberian worlds, settlers-or more accurately, *pobladores*, those who peopled Iberian colonies overseas—were often anything but white or European.[19]

My reading of Dieguito's role as *de facto* "colonist" or migrant – as gleaned from how I historicize the perceived literary fiction of his letter to Guiomar – is predicated on his mother's agency and subjectivity as an African woman who (re)traces her royal African lineage. Just as Dieguito's narrative undercuts the primacy of white settlers as the dominant figures presented in historical narratives and complicates the very notion of European colonization of the Americas,[20] Guiomar's role in *Los engañados* is anything but marginal or passive. As a mother, Guiomar's *habla de negros* language corroborates her "Berbasina" and "Biafra" genealogies – ethnonyms we can thread historically to the Rivers of Guinea and the Bight of Biafra.

The categories of mothers and motherhood also cannot go overlooked in my reading of Guiomar. She heralds her self-definition and subject position by recounting *her* sub-Saharan African matriarchs: Queen Berbasina (her aunt) and Lady Bialaga (her mother). Guiomar's memory of them, as created by Rueda, weaves a narrative of matrilineal authority and power captured by those textual moments when she talks back to Julieta and self-defines her role as a non-passive subject in the play. As the skit closes, Rueda leaves us with the following exemplary message: unlike Guiomar's co-star Julieta, whom Rueda, I suggest, constructs as a divisive force in the *Los engañados*, Guiomar *unites* women. Clavela shows sympathy for Guiomar by telling her not to cry about Dieguito's transatlantic absence ("No llores, Guiomar, no llores") and reassures her of his well-being overseas ("Bien está," she says).

Conclusion

In this chapter, I have examined Lope de Rueda's Black woman character Guiomar's agentive voice via her contestatory speech acts. I have proposed that her subversive *habla-de-negros* speech events serve not only to redirect critical attention on Black women literary characters but also to elevate the theoretical apparatus employed in Hispanic Studies. Black women characters – or the "negra," as they are commonly called in early modern Spanish theater studies – also fight to protect their womanhood and social standing in early modern Spanish society. Just as their white female counterparts represented in theatrical works written by men – let us consider, for example, Gil Vicente's *Auto de la síbila Casandra*, Calderón's *La vida es sueño*, or Lope de Vega's numerous plays – or plays written by women about women – I am thinking of Ana Caro de Mallén, María de Zayas y Sotomayor, and Sor Juana Inés de la Cruz – Black women, too, offer us complex and multivalent roles to examine. Rueda's Guiomar is indeed a force with which to be reckoned and to be taken seriously in our scholarly criticism.

To that end, Guiomar is not the only Black woman character who speaks assertively and subverts power dynamics in her scenes with white actors. In Diego Sánchez de Badajoz's *Farsa teologal*, for example, the work closes with a Black woman who defends herself from a shepherd's countless vicious attacks. The Aragonese dramaturge Jaime de Güete, in *Tesorina*, showcases the slave Margarita, who fights against male chauvinism and misogyny. Margarita's role in *Tesorina* ought to capture more widespread critical attention, for she safeguards not just her Black womanhood but the womanhood of *all* women. When Margarita refuses to tell her master Timbreo and his shepherd Giliracho the whereabouts of the women who have disappeared on set, she angrily replies: "Tú Xaber y digir no" [You know where they are; I'm not saying a word!] [v. 2369], which, as a result, provokes Timbreo's wrathful retort: "¡Valgaos el diablo, morruda!" [Go to Hell, you smashed-in-faced bitch!] (v. 2370). The heated exchange then escalates with back-and-forth expletives, in which Margarita exclaims to Giliracho: "patanax, viyaca, borde" [Boor!

Scoundrel! Scumbag!] [v. 2414], "viyaco" [Villain!] [v. 2532], and "don boraxo" [Mr. Drunkard!] [v. 2547].

What angers her is Giliracho's devious neglecting to reveal where he has seen the missing women. To him, she shouts: "Dale, xux, / te yuro esta crux / qui yo te quibraré el dente" [Come here, you! I swear on this cross that I'll break your teeth] [vv. 2542–4]. Recycling lines from the heated exchange between Jorge and Comba in Reinosa's "Gelofe, Mandinga," Güete also positions Margarita in a non-passive role. The work ends with Sircelo, Giliracho's lackey, intervening with an attempt to make peace between Giliracho and Margarita.

The variety of textual examples showcasing the presence of Black women in the theater of Lope de Rueda allows us to affirm that early modern Spanish theatrical representations of these women did not solely position them as inferior to whites. If anything, these depictions in drama treat them as subjects knowledgeable and proud of their presence and skills; their royal origins and wealth of lands; their previously acquired education and decorum. Guiomar, or otherwise, these Black women know they are gifted with wisdom and the resolve to subvert a variety of circumstances that others could not, however white they might be.

Notes

1 See *The Global City: On the Streets of Renaissance Lisbon*, eds. Lower, K.J.P. and Annemarie Jordan Gschwend.

2 The Flemish humanist, Nicholas Cleynaerts, visited Portugal between 1533 and 1538. His correspondence appears in *Correspondance de Nicholas Clénard*, ed. Alphonse Roersch, 3 vols. (Brussels, 1940–1) and Manuel Gonçalves Cerejeira's *O Renascimento em Portugal: Clenardo e a Sociedade Portuguesa* (Coimbra, 1974). See also Jorge Fonseca, "Black Africans in Portugal during Cleynaert's visit (1533–1538)," in *Black Africans in Renaissance Europe*, 113–21.

3 Quoted from A.C. de C.M. Saunders, *A Social History of Black Slaves and Freedmen in Portugal, 1441–1555*, 77. The sixteenth-century Portuguese writer António Ribeiro Chiado reprises these themes in his *Auto das Regateiras*.

4 For more on these women, see chapter 4 in David Wheat's *Atlantic Africa and the Spanish Caribbean, 1570–1640* (Chapel Hill, NC, 2016), 142–80. On Black women and solidarity in late-medieval and Renaissance Valencia, see Debra Blumenthal, "'La Casa dels Negres': Black African solidarity in late medieval Valencia," in *Black Africans in Renaissance Europe*, 225–46.

5 The original Spanish reads: "Yo la conocía en mi puecia y me iba tras ella pareciéndome gran novedad ver una negra muy aseada y compuesta, con dos criadas blancas detrás de ella," 260, in *Historia eclesiástica de Granada*. The modern edition, from which I cite, was published in 1989. Also, unless otherwise noted, all English translations are mine.

6 The original Spanish reads: "atrajo un público de muchas gente [que] ocorrían a ella pidiendo les anunciase cosas ocultas y secretas que se deseavan saber" (AHN, fol. 100v–101r). On Sunday June 19, 1588, a date that both encapsulates and recounts Catalina's spiritual activity, the Inquisitors of Valencia, Spain, Don Pedro Girón, Don Pedro Pacheco, and Doctor Frexal, found Catalina guilty of heresy and having a *pacto diabólico* (pact with the Devil). For further study on Catalina Muñoz, see Nicholas R. Jones, "Valencia's miraculous prophet: The Inquisition dossier of Catalina Muñoz (1588)," *postmedieval: a journal of medieval cultural studies* 10.1 (2019): 36–49 and Benjamin Ehlers, "La esclava y el patriarca: las visiones de Catalina Muñoz en la Valencia de Juan de Ribera," *Estudis* 23 (1997): 101–16.

7 See Baltasar Fra-Molinero's *La imagen de los negros el teatro del Siglo de Oro* and Antonio Santos Morillo's "Caracterización del negro en la literatura española del siglo XVI." For an alternative perspective, refer to chapter 3 in Nicholas R. Jones's *Staging Habla de Negros: Radical Performances of the African Diaspora in Early Modern Spain* (University Park, PA: Penn State University Press, 2019), 119–58.

8 While this chapter only focuses on Lope de Rueda's *Los engañados*, it is important to note that the playwright features Black women in his *Comedia Eufemia*, *Coloquio de Tymbria*, and *Coloquio de Gila*.

9 Lipski expounds this idea more fully in *A History of Afro-Hispanic Language*. Refer specifically to chapters 2 and 3.

10 Jones, *Staging Habla de Negros*, 6.

11 Original Spanish in Lope de Rueda, *Las cuatro comedias*, 182–3.

12 Wheat, *Atlantic Africa and the Spanish Caribbean*, 34. For additional archival records on this subject, see footnote 15.
13 Rueda, 182.
14 Ibid., 183.
15 Ibid., 182.
16 See Herman L. Bennett, *Colonial Blackness: A History of Afro-Mexico* (Bloomington, IN: Indiana University Press, 2009), Kathryn Joy McKnight and Leo Garofalo, *Afro-Latino Voices: Narratives from the Early Modern Ibero-Atlantic World, 1550–1812* (Indianapolis, IN: Hackett, 2009), and David Wheat, *Atlantic Africa and the Spanish Caribbean, 1570–1640*.
17 Wheat, *Atlantic Africa and the Spanish Caribbean*, 7.
18 Ibid., 7.
19 Ibid., 7. Refer specifically to the book's introduction, 5–19, and chapter 1 "The Rivers of Guinea," 20–67.
20 Ibid., 8.

Bibliography

Bennett, Herman L. *Colonial Blackness: A History of Afro-Mexico.* Bloomington, IN: Indiana University Press, 2009.

Earle, T.F. and K.J. Lowe, eds. *Black Africans in Renaissance Europe.* Cambridge: Cambridge University Press, 2005.

Fra Molinero, Baltasar. *La imagen de los negros el teatro del Siglo de Oro.* Madrid: Siglo Veintiuno, 1995.

Johnson, E. Patrick, ed. *No Tea, No Shade: New Writings in Black Queer Studies.* Durham, NC: Duke University Press, 2016.

Jones, Nicholas R. *Staging Habla de Negros: Radical Performances of the African Diaspora in Early Modern Spain.* University Park, PA: Penn State University Press, 2019.

Jones, Nicholas R. "Valencia's miraculous prophet: The Inquisition dossier of Catalina Muñoz (1588)." *Postmedieval: A Journal of Medieval Cultural Studies* 10.1 (2019): 36–49.

Kathryn, Joy McKnight and Leo Garofalo, eds. *Afro-Latino Voices: Narratives from the Early Modern Ibero-Atlantic World, 1550–1812.* Indianapolis, IN: Hackett, 2009.

Lipski, John M. *A History of Afro-Hispanic Language: Five Centuries, Five Continents.* Cambridge: Cambridge University Press, 2005.

Martín Casares, Aurelia and Rocío Periáñez Gómez, eds. *Mujeres esclavas y abolicionistas en la España de los siglos XVI al XIX.* Madrid: Iberoamericana, 2014.

Morgan, Jennifer L. *Laboring Women: Reproduction and Gender in New World Slavery.* Philadelphia: University of Pennsylvania Press, 2004.

Omise'eke Natasha Tinsley. "To Transcend Transgender: Choreographies of Gender Fluidity in the Performances of MilDred Gerestant." In *No Tea, No Shade: New Writings in Black Queer Studies.* Ed. E. Patrick Johnson. Durham, NC: Duke University Press, 2016. 131–46.

Pike, Ruth. "Sevillian Society in the Sixteenth Century: Slaves and Freedmen." *Hispanic Review* 47 (1967): 344–59.

Rueda, Lope de. *Las cuatro comedias.* Ed. Alfredo Hermenegildo. Madrid: Cátedra, 2001.

Sánchez de Badajoz, Diego. *Farsas.* Ed. José María Díez Borque. Madrid: Cátedra, 1978.

Santos Morillo, Antonio. "Caracterización del negro en la literatura española del XVI." *Lemir* 15 (2011): 23–46.

Saunders, A.C. de C.M. *A Social History of Black Slaves and Freedmen in Portugal, 1441–1555.* Cambridge: University of Cambridge Press, 1982.

Weber de Kurlat, Frida. "Sobre el negro como tipo cómico en el teatro español del siglo XVI." *Romance Philology* 17 (1962): 380–91.

Wheat, David. *Atlantic Africa and the Spanish Caribbean, 1570–1640.* Chapel Hill, NC: University of North Carolina Press, 2016.

6

The legend of Lucy Negro

Joyce Green MacDonald

The historical Lucy Negro – also known as Black Luce, or Luce Baynam – was a notorious madam who ran a series of floating brothels in Clerkenwell, to the northwest of Renaissance London, from the mid-1570s through about the end of the sixteenth century. With a clientele that included aristocrats, court figures, and wealthy city merchants, she was well enough known to be invited, along with some of her girls, to serve as entertainment at the Christmas festivities staged by the law students of Gray's Inn on December 28, 1594.[1] Another part of the revels that evening was a performance of a play called "a Comedy of Errors," whose description as being "like to *Plautus* his *Menechmus*" indicates that it was Shakespeare's very early *The Comedy of Errors*.[2]

No irrefutable evidence survives that reveals Shakespeare was at Gray's Inn that night or that he and Lucy Negro actually knew each other, although sex workers and theatre people freely crossed paths in Clerkenwell and other city neighborhoods. The lives of most Renaissance Londoners, including Shakespeare himself, seem shockingly under-documented by modern standards. Lucy Negro left no papers of her own; we don't know where she was born or to whom, when she entered her trade, what she thought about it, or when she died. This lack of rich life records for her, combined with the fact that she and Shakespeare *may* have been in the same place at the same time for at least one night, fuels the claim this chapter studies: that she was the life model for the so-called "Dark Lady" of his last 28 sonnets. I'll be arguing here that we should treat this assumption with suspicion. Appropriating the historical Lucy Negro to the legend of Shakespeare, the national poet, by identifying her as the Dark Lady is an early example of the erasure of Black women and of how their stories, their bodies, their sexualities come to figure in the narratives that white society constructs and imposes on them. Critical speculation that Shakespeare fell catastrophically in love with her, was emotionally destroyed when their affair ended, and turned his pain into powerful art is actually a story about him and not her.

I should probably say here that I'm not particularly interested in whether Lucy Negro or any other real woman was actually the life model for the Dark Lady, or whether she and Shakespeare were lovers. I don't know that such claims can actually be proved one way or the other from the materials now available to us. More importantly, remembering a woman only because of the most famous man she *might* have slept with memorializes patriarchal readings of history more than it memorializes *her*. Rather, in what follows, I want to revive the notion of her blackness (none of the 28 poems describes her as "dark," and none calls her a "lady"), to think about what and how it meant in its Renaissance moment, and how it entered into the cultural legends of her time in ways that reverberate into our own.

Black women in the early modern imagination

Lucy Negro's name itself suggests that she was indeed one of the several hundred African-descended people living in England in the last decades of the sixteenth century.[3] She and William Shakespeare lived and worked in a city that was well on its way to becoming a capital of global empire, and virtually from the beginning, England's global might was intimately bound up with the Atlantic slave trade. In 1564, the year Shakespeare was born, Sir John Hawkins mounted the first English slaving voyage when he sailed to the Guinea coast to capture hundreds of Africans and then crossed the Atlantic to sell them in Venezuela. (The Crown furnished his ship and received a cut of the profits.)[4]

Part of the discourse that represented colonial enterprise to its English consumers deeply relied on tropes of gender and gendered sexuality.[5] Soliciting investors to support a planned return voyage to the Guyana region on the cost of Venezuela, Sir Walter Raleigh assured readers that the country was full of wonders: fabulous beasts, tribes of Amazons, great stores of gold, whole nations of people who "have their eies in their shoulders, and their mouthes in the middle of their breastes." He strikingly concluded that "*Guiana* is a Countrey that hath yet her Maydenhead, never sackt, turned, nor wrought, the face of the earth hath not been torne, nor the vertue and salt of the soyle spent by manurance."[6] The fact that the country had never been conquered by Europeans rendered it virginal and implicitly cast the adventurers who would heed his call as that virgin's first lover, the one who would tear her and use her until they exhausted her fertility – the "vertue and salt" of her "soyle." Raleigh's invitation invokes a predatory, aggressive relationship to the foreign landscape, which in a colonial order, he seems to assume is inevitable. He narrates his invitation to colonial plunder in terms of the plunder of women's passively available bodies.

Raleigh's account has a surprising amount to say about the women of Guiana – not only the Amazons he claimed lived in the interior, who "do accompanye with men but once in a yeeare," (p. 23) but the beautiful wife of a local chieftain with her hair "tied up ... in prittie knots." Except "for the difference of colour," he would have sworn she could have been the twin of "a Lady in England" he'd seen (p. 55). Raleigh's *Discoverie* is very conscious of its rhetorical obligation to incite appetite and wonder in an audience of English readers and potential supporters; we can see this in the language he uses to describe the richness of Guiana's territory and the limitless bounty it contains, free for the taking by the sufficiently enterprising. But that appetite does not extend so clearly to the women he says he finds there. His text is content to leave them in the realm of fantasy, as in the case of the Amazons, or to assure his audience that they are fundamentally not really foreign at all and that they – and the land he associated with their bodies – can be easily known and possessed.

Colonial writing about African women, however, focused much more closely on bodily and behavioral difference. The new travel narratives of the last decades of the sixteenth century inherited earlier decades' penchant for mostly fact-free tales of wonder deriving from earlier chroniclers like Sir John Mandeville, repeating familiar stories about Africans' blackness, nakedness, and savagery. For Andrew Thevet, Ethiopia's hot climate was not only responsible for the white teeth and curly hair of the "*Neigers*" who lived there but also made the women "unconstant, with many other vices."[7] Pieter de Marees insisted that women of the Guinea coast were "given to Lust and uncleannesse" from their youth, and when they grew old enough to begin covering their nudity, they "then begin to be lecherous." In his account, they were thus inevitably eager "to have carnal copulation" with the Dutch traders who began arriving in West Africa in the seventeenth century, and tried their best to attract them.[8] Without modesty – give a woman from Zaire or Angola "a piece of bread," and "she will immediately discover her pudenda" in thanks – their bodies were as distorted as their morals: "The women give their infants suck as they hang at their backs, the uberous dug stretched over her shoulder."[9]

But recirculating during a period when the economic potential of a transatlantic slave trade was becoming apparent, and when actual Africans were beginning to arrive in greater numbers at least in England's largest cities, travelers' tales about African women took on new ideological force.[10] Jennifer L. Morgan writes that sixteenth-century "racialist discourse was deeply imbued with ideas about gender and sexual difference that, indeed, became manifest only in contact with each other."[11] Such mutually reinforcing notions of blackness and womanhood would become deeply useful in producing and justifying notions of Europeans' right to exploit the physical and reproductive labor of African women.

In early modern literature, we can see emerging notions of links between blackness and womanhood being laid over existing English cultural connections of femininity with color, so that white English femininity was increasingly understood as existing in opposition to blackness. Elizabeth Cary's *The Tragedy of Mariam, the Faire Queene of Jewry* (1613) is a useful example here.[12] Cary's play tells the story of Mariam, last heiress of Judaea's royal family, who had been displaced when the Romans took over the territory and installed Herod as their client king. Herod married Mariam, but Mariam's mother Alexandra is still angry that the Romans killed her own father as well as Mariam's brother in order to settle Herod's claim. Alexandra believes that if she had only succeeded in getting the Roman triumvir Mark Antony interested enough in Mariam to marry her instead of Cleopatra, their family's position would now be secure; Antony would have killed Herod "and left the browne *Egyptian* cleane forsaken."[13] Herod – desperately in love with Mariam but also wildly suspicious that she doesn't love him back – rejects the doubt his sister Salome tries to cast on Mariam's trustworthiness, castigating Salome in deeply racialized terms. She has no right to criticize his wife, since when she stands next to her, he has "often tane [her] for an Ape … You are to her a Sun burnt Blackamore" (G2v). After having Mariam executed, Herod immediately regrets it, implying that her moral and physical fairness made her too delicate to survive in a corrupt world: "If she had bene like an *Egiptian* blacke, / And not so faire, she had bene longer livde" (Ii).

Cary's Salome is so far from Mariam's womanly ideal that she is not only Black but virtually subhuman. The play's characters routinely draw the line between "fair" women and bad ones in terms of color, extracting moral qualities from Mariam's fairness as well as from Cleopatra's darkness. *Mariam's* example suggests some of the ways in which skin color as a racial marker was gendered in the Renaissance, working to produce white womanhood as rigorously as it defined what was Black and unworthy in other women.

Literary histories of blackness and beauty

Early modern literature offers its most extensive archive of the literary links it established between color and womanhood in the Petrarchan color vocabularies of Renaissance lyric. Kim Hall's seminal discussion has analyzed the degree to which these poems' traditional anatomization of feminine beauty – alabaster skin, golden hair, lips like rubies, teeth like ivory or pearls – reads racially in their colonial moment.[14] As Petrarchan lyric participated in the large-scale cultural production of feminine beauty in terms of whiteness, it also indirectly invoked the

Black female object of early modern racial discourse, an object against which values of white female beauty and virtue could become more visible.

Typical of this style is Sonnet 9 from Sir Philip Sidney's sequence *Astrophel and Stella*:

> Queen Vertues Court, which some call *Stellas* face,
> Prepar'd by Natures cheefest furniture:
> Hath his front built of Alabaster pure,
> Golde is the couering of that statelie place.
> The doore, by which sometimes runnes forth her grace,
> Red Porphire is, which locke of Pearle makes sure:
> Whose Porches rich, with name of chekes indure,
> Marble mixt red and white, doe interlace.[15]

Here, Stella's features are compared to the colors of various inanimate objects, as fixed in their value as is the "Virtue" which shines forth in her face.[16] Colonial expansion, with the influx of luxury trade goods it introduced into the country, amplified and materialized the range of meanings readers could attach to the things that offered corollaries to a sonnet lady's beauty. For Hall, reading Petrarchan poems in a colonial moment also amplified the field of meanings readers could attach to the poems' invocation of color and morality – drawing on and responding to the ways travelers' writings and explorers' exhortations talked about the blackness and degraded moral status of African women, as we've already seen in motion on the dramatic side in Cary's *Mariam*.

More than merely racial identity, then, Renaissance vocabularies of blackness and whiteness also indicated moral quality. The body was an index to ethical standing, to a person's probity and virtue. That color indicates race, and that race implies moral standing, are ideas that survived long after the premodern moments in which they were generated, as is the Renaissance linkage between race and a specifically sexual morality.[17] Hyder Rollins, the editor of the volumes on the sonnets in the Modern Language Association's *New Variorum Edition of Shakespeare*, noted that in 1861, a German scholar speculated that the "Dark Lady" was actually West Indian, a creole with "an admixture of African blood. Was she not a mulatto or a quadroon?" (This German scholar apparently also read Shakespeare's sonnets colonially.) Rollins responded to this speculation in a footnote: "No doubt this would explain why Sh.'s eyes didn't love the dark woman, and why … they in her 'a thousand errors' noted."[18]

To be sure, Rollins is impatient with all critical speculation about the real identity of the Dark Lady, since he didn't believe any such identification could be made beyond the shadow of a doubt. But his distaste for the idea that the "real" Dark Lady may have been Black is palpable. In 1933, only 11 years before the publication of Rollins' work, British scholar G. B. Harrison was the first to advance Lucy Negro as the model for the Dark Lady, citing the account of her presence at the 1594 Gray's Inn Christmas revels noted at the beginning of this chapter.[19] Rollins notes that a second scholar, E. I. Fripp, repeated Harrison's claim in 1938, "calmly … as if the matter was proved." "Thus, seventy-seven years after the German translator … had provided a negro mistress for Sh., two distinguished Englishmen, adopting and expanding his ideas, assigned her a name and an excessively squalid locale" (p. 272). Twenty years after Rollins, Leslie Hotson is even more explicit in his rejection of the possibility that the Dark Lady was actually a Black woman. For him, Harrison's conjecture had permanently earned him "the discredit of believing Shakespeare's fair enslaver a blackamoor."[20]

For the speaker to be enslaved by their love for a distant and indifferent beloved is a common idiom in Renaissance sonnets. Shakespeare's Sonnet 133, for example, laments that his cruel and promiscuous mistress, finding it "not enough to torture me alone," must also make a "slave to slavery" (i.e., helpless love) out of his "sweet'st friend."[21] The speaker goes on to eroticize his double torment; since he is "pent in" her, he "and all that is in me" are irretrievably hers (lines 13, 14). To be "pent" is to be confined, whether in a slave's chains or in his dark mistress' body. That she is "black," as this subgroup of sonnets repeat (see 127, 131, 132, and 144), re-racializes both the conventional trope of the lover's enslavement to a fair cruel beauty and the position of master and slave beginning to unfold in the New World during Shakespeare's lifetime.

It's possible, but not certain, that Shakespeare was at Gray's Inn with Lucy Negro that December night, possible even that he knew her more intimately. But Rollins' flat rejection of the notion that Shakespeare had "a negro mistress," and Hotson's disgust at the idea that he'd been sexually obsessed with "a blackamoor," seem to me to be more about race than about the status of the evidence. Hotson even advances an alternative candidate for the Dark Lady – a former Maid of Honor to Queen Elizabeth named Lucy Morgan, who he believed was dismissed from court under mysterious circumstances in the early 1580s, apparently ended up running a brothel, and was eventually imprisoned in Bridewell (Duncan Salkeld skeptically reviews Hotson's findings; p. 134). But at least she was white.

The implications of counting blackness fair

I do not believe that establishing correlation between what happens in a work of art and what happens in the artist's real life really gets us any closer to fully grasping what the art is about. Art is refracted through an artist's lived experience, but a poem isn't the same kind of thing as a journal entry. I think that the impulse to make the Dark Lady sonnets tell us a coherent, factually based story derives from the compelling emotional power of the poems themselves. They *feel* true. Whatever was going on in Shakespeare's life during the composition of these poems, they participate fully in their period's recognition of the links between color, race, gender, and sexuality, and this contemporary recognition is heightened through his masterful exploitation of the features of Petrarchan style. We can't prove that the real Lucy Negro has anything to do with these poems, but in the next section of this chapter, I would like to discuss the possibility that the symbolic value of Lucy Negro – "blackamoor," madam, "negro mistress" – reverberates through them, shaping their meanings and directing their impact.

Consider Shakespeare's Sonnet 127, where the Dark Lady first enters the sequence:

> In the old age black was not counted fair,
> Or if it were it bore not beauty's name;
> But now is black beauty's successive heir,
> And beauty slandered with a bastard shame:
> For since each hand hath put on Nature's power,
> Fairing the foul with Art's false borrowed face,
> Sweet beauty hath no name, no holy bower,
> But is profaned, if not lives in disgrace.
> Therefore my mistress' eyes are raven black,
> Her brows so suited, and they mourners seem
> At such who, not born fair, no beauty lack,
> Sland'ring creation with a false esteem.
> Yet so they mourn, becoming of their woe,
> That every tongue says beauty should look so.

The poem opens by directly acknowledging the color conventions embedded in the Petrarchan style, conventions that valorized whiteness as the sign of female beauty and at least implicitly, therefore, devalued its dark opposite. It also invites us into what feels like the imminent demonstration of another of that style's common features, its love of paradox. "People used to think that black wasn't beautiful," it says, "but wait until you see what I'm going to do next."

Almost immediately, though, the sonnet switches into a new register that refers back to earlier poems in the sequence and not to the rules of its style. The first 17 poems in the whole group encourage a young man who is the object of the poet's affection to marry and reproduce so that his beauty will not disappear from the world when he is gone: "From fairest creatures we desire increase, / That thereby beauty's rose might never die" (1: 1–2). "[U]nless thou get a son," the poet warns, "thou … [u]nlooked on diest" (7: 14, 13). But Sonnet 127 heightens the reproductive mood of the sequence's opening by splicing it to its new subject of the desirability and erotic power of blackness ("every tongue says beauty should look so"). In this new age of poetic possibility, blackness "is … beauty's successive heir."

Shakespeare's sonnets were first published in 1609, by which date the circulation of travelers' tales detailing Black women's social and sexual deviance, and their biological difference from European women, was well underway. The first of England's mid-Atlantic colonies was permanently established at Jamestown in 1607, and Virginia's history shows how this sense of deviance gradually became embedded in the colony's laws. The colonies followed English common law by condemning fornication for all and by tending to punish guilty women more harshly than their male partners. But early on, race as well as gender came to mark the colony's reaction to crimes of sexual behavior. In 1640, a white man named Robert Sweatt was forced to apologize before his local parish for the crime of fornicating with a Black woman; his unnamed pregnant partner was publicly whipped. The Virginia House of Burgesses passed a law in 1662 that fined interracial couples guilty of fornication twice the amount that would be due from unmarried couples of the same race, and any white female servant who gave birth to a child by a Black or mixed-race man would either have five years added to her period of indenture or pay a 15-pound fine to the churchwardens. (No servant would have ready access to that kind of money.) When Maryland made interracial marriage illegal in 1664, it expanded existing assumptions that intimate behaviors mattered to public order by racializing the sexual domain over which it already exercised civic control.

In the early colonies, interracial sex was regarded as an economic and legal problem as well as a social one. Many of the white women who participated in such unions were largely indentured servants, and some historians have read legal prohibitions against these women's intermarriage with Black men – who may have been indentured or enslaved themselves – as a response to the problems created by the children born to them. Would the women's masters have to support these minor children? Who would have the right to the children's labor when they became old enough to work, the women's masters or the men's? In another marked departure from English common law, Virginia settled such vexed labor and economic issues in 1662 by declaring that all children born in the colony would henceforth hold the condition of their mother instead of their father; any child born to an enslaved woman would also be a slave. Slavery's social hold over the colony and the racialization of its public order was such that when Virginia finally outlawed interracial marriage in 1691, nearly 30 years after Maryland, economic considerations were absent from the statute. Rather, its language cited the colony's desire to prevent the spread of "that abominable mixture and spurious issue" which miscegenous relationships inevitably caused. Any Virginians who married interracially would have to leave the colony within three weeks of the ceremony.[22] The racially mixed offspring of such unions would provide living evidence of a sexual crime against the colony's regulation of contact between the races.

Such colonial changes lay in the future, beyond the date of the sonnets' publication in 1609. But what we do see in them, beginning with number 127, is a similar sense of concern with interracial sex and its reproductive and social consequences. The speaker in the first group of sonnets urges the young man to marry and have legitimate children who will replicate and preserve his beauty in the world. In Sonnet 127, however, blackness has become beauty's "successive heir" – its child, its beneficiary. As a result, beauty has been "slandered with a bastard shame," since the only way beauty – poetically and socially denominated as white – could give birth to a Black heir is through an act of miscegenous infidelity. One scholar characterizes the Dark Lady sonnets' embrace of a cross-racial attraction as their true "scandal," perhaps even more so than the earlier poems' matter-of-fact proposal that the young man the poet loves should marry and have children.[23]

The poet's love for the Dark Lady cannot be accommodated by existing social custom; there is no way it can be made to fit within received rules of inheritance, as Sonnet 142 acknowledges. There, the poet knows that "[l]ove is my sin" (line 1) but declares that any sin he has committed in desiring her "merits not reproving" (line 4) in comparison with her own corrupt deeds. She is the one who has "sealed false bonds of love"; she is the one who has "[r]obbed others' beds' revenues of their rents" (lines 7, 8). Putting a wax seal to a legal document formalized its status, but her "bonds of love" are false, because she loves no one. If others' beds are "revenues," or the income from landed estates, she has "robbed" the owners of those beds of the sexual energy that should have been reserved to pay the marital debt they legally owed.[24]

Lines 5–8 of Sonnet 127 expand on this idea of legitimacy through a discussion of face-painting and its attempt to counterfeit true beauty. The white complexion prized by Renaissance beauty standards, often secured through the use of cosmetic pastes containing lead or mercury, was derided as a foreign affectation more suited to whores than to honest women.[25] Moralists condemned face-painting as women's arrogant attempt to improve on God's creation: "Sure there is a wrong done to God, whose workmanship they would seeme to mend, being discontented with it."[26] In Sonnet 127, the eyes of the speaker's "mistress" are black as though in mourning, because she grieves that God's "creation" has been slandered by a cosmetic application of unguents designed to elicit a "false esteem."

The notion of women currying "false esteem" through face-painting also carries a racial charge. In Cary's *Mariam*, Herod tells his sister Salome that even with all her "paintings," she "can never equall Mariam's praise" (Giii) – never, that is, achieve true beauty or hide her true corruption. Awaiting execution, Mariam comforts herself by boasting that despite all the artifice at the command of "the browne *Egyptian*," Cleopatra could not seduce Herod away from her side. The moral economy that inveighed against women's face-painting held that it was trying to hide the truth of what women actually looked like by counterfeiting whiteness with all of its implied beauty and moral probity. Beginning with Sonnet 127, the Dark Lady sonnets simply refuse the equation between whiteness, beauty, and virtue. The truth embodied in the mistress's black beauty, a beauty that cannot be disguised or misrepresented, challenges both the period's aesthetic and moral judgments and the racial language used to express them. Simply, the speaker tells us, his lady's black "is fairest in my judgment's place" (131: 12).

Conclusion: racial hauntings

The beauty and integrity of blackness remains a subject elsewhere in Shakespeare's early works.[27] And yet it must also be said that with the possible exception of his Cleopatra, there are no non-white female characters in his plays. His characters talk about Black women: they mention a dark-skinned maid named Susan in *The Comedy of Errors*; the clown Lancelot Gobbo in *The*

Merchant of Venice is accused of having got the heroine's Black maidservant pregnant; the maid of Desdemona's mother was named Barbary. But none of these women come onstage. Rather, they exist in the background, as subordinates and sex partners, part of the main characters' histories but never as characters in their own right. We don't know the stories they would have told about themselves or what would have happened to them next.

Lucy Negro occupies this same shadowy space, instrumental to a story that others want to tell, or want to refute, about Shakespeare. The scattered mentions of her name – Lucy Negro, Black Luce – that survive in the testimonies collected in the Bridewell minute books provide one kind of record about her. But entering legend as the Dark Lady, if indeed Shakespeare had her in mind as he wrote (and if he knew her, and if he'd loved her), she survives more surely in others' stories than in the records we have that mention her name.

Notes

1 Duncan Salkeld, *Shakespeare Among the Courtesans: Prostitution, Literature, and Drama, 1500–1650* (Farnham: Ashgate, 2012), describes Black Luce's business, 135–41. His book is largely based on his research in the sixteenth-century Minute Books of London's Bridewell Hospital, which was actually a combined court and prison rather than a hospital in the modern sense.

2 *Gesta Grayorum: Or, the History of the High and Mighty Prince, Henry Prince of Purpoole* (London, 1688), 22.

3 Imtiaz Habib, *Black Lives in the English Archives, 1500–1677: Imprints of the Invisible* (Farnham: Ashgate, 2008), notes the "racial etymology" (p. 12) behind the names in early modern parish registers and other archival sources assigned to people he believes were Black, pointing to records of people called "Thomas Blackmore," "George Blackmore," "Peter Negro," "Dinah the Black," and "Christen Ethiopia."

4 Richard Hakluyt, *The Principall Navigations, Voiages and Discoveries of the English Nation* (London, 1589), describes Hawkins' 1564 voyage, pp. 523–43.

5 Louis Adrian Montrose, "The Work of Gender in the Discourse of Discovery," *Representations* 33 (1991): 1–41.

6 *The Discoverie of the Large, Rich, and Bewtiful Empire of Guiana* (London, 1596), 70, 96.

7 *The New Found Worlde, Or Antarctike* (London, 1568), 25.

8 De Marees' *A Description and Historicall Declaration of the Golden Kingdome of Guinea, Otherwise Called the Golden Coast of Myna* is included in Samuel Purchas' compilation *Purchas His Pilgrimes In Five Bookes* (London, 1625), 927.

9 Ania Loomba and Jonathan Burton, eds., *Race in Early Modern England: A Documentary Companion* (New York: Palgrave, 2007) quote Sir Thomas Herbert's 1634 travel narrative on their pp. 227 and 228.

10 See Winthrop Jordan, *White Over Black: American Attitudes Toward the Negro, 1550–1812* (Chapel Hill: University of North Carolina Press, 1968), 3–11.

11 "'Some Could Suckle Over Their Shoulder': Male Travelers, Female Bodies, and the Gendering of Racial Ideology, 1500–1770," *William and Mary Quarterly*, 54, no. 1 (1997): 169.

12 This section draws on Joyce Green MacDonald, "Reading Race in *Women Writers Online*: Thirty Years On," https://wwp.northeastern.edu/context/#macdonald.30race.xml, pars. 9–19.

13 *The Tragedie of Mariam, the Faire Queene of Jewry* (London, 1613), B1v. I'll include subsequent references parenthetically in my text.

14 In *Things of Darkness: Economies of Race and Gender in Early Modern England* (Ithaca: Cornell University Press, 1995), 62–122.

15 *Syr P. S. his Astrophel and Stella* (London, 1591), 4.

16 "Virtue" is a rich term here; its sixteenth-century meanings include an object's essential nature or identity as well as a person's moral quality.

17 This is the argument of Marvin Hunt, "Be Dark, But Not Too Dark: Shakespeare's Dark Lady as a Sign of Color," in *Shakespeare's Sonnets: Critical Essays*, ed. James Schiffer (New York Garland, 2000), 369–90.

18 Vol. 25 (Philadelphia: J. B. Lippincott, 1944), 243. The phrase "a thousand errors" appears in Sonnet 141, line 2.

19 *Shakespeare at Work, 1592–1603* (London: Routledge, 1933), 64, 310–11.

20 *Mr. W. H.* (New York: Knopf, 1964), 244.

21 I cite *The Complete Sonnets and Poems*, ed. Colin Burrow (Oxford: Oxford University Press, 2002); here, lines 3 and 4. I will provide future citations parenthetically in my text.
22 See Kevin Mumford, "After Hugh: Statutory Race Segregation in Colonial America, 1630–1725," *American Journal of Legal History* 43, no. 3 (1999): 280–305.
23 Margreta De Grazia, "The Scandal of Shakespeare's Sonnets," in *Shakespeare's Sonnets: Critical Essays*, 105–6.
24 This financial and legal language is also visible in sonnets 134, 135, 136, 142, and 146.
25 See Farah Karim-Cooper, *Cosmetics in Shakespeare and Renaissance Drama* (Edinburgh: Edinburgh University Press, 2006).
26 Thomas Tuke, *A Discourse Against Painting and Tincturing of Women* (London, 1616), 2.
27 See Karim-Cooper, 142–7.

7

(Anti-)colonial assemblages
The history and reformulations of Njinga Mbande

Daniel F. Silva

Njinga[1] Mbande, or Ana de Sousa, the Christian Portuguese name she took on following her strategic christening, ruled the Ndongo and Matamba Kingdoms (geographically spanning what is today northern Angola) from 1624 to her death in 1663. During this time, in a complex way, she balanced diplomatic collaboration with, and military opposition to, the Portuguese crown in addition to military tensions with neighboring kingdoms and other encroaching European forces. By sifting through the colonial documents from the Portuguese authorities and other European travelers and missionaries, as well as her own letters written to the Crown and the Vatican, we get a sense of how Njinga was articulated via colonial discourse and how she challenged the forces and epistemologies of Western imperialism. Njinga's life coincides with a particular moment of racial capitalism in which taxonomies of racial, gender, and sexual difference were negotiated and trafficked by the forces of Empire as undergirding and informing its expansionist and extractive desires and processes. During and after her life, her body and political stature served, as I shall consider ahead through the framework of assemblages, as racialized texts and fantasies of gendered abjection, sexual deviance, and psychological pathos. While these have continued to inform the continuity of Empire after her political and military resistance to it, her defiance toward imperial forces is also recovered and integrated into radical cultural production and meaning-making across the African diaspora and within anti-colonial epistemologies.

Life and political rise of Njinga

Prior to her reign, all known rulers of the Ndongo and Matamba Kingdoms had been men. As Stephen O. Murray and Will Roscoe point out, the Kimbundu term for ruler, *ngola*, was not gendered as in European languages and political models. Therefore, the title of "queen" is both a translation into European gendering systems and an erasure of the complexities of Njinga's rise to power and struggle against colonizing forces. As I shall expound upon further ahead, Murray and Roscoe perform the important decolonial work of placing Njinga into an African queer history, an archive of life beyond the European gendered order of bodies. Historian Linda Heywood, author of *Njinga of Angola: Africa's Warrior Queen* (2017), would disagree with Murray and Roscoe's assertion that Ndongo society was matrilineal.[2] Though gender expectations at the level of the body and its everyday performativity were blurred to some extent within a particular binary, Ndongo division of power followed patrilineal orders, as indicated by Njinga's suspicion of male claims to the throne.

Njinga's lineage could be traced back to the founders of the Ndongo Kingdom, over a century prior to her birth.[3] The reign of her grandfather (1575–92), Ngola Kilombo kia Kasenda, saw substantial incursions of the Portuguese and military conflict, with resounding defeats on both sides. Her father, Mbande a Ngola, was elected in 1592 and ruled until 1617. His reign was plagued by internal discord between himself and local officials of the kingdom, known as *sobas*, which would carry serious military consequences as Portuguese armies seized significant portions of Ndongo territory.

This Portuguese encroachment also coincided with the expansion of the slave trade across Ndongo and Kongo spheres of influence (located to the north of Ndongo). As a result of these dire consequences and compounded dissatisfaction among regional leaders known as *sobas*, Mbande a Ngola was ultimately murdered by his own military. The years immediately following his death left the decimated kingdom without a successor. In the meantime, court officials and *sobas* were responsible for electing the next ruler from several different eligible lineages and from candidates holding important local positions of power. Ngola Mbande, son of Mbande a Ngola and his favorite concubine, Kengela ka Nkombe, and full brother of Njinga and her two sisters, Kambu and Funji, ultimately seized power by preemptively proclaiming himself king with the help of his supporters moments before many Ndongo electors arrived at the voting location. He did so by arguing that Mbande a Ngola's legitimate heir – the latter's son with his principal wife – was, in fact, ineligible because his mother had been convicted of adultery. He went on to enact violent retribution against much of his opposition, including family members. He ordered the sterilization of his sisters and killed Njinga's son (the offspring of one of her male concubines)[4] in order to secure his line of succession.

As Linda Heywood and other historians have argued, her brother saw Njinga as a threat to his political aspirations before he even took power. Njinga spent the early years of her brother's reign living in the neighboring and incorporated Matamba Kingdom. In 1621, as a result of growing Portuguese military expansion into Ndongo territory and a subsequent need for re-establishing diplomatic relations with the Portuguese Crown, Ngola Mbande invited Njinga to be Ndongo's official envoy to the Portuguese. She and a vast Ndongo delegation met with the Portuguese in Luanda – the first African delegation to receive such an invitation and grandiose reception by the Portuguese governor and local colonial elites, thus highlighting Portuguese recognition of the Ndongo Kingdom as a major power in the region.

The establishment of Portuguese and Dutch colonial presence in the region hinged on tensions and conflict between local kingdoms, and when Njinga took power in 1624, the Portuguese had seized control of coastal and inland territories between the Lifune and Kwanza rivers. Njinga, like her predecessors and counterparts, leveraged power and political relationships with European envoys and militaries to consolidate and in some cases, expand her influence and the Ndongo sphere of control. As Heywood notes in the case of Njinga, these relationships entailed land concessions, continued acceptance of Christianity and the presence of Catholic missionaries, military alliances with both the Portuguese and the Dutch as well as against one another, and the exchange of enslaved bodies to the Portuguese and Dutch.[5] These local power dynamics and practices at the dawn of European colonization in southern Africa were common in the region before Njinga's reign.

Njinga accepted baptism as a diplomatic tool during her meeting in Luanda with Portuguese governor Correia de Sousa. Njinga and Correia de Sousa came to a peace agreement of sorts whereby Portugal and Ndongo would accept the current borders and support one another in the fight against common enemies. She refused several Portuguese demands in the process, however, most notably that of paying an annual tribute to the Portuguese in enslaved Ndongo citizens. Njinga was steadfast on her position, reminding Correia de Sousa that Ndongo remained a sovereign kingdom and thus had no need to pay any tribute to the Portuguese. In response to Portuguese insistence on this matter, she agreed to be baptized, and a public christening ceremony in Luanda ensued. Njinga also saw her baptism as strategic from a military standpoint, considering that Ndongo nemeses would now be Portuguese nemeses under the Ndongo–Portugal alliance, but the Portuguese used the opportunity to claim the land for themselves. Ngola Mbande subsequently fell into depression with the reality of the ever-dwindling Ndongo Kingdom and died after ingesting a supposedly poisoned beverage. According to different chroniclers, most notably the Portuguese António de Cadornega, Njinga was behind the poisoning.[6]

Njinga immediately assumed power and was driven, like her predecessors, to revive the Ndongo Kingdom to its former glory prior to Portuguese colonial expansion. She shared a deep distrust and hate toward the Portuguese, not only for the loss of Ndongo territories but also for the underhanded diplomatic tactics and brutal military strategy they employed, leading to the death of several of her family members and ancestors. For the duration of her nearly 40-year reign (1624–63), she achieved her goal of resisting Portuguese expansion in the region and regrowing the Ndongo Kingdom.

She quickly worked to mobilize military support from *sobas*, and so for the first time since the arrival of the Portuguese in the region, their growing power was threatened by a possible uprising. However, the Portuguese preempted any uprising by defeating Njinga's armies and forced her court to flee from Ndongo lands, subsequently installing Ngola Hari, a distant descendent of Ndongo founder Ngola Kiluanje kia Samba, as puppet ruler of the Kingdom. In addition to military intervention, the Portuguese attempted to convince regional officials of the Ndongo that Njinga was unfit to rule because she was a woman.

The racial, gendered, and sexual discourses that impacted her identity and informed the inscription of her body in various ways came from both European and Ndongo modes of knowledge and gender norms. As she told her biographer, Antonio Gaeta, regarding her childhood, she caused significant concern and consternation among elders and wider society by learning political, judicial, and military practices that were reserved for the sons of rulers. At the same time, she was known for outshining her brother and other young men with whom she circulated in the acquisition of knowledge.

Her challenging of prescribed gender norms caused further alarm as she got older. As Heywood notes,

> she made clear through her actions that her gender did not preclude her from enjoying the same liberties as her male counterparts. In addition to having in her service a coterie of female attendants and slaves, she kept a large number of young male consorts (concubines), and she is reported to have had multiple lovers throughout her long life.[7]

Her sexual relationships and performance of power via sex drew disapproval from Ndongo elites and horror from Portuguese administrators and chroniclers.

Portuguese imperial signification of Njinga in positing her as an unfit ruler to her Ndongo rivals reveals much of the contradictory discourses inscribed on Black women's bodies, already in the early centuries of Western expansion. On the one hand, her perceived gender inscribed her as unfit to rule due to a deficit in the signifiers of masculinity – itself always signified through the performance of domination over othered bodies. On the other hand, her alleged poisoning of her own brother, as recorded by Portuguese chroniclers, allowed the Portuguese to signify her to Ndongo officials as an abject subject that carries out power by way of treacherous excess. In other words, Njinga was posited by the Portuguese as both deficit and excess of the white imperial standards of normative personhood and masculine ideals of leadership. A political imperial textuality and imagery surrounding Njinga was thus in formation. Under this growing imperial narrative of Njinga's alterity was the Portuguese Crown's fundamental fear of Njinga's political power and military shrewdness. Unlike her sibling predecessor, Njinga was revered and respected by many of the Ndongo elites, and the Portuguese would have a harder time taking political advantage of internal fractures in Ndongo power structures.

Njinga would remain peripheral to the Ndongo during Ngola Hari's reign until 1657, when the Portuguese signed a new peace treaty with Njinga in 1657, thus recognizing her as ruler of the Ndongo once again. By this time, and in the over 30 years that had elapsed since her removal, Njinga and the Portuguese had had no shortage of conflicts. They had excommunicated her from the Catholic Church and kidnapped her sisters, eventually murdering one of them – Funji – and destroying her base in 1646. These violent and political initiatives were nonetheless insufficient to erase or limit Njinga's power in the region. After her military losses to the Portuguese in 1626 and 1629, she began her conquest of the neighboring Matamba Kingdom, ultimately establishing herself as ruler of both Ndongo and Matamba in 1648.

In this same year, and as the Portuguese reconquered Luanda from the Dutch, Njinga began correspondence with the Vatican with the goal of gaining the Vatican's formal political recognition as ruler of the Ndongo and Matamba Kingdoms. In exchange for recognition, the Vatican sent missionaries to Njinga's court and established churches in her kingdoms, beginning in the 1650s. From then until her death in 1663, she corresponded extensively with the Vatican to ensure sovereignty while also working to reintegrate people formerly enslaved into Ndongo-Matamba societies. During this final period of her life, she reinitiated direct diplomatic relations with the Portuguese and eventually signed the aforementioned peace treaty of 1657. Peace with the Portuguese temporarily secured Ndongo-Matamba sovereignty until 1671, when the kingdom was invaded and integrated into Portuguese Angola. One can argue that Njinga's unrelenting resistance to Portuguese imperialism played a significant part in postponing European encroachment and colonization of southwestern Africa beyond coastal regions until the late nineteenth century.

Njinga in Western imperial representation

As Njinga resisted colonization, her body and its actions were in many ways semantically ensnared by binary thinking and racialized modes of imperial signification. Her transgressive use of masculine behaviors (in other words, those sanctioned only to cisgender men) within her repertoire of performativity[8] led to racialized European images and narratives of a volatile, unstable, and abject ruler who was to be distrusted and ultimately removed from power. These actions included access to sexual exploitation over subalternized bodies, use of male attire, and enactment of physical violence in battle. Equally important, and perhaps most substantially transgressive, Njinga accessed a sphere of knowledge and privilege afforded nearly exclusively to men. By entering these spaces and challenging their foundational racist and misogynistic discourses surrounding African women's roles and bodies, she presented a greater threat to patriarchal and European systems of representation and concentrations of power.

Due to her powerful role in southwestern African politics and resistance to European imperialism, Njinga figured prominently in European imperialist cultural production and historiography. Through deeply racialized, sexualized, abjectified, and gendered imagery and discourses, her body and actions came to be a text within what T. Denean Sharpley-Whiting has called "a totalizing system of representation"[9] at the heart of Western imperialism's epistemology and mechanisms of signification. I use the term "assemblage" – as indicated in this chapter's title – to designate and frame the myriad, conflicting, and overlapping discourses, images, and narratives that have signified Njinga's life and body. These draw on her many notable accomplishments and the complexities of her legacy – anti-colonial resistance, shrewd political and military decisions, and strategic negotiations with European colonial powers, including the slave trade to the Americas and Europe. Njinga has been integrated into and rendered via an assortment of assemblages that span spectrums of political ideology, historiography, and public memory.

European travelers, historians, politicians, and artists have notably rendered Njinga through discourses that have informed the inscription of Black women in the *longue durée* of Western imperialism through white masculine gazes. As Jennifer Morgan underscores in her exploration of imperial male travel writing, "Europe had a long tradition of identifying Others through the monstrous physiognomy or sexual behavior of women."[10] Njinga's body, political actions, and sexual life were thus imperially translated into the racialized lexicon and textuality of imperial meaning and claims to knowledge while becoming part of an "iconography of danger and monstrosity."[11] Some of the earliest examples of European writing and painting on Njinga came from Antonio Giovanni Cavazzi de Montecuccolo, one of the Capuchin missionaries who resided in her court from 1654 until her death in 1663. Although he also came to be her chronicler, Cavazzi took biased liberties in reframing her endeavors and legacies through a white supremacist gaze that discredited, abjectified, and vilified Njinga to his European audiences. His paintings and poetry on Njinga provided Europeans with an assembled story of an African queen who ruled with treachery and moral corruption toward her own people as well as her enemies, thus rendering the implied European self *vis-à-vis* the Black other as both the apex of valid personhood and the more benevolent ruler of bodies to be colonized. His paintings include a visual rendering of Njinga's diplomatic visit to the Portuguese governor in Luanda in 1662 in which, due to lack of seating, Njinga orders one of her servants to get on all fours and serve as her chair. In another painting, Njinga sits on a lavish rug surrounded by her servants and orders a woman to be punished – a ruling executed by two men who, in the painting, can be seen grabbing her breasts with objects while her hands appear to be tied behind her back.

His poetry on Njinga designates a racialized place, marked by excess, for her among earlier historical and mythological female figures who, in Cavazzi's eyes, attained notoriety via treacherous means. These include Medea, Agrippina, and Helen of Troy, who challenged gender roles, political structures, or patriarchal orders of power to varying degrees, but whose actions have also been renarrativized within imperial patriarchal matrices of power. For Cavazzi, Njinga surpasses all of these earlier figures in supposed brutality toward her own people and unethical transgressions. He labels Njinga "a most cunning thief" who instead of rallying together a nation as Helen did with Troy, or Agrippina with Rome, "overturned, destroyed, and ruined Ethiopia"[12] – Ethiopia being the early modern European term for nearly all regions of sub-Saharan Africa. In other words, according to Cavazzi, her resistance to European imperialism did not save Ndongo and Matamba but rather contributed to their downfall.

Another missionary of her court, Antonio Gaeta, went on to write a biography of Njinga's life, political endeavors, and ties to the Catholic Church, titled *The Marvelous Conversion to the Holy Faith of Christ of Queen Njinga and her Kingdom of Matamba in Central Africa*, and published in 1669. Like Cavazzi, Gaeta also compares Njinga to female political figures of Antiquity but nonetheless articulates her difference in terms of a "warlike Amazon," "pagan idolater," and practitioner of "diabolic ceremonies."[13] Following Cavazzi and Gaeta, other European missionaries, colonists, chroniclers, and cultural producers wrote extensively on Njinga in the eighteenth and nineteenth centuries, reproducing similar tropes while describing her as cannibalistic and sexually deviant, ultimately becoming a prominent reference for French libertine writers. The latter would posit her into an assemblage of European imagery and narratives on Black women as a profoundly racialized and eroticized image of transgression against sexual norms – a corporal site of sexual difference and fantasy for European consumption and negotiation of European sexual identities.

French writer Jean-Louis Castilhon's *Zingha, Queen of Angola*, published in 1769, the first fictional work in which Njinga figures as a subject, renders Njinga through the author's racialized fantasies of her, themselves drawn from the aforementioned works of missionaries. In Castilhon's novel, Njinga escapes cannibalistic desire through her thirst for power. Marquis de Sade and other libertine French authors would retake the racist trope of a cannibal Njinga, most notably in his *Philosophy in the Bedroom* (1795). In defense of his argument for a society that privileges sexual pleasure above all sorts of social order and of his definition of sexual pleasure as the sole aim of human existence, he renders and deploys an image of Njinga and her kingdom as the political example *par excellence* of a debased ruler and a society free of all sexual norms that were foundational to European claims to civilization. In Sade's view of an ideal society, all actions in search of sexual pleasure, as violent as they may be, are fully justified and should not be punished.

His portrayal of Njinga went far beyond his arguments in favor of the primacy of sexual pleasure, articulating her as a hypersexual ruler who effectively ruled, and was ruled by, her sexual desires, with no allusion to her political life and complex diplomatic maneuvers. As a sexual tyrant, Sade's Njinga exploited and killed her sex partners, men and women; killed pregnant women; and legally established prostitution. In promoting libertinism in Europe, Sade utilized and further exoticized a version of Njinga he had encountered in Cavazzi, Gaeta, and Castilhon as an example of a "far-away" society that had taken his tenets to excess. In other words, despite looking to challenge European norms, Sade nonetheless did so within a framework of European civilization built on imperial projects and held on to claims of white supremacy. This libertine European society he envisaged would still represent the core of normative personhood and knowledge despite challenging the sexual discourses that traditionally othered colonized bodies.

Also at the turn of the nineteenth century, German philosopher GWF Hegel used this colonial image of Njinga in teaching his philosophy of history. More specifically, in his lectures on the "geographical basis of history,"[14] he alludes to her without naming her specifically when discussing an African "state composed of women" from "a former time" and "whose head was a woman." He goes on:

> She is said to have pounded her own son in a mortar, to have besmeared herself with the blood, and to have the blood of pounded children at hand. She is said to have driven away or put to death all the males, and commanded the death of all male children.[15]

He utilized this imagery of Njinga as part of his European supremacist and colonialist argument, which posited Europeanness as the core of history and that Africa and other colonized spaces were to be objects of European history. This argument hinged on discrediting and erasing non-European forms of knowledge as they pertained to economic development of the land and political structure. For Hegel, Njinga's rule confirmed his view that normative European gender norms and patriarchal orders of power were abjectly corrupted in Africa, further condemning the continent to historylessness, from which European colonization had to save it. Hence his narrativization of Njinga's rule: "These furies destroyed everything in the neighbourhood, and were driven to constant plunderings, because they did not cultivate the land. Captives in war were taken as husbands."[16]

European paintings and drawings of Njinga also emerged in the centuries after her death and building on the tropes found in Cavazzi's paintings. The most widely circulated of these is Achille Devéria's from 1830 – a drawn portrait in which Njinga wears a crown on her head, while her torso is covered by only a cloak held up over her shoulder by a pin resembling a jeweled rose. Around her neck is what appears to be a pearl necklace. Despite the seemingly unassuming regal attire, characteristic of European royalty, her exposed breast serves to render her as a sexual other – an integral component to the consistent racialization of women of African descent in European imperial imaginaries, past and present. In this sense, the painting enacts the colonial discursive confluence of hypersexuality or sexual accessibility with epistemic deviance that has marked colonized bodies in general and Black women in particular.

Anti-colonial and diasporic assemblages

Njinga did not exist solely in European imperial systems of representation, however. Anti-colonial movements and sentiment during the last century of Portuguese colonialism kept alive, or in some cases recovered, a version of Njinga's life and actions more similar to her documented biography. After the fall of Ndongo, Matamba, and other Kimbundu-speaking kingdoms in the northwestern region of current-day Angola, stories of Njinga's resistance to the Portuguese endured among residents living under Portuguese rule. As organized anti-colonial movements emerged in the mid-twentieth century, so too did consolidated anti-colonial systems of representation and national discourse that also looked to undergird a unified struggle against the Portuguese that traversed regions, ethnic groups, and language.

Angolan political sovereignty, won and declared in 1975, saw the integration of anti-colonial recoveries of Njinga into official national discourse and disseminated in public education and state-run media. A host of prominent cultural producers with ties to the postcolonial ruling party, the People's Movement for the Liberation of Angola (MPLA), also released different products revolving around Njinga's resistance against the Portuguese. As cultural scholar Inocência Mata argues, this postcolonial articulation of Njinga in the MPLA-ruled public sphere was about more than fomenting a decolonial system of historical signifiers; it was also "a strategy of constructing a 'grandiose narrative,' characteristic of nationalist ideologies."[17] She points out notable cases, including a 1960 poem by Angola's first president and MPLA leader, Agostinho Neto, shortly after his arrest by Portuguese authorities on suspicion of political dissidence. In the poem "The Raising of the Flag," the poetic "I" dreams of liberation from prison and returning to an Angola fighting for independence.[18] The poem effectively utilizes Njinga and Ngola Kiluanje kia Samba, founder of Ndongo, as early ancestors of a precolonial sovereignty and an anti-colonial lineage of resistance of which MPLA fighters are the heirs. Though the poem does not make explicit reference to the MPLA over other movements, the combination of "soldiers" and "poets" in the stanza mentioned conveys the makeup of the MPLA movement, formed by urban colonized elites (including colonial literati) and white colonists in favor of Angolan independence.

Ties between Njinga and the MPLA were made more explicit in Manuel Pedro Pecavira's novel *Nzinga Mbandi*, published in 1975. Mata considers that "based on the novel's title, one can surmise that its intention was to initiate an inversion of the Portuguese colonial image of an African queen bordering the sub-human based on her supposed cannibalism and cruelty."[19] For her, this apparent intervention against imperial historicity and knowledge is complicated by the novel's paratext – its epigraph. In this regard, Mata highlights Pecavira's dedication of the novel to the MPLA army, known as FAPLA (People's Armed Forces of Liberation of Angola), which establishes a historical connection between MPLA anti-colonial resistance and that of Njinga three centuries earlier. This connection notably leaves out the numerous other anti-colonial movements in Angola that resisted the Portuguese, thus positing and legitimizing the MPLA, the postcolonial ruling party, as the principal agent of liberation and revolutionary heirs to Njinga. Therefore, Njinga became part of a postcolonial revolutionary mythology allied to the party's promises and initial policies of nationalization, wealth redistribution, and worker rights.

In the decades following independence, Njinga would continue to be a prevalent symbol of precolonial national glory and resistance against the forces of Empire (whether colonialism or late capitalism). MPLA rhetoric and initiatives have foregrounded Njinga's legacy (while placing the party as part of this legacy) at exceptional moments of Angolan post-independence history, in triumph and to combat insurgency against a party that has since abandoned Marxist policies in practice, giving rise to a small urban millionaire/billionaire class with close and often familial ties to MPLA leadership. In 2002, a large statue of Njinga was erected in downtown Luanda, funded by the MPLA, to mark the 27th anniversary of independence. The year is also relevant because it marked the end of an almost 30-year civil war (beginning before independence) following the death of Jonas Savimbi, leader of UNITA (Union for the Total Independence of Angola), formerly supported by the United States and apartheid South Africa, and long posited by the MPLA as an enemy of Angolan independence and ally of Western capitalism.

As the twenty-first century has seen the growth of economic inequality in Angola and state-backed monopolies, protest and unrest against the MPLA has also intensified. With this have come severe cases of state repression and incarceration of dissidents, which have overlapped with continued national narratives of anti-colonial lore. It is in this context that Njinga has once again been highlighted in the public sphere, in the shape of the 2013 film *Njinga: Rainha de Angola* [*Njinga: Queen of Angola*]. The film's production has notable ties to the MPLA and directly to then president José Eduardo dos Santos, who served from 1979 to 2017 and whose family members have accumulated substantial wealth and international political power. His son, José Paulino dos Santos, better known by his artist name, Coreón Dú, produced *Njinga: Queen of Angola*, and through his own production company, Semba Comunicações. Therefore, the MPLA's articulation of national history temporarily dovetails with, and arguably occurs in relation to, the growing public unrest from an economically disenfranchised majority.

In addition to being produced and released via political ties to the ruling party, *Njinga: Queen of Angola* deploys colonial stereotypes of precolonial African societies and cultural practices while simplifying otherwise complex structures of Ndongo government. The film nonetheless offers an important and highly disseminated revision of colonial representations of Njinga. An early battle scene against a Portuguese brigade shows Njinga leading her military to victory from the front lines, attacking soldiers with an axe and shield. The film begins with the death of her father, Mbande a Ngola, at the hands of traitors whom she suspects of having conspired with the Portuguese and her brother's rise to power. As her brother and eventual king, Ngola Mbande, lays claim to the throne, arguing that Ndongo needs a man with a warrior spirit to fight the Portuguese, one of the leaders retorts: "What about Njinga? She is a greater warrior than Mbande."[20] In this regard, whereas European accounts of Njinga posited her gender insubordination[21] as a sign of racialized monstrosity, the film's writers incorporate such transgressiveness into the formation of a national hero. Similarly, the cruelty that had been such an integral component of European representations is transformed in the film, as she is configured as a noble savior of the kingdom with "purity and honesty of heart."[22] Even her brother and the Portuguese laud her noble character traits. Furthermore, she is alibied from any involvement in her brother's death, though not without suspicions after she assumes power.

Also of note is the film's treatment of her sexuality, particularly with regard to historical accounts of her possession of male concubines. Instead, the film develops a romantic relationship between Njinga and Ngola Mbande's fictionalized assistant, Jaga Kasa Kongola. The relationship develops in the film through performances of heterosexual masculine chivalry by which Kasa Kongola courts Njinga, offering gifts as the film's score introduces light piano keys for romantic effect. On the one hand, one can argue that this screenwriting choice undoes colonial inscriptions of Njinga as a hypersexual and abject threat to masculinity. On the other hand, this decision places Njinga into a matrix of compulsory cisgenderism, monogamy, and heterosexuality that is at the core of imperial notions of valid personhood. This revision of her sexual life thus appears to be a prerequisite for the construction of a Black female hero in an articulation of modern postcolonial nationhood that does not disturb patriarchal orders of power and bodies. In this regard, the film's radical potential is limited to the inscription of a figure of anti-colonial resistance while nonetheless mitigating Black women's agency into the confines of imperial patriarchal notions of valid personhood. Although their romance does not last long after Kasa Kongola accuses her of killing Ngola Mbande and the latter's son in order not to threaten her right to the throne, the romance is once again reestablished during the film's final scene, when they lock eyes from afar during the celebration marking Njinga's defeat of Ngola Hari and reassumption of control over Ndongo.

The film aims at a decolonial epistemology that nonetheless forecloses particular revisions of race, gender, and sexuality as they intersect with one another. In this sense, one can argue that the film, in reshaping Njinga's sexuality and gender performativity, prevents her from operating as a site of a more radical Black feminist epistemology whereby repertoires of racialized and gendered behaviors can be revised, acting as a fomenter of "knowledge that fosters empowerment and social justice."[23] Such hegemonically sanctioned repertoires continue to inform the pathologization and systemic oppression of particular identities.

Conclusion

Njinga has also been recovered and maintained within diasporic Black feminist archives over the last century, in which her life and legacy have been circuited toward a deeper dismantling of Empire and the articulation of decolonial knowledge production. This is best exemplified by the poem "Song of Love and Respect for Queen Ana de Souza," by Afro-Cuban poet Georgina Herrera, published in 1978. Herrera opens more radical possibilities for future inscriptions of Njinga by focusing on her relentless struggle against Empire.[24] In centralizing Njinga in her articulation of the African diaspora, Herrera conveys diaspora as a space of counter-hegemonic renegotiation and reinvention, utilizing Njinga in her own development of a Black feminist epistemology that is global and trans-temporal. Herrera's poem also intervenes in a particular historical moment in which the Cuban nation-state resists the forces of Empire at home and through military, social, and infrastructural collaboration with recently independent Angola, supporting the MPLA independence movement and nation-building process against the US-backed and South Africa–backed UNITA during the 1970s, 1980s, and 1990s. Herrera renders Njinga's legacy through a lexicon of unfixity tied to resistance against overlapping forces of Empire and patriarchy, with "strong wind," "furious flame," and "never prisoner" marking resistance to both the physical and economic apparatuses of Empire as well as against its epistemological mechanisms that endeavor to confine the body and being of Herrera's evoked Black female subject. While the archives of European imperialism have contorted her life and body into its racialized and gendered tenets of white supremacy, anti-colonial and diasporic archives of her life and legacy have emerged in the last century. The latter continue to grow and are constituted by different images varying in degrees of radical potential. These can be found not only in the realms of cultural production but also in scholarly interventions reclaiming African queer histories and epistemologies.

For instance, the aforementioned work of Murray and Roscoe places Njinga as a key figure in the articulation of a queer African history and a radical queering of how gender and sexuality have been understood in different times and spaces across Africa, especially through the Western imperial lens of heteronormativity and cisgenderism. Though their assertion of the Ndongo Kingdom as a matrilineal society is a topic of debate among historians, and the European travel narratives cited can be further problematized, Murray and Roscoe's analysis of Njinga's life sheds important light on how Njinga's insubordination toward European gender norms "was not some personal idiosyncrasy but was based on beliefs that recognized gender as situational and symbolic as much as a personal, innate characteristic of the individual."[25] The reconfiguration of Njinga's life through queer critiques and epistemologies delinks gender performance from European imperialist knowledges and reclaims gender as a fluid everyday social practice rather than a fixed and essentialized trait as trafficked by Empire. In becoming part of different colonial and anti-colonial assemblages, Njinga has been repeatedly translated from reality and into narratives and images that serve both the reproduction of Empire as well as different models of resistance and emergent epistemologies of radical engagement.

Notes

1 Throughout this chapter, I will use this spelling of her name, as it corresponds to the orthographic rules of Kimbundu placed in effect in Angola in 1980.
2 Stephen O. Murray and Will Roscoe, *Boy-Wives and Female-Husbands: Studies in African Homosexualities* (New York: Palgrave Macmillan, 1998), 1.
3 For the most thorough historical interrogation of Queen Njinga's life and legacies, see Linda M. Heywood. *Njinga of Angola: Africa's Warrior Queen* (Cambridge, MA: Harvard University Press, 2017).
4 Heywood, *Njinga of Angola*, 45.
5 Ibid., 12.
6 António de Oliveira de Cadornega. *História Geral das Guerras Angolanas*, ed. José Delgado, 3 vols (Lisbon: Agência Geral do Ultramar, 1972), 1:161.
7 Heywood, *Njinga of Angola*, 59.
8 Judith Butler, *Bodies that Matter: On the Discursive Limits of "Sex"* (New York: Routledge, 1993).
9 T. Denean Sharpely-Whiting, *Black Venus: Sexualized Savages, Primal Fears, and Primitive Narratives in French* (Durham: Duke University Press, 1999), 22.
10 Jennifer Morgan, "Male Travelers, Female Bodies, and the Gendering of Racial Ideology, 1500–1770," in *Bodies in Contact: Rethinking Colonial Encounters in World History*, Tony Ballantyne and Antoinette Burton (eds) (Durham: Duke University Press, 2005), 57.
11 Ibid.
12 Giovanni Antonio Cavazzi da Montecuccolo, "Missione evangelica nel Regno de Congo" (Volume A. Private collection, Araldi Family, Modena, Italy, 1668), 213–14.
13 Gaeta, *Meravigliosa*, 228.
14 GWF Hegel, *Lectures on the Philosophy of History* (London: Henry G. Bohn, 1861), 101.
15 Hegel, *Lectures*, 101.
16 Ibid.
17 Inocência Mata, *A Rainha Nzinga Mbandi: História, Memória, e Mito* (Lisbon: Edições Colibri, 2010), 24.
18 Agostinho Neto, "O Içar da Bandeira," *Sagrada Esperança* (Lisbon: Sá da Costa Editora, 1987).
19 *Njinga: Rainha de Angola*. Directed by Sérgio Graciano. Luanda: Semba Comunicações, 2013, min. 8.
20 Ibid, min. 26.

21 Butler, *Bodies that Matter*.
22 *Njinga: Rainha de Angola*, min. 8.
23 Patricia Hill Collins, *Black Feminist Thought: Knowledge, Consciousness, and the Politics of Empowerment* (New York: Routledge, 2000), 269.
24 Georgina Herrera, *Granos de Sol y Luna* (La Habana: Unión de Escritores y Artistas, 1978), 10.
25 Murray and Roscoe, *Boy-Wives*, 2.

8

Preserving the memories of precolonial Nigeria

Cultural narratives of precolonial heroines

Aje-Ori Agbese

When it comes to Africa's precolonial history, debates persist on whether women played an active role beyond the domestic sphere.[1] Western and African men who told of Africa's past largely "celebrated male sectors of society to the neglect of female contributions. Most chroniclers ignored women's economic, religious, or social activities."[2] But recent studies, driven by the popularity of feminism, have pushed for a retelling of African women's histories. According to Ogbomo and Ogbomo, we need to continue challenging "the myth that African women have been among the most oppressed in the world."[3] In African countries where patriarchy and long-held gender stereotypes have further oppressed women, challenging this myth is even more urgent.

So far, historians have found and used folklores/tales, oral accounts, written records, proverbs, and myths to reveal women's invaluable contributions. Another way is to engage the past through popular mass media/communication forms like film, novels, theatre, and television. According to Mike Kirkup, historical media are popular ways of engaging audiences with the past because they bring history "to life, inspire lively debates, arguments and discussions around a range of topics."[4] Historical media can also help audiences "renegotiate cultural memory and their understanding of how the past shapes the present."[5] Yet, communication aspects in the areas of empowerment and gender equality "remain largely unrecognized and understudied, even by scholars in feminist communication, development communication, persuasion and other forms of social change."[6] Scholars must acknowledge that "writing women out of history has not only discouraged or punished women who challenged the status quo, it has also ignored and reduced their accomplishments."[7] Moreover, historical films "offer a privileged site for scholars of cinema, media, history, and many other disciplines to interrogate a nation's relationship with the past."[8]

The purpose of this chapter, therefore, is to describe and discuss how Nigerians are using mass media and theatre to preserve and share the memories and contributions of precolonial Nigerian women to nation-building, thus contributing to a new image of Nigerian women. Specifically, it examines those works that celebrate and portray the heroism of three women – Queen Moremi Ajasaro of Ife Kingdom, Queen Amina of Zaria, and Princess Inikpi of Igala Kingdom. Nigeria is home to the world's second largest movie industry, Nollywood, and has used media and theatre for national development and social orientation since the 1940s, which makes it a good site for this study.

This discussion is also important because since 2009, Nollywood and theatrical works on historical events and figures have increasingly focused on notable women. The current global push for women's empowerment and gender equality in all spheres of life may be responsible for this focus. However, this push will be incomplete if past efforts of women are not considered. Moreover, scholars have contended for decades that the messages people receive about gender roles play a critical role in how women see themselves and how society views women.[9] Nigerian state and local governments are also investing in these projects. One example is the Kogi State Diaries, "which seeks to harness the media as a tool for telling the story of the people of the state and showcasing their cultural diversity to a global audience."[10] For Nigerian women especially, stories about historical women are relevant today because they "suggest that we should give womenfolk their pride of place."[11]

This chapter provides a background on each woman named and discusses some works available about them. As Nigeria is home to more than 250 ethnic groups, these women are symbolically more popular within their ethnic groups than the nation in general. Therefore, apart from Queen Amina, people of the same ethnicity as these women have sponsored or spearheaded the projects. The discussion begins with Moremi of Ile-Ife (Ife town) in present-day Osun state.

Queen Moremi Ajasaro of Ife

Queen Moremi Ajasaro of Ife is probably the most celebrated woman in Yorubaland. Ife, the recognized founding place of Yoruba kingdom, is in western Nigeria. Presumably, Moremi lived in the twelfth century and was born in Offa in present-day Kwara state. She later married Ooni Oranmiyan of Ife and had a son, Olurogbo. She was and is still renowned for her beauty.

As the story goes, another tribe, called Ugbo/Igbo, raided Ife for several years. According to Ibrahim Anoba, the people of Ife were afraid of the Ugbo because they appeared "completely covered in raffia leaves," which were used to separate people from oracles and the sacred forest.[12] Moremi consulted the Esimiri goddess, who advised her to surrender next time the Ugbo raided. She acquiesced and also married the king of Ugbo, Orumakin. With time, she gained his confidence and learned the secret of the Ugbo raiders – they were men, not spirits, who could be defeated with fire. Moremi later returned to Ife, divulged the secret, and devised a plan. The next time the raiders came, an ambush awaited and defeated them.

According to the current Ooni of Ile-Ife, Oba Adeyeye Enitan Ogunwusi, Moremi was the "real mother of liberty," whose actions and sacrifice saved Ile-Ife.[13] She is immortalized in music and art. In 2016, Oba Ogunwusi erected a statue in her honor, which is the third tallest statue in Africa and the tallest in Nigeria.[14] For her contributions to Yoruba history, there are also plays, about six Yoruba language films, and one English film titled *Moremi*. The movies are mostly about powerful, mythical, or modern women leaders, the exploits of beautiful women, or women creating wealth with a Moremi-like theme. Only one of them is about her.

In 2009, 1st Eye Productions released a historical epic called *Moremi Ajasaro*. The movie recounts Moremi's story, based on Chief Duro Ladipo's stage play *Moremi Ajasaro*. The storyline matches much of what is known about Moremi and how she saved Ife. The movie's morals are built on three principles – love, patriotism, and courage. In *Moremi Ajasaro*, viewers get a strong appreciation for Moremi's courage, her love for her husband and child, and her love for her people in Ife. The portrayal implicitly asks whether present Nigerian leaders will make heavy sacrifices for their people. However, "even as a film and its characters reflect the time when it was made, we are reinterpreting the film from our own perspective."[15]

One difference seen in the movie's interpretation of history is how it portrayed the Ugbo as savages who lived in the forest. This portrayal contradicts historical accounts that identify the Ugbo as the original inhabitants of Ife. They lost Ife when they could not produce a king and moved to Ilaje, also in present-day Ondo state. They also speak Yoruba. Another choice the filmmaker made was to show Moremi living into old age and still contributing to the community. However, the movie suggested she felt unappreciated following her husband's death.

Another way Moremi has been immortalized is through *Queen Moremi: The Musical*. It premiered on December 21, 2018 in Lagos, Nigeria and has sold out each time. This is the first play on Moremi with a musical component. Directed by Bolanle Austen-Peters, the story in many ways matches what is known of Moremi's legend with an injection of folklore, solos, and modern musical beats. However, unlike 1st Eye Productions' epic, the musical has a strong feminist theme that puts women at the center and as part of Ife's victory over Ugbo. According to Austen-Peters, the feminist perspective was selected because she believes in equal rights.[16] The musical emphasizes that women prevailed where men had failed. Kings had sacrificed virgins and animals for years against the Ugbo raids to no avail, but a woman succeeded. When Ife attacked Ugbo, its army included women. In their costume choices, the women are also shown wearing the clothes of warriors, which include shorts. Audiences see a community that succeeded because it included women in every aspect.

Moremi's husband is also portrayed as controlling and patriarchal, one who sees little value in women. When Moremi tells him of her mission, he calls her a "mere woman." He reminds her that as her husband, he owns her and forbids her, as her lord and master, from going on the mission. When she insists, he accuses her of infidelity and promises to marry another wife if she goes. These sentiments resonate with the patriarchal structure in Nigeria today, where husbands contend that they own their wives and can divorce and replace them at will.[17] The musical speaks specifically to the contemporary women's movement in Nigeria, which is mostly fought at home, where the supremacy of men is maintained culturally, traditionally, and religiously.

However, the musical shared some untold aspects of Moremi's history. For one thing, it portrayed the Ugbos as aborigines of Ife and the original inhabitants. This account matches recent historical discoveries contradicting long-held beliefs that Ife was the founding place of the Yoruba. New information suggests that the Yoruba immigrated to Ife.[18] The musical also differs in its portrayal of Moremi as a hunter and the daughter of a hunter; a warrior, and not a princess of Offa. This account suggests she married into royalty. That Austen-Peters chose hunting rather than another profession should not be disregarded. This is because hunting is a male profession. In Yoruba culture, hunters are also perceived as brave businessmen, capable of fighting spirits, and often serve as security and soldiers.[19] Therefore, portraying Moremi as a hunter suggested she was brave, economically independent (hunters sold meat to the community), and strong. If Moremi was a hunter, she was also a soldier. Perhaps Austen-Peters reframed Moremi as one who married into wealth rather than one who was born into it to explain why the raids disturbed her so greatly. If she had been royalty from the beginning, she would have been shielded from what regular people suffered. But as a woman who lived and worked among the people, she would know first-hand how the raids impacted non-royals and, as a hunter, would defend her people.

Another element the musical emphasized was Moremi's struggle to become a mother and her closeness to Olurogbo (called Ela here). He was the only child she conceived after years of childlessness. To eventually lose the child she had waited long to have in a culture where children solidify marriages highlights the immense sacrifice Moremi made for Ife. There is yet another controversial message in the musical – Moremi committed polyandry for Ife. She married the Olu of Ugbo without divorcing her first husband. This unexplored part of the story is critical, considering that many Nigerian cultures frown on the idea that a woman can marry more than one man, an idea that is unthinkable to some. But this heroine did, and then returned to her husband. It is telling that historical accounts emphasize that Oranmiyan accepted her and reinstated her as a queen, though he had married other women while she was gone.

Apart from the play and musical, in 2019, Akin Alabi released a short animated video on Moremi.[20] Titled *Moremi: The Legend*, the six-minute video tells the story of Moremi as others have, portraying her as courageous, wise, and beautiful (see Figure 8.1). Alabi said he chose animation so "our technology-driven generation can relate."[21] Unlike other popular narratives of Moremi, the animation depicted the king, not Moremi, consulting the oracle on the Ugbo problem and being told that a woman would solve it. Like the musical, the animation showed Moremi leading the battle against the Ugbo in the end.

Overall, these projects have renewed conversation and interest in Moremi's legend. A deeper examination of these works, especially 1st Eye Productions and Austen-Peters' musical, suggests that recent global movements on gender, especially from 2009 onward, may have affected the artistic differences and interpretations. In 2009, Nigeria was working toward achieving the UN Millennium Development goals (MDGs), which include gender equality and women's empowerment. Therefore, 1st Eye Productions' film, which came out in 2009, was in line with Nigeria's efforts to meet this MDG, because it suggested that women had played important roles in nation-building in the past and could do so in the present. By 2014, Nigeria was witnessing more discussions on gender issues, thanks to feminist literature (with authors like Chimamanda Ngozi Adichie, Ayobami Adebayo, and Lola Shoneyin), Boko Haram's kidnapping of 276 high school girls, online discussions and debates (such as #FemaleInNigeria), and women's empowerment movements such as #MeToo and #NoMore.

These events may have influenced Austen-Peters' decision to portray Moremi using a feminist lens. Austen-Peters' Moremi is one current Nigerian that women can relate to, because she wove in issues that Nigerian women face today. This Moremi worked and was financially independent, as are contemporary Nigerian women, even when married. Moremi's efforts to convince her husband to let her be captured suggest she was politically and socially active in her community, and also portray the patriarchal beliefs and systems that prevent women from participating in politics and social issues even today. The conversation she had with her husband about

Figure 8.1 Animated short *Moremi: The Legend*.

letting her join the fight redefined Moremi as an agent of history, a woman who wanted to act and not remain a victim. She also understood that her biggest obstacle lay in her home, in her husband's hands. Rather than go against him, she convinced him to work with and support her.

Fertility is also a serious issue in Nigerian marriages, and women are blamed when a couple cannot or does not conceive on schedule. Divorce, adultery, and polygyny are common for this reason, with the woman who has no children bearing the shame. To sacrifice a child without hope for another is indeed a powerful message in Moremi's story. Still, the musical's conclusion brought women back to a traditional perspective – a woman is nothing without children.

Queen Amina of Zazzau

Among Nigeria's many heroines, Queen Amina of Zazzau might be the most popular and most studied. This may be because written records of her feats exist.[22] Hers is probably a unique tale of a Hausa woman, because scholars have stressed the "subordination of women to men arising from an intersection of a patriarchal Islam and Hausa cultural values, which were in place before colonization," for years.[23] In his work, Balbasatu Ibrahim also contends that Hausa women had no rights before Usman Dan Fodio's jihad from 1804 to 1814 and were treated as slaves. But other scholars dispute this, arguing that the jihad actually challenged and ended the liberalism women had enjoyed as active members of all spheres of life.[24] These different perspectives make Amina's legend even more intriguing.

Amina was born in 1533, the oldest child and daughter of the ruler of Zazzau, Bakwa of Turunku. Her family was a wealthy one, as its members traded in various goods, including metal, cloth, and horses. Legend has it that Amina spent her days honing her fighting and military skills from a very young age. She led the Zazzau Cavalry and was admired for her swordsmanship. She also became a member of the royal cabinet at sixteen, when her mother named her Magajiya (female heir) of Zazzau. Upon her father's death, her younger brother Karama inherited the throne and reigned for 10 years. After Karama's death, Amina took over, and within three months, naturally, led the Zazzau army on a path of domination. During her 34-year reign, Amina expanded the kingdom and made it the center of trade in Hausaland.[25] She boosted her kingdom's wealth and power with gold, slaves, and agriculture (with new crops such as kolanuts). Because her people were talented metal workers, Amina introduced metal armor, including iron helmets and chain mail, to her army.[26] She also conquered and controlled large cities like Borno, Kano, and Katsina in the north and Idah and Nupe in the south.

Amina also introduced architecture to Hausaland, the most famous example being the "ganuwar Amina" (Amina's walls).[27] Amina made Zazzau the largest far-reaching kingdom in Nigeria due to her military assaults and prowess. In her personal life, it is said that she never married (she rejected all suitors from a young age) and had no children. Rather, she took a man from a land they invaded, had sex with him, and killed him the next morning so that "he could tell no stories."[28] Amina's history is memorialized in countless ways. There are stamps, books, and various sculptures commemorating her contributions to Hausaland. There are also plays and TV shows about her. One popular show that may be based on Amina is the American series *Xena: The Warrior Princess*.[29] Her story also featured in an episode of a popular 1980s Nigerian television series, *Magana Jari che*.

In 2008, Nollywood released a movie titled *Amina*, starring Genevieve Nnaji, about an Igbo princess adopted by a Hausa royal family. She was not a warrior, but she was strong and honest. The first Nigerian movie to explore Queen Amina's legend is director Izu Ojukwu's epic, *Amina: The Movie*, which was expected to debut in 2018 but was not released, despite intense global promotion. According to the executive producer, Okechukwu Ogunjiofor:

> The movie chronicles the many lives of this exceptional woman; the pain and the agony caused by the betrayal of cherished lovers; the ferocious savagery in the face of all battles and enemies; the cunning manipulation at will of the nobles and sovereigns of kingdoms; and the tender concern over the down-trodden Talakawasor common people.[30]

In an age of women's empowerment, the "film raises an important question on why there are not many female leaders in the world today when history is full of women who have excelled as leaders."[31] Cinematically, the trailers paint a powerful and beautiful image of Amina as a warrior and strategist and invoke different angles to explore her identity. However, it appears that the writers either chose a feminist perspective or worked from the stereotype that Hausa women were relegated to domestic duties during Amina's childhood and before, making Amina an exception. The movie's synopsis suggests the latter, stating that Amina's story is of a princess who "battles forces which have long relegated the female child to the background, to be seen and not heard; subjugated to remain under a man."[32] But this perspective may be far from the truth.

In 2019, YouNeek Studios released a different take on Amina using animation and comics.[33] Through a historical fantasy series called *Malika: The Warrior Princess*, YouNeek tells Amina's story.[34] Like Amina, Malika rules over the kingdom of Azzaz, and expands it, starting in the fifteenth century. She is from the Bakwa family and an undefeated warrior. The first page of the comic frames Malika as a girl who could wield a dagger at a young age. But unlike Amina, Malika has superpowers and also battles the Ming Dynasty to stop it from destroying her people and the world (see Figure 8.2). She also worked for 10 years to unite Azzaz following a civil war. There are other differences too.

Malika, unlike Amina, is the youngest sibling and has a sister called Nadia, who will take over when their father dies. The comic also suggests that both girls are formidable, contradicting the stereotype of Hausa women. The comic also portrays Malika as fiercely protective. For instance, on her way to battle, she rescues a boy from a leopard by killing the animal. In another instance, she engages in combat with General Ras of Bornu, nicknamed "The Savior." Ras is loyal to Malika's uncle, who he thinks deserved the throne instead. Following a battle between their

Figure 8.2 Malika: Warrior Queen.

armies, which she wins, Malika challenges him to single combat. He accepts, assuming he will win. Malika uses moves reminiscent of Neo's in *The Matrix* and triumphs. The trailer for the animated series was released on July 24, 2019. This is the first superhero animated series from Nigeria.

Overall, these stories of Amina have maintained her legacy as a strong, powerful, and capable woman. Amina's portrayals in recent times seem almost superhuman. Unlike Moremi, whose legacy is situated in her femininity and her ability to use it to her advantage, Amina is situated in her rejection of her femininity and her emphasis on her ability to not only challenge paternalistic notions of what women can do, but also take on masculine roles from a young age. Even her sexual history appears masculine, because it is rare to hear of Nigerian women using men only for sex as she did. The idea of whether a Nigerian woman can enjoy sex for the sake of pleasure and not to produce children is often debated on Nigerian Twitter. While Amina appears to have had no interest in anything feminine, none of the works portray her as wanting to become a man (she does not dress like one or speak like one), and they also emphasize her beauty. Perhaps this is to frame her as the total package. At the same time, this frame borders on fantasy and idealism.

Princess Inikpi of Igala Kingdom

The final woman I will discuss is Princess Inikpi of Igala Kingdom. Hers is a story known mostly to the Igala people, who are found in present-day Kogi state in south-eastern Nigeria. Princess Inikpi "was a beautiful and intelligent young woman, whose selfless sacrifice saved her people from doom."[35] Though it is not known when she was born, she existed between the late fifteenth and the sixteenth century. During this era, either the Igalas were at war with the people of Benin, or their kings had a disagreement that could have caused a war. Whatever the version, the gods requested that the Igalas sacrifice Inikpi to ensure victory. Inikpi willingly agreed to sacrifice herself for the kingdom. She, along with nine virgin maids, was buried alive by the bank of the River Niger in Idah. It is said that as the Bini people approached, they saw the entire town engulfed in fire, assumed there was no need to attack, and left.

According to Ahmed Yerima, "Her bravery of self- sacrifice, loyalty, dedication and love become the embodiment of Inikpi as a person, who has since been deified as a goddess."[36] To recognize her contribution, she is memorialized in a statue in Idah, the state capital. There are also two plays and three movies about her. The plays include *The Legendary Inikpi* by Emmy Idegu and *Inipki: The Warrior Princess* by Nath McAbraham-Inajoh. According to Yerima, the plays "deify the young innocent girl" and "can be used to affect, effect and appeal to the consciousness of the Igala people of now and of future generations."[37]

In terms of movies, the three that exist comprise director Dave Ibrahim's *Inikpi: Sacrifice of Redemption* (2013), director Chico Ejiro's *Inikpi: The Legendary Princess* (2017), and director Frank Rajah Arase's *The Legend of Inipki* (2020). The first two are publicly available, while the third premiered on January 24, 2020. Ibrahim's version framed Igalaland as a tributary of Bini, who raided them at will. The Igala were especially afraid of the Bini because among them was a young woman with supernatural powers who ensured Benin's victory in any war. Fearing their doom, the Attah and his chiefs consulted the gods, who asked for Inikpi if they wanted victory. Inikpi is portrayed as one of two children, both female, but she is her father's favorite. She is also very popular in the community and is framed as kind and fair. However, the 2017 version portrays the Attah and Oba as best friends who fight because the Attah mistakenly assumed that the Oba had seized and killed his servants. It also frames Inikpi as fearless, willing to go hunting with her four brothers and even challenging a man who beats his wife.

Figure 8.3 Inikpi's burial in *Inikpi: Sacrifice of Redemption.*

The movies also vary in how Inikpi was buried. The 2013 version shows her being buried while standing in the grave with nine virgin maids. The 2017 version depicts her buried with three teenage boys and nine virgin girls, lying down. Inikpi lies on top of the boys, who carry her as if on a lifter (see Figure 8.3).

Though the movies focused more on the relationships between the kings, both emphasized her sacrifice. A viewer will appreciate her humility and selflessness. Interestingly, Ibrahim compares her to Jesus, using John 3:16 at the end of the movie to signify how in laying her life down for her people, like Jesus, she saved them. But as the Bible verse refers to God's act of giving his only son, perhaps the director was also referring to Ayegba, who sacrificed either his only or his favorite daughter to save the people he loved. Her story is similar to biblical accounts of Jephthah, a judge who promised to sacrifice to God whatever came out to greet him first if he returned safely and defeated the Ammonites.[38] He is victorious, and his daughter and only child is the first person to welcome him. He regrets his vow, but his daughter tells him he must keep it and, like Inikpi, willingly offers herself. Like Inikpi, she died a virgin and is celebrated within certain Jewish sects today.[39] One also sees the significance of Inikpi, as she is not forgotten in Igala's history. Though not a political leader, Inikpi represents a popular saying that women are called on when men fail.

But Inikpi's legend is probably more dramatic and emotional because she was a princess and her father's favorite child. What if she had been a commoner? Would she have had a choice? Would she have tried to convince her father to let her be sacrificed? Would we know her story? After all, she was buried alive with nine virgins, who also sacrificed their lives and futures for Igalaland. Why are they not celebrated?

Conclusion

I looked at these works from a Nigerian woman's perspective, in that "arts and culture play a significant role in shaping the contemporary feminist agenda" because they "are sites where women can challenge male-dominance as a form of political and intellectual intervention."[40]

Women directed and/or produced only three of the works discussed here (*Moremi Ajasaro, Moremi: The Musical*, and *The Legend of Inikpi*).

In this regard, the works examined in this chapter raised issues on patriarchy and tradition. The works on Amina largely represented rather than challenged the status quo, because they focused on her extraordinariness, presented an example of a woman who did what men could do, and celebrated her legacy. Her legend is definitely inspiring. However, there are issues in contemporary Nigeria that the works could have used her legacy to explore, such as marriage/ love and sexuality. Of the three women, Inikpi's history is the most incomplete and as such, open to interpretation.

Ultimately, only Austen-Peters' *Moremi: The Musical* portrayed a heroine of the past with strong feminist undertones that challenged long-held beliefs on gender, gender roles, and issues like fertility and politics in contemporary Nigeria. The musical reframed Moremi as a woman who possessed bravery and strength long before she became a queen. Austen-Peters' decision to make her an active agent of change and to dramatize how she convinced her husband to let her act makes the home the deciding location where a woman can consciously construct who she is and how successful she can be outside it. This resonates with works by Nigerian female authors like Flora Nwapa, Zulu Sofola, and Buchi Emecheta that also identified and placed the struggle for women's rights within the home. Overall, these works are useful for preserving the memories of women who made great strides or sacrifices for their communities, thus serving as precolonial proto-feminist models.

Notes

1 Funmilayo Agbaje, "Reflections on the Challenges Facing Women," *Journal of International Politics* 1, no. 1 (2019).
2 O.W. Ogbomo and Q.O. Ogbomo, "Women and Society in Pre-colonial Iyede," *Anthropos*, 88 (1993): 431.
3 Ibid.
4 Mike Kirkup, "Representing History: Why Use Film?" (2003). Film Education. http://filmeducation .org/pdf/film/rephist.pdf
5 John Trafton, "The End of History in Jim Jarmusch's Only Lovers Left Alive" (2017). https://brightl ightsfilm.com/the-end-of-history-in-jim-jarmuschs-only-lovers-left-alive/#.XUhO9kxFzcu
6 Corrine L. Shefner-Rogers, Nagesh Rao, Everett M. Rogers, and Arun Wayangankar, "The Empowerment of Women Dairy Farmers in India," *Journal of Applied Communication Research*, 26 (1998): 322.
7 Anita Sarkeesian and Laura Hudson, "We Must Rewrite Women's Role in History" (2019). *Time*, March 8, 2016. https://time.com/4248910/women-in-history/
8 John Trafton. "Historical Film." www.oxfordbibliographies.com/view/document/obo-97801997 91286/obo-9780199791286-0239.xml
9 C. Giffard, S. Cunningham, and Nancy Van Lueven, "The Female Face of Poverty: Media and the Gender Divide in the Millennium Development Goals," 2006, Paper presented at the International Communication Association conference.
10 www.nollywoodlibrary.com/mercy-johnon-set-to-premier-new-igala-culture-movie-the-lamb-2/Th estategovernmentsponsoredthemovieoninikpi
11 *Punch*, "Without Moremi, the Yoruba Would Have Never Survived – Ooni," May 3, 2019. https://pu nchng.com/without-moremi-the-yoruba-would-never-have-survived-ooni/
12 Ibrahim Anoba. "African heroes of freedom: Queen Moremi Ajasaro." June 18, 2019. www.libertarian ism.org/columns/african-heroes-freedom-queen-moremi-ajasaro.
13 Gbenga Olarinloye, Ooni of Ife celebrates Moremi Ajasaro, November 11, 2016, www.vanguardngr .com/2016/11/ooni-ife-celebrates-moremi-ajasaro/
14 Abimbola Adegoke, Photos: Statue of Moremi Ajasaro, tallest in Nigeria, unveiled in Ile-Ife, November 22, 2016. https://lifestyle.thecable.ng/moremi-ajasaro-ile-ilfe-tallest-statue/

15 Paul B. Weinstein. "History Written with Lightning." http://faculty.washington.edu/momara/HIS
 TORY%20WRITTEN%20WITH%20LIGHTNING-1.pdf
16 This Day, "Queen Moremi the Musical as December Treat," November 16, 2018. www.thisdaylive
 .com/index.php/2018/11/16/queen-moremi-the-musical-as-december-treat/
17 Godiya Allanana Makama, "Patriarchy and Gender Inequality in Nigeria: The Way Forward," *European
 Scientific Journal* 9, no. 17 (2013).
18 Yemisi Thessy Akinbileje and Joe Igbaro, "Moremi Statue in Ile-Ife: A Symbol of Yoruba Aesthetics,"
 African Research Review 4, no. 1 (2010).
19 http://africa.uga.edu/Yoruba/unit_15/cultureunit.html
20 A trailer is available on YouTube and can be downloaded for $3 from www.moremithelegend.com
21 https://newsvila.com/news/akin-alabi-releases-short-animation-on-queen-moremi/
22 See H.R. Palmer, "The Kano Chronicle," Journal of the Royal Anthropological Institute, 38 (1908):
 58–98.
23 Catherine Coles and Beverly Mack, "Women in Twentieth Century Hausa Society," 6. In *Hausa
 Women in the Twentieth Century*, edited by Catherine Coles and Beverly Mack, 3–26. University of
 Wisconsin, 1991.
24 Coles and Mack, "Women." The *Kano Chronicle* also states that women were involved in politics and
 leadership. Also see Mahdi Adamu, *The Hausa Factor in West African History* (1978), Ahmadu Bello
 University Press.
25 Mirella Sichirollo Patzer, "Amina of Zaria." Accessed June 28, 2019. www.historyandwomen.com/2010
 /08/amina-of-zaria.html
26 Ibid.
27 Jone Johnson Lewis, "Amina, Queen of Zazzau." Accessed June 28, 2019. www.thoughtco.com/amina
 -queen-of-zazzua-3529742
28 Ibid.
29 https://thenerdsofcolor.org/2016/02/10/xena-was-black/
30 Funso Arogundade, "Queen Amina, BoI's Next Movie, Shoots in Jos," December 5, 2015. www.p
 mnewsnigeria.com/2015/12/05/queen-amina-bois-next-movie-shoots-in-jos/
31 http://aminaqueenofzazzau.com/about.php
32 Ibid.
33 See trailer at www.youtube.com/watch?v=ppGA3iMhdGs
34 Watch the creator's description on www.youtube.com/watch?time_continue=153&v=SUDsta2GktE
35 Editor, "Inikpi, Self-Sacrificing Igala Princess," 28 July 2019. https://guardian.ng/sunday-magazine/
 inikpi-self-sacrificing-igala-princess/
36 Ahmed Yerima, "Princess Inikpi and Culture of Sacrificial Leadership for National Development."
 file:///F:/Heroines/Inikpi.pdf
37 Yerima, "Princess Inikpi," 3.
38 See Judges 11:29–40.
39 For more information on Jephthah's daughter, see Elisheva Baumgarten, "'Remember That Glorious
 Girl': Jephthah's Daughter in Medieval Jewish Culture," *The Jewish Quarterly Review*, 97, no. 2 (2007):
 180–209.
40 www.msafropolitan.com/2018/10/nigerian-feminism-past

Bibliography

Adegoke, Abimbola. "Photos: Statue of Moremi Ajasoro, tallest in Nigeria, unveiled in Ile-Ife." November
 22, 2016. https://lifestyle.thecable.ng/moremi-ajasoro-ile-ilfe-tallest-statue/
Agbaje, Funmilayo I. "Reflections on The Challenges Facing Women in Contemporary Nigeria Politics."
 Journal of International Politics 1, no. 1 (2019): 32–8.
Akinbileje, Yemisi Thessy and Igbaro, Joe. "Moremi Statue in Ile-Ife: A Symbol of Yoruba Aesthetics." *African
 Research Review* 4, no. 1 (2010): 14–28.
Anoba, Ibrahim. "African heroes of freedom: Queen Moremi Ajasaro." June 18, 2019. https://www.libertar
 ianism.org/columns/african-heroes-freedom-queen-moremi-ajasaro
Arogundade, Funsho. "Queen Amina, BoI's Next Movie, Shoots in Jos." December 5, 2015. https://www
 .pmnewsnigeria.com/2015/12/05/queen-amina-bois-next-movie-shoots-in-jos/
Baumgarten, Elisheva. "Remember That Glorious Girl": Jephthah's Daughter in Medieval Jewish Culture."
 The Jewish Quarterly Review 97, no. 2 (2007): 180–209.

Coles, Catherine M. and Mack, Beverly B. "Women in Twentieth-Century Hausa Society." In *Hausa women in the Twentieth Century*, edited by Catherine Coles and Beverly Mack, 3–26. University of Wisconsin, 1991.

Editor. "Inikpi, Self-Sacrificing Igala Princess." *The Guardian*. July 28, 2019. https://guardian.ng/sunday-magazine/inikpi-self-sacrificing-igala-princess/

Giffard, C., Cunningham, S. and Van Lueven, Nancy. "The female face of poverty: Media and the gender divide in the Millennium Development Goals." Paper presented at the International Communication Association Conference. 2006.

http://aminaqueenofzazzau.com/about.php

http://www.nollylibrary.com/mercy-johnson-set-to-premier-new-igala-culture-movie-the-lamb-2/

Kirkup, Mike. "Representing History: Why Use Film?" *Film Education*. 2003. Accessed July 2, 2019. http://filmeducation.org/pdf/film/rephist.pdf

Lewis, Jone Johnson. "Amina, Queen of Zazzau." Accessed June 28, 2019. https://www.thoughtco.com/amina-queen-of-zazzua-3529742

Makama, Godiya A. "Patriarchy and Gender Inequality in Nigeria: The Way Forward." *European Scientific Journal* 9, no. 17 (2013):115–44.

Ogbomo, O. W. and Ogbomo, Q. O. "Women and Society in Pre-colonial Iyede." *Anthropos*, 88 (1993):431–441.

Olarinloye, Gbenga, Ooni of Ife celebrates Moremi Ajasaro, November 11, 2016, https://www.vanguardngr.com/2016/11/ooni-ife-celebrates-moremi-ajasoro

Patzer, Mirella Sichirollo. "Amina of Zaria." Accessed June 28, 2019. http://www.historyandwomen.com/2010/08/amina-of-zaria.html

Punch. "Without Moremi, the Yoruba Would Have Never Survived – Ooni." May 3, 2019. https://punchng.com/without-moremi-the-yoruba-would-never-have-survived-ooni/

Sarkeesian, Anita and Hudson, Laura. "We Must Rewrite Women's Role in History." *Time*, March 8, 2016. https://time.com/4248910/women-in-history/

Shefner-Rogers, L. Corrine, Rao, Nagesh, Rogers, M. Everett and Wayangankar, Arun. "The Empowerment of Women Dairy Farmers in India." *Journal of Applied Communication Research* 26 (1998): 319–337.

This Day. "Queen Moremi the Musical as December Treat." November 16, 2018. https://www.thisdaylive.com/index.php/2018/11/16/queen-moremi-the-musical-as-december-treat/

Trafton, John. "The End of History in Jim Jarmusch's Only Lovers Left Alive." 2017. Accessed June 24, 2019. https://brightlightsfilm.com/the-end-of-history-in-jim-jarmuschs-only-lovers-left-alive/#.XUhO9kxFzcu

Weinstein, Paul B. "History Written with Lightning: A Guide to Using Popular Film as a Tool for Historical and Cultural Investigation." Accessed June 24, 2019. http://faculty.washington.edu/momara/HISTORY%20WRITTEN%20WITH%20LIGHTNING-1.pdf

www.msafropolitan.com/2018/10/nigerian-feminism-past

Yerima, Ahmed. "Princess Inikpi and Culture of Sacrificial Leadership for National Development." Accessed May 12, 2019. file:///F:/Heroines/Inikpi.pdf

9

Nana Asma'u

A model for literate women Muslims

Beverly Mack

Nana Asma'u (1793–1864) spent her life in what is now known as northern Nigeria, never imagining that her reach would extend to a country that was the final destination for Africans transported there against their will in the Atlantic slave trade during the span of her lifetime. Raised in a literate, activist family of Qadiriyya Sufi Muslims, Asma'u established a program of women's education that has endured multiple political transmutations in Nigeria and jumped the ocean to flourish in twenty-first-century North America. In both places, Nana Asma'u personifies local resistance to oppression and fosters women's spiritual right to acquire knowledge. This chapter is an exploration of her life and how her legacy has impacted two continents.

Origins

Islam is as diverse in its practices and communities as any of the other Abrahamic religions. While most Muslims agree on Islam's foundations – the Qur'an, the five pillars of recommended behaviors, the Prophet Muhammad's life history – beyond those, there is much variation in interpretations, practices, and schools of law. The Sunni–Shi'a split occurred quite early in Islamic history's seventh-century origins. Throughout the subsequent unfolding of Islam, mystic philosophy, known as Sufism, has been practiced by Muslims in both Sunni and Shi'a communities. Just as Islamic practices are not monolithic, Sufism's particular practices also vary, depending on the interpretation of the brotherhood community to which one adheres. Nevertheless, a commonly held Sufi belief is that "the soul has no gender." Despite the Qur'an's clear message of human equity, many Muslims' interpretations deem Sufism heretical either for practicing gender equity or on the grounds that it advocates mystic union with God, which they feel allows for more human agency than is merited in theological matters. Nevertheless, in the twenty-first century, Sufi brotherhoods remain some of the fastest-growing branches of Islam.

Asma'u's family's particular brand of Islam was Sunni, and they were adherents of the Sufi Qadiriyya brotherhood that had spread from its twelfth-century Persian roots in the preaching of Abdul Qadir Gilani (1076–1166), which advocates free will.[1] Asma'u was born into the ethnic Fulani clan known as Fodiyo, which means "learned" in the Fulfulde language. Among the Fodiyos, both women and men were educated from an early age.[2] The Fodiyos originated from the Futa Toro region of West Africa, now known as Senegal. The clan consisted of ethnic

Fulani scholars and pastoralists who had resided there since the fifteenth century. They had long practiced Islam, which had spread westward along the North African coast and then south along the West African coast between the seventh and fourteenth centuries. Asma'u's grandparents were among those who had gradually migrated eastward from Futa Toro into the region now known as northwestern Nigeria by the early part of the eighteenth century. As they moved, they encountered ethnic groups that either were not Muslim or practiced syncretic forms of worship that combined traditional spirit possession (Hausa, *bori*) practices with aspects of Islam. Some of the rural Fulani migrants simply grazed their cattle, but others, who were scholars, settled in urban areas and acted as scribes for illiterate local kings.

The Fodiyo family of scholars had been actively involved in teaching, preaching, and producing written works since at least the eighteenth century, when Nana Asma'u bint Fodio's parents settled in the region. All four of Asma'u's grandparents were highly educated, literate scholars of Islam, whose reverence for the accumulation of knowledge set the standard for subsequent generations. Asma'u and her siblings were educated in their early years by their mothers and grandmothers, as was their father, the Shehu.[3] Asma'u was quadrilingual. Fulfulde was her first language, but Arabic was central to acquiring a deep knowledge of Islam, so she learned to read and write in both languages. In addition, Hausa was the language of the local Hausa majority, and Tamchek was spoken by itinerant Tuareg herders who moved around the region seasonally: Asma'u spoke both these languages and wrote in Hausa as well.[4] In Asma'u's family, prose narrative was the common means of communicating concepts of equitable social organization, while poetry was the familiar language of the Qur'an as well as the format for compositions of remembrance and admonition. As Qadiriyya Sufis, their aim was to study and preach Islam, freely, in a gender-equitable context. Asma'u's poetic productivity began when she was in her mid-twenties, following years of study based on the canon of classical Islamic works that comprised her father's library. Among these manuscripts were over 300 of the Shehu's own compositions in prose and poetry. Asma'u and her brother Bello wrote poetic works to each other whenever they were physically separated by battles or caliphate demands, commenting on current events and suggesting strategies.

The Sokoto jihad

Asma'u's father, Shehu Usman 'dan Fodiyo (1754–1817 CE), is renowned as the leader of the regional Sokoto jihad (1804–8, with skirmishes lasting until 1830) to reform Islamic practices. Plans for the jihad evolved over several decades, during which the Shehu's practice of preaching about Islam was met with increasing resistance by local Hausa kings. When he began to preach in about 1774, local kings tolerated his activities, but as his following grew, it became a threat to the status quo. With the death of an older, more deferential king and his ambitious son's succession, new laws prevented the Shehu's continued preaching and banned new Muslims' overt expressions of their faith, including public prayer and Islamic attire for both men and women. By 1804, the Shehu and his followers felt they had no recourse but to resist such oppression through jihad activities. They launched the first of several signal battles and years of itinerancy as they fled from Hausa non-Muslim enemies and fought back when they could. Against all odds, the Muslims' ultimate victory in the region resulted in the replacement of non-Muslim Hausa kings (called *Sarki* in Hausa) with Fulani Muslim leaders known by the Arabic term Emir. Nevertheless, the majority's Hausa language continued to be the lingua franca of the region, and the Hausa majority were not compelled to convert to Islam. The Sokoto jihad led to the establishment of the Sokoto Caliphate in what is now northern Nigeria and a pattern of ethnic mixing that resulted in contemporary Hausa-Fulani ethnicity. By the time the British arrived in northern Nigeria in 1903, they found extensive Islamic education systems, which they felt obviated the need to establish schools in the north as they had done in the southern part of the country.[5] Asma'u was instrumental in that change, but not because she orchestrated mass literacy. Rather, the extensive system of orally transmitted Islamic education among rural women that Asma'u established in the aftermath of the jihad laid the groundwork for the spread of Islam well beyond urban areas.

The jihad began when Asma'u was 10 years old. By then, she had been a student for more than five years and was expected to behave at a level of maturity far beyond what might be imposed on a child of that age in contemporary Western culture. Her father had personally overseen her education and that of her other siblings, both girls and boys, instilling in them the expectation that they would contribute to society through their intellectual as well as physical capabilities. Asma'u married Gidado, her brother's close friend, and began a life-long collaboration with them both as intellectual equals. Thus, throughout the jihad battles, Asma'u joined her father, uncle, brother, and husband in active involvement in the philosophical and practical aspects of the jihad, during which literary communiques among them featured prominently. Asma'u's opinions on strategies were respected, and she was revered as a stalwart supporter of jihad efforts.

In the aftermath of the jihad years, Asma'u sought to improve the quality of life for defeated rural Hausa women by creating a program through which they could learn the basic tenets of Islam through oral instruction. To this end, she established a program of women extension teachers, the *'Yan Taru*, "the Associates," in which her poetic works were the material through which social reform was effected throughout the region.[6] The aim of the *'Yan Taru* system was the transmission of Islamic cultural and spiritual knowledge; literacy was not the aim, nor was literacy a necessary skill for the women who became teachers in the system. They could easily have listened to the recitation of Asma'u's poems and memorized them. Then, they would teach rural women in the same manner. Although members of the Fodiyo family and those who studied with them were highly literate and skilled in composition, they lived in what was, for the masses, an oral culture. Memorization of verse has been integral to Islamic culture from its inception, as the devout are expected to internalize Qur'anic verses for daily prayers. The entire first chapter of the Qur'an, the Fatiha, is brief, easily memorized, and recited by all Muslims, regardless of whether they are literate, at least five times a day. It should be recalled that Islam was meant to be accessible to any and all – equality among the devout being a central founding principle – and ease of access to Qur'anic verses was a prime factor in accomplishing this end. Thus, the *'Yan Taru* system was never a literacy program but a means of spreading knowledge about Islamic culture and local history through the transmission of memorized verse suited to the needs of the time.

Asma'u's poetic works[7]

Of the works that Nana Asma'u wrote, approximately 60 have survived and been published in the twentieth century[8]; more may exist in the family library in Sokoto, in northern Nigeria. Most of her works were long rhymed poems, with a few in prose form. Her poetic style exhibits great literary talent, especially in the demonstration of acrostic style, and facility in producing *takhmis* (Ar.), a process of appending three lines to other poets' poems in couplets, rendering a new poem in quintains, in which the original rhyme and meter are faithfully maintained. Such poems were written as homage to the original author, whose work would be easily recognized, embedded in the new poem. Asma'u also wrote her poems in the particular language best suited to her audience: for scholars, Arabic was the lingua franca; poetry meant for her extended family members was written in Fulfulde. For the masses, and especially for *'Yan Taru* instruction, Asma'u wrote poems in Hausa.

Asma'u's works were devotional, instructional, and historical, as well as eulogies for those in her community. Devotional works advised spiritual rigor, instructional pieces taught normative Islamic practices, and historical works explained the jihad from her family's perspective. All three of these types of poems were in Hausa (as well as Arabic and Fulfulde) so that the masses could learn from them. The eulogies provided blueprints for ethical-personal behavior, focusing on individuals' spiritual characteristics rather than accomplishments in the socio-political context, and because many of these concerned Fulani individuals in her extended family, Asma'u wrote these in Fulfulde. Any works on deeply metaphysical topics or spiritual healing were in Arabic and thus available only to those sufficiently educated to make good sense of the material; these poems reflect her extensive study of classical Islamic scholarly works and intellectual discussions with others of like mind. Although Asma'u is known to have been in written communication with scholars across the Sahara, in Mali and Mauretania,[9] she was not averse to creating basic informative works for rural women as well. Any transmission of knowledge was worth her effort.

Asma'u's devotional poems are exemplified by her first known composition, "The Way of the Pious." She wrote it in prose when she was in her mid-twenties, in Arabic, a language facility that attests to her long years of study in her youth. In it, she speaks to an educated audience, and her topic conveys spiritual concerns that guide her every action. The poem advocates a demonstration of devotion to the *sunna* (the practice, the way) through the performance of charitable actions recommended in the Qur'an, like teaching and visiting the sick, and the development of character traits like humility and modesty. It is a concise rule book for appropriate spiritual behavior, divided into four distinct sections: 1) barriers between man and paradise; 2) personal traits that lead to damnation; 3) redeeming traits; and 4) ways in which one can demonstrate love for Muhammad in daily life. The work reflects her intimate knowledge of the Shehu's teachings and writings on these topics.

At the end of her life, Asma'u composed a similar work, "Reasons for Seeking God." This time, she wrote it in Hausa for the benefit of Hausa speakers, so that her *'Yan Taru* women teachers could use it for instruction in the rural regions. "The Way of the Pious" is one of the few works Asma'u produced in prose form. It is long. It would have been read and heard by those Arabic-speaking scholars who would have appreciated its content without needing to memorize it. "Reasons for Seeking God," however, consists of just 35 concise rhymed couplets instead of prose, for ease of memorization. In it, she advises:

16 Repent and obey God's commandments
For to desist from evil is to show repentance.
17 The *Shahada* and prayer are true
And the fast, alms, and the pilgrimage for those who have the means.

In verse 17 alone, she has named succinctly the five pillars of required behavior for Muslims: profession of faith, prayers, fasting, charity, and pilgrimage. These are among the first things a new Muslim learns about Islam. *'Yan Taru* teachers memorized and then taught this poem to their students in rural areas. The mnemonic devices of rhyme and meter, and of course its Hausa language, made it accessible to Hausa-speaking refugees still learning about reformed Islam in the region, easy to memorize, and informative. That Asma'u wrote this work at the end of her life indicates that her spiritual seeking was a consistent trait, which she sought to share with everyone, regardless of their level of education, ethnic background, or preferred language.

"Fear of the Hereafter" (1860) is an example of eschatological poetry that Asma'u felt contained an urgent message for both her Hausa and Fulfulde-speaking audiences, so she wrote it in both languages during the same year. The poem comprises a manageable 54 couplets that could easily have been memorized. Written at the end of her life, this work consolidates Qur'anic descriptions of the hereafter, discussing how the world will end, and contrasting fates of the wicked and the pious:

> 8 The sun and the moon will merge
> And darkness will descend over everything
> 9 The heavens will split asunder and angels will descend
> To find the populace huddled together …
> 12 The noise of the roaring and crackling will exceed
> Any noise we know like thunder …
> 23 Mankind will be divided into two, those for Hell
> And those for Paradise and joy.

These issues were on Asma'u's mind in her old age, and she likely felt that it was important to write this poem in Hausa for instructional purposes but also in Fulfulde to remind those among her clan-members who might become lax in their spiritual practices.

Asma'u wrote an especially important instructional poem called "The Qur'an" in Fulfulde (1829), Hausa (1838), and Arabic (1850). The Fulfulde and Arabic speakers, being familiar with the Qur'an, would have appreciated this poem, which includes the names of all 114 chapters of the Qur'an:

> 1   I pray to God the Glorious,
>   Through the honor of Ahmadu and the Sura Bakara.
> 2   And Ali Imrana and Nisa'u and Ma'idatu
>   Lan'ami, La'arafi, and Lanfali and Bara.

These two verses include the Hausa language forms of the names of the first nine chapters of the Qur'an: Fatiha, al-Baqarah, al-Imran, An-Nisa, Al-Maidah, al-Anam, al-A'raf, Al-Anfal, and al-Taubah; the rest of the Qur'anic chapter names are included in the remainder of the poem. It is for the Hausa speakers that this poem would have been most instructive. It contains a mere 30 couplets, easily memorized. In 1838, the *'Yan Taru* were actively engaged in teaching rural women normative Islamic practices. This poem provided a succinct outline of the entire Qur'an, allowing the *'Yan Taru* teachers to "unpack" it, explaining the messages contained in each Qur'anic verse. When the teachers left the area, the women who had participated in the classes retained their memorized list of Qur'anic chapter names and explanations about the message of the Qur'an.

Some instructional poems were focused on jihad victories. Asma'u wrote "Caliph Aliyu's Victory" in both Fulfulde and Hausa in 1844 to spread the word about this particular jihad success. While these two poems cover the same material, their tones are different: for her Fulfulde-speaking family members, Asma'u focused on their spiritual strength as the cause of victory, while for the defeated Hausa speakers, she emphasizes that it was their lack of spirituality that caused the defeat. The two short works – 25 couplets each – are news flashes, written in urgency to explain to separate audiences the reasons for victory or defeat, and urging the Hausa speakers to realize the error of their ways.

Other instructional works in Hausa include two long compositions: "Yearning for the Prophet" (vv 316) and "Signs of the Day of Judgment" (75 vv). Neither has a date of composition. The first is a detailed biographical account of the Prophet's life, but with emphasis on events that can be viewed as parallel to events in the Shehu's life. Likely too long for rural women to memorize, it was sufficient for them to hear this song and recognize the similarities implied in it between the Prophet and the Shehu. The 'Yan Taru teachers are known to have recited this long poem during their procession to villages — some of these journeys involved several days' worth of travel on foot.[10] This gave credibility to the Shehu's jihad and was meant to foster loyalty among those who were adjusting to the newly reformed Islamic Caliphate. "Signs of the Day of Judgment" is a terrifying account of the Last Days, straight out of the Qur'an. If anyone had doubts about the importance of repenting and becoming devout, this poem would surely have frightened them into rigorous prayer and right behavior.

Pittsburgh, Pennsylvania

Two centuries and an ocean away, in Pittsburgh, American 'Yan Taru students replicate the 'Yan Taru program in a way that suits their own socio-economic conditions. These members of the Light of the Age Islamic community do not speak Hausa or Fulfulde, and their Arabic facility is limited. They study English translations of Asma'u's instructional poems, like the one listing Qur'anic chapters, and her historical works. These American women have other concerns as well: their curriculum is fluid and includes as much Arabic language instruction, Sufi thought, and Islamic history as an individual's time allows. In this way, they straddle the approaches of the Fodiyo scholars and rural illiterate women of Asma'u's day. Some of the Arabic-speaking women at the Light of the Age teach separate Arabic classes for children. Social welfare work is integral to the curriculum as well: the homeless and refugees in America need to be aided. To this end, the entire membership of the Light of the Age community regularly distributes food and clothing to the homeless in Pittsburgh, and these modern-day 'Yan Taru women have funded a homeless shelter for local women in need.[11] Just as nineteenth-century women teachers in Nigeria took a practical approach to the conditions of the women they needed to reach, so too do the twenty-first-century women in Pittsburgh hearken to the activist example of Nana Asma'u to educate however and wherever they can. The Light of the Age community exemplifies gender, race, and ethnicity equity as it is meant to be practiced in Islam.

The Light of the Age mosque was founded in the late twentieth century by an American Muslim, Shaykh Muhammad Shareef, who had studied with Fodiyo scholars in Africa and sought to carry on their Qadiriyya Sufi teachings in an American context with African heritage ties.[12] He sought to bring orthodox Islamic practices to Pittsburgh because it was known as the site of the first African American mosque community,[13] the first African American Sunni Muslim community in the United States (Hakim 1992: 157).[14] Shareef explains:

with the [circa 1930] emergence of the ... [African Moslem Welfare Society of America], we witness a direct connection between the African American community and African Sunni Islamic traditions. This was the reason that as *Amir* of the [American] *Jama'at* [community] of Shehu "Uthman ibn Fuduye," I decided to centralize the national community in Pittsburgh.[15]

Thus, the explicit aim of the Light of the Age mosque was to recreate the ideal social context of the Sokoto Caliphate and live by its values. In subsequent years, Shareef's leadership role fell to a young Latino hip-hop singer and convert, Imam Hamza Perez, who focuses on teaching that jihad is an internal spiritual struggle against the negative self, assists Shareef remotely in the publication of Shareef's translations of Shehu Usman 'dan Fodiyo's works, and writes his own poetry exploring Sufi concepts (Taylor 2009). The community continues its classes and social welfare work, mobilized by women's involvement.

Conclusion

In a time when groups like Boko Haram – in the same country as the Fodiyos – engage in horrific acts in the name of Islam, specifically in regard to prohibiting women's education, it is an uphill battle for Muslims to garner credibility. Nevertheless, living by Sokoto Caliphate values is an achievable goal. In Pittsburgh, Light of the Age congregants, both women and men, work outside the home as insurance sales people, art teachers at local schools, tree trimmers, and accountants, among other jobs. Their discretionary time is devoted to social welfare work organized through consensus among mosque members. Communal prayer is enjoyed in private, gender-specific spaces, in adjacent sides of a large partitioned room, with the imam speaking the sermon to both sides. They share group celebrations of Islamic holidays, educational lectures, and planning meetings at the mosque, for which potluck meals are provided, and cleanup duties are shared. But always, education classes for all are an important focus.

Women's right and obligation to pursue education, both inside and beyond the home, always has been a central precept among the Fodiyos and was promoted in the structure and subject matter of the original *'Yan Taru* women's education system. Asma'u, her sisters, and other women of the Fodiyo extended family were expected to study to the best of their abilities, just as was the case for men in the family. They studied the same texts, composed prose and verse, and taught others, as did the men in the family. When Shareef settled in Pittsburgh at the end of the twentieth century, he began to teach in the manner of and with the curriculum familiar to scholars in Sokoto, thereby establishing an atmosphere of egalitarian worship and behavior. He encouraged the women of the community to develop their own *'Yan Taru* study group, based on Asma'u's example; because Muslim women in Pittsburgh have a long history of community activism and appreciation for education, this was not a hard sell. The Light of the Age women operate autonomously according to their needs.

The philosophy of the Light of the Age mosque has endeavored to be egalitarian from the outset, and while this aim is not perfectly executed, it harkens back to overt Fodiyo support of women's autonomy in educating women; it also has adhered to the Qur'anic assertion that the "best among you is the most devout" (49:13) without regard to gender, nationality, or ethnicity. This foundational precept of equality dovetails with the American democratic ideal of equality, especially with regard to women's rights; the intention of this community is to put that ideal into practice. For members of the Light of the Age community, social activism and education are the driving forces, embraced in a context of gender equality. This manner of social organization follows that of the original Fodiyo community and Nana Asma'u's philosophical foundation for her *'Yan Taru* system of educating women. It is a system whose merits continue to benefit women in its country of origin and beyond.

Notes

1 Qadiriyya Sufism is arguably the most widely spread of all Sufi brotherhoods.
2 Evidence of girls and women being educated in Asma'u's family is available for three generations prior to her birth.

3 The Shehu's life and times have been discussed extensively, but principally by Murray Last and Mervyn Hiskett: Murray Last, *The Sokoto Caliphate* (Ibadan, Nigeria: Longman, 1967) and Mervyn Hiskett, *The Sword of Truth* (London: Oxford University Press, 1973), both of whom drew heavily on the Arabic writings of the Shehu himself as well as works by his younger brother Abdullahi, his son Muhammad Bello, and his son in law Gidado 'dan Laima. What is known to date about Nana Asma'u and her active role in the history of her times is found in four recently published books, including a biography, the text and translations of her collected works, and two other books on Asma'u's life and times: Jean Boyd, *The Caliph's Sister* (London: Frank Cass, 1989); Jean Boyd and Beverly Mack, *The Collected Works of Nana Asma'u, Daughter of Usman 'dan Fodiyo (1793–1864)* (East Lansing, Michigan: Michigan State University Press, 1997); Beverly Mack and Jean Boyd, *Nana Asma'u, Scholar and Scribe* (Bloomington, Indiana: Indiana University Press, 2000); and Jean Boyd and Beverly Mack, *Educating Muslim Women: The West African Legacy of Nana Asma'u 1793–1864)* (Oxford: Interface Publications, 2013).

4 Until the onset of the British colonial era in the twentieth century, Hausa had been written in Arabic script, a process known as *ajami*.

5 British colonial intervention in the region, beginning in 1903, resulted in significant changes in education systems, including the establishment of secular schools for boys, and eventually girls' schools and women's teacher training colleges. Much has been written about this process elsewhere. For more on this topic, the reader is directed to my "Islamic Cultural Socialization and Education in Nigeria" (with Omiunota Ukpokodu) in *Voices from the Margin: African Educators on Africa and American Education*, eds. O.N. Ukpokodu and P. Ukpokodu (Charlotte, NC: Information Age Publishing, 2012), pp. 85–107. For more on the topic of Muslim women's traditional education programs, see my "Muslim Women's Knowledge Production in the Greater Maghreb: The Example of Nana Asma'u of Northern Nigeria" in *Gender and Islam in Africa: Rights, Sexuality, and Law*, ed. Margot Badran (Seneca Falls, NY: Woodrow Wilson Press co-publishing with Stanford University Press, 2011), pp. 17–40.

6 It is indicative of her sensitivity to the needs of students that these terms are in the Hausa language of the majority population.

7 For a supplement to this section, see my "Nana Asma'u: 19th C West African Poet and Educator" in *New Studies in African Literature*, eds. Umar Abdulrahman (Ibadan, Nigeria: Kraft Books Limited, 2018), pp. 101–36.

8 These are available in Boyd and Mack, 1997. Any works cited here may be found in that volume.

9 Asma'u's letter to a Mauritanian scholar is but one indication of her communiques; see Boyd and Mack, 1997: 282–4.

10 In *The Caliph's Sister*, Boyd notes that these women were never set upon by highway robbers or wild animals, although those dangers did indeed exist in that time and place.

11 The Few of a Kind Store in Pittsburgh supports the women's shelter, which serves any woman in need.

12 His intentional modelling on the Fodiyo format is evident in his choice of the community's name: *Zamman Nur* honors Shehu Usman 'dan Fodiyo's sobriquet, *Nuru-l-zaman* "the light of the time" in Seyni Moumouni "Uthman (Osman) dan Fodio (1754–1817)" in *Oxford Research Encyclopedia of African History* (forthcoming).

13 This is al-Masjid al-Awwal, located at 1911 Wylie Ave. in Pittsburgh.

14 For more on this community, see my "Fodiology: African American Heritage Connections to West African Islam" in *Journal of West African History*, Vol. 4, No. 2, Fall 2018, 103–30.

15 Personal communication to the author, August 2014.

References

Boyd, Jean. *The Caliph's Sister: Nana Asma'u Teacher, Poet, and Islamic Leader.* London: Frank Cass, 1989.

Boyd, Jean and Beverly Mack. *The Collected Works of Nana Asma'u, Daughter of Usman 'dan Fodiyo (1793–1864).* East Lansing: Michigan State University Press, 1997.

Boyd, Jean and Beverly Mack. *Educating Muslim Women.* Oxford: Interface Publications, 2013.

Hakim, Jameela A. "History of the First Muslim Mosque of Pittsburgh, Pennsylvania." In *Islam in North America: A Sourcebook*, edited by Michal A. Koszegi and J. Gordon Melton, 153–163. New York: Garland Publishing, 1992.

Hiskett, Mervyn. *The Sword of Truth: The Life and Times of Shehu Usman 'dan Fodio.* London: Oxford University Press, 1973.

Last, Murray. *The Sokoto Caliphate.* London: Longman, 1967.

Mack, Beverly. (with Omiunota Ukpokodu) "Islamic Cultural Socialization and Education in Nigeria." In *Voices from the Margin: African Educators on Africa and American Education*, edited by O.N. Ukpokodu and P. Ukpokodu, 85–107. Charlotte, NC: Information Age Publishing, 2012.

Mack, Beverly. "Fodiology: African American Heritage Connections to West African Islam," *Journal of West African History* 4, no. 2 (Fall 2018), 103–130.

Mack, Beverly. "Nana Asma'u: 19th C West African Poet and Educator." In *New Studies in African Literature*, edited by Umar Abdulrahman, 101–136. Ibadan: Kraft Books Limited, 2018.

Mack, Beverly. *Following Asma'u: Women's Authority and Islamic Scholarship in Northern Nigeria and North America*. Oxford: Bloomsbury/Oxford Press, in production.

Moumouni, Seyni. "Uthman (Osman) dan Fodio (1754–1817)". In *Oxford Research Encyclopedia of African History*, forthcoming.

Taylor, Jennifer Maytorena, Director. *New Muslim Cool*. Specific Pictures, 2009.

10

Finding "Fatima" among enslaved Muslim women in the antebellum United States

Denise A. Spellberg

In 2008, the historian Mary Elizabeth Perry wrote: "Because we find Fatima in a single document, much of her identity remains lost to us …"[1] Perry referred to a woman named Fatima in sixteenth-century Spain. A decade later, Juliane Hammer observed of American Muslim female slaves: "It speaks to the erasure of women as subjects, their lack of literacy, and the limited imagination of American society that we do not have any literary sources for the lives of African Muslim slave women."[2]

When Perry wrote about Fatima in 2008, she described a woman who lived in Malaga, Spain, in 1584. The historian documented the significance of "finding" Fatima from a single piece of evidence: an Inquisition account. The Fatima she discovered claimed to be a Muslim. She had the misfortune to be charged by the Inquisition with apostasy after a supposed conversion to Christianity in which she allegedly took another name, Ana. In the only record of her existence, Fatima insisted to her Catholic clerical interrogators that even if she had converted, she had done so while ill with the plague, in an altered state of mind, which she described as "crazy and without sanity and without judgment."[3] For refusing to renounce Islam, and her Muslim name, the Inquisition decreed Fatima's punishment: 200 lashes.[4] Did she survive this possibly lethal sentence? No evidence reveals her final fate.[5] Originally from North Africa, the second uncontested piece of evidence about Fatima recorded by the Inquisition is that she remained – throughout her legal ordeal – a slave.[6]

A decade after Perry's attempt to "read against the grain" in recovering the significance of one enslaved Muslim woman's life, Juliane Hammer opined about the "erasure of women as subjects," duly noting the absence of Arabic literary documents by West African enslaved women or even contemporary English observations about their lives. Without such sources, what is the historian to do?

Hammer's apt observation challenges historians to confront this presumed erasure of female lives. But how? Definitive evidence written by enslaved Muslim women may be found one day. Until that time, this presumed lacuna proves *nothing* about the state of Muslim female literacy in either Arabic or English; it merely underscores the different gendered demographic realities for enslaved Muslim men and women in North America.[7] Did enslaved Muslim women leave their mark in America, even without surviving textual examples of their literacy? The short answer is yes.

What follows is a first attempt at the documentation of the lives of enslaved women, all named "Fatima," an explicitly Islamic name, which appears repeatedly in legal documents, now preserved online in databases. Separated by the Atlantic, enslaved North American women named Fatima may be the Islamic sisters of the sixteenth-century Spanish slave with whom they share a distinctly Muslim moniker and possibly, a faith. What, if anything, about their lives may we learn from their presence in West African and North American legal documents? Unlike the Spanish Fatima, who asserted her Islamic faith in the face of Catholic legal prosecution, multiple enslaved women identified by this same name in North America share an avowedly Islamic moniker, but legal sources that record their presence as property seldom indicate their faith. Thus, while it is possible to presume that these women may be Muslim, or descendants of enslaved persons of Islamic heritage, it is also important to recognize the uncertain nature of their religious identity.

Literacy differently manifested according to gender

Islam is an American religion, but most of its earliest practitioners since the seventeenth century arrived in bondage from West Africa, and the vast majority were men. In select Islamized zones within West Africa, children, both boys and girls, were taught Arabic. They wrote and read in the sacred script, as well as memorizing Arabic passages of the Qur'an. Girls in these original learning environments were once again in the minority, their presence estimated at a mere 20 percent.[8] Although one scholar asserts that enslaved Muslims in North America would have been visibly identified due to their "diet, clothing, names, prayer beads, and rituals," such markers of religious identity do not support her hyperbolic insistence about their literacy: "Most Muslim women were able to read, write, and speak fluent Arabic."[9] (Fluency in the many spoken dialects of West African languages, certainly, but not necessarily in spoken or written Arabic.) Instead, the reduced presence of girls in West African schools that taught Arabic strongly suggests one reason why evidence of Muslim female literacy has not been attested in the antebellum United States. Moreover, the same author insists that Muslim women "also stood out because of their literacy skills."[10] If they did, these skills were not noted or recorded by those white enslavers who exercised complete control over the fates of enslaved Muslim women.

The single exception to date emerging in opposition to this lacuna in African American literature may be the exceptional eighteenth-century poet Phillis Wheatley (1753–84), who was abducted from West Africa at the age of five or six and sold to a couple in Boston as a girl.[11] Scholars now advance the argument that Wheatley's early attempt to write on walls as a child may reflect her desire to demonstrate previous Arabic literacy, learned in her West African childhood.[12] No Arabic details, however, survive. Solid speculation about Wheatley's possible Fulani tribal origins creates a likely link to the Senegambia region of West Africa, known for its significant Muslim population.[13] Beyond this, the poet's invocation of the phrase "Thou glorious king of day" in three poems, one scholar suggests, directly evokes the *Fatiha*, the opening chapter of the Qur'an.[14] The Arabic phrase "*Malik yawm al-din*" (Qur'an 1:4) found therein could be rendered literally as "King of the Day of Judgment," but the pivotal Arabic word *malik* has been defined by Muslim commentators more consistently as "Owner" or "Master." The latter term in particular denotes a singular divine omnipotence rather than mere earthly sovereignty.[15] While suggestive, there are problems with tying Wheatley's poetic verse to the Qur'an, for as a practitioner of Christianity, she may have found inspiration for God/Jesus enthroned on the Day of Judgment in 2 Corinthians 5:10 or in Revelation 20:11–15.[16]

Ironically, Thomas Jefferson, who read Wheatley's poetry, could not dismiss her literacy along with his determined disparagement of the intellects of all other enslaved Africans. Instead, he condemned Wheatley's poetry as "below the dignity of criticism."[17] The attention Wheatley received for her published poems, including one about the evangelical British minister George Whitefield, in London and the American colonies did not gain her immediate freedom. She was trained to write English while still enslaved, and her bondage ended only with the death of her male enslaver in 1778. After her emancipation, Wheatley married a free man of color in Boston, but her literary efforts could not support her family or protect her from the drudgery of employment as a maid. She died in poverty after six years of freedom.[18]

Wheatley received special attention because of her literacy and creativity in English while still a child, enslaved in an urban, relatively affluent household. She could not have done so without the knowledge and support of her enslavers. However, most enslaved girls and women had neither the leisure of time, nor material access to pen and paper, with which to demonstrate literacy. Other, non-Muslim enslaved women credited with autobiographical accounts wrote these only *after* their emancipation, which further narrowed the possibility of Muslim women memorializing their enslaved existence.[19]

In contrast, antebellum male Muslim slaves, such as Ibrahima Abd al-Rahman (d. 1829) and Omar ibn Said (d. 1863), garnered rewards for their public demonstrations of Arabic literacy. Fame for Ibrahima resulted, finally, in his emancipation, and for Omar, in better treatment but not his freedom.[20] Recently identified Arabic writing, attributed to two male Muslim fugitive slaves and brought to the attention of President Thomas Jefferson in 1807, resulted in a request for their emancipation. However, the fate of the enslaved remains unknown.[21] Of course, these few famed examples are exceptional by definition, for we have no extant evidence that possibly, other literate enslaved Muslim men demonstrated their Arabic skills only to elicit punishment rather than reward. However, as one analyst of antebellum Islam reminds us, "The vast majority of Muslim slaves, despite their faith, did not garner the attention their more notable counterparts attracted."[22] The dangers of focusing on "these notable slaves overlooks the distinct experiences of the anonymous masses," including undocumented Muslim women.[23]

Why Fatima? Or, what's in this name?

Without examples of Muslim women's literacy, how do we identify them and study their presence in North America? Islamic names endured in North America throughout the antebellum period, even though they were not common. Fatima, as a moniker searched in slave databases, may be among the most frequently recorded Islamic female names for enslaved women. It represents a clear case of Arabic linguistic derivation, linked to a famed Muslim founding female figure: the Prophet Muhammad's daughter, Fatima bint Muhammad (d. 633). She is a Muslim exemplar revered by the Sunni majority, who under the eleventh-century Almoravid dynasty based in Morocco, spread Islam into sub-Saharan West Africa as far south as Ghana.[24]

Not only was Fatima the only one of four daughters to survive her father's death, albeit only by six months; her father also arranged her marriage to his closest male relative, his first cousin, Ali ibn Abi Talib (d. 661). Ali became the fourth caliph, or successor to the Prophet, in 656. Fatima and Ali's union remained monogamous at the Prophet's protective insistence. It produced two grandsons, who remain the only direct male heirs to the Prophet, none of whose sons survived him. In a patrilineal Arab tribal society, Fatima exemplifies an exceptional feminine genealogical link in an entirely masculine chain of sacred Islamic descent.[25]

Before Fatima became the name of a slave in sixteenth-century Spain or eighteenth- or nineteenth-century North America, it was already well known in Sunni Muslim West Africa. In Arabic, the name Fatima literally means a woman "who has weaned a young female offspring," and it proved "generally popular" among Muslim women, whether free or enslaved, in both North and West Africa.[26]

Did early white Americans know Fatima as a Muslim name?

Fatima's name appears in more than 30 English early modern books, most concerning the history of the Islamic world and the Europeans who traveled through it during the seventeenth century.[27] Some of these texts were translated into English from French, Italian, Spanish, and Portuguese.[28] An additional few were fictional, plays and romances, featuring a protagonist named Fatima or "Fatyma."[29] However, among these printed works, only three notable tomes crossed the Atlantic to North America.

In the 1649 first English translation of *The Alcoran of Mahomet*, Fatima appears as "Fatione," the Prophet's "eldest" child, a fact Islamic sources dispute.[30] This errant spelling would not have set a precedent for slave names. Forty-eight years later in London, the Anglican cleric Humphrey Prideaux produced a polemical biography of the Prophet, which referenced Fatima. Prideaux depicts "Mahomet" as an arch-impostor but records praise for his daughter, asserting that "Fatima," spelled correctly, "survived" her father and that "he exceedingly loved" her.[31] He describes her sacred maternity correctly: "From her all that pretend to be of the race of Mahomet, derive their descent."[32] He does emphasize, however, the Prophet's "great commendations" of Fatima, "reckoning her among the perfectest of women."[33] This work became exceedingly popular in eighteenth-century America, with local editions in Philadelphia, Connecticut, and Vermont.[34] The circulation of this tome in the northeast, however, did not extend to slaveholding southern states.

Unlike Prideaux, the Englishman George Sale offered a more informed and balanced depiction of Islam in his 1734 translation of the Qur'an, the first directly from Arabic to English. Thomas Jefferson purchased Sale's Qur'an in 1765 while studying law in Williamsburg, Virginia.[35] However, this version of the Qur'an was not popular in the British colonies. Whether Jefferson or any other white American enslaver equated "Fatema" with enslaved Muslims remains unknown but unlikely. However, in West Africa, the name has been frequently attested.

Fatima found in the African Names Database and the North American historical record

Women and girls named Fatima were swept up in the slave trade, but some were rescued by abolitionists and returned, against all odds, to their West African homes. The African Names Database, part of the larger Slave Voyages Database, contains the name of 91,491 souls rescued from the slave trade. Between 1808 and 1822, 39 people named Fatima are recorded as enslaved, then saved and returned to Freetown, Sierra Leone. Among these female Fatimas, three are designated as boys.[36]

Most women named Fatima were not rescued by abolitionists; they arrived and remained enslaved in North America. Two pioneering historians, Michael Gomez and Sylviane Diouf, first located in newspapers and archives women named after the Prophet's daughter.[37] Gomez mentions 11 distinct Fatimas between 1786 and 1901, six on a single large plantation, most concentrated along coastal Georgia and South Carolina.[38] Even so, he argues, "incontestably Muslim names" are "relatively infrequent" even in runaway slave advertisements.[39] He theorizes that one Fatima born in North America may have converted or may have been "the child of at least one Muslim parent."[40] As late as 1901, a former slave of Sapelo Island, Georgia, described herself as the granddaughter of a Muslim father.[41] Possibly, these enslaved Muslims influenced conversion to Islam.[42]

No extant study of slave names focuses exclusively or systematically on Islamic monikers. However, one that analyzes slave naming patterns in both the Carolinas in the antebellum era suggests that while the enslaved may have "remained nameless entities, only part of a mass of cargo, from their time of capture,"[43] nevertheless, "as many as 15 to 20 percent of the slaves in the two Carolinas had African names."[44] The same study demonstrates that "African names never died out."[45] Of significance also is evidence about who controlled naming in the first American-born generation, when "slaves for the most part freely chose whatever names they liked for their children."[46] In this pivotal choice, maternal influence predominated: "The testimony of ex-slaves confirms that most were named by their mothers, with or without consultation with their fathers."[47] Thus, the repetition of the name Fatima may indeed be a sign of maternal agency, an assertion of the survival of Islamic heritage, as Gomez first suggested.[48]

Finally, unlike North and West Africa, where Fatima proved a popular name for *both* enslaved and free Muslim women of every hue, in North America, free white women were *not* named Fatima by their parents. Yes, a few white enslavers may have encountered the name in a text about Islam, but such books were not commonly found in most American homes. It is therefore unlikely that whites opted for Fatima as an Orientalist naming option for the enslaved. In contrast, the survival of numerous women named Fatima among the enslaved provides evidence, at least, that "slaves continued to differ" from whites "in their naming practices."[49] And, at most, if the name Fatima reflects a moniker chosen by an enslaved mother for her child, then this act preserved a pivotal aspect of shared identity, whether the faith of Islam continued to be practiced or not.[50] All these patterns may be tested with greater numbers in this study of three North American databases.

Seeing double: evidence of two Fatimas in one legal document

George Washington owned two slaves named "Fatimer" and "Little Fatimer."[51] Both names appear as part of a list of his more than 300 "taxable" slaves, recorded in 1774. Clearly, this is a mother–daughter duo, a vivid proof for the maternal preservation of Islamic heritage over a generation. Washington's 1801 will manumitted 123 of his slaves.[52] We do not know whether either Fatima found freedom by this act.

Washington's slave list is preserved in plantation records, but the Race and Slavery Petitions Project of the University of North Carolina, Greensboro, database offers additional instances of more than two slaves named Fatima on a single plantation. In Georgia in 1828, the white heirs to an estate of 200 slaves pressed for more revenue from a prior sale, which they demanded be declared "null and void." Among saleable items, one Fatima appears, along with another Fatima, whose name is spelled three different ways: *Fortimore* [*Fatemore*] [*Fatemage*].[53] Varied mispronunciations of an Islamic name, here, led to orthographical variations. These suggest that white enslavers or overseers never recognized the name's origin.

A third instance of a large plantation with two slaves named Fatima appears in South Carolina in 1856. Both women are listed among 120 slaves scattered over six plantations. Were these doubled-Fatimas a reflection of a mother–daughter bond, as on Washington's plantation? A likely and enticing but unprovable possibility.[54]

George Washington was not the only famous member of the founding white American generation to own a Muslim female slave named Fatima. Thomas Pinckney (d. 1842), the son of the man President Washington appointed ambassador to Great Britain in 1792, inherited over 300 slaves from his father.[55] The elder Thomas Pinckney (1750–1828), a wealthy South Carolina enslaver, fought in the American Revolution, served as governor of South Carolina, and presided over South Carolina's convention to ratify the U.S. Constitution.[56]

In 1843, a year after the junior Thomas Pinckney died, a dispute over his property ensued. Among the valuables contested in his will were "several plantations" as well as "fine furniture, paintings, and debts." Among the 120 slaves listed as property, there appeared one woman named Fatima, next to the number 114 in the tally.[57] Her fate among the contentious Pinckney clan remains unknown.

Disputes over slaves owned by less famous southerners also changed the lives of women named Fatima. Many lived along the Georgia–South Carolina coast, the geographical nexus Gomez first noted as a key site for enslaved West Africans of Islamic heritage.[58] Databases reveal three more women named Fatima documented in South Carolina, one in a 1792 dispute over a will[59] and another in a case from 1821.[60] A third in Charleston appears in a petition to sell 53 slaves in 1824. In this handwritten list, Fatima is grouped with other slaves collectively valued at $2500.[61] Was her individual worth then appraised at $625?[62] The fates of all three remain a mystery, as does that of one Fatima sold in Mississippi in 1852.[63]

Fatima finds freedom: serial emancipation among free people of color in New Orleans

More Fatimas than can be analyzed here may be found on the Afro-Louisiana History and Genealogy, 1718–1820, website,[64] established in 1984 by the extraordinary historian Gwendolyn Midlo Hall, who also created in 1999 the first database dedicated to "Islamic Female Names."[65] Hall's long labors documented 100,000 enslaved lives. More women named Fatima may be found on this database than on any of the other three searched in this study. The only catch? The search must be in two languages. In English, Fatima reveals 16 names,[66] and in French, "Fatime" yields 22 more names.[67] Why? Because the original documents were written in French. As a result, there is often unstated overlap between individuals found in the Afro-Louisiana History and Genealogy website and both the Race and Slavery Petitions Project and the ProQuest Slavery and the Law databases.

The marked presence of women named Fatima in Louisiana speaks not only to the depth of the records preserved but also to the unique features of the territory's history prior to U.S. statehood in 1812. Spanish legal precedents sympathetic to the plight of the enslaved impacted French laws, which preserved unique pathways for their emancipation through 1822.[68] As a result, by the census of 1805, 1565 free persons of color lived in New Orleans center, with two-thirds of these households headed by women.[69] The agency of such free people of color in New Orleans, including a woman named Fatima, may be found in a series of interconnected emancipation cases.

The process begins with the petition of Francois Buteau, a free man of color, to purchase from a free woman of color, named Marie Magdelaine Labatut, a slave named Fatime. She was then 30 years old. The petition formally applauds the enslaved woman's good conduct, a legal formality. Francois emancipated Fatime/Fatima in 1817.[70]

Two years later, we find Fatime Buteau, now identified as a free woman of color, who chose the surname of her male emancipator. Presumably, Francois Buteau still mattered in Fatima's life as either a husband or a sibling. The likelihood that they had been related while both were enslaved cannot be ruled out. Unfortunately, neither can it be proved.

What can be known for certain is that after two years of freedom, Fatime Buteau emancipated a 50-year-old enslaved woman named Fillette in 1819.[71] This case doesn't exist in the Afro-Louisiana database; rather, it can be found by searching for "Fatime" on the Race and Slavery Petitions Project and ProQuest's Slavery and the Law database. The day following Fatime's petition, the slave Fillette became a free woman of color.

A single detail found only on the Afro-Louisiana database about Fatime's emancipation reveals a pivotal link between Fatime and Fillette. Buteau's original purchase of Fatime in 1817 contains the proviso that she be purchased "under the condition that the slave be immediately freed." Then follows a key sentence: "Slave's mother is slave named Fillette nation Nago acquired by act under private signature 10 July 1791."[72] Fatime had emancipated her own mother, Fillette, in 1819. The latter had been enslaved since 1791, at least. Fillette's tribal affiliation as "Nago" confirms an Islamic origin.

The single salient detail about her mother's linguistic/tribal origin allows us to identify Fillette as the first generation to arrive from West Africa. Her original African and Islamic name we will never know. But her imposed French moniker "Fillette," meaning "Young Girl," reveals the tale of an enslaved child. This would explain why she could not retain her own name but had one assigned to her by a white, French-speaking enslaver instead.

The term "Nago" for slaves appears in Louisiana as early as the 1770s, but it was also well known as the term for a Yoruba-language speaker in the British West Indies and Brazil.[73] In 1835, the Nago played a crucial role in a major Muslim slave uprising in Bahia, Brazil. One non-Muslim slave involved in the rebellion "complained of the air of superiority of literate (Muslim) Nagos"; he described them as people "who can read, and who took part in the insurrection …"[74]

Here, at last, there is a direct reminder of West African Muslim literacy in Arabic. We cannot know whether Fillette's original African name was Islamic, but we do know that she chose to link her own child to the Prophet's perfect daughter. Even without evidence of Arabic literacy, which she may have preserved as Wheatley had done from her African childhood, Fillette found maternal agency in inscribing her Muslim identity upon the next generation. And Fatima proved her capacity to honor her mother, as the Qur'an instructs, with the ultimate gift: freedom.

A final Fatima and her self-emancipation, Washington, DC, 1862

Forty-one years later, in Washington, DC, another Fatima took the matter of her manumission into her own hands during the Civil War. She filed a petition for self-emancipation in the wake of the District's abolition of slavery on April 16, 1862, and the subsequent Supplemental Act of July 12, 1862, which decreed that slaves could file certificates of freedom for themselves.[75] The document states that her enslaver, one Jesse D. Bright of Indiana, knew of her presence in Washington, DC, and posed no opposition to her emancipation. But it omits that Fatima had triumphed over one of the most powerful men in the nation: disgraced former Indiana Senator Bright, who had been expelled from the Senate for "disloyalty" six months before. Only 11 days after she could legally proceed, she became a free woman of color. Her petition vividly preserves her physical presence, documented by white government officials. She was "46," a "female," "dark brown," and "5 ft 6 inches high."[76]

Tellingly, the clerk spelled her name twice, differently: "Fatimey" Milton first, and below, "Fatima." The latter version precedes the "X" she marked between her Islamic given name and her surname at the end of the document. But on closer inspection, the final "Fatima" recorded seems to have been changed from what may have been "Fatimey" originally.[77] Whichever pronunciation and spelling she preferred, she acted upon new laws to emancipate herself when her enslaver failed to do so. Her voyage from slavery to freedom, this Fatima charted for herself. Illiterate though she was, she had made her mark.

Finding Fatimas: the advantages and disadvantages of slave databases

Simply entering the name Fatima into a search on four databases reveals more possible Muslim women's names than previous scholarship based on archival research alone. This unique name for the Prophet's daughter survived against long odds in North America. It appears as an Islamic marker, which connected mothers and daughters on the same large southern plantations. In the city of New Orleans, finding Fatima led not only to her emancipation but to her mother's. However, while we may presume Islamic heritage for those named Fatima, what we cannot know includes whether these women were literate and how they practiced their faith. What can be proved from this initial foray is that legal records in North America, from Louisiana to Washington, DC, from 1774 to 1862, preserve repeatedly the name of the Prophet's daughter. This offers a corrective to legal scholars who opine about the "erasure of Muslim slaves from legal scholarship."[78] Databases focused on white legal disputes about the enslaved and cases concerning Black-powered emancipation reconnect the supposed rupture of "Black and Muslim identity" alleged by legal scholars of the antebellum era.[79]

Deprived of freedom, many women clung to their Muslim name as the sole marker of an African and Islamic past, a memory of former freedom. Even in this sample of fewer than 100 names, what is certain is that there are many more lives still unrecovered. Of those Fatimas forced to renounce their names, we know nothing.

Clearly, research with multiple databases offers better results than devotion to one; such an approach offers new access to previously discrete, now combined plantation and archival records. Myriad orthographical variations present challenges. This foray serves as the beginning of a larger digital venture, in which I plan to recover the names of other enslaved Muslim women. For now, perhaps the most important lesson about the past still awaits our students, who embrace the digital world daily. They may be thrilled to discover that a simple search provides visceral evidence for the American lives of more than a single enslaved Muslim named Fatima.

Notes

1 I am grateful to Janell Hobson for insightful comments, which strengthened this essay. My thanks to Daina Ramey Berry, a treasured colleague, who first suggested searching databases for enslaved Muslim women. My title pays homage to the path-breaking article of Mary Elizabeth Perry, "Finding Fatima, a Slave Woman of Early Modern Spain," *Journal of Women's History*, vol. 20, no. 1 (2008): 152.

2 Juliane Hammer, "Islam and Race in American History," in *The Oxford Handbook of Religion and Race in American History*, eds. Kathryn Gin Lum and Paul Harvey (New York: Oxford University Press, 2018), 211.

3 Perry, "Finding Fatima," 152.

4 Ibid., 154, 163.

5 Ibid., 163.

6 Ibid., 152.

7 Denise A. Spellberg, "Islam in the Atlantic," in *The Atlantic World, 1450–1850*, eds. D'Maris Coffman, Adrian Leonard, and William O'Reilly (London: Routledge, 2015), 387.

8 Sylviane Diouf, *Servants of Allah: African Muslims Enslaved in the Americas* (New York: New York University, 1998), 7.

9 Bayyinah S. Jeffries, "Islam," in *Enslaved Women in America: An Encyclopedia*, eds. Daina Ramey Berry and Deleso A. Alford (Santa Barbara, CA: Greenwood Press, 2012), 145.

10 Ibid.

11 Frances Smith Foster, *WRITTEN BY HERSELF: Literary Production by African American Women, 1746–1892* (Bloomington, IN: Indiana University Press, 1993), 31.

12 Most recently, Will Harris, "Phillis Wheatley: A Muslim Connection," *African American Review*, 48:1/2 (Spring–Summer 2015): 1. Harris builds upon arguments by John C. Shields, *Phillis Wheatley's Poetics of Liberation: Background and Contexts* (Knoxville, TN: University of Tennessee Press, 2008), 102–3.

13 Shields, *Phillis*, 198–203.

14 Harris, "Phillis," 5–6, based on his reading of "A Farewell to America, to Mrs. S.W." (sec. 10, line 40); "An Hymn to Morning" (l. 17); and "An Hymn to Evening."

15 For variations on the term *malik* in the *Fatiha*, see *The Meaning of the Glorious Qur'an: Text and Explanatory Translation*, trans. Muhammad M. Pickthall (Mecca: Saudi Arabia, 1977), where the term is "Owner," 2; *The Qur'an: Translation*, trans. Yusuf Ali (Elmhurst, NY: Tahrike Tarsile Qur'an, Inc.: 2005), where it's translated as "Master," 1; and for "Master" as a sign of God's "Power of disposal over all things," *The Study Qur'an: A New Translation and Commentary*, ed. and trans. Seyyed Hossein Nasr et al. (New York: Harper Collins, 2015), 5, 7.

16 Harris, "Phillis," 4; Shields, *Phillis*, 101. Both refer to her pouring water before sunrise as proof of Islamic ablutions, but this action may simply be African, rather than Islamic, or purely hygienic.

17 Thomas Jefferson, "Notes on Virginia," in *The Life and Selected Writings of Thomas Jefferson*, eds. Adrienne Koch and William Peden (New York: The Modern Library, 1998), 240.

18 Timothy R. Buckner, "Phillis Wheatley," in *Enslaved Women in America: An Encyclopedia*, 335–7.

19 The classic account is Harriet Jacobs, *Incidents in the Life of a Slave Girl*, eds. Frances Smith Foster and Richard Yarborough (New York: W.W. Norton and Company, 2019 [1861]), xiii.

20 Michael A. Gomez, *Black Crescent: The Experience and Legacy of African Muslims in the Americas* (New York: Cambridge University Press, 2005), 169–72, 176–9, 181–2, on Ibrahima; 168, 172, 176–9, for Omar. See also Terry Alford, *Prince among Slaves* (New York: Harcourt Brace Jovanovich, 1977); and Ala Alryyes, ed. and trans., *A Muslim American Slave: The Life of Omar ibn Said* (Madison: University of Wisconsin, 2011).

21 Jeffrey Einboden, *Jefferson's Muslim Fugitives: The Lost Story of Enslaved Africans, Their Arabic Letters, and an American President* (New York: Oxford University Press, 2020), 10, 253.

22 Quoted in Khaled Beydoun, "Antebellum Islam," *Howard Law Journal* 58: 1 (2014): 153.

23 Beydoun, "Antebellum Islam," 153.

24 Hugh Kennedy, *Muslim Spain and Portugal: A Political History of al-Andalus* (London: Longman, 1996), 155, 163.

25 Jane Dammen McAuliffe, "Fatima," *Encyclopaedia of the Qur'an*, ed. Jane Dammen McAuliffe, 5 vols. (Leiden: E.J. Brill, 2002), 2: 192–4.

26 J. G. Hava, S.J., *Al-Fara'id, Arabic-English Dictionary* (Beirut: Dar al-Mashriq, 1970), 568. For Fatima's popularity among enslaved Black and free Muslim women in Egypt and Morocco, see Hekmat Dirbas, "Naming of Slave-girls in Arabic: A Survey of Medieval and Modern Sources," *Zeitschrift für Arabische Linguistik* 69 (2019): 33.

27 For example, the following identify "Fatima" as the daughter of the Prophet: John Chardin, *The Travels of John Chardin into Persia and the East Indies* (London, 1686); Peter Heylyn, *Cosmographie in four books* (London, 1652); and John Ogilby, *Asia. Being an accurate description of Persia* (London, 1673).

28 Antoine Galland, *The Remarkable Sayings, apothegms and maxims of Eastern nations, abstracted and translated out of their books written in Arabian, Persian, and Turkish language* (London, 1695); Johannes Maurus, *The confusion of Muhamed's sect, or a confutation of the Turkish Alcoran* (London, 1652); Giovanni Botero, *The travelers breuiat, or, An historical account of the most famous kingdomes in the world* (London, 1601); and Manuel de Faria e Sousa, *The History of Portugal* (London, 1698).

29 "Fatyma" is a protagonist in a play by English poet laureate John Dryden, *An Evening's Love, or, The mock-astrologer* (London, 1671), and in an eighteenth-century romance by the lesser-known T. Wright, *Solyman and Fatima; or the Sceptic Convinced. An Eastern Tale* (London, 1791), 12, where Fatima is described as "fair as the snow" with "blue eyes."

30 Alexander Ross, trans., *The Alcoran of Mahomet* (London, 1649), Gareth and Dunleavey Collection, Library of the University of New Hampshire, www.library.unh.edu/find/digital/object/digital%3A 00013, accessed February 12, 2018. Reference to Fatima in section on "Life and Death of the Prophet," 407.

31 Humphrey Prideaux, *The life of Mahomet* (Glasgow, Scotland: E. Miller for Wm. Stewart, 1799 [1697]), 73.

32 Ibid., 74.

33 Ibid.

34 Robert J. Allison, *The Crescent Obscured: The United States and the Muslim World, 1776–1815* (Chicago: University of Chicago Press, 2000 [1995]), 41.

35 Denise A. Spellberg, *Thomas Jefferson's Qur'an: Islam and the Founders* (New York: Knopf, 2013), 80.

36 Slave Voyages Database, www.slavevoyages.org/resources/names-database, accessed September 28, 2019.

37 Diouf, *Servants*, 83–4, 86.

38 Gomez, *Crescent*, 149, 151–2, 155; Michael A. Gomez, "Muslims in Early America," *The Journal of Southern History*, 60: 4 (November 1994): 695–6.

39 Gomez, *Crescent*, 149.

40 Gomez, "Muslims," 695.

41 Gomez, *Crescent*, 155.

42 Gomez, "Muslims," 695.

43 John C. Inscoe, "Carolina Slave Names: An Index to Acculturation," *The Journal of Southern History*, 49: 4 (November 1983): 527.

44 Ibid., 532.

45 Ibid., 534.

46 Ibid., 527.

47 Ibid., 530.

48 Gomez, "Muslims," 695.

49 Inscoe, "Carolina," 539.

50 The emphasis on agency in naming found in Inscoe, "Carolina," 554.

51 Mary V. Thompson, "Mt Vernon," *Encyclopedia of Muslim-American History*, ed. Edward E. Curtis IV, 2 vols. (New York: Facts on File, 2010), 2: 392. For further evidence of naming "Young and Old or Big and Little" among the enslaved, see John C. Inscoe, "Generation and Gender as Reflected in Carolina Slave Naming Practice: A Challenge to the Gutman Thesis," *The South Carolina Historical Magazine*, 94: 4 (October 1993): 259.

52 Thompson, "Mt Vernon," 2: 393.

53 "Race and Slavery Petitions Project at the University of North Carolina Greensboro," PAR# 20682920; Chatham County, Georgia, Jan 1, 1828–Dec 31, 1828. Accession #009061-002-0874, https://congressional.proquest.com/histvault?q=009061-002-0874, accessed March 26, 2018.

54 "Race and Slavery Petitions Project," PAR# 2138568; Sep 19, 1856–September 27, 1856, Darlington District, South Carolina, South Carolina Department of Archives and History, Columbia, South Carolina, Accession #01645-022-0801, https://congressional.proquest.com/histvault?q=016455-022-0801, accessed March 26, 2018.

55 "Race and Slavery Petitions Project," PAR #21384356; Record of the Equity Court, South Carolina Department of Archives and History, Feb 3, 1843–Dec 31, 1843, Accession #016455-016-0841, https://congressional.proquest.com/histvault?q=016455-016-0841, accessed March 25, 2018. For Thomas Pinckney, the elder, see Marvin R. Zahniser, *Charles Cotesworth Pinckney: Founding Father* (Chapel Hill, NC: University of North Carolina Press, 1967), 113.

    Charles Cotesworth Pinckney, Jr., *The Life of General Thomas Pinckney* (Boston: Houghton Mifflin, 1895), 21, 26–88, 89, 97.

56 Pinckney, *Life of General Thomas Pinckney*, 21, 26–88, 89, 97.

57 "Race and Slavery Petitions Project," PAR #21384356; Record of the Equity Court, South Carolina Department of Archives and History, Feb 3, 1843–Dec 31, 1843, Accession #016455-016-0841, https://congressional.proquest.com/histvault?q=016455-016-0841, accessed March 25, 2018.

58 Gomez, *Crescent*, 153.

59 "Race and Slavery Petitions Project," PAR #11379211; Oct 4 1792–Dec 31, 1792. Accession #001542-008-0276, https://congressional.proquest.com/histvault?q=001542-008-0276, accessed March 20, 2018.

60 "Race and Slavery Petitions Project," PAR# 21382118; County Courts, Charleston District, South Carolina, 1784–1867, South Carolina Department of Archives and History, Columbia, South Carolina, Mar 1, 1821–Dec 31, 1821. Accession #016455-010-0898, https://congressional.proquest.com/histvault?q=016455-010-0898, accessed March 25, 2018.

61 "Race and Slavery Petitions Project," PAR# 21382426; Charleston, District, South Carolina, South Carolina Department of Archives and History, Columbia, South Carolina, Nov 3, 1824–December 31, 1824. Accession #016455-011-0707, https://congressional.proquest.com/histvault?q=016455-011-0707, accessed March 26, 2018.

62 Daina Ramey Berry, *The Price for Their Pound of Flesh: The Value of the Enslaved, from Womb to Grave, in the Building of a Nation* (Boston: Beacon Press, 2017), 10–33.

63 "Race and Slavery Petitions Project," PAR# 21085212; Apr 7, 1852–Jul 5, 1852, Wilkinson County, Mississippi, Wilkinson Country Courthouse, Woodville, Mississippi, Accession #009061-017-0459, https://congressional.proquest.com/histvault?q=009061-017-0459, accessed March 26, 2018.

64 "Afro-Louisiana History and Genealogy," www.ibiblio.org/laslave/introduction.php, accessed March 26, 2018.

65 "Afro-Louisiana," www.ibiblio.org/laslave/calcs/islamicnames.html, accessed March 26, 2018.

66 "Afro-Louisiana," www.ibiblio.org/laslave/individ.php?sid=3620; the following cases are from the same site but a different final case number: 3773, 3910, 3912, 12483, 12992, 13039, 13741, 18178, 20765, 33510, 33511, 41727, 42735, 58081, and 58230, accessed March 25, 2018.

67 "Afro-Louisiana," www.ibiblio.org/laslave/individ.php?sid=4284; the following cases are from the same site but a different final case number: 4294, 4501, 23194, 25500, 27297, 28325, 28654, 55691, 58545, 59634, 60418, 67647, 69615, 70010, 71595, 72846, 74568, 79129, 80705, 81868, 84115, accessed March 25, 2018.

68 Judith Kelleher Schafer, *Slavery, the Civil Law, and the Supreme Court of Louisiana* (Baton Rouge, LA: Louisiana State University Press, 1994), 2–3. Inscoe observes in the Carolinas "the frequent use of Spanish and Portuguese names retained by slaves brought from the Caribbean Islands or South America," 529.

69 Thomas S. Ingersoll, "Free Blacks in a Slave Society: New Orleans, 1718–1812," *The William and Mary Quarterly*, 48: 2 (April 1991): 198–9.

70 The same record may be found in three databases: "Afro-Louisiana," www.ibiblio.org/laslave/individ .php?sid=70010, accessed March 20, 2018; also at "ProQuest, History Vault, Slavery and the Law," PAR #20881761, https://congressional.proquest.com/histvault?q=101693-002-0488&accountid=7118, accessed January 30, 2020, and the "Race and Slavery Petitions Project," Petition 20881761, https://li brary.uncg.edu/slavery/petitions/pDetailsNew.aspx?pID=66087&s=2, accessed January 30, 2020.

71 "ProQuest, History Vault, Slavery and the Law," PAR 20881970, https://congressional.proquest .com/histvault?q=101693-003-0071&accountid=7118; and "Race and Slavery Petitions Project," # 20881970. https://congressional.proquest.com/histvault?q=101693-003-0071&accountid=7118 accessed March 21, 2018.

72 "Afro-Louisiana," www.ibiblio.org/laslave/individ.php?sid=70010, accessed March 21, 2018.

73 Robin Law, "Ethnicity and the Slave Trade: 'Lucumi' and 'Nago' as Ethonyms in West Africa," *History in Africa*, 24 (1997): 2018.

74 Quoted in Olatunji Oro, "The Root Is Also Here: The Nondiasporic Foundations of Yoruba Ethnicity," in *Movements, Borders, and Identities in Africa*, eds. Toyin Falola and Aribidesi Adisa Usman (Rochester, NY: University of Rochester Press, 2009), 54. For the role of Nago Muslims in Bahia, Brazil, see Joao Jose Reis, *Slave Rebellion in Brazil: The Muslim Uprising of 1835 in Bahia*, trans. Arthur Brakel (Baltimore: Johns Hopkins University Press, 1993), 127, 134.

75 "An Act for the Release of certain Persons held to Service or Labor in the District of Columbia," April 16, 1862, www.archives.gov/exhibits/featured-documents/dc-emancipation-act/transcription.h tml, accessed January 29, 2020, 94. "The Supplemental Act of July 12, 1862," www.archives.gov/exh ibits/featured-documents/dc-emancipation-act/supplemental-act.html, accessed January 29, 2020.

76 "Race and Slavery Petitions Project," PAR #20486217; Records of the United States Circuit Court, Slavery Records, Emancipation Papers, National Archives, Washington, DC, 1862, Accession # 008967-016-0189, https://congressional.proquest.com/histvault?q=008967-016-0189, accessed March 26, 2018. Original document at ProQuest, History Vault, Slavery and the Law, PAR #20486217, https ://congressonal.proquest.com/histvault?q=008967-016-0189&accountid=7118, accessed December 14, 2019. On the 32-14 Senate vote to expel Bright in February 1862, because he had written to Jefferson Davis, President of the Confederate States, a month before the Civil War began, see Matthew N. Vosmeier, "Jesse D. Bright," Indiana Historical Bureau, www.in.gov/history/3998.htm, accessed November 12, 2020.

77 Ibid., "Race and Slavery Petitions Project," PAR #20486217.

78 Beydoun, "Antebellum Islam," 144.

79 Ibid.

11

Phillis Wheatley and New England slavery

Jennifer Thorn

With her 1773 book *Poems on Various Subjects, Religious and Moral*, Phillis Wheatley became the first African American to publish a book of poems. Wheatley was, for a few years, an international star – clearly exceptional. At the same time, her experience resembled that of other enslaved Africans in New England in the constant tension she lived with between "family" (meaning those from whom she was kidnapped by enslaving foreigners) and the "family" of New England family slavery. Seized into slavery in 1761 as a child of about six, Wheatley was manumitted in 1774 on the death of her slaveholder mistress, Susanna Wheatley.

Wheatley returned to Susanna's sickbed from London, where she had tended to matters relating to the publication there of *Thoughts on Various Subjects* and where she could have remained, a free woman. She lived with the Wheatley family until the death of John Wheatley, Susanna's husband, in 1778. Later that same year, she married John Peters, a free Black man who worked, over the course of his life, as a shopkeeper, laborer, and entrepreneur. This marriage may reflect acquaintance with Peters about which we know little; it may reflect economic need borne of the reality that neither Susanna nor John Wheatley had provided for her in their wills. With John Peters, Wheatley had, and buried, three children in the next six years. Her efforts to secure subscribers in Boston for a second volume did not succeed, nor did Peters' business ventures in the economically challenging Revolutionary years, in a Boston in which there were legal limits to the potential economic rise of non-whites; the family slid steadily into poverty. We do not know the names of Wheatley's children or where they are buried, and the manuscript of her second book is lost. She died at age 31, an early death considered in more detail in this chapter.

Wheatley's place in this *Companion to Black Women's Cultural Histories* is self-evidently assured by her place among the historic "firsts" of African American history. But the importance of taking Wheatley's life and works as a "companion" also lies in the assistance to the urgent and ongoing project of understanding and dismantling racism that can be derived from reflection on the implications of regarding Wheatley, enslaved poet and transatlantic celebrity, as exceptional. Indeed, to equate Wheatley's significance with the historic publication of her book carries with it a certain potential, even grave, peril. This chapter suggests that Wheatley's exceptionality exists on a continuum with her typicality, the ways she did not transcend the material and ideological realities of her region and era. My allegiance here is to Wheatley's "complex personhood," Avery Gordon's recommended goal to historians entering archives in pursuit of understanding

120

people of the past whose lives are recorded, directly and indirectly, by others and of those who enter history by virtue of their own textual production.[1] "[E]ven those who live in the most dire circumstances possess a complex and oftentimes contradictory humanity and subjectivity that is never adequately glimpsed by viewing them as victims, or, on the other hand, as superhuman agents," she writes:

> Complex personhood means that all people (albeit in specific forms whose specificity is sometimes everything) remember and forget, are beset by contradiction, and recognize and misrecognize themselves and others. ... At the very least, complex personhood is about conferring the respect on others that comes from presuming that life and people's lives are simultaneously straightforward and full of enormously subtle meaning.
>
> *(4–5)*

The conditions in which Wheatley came to be literate and to write pious encomiums in iambic pentameter are profoundly imbricated with her enslavement, the damaging force of which must be probed concomitantly with the task of recognizing Wheatley's resilience and agency. This latter task also requires closely reading the poems in *Thoughts on Various Subjects, Religious and Moral*, which have often been understood as a homogeneous monolith, proof of the rightness of the abolitionist cause, of the full humanity of Africans, of the improvement that education can bring, or, for a period in the mid-twentieth century, of Wheatley's false consciousness. Wheatley's "complex personhood" can be discerned both in the writerly departure from familiar norms that she made even as a child author and in the skill with which she cultivated a network of white women supporters to develop as a poet and to publish her book. Wheatley's value to a *Companion to Black Women's Cultural History* includes, I'll suggest, attending both to the "complex personhood" of her life in an elite white Bostonian household and to the "complex personhood" of the last six years of her life, the years in which she lived as a free Black woman and fell precipitously into archival obscurity.

The world of New England slavery

New England's practice of "family slavery" saw enslaved people living under the same roofs as their enslavers – typically one to four enslaved people per elite household – and thus lacking the opportunity to develop a sense of the distinctness of their condition relative to their enslavers that came, on Southern plantations, with separate quarters for enslaved people. The difference between this way of housing, supervising, and disciplining enslaved people and Southern and Caribbean practices of enslavement has in the past led observers to present New England slavery as quasi-slavery, such as in the view of one historian that "the brutality of the system" of New England slavery was "lessen[ed]" by the side-by-side work and shared living quarters of enslavers and enslaved.[2]

With the significant exception of the plantations of Rhode Island, enslaved people in eighteenth-century New England typically labored in elite households that were steadily shifting from household economies toward diversification for exchange and trade. Recent scholarship on New England slavery stresses that its economic value to slaveholders often lay in its enabling travel away from home, for work, of the male heads of slaveholding households. Elise Lemire, for example, finds lawyers, clergymen, doctors, and merchants among slaveholders of eighteenth-century Walden, Massachusetts; in 1772, 10 of the 15 known slaveholders of the town "had a professional, military, or civic title," as "an ambitious man with sufficient education and wealth to pursue a title typically used slave labor and the prestige of owning slaves to ensure his rise."[3]

These households were predominantly based along the coast, in cities like Boston that were tied to ocean trade, entwining the New England economy with those of the South and the Caribbean.[4]

Though Susanna Wheatley, like most other elite women of eighteenth-century Boston, could not participate in public, remunerated labor as a lawyer, doctor, or merchant, the work done for her by Phillis Wheatley was nonetheless of economic value that accords loosely with this model. Susanna Wheatley's championing of the poetry of the enslaved person she owned for 14 years advanced the status and efficacy of the evangelical and missionary projects in which she was involved. With, and on behalf of, Phillis Wheatley, she became known to such evangelical luminaries as George Whitefield and Selina, Countess of Huntingdon. As Joanna Brooks has shown, Wheatley's literary fame was the consequence of her cultivation of "a network of white female supporters" in whose private homes she performed her poetry, who "purchased her books for themselves and commissioned original works on personal or occasional topics" – women who circulated her manuscript poems "as a currency of friendship, familial relationship, education, and consolation."[5] In a sense, then, Wheatley herself was a kind of "currency" in an economy productive of pious and cultured gentility, an economy in which Susanna could regard herself, and be regarded, as central even as the public nature of that centrality could be understood both as feminine piety and as compliance with the duty of Christian householders to attend to the religious instruction of the subordinates of the household.

Religion and understandings of racial and class identity were intimately associated in early New England, a complex culture that persisted through the Awakenings into the eighteenth century. The most prominent early articulation of the duty of Christian householders to work actively to protect all dependents from "the Rage of Sin, and Wrath of God" was Cotton Mather's 1706 "The Negro Christianized: An Essay to Excite and Assist that Good Work, the Instruction of Negro-Servants in New England," an important text for understanding Wheatley's enslavement and piety, even as the cultures of Puritanism and the Congregationalism that it became are not identical. Mather's essay rejects the "Brutish insinuation" that "Negroes" lack "Rational Souls" even as it unquestioningly accepts that slavery is fully compatible with church and civil law, as did the Wheatleys; Mather himself was an enslaver.[6] "Thy Negro is thy Neighbour … he is thy Brother too. No canst thou love thy Negro, and be willing to see him ly under the Rage of Sin, and Wrath of God?" (Mather, 5–6): here, both "love" and privilege require the conversion of all dependents. This framing of coercion as generosity is of a piece with the blurred kind of agency implied by Mather's instructing of the elite. Householders' personal salvation requires their active protection of all dependents from eternal damnation: "[t]he Blood of the Souls of your poor Negroes, lies upon you" (Mather, 16). If the fate of enslaver and enslaved are bound together here, elsewhere the two roles are starkly differentiated, as in Mather's declaration that the piety of the enslaved accrues not to them but to their enslavers. Both kinds of subject–object relations share the assumption that the enslaved object can possess neither identity nor virtue except as these are projected by the enslaving subject: the two are one, and the one is the householder.

Indeed, religious instruction was central to the legal definition of "family" put in place in New England with the 1620 founding of Plymouth and the 1630 founding of the Massachusetts Bay Colony. "Family" was then legally defined as a household headed by a householder, including his wife, his children, other relatives, and all hired servants, indentured servants, enslaved people, and apprentices. These laws required unattached newcomers to affiliate themselves with a family in order to receive, within the "family," legally required religious instruction. In this early era, most towns required household catechizing by law; many wrote their own catechisms. "Family" thus indicated a civic entity central to religious instruction and regional governance.

Phillis Wheatley was received into Boston's Old South Church on August 18, 1771, by Dr. Joseph Sewall. She was 16 years old and had been part of the Wheatleys' household for a decade, since their purchase of her in 1761. As Joanna Brooks has described, Wheatley's attendance at Old South Church with her enslavers introduced her to elite women who would become her supporters, hosting poetry performances in their home, hand-copying and circulating her manuscripts, commissioning poems on particular topics, and in time, seeking subscribers to the proposal for the publication of a book manuscript, which would become *Poems on Various Subjects, Religious and Moral* (1773) (Brooks, 10–13). As Brooks notes, "twenty-one of the thirty-nine poems in the 1773 volume are elegies or occasional poems, and at least twelve of them are written about or for white women" (Brooks 11) – women encountered at Old South Church and in the genteel coteries devoted to the exchange of poems in manuscript with which that circle overlapped. Wheatley's piety, then, reflects the highly gendered nature of her experience of enslavement. The white people who most significantly shaped her career and life are not the men (half of them, ministers) whose names preface *Poems on Various Subjects*, their signatures confirming her authorship of the poems, but women who encountered Susanna's "little black genius," in William Robinson's phrase, as the two circulated in Boston's pious and literary circles of elite women.[7]

These experiences might seem to mark Wheatley's specific circumstances as emphatically different from those of other enslaved people in the North, but there is important continuity, too, with the qualities of face-to-face encounters that Eugene Genovese and Elizabeth Fox-Genovese have seen in the South, interactions reflective of both "planters' needs to think well of themselves and slaves' needs to foster and manipulate planters' feelings in order to encourage care and limit abuse."[8] The benefits, if they should be called such, that Wheatley received through her membership in Old South Church also coexist with realities less amenable to perception as potential benefits. Wheatley shared with other New England Christians of African descent, enslaved and free, the reality of race-based discrimination in worship and church governance, policies that included, in most Protestant churches and for most services, being required to receive the sacrament only after white congregants had done so, baptism after the regular service was over and white congregants had largely left, the refusal by some white ministers to hold Black babies as they baptized them, exclusion from church governance and leadership, racially segregated church seating, and after death, burial in racially segregated cemeteries rather than in cemeteries affiliated with the churches they had attended.[9] For all Wheatley's fame, for all her accomplishments, we don't know for sure whether she is buried in the part of Copp's Hill Burying Ground in which people of African descent were buried or in an unmarked grave in the Granary Burying Ground, where John Wheatley is buried.

Phillis Wheatley's life and poetry

From the perspective that this end of life offers to the consideration of Wheatley's socialization with elite white women and the transatlantic fame that it enabled, let us turn to the beginning not of Wheatley's life, but of her life in America. Her name marks her as enslaved in two ways. Her first name commemorates the ship, the *Phillis*, on which she was brought to Boston in July 1761. The size of the *Phillis*, requiring only an eight-man crew, was typical of the slaving ships that comprised a considerable part of New England's economy. During the eight-month voyage to Boston, 75 of the 96 enslaved people on board died, twice the expected death rate for the Middle Passage.[10] In Boston, the child who would be renamed Phillis Wheatley was purchased by John Wheatley, a prosperous tailor, merchant, and city official, and his pious wife, Susanna, then 58 and 52 years old, to be Susanna's personal servant. The purchase of children to attend to the personal needs of adults and to act as companions was typical of Northern enslavement. Also living in the Wheatley mansion on King Street were the Wheatleys' children, the 18-year-old twins Mary and Nathaniel (the only two of the Wheatleys' five children to survive to adulthood), and three or four enslaved people.

A descendant of Susanna Wheatley opined in an 1834 memoir of Phillis Wheatley that "the chains which bound [Wheatley] to her master and mistress were the golden links of love, and the silken bonds of gratitude"; Susanna is to this day described as having acted "like a mother" to Phillis Wheatley.[11] "Love" may perhaps have motivated Susanna in the years in which the child she had purchased grew to womanhood, piety, and literary fame, but that love, that intimate relationship, is profoundly shadowed by Susanna's slowness to manumit her and by the lack of provision made for her life after manumission, almost as if such a life were unimaginable by her enslavers. Susanna's love for Phillis as a "daughter" is not like her love for Mary, who was prepared by her family life to marry well, enabled by their social circles to meet and marry the prominent minister John Lathrop, and included in her parents' will. In contrast, Susanna made no provision for the life that her "daughter" would live after her (Susanna's) death, such as marriage, a bequest in her will, or even training in domestic skills that might allow her to support herself.[12] The self-deception infusing this "love" is not specific to New England; the "fatal self-deception" of Southern enslavers was also evidenced in their self-styling as "the best, the sincerest, indeed, the only friends that American blacks ever had" (Genovese and Fox-Genovese, 3).

Children learning to read in early New England did so with texts that taught Christianity: hornbooks, primers, psalters, and Bibles. The omnipresence of these texts can hardly be overemphasized: the most popular psalter in eighteenth-century New England, Isaac Watts' *Divine Songs for Children*, was "part of English-speaking childhood for two centuries," and the *New England Primer* was, "well into the nineteenth century, the USA's most popular book after the Bible."[13] It was Mary Wheatley who taught Phillis Wheatley to read, on her mother's instruction, instructing her in Christianity and the Bible and also exposing her to Greek and Latin classics by Virgil, Ovid, Terence, and Homer; the poetry of John Milton and Alexander Pope; and history, geography, and astronomy. The Christian texts with which it is likely Wheatley was taught to read offered a model of rhetorical authority, the pious child, as well as metaphors, rhythms, allusions, and themes that she would adapt and respond to in her poems. Wheatley's poetry is usefully approached in relation to the *New England Primer* and the so-called juvenile death literature that it partially exemplified. In these narratives and poems, pious children instruct, criticize, and warn their backsliding elders – a highly specific and scripted disruption of social hierarchy in the name of its preservation. The *New England Primer* differs from the *Negro Christianized* in that the former empowers children and adults to imagine children's authority over adults and the latter urges spiritual care of alleged inferiors in order to be spared the guilt of their damned souls; but they are alike in blurring the boundaries between subject and object and the specific, provisional kinds of individual agency and responsibility that they sanction and imagine.

The role of pious child, and the kinds of provisional authority granted to the pious child to preach to social superiors, could not but have helped make Wheatley legible, and acceptable, as a poet to her elite white audiences. Of the 39 poems included in *Poems on Various Subjects*, five are elegies to infants and children, first-person laments that sometimes assume the point of view of the recently deceased offspring, looking down from Heaven to tell their parents to stop crying and repent. In "A Funeral Poem on the Death of C.E. an Infant of Twelve Months," Wheatley makes double use of this role, gently chastising the parents who long for their lost baby ("Why this unavailing moan? / ... To Charles, the happy subject of my song, / A brighter world, and noble strains belong," lines 25, 27–8) – and then ventriloquizing the dead child as he explains to his parents why he prefers Heaven ("Thrones and dominions cannot tempt me there," line

35).[14] Wheatley's skills in writing and in performing "emotional labor of condolences and sympathy" are evident in this poem and its reception (Brooks, 8). At least two occasional poems in the book assume the persona of a Christian advising members of the elite to repent; in "To the University of Cambridge, in New-England," for example, the speaker commands students in the college that would become Harvard to suppress sin – "An Ethiop tells you 'tis your greatest foe" (Carretta, 2001, 12). Other poems in the book make use of Bible verses included in primers and children's Bibles ("Goliath of Gath," Isaiah lxiii.1–8).

Phillis Wheatley's first published poem, written and published while she was still a child, makes use of the rhetorical authority of pious children and presages the complexity of her later poems. She was 13 years old and had been living in Boston for only six years when "On Messrs. Hussey and Coffin" appeared on December 21, 1767, in the *Newport Mercury*, a weekly Rhode Island newspaper. "Hussey and Coffin" shares with other poems by Wheatley a depiction of the ocean's power and unpredictability – suggestive, perhaps, of a memory of her own experience of the Middle Passage. That Wheatley's appeal as a poet rested initially on her legibility as a child is also suggested by the preface, probably written by Susanna, foregrounding Wheatley's enslavement even as it asserts, and values, her precocity. "To the Printer. Please to insert the following Lines, composed by a Negro Girl (belonging to one Mr. Wheatley of Boston)," the statement begins, going on to note that the poem is the product of an overheard conversation in the Wheatley household. "[W]hile at Dinner" at the Wheatleys,' Hussey and Coffin "told of their Narrow Escape, this Negro Girl at the same Time 'tending Table, heard the Relation, from which she composed the following Verses" (Carretta, 2001, 73). This preface mediates the reader's potential engagement with the poem that follows, just as family slavery mediates the vision of domestic intimacy – the child and the enslaving family in a room together – that it provides.

The iambic pentameter, tone, and allusions of "On Messrs. Hussey and Coffin" can make it easy to miss the ambiguities and ambivalences that it conveys. Comprised of a single stanza, it can be understood as having three parts, each directing a specific audience, "you." The first 10 lines address Hussey and Coffin directly in a series of questions that ask them how they felt in the storm and how they understood it. Did "Fear and Danger" in the "whistling Wind" confuse you?, the speaker asks (Carretta, 2001, 74). Did you think that the wind – "Boreas" – was "Against you," and did you wonder if a malicious Eolus "with Contempt look[ed] down" on your terror? This section ends with an admonition to Hussey and Coffin to disregard such fears and affirm the divine plan, "something hidden from our Eyes."

The poem then addresses the audience as "you," asking questions that seem to be also directed to the speaker herself and that take us back into the ambivalence and uncertainty of the poem's opening. Here, the poem imagines things going quite badly for Hussey and Coffin: "the groundless Gulph" could have "snatch'd [them] away." The poem then asks, "Where wou'd they go? where wou'd be their Abode?" – repeated questions at odds with the poem's earlier promise of divine protection, "something hidden from our Eyes." The violent storm might mean that the dead seamen "ma[k]e their Beds down in the Shades below, / Where neither Pleasure nor Content can flow" – a frank openness to suffering then countered, again, by pious aphorism: "To Heaven their Souls with eager Raptures soar, // Enjoy the Bliss of him they wou'd adore." The verb here is conditional; "him they *do* adore" would scan as iambic pentameter just as well.

In a kind of breaking of the fourth wall, two italicized sentences then shift the target under consideration from the threatened captains and the existential questions they face to the speaker's personal wish for eloquence: "Had I the Tongue of a Seraphim, how would I exalt thy Praise; thy Name as Incense to the Heavens should fly, and the Remembrance of thy Goodness to the shoreless Ocean of Beatitude? – Then should the Earth glow with seraphick Ardour." These lines address an audience of God so intensely and personally that the two sea captains seem entirely irrelevant. Here is a declaration of submission that at the same time draws attention to the personal aspirations and abilities of the speaker as an individual. All this interesting complexity is left unresolved in the poem's ambiguous final couplet, lines closely evocative of Isaac Watts' hymns for children: "Blest Soul, which sees the Day while Light doth shine, / To guide his Steps to trace the Mark divine" (Carretta, 2001, 74). Whose soul? Which "he" has steps that need "guid[ing]"? Which "Mark divine," on what or whom? The couplet's use of the cadences and vocabulary of evangelicalism leave unresolved the two stories of hope unfulfilled that the poem has told: the sea captains who want to live and to know that the sea does not mean them harm, and the speaker who wants to make the "Earth … glow" with the power of eloquence.

Marissa Fuentes reminds us that the "ethics of history" require that we attend steadily to "the consequences of reproducing indifference to violence against and the silencing of black lives" and that we "acknowledge and actively resist the perpetuation of their subjugation and commodification in our own discourse and historical practices."[15] The material comfort in which Wheatley lived during her 17 years in the Wheatley household and the records of Wheatley left by white people who understood themselves as her loving champions can make it seem counterintuitive to see "violence" as characteristic, even constitutive, of her life and her achievement in publishing *Thoughts on Various Subjects*. Even more unlikely might seem to be the description as a kind of "silencing" of the publication of a book that brought Wheatley transatlantic fame. This chapter has framed Wheatley in relation to violence and silencing both to attend to her "complex personhood" and to recognize both the complexity and the contingency of "violence" and "silence" and their imbrication with conditions and effects that can appear to be their opposites. To "companion" Wheatley, that is, is to be pushed to articulate with greater precision the ways that racism thwarts Black lives and the ways that Black lives persist in, with, and through it.

To learn about Wheatley is to grapple with the fact that the "deep prejudice against blacks that was typical of eighteenth-century New England" took forms that can be surprising and hard to see – forms not unrelated to the microaggressions of today.[16] Joanne Pope Melish vividly describes the "terrible psychological burden" of the New England slave system, the autonomy that it sometimes seemed to offer, and steadily withheld from, enslaved people: this system "in practice demanded agency and feared it, demanded passivity and was disgusted by it," "impos[ing] upon slaves the obligation to be exactly like whites while remaining absolutely unlike them" (Melish, 26). Wheatley's life in the family, yet not of the family – and in the coterie of literary and pious white women, yet not of this coterie – is just of this kind, a "now you see it, now you don't" of enslavement that is of a piece with the persistent erasure of New England slavery. Her life and her poetry challenge us to rethink assumptions about the nature of resistance and complicity, the relation of emotion to enslavement and disenfranchisement, and the value and cost of exceptionality.

Notes

1 Avery Gordon, *Ghostly Matters: Hauntings and the Sociological Imagination* (Minneapolis: University of Minnesota Press, 2008), 4.

2 On the term "family slavery," see William D. Piersen, *Black Yankees: The Development of an Afro-American Subculture in Eighteenth-Century New England* (Amherst: University of Massachusetts Press, 1988), 25–36.

3 Elise Lemire, *Black Walden: Slavery and Its Aftermath in Concord, Massachusetts* (Philadelphia: University of Pennsylvania Press, 2011), 187.

4 Wendy Warren, *New England Bound: Slavery and Colonization in Early America* (New York: Liveright Publishing, 2016), 243–52.

5 Joanna Brooks, "Our Phillis, Ourselves," *American Literature* 82. 1 (2010): 8.

6 Cotton Mather, "The Negro Christianized: An Essay to Excite and Assist that Good Work, the Instruction of Negro-Servants in Christianity" (Boston: Printed by B. Green, 1706), 23.

7 The phrase "little black genius" is William H. Robinson's: "Several visitors to the Wheatley home would be obliged by a persuasive Mrs. Wheatley to listen to her little black genius recite an original poem, or two, or three." *Phillis Wheatley and Her Writings* (New York: Garland, 1984), 23. For a discussion of the role of white women in the publication of Wheatley's poetry, see Caroline Wigginton, *In the Neighborhood: Women's Publication in Early America* (Amherst: University of Massachusetts Press, 2016), 97–100.

8 Eugene Genovese and Elizabeth Fox-Genovese, *Fatal Self-Deception: Slaveholding Paternalism in the Old South* (New York: Cambridge University Press, 2011), 3.

9 Julius Bailey, *Down in the Valley: An Introduction to African American Religious History* (Minneapolis: Augsburg Fortress Press, 2016), 53.

10 Vincent Carretta, *Phillis Wheatley: Biography of a Genius in Bondage* (Athens: University of Georgia Press, 2014), 4–5.

11 Margaretta Matilda Odell, *Memoir and Poems of Phillis Wheatley, A Native African and a Slave* (Boston: George Light, 1834), 34.

12 Chloe Spear (c. 1767–1815), who, like Phillis Wheatley, was kidnapped as a child and enslaved to elite Bostonians, earned enough money by working as a laundress and keeper of a boarding house to purchase a home in Boston's North End; she left a will bequeathing $1500 to relatives in nearby towns. In the last few decades of the eighteenth century, it became more common in New England for enslaved favorites to be left money, property, or goods to assure them of support. See Melish, 89–114, and see Robinson, 52–4, for discussion of the non-inclusion of Phillis Wheatley in the wills of John and Nathaniel Wheatley.

13 Margaret Kinnell notes that Isaac Watts' *Divine Songs for Children*, first published in 1715 and abounding in associations of childhood and death, was similarly "part of English-speaking childhood for two centuries" ["Publishing for Children: 1700–1780," in *Children's Literature: An Illustrated History*, ed. Peter Hunt (New York: Oxford University Press, 1995), 47]. Paul Leicester Ford tracks the tremendous popularity of the *New-England Primer* in *"The New-England Primer": A History of Its Origin and Development* (New York: Teachers College Press, 1962), 17.

14 Vincent Carretta, ed., *Phillis Wheatley: Complete Writings* (New York: Penguin, 2001), 125. All quotations of Wheatley's poetry in this paragraph refer to this edition.

15 Marissa Fuentes, *Dispossessed Lives: Enslaved Women, Violence, and the Archive* (Philadelphia: University of Pennsylvania Press, 2016), 13.

16 Joanne Pope Melish, *Disowning Slavery: Gradual Emancipation and "Race" in New England, 1780–1860* (Ithaca: Cornell University Press, 2000), 25.

Bibliography

Bailey, Julius. *Down in the Valley: An Introduction to African American Religious History*. Minneapolis: Augsburg Fortress Press, 2016.

Brooks, Joanna. "Our Phillis, Ourselves." *American Literature* 82, no. 1 (2010): 1–28.

Carretta, Vincent, ed. *Phillis Wheatley: Complete Writings*. New York: Penguin, 2001.

Carretta, Vincent. *Phillis Wheatley: Biography of a Genius in Bondage*. Athens: University of Georgia Press, 2014.

Ford, Paul Leicester. *"The New-England Primer": A History of Its Origin and Development*. New York: Teachers College Press, 1962.

Fuentes, Marissa. *Dispossessed Lives: Enslaved Women, Violence, and the Archive*. Philadelphia: University of Pennsylvania Press, 2016.

Genovese, Eugene and Elizabeth Fox-Genovese. *Fatal Self-Deception: Slaveholding Paternalism in the Old South*. New York: Cambridge University Press, 2011.

Gordon, Avery. *Ghostly Matters: Hauntings and the Sociological Imagination* Minneapolis: University of Minnesota Press, 2008.

Lemire, Elise. *Black Walden: Slavery and Its Aftermath in Concord, Massachusetts*. Philadelphia: University of Pennsylvania Press, 2011.

Melish, Joanne Pope. *Disowning Slavery: Gradual Emancipation and "Race" in New England, 1780–1860*. Ithaca: Cornell University Press, 2000.

Odell, Margaretta Matilda. *Memoir and Poems of Phillis Wheatley, A Native African and a Slave* Boston: George Light, 1834.

Piersen, William D. *Black Yankees: The Development of an Afro-American Subculture in Eighteenth-Century New England.* Amherst: University of Massachusetts Press, 1988.

Robinson, William H. *Phillis Wheatley and Her Writings.* New York: Garland, 1984.

Wigginton, Caroline. *In the Neighborhood: Women's Publication in Early America.* Amherst: University of Massachusetts Press, 2016.

Primary sources

Mather, Cotton. "The Negro Christianized: An Essay to Excite and Assist That Good Work, the Instruction of Negro-Servants in Christianity." Boston: Printed by B. Green, 1706.

12

Sally Hemings
Writing the life of an enslaved woman

Annette Gordon-Reed

In 1802, James Callender, the notorious Scottish émigré who made a name for himself in the American political maelstrom of the 1790s by writing with extreme aggression about leading political figures of the day, wrote a story about the then-president Thomas Jefferson that would go down in history. Although rumors that Jefferson was "co-habiting" with an enslaved woman had been circulating in the 1790s – blind items and verbal gossip – Callender was the first to write openly about it in a newspaper and to use the name "Sally," though he did not give her last name.[1] He predicted in another piece about the president that the name "Sally" would go down in history with Jefferson's. Although it may have seemed like hyperbole at the time, it turns out that Callender was right about this, as he was right about the basic substance of the Jefferson–Hemings story.

During the first part of the nineteenth century, Sally Hemings was likely the most famous enslaved person in America. She figured in the political battles from the beginning of Thomas Jefferson's presidency in 1801 and remained a topic of discussion long after he left office in 1809. When the name "Sally" was mentioned in relationship to Jefferson, people knew who "Sally" was. In 1807, President Jefferson invited Native American leaders to the President's House for dinner. Breaking with tradition, he invited the wives of the delegation to attend, which made it look like a social engagement among equals. The wives of the government officials were aghast. Louisa Adams, the wife of then senator John Quincy Adams, wrote in her diary: "Perhaps this is the first *step* toward the introduction of *the incomparable Sally*" (emphasis in original).[2] The talk about Hemings was really talk about Jefferson; what did his connection to her say about *him*? One newspaper editor asked the question that seems to have been on many people's minds about the long-term connection to Hemings: "Why have you not married some worthy woman of your own complexion?"[3]

Given the racial and status hierarchy in the United States, and Jefferson's prominence, there is no wonder that most of the focus on Hemings and Jefferson has been on Jefferson – how the relationship fit, or did not fit, into his life. There is no record, to date, of Hemings having anything to say about Jefferson to outsiders. The modern notion of interviewing a subject did not exist: who could go to Monticello and try to talk to her? James Callender did spend time in Richmond and Charlottesville gathering information about Hemings and Jefferson from residents, but he would not have dared to try to make contact with Hemings herself. Had he been able to speak with her, it would be hard to trust what the rabidly racist Callender might have conveyed about the interaction.

Sally Hemings is often described as a blank slate upon which people write whatever they need or desire her to be: "slut" (as per Callender), lover, mistress, "substitute for a wife" (as per one of Jefferson's friends), rape victim, or sex slave. Changing times and changing mores have shaped people's understanding about her. During the initial firestorm that the Callender stories provoked, commentators used Hemings's race to ridicule Jefferson's attentions to her, suggesting that it was absurd for a man of his race and stature to be involved with such a person. Later in the nineteenth century, Hemings was used to decry the abuse of enslaved women in the South.

Things had changed enough by the early twentieth century that in a feature about their son Eston, the story of the Hemings–Jefferson connection could be described in a white newspaper as "romantic."[4] In 1968, the historian Winthrop Jordan, in his magisterial work *White Over Black: American Attitudes Toward the Negro 1550–1812,* wrote about Hemings and Jefferson in an even-handed fashion that disconcerted some who felt he should have debunked the story totally. But it was Fawn Brodie, in her 1974 biography of Jefferson, *Thomas Jefferson: An Intimate History,* who provoked the most intensely negative reaction. Brodie was the first Jefferson biographer to openly state that Hemings and Jefferson had had children together and to write as extensively as she could about Hemings. What incensed people most of all was her suggestion that Jefferson loved and needed Hemings. The book became an instant bestseller and has never been out of print.

Four years after Brodie's biography, Barbara Chase-Riboud's *Sally Hemings*, a novel written from Hemings's perspective, switched from the omniscient voice to the first-person voice of Hemings herself. Chase-Riboud made the crucial decision not to use what people take to be Black dialect during slavery when presenting Hemings's inner monologue. As a result, Hemings appeared more real and understandable, which allowed readers of all types to have instant empathy with her. The book became an international bestseller.

As a novelist, Chase-Riboud was interested in portraying Sally Hemings's humanity through a focus on Hemings as an individual, drawing on the particulars of her known biography to fashion a character who could be believable to readers. The time in which the novel appeared allowed this type of presentation. It is highly unlikely that *Sally Hemings* would be received in the same way today. At that moment, the Hemings–Jefferson story was seen largely through a racial lens. The open hostility toward the story, among at least some white historians, seemed rooted in anxiety about a "founding father" being involved in race mixing. After all, it was not until 1967 that the US Supreme Court, in the case of *Loving v. Virginia*, declared laws against interracial marriage unconstitutional. Virginius Dabney, a famous journalist and a Jefferson descendant, wrote an entire book attempting to refute Brodie's history and, strangely enough given that it was fiction, Chase-Riboud's novel. Dabney was so upset that he pronounced *Sally Hemings* "pornography," even though the book merely hints at the sex between Jefferson and Hemings rather than describing it.

The racial lens through which the story was seen allowed Hemings and Jefferson to be portrayed as star-crossed lovers kept from a true union by the laws and prejudices of their time. As long as Jefferson scholars were passionate to the point of irrationality in their resistance to the story, there was reason to suspect that concerns about race mixing played a role in the response. When my book *Thomas Jefferson and Sally Hemings: An American Controversy* was published in 1997, there appeared to be a large disconnect between the public and historians on the question of whether Hemings had had children with Jefferson. The general public, no doubt influenced by Brodie and Chase-Riboud, believed, or was prepared to believe, that the story was true, and most Jefferson scholars were still insisting it was not. My aim was not to prove or disprove the connection between the pair, but to show the ways in which white historians had weighed evidence incorrectly and in the process produced subpar historiography on the subject. When DNA testing corroborated my findings, and the Thomas Jefferson Foundation issued a report in 2001 agreeing with the conclusions of my book and the DNA, the balance shifted in the historical community and caught up with the public.

Sociology or biography?

It is a commonplace that historical issues are seen through the prism of the time in which the subject is addressed. Once the debate about whether Hemings bore children by Jefferson was resolved, the question shifted to thinking about the nature of the relationship. What had been, primarily, an issue about race and slavery became an issue about gender and slavery. Hemings and Jefferson as star-crossed lovers? What about the matter of consent? The law of slavery, which made Hemings Jefferson's property, meant that she could not legally refuse to have sex with him. If she could not refuse, how could it be said that she had consented to him?

This question has taken on even greater urgency in what has been called the "Me Too" era. In the wake of revelations about the alleged sexual depredations of the movie mogul Harvey Weinstein, and the ensuing information about other powerful men who used their positions to abuse women, what are we to make of sexual relations between enslavers and the enslaved? The power Weinstein had over the women who came into his orbit was nothing like the power Jefferson had over Hemings. Although "Me Too" is a modern-day phenomenon, born of our current sensibilities, it is natural that this heightened awareness would prompt a closer look at Hemings and Jefferson.

A *Washington Post* story on the archaeological excavations that found what researchers at Monticello took to be one of the places Sally Hemings lived for a time drew a storm of protest because the article referred to Hemings as Jefferson's "mistress." Critics insisted that "mistress" implied that the woman involved had consented to the connection, even though the adjective "enslaved" before the word "mistress" apprises the reader of what the phrase means. Objections have also been raised to the word "relationship," because some feel it suggests something positive, as if all "relationships" were necessarily good. In this new dispensation, Hemings should be described only as a rape victim or a "sex slave."[5]

The question of how to view the life of an individual enslaved woman requires thinking about the relationship between sociology and biography. Because the details of the lives of the vast majority of enslaved women are and will remain unknown, when making pronouncements about them, it makes sense to speak in sociological terms, referencing the experiences of the group. What happens, however, when information is actually known about a particular woman? Do we seek to explicate her life based upon known information, or do we resort to sociology, as if the experiences of the outside larger "group" should take precedence over the things that happened in the individual's life? What is the purpose of historical research into the lives of individual enslaved people, if the answers to every question are to be found in our general knowledge about slavery overall?

Sally Hemings is not a complete mystery. We know a good deal about her that should have some bearing on our understanding of her connection to Jefferson and what we write about it. First, what we know: Hemings was the daughter of the enslaved Elizabeth Hemings, herself the daughter of an enslaved African woman and an English ship captain whose last name was Hemings. Sally Hemings's father, John Wayles, was an Englishman brought to the United States as a servant who became a prosperous lawyer and planter. Wayles's daughter, and Hemings's half-sister, Martha married Thomas Jefferson. Hemings and her family were inherited by Martha and

Thomas when John Wayles died in the year Hemings was born, 1773. She, along with the rest of her Hemings-Wayles siblings and her enslaved half-siblings, came to live at Monticello when she was around three years old.

The Hemings siblings were installed as personal servants to Thomas and Martha, which suggests Martha's level of comfort with her enslaved half-siblings. Robert Hemings, at age 12, replaced Jupiter Evans, aged 30, as Jefferson's personal valet. The historian Deborah Gray White has noted that many white women in similar situations insisted that the children of their fathers, brothers, or husbands be sold or at least, put out of sight. The opposite happened at Monticello, and that would not have been lost on Sally Hemings. She grew up with male siblings who often left Monticello to hire themselves out and keep the money they made. The brothers understood, as we do, that the legal relationship to Jefferson remained despite all of this. But their capacity to move about had to make a difference to the inner lives of those young men, and to young Sally Hemings, who witnessed this and may have benefited from it. She had brothers who could do things that the other enslaved men on the plantation could not do. As for Hemings and her female siblings, they only did what can be described as "women's work," keeping house – sewing, knitting, tending to children. They did not go to the fields and were the only enslaved people spared from participating in the harvest. When Martha Jefferson was on her deathbed, her female Hemings half-siblings and their mother attended her along with Jefferson and another of her white sisters and one of Jefferson's sisters. According to Hemings family lore, just before she died, Martha extracted a promise from Jefferson that he would never marry again. She also gave Sally Hemings a hand bell as a memento.

Of course, none of the things the Hemingses were allowed to do, or did not have to do, changed the basic nature of slavery in Virginia. But the things that happen to any individual family – even our own – do not matter in the grand scheme of things, however important and urgent they may seem to us. Human beings do not live their daily lives in the big picture, and historians writing about the lives of individual people should not pretend that they do. In thinking of a young Sally Hemings's life, it is necessary to consider how her actual experiences at Monticello helped to shape her self-identity and what she would want and/or expect out of life. One thing Hemings would have learned early on is that genealogy mattered. Her connection to Jefferson's wife made a difference in her family's life. Looking at the matter sociologically, we would see that across the large swath of enslaved people who had biological connections to white people, those connections resulted in no change in their day-to-day lives. Either the connection meant nothing to their white relatives, or it meant something deeply negative. In Hemings's case, however, her biological tie to John Wayles clearly meant something to Martha and Thomas.

Hemings learned something else early on, too. Her father was a white man, and her grandfathers had all been white men. Although we cannot be sure of the racial makeup of all of those enslaved at Monticello, it is very likely that Hemings was phenotypically different from the majority of other enslaved people on the plantation. This had no bearing on her legal status, and Virginia law kept her in the category of "mulatto," meaning that she was not "white." Modern-day considerations of Hemings should be wary of assuming that our conceptions of racial solidarity, developed over the near two and one-half centuries after Hemings was born, would have been in her mind. Her grandmother, mother, and sisters had all had children with white men. There would be no reason for Hemings to think that a Black man would be her partner.

At age 14, Sally Hemings experienced a life-defining change. She sailed to Europe in 1787, accompanying Jefferson's youngest daughter, nine-year-old Mary (Polly). After spending time in the home of John and Abigail Adams in London, she went to Paris in July. There, she joined her brother James, who had come over in 1784 with Jefferson and his eldest daughter, Martha

(Patsy). After enduring a 40-day quarantine after being inoculated by the celebrated doctor Robert Sutton, she returned to live at Jefferson's residence in the Hotel de Langeac. By then, her brother James was the chef de cuisine Langeac. It is not known when she learned this, but it was likely her brother who let her know that in France, freedom was simply a matter of filing a petition. Every enslaved person who had done so in Paris in the eighteenth century had had their petitions granted. Jefferson was on the defensive about this, having written to a correspondent that the laws were "so far of the side of the slave" that there was nothing that a person claiming ownership could do. This may have accounted for his decision to pay wages to James and Sally Hemings. The siblings were paid near the highest rate for servants performing their assigned tasks.

Sally Hemings had arrived in what was pre-Revolutionary France. Riots were taking place. People were marching, sometimes right outside her home, shouting about freedom and the new world that was to come. There is no reason to doubt that the Hemings siblings noticed this. The neighborhood where the Hemings lived had the largest concentration of people of color in the city, though the numbers were small. It is probable that after five years and about two and a half years, respectively, James and Sally Hemings made contact with some of the people of color in their neighborhood.

At some point, Sally Hemings's relationship to Thomas Jefferson changed. In his recollections, their son Madison said, "During that time, my mother became Mr. Jefferson's concubine." It is common when discussing Hemings to say that she was 14 when this occurred. In my first book, I mentioned that it was a debate tactic, used by those who denied that Jefferson fathered Hemings's children, to push her age as low as possible in order to make the idea so unpalatable that people would not believe the story. Today, after the ground has shifted, people continue to assert confidently that Hemings was 14, positing that as soon as she walked into the Hotel de Langeac, Jefferson assaulted her. Some write of this as statutory rape, thinking of the modern-day category, though the age of consent in Virginia during the 1780s was 10.

The truth is that we do not know, and will likely never know, when Hemings became Jefferson's "concubine." The sociological approach to the question focuses on the fact that Jefferson was, under Virginia law, the enslaver of Hemings. Under that law, he could have assaulted her upon her arrival at the Hotel de Langeac in Paris; therefore, he did. And we do not have to worry about being wrong about this specific fact, because saying that Jefferson assaulted Hemings when she was 14 expresses a fundamental truth about slavery: enslavers had the power to, and often did, rape the women they enslaved. In this formulation, Jefferson and Hemings are symbols of the institution of slavery, not individuals. The actual details of Sally Hemings's life (the person who should most engage our sympathy) are subordinated to that larger truth about the vulnerability of enslaved women encoded in the institution of slavery.

The biographical approach recognizes that Hemings was enslaved but focuses on the specific things that happened to Hemings the individual. Given the scanty record, adherents to this approach must acknowledge the limits of the available information while assessing the value and meaning of the information that is known. We know that Abigail Adams, who saw Hemings when she arrived from the United States, thought she was 16 years old. Scholars have determined that the average age of menarche at this time was 15. Adams's observation that Hemings was 16 suggests that she may have had physical attributes indicating she had gone through puberty, such as breasts. If she had, it would seem unlikely that she could have been having sex with Jefferson for over two years but did not get pregnant until the end of her stay. Perhaps she had miscarriages? But there is no evidence of that, and that possibility cannot be converted into a probability, let alone a certainty, for historical purposes. On the other hand, there is documentary evidence that Jefferson's behavior toward Hemings changed markedly in 1789; behavior that is consistent with a show of a male's romantic or sexual interest in a female. That year, when Hemings was 16, Jefferson began buying her clothing, even though she had her own money from the wages he was paying her.

The story of Hemings and Jefferson in France comes from their son, Madison Hemings. Only two people, or someone they had talked to, could have possessed the information that he relayed: his mother or his father. Although there is no reason to doubt that Madison Hemings talked to his father, it seems more likely that these details came from his mother. While we have no letters from Sally Hemings that tell us what she thought of her life, we do have the vision of her life that she imparted to her son. It was a vision that she felt it important to pass down to her family. Historians, myself included, have not made enough of this. Instead, we have focused on all the things we do not know about Hemings and all that we know about enslaved women as a group, and neglected to consider the importance of what she said to her son about her life.

Above all, the Sally Hemings of her son's narrative is a person who believed that residence in France changed the dynamic between her and Jefferson. Law made her an enslaved person in Virginia. Law made her a free person in France. It did not make her Jefferson's equal, but it gave her leverage that she did not have in Virginia. His decision to pay her and her brother betrayed his anxiety about their status and his capacity. If things were exactly as they had been in Virginia, he would not have felt compelled to do this. When Jefferson wanted to return to the United States and to drop his daughters and Hemings off with Hemings's half-sister and his sister-in-law Elizabeth Eppes, Hemings balked. She was just getting comfortable there, had learned to speak French well, and did not want to be "re-enslaved." Jefferson's overseer, Edmund Bacon, remembered Hemings "often" talking about her trip to France. Bacon came to Monticello 16 years after Hemings returned from France and stayed until she was nearly 50. Madison Hemings's recollections and Bacon's statements make it clear that she looked upon her time in France fondly and considered those years transformative.

A point of context: Hemings was not alone in her feelings about going back to the United States. None of the young people living at the Hotel de Langeac wanted to return. Her brother James hired a tutor near the end of their stay to teach him proper French grammar, as if he was serious about mixing into French society. Patsy Jefferson spoke about renting rooms in her convent school while Jefferson dealt with his business affairs. William Short, Jefferson's Virginian protégé, declined to return and indeed, stayed in Europe for many years. As for Polly Jefferson, Nathaniel Cutting, who saw the Hemingses and Jeffersons in Le Havre just before they set sail, said that the young girl complained repeatedly that things were not being done the way they did them in Paris. The idea of remaining in France was on everyone's mind but Jefferson's.

Significantly, Hemings was pregnant, likely in the early stages. She understood that if she returned to Virginia, the child she was carrying would be enslaved, because the status of the child followed the status of the mother. That potential fate for her offspring evidently alarmed Hemings enough that she was willing to contemplate claiming her freedom in France. Could a 16-year-old have taken such a position? A sociological approach to the question would think of 16-year-olds in general and determine that such a person would be too afraid, too chastened by the power of slavery, to do so. The approach would also fixate on the likely bad outcomes, positing that they would have naturally deterred the person from the thought of remaining, rather than considering the personality and specific circumstances of the individual in question.

The problem with such an approach is that enslaved people escaped slavery under far more daunting circumstances than those Sally Hemings faced in Paris. They ran away knowing they would never see their families again. They ran with hounds in close pursuit, living in forests and swamps. Hemings and her 24-year-old brother had been working for wages for years, with ample opportunity to save and prepare for taking their leave of the Jeffersons. Both had opportunities to make friends who could have been helpful to them. The Jeffersons made friends during their stay. Why could not the Hemingses have done so? When Jefferson was in other towns away from Monticello, the enslaved people who worked for him made friends in the neighborhoods where they lived. There was a language barrier in France, but not an insurmountable one. Human beings, particularly young people in residence in a place for years and daily surrounded by people speaking another tongue, can learn a new language.

Sally Hemings presented herself as one who knew law and successfully, used the law to negotiate with Jefferson. She made her return to Virginia contingent on his promising to provide a certain type of life for her at Monticello and that her children would be free when they reached the age of 21. Madison Hemings, when talking about the fact that his father fulfilled his promises, very interestingly refers to the "treaty" between his parents that put all of this in motion. He places his parents on an equal footing for purposes of negotiating the "treaty," no doubt because he accepted the idea that the law in France gave his mother power that she would not have had in Virginia.

This was all extremely risky. Jefferson could have decided not to abide by his promises. He could have died with no assurance that his daughters would fulfill his wishes on the matter. And then there is the troublesome notion that Hemings "implicitly relied" on Jefferson's promises. I have often noted the difficulty I had with this idea. Falling back on the sociological approach to the question, I thought of the dangers that enslaved people put themselves in if they trusted an enslaver. Here, too, however, the details of biography may provide an answer. Sally Hemings and Thomas Jefferson cannot not be usefully considered just one on one. They were part of a web of relationships between mothers, fathers, brothers, full siblings, and half-siblings that went back far beyond their time in France. They would have seen each other through the prism of those relationships. The sociology of slavery would tell us that those relationships meant nothing to the vast majority of people in similar situations. But the biographies of Hemings and Jefferson suggest that they meant something to them.

Once Hemings returned to Virginia, she had no legal leverage over Jefferson. He could do as he pleased. She spent the rest of her life taking care of Jefferson's rooms and wardrobe, looking after her children, and doing "light-sewing" for her family. Although one of Jefferson's enemies called her "pampered and spoiled," it is likely that any positive treatment above the norm for an enslaved woman would be considered pampering. Another observer said that she was treated as "much above" other enslaved people, but that vague statement does not say how. Unlike other enslaved women, when Hemings was having her first child, a young girl was moved into her residence to help look after the child, while the children of other enslaved women were looked after communally. Jefferson's records also show that every adult member of the enslaved community at one time or another sold vegetables or fruit to Jefferson or his family, save for Sally Hemings. This would suggest that she had access to money from Jefferson without having to sell anything to him or his family. The biggest evidence of favored treatment was, of course, the freedom of all four of her children when they were adults or approaching adulthood.

Conclusion

What do we make of all this? Sally Hemings's version of the important events of her life, and her son's depiction of his family life, do not comport with the designation of Hemings as a "sex slave." Whatever generalizations from the sociology of slavery might tell us, Madison Hemings's recounting of his biography clearly indicates that he saw his mother, father, and siblings as existing in a family. He calls Sally Hemings "Mother," and he calls Jefferson "Father." He draws a circle around this group of six, differentiating their circumstances from those of everyone else on the plantation, white and Black.

As for Sally Hemings, her primary identity was that of a woman who used an available tool, the law, to calculate and negotiate the terms of her connection to a man whom we know only through documents and our understanding, and natural abhorrence, of the legal role he played in her life. She knew him personally. The end result of Hemings's calculation was that she could be with her family in Virginia and ensure that slavery, in her line, would end with her. What was a woman's life in the eighteenth century other than being attached to a man (white women could be married) and hoping that he would treat her well and provide for the success of her children to the extent that he could? It was a gamble, to varying degrees, but always a gamble nevertheless. While some may be loath to make any comparison between the situation of enslaved women and free women, there is no reason to doubt that actual enslaved women compared their lot with those of free white women. As sentient beings, they saw what their oppressors had relative to their own deprivations. They knew the state of slavery versus the state of freedom.

At the same time, Sally Hemings knew a world in which the lives of *all* women were more circumscribed than those of males. She watched as her sister Martha, who was not equipped for childbearing, suffered with each pregnancy and eventually died from complications of childbirth. Because of the marriage contract, which created perpetual consent, Martha could not refuse sex to her husband and could not protect her own life. The "privilege" given to the Hemings brothers was to go out in the world and work for themselves. The "privilege" given to Hemings and her sisters was to be kept in the home doing things that only the wives of white farmers would be doing – and not poor white farmers, whose wives often did work in the fields.

Sally Hemings is a figure of history whose life deserves to be considered on its own terms. Making judgments or pronouncements about her life based upon our understandings about slavery in general, while ignoring the context of her specific world, does an extreme disservice to her and to the historiography of slavery. We have so few opportunities to train the microscope to look closely at the facts of an individual enslaved person's life. As tempting as it is to see Hemings as a symbol and ignore her own and her family's understanding of who she was, we risk replicating, albeit in a small measure, the denial of humanity that warped her life when she was alive.

Notes

1 James Callender, *The Richmond Recorder*, September 1, 1802.
2 Louisa Catherine Adams to John Quincy Adams, June 11, 1807, Adams Family Papers MHi, cited in Annette Gordon-Reed, *The Hemingses of Monticello: An American Family*, (New York, 2008), at page 583.
3 *Richmond Recorder*, November 3, 1803.
4 "A Sprig of Jefferson was Eston Hemings – Then Gazette's Delver into the Past Brings Up a romantic Story…Was the Natural Son of the Sage of Monticello…Had the Traits of Good Training," *Daily Scioto Gazette*, August 1, 1902, cited in Annette Gordon-Reed, *Thomas Jefferson and Sally Hemings: An American Controversy* (Virginia, 1997), 15.
5 Britni Danielle, "Sally Hemings Wasn't Thomas Jefferson's Mistress. She Was His Property," www.washingtonpost.com/outlook/sally-hemings-wasnt-thomas-jeffersons-mistress-she-was-his-property/2017/07/06/db5844d4-625d-11e7-8adc-fea80e32bf47_story.html

13

The persistence of Félicité Kina in the world of the Haitian Revolution

Kinship, gender, and everyday resistance

Nathan H. Dize[1]

Since the early 1990s, studies of the Haitian Revolution and its multiple theaters have shifted from the realm of silence to open and public discourse.[2] However, the study of the 13-year period from August 1791, when plantations in the northern plain of the French colony of Saint-Domingue were set ablaze, until General Jean-Jacques Dessalines declared Haiti independent on January 1, 1804, has still led to challenges in assessing the lives and conditions of Black women, enslaved and free, in the world of the Haitian Revolution.[3] Scholars have shown that it can be rewarding to examine the ways that women participated in and shaped the history of the revolution through the figure of Cécile Fatiman, the *manbo* or Vodou priestess who, along with Boukman Dutty, animated the Ceremony of *Bwa Kayiman* (Bois Caïman), which launched the 13-year revolution.[4] Others, like Colin Dayan, have looked to Ezili, the Vodou *lwa*/goddess, as a narrative mode for telling women's stories in Haiti.[5] Furthermore, Haitian literary historian Marlene L. Daut asserts that women's narratives in the eighteenth- and nineteenth-century Caribbean often slip from view, not only because women are either assumed to be actors only when it entails willing or forced sexual encounters but also because in the history of slavery "what often counts as rebellion is violent armed resistance."[6]

In her search for Jean-Louis le Baron de Vastey's mother, Élisabeth "Mimi" Dumas, Daut demonstrates how difficult it can be to trace family histories during the Haitian Revolution, not only due to the colonial dispersal of archival documents but also as a result of the "tensions involved in representing one's self as connected to enslavers in the post-slavery society" (Daut 2017, 31). Similarly, Lorelle Semley and Nicole Willson have shown how the stories of individual women – Anne and Marie-Adelaïde Rossignol and Catherine Flon, respectively – are able to provide critical perspectives on what constitutes resistance, mobility, and citizenship in a period where the political terrain on which they stood shifted daily.[7] For instance, how might physical movement through the Atlantic world or the material histories of flag-making assist in the recovery of occluded narratives of women at the turn of the nineteenth century in the revolutionary Caribbean? To be sure, the veiled nature of Black women's histories during and after the Haitian Revolution requires scholars to rethink how rebellion is constituted as well as the spaces in which history is said to be made.

Figure 13.1 Fort de Joux prison, where Jean and Zamor Kina were held. (Photo credit: Nathan H. Dize)

For that reason, this chapter follows Stephanie M. H. Camp's assertion that "spaces matter" when considering women's acts of resistance to enslavement and dispossession and that in order to account for women's stories, we must turn toward everyday forms of resistance. Camp argues that "turning our attention to the everyday, to private, concealed, and even intimate worlds, is essential to excavating bondwomen's [and precariously free women of color's] resistance to slavery because women's history does not merely add to what we know; it changes what we know and how we know it."[8] This chapter draws on these methodological lessons from Camp, Daut, and others in order to tell the story of how Félicité Adelaïde Kina resisted the Napoleonic government's attempts to tear apart her family by imprisoning her husband Jean and stepson Zamor in a medieval French prison high in the Jura mountains of France.

Martinique, Guadeloupe, and Félicité Kina in the world of the Haitian Revolution

Before the news of the toppling of the Bastille and the outbreak of the French Revolution reached Martinique, in August 1789, a rumor circulated that Louis XVI had abolished slavery in the colonies. As a result, groups of enslaved people gathered between two plantations near the town of Saint-Pierre, armed with the tools used to cut sugar cane, declaring their freedom. The colonial Governor Charles du Houx de Vioménil immediately ordered the colonial militia to disperse the crowd of rebels, capturing 200 maroons, punishing 23, and executing eight.[9] While this revolt may seem minor, it provides a way of accounting for the revolutionary shifts that began to take place in Martinique as well as in Guadeloupe in the 1790s in the world of the Haitian Revolution.

After the Saint-Pierre revolt, colonial Martinique entered a period of "civil war" in 1790, when a polarized white enslaving class made of *grand blancs* and *petit blancs* (*big whites* and *little whites*) vied for political power with the *gens de couleur* (*free people of color*) and enslaved Blacks seeking citizenship and legal rights. In June of that same year, 14 *gens de couleur* were killed, according to the *Gazette de la Martinique*, for "[aspiring] to the quality of citizens."[10] By March 1791, the French had sent troops to quiet the civil war in Martinique, but it was clear that any peacetime would be short-lived.

From 1792 to 1794, revolts broke out between white republican and royalist factions in Martinique and Guadeloupe as they also recruited enslaved and free people of color to their causes. As the cracks in the colonial order began to emerge, the French National Convention issued a decree on February 4, 1794, granting universal emancipation in French Guyana, Guadeloupe, Martinique, and Saint-Domingue. Given the local instability in the Caribbean and the lack of metropolitan control from mainland France, the British seized on the chance to lay siege to both Martinique and Guadeloupe in February 1794 and later, Saint-Domingue in mid-September of the same year.[11] The British not only relied on their own troops and reinforcements from their colonies of Dominica and Jamaica, but they also managed to recruit formerly enslaved soldiers like Jean Kina to lead enslaved battalions in fighting both royalist and republican French fighters. Jean Kina's military career, as historian David Geggus carefully traces, led him to Fort-Royal, Martinique, where on October 28, 1800, he married the daughter of a free Black mason, a 14-year-old girl named Félicité Adélaïde Quimard.[12] On May 20, 1802, two months after signing the Treaty of Amiens establishing peace between the British and the French, Napoleon Bonaparte re-instituted slavery in Guadeloupe, French Guyana, and Martinique.

In January 1803, the 16-year-old Félicité Adelaïde Kina traveled from Paris to Pontarlier to protest the imprisonment of her stepson Zamor and her husband Jean for allegedly inciting revolution in British-occupied Martinique two years earlier. All three had been deported from the Caribbean island to England in 1801 and then detained in France in December 1802. In the late stages of pregnancy, Félicité obtained a passport from Parisian officials to be reunited with Jean and Zamor in the town of Frambourg, the closest town to the Fort de Joux prison. Once she arrived, Félicité presented herself before the commander of the prison and refused to leave Frambourg or the adjacent city of Pontarlier until Jean and Zamor were released.[13] Unsure how to receive Félicité Kina, the commander refused to allow her to see her husband and sent her back to town.

Due to her pregnancy, Félicité negotiated with a female innkeeper in Frambourg early during her stay and later in a hospice for women in Pontarlier, where she gave birth to her child.[14] Eighteen months later, Jean and Zamor consented to serve the Napoleonic army in Italy as a condition of their release. Both men had fought in the insurgent army battling against the French in Saint-Domingue (present-day Haiti) as well as for the British in southern Saint-Domingue and Martinique, for which they won their freedom.[15] Once again, the pair were forced to negotiate freedom from captivity with military service once their request to serve as carpenters in a French port city was denied. In order to keep their family and kinship ties together, Félicité, along with her infant, accompanied Jean and Zamor to the French town of Menton along the Italian border to prepare for another war.

Stories of Félicité and the Kina family tend to revolve around the military careers of Jean and Zamor, recounting their service with insurgent forces in Saint-Domingue and the British army in both Saint-Domingue and Martinique, their arrest and deportation to England and France, and their conscription into the battalions of Free People of Color sent to fight in Napoleon's Italian campaigns in 1805 (Geggus 2002, 137–47). These tellings, however, overshadow Félicité's story: the way that she navigated the Napoleonic legal system in order to keep the Kina family intact through imprisonment, dispossession, and liberation from captivity. So much of what we know about the Kina family's time in France from January 1803 until September 1804 is recorded in the carceral records of the Fort de Joux collected in the appendix of Alfred Nemours' 1929 *Histoire de la captivité et de la mort de Toussaint Louverture*, the manuscript of which was typed by his wife "Madame Nemours."[16] Although Félicité was never imprisoned with Jean and Zamor, these documents provide a record of her intimate and political maneuverings within a racially codified, imperial French space. On the one hand, these 18 months represent a period of spatial stasis for Jean and Zamor, who despite sharing the same prison cell, remained inside the walls of the medieval fortress overlooking the Swiss border, interacting only with the fort's commander and the maids who cleaned the cells and brought them sustenance. On the other hand, Félicité's movement was physically unencumbered as she freely traveled from Paris to Frambourg to the prison, made routine trips between the Fort de Joux and the surrounding towns and villages, and gained access to philanthropic networks that assisted her with childbirth and charitably provided her with shelter and food.

Félicité Kina understood that in order to preserve her family ties, she had to follow Jean and Zamor to the Fort de Joux and physically present herself before the French government to protest their detention. She did just that. On New Year's Day, 1803, Félicité obtained a passport to travel from Paris to the prison at Fort de Joux to reunite with her husband and stepson. On January 18, the prison's commander wrote to his superiors in Paris that Félicité traveled the distance of over 400 kilometers pregnant and alone. Félicité informed the commander of the fort that she would not leave her husband and stepson, and she planned to give birth in a nearby town. Before leaving the prison, she demanded to see her husband. The commander refused, and Félicité left the fort to seek refuge at an inn, where she stayed on credit (Nemours 1929, 254). Félicité's very presence was unprecedented, causing Amiot, the commander of the fort, to write to his superiors:

> I kindly ask of you […] to inform me as to the conduct that I must keep with regards to this woman who has already asked me to see her husband (and) whom I have denied the right until I have received orders from you or the government [Je vous prie […] de me faire savoir la conduite que je dois tenir envers cette femme qui m'a déjà demandé à voir son mari que j'ai refusé jusqu'à ce que j'aie reçu des ordres de vous ou du gouvernement]
>
> *(Nemours 1929, 254)*

On February 3, Félicité returned to the prison to collect the family's luggage, including a number of her dresses, since for some time she had only possessed the clothing on her back. In order to recuperate the family's belongings, Félicité had to receive permission not only from Amiot but also from her incarcerated husband (Nemours 1929, 257). When they were arrested, the Kinas were in possession of three trunks, which contained clothing for all three, including a number of Félicité's dresses, decorative headscarves, and other articles like a taffeta parasol. Records show that the contents of the other two trunks were either to be confiscated and used to clothe Jean and Zamor while they were imprisoned or to be sold by the Napoleonic state in order to subsidize the Kinas' imprisonment (Nemours 1929, 254).

While the French government clearly could have confiscated and sold the contents of all three trunks to the profit of the state, Félicité's presence and her pregnancy tested the limits of Napoleonic carceral protocols. The deputy prefect, Citoyen Micaut,[17] of the department of Doubs, wrote to his superiors on her behalf:

> I would be charmed if you were to inform me if it would be possible to return to the Kina woman the suitcase that contains merely the effects of her own personal use […] this

woman who has reached the term of her pregnancy has been welcomed with all possible humanity by the administrators of the hospice of Pontarlier ... [je serais charmé que vous voulussiez bien me faire connaître s'il conviendrait de remettre à la femme Kina la malle qui ne contient que des effets à son usage [...] cette femme qui touche au terme de sa grossesse a été accueillie avec tout l'humanité possible par les administrateurs de l'hospice de Pontarlier.

(Nemours 1929, 257)

Numerous letters circulated between administrators, prison officials, and local judges to resolve Félicité's request for her property. This not only helped her to maintain a partial yet indirect contact with her husband and stepson, but also successfully kept the Kina name in the front of local officials' minds. While the records Nemours includes in the appendix to *Histoire de la captivité et de la mort de Toussaint Louverture* do not definitively show that Félicité was able to recover her or her family's belongings, as a free woman of color, she was able to petition the government for a number of weeks on this very subject (Nemours 1929, 258).[18] At the same time, Félicité's inability to collect her belongings is entwined with the incarceration of her formerly enslaved next of kin, Jean and Zamor. As people with intimate ties to slavery, it appears that in mainland France, the Kinas would have to, as Saidiya Hartman writes, "[fashion] themselves again, making possibility out of dispossession."[19]

Petitions, escape, and conscription: the Kinas' military path to freedom

According to the local government ministers, by March 25, Félicité had given birth to her child and had overstayed her welcome at Pontarlier's hospice. The two ministers wrote that Félicité had to leave because she had a child and was without either a profession or financial means to pay for her room and board (Nemours 1929, 258). Félicité, nonetheless, remained. We can only speculate as to how Félicité managed to negotiate her stay at the hospice, because there is a gap in the archival record.[20] The ministers' letter concluded only that "[Félicité] stayed thanks to the gifts of a few well-meaning people" (Nemours 1929, 262).[21] It appears that the midwives and the charity of women innkeepers in Pontarlier allowed Félicité to safely give birth to her child and remain close to Jean and Zamor until they were released from prison. After receiving authorization from the Napoleonic army, the four Kinas left for Menton on August 20, 1804.

However free Félicité's movement was, the department of Doubs was still part of a Napoleonic France that had already re-instituted slavery in Martinique and Guadeloupe and that was still embroiled in an expeditionary invasion of Saint-Domingue to attempt to restore the colonial order and re-enslave or eradicate the Black insurgent soldiers of the Indigenous Army.[22] A letter written by J. de Bry, the prefect of the department of Doubs, wrote that the Kinas were arrested by the English in Martinique for "having placed themselves at the helm of a negro insurrection that has broken out on this island [pour s'être mis à la tête d'une insurrection des nègres qui éclata dans cette isle]" and that once they had been transferred to the fort, they must not "be informed of the presence of Toussaint-Louverture [sic] [informés de la présence de Toussaint-Louverture]" (Nemours 1929, 250–1). By 1803, the palpable "fear of French negroes" in the Caribbean had indeed reached the depths of the mainland French administration, so much so that an interior department on the Franco-Swiss border was aware of Black rebellion and its challenges to the colonial status quo.[23] In this space and in the eyes of the Napoleonic legal system, Jean and Zamor were seen as rebels and fugitive slaves whose precarious hold on freedom made them subject to labels marked by enslavement, such as "nègre," meaning simultaneously "negro" and enslaved person of African descent, in the legal records of the Fort de Joux. Despite the terminology "Men of color [Hommes de couleur]" used on many of the letterheads accounting for Jean and Zamor's provisions, the government officials and various commanders of the Fort de Joux continued to refer to them as "nègre" in the body of their correspondence, implying that the Kinas' hold on freedom was both tenuous and precarious in the eyes of the local French administration (Nemours 1929, 252–3).

After 19 months in French custody, in July 1804, Jean and Zamor Kina petitioned the local government seeking clemency for the rest of their prison sentence. Even though the Kinas seemed to have been imprisoned indefinitely, they offered via the prefect of the department of Doubs to serve the Napoleonic government as ship makers and carpenters in any of the ports of the French Republic (Nemours 1929, 261–2). These initial proposals were apparently rejected, because a document titled "Freeing of Kina, father and son [Mis en liberté de Kina père et fils]" states that the two men were freed exclusively to serve in the Free Colored battalions of the Napoleonic Army in the 1805 invasion of Italy (Nemours 1929, 262). The two were to report to the French town of Menton, on the Franco-Italian border along the Mediterranean Sea; however, it was not initially certain that Félicité could follow the two men to war. Set to depart for Menton at the end of August 1804, Félicité was told that she must produce the passport that had enabled her legal passage from Paris to the Fort de Joux nearly two years prior. At some point, however, Félicité had lost the passport and declared it missing, requiring the French government to inquire with the Police prefecture in Paris to validate her story (Nemours 1929, 264).

At this point, the prefect and deputy prefect of Doubs were quite familiar with the Kinas' case and seemed to be intent on helping to keep the Kina family together, especially since Félicité had so frequently interfaced with local officials in Doubs, Pontarlier, and at the Fort de Joux. By the time the Kinas finally left the Fort de Joux for Menton, the prefect of Doubs managed to outfit the family with a stagecoach and a pension for Félicité and her child of 15 centimes per league traveled due to French law dating back to June 13, 1790 (Nemours 1929, 265–6). From the moment Félicité Kina arrived in Pontarlier, pregnant with child, to the moment she left with Jean, Zamor, and her newborn child, she managed to navigate a racially hostile space and government that sought to separate her from the only family she had; her persistence and

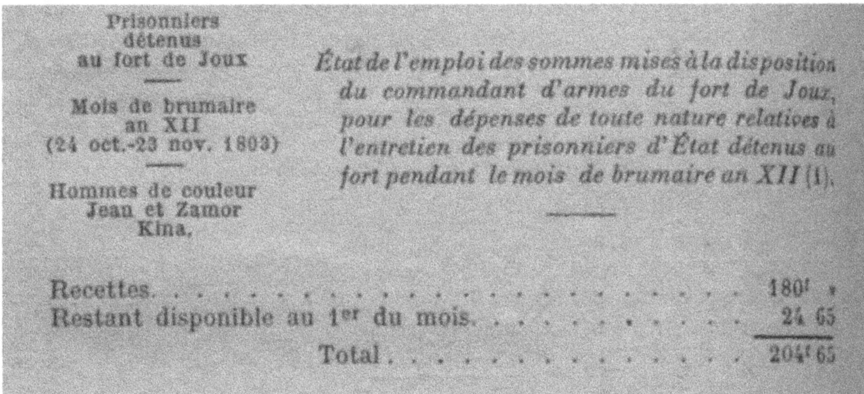

Figure 13.2 Letter head from Alfred Nemours's documentary appendix in Histoire de la mort et de la captivité de Toussaint Louverture, where Jean and Zamor Kina are referred to as "Hommes de couleur." (Image credit: Bibliothèque Numérique Caraïbe, Amazonie, Plateau des Guyanes, Public Domain)

pursuit of legal action must be considered as acts of resistance that ultimately resulted in the reunion of the Kina family.

In perhaps the most comprehensive English-language narrative of the life of Jean Kina, David Geggus recounts Jean's heroic journey from an enslaved soldier in the southern province of Saint-Domingue to a French prisoner for presumably spreading insurrection in the neighboring French colony of Martinique. While Geggus mentions Félicité Kina, he grants her little subjectivity apart from her role as wife and mother. Sociologist of slavery Stéphanie Mulot refers to this process as a political and scientific discourse in which "the bases of colonial domination are reinforced by their relationship to sexual domination."[24] In short, to account for the stories of free and enslaved women of color is to understand the way that sex and gender shape colonization, enslavement, and other forms of dispossession. To tell these stories, we must engage with the full spectrum of personal and political acts that make up women's lives. Unlike her husband and her stepson, Félicité Kina did not have a military career; however, her actions while Jean and Zamor were imprisoned acutely constituted acts of resistance. Scholars also overlook Félicité's time in France because it coincided with the imprisonment of one of the most famous leaders of the Haitian Revolution, Toussaint Louverture, who died in a French prison only three months after Félicité arrived to protest her own family's captivity.

Conclusion: Félicité Kina and Black women's military lives in Napoleonic France

When Félicité married Jean Kina in October 1800, she became a military wife. As Jean's wife, Félicité was subject to the movement and maneuverings of her husband in addition to the manipulation of whichever military corps he joined. In marrying Jean, Félicité made the transition from a civilian life to a military one. She was now subject to the same laws and constraints as Jean, including arrest and his precarious hold on freedom as a formerly enslaved Black man. In looking at her travels from Fort-Royal to London and from Paris to Pontarlier, it is clear that Félicité's political and legal acumen was sharp. She understood how to maneuver the French legal system, locate her kin, and navigate the networks of white women in the villages surrounding the Fort de Joux prison in order to successfully give birth and remain in proximity to her imprisoned husband and stepson. Félicité also managed, by her presence alone, to secure a pension and subsidized travel for the entire family from Pontarlier to their new military training post along the Côte d'Azur in Menton, France. Félicité's story provides a salient example of how militarization impacted Black families within the wider frame of the Haitian Revolution and how Black women navigated their position as military wives, "straddling," as Cynthia Enloe argues, "military and civilian positions."[25]

Months before the Kinas were transferred to French custody, Napoleon Bonaparte's government re-instituted slavery in Martinique. Growing up in the colony, this was a legal reality that Félicité had navigated for the majority of her life prior to her marriage to Jean. Before, as a girl of color in Martinique, she was subject to the legal whims of a militarized French colony that had been living under war-like conditions in the revolutionary Caribbean for nearly 10 years. After her marriage to Jean, she was subject to the whims of the British army and later the French Imperial army as her mobility was conscripted not only to Jean but to the military. Félicité's story allows us to see what Enloe characterizes as "the military's intimate relationship with the state – with the central government and the laws and ideologies which sustain its authority," especially as it pertains to Black soldiers and their families in the First French Empire (Enloe 1983, 11). To some degree, Félicité was contained behind a "double-locking door" of Black civilian life in a French slave society and the military life in the First Empire, but her story also shows how a careful navigation of French laws and ideologies surrounding the military family enabled the Kinas to remain united in the face of enslavement and/or coerced military conscription (Enloe 1983, 15).

In looking closer at the Black military family in the era of the Haitian Revolution, in particular, we might also turn to stories of failed or denied reunification – like Toussaint Louverture's family, who were interned and dispersed throughout France before and after Toussaint's death in April 1803 – for what they might say about the differing experiences between Black military leadership and the rank and file. It is clear that Toussaint Louverture's status as a general in the French army resulted in a heightened profile for his wife, Suzanne, and their children, causing them to be placed under arrest and to experience imprisonment.[26] But was Félicité's mobility, in part, a result of Jean's subaltern status within the military? Did other Black military families face similar experiences? In the end, Félicité's story reveals the importance of examining the Black military family in the Age of Revolutions, because within these family experiences, we gain a fuller understanding of the contours of Black citizenship as well as the (un)willing participation in military life.[27]

Notes

1 Versions of this chapter have appeared on Nursing Clio, a collaborative, peer-reviewed blog focusing on the history of gender and medicine, as well as in the *Haitian History Journal*. Nathan would like to thank these venues for the permission to reprint portions of this chapter. For the original post, see Nathan H. Dize, "The Persistence of Félicité Kina: Kinship, Gender, and Everyday Resistance," Blog. Nursing Clio, July 26, 2018. https://nursingclio.org/2018/07/26/the-persistence-of-felicite-kina-kinship-gend er-and-everyday-resistance/.

2 In his foundational study, *Silencing the Past: Power and the Production of History*, Michel-Rolph Trouillot articulates how the Haitian Revolution remained "unthinkable" to U.S. and European intellectuals during and after the revolution, because it challenged the very ontological and political roots of the Enlightenment.

3 For studies of women and families before the Haitian revolution, see Eddins, Crystal Nicole, "African Diaspora Collective Action: Rituals, Runaways, and the Haitian Revolution," PhD, Michigan State University, 2017; Taber, Robert D., "The Issue of Their Union: Family, Law, and Politics in Western Saint Domingue, 1777 to 1789," PhD, University of Florida, 2015. For studies that center gender during and after the Haitian Revolution in Haiti, see "La Femme dans la guerre de l'indépendance d'Haïti," *Le Document* 1, no. 2 (February 1940): 77–129; Sheller, Mimi, *Citizenship from Below: Erotic Agency and Caribbean Freedom* (Durham: Duke University Press, 2012).

4 Ulysse, Gina Athena, "Why Representations of Haiti Matter Now More than Ever," *NACLA Report on the Americas* (July 2010): 37–43.

5 Dayan, Joan (Colin), "Erzulie : A Women's History of Haiti," *Research in African Literatures* 25, no. 2 (1994): 5–31.

6 Daut, Marlene L., *Baron de Vastey and the Origins of Black Atlantic Humanism* (London: Palgrave, 2017), 28–31.

7 Semley, Lorelle, *To Be Free and French: Citizenship in France's Atlantic Empire* (Cambridge: University of Cambridge Press, 2017); Willson, Nicole, "Unmaking the Tricolore: Catherine Flon, Material Testimony and Occluded Narratives of Female-led Resistance in Haiti and the Haitian *Dyaspora*," *Slavery & Abolition* 41, no. 1 (2020): 131–48. For other important contributions to the intellectual history of Haitian women, see the digital humanities projects *Mémoire de Femmes* by Jasmine Narcisse (http://jasminenarcisse.com/memoire/index.html), *Fanm Rebèl* (https://www.fanmrebel.com/) by Nicole Willson, and *Rendering Revolution* (https://renderingrevolution.ht/about) by Siobhan Meï and Jonathan Michael Square. See also Germain, Félix, and Silyane Larcher, eds., *Black French Women and the Struggle for Equality, 1848–2016* (Lincoln: University of Nebraska Press, 2018); Mitchell, Robin, *Vénus Noire: Black Women and Colonial Fantasies in Nineteenth-Century France* (Athens: University of Georgia Press, 2020); Joseph-Gabriel, Annette K., *Reimagining Liberation: How Black Women Transformed Citizenship in the French Empire* (Champaign, IL: University of Illinois Press, 2020).

8 Camp, Stephanie M.H., *Closer to Freedom: Enslaved Women & Everyday Resistance in the Plantation South* (Chapel Hill, NC: University of North Carolina Press, 2004), 1–3.

9 Dubois, Laurent, *A Colony of Citizens: Revolution & Slave Emancipation in the French Caribbean, 1787–1804* (Chapel Hill: University of North Carolina Press, 2004), 85.

10 Cormack, William S., *Patriots, Royalists, and Terrorists in the West Indies: The French Revolution in Martinique and Guadeloupe, 1789–1802* (Toronto: University of Toronto Press, 2019), 64–6, 84–5.

11 For a survey of the impact of these rebellions and political tensions, see Dubois, 124–71.

12 Geggus, David Patrick, "Slave, Soldier, Rebel: The Strange Career of Jean Kina," in *Haitian Revolutionary Studies* (Bloomington: Indiana University Press, 2002), 147. Émile Huyot identifies Antoine Quimard as Félicité's father: Huyot, E., *Les Gens de couleur libres du Fort-Royal, 1679–1823* (Paris: Société Française d'Histoire d'Outre-Mer, 1971), 28.

13 Nemours, Alfred, *Histoire de la captivité et de la mort de Toussaint Louverture : Notre pèlerinage au Fort de Joux* (Paris: Berger-Levrault, 1929), 254.

14 This story is adapted from the narrative woven by the Haitian historian Alfred Nemours and the archival documents he collected and published in Alfred Nemours, *Histoire de la captivité et de la mort de Toussaint Louverture : Notre pèlerinage au Fort de Joux* (Paris: Berger-Levrault, 1929).

15 See Geggus, "Slave, Soldier, Rebel: The Strange Career of Jean Kina," 137–51.

16 Alfred Nemours, a Haitian diplomat and retired general, was the first to provide evidentiary proof of how the Napoleonic regime denied Toussaint Louverture the resources he needed to survive in the Fort de Joux prison, amounting to a torturous execution over the course of eight months from August 1802 until his death on April 7, 1803. See also Gutarra, Dannelle, "Toussaint Louverture's Captivity at Fort de Joux," *Journal of Caribbean History* 49, no. 2 (2015): 145–59.

17 This official's name is also occasionally spelled "Micaux" as well as "Micaud" in Nemours' appendix.

18 A subsequent letter reiterating Félicité Kina's request was sent to the Grand Judge in Pontarlier.

19 Hartman, Saidiya, *Lose Your Mother: A Journey Along the Atlantic Slave Route* (New York: Farrar, Straus, and Giroux, 2007), p. 7.

20 Speculation or "critical fabulation," as Saidiya Hartman calls it, might be the best way to cope with the missing links in the evidentiary gaps in Félicité's story. See Hartman, Saidiya, "Venus in Two Acts," *Small Axe: A Caribbean Journal of Criticism* 12, no. 2 (June 1, 2008): 1–14. https://doi.org/10.1215/-12-2-1.

21 Nemours acknowledges the women and men who aided Félicité Kina only by profession, like the midwife and male functionary who helped process her passport documents.

22 See Dize, Nathan H., "Haiti and the Colonial Predicament of Language in Zamoyski's *Napoleon, A Life*," *Age of Revolutions* (blog), August 19, 2019. https://ageofrevolutions.com/2019/08/19/haiti-and-the-colonial-predicament-of-language-in-zamoyskis-napoleon-a-life/.

23 Johnson, Sara E., *The Fear of French Negroes: Transcolonial Collaboration in the Revolutionary Americas.* (Berkeley, CA: University of California Press, 2012), xv–xxii.

24 Mulot, Stéphanie, "Quand la race croise le genre : le fondement des sociétés antillaises," *Chemins Critiques* 6, no. 1 (2017): 147–62.

25 Enloe, Cynthia. *Does Khaki Become You? The Militarization of Women's Lives* (Boston: South End Press, 1983), 9.

26 See Nemours, Alfred, *Histoire de la famille et de la descendance de Toussaint Louverture* (Port-au-Prince: Edition Presses Nationales d'Haïti, 2008).

27 Tozzi, Christopher, *Nationalizing France's Army : Foreign, Black, and Jewish Troops in the French Military, 1715–1831* (Charlottesville: University of Virginia Press, 2016).

14

The then and now of subjugation and empowerment

Marie Benoist's *Portrait d'une négresse* (1800)

James Smalls

Marie-Guillemine Benoist's *Portrait d'une négresse* (1800) complicates matters of race, gender, and class. The portrait not only constructs racial otherness in the historical moment but relates that process to the assumed un-raced white and in this case, female rather than male self. In this undertaking, the Black woman depicted confuses rather than clarifies the expected function of the portrait genre as a marker of a person's subjectivity, social class standing, and occupation. Benoist's portrait is a complex painting with serious political implications around not only matters of race, gender, and class but also agency, the circuitry of male and female gazes, allegory, modernity, and exoticism. It is one of those rare images that have far-reaching implications for the past and present cultural histories of Black women and their primacy or impotence in the discourse over visual representation, agency, and cultural value as modernist subjects.

Over the past two decades, art historians and other scholars of late eighteenth- and early nineteenth-century French art have offered varying interpretations of this very complex and ambiguous work. The painting's subject matter and reception have provoked a variety of responses ranging from Hugh Honour's praise for it as a "warmly humane and noble image" to Griselda Pollock's criticism of the painter for shamefully putting her Black model on display, as on a slave auction block, to serve the cause of her own creativity (Honour 1989, 7–9; Pollock 1999, 300). Scholars such as Helen Weston and Darcy Grimaldo Grigsby, as well as myself, view the image as part of a dehumanizing tendency through the erasure of the sitter's identity, despite the fact that the Black woman is the primary focus of the painting and that she has been recently identified by her name.[1] It has been argued that dehumanization and objectification are furthered in the work by "the stark exposure of her [the Black woman's] body, and the deliberate emphasis on her skin color." As such, the painting "deprives the sitter of her individuality and reduces her to a generic, racial, and sexualized category – 'a negress'" (Bishop 2019, 2).

The Black woman in Benoist's painting can be taken as a symbol of modernity; a visible sign of simultaneous empowerment and subjugation. As David Theo Goldberg has pointed out, definitions of race and gender, along with their representational forms, emerge, develop, and change within the institution of modernity (Goldberg 1993, 1). Benoist's portrait demonstrates the extent to which gender, race, and class were significant to the articulation of the artist's subjectivity in the historical moment of French entry into the modern world. Through the image, we as viewers are forced to question these matters as defining aspects of the collective body politic in the building of French nationhood, in which women and Blacks were to be included in the abstract ideals of revolutionary liberation.

This chapter constitutes a rumination over the historical, aesthetic, and conceptual "then and now" of the painting in matters of race, gender, class, aesthetics, and the gaze. I want to consider the representation of the Black woman in Benoist's portrait as simultaneously empowered and subjugated – locked into an ambiguous state of affairs that confounds and disrupts while lending productive meaning to the image.

Due to the absence of firsthand accounts of art and writing by Black women from this period, it becomes necessary to analyze the conditions of the sitter's existence and the cultural ideologies surrounding the portrait, and to undertake a critical examination of the subject matter and style of the visual image itself. Many scholars who have examined this portrait tend to argue either pro or against its sympathetic portrayal. Either way, one must concede that the overwhelming context for considering the work is the phenomena of slavery and antislavery. In this instance, the conscientious representation of a Black figure by any artist would constitute a political and politicizing site/sight. I have contended, and continue to contend, that there is no such thing as a politically neutral representation of an *esclave* (slave), nègre/négresse (Negro/ Negress), or noir (Black), even though aesthetics and classicizing language often attempt to convince us otherwise.[2] Both the Black presence and absence in visual and literary representation speak to the political volatility Black people embody in the visual register, past and present. Benoist's portrait is no exception. With it, the artist scrutinizes a racialized sitter "to create an accurate likeness, [while] complicating the dynamics of agency, traditionally held by white male portraitists over their female sitters of any race" (Cresseveur 2015, 2).

As I have pointed out elsewhere, *Portrait d'une négresse* is less a likeness of the Black woman depicted and more a representational act of self-reflection by the artist on her own status and condition as a woman in early nineteenth-century France. Benoist's painting is powerful in its dual function as a focus of the simultaneous empowerment and subjugation of Black women; of the exploitive use of a Black woman by a white female artist to speak to the deplorable condition of women as enslaved in society. By virtue of its subject and the time period in which it was produced, the painting combines the volatile contemporary debates over slavery, antislavery, and the social status of women. Thus, the work is unquestionably political and politicizing, intentionally or not, if we accept the idea that fundamentally, "politics is about relationships among people and how they intersect with and are informed by dominant ideologies and systems of authority in the real world" (Amin 2014, 255).

In addition to race as a topic of consideration, Benoist's portrait can be viewed as a work of both consensus-building and "feminist" protest. In its thematic strategies, the portrait closely relates to early nineteenth-century feminism and the writings of women authors of the period, such as Olympe de Gouges (1748–93), Germaine de Staël (1766–1814), and Claire de Duras (1777–1828), all of whom wrote about slavery in relation to the oppression of women in society. Indeed, many of the processes and motivations of Benoist as a painter parallel the complications, ambiguities, contradictions, and ambivalences found in the written works of these antislavery authors.[3]

Portrait d'une négresse is unusual in many respects. For one, it deviates from standard representations of Blacks in European art, which typically show them as exotic additions to a portrait or a narrative scene in which a white master or mistress is the intended primary focus. Based on the physiognomic detailing of the model and the high degree of finish, Benoist's portrait was not a study for a larger project, as was the case with the majority of late eighteenth- and early nineteenth-century works in which Black women appeared and were typically shown in their expected roles as attending servants and exoticized complements to a white mistress. By depicting a Black woman in the traditional pose and situation of white women in portraiture, Benoist has turned the *Portrait d'une négresse* into something of an allegory of her own condition of subservience to patriarchy, thereby simultaneously empathizing with the oppressed condition of her sitter while subjugating her.

Clearly, in choosing to paint a woman of color as the sole rather than ancillary subject of the composition, Benoist embraced an unusual subject and knowingly engaged in intersecting and politically contentious issues (e.g. race, gender, class, slavery/antislavery). The only other portrait of an independent Black subject to be publicly exhibited around the same period was Anne-Louis Girodet's *Portrait of Citizen Belley, Ex-Representative of the Colonies* (Salon of 1798).[4] Girodet's work is a visualized manifesto for Black emancipation and was undoubtedly received in that way by visitors to the Salon (Waller 2018). It has been suggested, based on the fact that not only were Girodet and Benoist acquainted but the former was the teacher of Marie-Guillemine's sister, that Benoist's *Portrait* may have been not only inspired by Girodet's *Belley* but perhaps even a conscious response to it (Grigsby 2002, 57). Both works are similar in that they were produced during a period in which the slavery/antislavery debate remained at the core of determining who was and who was not to become a member of the French nation; who was to be a citizen and who was not worthy of that status.

Although both portraits are unusual in that they are not stereotypical images of Blacks, they differ in that the *Belley* is a large canvas depicting a recognizable historical male figure in the grand manner of portraiture (containing public and lofty ideas promoting the revolutionary democratic principles of liberty, equality, and brotherhood), while the *Portrait d'une négresse* is of modest size, intended for private consumption/contemplation, and showcases a Black female sitter used to communicate ideas about race, bondage, and liberation in a less demonstrative and more generalized manner. As is also the case with Girodet's image, Benoist's figure constitutes a combined allegorical and straightforward portrait containing elements of idealization and historical "truth" (Weston 1994, 98–99).

Benoist's portrait contains ambiguities and contradictions that are exacerbated by the biography of the artist and the historical context in which the work was painted. Ironically, the biographical details of the assumed focus of the painting, the Black woman, remain a mystery.

A painting, a history, and a life

Benoist's portrait shows a young Black woman seated in an armchair in a three-quarter position (see Figure 14.1). Her face is turned to the viewer with a facial expression described as "somewhere between defiance and melancholy" (Bishop 2019, 1). The treatment of her face suggests that this is a likeness of a particular individual rather than the representation of a generic racial type. She wears an elaborate white and crisply laundered headwrap along with a white garment and red sash, the former of which slips from her shoulders, exposing her right breast. The background is plain, and the chair in which she sits suggests that she is in a privileged domestic space. The work is mostly monochromatic with hints of bright red and blue. It has been proposed by several scholars that the red, white, and blue palette is conscientiously suggestive of the democratic tricolors of the French revolutionary flag.

Both the biographical details of Benoist and the historical context in which the portrait was painted are critical to the work's actual and potential meaning. *Portrait d'une négresse* was painted between 1794 and 1802, during a time in which the transatlantic slave trade was thriving, even though France had (temporarily) abolished slavery in its colonies in 1794, only to have it reinstated by Napoleon Bonaparte in 1802.[5]

Figure 14.1 Marie-Guillemine Benoist – *Portrait d'une négresse.* (Art Collection / Alamy Stock Photo)

The painting reveals much about the life and career of Benoist but uncovers nothing about those of the Black sitter, thereby leaving her subjectivity to speculation. Benoist's biographical details provide some clues as to why she chose to paint this subject. Marie-Guillemine Benoist, born Marie-Guillemine de Laville-Leroulx in 1768 (died 1826), was from a middle-class family. She and her sister, Elisabeth de Laville-Leroulx, first studied painting with Elisabeth Vigée-Lebrun (1755–1842) and later were among a handful of women artists whom the famed neoclassical painter Jacques-Louis David (1748–1825) took into his studio in the Louvre. Before she married, Marie-Guillemine made her debut at the Salon of 1791, when the revolutionary government opened the exhibition to women and non-French artists for the first time. She was ambitious and exhibited history paintings, which were considered at the time beyond women's capacities and not a suitable pursuit. In 1793, during the most violent phase of the French Revolution, she married Pierre-Vincent Benoist (1758–1834), a lawyer of noble birth who fostered connections with the royal family (Ballot 83, note 2). He was from Angers and an avowed monarchist. The political circumstances of the period forced the couple into hiding until moderate revolutionaries overthrew the government in 1794, the same year that slavery was temporarily abolished in the colonies (Weston 2000, 56). By 1800, however, Napoleon had staged a coup d'état and installed himself as First Consul of the Directory. With the change of government, Benoist continued to work as a professional artist for much of her marriage. She used her contacts in the art world to assist her husband's rise in status during the Consulate, First Empire, and Bourbon Restoration. In 1814, Louis XVIII appointed her husband to the position of Conseiller d'État, a position that provided him with a substantial income (Cresseveur 2015, 8). During the period, it was frowned upon for wealthy women to hold paid employment in the public sphere. As a result, Benoist was forced to forego her career as a painter in deference to her husband and to societal norms.

It has been pointed out that although Benoist's husband had royalist connections, "we cannot determine the artist's political sympathies by considering those of her husband." However, "we can conclude that her role in his rise in status necessitated her conformity to contemporary political conventions, which would foreclose any attempts to effect social change" (Cresseveur 2015, 8–9). This state of affairs bears strongly on Benoist's representation of the Black sitter. It is my contention that Benoist's portrait was an aesthetically sanctioned attempt by the artist to effect social change as far as the status of women was concerned. The painting manifests the artist's endeavor to exercise as much agency as she could get away with in the face of insurmountable odds that restricted her actions because of her gender. The portrait speaks powerfully to the artist's desire to assert her own agency as a woman and professional artist in contemporary patriarchal society and debatably, that of her Black sitter as well.

Available documents reveal that Benoist's Black sitter was a formerly enslaved woman brought to France in 1794 from the island of Guadeloupe by Benoist's brother-in-law, Auguste Benoist-Cavay, a ship's purser and civil servant (Ballot 1914, 151).[6] Whether she was brought to France under enslaved or servant status, she, unlike fashionable women who commissioned their portraits, would have had little influence or say in how she was depicted (Smalls 2004; Waller 2018). Nevertheless, it is true that "portraits of 'free' Black servants were [often] used as status symbols for wealthy and haut bourgeois families at the time" (Pollock 1999, 287; Cresseveur 2015, 10–11). *Portrait d'une négresse* may well have served this purpose.

Accessible sources also confirm that Benoist "never travelled outside Paris and never witnessed the conditions [that] slaves were forced to endure in French and other European colonies" (Cresseveur 2015, 10; Cameron 1997, 245). There are scholars who suspect that the male members of Benoist's family, namely her husband and brother-in-law, held abolitionist sentiments that Benoist shared. Unfortunately, there is no credible evidence to support this claim. The historian Helen Weston has categorically ruled out abolitionist intentions on the part of the artist, noting that it was Benoist's connections with Napoleon's brother, Lucien, that guaranteed Benoist's husband a coveted government position and that socially, the families of both the artist and her spouse were deeply imbricated in Napoleonic circles of influence and power. Thus, Weston concludes, and I fully concur, that

> [i]t is out of the question that she [Benoist] would have exhibited or been allowed to exhibit a painting of a black woman which celebrated liberty and equality when the men in power in the circles in which she and her husband moved were actively ordering the suppression of slave rebellion, and setting in motion the mechanisms to reintroduce slavery.
>
> *(Weston 2000, 57)*

I do not, however, doubt the conscientiously political implications of Benoist's painting. I believe that the artist was cautious yet savvy enough to use the portrait as subtle protest and that its original title, *Portrait d'une négresse*, was intended to guarantee that the Black woman would remain an anonymous, innocuous type and not a named, identifiable threat. As the portrait suggests, the Black woman is locked into a state of "objecthood" as enslaved/servant, forever subordinated within bourgeois domestic space. The portrait, however, whether considered in its own historical context or in ours today, remains an ambiguous and complicated image in its capacity to elicit intersectional readings and meanings, be they actual or implied. It is the painting's productive ambiguity that constitutes the attraction and power of the portrait, regardless of whether the subject is designated a "negress" or Madeleine.

The painting can be viewed as "an antithesis of the artist" in which the representation is simultaneously empathetic and elitist (Cresseveur 2015, 11–12). As such, *Portrait* complicates, that is, it makes more ambiguous, the aspects of gender and race embodied in the image. I contend that for Benoist, the Black woman served as a reflection of the artist's own disempowered status as a woman and an artist in a patriarchal culture. Such a condition did not allow the painter "to change her sitter's situation" but afforded an opportunity "to create her sitter's likeness in her own image as an unconscious attempt to empathize" (Cresseveur 2015, 12). There is irony here when taking into account that Benoist may have intended her portrait to serve as an allegory of freedom, a possibility suggested both by the obvious reference to abolition connoted by the Black woman's racial identity and by the blue, white, and red pattern of colors used throughout the painting. The image remains intriguing because on the one hand, it speaks to emancipation and gives a nod to recognizing this Black woman's individuality, while on the other, it exploits the sitter's condition of servitude. So, "what emerges is not a relation of opposition between freedom and enslavement, or between subjecthood and objecthood, but rather one of complementarity and interdependence" (Bishop 2019, 8). The portrait offers a vision in which enslavement and emancipation coexist, merge, and become inextricably linked, producing ambiguous and unfixed meaning around matters of race, gender, class, and nationhood (Bishop 2019, 8–9).

Disrupting portraiture

Benoist's image adheres to the stylistic and compositional conventions of neoclassical portraiture in 1800. However, it is Black woman as subject matter that undermines those codes. The contrast of colors, fabric, and skin is consistent with protocols of European portraiture of the period, in which the convincing rendering of flesh tones was crucial. In painting the portrait, one of Benoist's goals was to demonstrate her technical prowess as a painter with an accurate rendering of likeness and skin tone. She did not set out "to revolutionize portraiture"; rather, it was ambiguity that was the best choice for a woman portraitist of an exotic sitter to take when navigating the cultural and political norms of the early nineteenth century (Cresseveur 2015, 31).

It was during this period that portraiture, along with still life and decorative painting, was deemed a pastime best suited for women, as opposed to history painting, which was considered a male pursuit. Jean-Baptiste Boutard (1771–1838), a conservative critic for the *Journal des débats* and hostile toward Benoist's portrait, held a widespread chauvinistic opinion that art was the purview of males and that women should pursue painting as a hobby, not a profession. As well, he dismissed finding attraction in a Black subject, believing black skin color to be anathema to Western aesthetics of beauty (Weston 2000, 57).

At the Salon, some reviewers read the portrait as a statement on the issue of slavery and liberation, while others, such as Boutard and Charles Thénevin (1764–1838), held some deep-seated racist attitudes and were not impressed. Boutard condemned the painting and its creator in this way: "Whom can one trust in life after such horror! It is a white and pretty hand which has created this black horror (noirceur)" (Boutard 1801; Ballot 1914, 150; Honour 1989, 12). Thévenin referred to the subject of the painting as "a sublime blurred tache (stain)" (Thévenin 1801). Boutard and Thévenin attacked Benoist and her painting based on their opinion that the artist had violated contemporary conventional notions of aesthetic propriety. Both critics held prevalent racist views that Blacks were set apart biologically, racially, culturally, and intellectually from Frenchness and whiteness; unworthy as the primary subject of art. The negative shock of blackness – the *stain* as visible sign and marker of racial difference, ugliness, and horror – was set in opposition to the virtuous attributes ascribed to white female purity and beauty. Benoist's portrait raised the question of not only what subjects were worthy of representation but more specifically, what subjects were appropriate for white women artists of high social standing to engage.

It has been suggested that humanist versus dehumanizing approaches to Benoist's painting have not only led to "contrasting conclusions" but have too heavily relied on the "structured binaries of subjecthood versus objecthood, agency versus passivity, individual versus racial type" (Bishop 2019, 2). My own 2004 critique of the Black woman's lack of agency has been recently taken to task for my resting on the assumption that somehow, "portraiture should convey a form of autonomous, individual subjectivity" (Bishop 2019, 2). Cécile Bishop has pointed out that we should not blame Benoist "for offering only a partial, reductive representation of her sitter," because to do so "implicitly measure(s) the portrait against an ideal of subjectivity, which is in fact a fantasy elicited by the portrait" (Bishop 2019, 2). Instead, it is more productive to view the painting as posing "a deeper structural challenge," that is, one that counters the very notion and structure of portraiture defined as the privileged form "through which European culture has visualized individual subjectivity," and that "blackness is the sign through which Europe has identified those it confined to servility and objecthood" (Bishop 2019, 2). In this respect, blackness in European portraiture is technically an aberration, which renders Benoist's portrait an unusual one for the period as well as an anomaly in the context of her body of works.[7]

Conclusion: what's in a name?

What's in a name? Everything and nothing at all. Taking into account the original title ascribed to *Portrait* when it was first exhibited, I am interested in how racializing designations such as "négresse" or "femme noire" operate as forms of exercising/exorcizing political and ideological forms of empowerment and subjugation for both the subject depicted and the artist. Benoist's *Portrait* is one of a few images that reflect the polarizing dynamic between slavery and antislavery, between investment in racial discourse and strategies of distancing from it.

Although the frequency of employing the term "negress" has diminished in the twentieth and twenty-first centuries, its potency increases as a term and concept of agency and empowerment by those who were once the "victims" of such racializing schemes. Today, "negress" has become somewhat popular as a term of appropriation by some contemporary artists, who have employed it as a form of empowerment in the act of (re)naming.[8] The "negress" as both a term and an idea has, in the contemporary moment, come to signify a fierce Black agency – a recouped designation and notion that catalyzes a probing of the racialized self in relation to history, memory, and the search for identities beyond those dictated solely by skin color and racial typologies.

In providing the name of the Black sitter and the historical context of the representation of Black women in nineteenth- and twentieth-century works of art when these are known, it becomes clear that "what is at stake is an art-historical discourse, posed as an intervention to the prevailing historical silence" about the "significance of the black female muse to the formation of modernism" (Higonnet in Murrell 2019, xviii). Moreover, the naming and interrogation of the legacy of Black women represented in works such as *Portrait d'une négresse* allows art history to reimagine the roles played by the Black female figure in the history of art. Benoist's *Portrait* may deservedly constitute an important precursor to how elements of race, gender, and class come "to structure our modern lives" (Higonnet in Murrell 2019, xviii).

More than two centuries after Benoist brought her "negress" into the visible world, the experiential and representational complex intersections of race, gender, class, and culture that the painting reflects live on today in the realm of popular culture. In 2018, the entertainer Beyoncé Knowles and her husband, Jay-Z, exploited the ambiguities of race, gender, and culture in a music track and accompanying six-minute video titled *Apeshit* from their first joint album as a married couple, called *Everything Is Love*. The video, characterized as provocative and radical at the level of gender, was filmed in the hallowed cultural space of the Louvre Museum and begins with fragments and close-ups of European paintings, including Benoist's *Portrait d'une négresse* (King 2018, 14).

Although Benoist's "negress" is a portrait of an enslaved woman-cum-servant, she has nonetheless attained a degree of nobility by virtue of her unique presence in the Louvre specifically and in Western art in general. She holds her own as an independent Black presence among all the other paintings in that hallowed institution. As one commentator has noted, it is for this reason that the Black woman is "[t]he only figure … that can withstand the unstoppable force that is Beyoncé" (Grady 2018). Given the painting's clear racial presence, the portrait has been reinterpreted, given a new context, and as such, remains relevant to the present. The painted "negress" of subjugation has been upstaged by a contemporary one of assertive presence and star power. In her co-opting of Benoist's painting, Beyoncé has made some highly selective choices of representation in order to deliver a powerful message about the potential of Black women's agency in the contemporary world.

As I have tried to make clear throughout this chapter and in previous writings, Benoist's portrait is a highly complex and ambiguous painting with many things happening in it across the domains of politics, race, gender, and class, and in the formation/deformation of Black subjectivity (Smalls 2004; Smalls 2018). As such, it continues to influence, provoke, and beckon reinterpretation. In the *Apeshit* video, Benoist's Black woman is not directly visually paired with Beyoncé, but the relationship between that Black woman of the past and this one of the present is implied. Beyoncé's act of appropriation is put to productive use as a visual and performative means of speaking to the then and now of Black women's subjugation and empowerment.

Notes

1 *Portrait d'une négresse* was exhibited in the Salon of 1800 under the title *Portrait d'une négresse*. In the twentieth century, the work was retitled by the Louvre as *Portrait d'une femme noire* (*Portrait of a Black Woman*). More recently, as a result of art-historical research, the portrait has once again been renamed *Portrait de Madeleine* (*Portrait of Madeleine*), in reference to the uncovered name of the sitter. This discovery has called to task art history's role in perpetuating a dehumanizing project by using racialized terms such as "négresse" or "noire," considering the figure only as a racial type and not as an individual. Although I acknowledge this state of affairs and have more to say about it later, I have chosen throughout this chapter to keep the original title, *Portrait d'une négresse*, under which the work was first displayed and critically received.

2 Over the course of the eighteenth and nineteenth centuries, the definitions of these terms tended to shift according to historical and political circumstances. The words "nègre" and "négresse" were employed with frequency as scientific terms of classification with the development of the African slave trade and the proposition of various racial theories. On the history and French etymology of these racial designations, see Serge Daget, "Les mots *esclave, nègre, noir* et les jugements de valeur sur la traite négrière dans la littérature abolitionist française de 1770 à 1845," *Revue française d'histoire d'outre-mer* 60 (1973): 511–48; Simone Delesalle and Lucette Valensi, "Le mot 'nègre' dans les dictionnaires français d'ancien régime: Histoire et lexicographie," *Langue française* 15 (September 1972): 79–104.

3 The relationship between the literary content and the ideological ambitions of these three women writers has been assessed recently by Stacie Allan. See Allan 2019, 1–15.

4 For a thorough discussion of the unique racial politics and aesthetics of this painting, see Grigsby 2002, 9–63.
5 Slavery on French soil proper had been banned in 1315, per an ordinance issued by Louis X. Colonial slaves who entered the metropole underwent automatic change in status to "servant" and were eligible to petition for emancipation while within the country's borders. For a critical examination of this law, see Samuel L. Chatman, "'There Are No Slaves in France': A Re-Examination of Slave Laws in Eighteenth-Century France," *The Journal of Negro History*, vol. 85, no. 3 (Summer 2000): 144–5.
6 This hypothesis was first offered by Ballot in 1914 and has been accepted by most critics. See Ballot 1914, 151.
7 In her early discussion of the painting, Marie-Juliette Ballot, who does not take into account the ideological complexity of race in conjunction with visual representation, describes Benoist's portrait as unique only in terms of its neoclassical style and Davidian influence. See Ballot 1914, 149.
8 Today, contemporary artists such as Kara Walker and Alison Saar have selectively chosen to use the term "negress" in the titles of some of their works. Likewise, in 2013, a collective of Black women filmmakers banded together in New York City to form the New Negress Film Society. Their choice of name was intended as a riff on the empowering alignment of the New Negro and the negress.

References

Allan, Stacie. "Female Bodies of (Inter)National Significance: Marie-Guillemine Benoist, Germaine de Staël, and Claire de Duras," *Journal of the Society of Dix-Neuviémistes*, vol. 23, no. 1 (2019): 1–15.

Amin, Takiyah Nur. "Girl Power, Real Politics: Dis/Respectability, Post-Raciality, and the Politics of Inclusion," in Melissa Blanco Borelli, ed., *The Oxford Handbook of Dance and Popular Screen* (New York: Oxford University Press, 2014), 255–267.

Ballot, Marie-Juliette. *Une Élève de David. La comtesse Benoist, l'Emilie de Demoustier 1768–1826* (Paris: Plon, 1914).

Bishop, Cécile. "Portraiture, Race, and Subjectivity: the Opacity of Marie-Guillemine Benoist's Portrait d'une Négresse," *Word & Image*, vol. 35, no. 1 (2019): 1–11.

Boutard, Jean-Baptiste. *Arlequin au Muséum, ou Critique des tableaux, en vaudevilles* (Paris, 1801).

Cameron, Vivian. "Benoist, Mme, French Painter, 1768–1826," in Delia Gaze, ed., *Dictionary of Women Artists*, vol. 1 (Fitzroy: London, 1997), 244–247.

Cresseveur, Jessica. "'It Was a White and Pretty Hand/Who Made This Blackness for us': The Politics of Gender and Culture in Early Nineteenth Century French Portraiture," *Rebus*, vol. 7 (Summer 2015): 1–35.

Goldberg, David Theo. *Racist Culture: Philosophy and the Politics of Meaning* (Oxford: Blackwell, 1993).

Grady, Constance. "The Meaning Behind the Classical Paintings in Beyoncé and Jay-Z's 'Apeshit'," *Vox*, June 19, 2018, https://www.vox.com/culture/2018/6/19/17476212/apeshit-video-beyonce-jay-z-carters-portrait-negresse-benoist.

Grigsby, Darcy Grimaldo. *Extremities: Painting Empire in Post-Revolutionary France* (London: Yale University Press, 2002).

Higonnet, Ann. "Introduction: The Gift of *Olympia*," in Denise Murrell ed., *Posing Modernity: The Black Model from Manet and Matisse to Today* (New Haven: Yale University Press 2019), xiv–xvii.

Honour, Hugh. *The Image of the Black in Western Art*, vol. 4 (Cambridge, MA: Harvard University Press, 1989).

King, Jason. "Stuck in a Time Loop: Notes on APES★★T," in *Journal of Popular Music Studies*, vol. 30, no. 4 (2018): 14–18.

Pollock, Griselda. *Differencing the Canon: Feminist Desire and the Writing of Art's Histories* (Routledge: London, 1999).

Smalls, James. "Slavery Is a Woman: 'Race', Gender, and Visuality in Marie Benoist's *Portrait of a Negress* (1800)," *Nineteenth-Century Art Worldwide: A Journal of Nineteenth-Century Visual Culture*, vol. 3, no. 1 (Spring 2004): http://www.19thcartworldwide.org/component/content/article/70-spring04/spring04article/286-slavery-is-a-woman-race-gender-and-visuality-in-marie-benoists-portrait-dune-negresse-1800.

Smalls, James. "Crazy in the Louvre: How Beyoncé and Jay-Z Exploit Western Art History to Ask Who Controls Black Bodies," *Frieze Magazine*, June 29, 2018. https://frieze.com/article/crazy-louvre-how-beyonce-and-jay-z-exploit-western-art-history-ask-who-controls-black-bodies.

Thévenin, Charles. *Le Nouveau Arlequin et son ami Gilles au museum*, vol. 22, no. 624 (1801).

Waller, Susan. "Marie-Guillemine Benoist, Portrait of Madeleine," in *Smarthistory*, September 26, 2018, accessed July 7, 2019, https://smarthistory.org/benoist-portrait/.

Weston, Helen D. "'The Cook, the Thief, His Wife, and Her Lover': LaVille-Leroulx's Portrait d'une négresse and the Signs of Misrecognition," in Valerie Mainz and Griselda Pollock, eds., *Work and the Image I: Work, Craft and Labour, Visual Representations in Changing Histories* (Ashgate: Aldershot, 2000), 53–74.

Weston, Helen D. "Representing the Right to Represent: The Portrait of Citizen Belley, Ex-Representative of the Colonies by A.-L. Girodet," *RES: Anthropology and Aesthetics*, no. 26 (Autumn 1994): 83–99.

Part III
Gendered lives, racial frameworks

15

A history of Black women in nineteenth-century France

Robin Mitchell

Nineteenth-century French cultural representations of Black women reflected historical events going back to the establishment of France's Caribbean colonies in the seventeenth and eighteenth centuries. Conditions of slavery generated pervasive tropes about Black women that migrated to metropolitan France, where they provided an attractive canvas for the subjects and citizens of a traumatized country digesting their political, military, and social losses in places such as Haiti.[1] Yet the historical presence of and discursive focus on Black women in the metropole remains under-examined.

I suggest a few reasons why this might be the case. One of the reasons could be the lack of substantial numbers of Black women in France during the nineteenth century.[2] A second reason, I argue, is because of the difficulties in separating out the tropes and stereotypes about Black women from the historical silences in the archives about these women and their actual lives. Finally, it helps to unpack the psychic and actual trauma of the loss of the Haitian Revolution and its aftermath on French citizens, as well as a tendency to "read" Revolution as a predominantly male sphere.

Representations of Black women in nineteenth-century France – how they were seen, perceived, produced, and imagined – suggest that French elites were deeply unsettled by the consequences of the Haitian Revolution. Focusing on both the representations and the realities of Black women such as Sarah Baartman, Ourika, and Jeanne Duval not only provides a history of these women but also illuminates the cultural histories of the white Frenchmen and Frenchwomen looking at them. They worked as artist models, domestic servants, sex workers, actors; they were enslaved and free, spectacles, performers, lovers, wives, and sometimes even French. Black women mattered in France for myriad reasons.

This can be seen by the zeal of legislators, administrators, writers like Charles Baudelaire and Victor Hugo, artists such as Louis-Léopold Boilly and Marie-Guillemine Benoist, and laypeople trying to convince themselves that these women lacked importance – often denying them their own names. According to its own self-definition of Frenchness, Black women were not supposed to be in France. Yet they were. And that anxiety needed to be managed. The trauma of losing the crown jewel of colonies, Saint-Domingue, was displaced onto a body and in a manner that appeared to simplify a far more complex range of experiences and identities. It is this event where representation converges with these women's actual lives and where any understanding of Black women in nineteenth-century France needs to begin.

The impact of the Haitian Revolution

A sustained analysis of the Haitian Revolution reveals that this event was cataclysmic, sending shock waves throughout the entire Atlantic world.[3] Even before France's own 1789 revolution, the nation had been struggling with a series of imperial losses that began in Canada and India in the 1760s. And as France was grappling with the thorny issues of citizenship and national identity brought on by the revolution, it had to contend not only with the loss of its most important colony, Saint-Domingue, but also with the 1803 sale of Louisiana to the United States (which some historians would argue was the result of financing the continued but eventual loss of the war with Haiti).

Even standard terms used to describe French constitutional history since 1799, such as the *Empire* and the *Second Empire*, elide the true imperial history and legacy of defeat. The loss of Haiti and the collapse of Napoleon's empire threatened France's self-perception as an imperial power (with its connotations of racial superiority) and its image of its masculine prowess. The vast majority of the migrants from Saint-Domingue were white settlers, with only about 800 Blacks fleeing the colony.[4] Yet when Saint-Domingue violently and permanently unyoked itself from France, the cultural reverberations both fueled and haunted the ongoing discursive construction of race and gender. In particular, the representations of Black women (who comprised a small minority among the influx) illuminate these tensions.

Tropes emerged in response not only to the presence of particular Black women but also to the convulsive changes in French culture and society, only to take on a life of their own, circulate widely, and be re-deployed again and again, slightly altered or fully resurrected in new historical contexts. Part of the complication for white Frenchmen and women was that real Black women were also on French soil, however, and not completely containable in those tropes and representations. Black women, seen as Other by the new republican definition of *citoyenneté*,[5] are a particularly rich focal point to study in exploring how France grappled with both race and gender. Looking at them as both representation and actual people opens up new spaces to understand their overall importance to French ideas about race, class, gender, sexuality, and nationality. Black women exist in nineteenth-century France, in ways not always expected or comfortable. But they exist. And they can teach us how France (mis)managed the myriad tensions that their presence engendered.

Portraits of Black womanhood

Although some scholars have studied Black female representations in France, particularly in literature and art, less attention has been paid to analyzing these representations within a larger historical framework. Historical studies of the presence of Blacks in the colonies and in France have lacked a sustained focus on Black women. Some scholars of literature, critical theory, gender, and art history have studied images of Blacks in France and the meaning of such depictions.[6] But tensions exist between these types of scholarship: history seeks to recover an accurate and changing past, while theories of representation look for the ways that enduring power relations, especially those built on binaries, operate as abstractions. Scholarship that seeks to incorporate both types of analytical models can be challenging: one tries to access a stable "truth" through documents, while the other insists that all documents, texts, images, or representations are distorted by powerful discourses of the dominant culture.

Historian Marisa Fuentes investigates the "'mutilated historicity' of enslaved women (the violent condition in which enslaved women appear in the archive disfigured and violated),"[7] which often causes the women themselves and their histories to disappear. Historically, many of the women in nineteenth-century France enter the historical archives in degraded ways. The tropes of Black women from France's Black colonies – as hypersexual, hyperviolent, and/or defeminized – makes uncovering their lives difficult. The loss of the Haitian Revolution (rhetorically at the hands of Black men) was also placed at the feet of so-called vicious Black women, like Marie-Jeanne Lamartiniére and Suzanne Béliar, who were implied not to have been women at all.[8]

This national embarrassment for France was also a blow to national identity – gendered as well as racial – and shifted some of the tensions of that loss onto Black women's bodies. So, we must bear this in mind when understanding that while Black women of course existed outside those representations, some of the rhetoric followed them into France proper. Many of them enter the historical archives in a multitude of guises: as domestiques, as sex workers, as fads, as spectacles, as artist models, actors, lovers, as prisoners, as nuns, and sometimes as wives. The nature of their lives was often precarious, based upon their race and gender. And we know that they had a cultural power that far outweighed their actual numbers in France, which were quite small until the mid- to late nineteenth century.

But we do know some of their names and their occupations, and this helps to show both that they were present in France, and why French men and women were often pre-occupied with them. Sarah Baartmann (c. 1770–1815/6), called the "Hottentot Venus," was born in South Africa, 50 miles north of the Gamtoos River. It is possible that she was married and had children before her arrival in London in 1810, but documentation regarding the earlier years of her life is scarce. According to musicologist Percival Kirby, Baartmann was smuggled out of British-occupied Cape Town by Hendrik Cezar (the brother of her old master, Peter) without the colonial governor's knowledge. The only female on board the HMS *Diadem*, Baartmann sailed with them on April 7, 1810, and they arrived in Chatham, just 30 miles from London, in July.

Alexander Dunlop – a surgeon with a penchant for exporting "museum specimens" from South Africa – had first seen Baartmann in Capetown around 1809 and at some point entered a partnership of sorts with Cezar. According to an alleged contract between the two men and Baartmann, she would be exhibited in England and Ireland as well as performing domestic duties, and a portion of her earnings would fund her repatriation to South Africa after two years. Because she was considered an oddity, her handlers hoped that European fascination with certain types of human curiosities would garner income and fame.[9] Baartmann was then brought to France in 1814. Her true status (as an enslaved performer or as a willing participant earning a salary) remains controversial.

Given her enslaved status in South Africa, there is little doubt that her life was governed by the whims of both her enslaver and then her handler in France. Though only in Paris for a short time, she cast a wide cultural shadow, inspiring fashion, theatrical works, and scientific scrutiny. Even in her death, Baartmann still remained the object of scientific investigation. Baartmann's physical body – specifically her genitalia – was an obsession in France, and this is perhaps most evident in George Cuvier's dissection of her cadaver. Given Cuvier's role in Napoleon's expedition to Egypt, it is not surprising that he too needed to reassert his white masculine dominance through the sexual and colonial conquest of the Black female body.

As well as Baartmann, a young Senegalese girl named Ourika (c. 1780–99), gifted to a French noble family in the late eighteenth century, inspired a fad in the 1820s that I call "Ourika Mania," which entailed a novel, plays, poetry, food, fashion, and colors named after her. Similarly to the colonial conquest of Baartmann's blackness, the Duchess de Duras appropriated the voice of an imagined Ourika in her overwhelmingly popular novel of the same name. In the novel, "Ourika" herself states that the revolution of Saint-Domingue further authenticates the savagery and barbarity of blackness.

Literary scholar Roger Little believes that Ourika was from Fouta-Djallon, in what is now southeastern Senegal, and that she was likely of Peul origin. In early 1786, the governor of Senegal, Stanislas Jean, the Chevalier du Boufflers, purchased a two- or three-year-old Senegalese girl for the Duchesse d'Orleans. This little girl, Zoé, is often confused with Ourika but was raised as a servant in the home of another aristocratic family. Boufflers described the girl as follows: "She is pretty, not like the day, but like the night … Her eyes are like little stars … She does not speak yet, but she understands what we say to her in Wolof."[10] Victor Hugo saw fit to write about the ramifications of the Duchess de Duras writing about the Black girl in an early edition of his novel, *Les Miserables*.

Another Black woman fueling the French imagination was Jeanne Duval (c. 1820–70s), who was the product of a mixed-race mother and a white French father. She lived on and off with the French writer and icon Charles Baudelaire for over three decades as his common-law wife. As is the case for Ourika and Baartman, many of the details about Jeanne Duval's life are the product of hearsay, at times both vague and contradictory. Her claim to fame (or infamy) came from Baudelaire's literary writings describing her as his "Vénus noire" and his copious letters about her. Baudelaire's 1857 publication of *Les Fleurs du mal*, a poetic cycle in which numbers 22–39 are influenced by or about Duval, forever bound her to him. The book was quickly denounced on grounds of obscenity.

Duval has been associated with several surnames, including *Prosper* as well as *Lemer* and *Lemaire*. In addition, she often performed under the stage name *Berthe*. Her grandmother, Marie Duval, may have been from Saint-Domingue and of African descent. Jeanne's mother, whose name may have been Jeanne-Marie-Marthe Duval, Jeanne Lemaire, or Jeanne Lemer, was "an old, respectable-looking negress, with thick, greasy hair which tried in vain to twirl over her cheeks and ears," and although it is unclear whether she immigrated or was born in Nantes, she is generally considered to have had ties there. She may have been a prostitute, and both Jeanne Duval's father and grandfather were almost certainly white Frenchmen, though it is not known whether they were planters, slave owners, or members of the working class, and as far as the documents indicate, she had no contact with either man.[11]

Other Black women emerge in the imagination of French nineteenth-century culture. In art, a Black woman named Madeleine is the model in *Portrait of a Negresse* by Marie-Guillemine Benoist. A Black woman named Laure appears in several paintings by Manet, such as *Olympia*, *Children in the Tuileries Gardens*, and *La négresse (Portrait of Laure)*. A Black woman named Esther is present in Louis-Léopold Boilly's painting *The Galleries of the Palais-Royal*. Miss LaLa appears in the painting of Edgar Degas called *Miss La La at the Cirque Fernando*; Jean Frédéric Bazille's *Young Woman with Peonies* features a Black woman in a tignon; and Henri Matisse used Black women as models. This list is by no means exhaustive. Photographer Nadar also centered Black women in his work, as did sculptors Charles Henri Joseph Cordier and Jean-Baptiste Carpeaux.

Blackness was racialized and gendered in nineteenth-century France. Gustave d'Eichthal, the secretary of the Société Ethnologique, wrote in his 1839 *Lettres sur la Race Noire et la Race Blanche* that Blacks were a "female race." "Just like the woman," he pontificated, "the black is deprived of political and scientific intelligence … Like the woman he also passionately likes jewelry, dance, and singing."[12] Eichthal's assignment of a discursive gender to an entire race at the beginning of the colonial project in Africa helps illustrate how the failure in Haiti, taken as a defeat at the hands of Black men, facilitated a reordering of French national identity via the Black female body, which was represented as savage, hypersexual, and above all, an existential threat to the purity of the French nation. To recover from this defeat by a Black nation, the French shifted their focus to a Black continent – Africa – where they could reassert their racial superiority and continue their "mission to civilize."

The prevailing narrative of these gendered representations, which transcends the vastly different political and cultural structures of multiple French regimes, established and reinforced the inability of Black women to be French, regardless of their individual stories or backgrounds. That France continued to exert ownership of Black bodies in the form of slavery until 1848 does not mean that they extended citizenship when slavery officially ended. Yet the representations of these women also reveal fissures in the definition of what it meant to be French, challenging existing gender and racial boundaries within white society.

Constituting race, gender, and nation

It was into this political, cultural, and racialized environment that a mix of émigrés, exiles, and colonial refugees returned to France in 1802. William Cohen states that

> in the nineteenth century, race became the main explanation of human variety. The tradition of attributing social differences between the nobility and the third estate to descent from distinctive "racial" groups was already evident in France; it continued in the nineteenth century.[13]

The influx of refugees from Haiti who had fled the "troubles" and who, by their very presence and need for assimilation, already testified to the colonial failure brought with them their own notions of proper French behaviors and culture. White French women dressed in blackface to play Black women on the stage. Caricatures, plays, poems, and novels were utilized to highlight and instruct white French men and women on how dangerous these behaviors were.

And white Frenchmen employed types of racial ventriloquism to hide behind Black women in order to speak about compelling issues of the day, to highlight unacceptable white French behaviors, or to silence moving too far beyond acceptable gender boundaries. Elite white French women were playing with racial drag – mimicking blackness in their clothes and in some of their attitudes – which was reflected in cultural movements such as the previously mentioned "Hottentot Venus" and "Ourika Mania." At the same time, white French men were still "playing" with Black female bodies, setting them at odds with many in the metropole.[14] Moreover, accusations of so-called colonial blood were discussed in elite circles, and tainted ancestry – and thus illegitimate Frenchness – became a powerful insult, which was the case against Napoleon's wife, the Creole Empress Josephine, who was born in Martinique in 1763, and aristocrat Claire de Duras, who was born to a plantation owning family in 1777. This was a shorthand way of genetically linking whites from the colonies with Blacks. For instance, Creoles like Empress Josephine and aristocrat Claire de Duras, with origins in France's Black colonies, tried to ignore or brush aside innuendoes that they had "impure blood."

If the various French classes could not agree on who and what they were, they could come together around what they were not. In the case of émigrés and some foreigners, it was race that allowed the possibility of incorporation into the idea of citizen and thus Frenchness, something that eluded Blacks, regardless of their gender. The identification of an Other facilitated the notion that previously excluded bodies could now be (re)incorporated. The presence of individuals designated as different allowed codification of a cohesive French identity. By holding themselves up against a specifically defined and racialized Other, elites could still claim cultural, racial, and political dominance, while the lower classes could throw off the shackles of a formerly perceived racial difference to be incorporated into the definition of French. Coming together to rally for a common good – Frenchness – would afford greater opportunity to consolidate collective ideologies and national unities.

Conclusion

The rapid changes in France in the nineteenth century, with the tensions between modernity and tradition, enrich the potential for exploring the idea of blackness during this time. The shoring up of Frenchness predicated upon whiteness and maleness, concomitantly incorporating blackness and femaleness into the antithesis to that definition, is what places Black women squarely in the center of my exploration. While legislation was important in early nineteenth-century France, the importance of science as a field of expert male knowledge gave ground to scientific racism. The Black female body became an important canvas on which to apply that new-found expertise, as seen with Cuvier's fixation on Baartmann, while at the same time firming up normative behaviors. Volatile political and social tensions figured prominently in the construction of self and the presentation of a French national identity. How these constructions were articulated shows much about what was at stake in a unified collective identity. What differentiated France from other nations in Europe in the early nineteenth century were new types of conversations about race powered by the Haitian Revolution and bolstered by science. One of the ways France did this was by demanding in 1825 – with ships – that Haiti compensate France for its lost property (including lost "slaves") in order to recognize Haiti as a sovereign nation; in 1838, it would reduce those payments.[15]

On the Left Bank in Paris, a candle shop – founded in 1643 – continues to reproduce works of French icons in wax. *Cire Trudon*, the world's oldest candle maker still in operation, has made candles for French monarchs, fashion houses, and discerning Parisians for nearly four centuries that span extraordinary shifts in government and culture. Among its collections, *Cire Trudon* includes one called *Les bustes de cire*, which is a series of oversized busts that "tries to revive the faces of those who marked its history and the history of France."[16] There are currently three candles in this *collection*: Marie-Antoinette (1789), Napoleon (1803), and the third, titled "*L'Esclave*" (1867).[17] It is identical to the terra cotta bust, *La Négresse*, created in 1872 by Jean-Baptiste Carpeaux. Not only does the candle depict the importance of slavery, then, but also its eventual end. Although my work has argued that slavery very much "marked the history of France" (and continues to do so), the inclusion of *L'Esclave* is a stunning recognition. The Haitian Revolution shifted the focus of France to redirect its imperial impulse in Africa while also heralding "revolutionary" ideals of championing the abolition of slavery, yet still pushing for the colonizing of African subjects, whom the French viewed as inferior.

Regardless of who they were or where they came from, the overarching narratives for Black women served to reinforce the inauthenticity of their Frenchness. Within the realm of vastly different political and cultural structures, their inappropriateness was foregrounded. Yet in almost every case, these *femmes noires* – not only apparitions from Saint-Domingue, but all those carrying the racial legacy of slavery – reveal through their narratives a chipping away, however slight, of racial and gender boundaries designed to constrain them.

Notes

1 It is important to clarify that Haiti and Saint-Domingue are considered one and the same by France and were often used interchangeably before the Revolution. France took great strides to continue to refer to Haiti as "San Domingue," however, even after it was declared a republic.

2 In the eighteenth century, metropolitan France had a tiny nonwhite population—about 3000 people out of a population of more than 25 million as of 1777; Pierre H. Boulle, *Race et esclavage dans la France de l'ancien régime* (Paris: Perrin, 2007), 109.

3 Jeremy D. Popkin, *Facing Racial Revolution: Eyewitness Accounts of the Haitian Insurrection* (Chicago: University of Chicago Press, 2007).

4 Darrell Meadows, "The Planters of Saint-Domingue, 1750–1804: Migration and Exile in the French Revolutionary Atlantic," PhD diss., Carnegie Mellon University, 2004.

5 Female citizenship.

6 For representations of Black women in literature, see, for example, Léon-François Hoffmann, *Le Nègre romantique: Personnage: littéraire et obsession collective* (Paris: Payot, 1973); Léon Fanoudh-Seifer, *Le Mythe du nègre et de l'Afrique noire dans la littérature française de 1800 à la deuxième guerre mondiale* (Paris: Klincksieck, 1968). For art, see Gen Doy, "More Than Meets the Eye: Representations of Black Women in Mid-19th-Century French Photography." *Women's Studies International Forum* 21, no. 3 (May 1998): 305–19; Darcy Grimaldo Grigsby, *Extremities: Painting Empire in Post-Revolutionary France* (New Haven: Yale University Press, 2002), and "Revolutionary Sons, White Fathers, and Creole Difference: Guillaume Guillon-Lethière's 'Oath of the Ancestors' (1822)." *Yale French Studies* 101 (2001): 201–26.

7 Marisa J. Fuentes, *Dispossessed Lives: Enslaved Women, Violence, and the Archive* (Philadelphia: University of Pennsylvania Press, 2016), 7.

8 Lamartiniére and Béliar were both female soldiers during the Haitian Revolution and were masculinized in their representation because they fought in battle, something considered to be a male space. Women like this helped perpetuate the idea of masculine Black women in the French imagination.

9 Robin Mitchell, *Vénus Noire: Black Women, Colonial Fantasies, and the Production of Race & Gender in France, 1804–1848* (Athens: The University of Georgia Press, January 2020), 30.

10 Mitchell, *Vénus Noire*, 22.

11 Ibid., 42.

12 Gustave d'Eichthal, and Ismayl Urbain. *Lettres sur la race noire et la race blanche* (Paris: Paulin, 1839).

13 William B. Cohen, *The French Encounter with Africans: White Response to Blacks, 1530–1880* (Bloomington: Indiana University Press, 2003), 215.

14 See Sharpley-Whiting, *Black Venus: Sexualized Savages, Primal Fears, and Primitive Narratives in French* (Durham: Duke University Press, 1999), and Janell Hobson, *Venus in the Dark: Blackness and Beauty in Popular Culture* (New York: Routledge, 2005), for a discussion on the ways in which the plays and poems engage these representations. In the case of Sarah Baartman, a plaster cast was made of her body after she died, and her genitalia were studied to contrast her Black women's body with those of white French women.

15 The debt was finally paid off in 1947; in 2005, Haiti demanded repayment of the original payments. France declined to do so.

16 www.ciretrudon.com/en/index.html (accessed October 22, 2010).

17 While it appears that the copy precedes the original, as with many pieces of sculpture, the "final" piece went through many iterations over several years. It was originally created by Carpeaux in 1867 for a fountain; many variations were done in marble, bronze, and plaster. www.artquid.com/artwork/5836/2826/captive-negress-carpeaux.html (accessed October 27, 2010).

Further reading

Albigès, Luce-Marie. "Portrait d'une négresse." *Histoire par l'image* (February 2007), http://www.histoire-image.org/etudes/portrait-negresse.

Birkett, Mary Ellen, and Christopher Rivers, eds. *Approaches to Teaching Duras's Ourika*. New York: Modern Language Association, 2009.

Blachère, Jean-Claude. *Le Modèle Nègre: Aspects littéraires du mythe primitiviste au XXe siècle chez Apollinaire, Cendrars, Tzara*. Dakar: Nouvelles Editions Africaines, 1981.

Boulle, Pierre H. *Race et esclavage dans la France de l'ancien régime*. Paris: Perrin, 2007.

Boulle, Pierre H., and Sue Peabody. *Le Droit des noirs en France au temps de l'esclavage: Textes choisis et commentés*. Paris: L'Harmattan, 2015.

Chalaye, Sylvie. *Du Noir au nègre: L'Image du noir au théâtre, de Marguerite de Navarre à Jean Genet (1550–1960)*. Paris: L'Harmattan, 1998.

Chalaye, Sylvie. *Nègres en Images*. Paris: L'Harmattan, 2002. For representations of black women in literature, see Hoffmann, Nègre Romantique; Fanoudh-Seifer, Mythe du Nègre; Jean-Claude Blachère, Modèle Nègre; Sharpley-Whiting, Black Venus. For art, see Doy, "More Than Meets the Eye"; Chalaye, Nègres en Images. See also Grigsby, Extremities; Grigsby, "Revolutionary Sons."

Chalaye, Sylvie. *Les Ourikas du boulevard*. Paris: L'Harmattan, 2003.

Cohen, William B. *The French Encounter with Africans: White Response to Blacks, 1530–1880*. Bloomington: Indiana University Press, 2003.

Crais, Clifton C., and Pamela Scully. *Sara Baartman and the Hottentot Venus: A Ghost Story and a Biography*. Princeton: Princeton University Press, 2011.

Cuvier, Georges. "Extrait d'observations faites sur le cadavre d'une femme connue à Paris et à Londres sous le nom de Vénus hottentotte." *Mémoires du Muséum d'histoire naturelle* 3 (1817): 259–74.

Debrunner, Hans. *Presence and Prestige, Africans in Europe: A History of Africans in Europe before 1918*. Basel: Basler Afrika Bibliographien, 1979.

De Groot, Joanna. "'Sex' and 'Race': The Construction of Language and Image in the Nineteenth Century." In *Sexuality and Subordination: Interdisciplinary Studies of Gender in the Nineteenth Century*, ed. Susan Mendus and Jane Rendall. New York: Routledge, 1989.

De Raedt, Thérèse. "Ourika : l'inspiration de Mme de Duras." *Dalhousie French Studies* 73 (Winter 2005): 19–33.

Dolan, Therese. "Skirting the Issue: Manet's Portrait of Baudelaire's Mistress, Reclining." *Art Bulletin* 79, no. 4 (December 1997): 611–29.

Doy, Gen. "More Than Meets the Eye: Representations of Black Women in Mid-19th-Century French Photography." *Women's Studies International Forum* 21, no. 3 (May 1998): 305–19.

Duras Claire de Durfort, Duchesse de. *Ourika*. Trans. John Fowles, intro. Joan DeJean and Margaret Waller. New York: Modern Language Association of America, 1994.

Eichthal, Gustave d', and Ismayl Urbain. *Lettres sur la race noire et la race blanche*. Paris: Paulin, 1839.

Eliel, Carol S. "Louis-Léopold Boilly's 'The Galleries of the Palais-Royal.'" *Burlington Magazine* 126, no. 974 (May 1984): 269–70, 275–76, 279.

Everist, Mark. *Music Drama at the Paris Odéon, 1824–1828*. Berkeley: University of California Press, 2002.

Fanoudh-Seifer, Léon. *Le Mythe du nègre et de l'Afrique noire dans la littérature française de 1800 à la deuxième guerre mondiale*. Paris: Klincksieck, 1968.

Fauvelle-Aymar, Francois-Xavier. *L'Invention du hottentot: Histoire du regard occidental sur les Khoisan, XVe–XIXe siècle*. Paris: Publications de la Sorbonne, 2002.

Ferrier, Michaël. "Histoire de Jeanne Duval, la 'Belle d'Abandon.'" In *Sympathie pour le fantôme*. Paris: Gallimard, 2010.

Fuentes, Marisa J. *Dispossessed Lives: Enslaved Women, Violence, and the Archive*. Philadelphia: University of Pennsylvania Press, 2016.

Grigsby, Darcy Grimaldo. *Extremities: Painting Empire in Post-Revolutionary France*. New Haven: Yale University Press, 2002.

Heuer, Jennifer Ngaire. *The Family and the Nation: Gender and Citizenship in Revolutionary France, 1789–1830*. Ithaca: Cornell University Press, 2007.

Hobson, Janell. *Venus in the Dark: Blackness and Beauty in Popular Culture*. New York: Routledge, 2005.

Hoffmann, Léon-François. *Le Nègre romantique: Personnage littéraire et obsession collective*. Paris: Payot, 1973.

Kadish, Doris Y., and Françoise Massardier-Kenney, eds. *Translating Slavery*. 2nd ed. Kent, OH: Kent State University Press, 2010.

Kirby, Percival. "The Hottentot Venus." *Africana Notes and News* 6, no. 3 (1949): 55–62.

Kirby, Percival. "More about the Hottentot Venus." *Africana Notes and News* 10, no. 4 (1953): 124–34.

"La France Noire du XVIIIe siècle à aujourd'hui." *L'Histoire* No. 457. Mars 2019.

Lindfors, Bernth. "'The Hottentot Venus' and Other African Attractions in Nineteenth-Century England." *Australasian Drama Studies* 1, no. 2 (1983): 83–104.

Lindfors, Bernth. "Ethnological Show Business: Footlighting the Dark Continent." In *Freakery: Cultural Spectacles of the Extraordinary Body*, ed. Rose-Marie Garland Thomson. New York: New York University Press, 1996.

Little, Roger. "Peau noire, masque blanc." In *Claire de Durfort, duchesse de Duras, Ourika*, ed. Roger Little. Exeter: University of Exeter Press, 1998.

Lowe, Kate. "The Stereotyping of Black Africans in Renaissance Europe." In *Black Africans in Renaissance Europe*, ed. T. F. Earle and K. J. P. Lowe. Cambridge: Cambridge University Press, 2005.

McCloy, Shelby T. *The Negro in France*. Lexington: University of Kentucky Press, 1961.

Meadows, Darrell. *The Planters of Saint-Domingue, 1750–1804: Migration and Exile in the French Revolutionary Atlantic*. PhD diss., Carnegie Mellon University, 2004.

Miller, Christopher L. *The French Atlantic Triangle: Literature and Culture of the Slave Trade*. Durham, NC: Duke University Press, 2008.

Mitchell, Robin. *Vénus Noire: Black Women and Colonial Fantasies in Nineteenth-Century France*. Athens, GA: University of Georgia Press, 2020.

Munford, Rebecca. "Re-Presenting Charles Baudelaire/Re-Presenting Jeanne Duval: Transformations of the Muse in Angela Carter's 'Black Venus.'" *Forum for Modern Language Studies* 40, no. 1 (2004): 1–13.

Murrell, Denise. *Posing Modernity: The Black Model from Manet and Matisse to Today*. Miriam and Ira D. Wallach Art Gallery, Columbia University in the City of New York, 2018.

Musée d'Orsay, Céline Debray, and Stéphane Guégan. *Le modèle noir: de Géricault à Matisse*. Paris: Coédition Flammarion, 2019.

Peabody, Sue. *There Are No Slaves in France: The Political Culture of Race and Slavery in the Ancien Régime*. New York: Oxford University Press, 1996.

Peabody, Sue, and Tyler Edward Stovall. *The Color of Liberty: Histories of Race in France*. Durham, NC: Duke University Press, 2003.

Pichois, Claude. "A Propos des 'Yeux de Berthe' du nouveau sur Jeanne Duval?" In *Baudelaire: Études et témoignages*. Neuchâtel: La Baconnière, 1967.

Pollack, Griselda. *Differencing the Canon: Feminist Desire and the Writing of Art's Histories*. London: Routledge, 2006.

Popkin, Jeremy D. *Facing Racial Revolution: Eyewitness Accounts of the Haitian Insurrection*. Chicago, IL: University of Chicago Press, 2007.

Richon, Emmanuel. *Jeanne Duval et Charles Baudelaire: Belle d'abandon*. Paris: L'Harmattan, 1999.

Sepinwall, Alyssa Goldstein. "The Specter of Saint-Domingue: American and French Reactions to the Haitian Revolution." In *The World of the Haitian Revolution*, ed. Norman Fiering and David Geggus. Bloomington: Indiana University Press, 2009.

Sharpley-Whiting, T. Denean. *Black Venus: Sexualized Savages, Primal Fears, and Primitive Narratives in French*. Durham, NC: Duke University Press, 1999.

Smalls, James. "Slavery Is a Woman: 'Race,' Gender, and Visuality in Marie Benoist's Portrait d'une négresse (1800)." *Nineteenth-Century Art Worldwide: A Journal of Nineteenth-Century Visual Culture* 3, no. 1 (Spring 2004). http://www.19thcartworldwide.org/spring04index?id=178.

Strother, Z.S. "Display of the Body Hottentot." In *Africans on Stage: Studies in Ethnological Show Business*, ed. Bernth Lindfors. Bloomington: Indiana University Press, 1999.

16

Living free

Self-emancipated women and queer formations of freedom

Vanessa M. Holden

Two women, separated by decades of history, make fleeting appearances in extant records pertaining to the lives of Black women in nineteenth-century Maryland. One appears in a jailor's pickup notice, an advertisement used to communicate to enslavers in and around Baltimore that she awaited pickup at a local jail. The other appears in her former enslaver's plea with local courts for compensation for human property lost during the War of 1812. In these heavily mediated sources, written with the intent of making chattels of two women intent on defining themselves as free, it is possible to glimpse how self-emancipated Black women fashioned freedom in ways historians, historical methods, and historical inquiry have rendered invisible.

A Baltimore justice of the peace committed Mary Ann Waters to jail in late September of 1851. Waters insisted, upon arrest, that she was free and had been born free in Elkridge, Maryland, just southwest of Baltimore. The jailor had probably heard similar stories. That someone purporting to be free had been apprehended by authorities, justly or not, was not remarkable. Mary Ann Waters's pickup notice is like thousands of others. The ad reveals another key reason why the jailor may have considered her unreliable. As far as the jailor was concerned, he had in his custody "a runaway, a Negro Man, who calls himself Mary Ann Waters." The jailor continues using only masculine pronouns for Waters throughout the remainder of the notice.[1] Her word did not hold against that of a justice of the peace, and like many others captured and reduced to chattels, the jailor dismissed her humanity and womanhood in two syllables: him-self.

Minty Caden lived nearly 40 years earlier as an enslaved woman on the farm of Susannah Rawlings in Calvert County, Maryland. The county is right on the Patuxent River, which leads north to the nation's capital. In the summer of 1814, Minty Caden would have been near enough to get early word of the U.S. Navy's defeat at St. Leonard's Creek and the two-pronged British amphibious assault that raged to either side of the county that summer. All around her, whole plantation quarters absconded to join the British in a bid for freedom.[2] Minty Caden and at least five other enslaved people from the farm owned by the Rawlings family joined the flood of freedom seekers.

The suit that Susannah Rawlings brought along with her granddaughter, to demand recompense for the human property, was like many others. The Rawlings family provided as much proof as possible that they had enslaved the six who had stolen themselves away. Depositions from neighbors included many of the details that runaway ads included at the time: physical descriptions, assessments of temperament, and possible sightings. But like Waters's pickup notice, Minty Caden's identifying information diverged from that of the thousands of other self-emancipated people who appear in lost property suits. More than one neighbor remembered that she had "formed an intimacy" with another enslaved woman, Philis Caden, and taken her name. Thereafter, a neighbor testified, Minty Gury went by the name Mrs. Minty Caden. And in Nova Scotia's Halifax List, a manifest used to count recent arrivals from the United States after the War of 1812, her name remained Minty Caden.[3]

Queering slavery / queering freedom

"What would it mean to queer slavery?" remains a question with multiple answers.[4] This chapter asks a related question: What might it mean to queer freedom? Both Mary Ann Waters's and Minty Caden's brief archival appearances posit new ways to understand how self-emancipated women shaped both definitions and practices of freedom.[5] Excellent work by Rachel Hope Cleves and Thomas A. Foster on early American history provides important methodological interventions upon which historians of slavery can draw. Clare Sears's chapter in *The Routledge History of Queer America* (2018), "Centering Slavery in Nineteenth-century Queer History (1800s–1890s)," makes an explicit argument for more interventions like theirs. Sears calls incisively for queer histories of American slavery and writes, "Queer historical studies of slavery are not only academically viable but also politically necessary to foreground the specificities of Black queer histories and center slavery's constitutive role in modern sexualities."[6] We must tend to the ways that enslaved people, particularly enslaved women and femmes, often through their actions, defined freedom and emancipation for themselves.[7]

E. Patrick Johnson poses this question in his essay, "'Quare' Studies, Or (Almost) Everything I Know About Queer Studies I Learned from My Grandmother": "what is the utility of queer theory on the front lines, in the trenches, on the street, or any place where the racialized and sexualized body is beaten, starved, fired, cursed – indeed, when the body is the site of trauma?"[8] Here, the histories of Black women and femmes is instructive. Scholars of enslaved women have been comfortable looking for and at different kinds of womanhood and various gender performances and gender expressions from the field's inception.[9] It is time for a queer of color reading of the history of American slavery that explores queering as integral to vernacular African American strategies for survival, liberation, and resistance. Both Waters and Caden self-emancipated. Their intersecting identities as Black women are integral to their own self-fashioned definitions of freedom.

The literary and interdisciplinary scholar Omise'eke Natasha Tinsley explores the possibility of queer Black femme history in her article "Black Atlantic, Queer Atlantic: Queer Imaginings of the Middle Passage." Her exploration of contemporary language and its history leads her to define the term *queer* not as same-sex sexual relationships but as "marking disruption to the violence of normative order and powerfully so: connecting in ways that commoditized flesh was never supposed to, loving your own kind when your kind was supposed to cease to exist." Tinsley defines an intimate community of survival centered on female intimacies, by which she suggests we should go about "marking disruption to the violence of normative order." The queer is an active disruption of the normative.[10]

In new studies that seek to queer the history of American slavery, queer sex and sexuality are often embedded in the violent sexual regimes that enslavers used to assert their power over enslaved bodies. Enslaved men and women endured homoerotic and homosexual sexual abuse. Through sexual abuse, assault, concubinage, and forced breeding, enslavers profited from the sexual and reproductive labor of enslaved people. This is an important facet of sexualized violence to explore. But it cannot be the only way that historians acknowledge same-sex sexuality during the period of American slavery.[11] We need to interrogate consensual relationships even as we critique what consent could mean within the context of the American slave regime.[12]

Furthermore, attending to the ways that self-emancipated women defined themselves and fought to possess themselves must include an exploration of queer sexuality and identities. Stealing themselves from enslavers, Mary Ann Waters and Minty Caden engaged in survival practices born of community. Their identities were not resistance in and of themselves; rather, their choices and actions, informed by their subject positions, were resistive. Waters and Caden accomplished their self-stealing by naming and flight. In the minds of authorities, the two practices were also connected.[13] The sources include glimpses of both women's own self-possession and their own self-definition: the most important of which was their identity as free women.

Fashioning freedom: Mary Ann Waters

According to the pickup notice a jailor placed in the *Daily National Intelligencer*, Mary Ann Waters was one of many women who had been "hiring out in the city of Baltimore as a woman for the last three years." Free women of color had limited employment options. In rural communities, they often found themselves in labor contracts performing field labor beside enslaved men and women.[14] In urban centers, large and small, free women of color faced labor competition from enslaved women and poor white women, while their gender restricted them from most skilled labor. Free women scraped by producing goods and foodstuffs for market, taking in washing, working in domestic service, and performing sex work. Poor women, white and Black, engaged in sex work for supplemental income in lean times and as their primary employment in antebellum cities.[15] Whether a domestic, laundress, seamstress, sex worker, or some combination of each, authorities committed Waters to jail as "a Negro Man."[16]

The jailor provided careful details of Waters's appearance. Without photographs to aid in identification, descriptions present in jailors' ads communicated details important to authorities and details that embedded criminality in phenotype and self-presentation. While the description provides a glimpse of how Waters appeared to white authorities, it also signals what other whites may have found remarkable about Waters. In C. Riley Snorton's reading of Waters's ad alongside other records, like Peter Sewally/Mary Jones, a sex worker convicted of larceny in 1830s New York, he writes:

> The praxis of emergence was most frequently criminalized such that (as Jones's narrative bears out) theft described the manner with which free blacks were seen as being in illicit possession of themselves and their perambulations, according to the logic of antebellum law, the press, and popular culture, requiring carceral containment as a response.[17]

Waters's self-possession was as transgressive as her gender presentation and claim to womanhood.

Her womanhood was, if the jailor is to be believed, lived and well coifed. The notice records her clothing in detail. She wore "a mousseline de laine dress, blue velvet mantilla, white satin bonnet, and a figured scarf."[18] Mousseline de laine, a fine, often printed textile made of either wool or wool and cotton, was used to make fashionable dresses in the period.[19] Blue velvet, white satin, and an ornamental scarf completed a sumptuous look meant to signal femininity and to potentially impress prospective employers or attract the attention of potential clients. Waters was at once conspicuous and invisible. Dressed to hire herself out, Waters worked as any number of free women did, to support herself.[20] Her labor, whatever form it took, was unremarkable in antebellum Baltimore. Her encounter with the authorities was just as common. But as Snorton points out in his analysis, her status as a potential runaway is deeply intertwined in her perceived gender transgression.[21]

The jailor's notice begins with physical attributes, sexing Waters's body before noting her chosen name. The text reads, "a runaway, a Negro Man, who calls himself Mary Ann Waters," leading with legal status, then race and sex, before noting how Waters identified herself. The notice moves on to physically describe Waters: "about twenty-eight years of age, 5 feet 2 1/2 inches high, stout build, very black complexion, and has a scar on his left ear."[22] The jailor hoped that Waters's body would betray her status as an enslaved person. Conspicuously absent from the jailor's ad is one key detail that could have instantly identified Waters to her former enslaver, if she had one: What name had Waters left behind?

It was possible for authorities to view and describe Waters's clothing and physical appearance without her input. The jailor's insistence that Waters was a man, using only male pronouns, suggests access to her body that went beyond what was described in the ad. His confidence suggests that either he, the justice of the peace, or even a denizen of Baltimore, discovered that Waters's body had sex characteristics consistent with antebellum definitions of the male sex. This implies access beneath Waters's clothing. Access to her body implies sexual access. This access allowed the jailor and authorities to insist that her careful gender presentation and years of living as a woman, her years of living free, were inconsequential.

The ad also includes descriptive information that the jailor learned from Waters. Her claim to freedom hinged on denoting that she was born in Elkridge. "Says he is free," reads the ad, "was born in Elkridge."[23] It is not possible to know whether officials held Waters as a fugitive in error. But, this passage of the notice provides a glimpse of how Waters defined herself: free, from Elkridge, and a woman. Waters would have needed someone white to back up the claim that she was free, a local official in Elkridge or a white person familiar with her family. Mentioning Elkridge may have been her best hope for help securing her release. But while she provided plenty of identifying information, she did not provide another name for herself. This suggests that those who knew her in Elkridge might not have known her by any other identity. That she was free and a woman, then, were also deeply intertwined social markers. For Waters, freedom was life as a free woman of color in Baltimore. Freedom and womanhood defined each other in inseparable ways.

Naming kinship, naming freedom: Minty Caden

In 1821, Minty Caden had lived in Nova Scotia, Canada, for six years. She was far away from Maryland, living among other formerly enslaved people. In that year, Susannah Rawlings, along with her descendants, began petitioning for reparations. Minty Caden had not been subject to their authority for some time, but they wanted it known that she and the others who had dared to abscond once had been. They believed that they deserved money in payment for property lost. Susannah Rawlings, her granddaughter Juliet, and her grandson, Issac Rawlings, Jr., each petitioned for compensation through her son, Dr. Issac Rawlings. In order to build a case for each family member, their legal council took depositions from neighbors who could confirm that each had once held slaves who matched the ages and descriptions of those for whom they sought recompense. The identifying information that witnesses and both Rawlings women provided suggests ways that the community identified each missing enslaved person. It is from these depositions that we learn about the family structures of those who ran from the Rawlings family.

Susannah Rawlings did not survive to see her claims satisfied. She died in October 1826.[24] But her family continued to build their case and make their claim for recompense. In July 1828, 14 years after Minty escaped from Calvert County, the family filed depositions given by Colonel Brook in regard to Susannah Rawlings's claim. Brook stated plainly that "Minty was known by the name of Gury or Caden."[25] Colonel Brook corroborated a deposition from earlier that year. Mrs. Alletha Smith, a female neighbor, went into more detail about Minty's two names:

> Minty had two surnames Gury, and Caden that she had a husband by the name of Joe Gurry the property of Thomas Ireland that a short time after their marriage they fell out and parted. She then formed an intimacy with a negro woman the property of James Avis by the name of Philis Caden, they joined the Methodist Church, claimed a Sisterhood, and then adopted that name as Mrs. Minty Caden as such she went to the British while the fleet was in the Patuxent river.[26]

It does not appear that Minty Caden's story was a secret; rather, white community members knew about her "intimacy" with Philis Caden.

On the eve of the chaos that the War of 1812 visited on the Chesapeake region, two enslaved women formed an attachment to each other, solidified it in public, and named their relationship a sisterhood. Minty Caden renamed herself, taking Philis's surname. Those who traveled with her carried surnames too. Mary Mitchel took her husband's name. Alexander, called both Sawney and Sandy, took two nicknames and the surname Covington with him into the First Company of the Colonial Marines.[27] Monday took the name Golden. And Charles took the name Gray, as did his wife and daughter. Only Peter, a teenager, claimed no surname that white neighbors were aware of when he ran, though his father went by both the names Goler and Washington.[28] Not a single person in their group claimed the surname Rawlings. That was a name each hoped to leave behind them in the Patuxent River.

In Minty's case, the neighbor Mrs. Smith took her name to be a means of knowing. That she had two surnames would have been of interest to anyone hoping to identify her. But unlike others deposed for the Rawlings's claim, Smith provided additional information. Through her one-time surname, Gurry, Smith identified Minty as an enslaved man's wife. Joe Gurry, Mrs. Smith swore, gave Minty that name upon their marriage.[29] An expected legal, social, and religious convention for free white women, taking Joe Gurry's name may have had social significance but not legal significance. Enslaved people did not have the same claim to marriage as whites did. Their marriages could be broken apart by their enslavers. Marriages abroad could be thwarted by whites who refused to acknowledge or accommodate them. The Gurrys, though, did the work of sundering their own relationship: "a short time after their marriage they fell out and parted."[30]

Smith's deposition defines Minty and Philis Caden's connection through their shared surname and their public actions. First, though, she presents Minty's marriage to an enslaved man as analogous to her connection to Philis Caden. Right after testifying that the Gurrys had parted, Smith states, "She then formed an intimacy with a negro woman the property of James Avis by the name of Philis Caden" and begins to describe the public evidence of the Cadens' private connection, ending with "[Minty] adopted that name as Mrs. Minty Caden as such she went to the British while the fleet was in the Patuxent river."[31] The kinship that Minty fled with had a name: Mrs. Minty Caden.

Minty was an active agent in her own intimate life. Minty formed an intimacy traversing the distance between the Rawlings farm and the Avis property. Maintaining relationships between farms and plantations was as common a reality as it was a difficult one. Yet, enslaved people raised families and kept kinship ties, risking punishment by thwarting white surveillance. Minty and Philis would have had to do the same to form their intimacy, an active process, a set of choices made throughout the workday to ensure stolen moments of privacy later.

The Cadens' attachment was more than a clandestine partnership. Smith's deposition denotes careful acts of naming and public proclamation. Smith notes that women themselves termed their kinship "a Sisterhood." Minty and Philis did not just name themselves sisters, they "claimed a Sisterhood."[32] Smith's grammar suggests a semantics of intimacy. Their Sisterhood, not sisterhood, was a claimed status and not the result of their birth. Theirs was symbolic sisterhood, not literal blood-relation. Smith used Minty Caden's previous marriage to Joe Gurry and her previous adoption of his surname to explain her intimacy with Philis Caden. She did not use another close female friendship or Minty's relationship to a parent to do so. The women's Sisterhood was adjacent to their intimacy; it was their public claim to kinship and partnership.

Sisterhood, of course, figures in the women's other public proclamation and consummation of their attachment. Smith states, "they joined the Methodist Church," a denomination in which women and men commonly referred to each other as sister and brother.[33] The two enslaved women joined a denomination fraught with conflict over slavery.[34] Nevertheless, the women joined a local Methodist church and found fellowship. Smith may have hoped that the church had records of the two women. Their membership denotes the possibility of public and spiritual recognition of their attachment to one another.[35]

Minty Caden's agency went beyond declaring a spiritual home and claiming kinship with Philis Caden. The two shared a surname. Minty Caden, as Smith made sure to note in her deposition, went by the courtesy title "Mrs." Smith stated that Minty "then adopted that name as Mrs. Minty Caden." Philis did not give Minty her name; Minty adopted it. She was Mrs. Minty Caden and "as such she went to the British while the fleet was in the Patuxent River."[36]

These social markers, a surname, a courtesy title, a church membership, were outward signs of the personal private commitment the two women had to one another. Smith implied but did not detail her understanding that Minty and Philis were physically involved by defining their relationship alongside Minty's previous marriage. But the details of their intimacy remain just that: theirs. Minty Caden not only possessed herself; she held on to her intimacy with Philis too.

Conclusion

Caden was remarkable and remarked upon because she fled slavery; she deprived her owner of her labor and the wealth she embodied. Her "intimacy" with another enslaved woman helped to identify her, but it wasn't, as far as the suit was concerned, her biggest transgression or even a transgression at all. Her status as a runaway was far more remarkable. The women's relationship, the way that they consummated it, sanctified it, and renamed themselves to reflect it, posits possibility for future historical inquiry. They provide us with a new way to think about the possibility of liberation. They model a pursuit of freedom that was not predicated on their access to white gender, sexual, or racial norms – theirs was one foraged amidst the very tangible possibility of freedom through flight. For Minty Caden, liberation came in the form of relocation to Nova Scotia. But survival and a type of liberation came in her intimacy with Philis Caden too.

Waters's story has no tidy conclusion. Instead, her self-definition as a free woman remains in an ad meant to make her someone's chattel. Like Caden, her appearance hinges on naming and claiming place and space. Minty Caden took Philis Caden's name and then took to her feet. Decades later, Mary Ann Waters held fast to her name and provided the barest outline of her journey from Elkridge to Baltimore, where she lived and worked as a free woman. Minty Caden's same-gender intimacy and Mary Ann Waters's insistence that she was both free and a woman not only identified them to their neighbors and authorities but more importantly, remained key components of the type of freedom both women fashioned for themselves. And it is precisely that type of survival and liberation that future studies should not overlook, especially in pursuit of the queer in the history of the enslaved.

Notes

1 I first read this document as part of a Spring 2014 Queering Slavery Working Group document work-shop that included Jessica Marie Johnson (Johns Hopkins), Derrias Carter (University of Arizona), and Emily Owens (Brown). C. Riley Snorton also reads this document in his work, *Black on Both Sides: A Racial History of Trans Identity*, and provides a reading of this text that I have found invaluable in writing this chapter: C. Riley Snorton, *Black on Both Sides: A Racial History of Trans Identity* (Minneapolis: University of Minnesota Press, 2017) Chapter 2; pickup notice for Mary Ann Waters, *Daily National Intelligencer*, September 29, 1851, pg. 2. Collection of the Maryland State Archives. Accessed via: http://slavery2.msa.maryland.gov/pages/Search.aspx

2 I first encountered Minty Caden in the work of Alan Taylor. After I corresponded with him, he graciously shared with me his sources about the Cadens and directed me to Maryland's online repository of petitions, which greatly aided in the production of this chapter. For more on African Americans in the Chesapeake during the War of 1812, see Alan Taylor, *The Internal Enemy: Slavery and War in Virginia, 1772–1832*, 1st edition (W.W. Norton & Company, 2013). Record of the group of runaways can be found here: Claim of Susannah and Juliet Rawlings, Calvert County, Case No. 569, Case Files, Ca. 1814–28, entry 190, Record Group 76, National Archives, College Park. Accessed via: http://msa.maryland.gov/megafile/msa/speccol/sc5400/sc5496/002500/002512/html/002512bio.html. For more on African Americans and the War of 1812, see Gerard T. Altoff, *Amongst My Best Men: African-Americans and the War of 1812* (Put-in-Bay, OH: Perry Group, 1996); Donald R. Hickey, *War of 1812 : A Forgotten Conflict* (Baltimore, MD: University of Illinois Press, 2012), http://site.ebrary.com/lib/alltitles/docDetail.action?docID=10628099; Gene Allen Smith, *The Slaves' Gamble: Choosing Sides in the War of 1812* (Basingstoke: Palgrave Macmillan, 2013); Alan Taylor, *The Civil War of 1812: American Citizens, British Subjects, Irish Rebels, & Indian Allies* (New York: Vintage Books, 2011); Joseph T. Wilson and Dudley Taylor Cornish, *The Black Phalanx: African American Soldiers in the War of Independence, the War of 1812, and the Civil War*, 1st Da Capo Press edition (New York: Da Capo Press, 1994).

3 Claim of Susannah and Juliet Rawlings, Calvert County, Case No. 569, Case Files. Ca. 1814–28, entry 190, Record Group 76, National Archives, College Park. Accessed via: Archives of Maryland Biographical Series, *MSA SC 5496-050782*, War of 1812 Claimant, Calvert County, Maryland, https://msa.maryland.gov/megafile/msa/speccol/sc5300/sc5339/000243/000000/000002/restricted/msa_sc_5339_243_2-0031.pdf; "Halifax List: Return of American Refugee Negroes who have been received into the Province of Nova Scotia from the United States of America between 27 April 1815 and 24 October 1818," Nova Scotia Archives, Digitized List. Accessed via: https://novascotia.ca/archives/africanns/1812results.asp

4 "What would it mean to queer slavery?" In my work co-organizing the Queering Slavery Working Group with Jessica Marie Johnson (Johns Hopkins University), it has meant many things to different scholars. For some, it means an application of queer methods pioneered in other disciplines and interdisciplinary fields to historical work. For others, it means explicitly naming the system of slavery as queer and finding ways to engage the queerness of enslavement and slave holding. Others still wonder what fully engaging with Trans★ Studies might tell us about the chattel principle, the transformation of people into commodities. Most also want to know what Queer Studies has for the study of slavery and what Slavery Studies has for Queer Studies in return. Always lurking is a project of recovery, though, one in which theorizing the queer goes hand in hand with finding queer people, their lives and experience, among enslaved people. See also Daina Berry and Leslie Harris, eds., *Sexuality and Slavery: Reclaiming Intimate Histories in the Americas* (Athens, Georgia: University of Georgia Press, 2018).

5 I refer to Waters as a woman and by feminine pronouns (she/her) because there is no evidence that she identified as a man or used masculine pronouns (he/him). Pickup notice for Mary Ann Waters. Accessed via: http://slavery2.msa.maryland.gov/pages/Search.aspx

6 Clare Sears, "Centering Slavery in Nineteenth-Century Queer History (1900s–1890)," *The Routledge History of Queer America*, Don Romesburg, ed., 1st edition (New York, NY: Routledge, 2018), 39.

7 Henry Bibb's narrative provides an excellent and heart-wrenching example of how the self-emancipated valued heterosexual family structures and provided them as evidence of their humanity and fitness for freedom. Henry Bibb, "Narrative of the Life and Adventures of Henry Bibb, American Slave," in Yuval Taylor, ed., *I Was Born a Slave: An Anthology of Classic Slave Narratives* (Chicago: Lawrence Hill Books, 1999), 1–101. Tera Hunter explores the many family formations that enslaved people placed under the umbrella of marriage, including non-monogamous and polyamorous relationships: Tera W.

Hunter, *Bound in Wedlock: Slave and Free Black Marriage in the Nineteenth Century* (Cambridge: Belknap Press, 2017), 36–40.

8 E. Patrick Johnson. "'Quare' Studies, Or (Almost) Everything I Know About Queer Studies I Learned from My Grandmother," E. Patrick Johnson and Mae G. Henderson, eds., *Black Queer Studies: A Critical Anthology* (Durham, NC: Duke University Press Books, 2005), 129.

9 This idea of a "different kind of womanhood" comes from the seminal work by Deborah Gray White, *Ar'n't I a Woman?: Female Slaves in the Plantation South* (New York: Norton, 1999). Another important work in competing womanhoods from more recent scholarship would be Thavolia Glymph, *Out of the House of Bondage: The Transformation of the Plantation Household*, 1st edition (Cambridge; New York: Cambridge University Press, 2008).

10 Omise'eke Natasha Tinsley. "Black Atlantic, Queer Atlantic: Queer Imaginings of the Middle Passage," *GLQ: A Journal of Lesbian and Gay Studies*, Volume 14, Number 2–3, 2008, 192 and 199.

11 Thomas A. Foster, *Rethinking Rufus: Sexual Violations of Enslaved Men* (Athens, GA: University of Georgia Press, 2019); Vincent Woodard, Dwight McBride, and E. Patrick Johnson, *The Delectable Negro: Human Consumption and Homoeroticism within US Slave Culture*, ed. Justin A. Joyce (New York: NYU Press, 2014).

12 Woodard, *The Delectable Negro*, 105–25. Woodard spends a significant portion of his third chapter, "A Tale of Hunger Retold," discussing enslavers' sexual violence against enslaved women and how Black male abolitionists express this type of sexual violence as an affront to their masculinity. They often reduced Black women's sexuality to rape and abuse. Additionally, Woodard posits that leaders like Frederick Douglass use the stories of Black women being raped to obfuscate their own experiences with rape at the hands of white men and women. While his focus then turns to the lived experiences of Black men with rape and homoerotic experiences, I will pivot to broadening the scope of female sexuality beyond rape and abuse. The question of consent, and whether it could exist for an enslaved person, remains.

13 Snorton, *Black on Both Sides*, chapter 2.

14 Pickup notice for Mary Ann Waters. Accessed via: http://slavery2.msa.maryland.gov/pages/Search.aspx

15 For information about women's labor in early national and antebellum Baltimore, see Seth Rockman, *Scraping By: Wage Labor, Slavery, and Survival in Early Baltimore* (Baltimore: The Johns Hopkins University Press, 2009).

16 Pick up notice for Mary Ann Waters, *Daily National Intelligencer*, September 29, 1851, pg. 2 Collection of the Maryland State Archives. Accessed via: http://slavery2.msa.maryland.gov/pages/Search.aspx Many free people of color lived within white households, particularly in the uppers south and the west, where small to midsized farms and plantations relied on their labor to supplement the labor of relatively small enslaved populations. See, Berlin, Ira. *Slaves Without Masters: The Free Negro in the Antebellum South.* (New York: The New Press, 2007); Lebsock, Suzanne. *The Free Women of Petersburg: Status and Culture in a Southern Town, 1784-1860* (W. W. Norton & Company, 1985); Stevenson, Brenda E. *Life in Black and White: Family and Community in the Slave South.* 1st edition. New York: Oxford University Press, 1997.

17 Snorton, *Black on Both Sides*, chapter 2.

18 Pickup notice for Mary Ann Waters. Accessed via: http://slavery2.msa.maryland.gov/pages/Search.aspx

19 Elisabeth McClellan, *Historic Dress in America, 1800–1870* (G.W. Jacobs, 1910), 204 and 227; "Delaine, n." In *OED Online*, Oxford University Press. Accessed September 29, 2019 at: www.oed.com/view/Entry/49257; "Mousseline de Laine, n." In *OED Online*. Oxford University Press. Accessed September 29, 2019 at www.oed.com/view/Entry/254601.

20 Pickup notice for Mary Ann Waters. Accessed via: http://slavery2.msa.maryland.gov/pages/Search.aspx

21 Snorton, *Black on Both Sides*, chapter 2.

22 For more on the many meanings of the term "complextion," see Sharon Block, *Colonial Complexions: Race and Bodies in Eighteenth-Century America* (Philadelphia: University of Pennsylvania Press, 2018). Quoted text from pickup notice for Mary Ann Waters. Accessed via: http://slavery2.msa.maryland.gov/pages/Search.aspx

23 Pickup notice for Mary Ann Waters. Accessed via: http://slavery2.msa.maryland.gov/pages/Search.aspx

24 "Susannah Rawlings." Middleham Cemetery, Lusby, Calvert County, Maryland. Find a Grave, Inc. www.findagrave.com.

25 Claim of Susannah and Juliet Rawlings.
26 Ibid.
27 Information on Alexander Covington can be found via the Maryland State Archives' official biography of him at:http://msa.maryland.gov/megafile/msa/speccol/sc5400/sc5496/002500/002512/html/002512bio.html. The biography sites the following for further information on the fate of the First Company of Colonial Marines: John McNish Weiss, *The Merikens: Free Black American Settlers in Trinidad: 1815–1816* (London, UK: McNish & Weiss, 2002), 25.
28 Ibid.
29 Claim of Susannah and Juliet Rawlings.
30 Ibid.
31 Ibid.
32 Ibid.
33 J. L. Gorman, "Evangelical Revivalism and Race Relations in the Early National Era," *Slavery's Long Shadow: Race and Reconciliation in American Christianity* (William B. Eerdmans Publishing Company, 2019), 21–6; Paul Harvey, *Through the Storm, Through the Night: A History of African American Christianity* (Rowman & Littlefield, Plymouth, 2011), 37.
34 Tera W. Hunter, *Bound in Wedlock*, 58–9.
35 Claim of Susannah and Juliet Rawlings. http://site.ebrary.com/lib/alltitles/docDetail.action?docID= 10628099; Gene Allen Smith, *The Slaves' Gamble*; Alan Taylor, *The Civil War of 1812*; Joseph T. Wilson, and Dudley Taylor Cornish, *The Black Phalanx*.
36 Claim of Susannah and Juliet Rawlings. http://site.ebrary.com/lib/alltitles/docDetail.action?docID= 10628099

17

"Blood, fire, and freedom"

Enslaved women and rebellion in nineteenth-century Cuba

Michele Reid-Vazquez

In Cuba's public history of rebellion, Carlota Lucumí dominates the narrative at the Triunvirato sugar mill archeological site in Matanzas. At the signal to start the revolt in November of 1843, she retrieved a machete hidden inside the slave barracks. With the dramatic cry of "Blood, fire, and freedom!" Carlota raised the blade, broke the chained door, and freed the rebels. Authorities linked her actions to a series of uprisings in March, May, June, and July of that year.[1] Carlota Lucumí, however, was not the only woman who led or participated in the uprisings. Rather, she represents one end of a continuum in the multidimensional contributions that women of African descent made in the struggle to end Cuban slavery during the nineteenth century. Exploring their roles expands our understanding of gendered resistance in the colonial context and lays the foundation for insights into contemporary forms of collective and individual agency at the intersection of race, gender, and power.

The actions of enslaved women in revolts varied from the visible to the clandestine. Some led their comrades into battle, like Carlota Lucumí and other insurgent figures across the Caribbean.[2] Many took on less visible parts as informants, messengers, munitions suppliers, and confidants. If trials ensued, officials demanded that women testify as witnesses to rebellious plots.[3] The growing scholarship on this subject has sought to shift Black women from the margins to the center in areas ranging from community and family structures to resistance and nation-building.[4] Such works shed light on the servitude that produced women's "dual burden" of manual and reproductive labor within plantation economies. Furthermore, their opposition to enslavement reinforces the reality that revolts required shared efforts. The inhumanity of slavery fostered what Angela Davis called "a profound consciousness of resistance."[5] Scrutinizing these tumultuous spaces upends notions of African-descended women's subservience to reveal their inherent abilities to foment insurgency, lead combatants, and conceal conspiratorial knowledge.

Women and slave rebellion in Cuba

In the early nineteenth century, the Atlantic slave trade funneled thousands of Africans into Cuba. In defiance of Britain's abolition of the slave trade in 1807 and Anglo-Spanish treaties in 1817 and 1835, Cuba expanded its imported workforce. Enslaved women had numbered 37,166 in 1792. By 1817, this sector had more than doubled to 74,821, and it escalated to 103,652 in 1827. By 1841, African and Cuban-born bondswomen had multiplied again to 155,245.[6] Comprising approximately 30 percent of the enslaved sector, they proved vital as agricultural workers, domestics, street vendors, and midwives. Many of those who hailed from West and West-Central Africa arrived fully enmeshed in a skill set involving oral transmission, spiritual rituals, and warfare.[7] As a result of their demographic size, African women played a significant role in Cuba's cycle of revolt.

Organizations known as *cabildos de nación* helped sustain African ethnic affiliations during enslavement, such as Arara, Gangá, Mina, Kongo, and Lucumí, as the Yoruba were known in Cuba. These sociocultural mutual aid associations brought together captive Africans as well as free people of African descent. They supported the cultural transition of new arrivals and maintained traditions and adaptations in the diaspora, including the development of Santeria and other syncretic religions. The organizations also offered a variety of services, ranging from artisanal apprenticeships, loans, celebrations, and housing to buying the freedom of enslaved participants. Groups also elected kings and queens as leaders. Because women often comprised a larger proportion of the membership, they typically directed organizational priorities as officers. Moreover, authorities implicated numerous association members in insurgencies. The lexicon of sovereignty within *cabildos de nación* provided the context for the roles of enslaved women in armed revolt.[8]

Cuba experienced major uprisings between 1812 and 1843, yet the scholarship on women rebels is sparse. During the 1812 Aponte rebellion, officials arrested 32 women, including Isabel Infante, a slave, who garnered a punishment of 150 lashes and six years in prison, and Maria Merced Llanes, a free woman of color, who was sentenced to a four-year incarceration.[9] The revolt of 1825 implicated Ana Gangá, wife of conspiratorial leader Frederico Carabalí, when rumors circulated that she had helped plan the uprising. Given that accused men faced death, Ana Gangá denied these allegations.[10] Following upheavals in 1835, authorities apprehended a free woman of African heritage, known as "La Reyna" (queen), for hiding weapons on her property.[11] This sparse data suggests that women's shared subjugation enabled them to forge personal, cultural, and political alliances to incite revolt. They facilitated clandestine meetings and arms, but also disavowed knowledge when confronted with prosecution. These glimpses into women's actions in the early nineteenth century underscore the reality that agitated resistance required their explicit and implicit participation.

Women in the Conspiracy of La Escalera

Leaders and insurgents

The rebellions of 1843, known collectively as the Conspiracy of La Escalera (The Ladder), named for the instrument of torture used to extract confessions, shed light on women as principal agitators.[12] Carlota Lucumí and Fermina Lucumí became the most well-known enslaved women insurgents. Both had been born in Africa, shared the same ethnicity, and labored in the Matanzas sugarcane fields; Carlota on the Triunvirato plantation, and Fermina at the neighboring Ácana estate. Although additional data on Carlota remains shrouded, records on Fermina indicated that she had served as a primary organizer of a summer uprising and facilitated contact with the Triunvirato sugar mill in preparation for the ensuing revolts. For her actions, she suffered a vicious whipping and spent several months in iron shackles.[13] This sketch of Carlota and Fermina provides insight into how cultural heritage, ethnic allegiance, harsh labor conditions

– and in the case of Fermina, a history of agitated defiance – set the stage for the bold feats attributed to these women.

Testimonies characterized Carlota as a rebel leader. Following her battle cry of "Blood, fire, and freedom!" she ordered insurgents to set the Triunvirato fields ablaze and gather firearms abandoned by retreating planters and overseers. She then directed them to the nearby Ácana estate. Carlota's exploits became more personalized there, where she assaulted the plantation manager's daughter. She then guided fighters to four more sugar mills. While it is unknown when she succumbed to local militia forces, authorities found her dead body the next morning.[14]

Fermina Lucumí would also exact similar revenge while leading efforts at the Ácana plantation. Slave witnesses Filomena Gangá and Catalina Gangá declared that Fermina steered the combatants to the homes of white personnel and families living on the estate and instructed rebels to capture whites trying to escape. The groups at Ácana torched the fields and buildings, coerced hesitant slaves into battle, freed those who had been placed in irons, and killed six members of the slaveholding family. Officials imprisoned Fermina for several months and interrogated her. Although she denied having a leadership role, her rebuttal fell on deaf ears. Bondsmen and women from area plantations watched the display of colonial power as Fermina, along with seven accused men, suffered death by firing squad and had her body disfigured.[15]

Witnesses named additional women as front-line warriors. A dozen testimonies acknowledged Clotilde, a *criolla* (woman born in Cuba), for ordering rebels to scorch the La Purísima Concepción Echeverría grounds and proclaimed that she had targeted the overseer's wife. The attacks by Clotilde and Carlota on the plantation manager's spouse and daughter, respectively, suggest an antagonistic relationship between each pair that highlighted the gendered nuances of power and oppression that fueled retribution. Observers identified *criollas* Carmita and Juliana among those from the Triunvirato estate who fought against colonial troops. They also recognized Filomena Gangá and Lucia Lucumí as major conductors of the armed upheaval at the Ácana and La Concepción plantations.[16]

The unconscious privileging of men in slave unrest has offered little space for addressing women's leadership. Archival sources have traditionally recorded men at the center of revolts and attributed the expected acts of aggression and destruction to them. When women engaged in violent methods of resistance, their actions were often masculinized, masked, or reframed as mythical or extraordinary. The daring exploits of Carlota, Fermina, Clotilde, and numerous others, however, loosen the entrenched expectations of what a rebel leader looks like and what she is capable of doing.[17]

Colluders, queens, and confidants

Rebellion records from 1843 also offer alternate ways that women supported armed revolt. Authorities accused Antonia, a cook at the Buena Esperanza coffee plantation, of using her position to collude with bondsmen to poison their enslaver and asserted that her actions revealed a deep knowledge about the targets and goals of the plot. Her conspiratorial behavior could not be ignored, and consequently, Antonia faced execution.[18] In addition, investigations revealed that many women had gained an awareness of the rebellion based on the dual meaning of "queen." Beyond an elected office in a *cabildo de nación*, the title became a central designation of the insurrection. The testimony by Rosa, a queen from the Merced estate, exposed her vast understanding of the plot, from poisoning the enslavers and acquiring munitions and money, to using free men of color to circulate the movement.[19] In terms of tacit participation, authorities arrested María del Pilar Poveda, a free woman of color, for permitting rebel leaders like her son-in-law, renowned poet Plácido (Gabriel de la Concepción Valdés), to hold meetings in her house. As a skilled midwife, Poveda held a highly regarded position that garnered her social capital among the free, enslaved, and white populations. Judges assessed this as a dangerous combination and insisted that she must have had full knowledge of the rebellion and willingly hidden the gatherings from police. As punishment, officials banned Poveda from practicing midwifery under penalty of life in prison.[20] As these examples suggest, aiding revolts as colluders, queens, and confidants left women vulnerable to incarceration, employment bans, and execution.

Because harsh punishments befell women for knowing too much, some engaged in an innocent bystander strategy. Many testified that they had only "overheard" snippets of conversations and therefore, had no real information about insurgent plans. Cecilia Criolla affirmed that she had noticed intermittent subversive chatter among the male work gangs, but nothing more. Numerous women whose spouses had been selected as kings denied any awareness of the uprisings. The mental and emotional exertion required to keep such secrets reveals an important form of passive resistance crucial to the development of the rebellion.[21] State repression of the uprisings not only made knowing about the revolts a criminal act; it also entangled individuals within the larger conspiratorial framework. Ultimately, however, women's silences and actions empowered combatants in the quest to dismantle the slave system.

Conclusion

This chapter has sought to shatter the dominant refrain of slave rebellion as a fully masculine endeavor. Women's involvement, whether visible or obscured, should be situated as crucial in the panorama of slave unrest. Their perception of insurgency as a path to liberty would prove pivotal in collective efforts to end Cuban slavery and colonialism.[22] Since the time of Cuba's nationalist battle against U.S. neocolonialism in the mid-twentieth century, a public narrative has embraced historical women freedom fighters. In honor of Carlota Lucumí, Cuba launched Operation Carlota, an elite military force that supported the Angolan liberation struggle in 1975.[23] In 2015, the Rebel Slave Museum opened to venerate the cycles of revolt. A monument erected on the grounds of the Triunvirato plantation depicts three stages of enslaved Africans' agency, from despondent to resolute to triumphant, and features a woman in the center position. These tributes represent Cuba's efforts to acknowledge the ways that African peoples challenged colonialism and enslavement. Additional studies into the actions of women of African descent will craft a deeper understanding of the multifaceted ways in which they lived, fought, and died for freedom.

Notes

1 José Luciano Franco, *La gesta heroica del triunvirato* (Havana: Editorial de Ciencias Sociales, 1978), 23, 27; author's personal tour of the Rebel Slave Museum at Triunvirato Sugar Mill, March 13, 2019; Michele Reid-Vazquez, *The Year of the Lash: Free People of Color in Cuba and the Nineteenth-Century Atlantic World* (Athens: University of Georgia Press, 2011), 3, 47–8.
2 Aisha K. Finch, *Rethinking Slave Rebellion in Cuba: La Escalera and the Insurgencies of 1841–1844* (Chapel Hill: University of North Carolina Press, 2015), 147–8; Karla Gottlieb, *The Mother of Us All: A History of Queen Nanny, Leader of the Windward Jamaican Maroons* (Trenton, NJ: Africa World Press, 2000); Bernard Moitt, *Women and Slavery in the French Antilles, 1635–1848* (Bloomington: Indiana University Press, 2001), 127–8.
3 Barbara Bush, *Slave Women in Caribbean Society, 1650–1838* (Bloomington: Indiana University Press, 1990), 67, 80; Robert L. Paquette, *Sugar Is Made With Blood: The Conspiracy of la Escalera and the Conflict*

Between Empires Over Slavery in Cuba (Middletown: Wesleyan University Press, 1988), 214; Moitt, *Women and Slavery in the French Antilles*, 128; Finch, *Rethinking Slave Rebellion in Cuba*, 152.

4 Mary Kemp Davis, "What Happened in This Place? In Search of the Female Slave in the Nat Turner Slave Insurrection," in *Nat Turner: A Slave Rebellion in History and Memory*, ed. Kenneth S. Greenberg (Oxford: Oxford University Press, 2003), 162–78; Finch, *Rethinking Slave Rebellion in Cuba*; Gottlieb, *The Mother of Us All*; Moitt, *Women and Slavery in the French Antilles*; Teresa Prado-Torreira, *Mambisas: Rebel Women in Nineteenth-Century Cuba* (Gainesville: University Press of Florida, 2005); Digna Castañeda, "The Female Slave in Cuba during the First Half of the Nineteenth Century" in *Engendering History: Caribbean Women in Historical Perspective*, eds. Verene Shepherd, Bridget Brereton, and Barbara Bailey (New York: St. Martin's Press, 1995), 141–54; Karen Y. Morrison, "Slave Mothers and White Fathers: Defining Family and Status in Late Colonial Cuba," *Slavery & Abolition*, 31, no. 1 (March 2010), 9–55.

5 Barbara Bush-Slimani, "Hard Labour: Women, Childbirth and Resistance in British Caribbean Slave Societies," *History Workshop*, No. 36, Colonial and Post-Colonial History (Autumn, 1993), 83; Finch, *Rethinking Slave Rebellion in Cuba*, 143; Angela Davis, "Reflections on the Black Woman's Role in the Community of Slaves," in *Words of Fire: An Anthology of African-American Feminist Thought*, ed. Beverly Guy-Sheftall (New York: New Press, 1995), 89.

6 Robin Blackburn, *The Overthrow of Colonial Slavery, 1776–1848* (London: Verso, 1988), 311, 314; Paquette, *Sugar Is Made With Blood*, 92, 131; Kenneth F. Kiple, *Blacks in Colonial Cuba, 1774–1899* (Gainesville: University Press of Florida, 1976), 85, 86, 88–90, Censuses of 1792, 1817, 1827, and 1841.

7 Castañeda, "The Female Slave in Cuba," 144; Camillia Cowling, *Conceiving Freedom: Women of Color, Gender, and the Abolition of Slavery in Havana and Rio de Janeiro* (Chapel Hill: The University of North Carolina Press, 2013), 31; Michele Reid-Vazquez, "Tensions of Race, Gender and Midwifery in Colonial Cuba," in *Africans to Colonial Spanish America: Expanding the Diaspora*, eds. Rachel O'Toole, Sherwin Bryant, and Ben Vinson III (Chicago: University of Illinois Press, 2012), 188; Olaudah Equiano, *The Interesting Narrative of the Life of Olaudah Equiano or Gustavus Vassa, the African written by himself* (Norwich: 1794) in Henry Louis Gates, Jr. and William L. Andrews, eds., *Pioneers of the Black Atlantic* (Washington, DC: Civitas, 1998), 208; Aisha K. Finch, "'What Looks Like a Revolution': Enslaved Women and the Gendered Terrain of Slave Insurgencies in Cuba, 1843–1844," *Journal of Women's History* 26, no. 1 (Spring, 2014), 132, n. 18; Paul E. Lovejoy and David V. Troutman, eds., *Transatlantic Dimensions of Ethnicity in the African Diaspora* (New York: Continuum, 2003), 17, 21.

8 Matt D. Childs, *The 1812 Aponte Rebellion in Cuba and the Struggle Against Atlantic Slavery* (Chapel Hill: University of North Carolina Press, 2006), 16, 18, 96, 111–13; Christine Ayorinde, "Santería in Cuba: Tradition and Transformation," in *Yoruba Diaspora in the Atlantic World*, eds. Toyin Falola and Matt D. Childs (Indiana University Press, 2005), 210; Finch, *Rethinking Slave Rebellion in Cuba*, 159.

9 Childs, *The 1812 Aponte Rebellion in Cuba*, 1, 144, Appendix: 190–206.

10 Manuel Barcia, *The Great African Slave Revolt* (Baton Rouge: Louisiana State University Press), 2012), 3, 21, 174–7.

11 Reid-Vazquez, *The Year of the Lash*, 39; Luis Martínez-Fernández, *Fighting Slavery in the Caribbean: Life and Times of a British Family in Nineteenth Century Havana* (New York: Routledge, 1998), 42.

12 Reid-Vazquez, *The Year of the Lash*, 6, 23, 55–6; Finch, "What Looks Like a Revolution," 118.

13 Finch, "What Looks Like a Revolution," 90, 117–18, 147; Franco, *La gesta heroica del triunvirato*, 23–4, 26–7.

14 Franco, *La gesta heroica del triunvirato*, 28; Tour of the Rebel Slave Museum at the Triunvirato Sugar Mill, 2019; Franco, *La gesta heroica del triunvirato*, 29–30; Finch, "What Looks Like a Revolution," 117.

15 Finch, *Rethinking Slave Rebellion in Cuba*, 16, 90, 91, 145, 147; Paquette, *Sugar Is Made With Blood*, 210; Finch, "What Looks Like a Revolution," 117; Franco, *La gesta heroica del triunvirato*, 30–1.

16 Michele Reid-Vazquez, "Formidable Rebels: Enslaved and Free Women of Color in Cuba's Conspiracy of La Escalera, 1843–1844," in *Breaking the Chains, Making the Nation: The Black Cuban Fight for Freedom and Equality, 1812–1912*, eds. Aisha Finch and Fannie Rushing (Baton Rouge: Louisiana State University Press), 166; Franco, *La gesta heroica del triunvirato*, 27–30.

17 Jane Landers, "Maroon Women in Colonial Spanish America: Case Studies in the Circum-Caribbean from the Sixteenth through the Eighteenth Centuries," in *Beyond Bondage: Free Women of Color in the Americas*, eds. David Barry Gaspar and Darlene Clark Hine (Chicago: University of Illinois Press, 2004), 3; Reid-Vazquez, "Formidable Rebels," 156–60; Finch, *Rethinking Slave Rebellion in Cuba*, 145.

18 Reid-Vazquez, "Formidable Rebels," 165–67.

19 Finch, *Rethinking Slave Rebellion in Cuba*, 161, 165.

20 Reid-Vazquez, "Formidable Rebels," 165; Reid-Vazquez, *The Year of the Lash*, 3; Reid-Vazquez, "Tensions of Race, Gender and Midwifery in Colonial Cuba," 198.
21 Finch, *Rethinking Slave Rebellion in Cuba*, 152, 156, 157, 161, 165.
22 Reid-Vazquez, "Formidable Rebels," 172.
23 Piero Gleijeses, *Conflicting Missions: Havana, Washington, and Africa, 1959–1976* (Chapel Hill: University of North Carolina Press, 2002), 305.

Bibliography

Andrews, William L. *Pioneers of the Black Atlantic, 183–366*. Washington, DC: Civitas, 1998.

Ayorinde, Christine "Santería in Cuba: Tradition and Transformation," in *Yoruba Diaspora in the Atlantic World*, Toyin Falola, and Matt D. Childs, editors, 209–230. Bloomington: Indiana University Press, 2005.

Barcia, Manuel. *The Great African Slave Revolt*. Baton Rouge: Louisiana State University Press, 2012.

Bush, Barbara. *Slave Women in Caribbean Society, 1650–1838*. Bloomington: Indiana University Press, 1990.

Bush-Slimani, Barbara. "Hard Labour: Women, Childbirth and Resistance in British Caribbean Slave Societies," *History Workshop, No. 36, Colonial and Post-Colonial History* (Autumn, 1993): 83–99.

Castañeda, Digna. "Female Slave in Cuba during the First Half of the Nineteenth Century," in *Engendering History: Caribbean Women in Historical Perspective*, Verene Shepherd, Bridget Brereton, and Barbara Bailey, editors, 141–154. New York: St. Martin's Press, 1995.

Childs, Matt D. *The 1812 Aponte Rebellion in Cuba and the Struggle against Atlantic Slavery*. Chapel Hill: University of North Carolina Press, 2006.

Cowling, Camillia. *Conceiving Freedom: Women of Color, Gender, and the Abolition of Slavery in Havana and Rio de Janeiro*. Chapel Hill: The University of North Carolina Press, 2013.

Davis, Angela. "Reflections on the Black Woman's Role in the Community of Slaves," in *Words of Fire: An Anthology of African-American Feminist Thought*, Beverly Guy-Sheftall, editor, 200–218. New York: New Press, 1995.

Davis, Mary Kemp. "What Happened in This Place? In Search of the Female Slave in the Nat Turner Slave Insurrection," in *Nat Turner: A Slave Rebellion in History and Memory*, Kenneth S. Greenberg, editor, 162–78. Oxford: Oxford University Press, 2003.

Equiano, Olaudah. "The Interesting Narrative of the Life of Olaudah Equiano or Gustavus Vassa, the African written by himself (Norwich: 1794)." in *Pioneers of the Black Atlantic*, Henry Louis Gates, and William L. Andrews, editors, 183–366. Washington, DC: Civitas, 1998.

Finch, Aisha K. "'What Looks Like a Revolution': Enslaved Women and the Gendered Terrain of Slave Insurgencies in Cuba, 1843–1844." *Journal of Women's History* 26, no. 1 (Spring 2014): 112–134.

Finch, Aisha K. *Rethinking Slave Rebellion in Cuba: La Escalera and the Insurgencies of 1841–1844*. Chapel Hill: University of North Carolina Press, 2015.

Franco, José Luciano. *La gesta heroica del triunvirato*. Havana: Editorial de Ciencias Sociales, 1978.

Gleijeses, Piero. *Conflicting Missions : Havana, Washington, and Africa, 1959–1976*. Chapel Hill: University of North Carolina Press, 2002,

Gottlieb, Karla. *The Mother of Us All: A History of Queen Nanny, Leader of the Windward Jamaican Maroons*. Trenton, NJ: Africa World Press, 2000.

Kiple, Kenneth F. *Blacks in Colonial Cuba, 1774–1899*. Gainesville: University Press of Florida, 1976.

Landers, Jane. "Maroon Women in Colonial Spanish America: Case Studies in the Circum-Caribbean from the Sixteenth through the Eighteenth Centuries," in *Beyond Bondage: Free Women of Color in the Americas*, David Barry Gaspar, and Darlene Clark Hine, editors, 3–18. Chicago: University of Illinois Press, 2004.

Lovejoy, Paul E. and David V. Troutman, editors, *Transatlantic Dimensions of Ethnicity in the African Diaspora*. New York: Continuum, 2003.

Martínez-Fernández, Luis. *Fighting Slavery in the Caribbean: Life and Times of a British Family in Nineteenth Century Havana*. New York: Routledge, 1998.

Moitt, Bernard. *Women and Slavery in the French Antilles, 1635–1848*. Bloomington: Indiana University Press, 2001.

Morrison, Karen Y. "Slave Mothers and White Fathers: Defining Family and Status in Late Colonial Cuba," *Slavery & Abolition* 31, no. 1 (March 2010): 9–55.

Paquette, Robert L. *Sugar Is Made with Blood: The Conspiracy of la Escalera and the Conflict Between Empires Over Slavery in Cuba*. Middletown: Wesleyan University Press, 1988.

Reid-Vazquez, Michele. *The Year of the Lash: Free People of Color in Cuba and the Nineteenth-Century Atlantic World*. Athens: University of Georgia Press, 2011.

Reid-Vazquez, Michele. "Tensions of Race, Gender and Midwifery in Colonial Cuba," in *Africans to Colonial Spanish America: Expanding the Diaspora*, Rachel O'Toole, Sherwin Bryant, and Ben Vinson III, editors, 186–205. Chicago, IL: University of Illinois Press, 2012.

Reid-Vazquez, Michele. "Formidable Rebels: Enslaved and Free Women of Color in Cuba's Conspiracy of La Escalera, 1843–1844," in *Breaking the Chains, Making the Nation: The Black Cuban Fight for Freedom and Equality, 1812–1912*, Aisha Finch and Fannie Rushing, 158–177. Baton Rouge: Louisiana State University Press, 2019.

Teresa, Prado-Torreira, *Mambisas: Rebel Women in Nineteenth-Century Cuba*. Gainesville: University Press of Florida, 2005.

18

Black women and Africana abolitionism

Nneka D. Dennie

Over the course of four centuries, approximately 12.5 million people were forcibly removed from the African continent and sold into slavery.[1] Countries including Portugal, Spain, Britain, France, and the Netherlands relied on stolen labor, knowledge, and skills as they established new colonies. Slavery and white supremacy became the basis of colonial life as complex systems emerged to solidify slavery in the New World. On the Caribbean island of Barbados, for instance, the Slave Code of 1661 instituted brutal punishments, like being burned in the face, for enslaved people who were found guilty of crimes. Meanwhile, whites enjoyed legal protection for inflicting violence on the enslaved.[2] In 1662, a Virginia law established that children born to Black women would inherit their mothers' status as free or enslaved.[3] As such, Black women's reproductive labor became a market commodity. In 1685, the French government implemented the Code Noir, a detailed set of regulations that applied to all French American colonies. One restriction, presumably intended to quell slave rebellions, prohibited enslaved persons belonging to different enslavers from gathering at any time of day. Violators would be whipped, branded, or killed.[4] Throughout the Americas, Black people had common experiences of enslavement.

Despite similarities in how Black exploitation functioned across continents, differences in regional slave systems emerged based on factors such as demographics, death rates, the natural environment, and demand for colonial exports. Additional distinctions existed regarding the types of labor that the enslaved performed, the gendered division of labor, the rigidity of racial stratification, cultural norms, and the legal protections that were available to Black people, regardless of how unreliable those protections were. Given that slavery was not identical throughout the New World, abolition necessarily adopted multiple forms as well.

One such form was a Pan-Africanist process that I term "Africana abolitionism." I define Africana abolitionism as a shared set of practices that African-diasporic people deployed to dismantle systems of slavery throughout North America, the Caribbean, and Latin America. Africana abolitionism sought to eradicate not simply regional systems of slavery but also racialized epistemologies that justified the enslavement of African-descended peoples and Black people's global subjugation. Africana abolitionism bridges the particular and the universal by offering a framework for understanding how localized abolitionist movements facilitated global emancipation.

This chapter first describes how Africana abolitionism can enrich the study of abolitionist movements by interrogating two questions: How might we understand abolitionism differently if we decenter colonizers and the roles that European nations played in undoing slavery? How might we understand abolitionism differently if we frame the movement's internationalism not in relation to colonial powers but in relation to Black people's shared visions for and approaches to freedom? Next, it highlights Black women's participation in three arenas of Africana abolitionism: slave revolts, the Black press, and lecture circuits. To conclude, it describes how framing local and national struggles against slavery as Africana abolitionism can allow us to reevaluate the roots of Black transnationalism.

Africana abolitionism

Black people's actions, whether conscious or unintentional, and whether they spurred material change or held symbolic value, were the driving force of the international abolitionist movement. Viewing these actions as Africana abolitionism allows us to consider how informal and decentralized modes of resistance became absorbed into the international abolitionist imaginary. Rather than casting enslaved people as the inspiration for abolition and colonial powers as abolitionists who combated slavery on an international stage, Africana abolitionism allows us to account for how the actions and worldviews of enslaved Black people and free Blacks bolstered transnational abolition.

Because the slave trade developed internationally, so too did abolitionist movements. Abolitionism was international in scope not only because of its impacts on trade and foreign policy but also because abolitionists understood that they needed support across national boundaries. As Manisha Sinha explains in *The Slave's Cause: A History of Abolition*: "Black abolitionists insisted that their struggle receive an international hearing."[5] American abolitionists participated in European lecture tours and published their work abroad in attempts to garner sympathy for their cause. They also aligned the abolition of slavery with other progressive causes, including that of European working classes (Sinha 2016, 351).

As various scholars demonstrate in *Women's Rights and Transatlantic Antislavery in the Era of Emancipation*, feminists throughout the United States, France, Germany, and Britain – countries that were among the world's foremost colonial powers – framed their advocacy for women's rights in relation to slavery.[6] Anti-slavery activism offered some European women a first foray into the public sphere. This was also true of the white American women who organized the Seneca Falls women's rights meeting in 1848 when they were denied a voice in the international anti-slavery movement. By traveling, publishing, and speaking abroad, African American women like Mary Ann Shadd Cary and Sarah Parker Remond simultaneously criticized slavery and opposed racialized, gendered norms that restricted Black women's mobilization. As women participated in the abolitionist movement, they situated themselves as transnational figures.

Many historians have described how interracial coalitions of activists turned to international audiences to foster abolitionist sentiments abroad.[7] Scholars have also discussed the role that European actors played in campaigning against slavery. Audrey Fisch, for example, explains how white activist J. B. Estlin distributed Frederick Douglass's narrative in Britain "as part of a larger effort to inform the English public about American slavery and raise international support for American abolition" (Fisch 2009, 3). I take such contributions as my starting point for theorizing Africana abolitionism. The wealth of research on how abolition involved a diverse cast of actors who mobilized on a global stage has created two particular opportunities to expand the historiography of the international abolitionist movement.

First, existing scholarship can more fully investigate how empire shapes historians' conceptualization of internationalism within the abolitionist movement. Historians have successfully shown how a dynamic interplay of forces precipitated the downfall of transatlantic slavery. However, in examining the international abolitionist movement, some scholars have overemphasized white activists' efforts to influence how imperial power is manifested in the Americas. Consequently, their discussions of international abolitionism center the colonial powers that were responsible for the systematization of Black subjugation. Rather than framing internationalism as a liberation strategy that African-diasporic peoples used to confront their oppression, scholarship on abolitionism portrays internationalism as a strategy that predominantly white actors used not to redistribute power but to reinforce colonialism in service of abolition. For example, J. R. Oldfield writes that white British activist Thomas Clarkson "established important links with French abolitionists" and "reinforced his identification with the French Revolution" after visiting Paris in 1789 (Oldfield 2013, 37–9). Oldfield continues: "strangely, [Clarkson] seems to have made little effort to cultivate American abolitionists … Clarkson showed little interest in America or in the potential of American abolitionism" (Oldfield 2013, 39). Given that colonialism lay at the heart of slavery, locating colonialism at the core of abolitionist internationalism neglects how Black abolitionists advanced their own brand of internationalism.

Second, scholarship on Black abolitionists' internationalism frequently centers African American men. Historians and literary critics have deftly illustrated how Black abolitionists participated in global activism.[8] Yet, their discussions of Black internationalism rarely encapsulate how it was imagined and practiced by women and by activists outside the United States. While scholars have published texts on African American women abolitionists' internationalism, such works generally feature a single woman.[9] Furthermore, scholarship on Black abolitionist women's internationalism focuses on travel, speeches, and essays – forms of abolition that were more accessible to the Black elite and Black men than to the rest of the Black population. If we consider how abolitionist internationalism existed beyond formal, male-dominated modes of resisting slavery, this can reveal new entry points for examining Black women's abolitionist internationalism.

This chapter therefore centers Africana abolitionism as an alternative framework for enhancing our understanding of the international abolitionist movement. Black women's participation in three forms of opposition to slavery – slave revolts, the Black press, and lecture circuits – highlights how Africana abolitionism manifested in North America, the Caribbean, and Latin America. Each strategy demonstrates how Africana abolitionism encompasses Black people's internationally recurring liberation strategies, their conscious appeals to transnational abolition, and the global impacts of regional Black resistance. Slave revolts were the most consistent form of abolition throughout the Americas. Their reappearance across geographic boundaries showcases enslaved people's shared commitment to their liberation. The Black press, comprising Black-owned publications and the work of Black writers/editors, facilitated the transnational exchange of ideas. It provided sites for Black abolitionists to practice and publicly debate the merits of internationalism. Similarly, by lecturing to coed, interracial, and international audiences, abolitionists embodied the liberatory promises of their work. I emphasize women's participation in these three forms of resistance not because they were the only Africana abolitionists, but to normalize their participation in the international abolitionist movement.

Slave revolts

Violent resistance to slavery was as common as slavery itself.[10] Individual slave revolts belonged to a larger pattern of global anti-slavery mobilization. Slave revolts throughout the Americas did not exist in a vacuum; it was not unusual for reports of rebellions abroad to circulate to other countries. Enslavers in the United States and the Caribbean, for example, feared that news of the Haitian Revolution would incite local insurrections.[11] Slave revolts may be understood as a form of Africana abolitionism because they occurred throughout the New World, influenced international debates about slavery and abolition, and generated transnational racial solidarity. Such was the case with a thwarted slave revolt in Cuba.

In 1818, British businessman Joseph Marryat published a pro-slavery pamphlet about the causes of slave revolts and the effects of emancipation. Writing that "Domestic conspirators were also aided by foreign emissaries," Marryat claims that "natives of St. Domingo" attempted to provoke rebellions in Barbados and Cuba.[12] He asserts:

> In 1812, a conspiracy was set on foot in Cuba, by some emissaries from St. Domingo, who … contrived to evade the vigilance of the Spanish Government, and to enter into the city of the Havannah undiscovered. The slaves readily listened to their instigations, and engaged in the enterprize [*sic*] of obtaining their freedom by the assassination of their masters.
>
> *(Marryat 1818, 17)*

Marryat places responsibility for the intended rebellion with Haitian ringleaders. His preoccupation with foreign influence on enslaved people reflects enslavers' anxieties about the international impact of the Haitian Revolution. Regardless of whether such fears were substantiated or baseless, they illustrate that knowledge of international slave revolts circulated among enslavers and was thought to be accessible to the enslaved.

As Marryat describes the intended uprising, he claims that a Black woman informed the Spanish governor of the revolt, thus foiling the rebels' plans. According to Marryat, the woman "cohabited with one of the leading conspirators" and "felt alarmed lest she should be abandoned for a white rival." He concludes that "her jealousy became so violent, that she determined to give information of the plot to the Spanish Governor, only stipulating for the safety of her paramour" (Marryat 1818, 17). Marryat's discussion of Black women's fear and jealousy reinforces stereotypes that often preclude Black women from being understood as abolitionists. As Camilia Cowling explains, "Whether marronage, violent crime, or violent uprisings are the focus, we tend to find fewer women mentioned" in accounts of self-manumission.[13] Likewise, Marryat frames the unnamed woman as a bystander whose emotions trumped her desire for freedom. He ultimately relegates Black women to the peripheries of violent resistance to slavery.

Marryat's anti-abolitionist text contains insights about the international significance of slave revolts. First, it shows that enslavers feared the possibility of African-diasporic peoples collectively resisting slavery. Second, it highlights how pro-slavery advocates used slave revolts to influence public sentiment about slavery and abolition. Third, it suggests that enslaved and formerly enslaved peoples at times forged international connections in their efforts to abolish slavery.

Contrary to Marryat's analysis, women throughout the diaspora participated in violent struggles against slavery. In her discussion of women's roles in an 1843 rebellion in Cuba, Aisha K. Finch explains:

> traditional narratives of slave insurgency implicitly recount not only the collective passage from passivity to defiance, but also the passage from "slavehood to manhood." … Together the highly visible male icon and the masculinized rank-in-file become pivotal to the slave rebellion's conceptual existence and therefore part of the collective inheritance of slave rebellion histories.[14]

Despite masculinized portrayals of slave revolts, scholars have documented how women facilitated rebellions by spreading news of impending revolts, securing weapons, and taking up arms. Bernard Moitt explains that women joined a rebel army during an 1812 slave revolt in the French colony of Guadeloupe, while Rebecca Hall describes how women provided the impetus for revolts on slave ships; in a 1712 New York rebellion; and in an 1812 Virginia uprising that she terms "Celia's Conspiracy."[15] From the inception of the transatlantic slave trade, women were eager to challenge its existence.

The Black press

Black-owned publications, Black writers, and Black editors were vital to the international abolitionist movement. The Black press exemplifies the global significance of Africana abolitionism because it offered a forum for Black people to build community and for Black thinkers to shape discourse on racial oppression. Some newspapers, like the *Liberator*, were interracial publications that amplified the voices of Black writers. Others, like the *North Star*, targeted Black audiences and granted greater autonomy to Black writers and editors. Such was the case when Mary Ann Shadd Cary, an African American abolitionist and suffragist, founded the *Provincial Freeman*.

The United States Congress passed the Fugitive Slave Act in 1850, which ruled that African Americans who escaped slavery could be captured and returned to their enslavers, including in states where slavery was outlawed. This legislation endangered free Blacks who had never been enslaved because they were subject to heightened scrutiny, particularly if they could not prove their status as free. After 1850, fugitives from slavery and free Black people increasingly emigrated to Canada, some famously ushered across the border by self-emancipated abolitionist Harriet Tubman, a "conductor" on the Underground Railroad, who may not have been literate but would have accessed news from the Black press. The *Provincial Freeman* catered to emigrants like Tubman in addition to African Americans who remained in the United States. The newspaper regularly featured articles intended to facilitate the transition to Canada and articles supporting abolition. As Dann J. Broyld notes, Tubman and other new arrivals to Canada were occasionally disillusioned to discover that racism did, indeed, persist in the then-British colony.[16] The *Provincial Freeman* and Cary herself extolled the virtues of life in Canada rather than grappling with how the British crown was embroiled in the ongoing oppression of Black people.

Cary emigrated to Canada in 1853 and launched her newspaper shortly thereafter, making her the first Black woman newspaper editor in North America and the first woman editor in Canada. She published the *Provincial Freeman* in the United States and Canada. The newspaper was transnational in its publishing practices, content, and audience. Cary's written work and editorship of the newspaper exemplify how the Black press enacted Africana abolitionism. Like other abolitionists, and despite Britain's lengthy participation in the slave trade, Cary encouraged African Americans to leverage British influence in hopes that international pressure on the United States would advance abolition. However, she mobilized Africana abolitionism as she explained how emigration would promote abolition and pan-Africanist solidarity.

In 1852, Cary asserted that in the British West Indies, "Much has been done by the colored people of those islands to improve their condition, and much more may be done conjointly with emigrants from the States."[17] Two years later, Cary established that the *Provincial Freeman* "wish[es] to help create a sentiment in Canada, and out of Canada, that shall tell against Slavery."[18] An 1856 editorial encouraging readers to attend an upcoming emigration convention also explained that emigrationists "would be enabled to do Anti-Slavery work more effectually" by leaving the United States.[19] For Cary, emigration was intimately tied to abolition and transnational Black liberation.

In addition to facilitating transnational movement, the Black press galvanized the international abolitionist movement by publicizing Black resistance abroad. Just as slave revolts, whether real or imagined, shaped international attitudes towards slavery, so too did Black uprisings, whether they occurred pre- or post-emancipation. Symbols of Black resistance were vital to fostering Africana abolitionism throughout the diaspora. On January 28, 1842, the *Liberator* reported on a deadly uprising against police in Kingston, Jamaica. Although slavery was abolished in Jamaica in 1834, the *Liberator* framed this rebellion as aligned with the struggle against American slavery. An observer who witnessed the riot writes that on December 22, 1841, "a crowd of women, children, and half grown boys were assembled, and the women began to throw stones and broken bottles at the police, who were obliged to run for their lives."[20] The observer portrays women as the heart of the revolt, explaining that the crowd was further "incited by the gestures and inflammatory language of the women." To American abolitionist audiences, this uprising highlighted the global nature of enslaved and Black oppression. It was not simply a revolt in Jamaica but an inspirational symbol of resistance that abolitionists embraced around the world. As this insurrection demonstrates, Black women's local mobilization had international implications – some of which were unpredictable but nevertheless positioned Black women at the center of abolitionist internationalism.

Lecture circuits

Lecture circuits enabled the autonomous creation and circulation of an African American public discourse that connected Black speakers with Black audiences. They also granted African American speakers a platform to embody new narratives of race to white audiences, both domestically and internationally. Some Black women lecturers, like Maria Stewart, rose to prominence during the 1830s at a moment when individual women successfully accessed abolitionist circles. As Martha Jones explains, debates about women's participation in African American public culture from the 1840s to the 1860s circumscribed and later reimagined Black women's roles.[21] Against this backdrop, women such as Sojourner Truth fused their abolitionist speeches with religious ministry; Black women insisted on their inclusion in the male-dominated Colored Conventions Movement; and women like Sarah Parker Remond launched international lecture tours.

Remond was born to a free, wealthy family in Massachusetts in 1826. After beginning a European lecture tour in 1859, Remond eventually immigrated to Italy, where she became an obstetrician (Salenius 2016, 2). Having delivered anti-slavery lectures in the United States, Canada, England, Ireland, and Scotland, Remond exemplifies the internationalist impulses that existed among Black abolitionists.

In an 1862 speech delivered in London, "The Negroes in the United States of America," Remond advocates for British intervention to abolish slavery. She asserts that "the negroes and their descendants, whether enslaved or free, desire and need the moral support of Great Britain."[22] After informing listeners that approximately four million persons are enslaved in the United States, Remond implicates Britain in the perpetuation of slavery and attempts to foster camaraderie between the British and the enslaved. She explains that slavery is a transnational system, stating:

> The free operatives of Britain are, in reality, brought into most personal relations with slaves during their daily toil. They manufacture the material which the slaves have produced ... although three thousand miles of ocean roll between the producer and the manufacturer and the operatives.
>
> *(Remond 2017, 89)*

Remond portrayed abolition as an international imperative precisely because the products of slave labor were consumed around the world. Like Cary, who traveled abroad and argued that the British could be allies to the enslaved, Remond emphasized that nothing should "prevent the people of Great Britain from maintaining their position as the friend of the oppressed negro" (Remond 2017, 89). By criticizing British use of items produced through enslavement and emphasizing that British support would be indispensable to African Americans, Remond illuminated how slavery and abolition both depend on transnationalism.

Remond was not alone in embarking on international lecture tours; other notable abolitionists, including Frederick Douglass and William Lloyd Garrison, also employed this strategy. Remond's lectures demonstrate how Black abolitionists practiced and conceptualized internationalism in relation to slavery. As her work shows, lecture circuits are significant to theorizing Africana abolitionism because speakers' self-representation and the content of their lectures privileged Black people's knowledge production in the fight to end slavery.

Conclusion

Examining African-diasporic people's resistance to slavery through the lens of Africana abolitionism allows scholars to reconceptualize abolitionist internationalism. Slave revolts, the Black press, and public lectures were three anti-slavery strategies offering opportunities for Black people to mobilize transnationally. Marryat's pamphlet highlights how enslaved people's real or imagined collaboration with each other across geographic boundaries threatened the slaveholding order, while the *Liberator*'s discussion of a Jamaican riot demonstrates how uprisings offered important symbols of resistance to abolitionists abroad. Shadd Cary's work with the *Provincial Freeman* shows how the Black press provided abolitionists with a discursive space to debate transnationalism and an opportunity to practice transnationalism in their publishing strategies. Likewise, Remond's lecture analyzed slavery's internationalism, while Remond herself cultivated an internationalist presence.

Africana abolitionism includes, but is not limited to, slave revolts, the Black press, and the lecture circuit, and the examples contained in this chapter are not exhaustive. As such, future research might consider how Africana abolitionism was enacted through other anti-slavery strategies, such as filing freedom suits and participating in abolitionist associations. Future scholarship must also continue to explore the gendered dimensions of Africana abolitionism. Examining abolitionist internationalism differently can provide scholars with a new way to understand Black women's activism. While Black women were at times excluded from fully participating in organized abolition because of their race and gender, looking at Black women's Africana abolitionism can reveal how they advanced abolition internationally, albeit by participating in resistance strategies that are infrequently recognized as abolition, such as truancy, maintaining familial bonds, poisoning enslavers, or work stoppages.[23] In addition, future research on Africana abolitionism should evaluate the concept's implications in different eras. How may Africana abolitionism enrich the study of the twentieth-century movements for independence from colonial powers? Might Africana abolitionism influence the ways in which contemporary activists conceptualize and enact prison abolitionism? Answers to these questions, and more, illustrate how abolitionists' struggles against slavery have consistently mirrored Black people's resistance to racism, sexism, and class exploitation.

Further inquiry into how Africana abolitionism manifested in North America, the Caribbean, and Latin America has the capacity to reshape scholars' understandings of the origins and forms of African-diasporic people's transnationalism. It will enable historians to interrogate abolition's internationalism, not to reveal how Black and white abolitionists appealed to colonial powers but to uncover how Black peoples had common understandings of how transnational approaches to abolition would advance their cause. Africana abolitionism allows scholars to consider how Black people adopted a bottom-up approach to eradicating slavery, and it encourages us to center Black people's links to each other rather than white abolitionists' links to colonizers. Africana abolitionism locates internationalism within the African diaspora, not in the long freedom struggle's relationship to colonial powers. By shifting focus towards Africana abolitionism rather than abolitionist internationalism more broadly, scholars can center Black actors and their global struggles against anti-blackness.

Notes

1 Eric Nellis, *Shaping the New World: African Slavery in the Americas, 1500–1888* (Toronto: University of Toronto Press, 2013), 1.
2 Hilary Beckles, *The First Black Slave Society: Britain's "Barbarity Time" in Barbados, 1636–1876* (Kingston: The University of West Indies Press, 2016), 20.
3 Jennifer L. Morgan, *Laboring Women: Reproduction and Gender in New World Slavery* (Philadelphia: University of Pennsylvania Press, 2004), 93.
4 "The Code Noir (1685)", trans. John Garrigus, last modified February 2016, <https://s3.wp.wsu.edu/uploads/ sites/1205/2016/02/code-noir.pdf>.
5 Manisha Sinha, *The Slave's Cause: A History of Abolition* (New Haven: Yale University Press, 2016), 340.
6 Kathryn Kish Sklar and James Brewer Stewart, eds., *Women's Rights and Transatlantic Antislavery in the Era of Emancipation* (New Haven: Yale University Press, 2007).
7 J. R. Oldfield, *Transatlantic Abolition in the Age of Revolution: An International History of Anti-Slavery, c. 1787–1820* (Cambridge: Cambridge University Press, 2013); Audrey Fisch, *American Slaves in Victorian England: Abolitionist Politics in Popular Literature and Culture* (Cambridge: Cambridge University Press, 2009).
8 Richard J. M. Blackett, *Building an Antislavery Wall: Black Americans in the Atlantic Abolitionists Movement, 1830–1860* (Baton Rouge: Louisiana State University Press, 2002); Ivy G. Wilson, "On Native Ground: Transnationalism, Frederick Douglass, and 'The Heroic Slave,'" *PMLA* 121, no. 2 (2006): 453–68.
9 Sirpa Salenius, *An Abolitionist Abroad: Sarah Parker Remond in Cosmopolitan Europe* (Amherst: University of Massachusetts Press, 2016); Jane Rhodes, *Mary Ann Shadd Cary: The Black Press and Protest in the Nineteenth Century* (Bloomington: Indiana University Press, 1999).
10 Kellie Carter Jackson, *Force and Freedom: Black Abolitionists and the Politics of Violence* (Philadelphia: University of Pennsylvania Press, 2019).
11 Ada Ferrer, *Freedom's Mirror: Cuba and Haiti in the Age of Revolution* (New York: Cambridge University Press, 2014).
12 Joseph Marryat, *More Thoughts Still on the State of the West India Colonies, and the Proceedings of the African Institution: With Observations on the Speech of James Stephen, Esq. at the Annual Meeting of that Society, held on the 26th of March, 1817* (London: Hughes & Baynes, 1818), 16.
13 Camilia Cowling, *Conceiving Freedom: Women of Color, Gender, and the Abolition of Slavery in Havana and Rio de Janeiro* (Chapel Hill: University of North Carolina Press, 2013), 51.
14 Aisha K. Finch, *Rethinking Slave Rebellion in Cuba: La Escalera and the Insurgencies of 1841–1844* (Chapel Hill: University of North Carolina Press, 2015), 142.
15 Bernard Moitt, "Slave Women and Resistance in the French Caribbean," in *More than Chattel: Black Women and Slavery in the Americas*, eds. David Barry Gaspar and Darlene Clark Hine (Bloomington: Indiana University Press, 1996), 242; Rebecca Hall, "Not Killing Me Softly: African American Women, Slave Revolts, and Historical Constructions of Racialized Gender," *Freedom Center Journal* 1, no. 2 (2009): 5, 18, 30.
16 Dann J. Broyld, "Harriet Tubman: Transnationalism and the Land of a Queen in the Late Antebellum," *Meridians: Feminism, Race, Transnationalism* 12, no. 2 (2014).
17 Mary Ann Shadd Cary, *A Plea for Emigration, or Notes of Canada West, in its Moral, Social, and Political Aspect: with Suggestions Respecting Mexico, West Indies, and Vancouver's Island, for the Information of Colored Emigrants* (Detroit: George W. Pattison, 1852), 37.
18 Mary Ann Shadd Cary, "Anti-Slavery Relations," *Provincial Freeman*, March 25, 1854.
19 Mary Ann Shadd Cary, "The Emigration Convention," *Provincial Freeman*, July 5, 1856.

20 "The Jamaica Riot," *Liberator*, January 28, 1842.
21 Martha Jones, *All Bound up Together: The Woman Question in African American Public Culture, 1830–1900* (Chapel Hill: University of North Carolina Press, 2007), 7.
22 Sarah Parker Remond, "The Negroes in the United States of America," in *The Portable Nineteenth-Century African American Women Writers*, eds. Hollis Robbins and Henry Louis Gates, Jr. (New York: Penguin Books, 2017), 87.
23 Stephanie Camp, *Closer to Freedom: Enslaved Women and Everyday Resistance in the Plantation South* (Chapel Hill: University of North Carolina Press, 2004).

References

Beckles, Hilary. *The First Black Slave Society: Britain's "Barbarity Time" in Barbados, 1636–1876*. Kingston: The University of West Indies Press, 2016.
Blackett, Richard J.M. *Building an Antislavery Wall: Black Americans in the Atlantic Abolitionists Movement, 1830–1860*. Baton Rouge: Louisiana State University Press, 2002.
Broyld, Dann J. "Harriet Tubman: Transnationalism and the Land of a Queen in the Late Antebellum." *Meridians: Feminism, Race, Transnationalism* 12, no. 2 (2014): 78–98.
Camp, Stephanie. *Closer to Freedom: Enslaved Women and Everyday Resistance in the Plantation South*. Chapel Hill: University of North Carolina Press, 2004.
"The Code Noir (1685)". Translated by John Garrigus. Last modified February 2016. https://s3.wp.wsu .edu/uploads/ sites/1205/2016/02/ code-noir.pdf.
Cowling, Camilia. *Conceiving Freedom: Women of Color, Gender, and the Abolition of Slavery in Havana and Rio de Janeiro*. Chapel Hill: University of North Carolina Press, 2013.
Ferrer, Ada. *Freedom's Mirror: Cuba and Haiti in the Age of Revolution*. New York: Cambridge University Press, 2014.
Finch, Aisha K. *Rethinking Slave Rebellion in Cuba: La Escalera and the Insurgencies of 1841–1844*. Chapel Hill: University of North Carolina Press, 2015.
Fisch, Audrey. *American Slaves in Victorian England: Abolitionist Politics in Popular Literature and Culture*. Cambridge: Cambridge University Press, 2009.
Hall, Rebecca. "Not Killing Me Softly: African American Women, Slave Revolts, and Historical Constructions of Racialized Gender." *Freedom Center Journal* 1, no. 2 (2009): 1–44.
Jackson, Kellie Carter. *Force and Freedom: Black Abolitionists and the Politics of Violence*. Philadelphia: University of Pennsylvania Press, 2019.
Jones, Martha. *All Bound up Together: The Woman Question in African American Public Culture, 1830–1900*. Chapel Hill: University of North Carolina Press, 2007.
Moitt, Bernard. "Slave Women and Resistance in the French Caribbean." In *More Than Chattel: Black Women and Slavery in the Americas*, edited by David Barry Gaspar and Darlene Clark Hine, 239–258. Bloomington: Indiana University Press, 1996.
Nellis, Eric. *Shaping the New World: African Slavery in the Americas, 1500–1888*. Toronto: University of Toronto Press, 2013.
Oldfield, J. R. *Transatlantic Abolition in the Age of Revolution: An International History of Anti-Slavery, c. 1787–1820*. Cambridge: Cambridge University Press, 2013.
Remond, Sarah Parker. "The Negroes in the United States of America." In *The Portable Nineteenth-Century African American Women Writers*, edited by Hollis Robbins and Henry Louis Gates, 87–90. New York: Penguin Books, 2017.
Rhodes, Jane. *Mary Ann Shadd Cary: The Black Press and Protest in the Nineteenth Century*. Bloomington: Indiana University Press, 1999.
Salenius, Sirpa. *An Abolitionist Abroad: Sarah Parker Remond in Cosmopolitan Europe*. Amherst: University of Massachusetts Press, 2016.
Sinha, Manisha. *The Slave's Cause: A History of Abolition*. New Haven: Yale University Press, 2016.
Sklar, Kathryn Kish and James Brewer Stewart, eds. *Women's Rights and Transatlantic Antislavery in the Era of Emancipation*. New Haven: Yale University Press, 2007.
Wilson, Ivy G. "On Native Ground: Transnationalism, Frederick Douglass, and 'The Heroic Slave'." *PMLA* 121, no. 2 (2006): 453–468.

Primary sources

Cary, Mary Ann Shadd. *A Plea for Emigration, or Notes of Canada West, in its Moral, Social, and Political Aspect: with Suggestions Respecting Mexico, West Indies, and Vancouver's Island, for the Information of Colored Emigrants.* Detroit: George W. Pattison, 1852.

Cary, Mary Ann Shadd. "Anti-Slavery Relations." *Provincial Freeman*, March 25, 1854.

Cary, Mary Ann Shadd. "The Emigration Convention." *Provincial Freeman*, July 5, 1856.

"The Jamaica Riot." *Liberator*, January 28, 1842.

Marryat, Joseph. *More Thoughts Still on the State of the West India Colonies, and the Proceedings of the African Institution: With Observations on the Speech of James Stephen, Esq. at the Annual Meeting of That Society, Held on the 26th of March, 1817.* London: Hughes & Baynes, 1818.

19

Ethiopia's woke women
The nineteenth century re-imagines Africa

Barbara McCaskill

"Ethiopia shall soon stretch out her hands unto God" (Psa. 68:31) was a biblical verse invoked by nineteenth-century African American women from Maria W. Stewart to Frances Ellen Watkins Harper. It expressed the hope for Emancipation, for the redemption that awaited those who had suffered and sorrowed. It foreshadowed the retribution in store for those who had kidnapped, sold, and enslaved other human beings.[1] In nineteenth-century American culture, images of Africa, like public perceptions about African American women, were both sympathetic and cruel, connoting oppositional and often absurd meanings. Africa was imagined as menacing and wild, a burden to the orderly, Christian West, or as a lush, uncultivated, Edenic paradise relieved of civilization's inhibitions and constrictions.

Influential literature anthologies edited by Beverly Guy-Sheftall, Teresa C. Zackodnik, and Hollis Robbins and Henry Louis Gates, Jr. have depicted a vibrant literary scene in which Black women opined about Africa and themes of race, gender, class, and community.[2] Generative research by Andreá N. Williams, Shirley Moody-Turner, Joycelyn Moody, Noliwe M. Rooks, Sarah Ruffing Robbins, Eric Gardner, Kimberly Blockett, and Crystal J. Lucky has been attuned to nineteenth-century Black women's submissions to and editorships of periodicals and serials. Such scholars have mined local and regional archives housing Black women's print productions, and they have paid attention to sacred and secular spaces as sites of Black women's art.[3] This chapter examines how and why the later nineteenth-century writings of Gertrude Emily Hicks Bustill Mossell (1855–1948) and Frances Ellen Watkins Harper (1825–1911), and additional Black women's literary productions, press back against enslavers' and colonizers' caricatures of Africa and African people. At times they may seem to buy into stereotypes, yet they also invoke the continent to express the specific conditions of Black women's lives: their relationships to their family members and communities; their sense of themselves as intellectuals, educators, and advocates; and their roles as citizens and leaders.

Competing notions of Africa in nineteenth-century Black women's writings and speech

African American women writing after the Reconstruction telegraphed contradictory messages about Africa. They reflected antipodal attitudes towards the continent held throughout the United States and Britain. From the American antislavery movement, to Emancipation and Reconstruction, to the post-Reconstruction decades, they bundled oppositional meanings in their thoughts about Africa: intellect and savagery, authority and surrogacy, fecundity and lack, potentiality and despair.

During the antislavery movement, many antebellum African Americans had embraced the idea of repatriation to Africa in light of a nation that seemed at first too quick to roll back the freedpeople's protections and too committed, after Emancipation, to maintaining an uncompensated, involuntary, abused labor force. They were receptive to Black leaders such as Martin Henry Freeman (1826–89), president of Liberia College, who advised them to come to the continent. They could "bring up their children to be men and not creeping things."[4] Like Huck Finn lighting out to freedom in the West at the conclusion of his *Adventures* to escape his Aunt Sally's cloying attempts to civilize him (Twain 1912, 405), they were all for sailing east to Liberia's vistas of land, liberty, and self-governance in order to escape America's racism and anti-Black violence.

Founded in 1817, the American Colonization Society (ACS) kitted out voyages of free or manumitted African Americans to Monrovia, Liberia. Yet its motives were a mixed bag. Anxieties about bloody revolts of the enslaved against enslavers, and fears that racial intermarriage would corrode pure white bloodlines and diminish their physical and intellectual vitality, inspired the ACS to action as much as benevolence.[5] Matthew Spooner writes that its "rhetoric and premise – that black Americans do not belong in this country – were overtly racist and deserving of the derision … heaped upon the ACS since its inception." The ACS, according to Spooner, reflected discordant strains that pitted a growing free Black populace against free white Americans and gestured towards gradual abolition but were ineffective in achieving it.[6] These tensions notwithstanding, by the eve of the Civil War, an estimated 120,000 Black people had made the trek to Liberia.[7]

Replacing this goal of departure with the resolution to stay put, a discourse about the American Revolution appeared in African Americans' antislavery literature. While unable to prove direct connections between family members and the Revolution, African American women such as Harriet A. Jacobs (1813–97) cited this war to demonstrate their people's hard-earned place here in the United States where they had fought it.[8] Maria W. Stewart (1803–79), opposed to colonization, instead reminded African American audiences that "we sprang from a scientific people." Addressing Black women frequently, exuberantly, as "daughters of Africa" and "Afric's daughters," she urged them to aspire to public roles as intellectuals and educators.[9]

Similar crosscurrents coursed during and after antislavery days, from abolition to Emancipation to Reconstruction, as the project of countering negative racial policies, attitudes, and stereotyping continued. Black women and men who identified as patriotic, Protestant Americans claimed without irony two opinions at once. They assented to the idea that Africans would benefit from Christianity and other edifying, civilizing effects of Western culture, even as they proudly documented examples of Africans' achievements in governance, commerce, the arts, and the military. Their lack of concern about these blazing incongruities may be traced to their exposure, along with white Christians, to religious dogma and instruction that centered the theme of God's unconditional love yet supported white supremacist attitudes predicated upon a belief in the inferior and superior races of humanity. White abolitionist Christians such as Harriet Beecher Stowe (1811–96), for example, could argue for the end of slavery while in the same breath insisting that free African Americans were ultimately better off and perhaps more temperamentally suited to living apart from white people.[10]

African American women writers who at once admired and patronized Africa and Africans thus did so in the context of an educational or religious training inflected by such ideas. They also attempted to subvert them. By acknowledging some need for Africa's improvement requiring the West's intervention, some common ideological ground they shared with white British and American audiences and readers, such as evangelizing the continent and rooting out so-called superstitions, Black women gambled on winning a more favorable outcome in the long game of racial politics. Perhaps they would be heard and taken seriously if they enlisted white women in their campaigns against voter suppression, lynchings, the under-resourcing of Black schools and hospitals, inadequate housing and healthcare, and other signals of how U.S. society devalued them.

A through-line that both valorized and condescended to Africa and Africans continued among post-Reconstruction African American women writers. As the first president of the National Association of Colored Women, Mary Church Terrell (1863–1954) invited white suffragettes to "judge" Black women "by the depths" which they had overcome – i.e., an African past – to obtain education and other opportunities. At the same time, she redefined those "depths" by lauding the formidable intellect of the poet Phillis Wheatley (1753–84).[11] "On Being Brought from Africa to America" (1773) had expressed Wheatley's gratitude for her spiritual salvation while throwing shade on those so-called Christians who had kidnapped Africans like her into American bondage.[12] Terrell emulated Wheatley's double-edged strategy: she acknowledged white women's assistance while advancing Black women as capable daughters of Africa who had earned their plaudits.

How could Black women writers and speakers maintain such longstanding contradictions about Africa while at the same time resisting stereotypes and re-imagining different meanings? Slavery and then imperialism, in the United States and Great Britain, generated forces that were sympathetic to Africans and the African Diaspora, not always for flattering reasons, or else outright opposed to them. Black women writers and speakers responded with fierceness to the opposition but resisted elements of paternalism and colonialism to varying degrees. Not only did the strategy of forging alliances with white institutions and individuals figure into this calculus and explain such contradictions; so, too, did the pressures of partnering to create social change while serving cultural expectations that prioritized their roles in the domestic sphere. In their writings during the Reconstruction and post-Reconstruction eras and at the height of nineteenth-century American and British expansionism, Gertrude Bustill Mossell and Frances Ellen Watkins Harper offer examples of how such racial and gender politics informed Black women's perspectives on Africa. Mossell's commitment to Black women's public service that centers maternity and marriage is evident in how she defines Africa as both powerful and in need of rescue. Harper breaks more fully from this quandary, recasting the continent and its peoples as symbols of liberation and autonomy.

Africa, maternity, and patriarchy

A literature review by T. McCants Stewart in the October 1885 *New York Freeman* praised a sister periodical, the *A.M.E. Christian Recorder*, for bringing "to notice" African American literary women "whose learning challenges attention." They included "Cordelia Ray and Frazelia Campbell," "Frances E[llen].W[atkins].Harper, Betty Ashe Lee," and "Gertrude Mossell" (Stewart 1885, 2). A journalist and former teacher, Mossell epitomized the cohort of educated, outspoken, selfless African American women, just one generation removed from enslavement, who participated in the vanguard of turn-of-the-century Black leadership. She was a cultural influencer whom the *Freeman* had tapped to publish a biweekly column on domestic news, "Our Women's Department," which also reported business matters for respectable, engaged, middle-class Black women in the know.[13] Mossell's fellow teacher, Lucy Wilmot Smith (1861–90), lionized her for setting the standard "that sex is no bar to any literary work, that by speaking for themselves women can give the truth about themselves and thereby inspire the confidence of the people."[14]

Mossell's collective biography *The Work of the Afro-American Woman* (1894) was a subversive text because it championed Black women's contributions as writers and artists in resistance to assumptions about them as uneducable, immodest, selfish, and hypersexual.[15] *The Work* centered the aesthetic decisions and critical qualities of a Black woman editor like Mossell within a genre of Reconstruction era and post-Reconstruction race histories dominated by storied Black men. The works of these male authors included the novelist William Wells Brown's *The Black Man: His Antecedents, His Genius, and His Achievements* (1863); the Rev. William J. Simmons' *Men of Mark: Eminent, Progressive, and Rising* (1887); and the anti-lynching activist Rev. Peter Thomas Stanford's three editions of his *Tragedy of the Negro in America* (1897, 1898, 1901).[16] Monroe A. Majors' *Noted Negro Women* and L[awson]. A[ndrew]. Scruggs' *Women of Distinction* honored influential women as well as men.[17] In fact, Majors' and Scruggs' collective biographies may have motivated Mossell to pen her book one year later and to keep in mind the gender politics of being a Black woman artist and leader in patriarchal communities. Anticipating Mossell's balancing act between conforming to roles of motherhood and stretching beyond them, Majors' *Noted Negro Women* admired Mossell for finding "time to do her special work, and to surround her two interesting daughters with the watchful care of a mother's love" (Majors 1893, 130). Scruggs' *Women of Distinction* similarly noted the "literary work" Mossell juggled in spite of having "little time" to complete it because of her responsibilities to her daughters and husband (Scruggs 1893, 25).

As Joanne Braxton astutely concludes in her Introduction to *The Work* for the groundbreaking Schomburg Library of Nineteenth-Century Black Women Writers, Mossell exemplifies the perspective of a "prototypical black feminist" (Braxton 1988, xxix). According to Braxton, Mossell's selections of representative Black women demonstrate "strict adherence to a code of race conscious womanhood and black Christian motherhood" and deference to "masculine authority," while making space for a mutuality with Black men in marriage and public and political affairs (xxix, xxviii). Such partnerships after the Reconstruction between many African American men and women ran counter to how many white women were subordinated to men in their households.

The paratext of *The Work* bears out Braxton's argument. Mossell thanks both women and men who have helped with her book: such collective networks advocated as effectively for Black people as the singular endeavors she describes. Similar rhetoric is evident in her short letter to the editor for the January 5, 1893, *A.M.E. Christian Recorder*, published in what Frances E. W. Harper dubbed "the women's era."[18] Her letter both demurred to conventional ideas about Black women's public and domestic roles and opened vistas for different conceptions about their leadership. In "Will the Negro Share the Glory That Awaits Africa?" Mossell supported A.M.E. Bishop Henry McNeal Turner's project to convert people on the African continent from their perceived idolatry to Christianity.[19] His mission was the culmination of a decades-long campaign in which African American evangelists had traveled to African shores.

For example, during the Civil War, the fugitive slave William Craft (c. 1824–1900) had accepted a commission from British Quakers and abolitionists to travel to Dahomey, negotiate an end to the internal slave trade, and convert its citizens to Christianity.[20] During the Reconstruction, the formerly enslaved Baptist minister Rev. Peter Thomas Stanford had left Canada West's chilly climes to proselytize up and down England and promote his scheme for building schools to prepare African Canadian youth for missionary work saving African and Asian souls.[21] In 1893, as the curtain opened on the women's era, the formerly enslaved Mrs. Amanda Smith (1837–1915), her body "broken down in health," nevertheless uplifted souls by publishing her memoir of spreading the gospel in Liberia and Sierra Leone, both colonized by England and settled by freed slaves.[22] Craft, Stanford, and Smith are representative examples of Black evangelists who shared an affinity for Africa and Africans based on similar histories of cultural and linguistic erasure, geographical displacement, the trauma of racism, and creative resilience and resistance. They had envisioned a partnership between Africans and African Americans to spur the economic growth, political autonomy, and artistic blossoming of both constituencies. Yet, their correspondence and letters back to England, Canada, and the United States also projected their biases in favor of the veracity and superiority of Christianity compared with what was frowned upon as ignorance and myth in African religions.

Africa, freedom, and will

This criticism of the continent as a morally diminished place, buttressed at its peril against the one, true religion of Christianity, permeated nineteenth-century Black women's submissions to the *A.M.E. Christian Recorder* and other Afro-Protestant print productions. For instance, in a poem the *Recorder* published titled "America's First Cargo of Slaves," Katherine Davis Chapman Tillman memorialized the 1619 kidnapping of Africans to Jamestown during the transatlantic slave trade. She accused their enslavers of profiting from the uncompensated labor of these "lost souls" while preventing their exposure to "Christian light."[23] As another example of such discourse, in the Parsons, Kansas, *Blade*, the correspondent "Mrs. Pryor" commended the altruism and sacrifices of Black women who funded schools and orphanages and raised money for foreign missions "dispensing the gospel among the heathen."[24] Sarah Jane Early's address, "The Organized Efforts of the Colored Women of the South to Improve Their Condition," similarly stated how the efforts of A.M.E. church women helped uplift the impoverished, "benighted heathen" of West Africa.[25] Their religious auxiliaries took as guidance the New Testament parable of the widow's mite (Mark 12:41–4, Luke 21:1–4), in which the charity of the wealthy is overshadowed by the generosity of the destitute, a widow who owns less but offers more. By contributing small sums that added up to large donations to overseas missions, African American women demonstrated the modesty expected of their gender even as they engaged in global philanthropy.

Mossell frames her letter supporting missions in Africa with images of maternity that affirm received notions of African American women's proper social roles. Her "first sight of a native African," she writes after her letter's opening paragraph, is of "ten native African boys" introduced on-stage at an event on the historically Black campus of Lincoln University. "I loved those children from that day," she enthuses. She reports that "[y]ear after year" she reconnected with them until each and every one had matriculated from Lincoln. After three paragraphs encouraging the magazine's readers to rally in support of "uniting America and Africa" based on mutual Christian identity, Mossell returns to the children. She encourages individual A.M.E. churches to establish pen pal programs that connect their youth to "one little native boy or girl." "To the women and children," she underscores, "it would be but a widening of the loving influences they throw around their own home circle" (Mossell 1893,1).

This imagery of nurturance and compassion is countervailed by a masculinist rhetoric of discovery and domination. Her correspondence thus positions Black women's public writing as acceptable public advocacy as long as it sanctions direction from men and privileges women's domestic responsibilities. Yet, her missive appears against the cultural backdrop of late nineteenth-century African American women seizing national and international platforms for their voices and opinions to be heard beyond their homes and communities. In 1893 and 1894, Ida B. Wells would go global with her anti-lynching campaign by embarking on a two-year tour speaking and fundraising in England.[26] A few years later, in 1896, the National Association of Colored Women would form out of the merger of regional and local women's groups.[27] By 1893, the year of her letter's publication, Mossell, too, would have been familiar to the *Recorder's* audience not only as a correspondent to that publication but also as a regular columnist on women's and race issues for such widely circulating Black urban newspapers as the *New York Freeman* and *New York Age* (1884–7, 1887–1960), Philadelphia *Standard-Echo* (c. 1890–c. 1896), and Indianapolis *Freeman* (1888–1926).[28]

The word "unity" is the most repeated in Mossell's "Will the Negro Share the Glory That Awaits Africa?" Mossell at one point capitalizes its every letter. In the context of her larger body of work about opportunities for Black people, she endorses two points: the mutually satisfying collaborations between African Americans and Africans, and the mutual progress, rather than competition, posed to Black men by influential Black women like her. She directly requests that both women's and men's benevolent groups of the A.M.E. Church, "King's Daughters and Son's Circles," share in the work of evangelizing Africans (Mossell 1893, 1). On January 5, 1893, when her letter appears, another year has dawned. The new century, and the efforts of African Americans to make it a rewarding and prosperous one, has engendered hope. By closing her submission with "the times that are in his hands," an allusion to how God delivers the faithful from evil, Mossell invites African American women and men to join together in the race's project of economic, educational, and religious transformation.[29] Yet her vision of another strategic collaboration, one between Afro-Christians and Africans, stands in tension with her attitudes towards Africans who shrugged away the gospel and its messengers.

Published in or reprinted from her 1874 edition of *Poems on Miscellaneous Subjects*, Harper's "The Death of Zombi" and "The Dying Bondman" braid together the destinies of African Americans and Africans and assert their struggle against oppression at a moment when the promises of Emancipation were still unrealized (87–8, 180–1). "An "Afric chieftain" is the central figure of Harper's "Dying Bondman." He has been defeated in his fight to retain his freedom and has spent his remaining adult years enslaved. On his deathbed, he faces one final chance to be free. Rather than contend with the shame and disappointment of his ancestors, who would "shrink back" from him if he crossed into the afterworld resigned, victimized, and defeated, he successfully inverts the master–slave hierarchy, demanding and receiving his free papers. "Master! write it, write it quickly!" he commands, "Master! write that I am free!" (181). Similarly, "The Death of Zombi" features a South African leader who is hunted by enslavers and captured with his people after losing a bloody battle for liberation. Faced with the prospect of either "freedom in death or the life of a slave," the "warlike old chief" elects to fall to his death along with other defiant fighters (87, 88).

According to the *Oxford English Dictionary,* the word "zombie" once connoted a chief or authority figure in Angola and the Congo. Men, women, and children were marched from there by enslavers to coastal West Africa for transport to servitude in the Caribbean and coastal American South. By 1872, a different kind of zombie had staggered and lurched into southern lore: a soulless, ghoulish human deprived of willpower and speech.[30] Zombies have become post-9/11 twenty-first-century cultural fixations through media franchises such as *The Walking Dead* (2003–present), novels such as Colson Whitehead's *Zone One* (2011), and movies such as *Contagion* (2011) and *World War Z* (2013). What registers the humanity of the Africans of Harper's 1874 poems is not only their un-zombielike assertions of will but also their plangent writing or oration. Harper implies that Black women like her, through the productions of their pens and the chorus of their voices, share these imagined Africans' intransigence, strivings to live freely, and insistence on being heard.

The frail yet determined hero of "The Dying Bondman" triumphantly "grasp[s]" his freedom papers before expiring. The story of "The Death of Zombi" similarly empowers its African subject because it is narrated in first-person plural. It is narrated from the perspective of those Africans who together have survived the unspeakable, may or may not yet be free, but definitely have retained their prerogative to frame their own narratives of struggle and success rather than ceding them to white people who have decimated their kingdoms and cultures.

Conclusion: re-imagining Africa

Nineteenth-century African American women writers revisited and complicated meanings of Africa as part of a broader cultural project to affirm the value of their accomplishments and expand the possibilities of their lives. Whether they traveled to Africa as missionaries and teachers or encountered it indirectly through reading about its culture and history and meeting visitors to this country, they grasped its power as a canvas for expressing their family and community concerns, their exclusion from full citizenship in American society, and their aspirations for full enfranchisement and more expansive opportunities for their progeny. During the new century, they would helm publications of their own, such as the *Colored American Magazine*, edited originally by Pauline Elizabeth Hopkins (1859–1930), and the literary pages of *The Crisis*, curated by Jessie Redmon Fauset (1882–1961). They would raise their voices in this new century to attain the vote, to pursue courses in higher education, and to press for civil rights. The mixed messages about Africa in their writings during the difficult, transitional nineteenth-century decades may not square with their activism but do not tarnish it. At moments, they even succeeded in fully breaking free from the constraints that influenced their writings about the continent.

Notes

1 "Princes shall come out of Egypt; Ethiopia shall soon stretch out her hands unto God." Psa. 68:31, King James Bible Online, last modified 2019, www.kingjamesbibleonline.org/Psalms-Chapter-68/#31. Frances Ellen Watkins Harper's "Ethiopia" begins with a paraphrase of this quotation. She imagines God's "mighty hand" exacting vengeance on slaveholders and liberating the enslaved as a reckoning for Ethiopia's (enslaved African Americans') sufferings. *The Complete Poems of Frances E. W. Harper*, ed. Maryemma Graham (New York: Oxford University Press, 1988), 7–8.

2 Beverly Guy-Sheftall, ed., *Words of Fire: An Anthology of African-American Feminist Thought* (New York: The New Press, 1995); Teresa C. Zackodnik, ed., *"We Must Be Up and Doing": A Reader in Early African American Feminisms* (Peterborough, Ontario, Canada: Broadview Press, 2010); Hollis Robbins and Henry Louis Gates, Jr, eds., *The Portable Nineteenth-Century African-American Women Writers* (New York: Penguin, 2017).

3 Andreá N. Williams, "Recovering Black Women Writers in Periodical Archives," *American Periodicals: A Journal of History, Criticism, and Bibliography* 27, no. 1 (April 2017): 25–8; Shirley Moody-Turner, "'Dear Dr. Du Bois': Anna Julia Cooper, W. E. B. Du Bois, and the Gender Politics of Black Publishing," *MELUS: The Journal of the Society for the Study of the Multi-Ethnic Literature of the United States*, 40, no. 3 (Fall 2015): 47–68; Joycelyn Moody, "Where Are the Women in Black Print Culture Studies: Obscene Questions and Righteous Hysteria," *Legacy: A Journal of American Women Writers*, 33, no. 1 (2016): 1–7; Noliwe M. Rooks, *Ladies' Pages: African American Women's Magazines and the Culture That Made Them* (New Brunswick, NJ: Rutgers University Press, 2004); Sarah Ruffing Robbins, "'That My Work May Speak Well for Spelman': Messengers Recording History and Performing Uplift," in her *Learning Legacies: Archive to Action Through Women's Cross-Cultural Teaching* (Ann Arbor: University of Michigan Press, 2017), 37–78; Eric Gardner, *Jennie Carter: A Black Journalist of the Early West* (Jackson: University Press of Mississippi, 2007); Kimberly Blockett, "Disrupting Print: Emigration, the Press, and Narrative Subjectivity in the British Preaching and Writing of Zilpha Elaw, 1840s–1860s," *MELUS: The Journal of the Society for the Study of the Multi-Ethnic Literature of the United States*, 40, no. 3 (Fall 2015): 94–109; and Crystal J. Lucky, *A Mysterious Life and Calling: From Slavery to Ministry in South Carolina – Reverend Mrs. Charlotte S. Riley* (Madison: University of Wisconsin Press, 2016).

4 Martin Henry Freeman to Martin Robison Delany, 14 April 1858, Emigration & Colonization: The Debate Among African Americans, 1780s–1860s, The Making of African American Identity: Vol. 1, 1500–1865, National Humanities Center, http://nationalhumanitiescenter.org/pds/maai/identity/t ext10/emigrationcolonization.pdf.

5 Winthrop D. Jordan, *White Over Black: American Attitudes Towards the Negro, 1550–1812*, 2nd ed. (reprint 1968: Williamsburg, VA: Omohundro Institute of Early American History and Culture; Chapel Hill: University of North Carolina Press, 2013), 546–69.

6 Matthew Spooner, "I Know This Scheme is From God: A Reconsideration of the Origins of the American Colonization Society," *Slavery & Abolition* 35, no. 4 (2014): 560.

7 Eric Burin, *Slavery and the Peculiar Solution: A History of the American Colonization Society* (Gainesville: University Press of Florida, 2005).

8 Jacobs discusses her biracial grandmother's thwarted escape from slavery during the Revolution. *Incidents in the Life of a Slave Girl: Written by Herself*, ed. Jean Fagan Yellin, enlarged ed. (reprint 1987; Cambridge, MA and London: Harvard University Press, 2000), 5.

9 Maria W. Stewart, "An Address Delivered at the African Masonic Hall," in Robbins and Gates, *African-American Women Writers*, 33; Maria W. Stewart, "Religion and the Pure Principle of Morality, The Sure Foundation on Which We Must Build," in Guy-Sheftall, *Words of Fire*, 27; and Maria W. Stewart, "Lecture. Delivered at the Franklin Hall. Boston, September 21st, 1832," in Zackodnik, *"We Must Be Up and Doing,"* 129.

10 Sarah Ruffing Robbins, *The Cambridge Introduction to Harriet Beecher Stowe* (Cambridge, UK: Cambridge University Press, 2007), 41–4.

11 Mary Church Terrell, "The Progress of Colored Women," in Robbins and Gates, *African-American Women Writers*, 440.

12 Phillis Wheatley, "On Being Brought from AFRICA to AMERICA," Digital Schomburg: African American Women Writers of the Nineteenth Century, last modified 1999, http://digilib.nypl.org/d ynaweb/digs-p/wwm9728/@Generic__BookView.

13 Barbara McCaskill and Michelle Taylor-Sherwin, "Womanhood, Religion, and Slavery: Dialogues from the Readex African American Newspapers Series," *Readex Report*, Fall 2020.

14 Lucy Wilmot Smith, "Women as Journalists: Portraits and Sketches of a Few of the Women Journalists of the Race," *Freeman* (Indianapolis), February 23, 1889. Reprinted in Robbins and Gates, eds., *African-American Women Writers*, 607.

15 Mrs. N. F. Mossell, *The Work of the Afro-American Woman* (Reprint 1894; New York: Oxford University Press, 1988).

16 Only three African Americans profiled in Brown's *The Black Man* are women. Rev. Stanford lauds Wheatley and Harriet Tubman (1822–1913). Rev. Simmons includes no women at all. William Wells Brown, *The Black Man: His Antecedents, His Genius, and His Achievements* (New York: Thomas Hamilton; Boston: R. F. Wallcut, 1863); Rev. William J. Simmons, *Men of Mark: Eminent, Progressive, and Rising* (Cleveland, OH: Geo. M. Rewell and Co., 1887); Rev. Peter Thomas Stanford, *The Tragedy of the Negro in America: A Condensed History of the Enslavement, Sufferings, Emancipation, Present Condition and Progress of the Negro Race in the United States of America*, 1st ed. (Boston: Charles Wasto, 1897).

17 Monroe A. Majors, *Noted Negro Women: Their Triumphs and Activities* (Chicago: Donohue and Henneberry, 1893); and L[awton]. A[ndrew]. Scruggs, *Women of Distinction: Remarkable in Works and Invincible in Character* (Raleigh, NC: L. A. Scruggs, 1893).

18 Zackodnik, *"We Must Be Up and Doing,"* 231. Zackodnik notes that Black women's networks "had actually been underway for some time" on local and regional levels.

19 Mrs. N. F. Mossell, "Will the Negro Share the Glory That Awaits Africa?" *A.M.E. Christian Recorder*, January 5, 1893, 1. Reprinted in Robbins and Gates, *African-American Women Writers*, 529–30.

20 Barbara McCaskill, *Love, Liberation, and Escaping Slavery: William and Ellen Craft in Cultural Memory* (Athens: University of Georgia Press, 2015), 70–4.

21 Barbara McCaskill and Sidonia Serafini, with Rev Paul Walker, *The Magnificent Rev. Peter Thomas Stanford: Transatlantic Reformer and Race Man* (Athens: University of Georgia Press, 2020), 18, 66–7.

22 Amanda Smith, *An Autobiography; The Story of the Lord's Dealings with Mrs. Amanda Smith, the Colored Evangelist; Containing an Account of her Life Work of Faith, and her Travels in America, England, Ireland, Scotland, India, and Africa, as an Independent Missionary* (Chicago: Meyer and Brother, Publishers, 1893), 8.

23 Katherine Davis Chapman Tillman, "America's First Cargo of Slaves," in *The Works of Katherine Davis Chapman Tillman*, ed. Claudia Tate (New York: Oxford University Press, 1991), 195, 194.

24 Mrs. Pryor, "In Defense of Our Women. The Position of the Enterprise Severely Scored," *Parsons* (Kansas) *Weekly Blade*, December 9, 1893, 2.
25 Sarah Jane Woodson Early, "The Organized Efforts of the Colored Women of the South to Improve Their Condition," in *The World's Congress of Representative Women: A Historical Résumé for Popular Circulation of the World's Congress of Representative Women Convened in Chicago on May 15, and Adjourned on May 22, 1893, under the Auspices of the Woman's Branch of the World's Congress Auxiliary*, ed. May Wright Sewall, Vol. 1 (Chicago and New York: Rand McNally Company, 1894), 718–23. Reprinted in Robbins and Gates, *African-American Women Writers*, 380–5.
26 Zackodnik, *"We Must Be Up and Doing,"* 182.
27 Guy-Sheftall, *Words of Fire*, 384–5.
28 Smith, "Women as Journalists," 607.
29 "My times are in thy hand; deliver me from the hand of mine enemies, and from them That persecute me." Psa. 31: 15, King James Bible Online, last modified 2019, www.kingjamesbibleonline.org/Psalms-Chapter-31/#15.
30 *OED: Oxford English Dictionary*, last modified 2019, www-oed-com.proxy- remote.galib.uga.edu/view/Entry/232982?redirectedFrom=zombie#eid.

Bibliography

Blockett, Kimberly. "Disrupting Print: Emigration, the Press, and Narrative Subjectivity in the British Preaching and Writing of Zilpha Elaw, 1840s-1860s," *MELUS: The Journal of the Society for the Study of the Multi-Ethnic Literature of the United States* 40, no. 3 (Fall 2015): 94–109.

Brown, William Wells. *The Black Man: His Antecedents, His Genius, and His Achievements*. New York: Thomas Hamilton; Boston: R. F. Wallcut, 1863.

Burin, Eric. *Slavery and the Peculiar Solution: A History of the American Colonization Society*. Gainesville: University Press of Florida, 2005.

The Declaration of Independence: A Transcription. *National Archives and Records Administration*. https://www.archives.gov/founding-docs/declaration-transcript.

Early, Sarah Jane Woodson. "The Organized Efforts of the Colored Women of the South to Improve Their Condition." *The World's Congress of Representative Women: A Historical Résumé for Popular Circulation of the World's Congress of Representative Women Convened in Chicago on May 15, and Adjourned on May 22, 1893, under the Auspices of the Woman's Branch of the World's Congress Auxiliary*. Ed. May Wright Sewall. Vol. 1. Chicago: Rand McNally Company, 1894.

Frederickson, Mary E., and Delores M. Walters, eds. *Gendered Resistance: Women, Slavery, and the Legacy of Margaret Garner*. Urbana: University of Illinois Press, 2013.

Freeman, Martin Henry, to Martin Robison Delany. 14 April 1858. Emigration & Colonization: The Debate Among African Americans, 1780s-1860s. *The Making of African American Identity 1*, 1500–1865. National Humanities Center. http://nationalhumanitiescenter.org/pds/maai/identity/text10/emigrationcolonization.pdf.

Gardner, Eric. *Jennie Carter: A Black Journalist of the Early West*. Jackson: University Press of Mississippi, 2007.

Guy-Sheftall, Beverly, ed. *Words of Fire: An Anthology of African-American Feminist Thought*. New York: The New Press, 1995.

Harper, Frances Ellen Watkins. *The Complete Poems of Frances E. W. Harper*. Ed. Maryemm Graham. New York: Oxford University Press, 1988.

Jacobs, Harriet A. *Incidents in the Life of a Slave Girl: Written by Herself*. Ed. Jean Fagan Yellin. Enlarged ed. Reprint 1987; Cambridge, MA: Harvard University Press, 2000.

Jordan, Winthrop D. *White Over Black: American Attitudes Towards the Negro, 1550–1812*. 2nd ed. Reprint 1968: Williamsburg, VA: Omohundro Institute of Early American History and Culture; Chapel Hill: University of North Carolina Press, 2013.

King James Bible Online. 2019. https://www.kingjamesbibleonline.org/.

Lucky, Crystal J. *Mysterious Life and Calling: From Slavery to Ministry in South Carolina— Reverend Mrs. Charlotte S. Riley*. Madison: University of Wisconsin Press, 2016.

Majors, Monroe A. *Noted Negro Women: Their Triumphs and Activities*. Chicago: Donohue and Henneberry, 1893.

McCaskill, Barbara. *Love, Liberation, and Escaping Slavery: William and Ellen Craft in Cultural Memory*. Athens: University of Georgia Press, 2015.

McCaskill, Barbara, and Michelle Taylor-Sherwin. "Womanhood, Religion, and Slavery: Dialogues from the Readex African American Newspapers Series." *Readex Report*, 2020.

McCaskill, Barbara, and Sidonia Serafini, with the Rev. Paul Walker. *The Magnificent Rev. Peter Thomas Stanford: Transatlantic Reformer and Race Man.* Athens: University of Georgia Press, 2020.

Moody, Joycelyn. "Where are the Women in Black Print Culture Studies: Obscene Questions and Righteous Hysteria." *Legacy: A Journal of American Women Writers* 33, no. 1 (2016): 1–7. Project MUSE.

Moody-Turner, Shirley. "'Dear Dr. Du Bois': Anna Julia Cooper, W. E. B. Du Bois, and the Gender Politics of Black Publishing." *MELUS: The Journal of the Society for the Study of the Multi-Ethnic Literature of the United States* 40, no. 3 (Fall 2015): 47–68. JSTOR.

Mossell, Mrs. N[elson]. F[rancis]. "Will the Negro Share the Glory That Awaits Africa?" *A.M. E. Christian Recorder,* January 5, 1893, p. 1.

Mossell, Mrs. N[elson]. F[rancis]. *The Work of the Afro-American Woman.* Introduction by Joanne Braxton. Rpt. 1894; New York: Oxford University Press, 1988.

OED: Oxford English Dictionary. 2019. https://www-oed-com.proxy- remote.galib.uga.edu/view/Entry /232982?redirectedFrom=zombie#eid.

Mrs. Pryor. "In Defense of Our Women. The Position of the Enterprise Severely Scored." *Parsons (Kansas) Weekly Blade,* December 9, 1893, p. 2.

Robbins, Hollis, and Henry Louis Gates, Jr., eds. *The Portable Nineteenth-Century African American Women Writers.* New York: Penguin, 2017.

Robbins, Sarah [Ruffing]. *The Cambridge Introduction to Harriet Beecher Stowe.* Cambridge: Cambridge University Press, 2007.

Robbins, Sarah [Ruffing]. *Learning Legacies: Archive to Action Through Women's Cross-Cultural Teaching.* Ann Arbor: University of Michigan Press, 2017.

Rooks, Noliwe M. *Ladies' Pages: African American Women's Magazines and the Culture That Made Them.* New Brunswick, NJ: Rutgers University Press, 2004.

Scruggs, L[awton]. A[ndrew]. *Women of Distinction: Remarkable in Works and Invincible in Character.* Raleigh, NC: L.A. Scruggs, 1893.

Simmons, Rev. William J. *Men of Mark: Eminent, Progressive, and Rising.* Cleveland, OH: Geo. M. Rewell and Co., 1887.

Smith, Amanda. *An Autobiography; The Story of the Lord's Dealings with Mrs. Amanda Smith, the Colored Evangelist; Containing an Account of her Life Work of Faith, and her Travels in America, England, Ireland, Scotland, India, and Africa, as an Independent Missionary.* Chicago: Meyer and Brother, Publishers, 1893.

Spooner, Matthew. "'I Know This Scheme is from God': A Reconsideration of the Origins of the American Colonization Society." *Slavery & Abolition* 35, no. 4 (2014): 559–75. JSTOR.

Stanford, Rev. Peter Thomas. *The Tragedy of the Negro in America: A Condensed History of the Enslavement, Sufferings, Emancipation, Present Condition and Progress of the Negro Race in the United States of America,* 1st ed. Boston: Charles Wasto, 1897.

Stewart, T. McCants. "Literature Review." *New York Freeman,* October 24, 1885. p. 2.

Tillman, Katherine Davis Chapman. *The Works of Katherine Davis Chapman Tillman.* Ed. Claudia Tate. New York: Oxford University Press, 1991.

Twain, Mark. [Samuel Clemens]. *The Adventures of Huckleberry Finn (Tom Sawyer's Comrade).* New York: Harper and Brothers, 1912.

Wheatley, Phillis. "On Being Brought from AFRICA to AMERICA." *Digital Schomburg: African American Women Writers of the Nineteenth Century.* 1999. http://digilib.nypl.org/dynaweb/digs-p/wwm9728/@ Generic__BookView.

Williams, Andreá N. "Recovering Black Women Writers in Periodical Archives." *American Periodicals: A Journal of History, Criticism, and Bibliography* 27, no. 1 (April 2017): 25–28. Project MUSE.

Zackodnik, Teresa C., Ed. *'We Must Be Up and Doing': A Reader in Early African American Feminisms.* Peterborough, ON: Broadview Press, 2010.

20

Singing power/sounding identity

The Black woman's voice from hidden Hush Arbors to the popular

Maya Cunningham

The African American vocal tradition encompasses different genres and styles falling both within and outside the African American Music Timeline.[1] While there are many Black men who are widely recognized for their singing, African American women have a particular singing tradition that is especially emotionally powerful and virtuosic. Even in countries where there are few African Americans, gospel-influenced singers like Whitney Houston, for example, might be the only image and representation of African America. Aretha Franklin was named number one in *Rolling Stone Magazine*'s "100 Greatest Singers."[2] The Black woman's vocal tradition demarcates an African American identity that originates in the Black church, which began during slavery. It descends from the earliest days of African America, going back to the arrival of the first Africans. In order to understand the power of Black women's vocality in the contemporary, we must explore its beginnings.

Mother tongue

It may be possible to trace the "mother tongue" of Black vocality back to African Americans' ancestors who arrived in the United States from West, Central, and even Southern Africa. As such, Black women's vocality descended from African mothers. Lorenzo Dow Turner's discovery in the early 1900s of the *A waka* song in Amelia Dawley's Georgia Sea Island family is a powerful example of this.[3] *A waka* is a Mende funeral dirge from Northern Sierra Leone that is performed only by women. It was passed down in Dawley's family as a girl's hand-clap game. It is significant not only because it is the longest text in an African language discovered to date in African American culture[4] but also because it is an example of an African woman passing down her vocal tradition to her African American daughters. This kind of generational transmission is also in Maya Angelou's family story. She learned her singing style, and a huge repertoire of African American spirituals, from her paternal grandmother, Annie Henderson. We can assume, since Angelou watched her grandmother sing in church several times a week, that she absorbed and imitated her grandmother's singing style in her own performances. Angelou later discovered the Ewe lineage of her grandmother's vocal timbre when she traveled in the early 1960s to Keta, in the Volta Region of Ghana.[5] These examples offer a hint of the "mother tongue" that has passed

204

down through generations of Black women. Due to its African descendancy, the Black woman's vocal tradition is an ethnic identifier that powerfully "sounds" African American identity.

The aesthetics of Black women's vocality developed during slavery in Hush Arbors – secret meetings held by enslaved Blacks. Black women's vocality has been foundational to a music of resistance for African Americans since the tradition developed in these sites. I will first examine the space of the antebellum Hush Arbor as a site of resistance. Through this, we can understand how the music performed in those spaces was also used to resist racial oppression. I will then discuss how the internal Hush Arbor song tradition bridged into public spaces that led to the global impact of Black women's vocality in the twentieth century and beyond.

The African American Hush Arbor as resistance, or freedom spaces in slavery

Within the context of slavery, African Americans formed a culture of secrecy that existed outside the white gaze of slave holders and their allies. Hush Arbors were spaces of refuge, central in this secret culture. They were surreptitious night meetings that were usually held deep in the woods that abutted plantations. This practice was ubiquitous all over the South. During these meetings, words could be openly voiced for freedom: words that could reap violent consequences if uttered openly before slave holders. These meetings concealed, or "hushed," such words and other activities that resisted bondage. Survival sounds and silence are sometimes called coded language, *double entendre*, or the "hidden transcript," a term coined by James C. Scott. He defines the "hidden transcript" as the non-hegemonic, subversive discourse generated by subordinate groups and concealed from certain dominant others.[6] Scott juxtaposes the hidden transcript with the "public transcript," which is information that is deemed safe to reveal to the dominant group. The meetings, which were hidden from cultural outsiders, facilitated a powerful emotional release, which often happened through song. The music that was central in these meetings was grounded in liberationist Christian worship practices.

Secret Christian worship provided a way for enslaved African Americans to assert their humanity against slave holders' crushing view of them as chattels. The vocal music they created during these times gave expression to their humanity. In this environment, the first forms of African American music were developed. These were the spirituals and the ring shouts.

Hush Arbor meetings usually took place in a four-part format. "After the first hymn or spiritual came prayer, a major focus of the hush harbor service … (prayer) was an essential community action … prayer had overtones of liberation."[7] Many narratives revealed that "any member of the congregation could lead prayers, but the lesson and sermon were conducted by a preacher, chosen by the community for ability to interpret the sacred word."[8] "After the sermon came the ring shout." Silvia King was interviewed when she was 100 years old for the Works Progress Administration (WPA) Slave Narratives. During her interview, she described the ring shout: "Dey gits in de ring dance … (it was) jes' a kind of shuffle, den it git faster and faster and dey gits warmed up and moans and shouts and claps and dances … sometimes dey sings and shout all night."[9] One example of a slave-era ring shout still performed by the Seniorlites shouters of South Carolina is "You Gotta Right to the Tree of Life."[10] The song's main lyric "Run Mary run, Run Martha run, tell Mary run I say, You got the right to the tree of life." This was resistance – singing songs that asserted their right to be free.

Hush Arbor meetings also helped enslaved Blacks to reclaim freedom because they served as a way for them to exercise control over their own bodies. Slave owners attempted to exert complete control over them. Their secret lives directly defied this control: "Bondspeople, who had their own plans for their bodies, violated the boundaries of space and time that were intended to demarcate and consolidate planters' … power over plantation households."[11] Stephanie M. H. Camp calls these freedom spaces "enslaved people's rival geography." Toni Morrison gives a vivid image of this "rival geography" in her Pulitzer Prize–winning novel *Beloved*. Within the gruesome and violent picture of slavery presented in *Beloved*, hope and freedom come through the character of Baby Suggs, who preached in a Hush Arbor space called "the Clearing." During these meetings, Baby Suggs encourages the recently freed Black community in Ohio to celebrate themselves. In *Beloved*'s Hush Arbor, the "sacred word" was given by Baby Suggs, a woman preacher, in a role usually served by men. And her message? Love your body, love your heart.

> In the heat of every Saturday afternoon, she sat in the clearing while the people waited among the trees … After situating herself on a huge flat-sided rock, Baby Suggs bowed her head and prayed silently … They knew she was ready when she put her stick down. Then she shouted, "Let the children come!" and they ran from the trees toward her. "Let your mothers hear you laugh," she told them, and the woods rang. The adults looked on and could not help smiling. Then "Let the grown men come," she shouted. They stepped out one by one from among the ringing trees. "Let your wives and your children see you dance," she told them, and groundlife shuddered under their feet. Finally she called the women to her. "Cry," she told them. "For the living and the dead. Just cry." And without covering their eyes the women let loose. It started that way: laughing children, dancing men, crying women and then it got mixed up. Women stopped crying and danced; men sat down and cried; children danced, women laughed, children cried until, exhausted and riven, all and each lay about the Clearing damp and gasping for breath.[12]

With these admonitions, Baby Suggs was healing the psychological damage of chattel slavery by affirming her congregation's humanity. She was teaching them to love the very bodies which slave-owning whites had commodified and abused. This was the work of the Hush Arbor.

The Black woman's voice, the aesthetic of catharsis, and the Black revolutionary song

It is no wonder that these Hush Arbor meetings resulted in the powerful African American vocal tradition. Although both men and women participated, Black women's voices were central to the emotional power of these meetings. African American autobiography and the WPA slave narratives detail how women's voices were used to utter fervent prayers for protection and freedom. Their voices were used to utter prayers, praises, and songs, which became African American *spirituals* and other sacred song types.

Maya Angelou offers a striking testimony of Hush Arbor activity used to resist slavery. Her third autobiography details the oral history passed down by her paternal great grandmother: "my great-grandmother (who had been a slave), told me of praying silently under old wash pots, and of secret meetings deep in the woods to praise God … Her owner wouldn't allow his Negroes to worship God (it might give them ideas) and they did so on pain of being lashed."[13] William Ford III, a Texas-based African American minister, has a Hush Arbor "prayer pot" as a family heirloom:

> It begins with a 200-year-old black kettle pot, used by my Christian slave forbearers in Lake Providence, Louisiana. While used for cooking and washing clothes during the day, this kettle was secretly used for prayer. Forbidden to pray by their slave master, my ancestors were beaten unmercifully if found doing so. However, in spite of their master's cruelty,

and because of their love for Jesus, they prayed anyway. At night, sneaking into a barn, they carried this cast iron cooking pot into their secret prayer meeting. As others looked out, those inside prayed. Turning this pot upside-down on the barn floor, they propped it up with rocks – suspending the pot a few inches above the ground. Then, while lying prostrate or kneeling on the ground, they prayed in whispers underneath the kettle to muffle their voices. The story passed down with the kettle is that they were risking their lives to pray for freedom for ensuing generations. One day, freedom did come.[14]

The WPA slave narratives also document the stories of others who participated in these meetings. Amanda McCray testified that on her Florida plantation, there were praying grounds where "the grass never had a chance ter grow fer the troubled knees that kept it crushed down."[15] Andrew Moss remembered that on the plantation where he grew up, all the slaves had their private prayer grounds: "My Mammy's was a ole twisterd thick-rooted muscadine bush. She'd go in dar and pray for deliverance of de slaves."[16] Patsy Larkin recalled that on her plantation, the slaves would steal away into the cane thickets and pray in a prostrate position with their faces close to the ground so that no sound would escape.[17] On a Louisiana plantation, enslaved Blacks would gather in the woods at night, form a circle on their knees, and pray over a vessel of water to drown out the sound.[18] Richard Carruthers remembered:

> Us (negros) used to have a prayin' ground down in the hollow and sometime we come out of the field, between 11 and 12 at night, scorchin' and burnin up with nothin to eat, and we wants to ask the good Lawd to have mercy. We puts grease in a snuff pan or bottle and make a lamp. We takes a pine torch, too, and goes down in the hollow to pray. Some gits so joyous they starts to holler loud and we has to stop up they mouth. I see (negros) git so full of the lawd and so happy they draps unconscious.[19]

Kalvin Woods, a slave preacher, described how women would take old quilts and rags and soak them before hanging them up in the shape of a small room, "and the slaves who were interested about it would huddle up behind these quilts to do their praying, preaching and singing. These wet rags were used to keep the sound of their voices from penetrating the air."[20]

All these testimonies describe the cathartic function of the meetings. The praying, preaching, and singing provided those who participated with a powerful emotional release. Hush Arbor meeting initiated the emotional power of the Black woman's vocal tradition. A recording curated by Dr. Bernice Johnson Reagon of the Blue Spring Mississippi Baptist Delegation, called "Traditional Prayer with Moan,"[21] captures what sung prayers in these meetings might have sounded like. While a male leader speaks a prayer, the congregation hums in the minor mode. The women give impassioned responses with "yes" and "well" and "oh yeah." Reagon calls these responses "moans." The praying man sometimes sings his speech in a type of preaching that is called a "squall." After the prayer, the group repeats phrases like "Lord Have Mercy" and "Come by Here." In the women's singing, we hear the cathartic aesthetic, which is called *soul* in the contemporary. It is a singing style that comes from the heart, sounded with open, passionate vocals that are melodious, sometimes rough textured, and with wide vibratos. This recording demonstrates the way the collective prayers during Hush Arbor meetings might have sounded.

The songs of the women quilters of Gee's Bend, Alabama also exemplify the sound of prayers and moans. Gee's Bend is an isolated community of African Americans descended from enslaved Blacks who worked on an immense cotton plantation. Their vibrant quilts have been exhibited all over the world. When quilting together, the women often sing African American congregational songs. On *How We Got Over: The Sacred Songs of Gee's Bend*, we hear many *spirituals* in the way they may have been performed during slavery's Hush Arbor meetings. Just as Silvia King and Richard Carruthers reported, the Gee's Bend women also moan, clap, and shout when singing. The quilting and singing traditions were passed down by their mothers and grandmothers. Mary Lou Bendolph recorded a *moan* called "Oh, please (Lord, have mercy)"[22] that descends from the Hush Arbor. Like the "Traditional Prayer with Moan," Bendolph sings the prayer from the depths of her soul with broad, textured, and emotionally charged vocals.

The Black revolutionary tradition in song

Spirituals evolved from the prayer-moan. Levine suggests that postbellum accounts are contemporary evidence that attest to the "presence of a compelling communal ethos at slave religious meetings."[23] He also suggests that *spirituals* were collectively composed from the emotional fervor of prayer moans and worship. Clifton Furness witnessed this process on an isolated South Carolina plantation in 1926.

> In the midst of increasing intensity, a black man ... suddenly cried out: "Git right-sodger! Git right-sodger! Git right-wit Gawd!" Instantly the crowd took it up, moulding a melody out of half-formed familiar phrases based upon a spiritual tune ... A distinct melodic outline became more and more prominent, shaping itself around the central theme of the words, "Git right, sodger!" Scraps of other words and tunes were flung into the medley of sound by individual singers from time to time, but the general trend was carried on by a deep undercurrent, which appeared to be stronger than the mind of any individual present, for it bore the mass of improvised harmony and rhythms into the most effective climax of incremental repetition that I have ever heard. I felt as if some conscious plan or purpose were carrying us along, call it mob-mind, communal composition, or what you will.[24]

Spirituals like "Steal Away," "Swing Low Sweet Chariot," and many others were composed through this collective process of communal prayer and song. The lyrics of the songs, and the different ways they were used in resistance to slavery, signaled the start of the Black revolutionary tradition. In his study of Alabama Blacks' engagement in the Communist Party, Robin D. G. Kelley states that "party theorists ... not only described black spirituals as America's most potent strain of protest music, but they discovered that the Negro church had a rich history of revolutionary traditions."[25] He also observes that the Black working class "shared ... a grassroots understanding of exploitation and oppression based more on scripture than anything else." This understanding was "forged in yesterday's slave quarters ... this prophetic interpretation of Christianity had informed black resistance for nearly three centuries."[26] The *spirituals* formed the foundation of this theology of resistance, which paralleled enslaved Blacks to the "Hebrew Children" of the Biblical exodus story, implored God for deliverance like Daniel from the lion's den, and issued sonorous warnings to slave owners of the "final judgement." In addition to their worship function, these songs, like "Swing Low Sweet Chariot" and "Steal Away," are well known to have been used by enslaved Blacks as code songs to communicate plans for escape.[27]

Harriet Tubman's use of the *spirituals* to advance her liberation activities perfectly exemplifies the Black revolutionary tradition in song. Tubman, in a desperate attempt to signal to her friends and family her plans to escape, encoded the message by singing "Bound for the Promised Land":

I'm sorry I'm going to leave you,
Farewell, oh farewell;

But I'll meet you in the morning
Farewell, oh farewell;
I'll meet you in the morning.[28]

The Promised Land could mean either going to heaven or going to freedom in the North. Tubman also used *spirituals* with coded messages to help others escape during her return journeys South. She would sing an appropriate spiritual to warn her party of danger or to guide them to the next safe place.[29] She used different hymns and spirituals, including "Go Down Moses," to communicate that danger had passed by.[30] Tubman's use of the *spirituals* to help fugitives to freedom was the Black woman's voice enacting the Black revolutionary tradition through song.

The Black woman's voice: from hidden to public

The song tradition of emotional power and revolutionary action that was forged in Hush Arbors remained a hidden aspect of Black culture almost until the postbellum period. Only cultural insiders knew the songs. They were eventually revealed to cultural outsiders through three different streams: Harriet Tubman's public lectures, the Fisk Jubilee Singers, and the postbellum African American Church.

Shortly before the Civil War, Harriet Tubman began to give public lectures in 1859 to raise funds to support her parents, whom she rescued from slavery in Maryland. She told her abolitionist audience stories of her enslavement, escape, and eight journeys back to the South to free others.[31] She became well known for her storytelling ability. Biographer Kate Clifford Larson reports that Tubman also had a beautiful singing voice.[32] Larson's statement indicates that Tubman might have also performed *spirituals* and hymns during her public lectures. Tubman certainly sang *spirituals* during an intimate visit with Agnes Garrison and Eliza Wright Osborne in 1899. Encouraged by Osborne, Tubman told her "narrative" and "acted out parts of it" … "singing one of the old songs in a curious, nasal, mournful voice."[33]

While Tubman might have shared Black vocal traditions with abolitionist audiences, the Fisk Jubilee Singers shared them on a national and international scale. Fisk University was founded by John Ogden, Reverend Erastus Cravath, and Reverend Edward Smith to educate newly freed African Americans in 1865. The university faced major financial troubles early on. George L. White, the university's treasurer, who was also a musician, founded the choir in 1871 to raise funds, inspired by the "beautiful voices of the formerly enslaved."[34] The group initially performed popular songs of the day and repertoire from the European classical canon, but without success. However, the singers often gathered privately to sing *spirituals* like "Steal Away." Ella Sheppard, a student and assistant choir director, recalled:

> The slave songs were associated with slavery and the dark past and represented things to be forgotten … they were sacred to our parents … we did not dream of ever using them in public. It was only after many months that gradually our hearts were opened to the wonderful beauty and power of our songs.[35]

Sheppard confirms that up to this point in 1871, the *spirituals* had remained hidden within African American culture. Seven of the final group of nine that embarked on the first national tour along old abolitionist circuits had been slaves. On the tour, they initially performed European *cantatas* with a few *spirituals* as an encore. However, at an Oberlin College performance, they finally made the decision to give a full concert of the *spirituals*. Musicologist Horace Clarence Boyer offers insight on this turning point:

> At Oberlin College at a convention of influential ministers, they reached … back to the secret music they'd sung behind closed doors … the sacred songs of their mothers and fathers. They started to sing steal away – then all of the sudden there was no talking. Then they said you could hear soft weeping and the faces of people reddened. And I'm sure the Jubilee Singers were joining them in tears because if you are about what you're singing, particularly if you believe it, you can't help but be moved.[36]

Through prayer, George L White was inspired to name the group the Fisk Jubilee Singers. The group continued to perform concerts of spirituals to ever increasing popularity nationally and internationally.

The Fisk Jubilee Singers initiated the tradition of concertizing spirituals. It is important to note that the Fisk Jubilee Singers did not perform these songs using traditional Black vocality, like their forebears, but in the European operatic tradition. They sang with an operatic timbre, with pre-arranged vocal parts. The Jubilee Singers, and similar choirs at other Black universities, act as crucibles that preserve the songs performed in slavery's Hush Arbors.

The Black church continued Hush Arbor vocal traditions and gave rise to public performances by Black women. Known as the "invisible institution," the secret Hush Arbor congregations that comprised the Black church became visible during freedom. Congregations often met outdoors in "Brush Arbors" on Sunday mornings and sometimes joined Methodist congregations.[37] The emotional intensity, expressive singing, and soulful musicality that have become the hallmark of Black women's vocality passed down through the generations in the Black church, which became a fixed component of African American culture. The Black female specialist singer emerged out of church choirs and Sunday services. Spirituals and other congregational song forms connected to forms that emerged after slavery, like the blues.

Amiri Baraka discusses the development of the blues in the late 1800s as a storytelling form that gave voice to new freedom and individual expression, compared with forms that developed during slavery, which were an expression of African Americans' collective experience.[38] From the blues flowed all other forms of Black popular music. However, the musical life of many African American women singers still began in the Black church. Childhood experiences in the Black church nurtured the talents of the first Black female pop stars: blues women like Ma Rainey and Bessie Smith. It was Ma Rainey's pianist, Thomas Dorsey, who in the 1930s, fused the blues aesthetic with the Black spiritual tradition to develop a new genre known as gospel. The emotional expression of older forms of Black congregational music fused with Dorsey's gospel. Gospel offered new songs as storytelling vehicles for the individual singers. The Gospel music genre created one of the most powerful musical outlets for Black female vocality. While many Black women singers performed with the local church, many professionalized into both sacred and secular genres. These professional singers of different Black popular traditions, from jazz to rhythm and blues to soul, who trained in church-based gospel, are the Black women known all over the globe for their vocal prowess: Sarah Vaughan, Dinah Washington, Chaka Khan, Jennifer Holliday, Patti Labelle, Aretha Franklin, and many others.

These Black women's voices echo the songs of those first African mothers and the enslaved women's shouts and prayers for survival in those secret meetings in the woods. The vocal tradition for which they are so well known is a 400-year-old lineage, formed through the Black experience and the revolutionary traditions of old. For this reason, Black women's vocality still serves as a clarion call of Black freedom.

Notes

1 Portia K. Maultsby and Mellonee V. Burnim, eds, *African-American Music: An Introduction, Second Edition* (New York: Routledge, 2015), xvi.
2 Clarence Waldron, "Aretha Franklin Tops List of '100 Greatest Singers of All Time'," *Jet*, December 8, 2008, 1.
3 Lorenzo Turner, *Africanisms in the Gullah Dialect* (Columbia, SC: University of South Carolina Press, 2002).
4 Alvaro Toepke and Angel Serrano, *The Language You Cry In*, 1998.
5 Maya Angelou, *All God's Children Need Traveling Shoes* (New York: Vintage, 1991).
6 James C. Scott, *Domination and the Arts of Resistance: Hidden Transcripts* (New Haven: Yale University Press, 1990).
7 Janet D. Cornelius, *Slave Missions and the Black Church in the Antebellum South* (Columbia, SC: University of South Carolina Press, 1999), 11.
8 Ibid., 11.
9 *Born in Slavery: Slave Narratives from the Federal Writers' Project*, 1936–1938, Volume 16. Texas Narratives: Part 1 and Part 2 (Washington, DC: Library of Congress, 1972), 294.
10 *Wade in the Water Volume II: African-American Congregational Singing: Nineteenth Century Roots.* Smithsonian Folkways Recordings, 1996.
11 Stephanie M. H. Camp, "The Pleasures of Resistance: Enslaved Women and Body Politics in the Plantation South, 1830–1861," *The Journal of Southern History* 68, no. 3 (2002): 535.
12 Toni Morrison, *Beloved* (New York: Alfred A. Knopf, 1987), 43.
13 Maya Angelou, *Singin' and Swingin' and Gettin' Merry Like Christmas* (New York: Bantam, 1976), 28.
14 Ford, William, III, *Created for Influence* (Dallas, TX: Chosen Publishing, 2007); "The Prayers of My Forefathers (Former Slaves) Echo Today, 150 Years After the Civil War," Will Ford Ministries, updated November 29, 2015, https://willfordministries.com/2015/11/29/the-prayers-of-my-forefathers-for mer-slaves-echo-today-150-years-after-the-civil-war/
15 *Born in Slavery: Slave Narratives from the Federal Writers' Project, 1936–1938.* Volume 3 Florida Narratives (Washington, DC: Library of Congress, 1972), 49.
16 *Born in Slavery: Slave Narratives from the Federal Writers' Project, 1936–1938.* Volume 15 Tennessee Narratives (Washington, DC: Library of Congress, 1972), 212.
17 Lawrence W. Levine, *Black Culture and Black Consciousness: Afro-American Folk Thought from Slavery to Freedom* (Oxford: Oxford University Press, 2007), 42.
18 Ibid., 42.
19 Vol. 16 Texas, Part 1, 199.
20 John. B. Cade, "Out of the Mouths of Ex-Slaves," *The Journal of Negro History* 20, no. 3 (July 1935): 87.
21 *Wade in the Water Volume II*, 1996.
22 *How We Got Over: Sacred Songs of Gee's Bend*, 2002, Tinwood Media.
23 Levine, 2007, 27.
24 Ibid., 27.
25 Robin D. G. Kelley, *Hammer and Hoe: Alabama Communists During the Great Depression* (Chapel Hill: University of North Carolina Press, 2015), 135.
26 Ibid., 107.
27 *Underground Railroad: The William Still Story*, PBS, 2018.
28 Kate Clifford Larson, *Bound for the Promised Land: Harriet Tubman, Portrait of an American Hero* (New York: Ballantine, 2004), chap. 4, Kindle.
29 Ibid., chap. 5.
30 Ibid., chap. 9.
31 Ibid., chap. 8.
32 Ibid., chap. 8.
33 Ibid., chap. 13.
34 *American Experience: Jubilee Singers*, PBS, 2019.
35 Ibid.
36 Ibid.
37 Rev. Dr. Timothy Freeman, interviewed by author, July 13, 2019.
38 Amiri Baraka, *Blues People: Negro Music in White America* (New York: William Morrow, 1999).

References

American Experience: Jubilee Singers. PBS, 2019.

Angelou, Maya. *Singin' and Swingin' and Gettin' Merry Like Christmas*. New York: Bantam, 1976.

Angelou, Maya. *All God's Children Need Traveling Shoes*. New York: Vintage, 1991.

Baraka, Amiri. *Blues People: Negro Music in White America*. New York: William Morrow, 1999.

Born in Slavery: Slave Narratives from the Federal Writers' Project, 1936–1938, Volume 16.

Cade, John B. "Out of the Mouths of Ex-Slaves." *The Journal of Negro History* 20, no. 3, July 10, 1935: 294–337.

Camp, Stephanie M.H. "The Pleasures of Resistance: Enslaved Women and Body Politics in the Plantation South, 1830–1861." *The Journal of Southern History* 68, no. 3 (2002): 533–72.

Cornelius, Janet D. *Slave Missions and the Black Church In The Antebellum South*. Columbia, SC: University of South Carolina Press. 1999.

Ford, William, III. *Created for Influence*. Dallas, TX: Chosen Publishing, 2007.

Ford, William, III. "The Prayers of My Forefathers (Former Slaves) Echo Today, 150 Years After the Civil War." *Will Ford Ministries*, updated November 29, 2015. https://willfordministries.com/2015/11/29/the-prayers-of-my-forefathers-former-slaves-echo-today-150-years-after-the-civil-war/

How We Got Over: Sacred Songs of Gee's Bend. 2002. *Tinwood Media*.

Kelley, Robin D.G. *Hammer and Hoe: Alabama Communists during the Great Depression*. Chapel Hill: University of North Carolina Press, 2015.

Larson, Kate Clifford. *Bound for the Promised Land: Harriet Tubman, Portrait of an American Hero*. 1st ed. New York: Ballantine, 2004.

Levine, Lawrence W. *Black Culture and Black Consciousness: Afro-American Folk Thought from Slavery to Freedom*. 30th ed. Oxford: Oxford University Press, 2007.

Maultsby, Portia K., and Mellonee V. Burnim Mellonee, eds. 2015. *African-American Music: An Introduction*. 2nd ed. New York: Routledge.

Morrison, Toni. *Beloved*. 1st ed. New York: Alfred A. Knopf, 1987. – find pages.

The Language You Cry In, 1998. Directed by Alvaro Toepke and Angel Serrano, James C. Scott, *Domination and the Arts of Resistance: Hidden Transcripts*. New Haven: Yale University Press, 1990.

Rev. Dr. Timothy Freeman, Senior Pastor, Trinity AME Zion Church, Washington DC, interviewed by Maya Cunningham, July 13, 2019, Washington, DC.

Turner, Lorenzo. 1949. *Africanisms in the Gullah Dialect*. Columbia, SC: Univ. of South Carolina Press.

Underground Railroad: The William Still Story. PBS, 2018.

Wade in the Water Volume II: African-American Congregational Singing: Nineteenth Century Roots. Smithsonian Folkways Recordings, 1996.

Waldron, Clarence Waldron. "Aretha Franklin Tops List of '100 Greatest Singers of All Time.'" *Jet*, December 8, 2008, p. 1.

21

Jamettes, mas, and bacchanal

A culture of resistance in Trinidad and Tobago

Allison O. Ramsay

Urban Black working-class women (jamettes) have a long "herstory" of engaging in acts of resistance in Trinidad and Tobago. Within the context of Carnival and the wider society, jamettes did not allow their bodies, sexuality, or femininity to be policed by public criticisms but instead, became carriers of tradition and embodied resistance. Jamette women were members of stick-bands who rivaled and fought each other and were among protestors in the 1881 Canboulay Riots and the Water Riot of 1903. The scrutiny of female bodies, masquerade, and performance, as well as debate on the role and place of Black women within society, persisted in the nineteenth century and continued into the late twentieth century, particularly when women became the predominant players of mas during Carnival. The development and predominance of "pretty mas" and "skin mas," which focus on bikinis, beads, and feathers that reveal much of the female body – considered excessive by some – extends the historical discussion on decency, morality, sexuality, and gendered identities within the space of the modern Trinidad Carnival, a discourse which arguably began with jamette women of the nineteenth century.

Carnival in Trinidad and Tobago is a time that allows all to feel free and to "bring out de jamette inna me," according to Trinidad and Tobago soca artist, Denise "Saucy Wow" Belfon, who created the song "De Jammette" in 2002. Trinidad Carnival is a topic that has been explored from various perspectives. Scholars such as Errol Hill (1997); Pamela Franco (2007); Hollis Liverpool (2001); Andrew Pearse (1956); Bridget Brereton (1982); John Cowley (1996); Richard Burton (1997); Gordon Rohlehr (1990); and Susan Campbell (1988) have all focused on traditional masquerade, the historical development and practice of Carnival, and the socio-economic and political context of Carnival in Trinidad and Tobago from the nineteenth century. Some studies focus on national and cultural identities, gender, the diaspora, and Carnival, such as those by Philip Scher and Garth Green (2007); Milla Riggio (2004); and Patricia De Freitas (1999). Meanwhile, Keith Nurse (2004) addresses the creative and cultural industries and festival tourism of the Trinidad Carnival from the late twentieth century into the twenty-first century.

The literature also discusses women and Carnival from both a colonial and a postcolonial perspective (Frances Henry & Dwaine Plaza 2020). Belinda Edmonson (2003) examines female public performance with regard to women's rituals, behavior, and popular culture in the public sphere. Edmonson notes how Black women are consistently portrayed as not respectable and lewd. Samantha Pinto (2009) highlights the public debate on "indecent" behavior

213

of masqueraders and the issue of respectability as linked to blackness. Samantha Noel (2010) similarly states that jamette women were judged, disregarded, and disrespected and that they used their bodies in order to rebel. Anna Perkins (2011), too, examines notions of sexuality and women's bodily displays during Carnival, contrasting these to Christian notions of the body and sexuality. This chapter seeks to add to this literature with historical attention to jamette women and the ways in which they embodied protest and agency through cultural resistance.

Origins of the Jamette Carnival

In the late eighteenth century, French immigrants introduced Carnival to Trinidad at a time when Carnival was segregated by race, color, and class (Franco 1998, 62). Elaborate masked balls, house to house visiting, music, dancing, and street promenading were a major part of activities embraced by the white and free colored elites, who celebrated in exclusive circles, especially in the towns. The enslaved were onlookers or took part when requested by special favor, while Indians, who migrated to the island primarily from 1845 to 1917, did not participate (Pearse 1956, 179–81). Prior to emancipation in 1838, Carnival was mainly confined to the island's elites.

In the post-emancipation era, Carnival "denigrated into a noisy and disorderly amusement for the lower classes," according to one local elite member.[1] Carnival from 1860 to the end of the nineteenth century was referred to as Jamette Carnival by the French and then the English due to the acts of aggression and sexual themes displayed by Blacks during this period (Liverpool 2003, 253). Jamette Carnival retained some links to West African traditions, which included stickfighting, drumming, and singing, and represented African working-class culture adapting to a changing society (Liverpool 2003, 253).

The conditions of urban life in Port of Spain played a crucial role in the history of Carnival and to the emergence of jamette culture. During the nineteenth century, the sugar industry, the main source of income for the British West Indies, faced challenges after the abolition of slavery in 1834 and also due to the 1846 Sugar Duties Act, which equalized all sugar coming into Britain, and competition from beet sugar. In Trinidad, sugar factories closed down or were amalgamated, and jobs were lost. In 1880, 109 sugar estates were in operation, and by 1895, only 59 existed (Campbell 1988, 16).

Another response to the economic situation in the region was migration. Migrants from islands such as Barbados sought a better life in Trinidad. With many Trinidadians leaving the plantations or being forced to do so while migrants sought out better opportunities, the urban areas of the city of Port of Spain became crowded. In 1860, the population grew from 16,457 to 29,468; 40 percent of the latter figure were born outside Trinidad (Pearse 1956, 190). In the city, many of the laboring classes lived in barracks, which formed a barrack yard community. Barrack yards were back to back with the houses of the middle and upper classes (Pearse 1956 190, 192–3). There was little privacy, water and latrines were common facilities, and the yard in the center was a common living space (Pearse 1956, 190–2). Epidemics such as smallpox and cholera were prevalent. With competition for resources and space, sometimes rivalries would occur in the overcrowded city (Pearse 1956, 190–2). This continuous immigration placed increasing pressure on housing in the slum sections of the capital, which led to vagrancy, juvenile crime, and prostitution (Brereton 1982, 132).

Unsanitary conditions, competition for space, and unemployment were some of the factors that contributed to the formation of stickbands in the city, in addition to the increased numbers and heightened tensions between band members. By the 1870s, there were at least a dozen bands that signified different areas of the city (Campbell 1988, 10). For example, the Maribones were from Belmont Road and the Bakers from the streets behind the Market (Liverpool 2003, 282–3). Bands also represented occupations; for instance, the Coraille band was comprised of store clerks. Bands, namely the Free-Grammars, Bakers, and Maribones, fought each other for turf and rights on Carnival Day. On this day, bands would also attack the elites and the police (Liverpool 2003, 282). Yet another reason for fighting was status to be gained. Victors often won the sexual favors of matadors (madams) and other women in districts, and some were even considered to be leaders of their communities as a result of their victories (Liverpool 2003, 285).

The urban center was dominated by young unmarried women. In 1881, women made up more than 50 percent of the Port of Spain population. In 1891, 60 percent of the city's female population was born in Trinidad, and 31 percent was from another West Indian colony (Trotman 1984, 61). They were employed as domestics, seamstresses, shopkeepers, hucksters, and sex workers. Sex work was especially on the increase in the 1870s and 1880s, likely due to the economic distress of the 1880s (Trotman 1984, 69). As a result, jamettes emerged, that is, "black women in nineteenth-century urban Trinidad who were associated with the barrack yards, gangs and the streets" (Edmonson 2003, 5).

Carnival became controlled by "citizens of the underworld, petty criminals, prostitutes, thieves, pimps, who were called jamettes" (Green & Scher 2007, 17). The words "'Jamet and Jamette' were French-patois terms for male and female members of the unemployed and petty criminal … those beneath the 'diameter' (diametre) of 'decent society '" (Campbell 1988, 10). The word "diameter" or "diamet" referred to the "underworld," (Pearse 1956, 188) that of "prostitutes and their 'sweet men', gamblers, corner men … the celebrated stickfighters … and the notorious jamettes" (Campbell 1988, 10). Stickfighting was an art form that was practiced mainly by enslaved men across the Caribbean and was retained as part of a principal cultural expression of Carnival in the post-emancipation period in Trinidad and Tobago. Associates with the culture that revolved around barrack yards also included singers, drummers, dancers, matadors, bad-johns, obeah men, and corner boys (Brereton 1982, 134). This jamette class was organized into loose associations, bands, or gangs that took over Carnival in the 1860s and 1870s (Brereton 1982, 132). Subsequently, during this period, Carnival across the island "came to have a distinct character and significance for the society as a whole," and was described as "Jamette Carnival" (Pearse 1956, 188; Cowley 1996, 72).

For the participants, it was an opportunity to play off old grievances in ritualized conflict and to let off steam. In spite of attempts to regulate Carnival by officials and upper-class hostility, Blacks were successful in preserving some of their values and traditions (Brereton 1982, 135). In the 1850s, masques such as negres jardins, linked to plantation life and African enslavement, were popular. These featured Black participants, who carried baskets on their heads, being driven by a man with a long whip. Masques depicting death and demons, in which tar was used to cover the body, were also prevalent (Cowley 1996, 80).

Another activity that became identifiable with Jamette Carnival was Canboulay. By 1847, Canboulay was integrated into Carnival and became a primary opening feature. Canboulay, which is a derivation of Cannes Brulees, was said to have originated during African enslavement: "Whenever fire broke out upon an estate, slaves of the surrounding properties were immediately mustered to the spot, horns and shells were blown to collect them and the gangs were followed by their drivers cracking their whips and urging them with cries and blows to their work."[2] However, after emancipation, the formerly enslaved "began to represent this scene as a kind of commemoration of the change of their condition, and the procession of the 'cannes brulees' used to take place on the night of 1st August, the date of their emancipation."[3] They carried flambeaux (flaming torches) in procession throughout the streets (Campbell 1988, 10). Cannes Brulees, which featured stickfighters of bands who clashed with each other, in which the rules of single combat were forgotten, were accompanied by kalenda/kalinda music. Sticks, stones, and bottles also became the weapons of the bands and were used by both male and female followers (Liverpool 2001, 274; Pearse 1956, 192). Canboulay was a main form of Carnival for the Black working class.

However, stickfighting and stickbands were not understood or embraced by the wider society. Subsequently, in 1868, an ordinance was passed to authorize police to end Canboulay torch-bearing in the event that it became a public nuisance (Campbell 1988, 15). In 1884, there was an amendment to the Peace Preservation Ordinance of 1883, which "outlawed disorderly assemblies of ten or more people, as well as unauthorised dancing, processions and drumming" (Campbell 1988, 15). The enforcement of this law led to the imprisonment of many band members over time (Cowley 1996, 75).

Women and masquerade

Women contributed to the masquerade of Jamette Carnival in several ways, as subjects of masques and as masqueraders themselves. The female masqueraders, in the 1860s, depicted sexual themes. Bands of men and women portrayed "matadors," "prostitutes," and "jamettes." For instance, jamette women would startle bystanders by opening their bodices and exposing their breasts. These women were known to wear sexually revealing clothing and for dancing indecently in the streets. They would fight among themselves for the attention of men and openly solicit men, particularly of the middle class (Liverpool 2001, 276). Some of these jamettes of notoriety were Annie Coals, Myrtle the Turtle, Boadicea, Alice Sugar, Hard Back Doris, Petit Belle Lily, Baje, and Cariso Jane (Liverpool 2001, 276). The presence and performance of these women at Carnival reveals narratives between Carnival and racial and gendered identities, because their actions indicated that mainly Black working-class women would behave in an inappropriate and suggestive manner. They were at ease with flaunting their bodies publicly in a provocative manner in order to entice men, especially those of higher-income strata, for their benefit; men who may have been lured by their exoticism, directness, and freedom of sexuality.

During the age of the Jamette Carnival, some elements of masquerade parodied gender roles. From the 1860s, the masque "piss en lit"/"pisse-en-lit," "pisani" ("wet-the-bed" or "stinker" crossdressers for the day) featured men wearing long transparent night gowns, some replete with "menstrual cloths" that were appropriately stained: "Some carried chamber pots on their heads and 'washed' themselves on the streets" (Liverpool 2001, 277).[4] Furthermore, "the "pisse-en-lit" male masqueraders threw powder and flour on passers-by while pretending [to be] women [who] beautify and powder their faces" (Liverpool 2001, 278). It was noted in 1888 that "most of the bands of men dressed as women paraded the whole city from morning to night, repeating the same song, containing double entendres of the most obscene meaning and dancing in the lewdest manner."[5] Arguably, the very existence of masquerade such as pisse-en-lit signified how important women – both cis- and transgender – were to this masque. Women were the subject of their masque to be portrayed, because part of playing the pisse-en-lit was not only to dress and act like women of the lower class but to target elite women deliberately in order to make them uncomfortable.

The inversion of gender roles exemplified mediating trans spaces and those in-between. In 1888, it was noted that there was "the undoubted increase in the exchange of the dresses of the two sexes … as the cases of men dressed as women and women dressed as men … were far more numerous than we have ever seen before."[6] The state eventually intervened, and in 1896, "it became illegal for any male to appear dressed or disguised as female, or any female to be dressed or disguised as a male."[7] This decision underscored the fact that although Carnival allowed for freedom of expression, this type of masquerade that reversed, or queered, gender roles was viewed as obscene, was not appreciated, and would not be tolerated.

Jamettes as chantuelles

Black women were visible in Carnival not only through their bodies but also by their voices in the capacity of chantuels/chantuelles/chantwells/chanterelles. "Women were the chantwells who sang fighting songs to intoxicate male stickfighters as they prepared to do battle on Carnival and other days" (Trotman 1984, 68). The role of this soloist was "to boast the accomplishments of his, or more often her, band in song while pouring vituperation on rival gangs … in this period ca'iso, as calypso was called before the 1890s, was usually sung by women" (Campbell 1988, 12). Women first sang the "cariso," an erotic song, at kalenda sessions (Liverpool 2001, 521). The belair and the calinda/kalenda were the two main types of songs during Carnival. The belair "could be a song of praise or satire on an individual or a group; it could be a witty or humorous commentary on topical events; or it could record personal adventures, real or imagined, amorous or otherwise" (Hill 1997, 72).

The belair was deceptive, and the double entendre (phrase or word having two interpretations) was an important weapon. However, the tunes of the calinda employed a direct declarative statement. They were more frequently used and became the popular lavway/calinda chanted on Carnival days. These "chanterelles," or calypso singers, and their "carisos" were habitually castigated as being lewd and erotic and for allegedly instigating obscene dancing (Edmonson 2003, 5). Until the late 1890s, the songs were sung in Creole, and most were impromptu (Hill 1997, 72).

This style and genre of music, which produced "the vilest songs, in which the names of ladies on the island are introduced to be sung in the streets, and the vilest talk to be indulged in,"[8] was not welcomed by other races and classes in the society. In 1898, there was a suggestion for the police to be on the alert to stop these "songs of a grossly indecent nature" that were sung in patois, particularly by those "members of the force who understand the Creole dialect."[9] The use of patois as the language of expression was a cause for concern for the local British elite, who had little knowledge of the language. By the 1890s, a consequence of suppressing Carnival's jamette element was the decline of female singers and the increased male domination of calypso. Subsequently, the use of patois declined and was often only retained in refrain as English became the dominant language of calypso (Campbell 1988, 18–19).

Through their knowledge and creation of these various types of songs associated with kalenda and Canboulay, women were preservers of oral traditions, expressive culture, and social practices of the communities of Port of Spain. Singing these songs was a means of preserving their cultural identities and was also a way to make sense of experiences and their harsh realities. Furthermore, by their use of patois, and not English, the language of their then colonizer, they preserved this hybridized language, which contained phrasing, syntax, and words of African origin. Moreover, through the roles they played in performing these songs and the use of patois, women became the vessels that allowed cultural transmission of this aspect of intangible cultural heritage, that is, music and its role in the practices associated with the art of stickfighting.

Women's participation in stickbands personified a culture of resistance in many ways. Some West African musical traditions survived through the jamette women who sang belair, kalinda, and cariso, which became part of an identity associated with blackness. Women contributed immensely to the retention of West African characteristics of music, namely the statement/response form, the frequent use of repeated short phrases, and the occasional litany-like pattern, and transformed satirical songs sung during enslavement in the post-emancipation context

(Campbell 1988, 12). Their musical pursuits led to "cariso" – "the use of song for purpose of social comment and satire" becoming the "kalenda" songs, which developed into calypso. The latter did not start with cariso but existed alongside kalenda throughout the nineteenth century when kalenda was suppressed (Liverpool 2001, 321). Women were not only the carriers of the music and the engine for stickfighting, but practitioners of this art form as well, and engaged in many battles during the nineteenth century.

Jamette stickfighters

Black working-class women participated in organized violence as members of stick bands and as stickfighters during the nineteenth century. Bands devoted to drumming, drinking, and stick-fighting were part of life and culture in the barrack yards. Being a part of a stickband gave members a sense of belonging and community. Generally, bands rivaled each other during and outside Carnival. Women belonged to either bands that contained both sexes or women's bands. Some female-led bands included the Dahlias, the Mousselines, and the Don't care Dams (Campbell 1988, 10; Trotman 1984, 68).

Bands that comprised both sexes clashed with each other. During the Carnival of 1874, "herds of disreputable males and females … organised into bands and societies," caused the closing of dwelling houses and shops to keep out missiles such as stones and broken bottles that were "set in constant motion by the contending bands" (Pearse 1956, 188).

Women's bands also fought each other. In one instance in 1864, Clementina Millas,

> armed with a horsewhip, led a band of women, the "Mousselines" against another group called the "Don't care dams" whose leader carried a flag. Both groups carried stones in their aprons, and were armed with knives and razors. With their frocks tucked up, they fought each other in a battle which spread from George Street to an open field on the banks of the Dry River.
>
> *(Trotman 1984, 68)*

In another case, in 1868, the women of the Dahlias and the Mousselines, who had prior tensions, fought. On the morning of the cannes brulees, besides this particular "Dahlia Association," "there were also the Mousselines, Magneta, Mariburn, True-Blue, Black Ball and Don't-care-a Dam associations parading the streets in fantastic dresses."[10] The leaders of the bands were called queens, and the members were princesses. The Queen of the Mousselines was Clementina Mills, and the Queen of the Dahlias was Elizabeth Simmons. Both bands were armed with batons and baskets, but the Mousselines also had stones and broken bottles. Juliana Gomez and 18 other young women appeared in the Supreme Criminal Court, before his Honor Justice Warner, who charged them with having unlawfully assembled together in warlike manner in the public street and making an affray on February 24. The 19 women belonged to the "Dahlia Association."[11]

Jamette women, through their participation in Carnival as stickfighters, reconfigured gender dynamics and identity politics in Trinidad and Tobago. Some women gained a reputation as fighting women. Some of the most notorious women were "Annie Coals, Myrtle the Turtle, Alice Sugar, Alice's younger sister, Piti Belle Lily, and Boadicea"[12] (Trotman 1984, 69). Their pursuits and notoriety were kept alive through Carnival songs that extolled their prowess in combat and boasted of their sexual adventures and conquests (Hill 1997, 72). By embracing the culture of the barrack yards and practicing it by joining bands, jamette women collectively defied societal norms of respectable and acceptable behavior for women, especially as compared with the perceived delicate nature of white women and their Victorian norms, and the modesty and demure view of East Indian women within the same society.

Women and popular protest

During the nineteenth century, women were highly visible participants in popular protest and could be found in the forefront of affrays and riots (Trotman 1984, 68). They were especially present as protestors in two major riots: the 1881 Canboulay Riots and the 1903 Water Riots. Pertaining to the Canboulay Riots, in 1881, the bands, namely the "Maribone" Band of Upper Belmont and the "Bakers" of Market Street, which usually rivaled each other, united against the police on Carnival Sunday.[12] Captain Arthur Baker, who had been appointed in 1877, succeeded in controlling the Carnivals of 1878 and 1879. In 1880, he called on participants to surrender their drums, sticks, and flambeaux; they complied with this order, and their torches were extinguished. His attempt to do so again in 1881 led to the riot, which commenced on February 27[13] (Pearse 1956, 189; Liverpool 2001, 304–5; Cowley 1996, 77).

Men and women prepared for battle with the police to defend their tradition. Revelers had bottles and stones lined up in the yards of the city. Some wore overturned utensils over their heads as a means of protection, and "the fighters were encouraged as is the custom in the Kalenda – by prostitutes and female stickfighters such as Lucretia, Pegtop and Sarah Jamaica" (Liverpool 2001, 307). Kalenda singing and chanting was heard as bottles and stones were thrown towards the police (Liverpool 2001, 308). The battle spread across the streets of Port of Spain, namely Duke, Prince, Charlotte, Queen, and Duncan streets. In the aftermath, 38 policemen had been hurt, between 40 and 50 masqueraders were injured, 21 arrests were made, and street lamps were smashed[14] (Liverpool 309).

From the 1890s, Carnival was brought under more effective control by the police, which eventually led to the end of Jamette Carnival. Street parading before dawn on Monday morning was forbidden with regard to Canboulay. Bands of more than 10 men carrying sticks were forbidden, and pisse-en-lit bands, transvestism, and obscene words and actions were prohibited (Pearse 1956, 189).

Carnival, as a result of enforcement of regulations and policing, had changed, and it became accepted by the middle and upper classes. Nonetheless, in the early twentieth century, protests continued in which women were involved, namely the 1903 Water Riot. This was a violent confrontation that transpired between the residents of Port of Spain and the colonial police on March 23, 1903. The Waterworks Ordinance of 1902 aimed to stop the waste of water by installing meters to charge for use of water, charge rates for baths exceeding 60 gallons, and so forth. However, the Ratepayers' Association, which was founded in 1901 by some prominent businessmen with the objective of safeguarding the interest of Port of Spain rate payers, took up the specific issue of water (Brereton 1982, 149). The Ratepayers' Association called on its members and public to assert their political rights and urged the public to converge on Red House to prevent the passage of this bill. "…Deep political tensions between an emerging Creole intellectual class able to organise mass political opinion and a powerful colonial establishment in near absolute control of the political framework" (Pantin 2016, 61) also contributed to causing the Water Riot.

On March 23, a crowd, which included "women, children and younger men of the poorer section of Port of Spain," gathered outside the parliamentary building, chanting and shouting. Women from the diametre played a prominent part in the assault on the Red House. They were dancing and singing in the street as they approached the building before they threw stones (Cowley 1996, 162). During the delivery of a speech by His Excellency, the crowds all around the Red House had been growing more and more noisy and turbulent and several small fights … with the police occurred. For a long while however nothing serious happened though the singing of the National Anthem, Rule Britannia etc., the beating of the drum, the blows of whistles and the cries of women carrying flags were on the increase.[15]

The incident that sparked the riot occurred when "a woman on the lawn to the East of the Red House was arrested by a constable, who was immediately struck by a couple of stones flung by two small boys."[16] The officer released the woman, but she attacked him immediately as well. Several members of the crowd dragged back the woman and the boys, and "in a moment the stone throwing was widely taken up by the crowd and the stones were pelted in a terrible shower in the Council Chamber."[17]

In the aftermath, the Government House (the Red House) was burned to the ground, 16 people were killed by the police, and over 40 were injured (Pantin 2016, 150). The list of those wounded or killed comprised predominately men, but some women were among those wounded or killed, namely Emily Donald of George Street, Eliza Walker of Belmont, Louisa Sobers of Henry Street, and Mary Seymour of Charles Street.[18] None of the Ratepayers' Association were involved in the rioting, and the victims were nearly all lower-class urban residents (Brereton 1982, 150).

Conclusion

By their very existence, jamettes embodied resistance through their bodies, whether as sex workers, stickfighters, or protestors in the 1881 Canboulay Riots and the 1903 Water Riot. They articulated resistance as chantwells, through which patois flowed off their tongues and through their songs. Their retention and preservation of this tradition were essential for stickband culture and barrack yard life. Women played an instrumental role and contributed tremendously to the cultural and racial identities of the Black working class of the city. At every turn, when they sought to bring out the jamette from within, they faced opposition from members of the public and the colonial government. Jamettes, nonetheless, continued to rebel in order to maintain a heritage that was based on African cultural traditions and resisted respectability politics to assert a liberated sexuality beyond racial and colonial confinements. Indeed, jamette women were survivors, strategists, bold, dangerous, violent, promiscuous, and skilled fighters, who held steadfastly to who they were and not what society dictated that a woman should be.

Notes

1 Dennis Mahabir Collection, "Mr. Hamilton's Report on the Causes and Disturbances in Connexion with the Carnival in Trinidad," London, June 13, 1881.

2 Ibid., 2.

3 Ibid.

4 *Trinidad Royal Gazette*, January 16, 1896: 66.

5 *Port-of-Spain Gazette*, "The Carnival," February 11, 1888: 5; *Port-of-Spain Gazette*, "The Carnival," February 15, 1888: 3.

6 Ibid.

7 *Trinidad Royal Gazette*, January 16, 1896: 66.

8 Dennis Mahabir Collection, "Mr. Hamilton's Report on the Causes and Disturbances in Connexion with the Carnival in Trinidad," 3.

9 *Port-of-Spain Gazette*, "The Coming Carnival," February 17, 1898: 3.

10 *Trinidad Chronicle*, June 16, 1868: 3.

11 Ibid.
12 *The Trinidad Chronicle*, "The Carnival Disturbances in Port-of-Spain," March 2, 1881.
13 Dennis Mahabir Collection, "Mr. Hamilton's Report on the Causes and Disturbances in Connexion with the Carnival in Trinidad," 3.
14 Ibid.
15 *The Port of Spain Gazette,* March 25, 1903: 4–5.
16 Ibid.
17 Ibid.
18 Ibid.

Bibliography

Barnes, Natasha. "Body Talk: Notes on Women and Spectacle in Contemporary Trinidad." *Small Axe 4*(1), 2000: 93–105.

Brereton, Bridget. *A History of Modern Trinidad 1783–1962.* Exeter: Heinemann, 1982.

Burton, Richard. *Afro-Creole: Power, Opposition, and Play in the Caribbean.* Ithaca, NY: Cornell University Press, 1997.

Campbell, Susan. "Carnival, Calypso, and Class Struggle in Nineteenth Century Trinidad." *History Workshop 26*, 1988: 1–27.

Cowley, John. *Carnival, Canboulay and Calypso: Traditions in the Making.* Cambridge: Cambridge University Press, 1996.

Crichlow, Michaeline. *Carnival Art, Culture and Politics: Performing Life.* Oxon: Routledge, 2012.

Edmonson, Belinda. "Public Spectacles: Caribbean Women and the Politics of Public Performance." *Small Axe 13*, 2003: 1–16.

Franco, Pamela. "Dressing up and Looking Good: Afro-Creole Female Maskers in Trinidad Carnival." *African Arts 31*(2), 1998: 63–67; 91–96.

Franco, Pamela. "The Invention of Traditional Mas and the Politics of Gender." In *Trinidad Carnival: The Cultural Politics of a Transnational Festival*, edited by Garth Green and Philip Scher, 25–47. Indiana: Indiana University Press, 2007.

Freitas, Patricia De. "Disrupting the Nation : Gender Transformations in the Trinidad Carnival." *NWIG 73*(1&2), 1999: 5–34.

Green, Garth and Philip Scher. "Introduction : Trinidad Carnival in Global Context." In *Trinidad Carnival: The Cultural Politics of a Transnational Festival*, edited by Philip Scher and Garth Green, 1–24. Indiana: Indiana University Press, 2007.

Henry, Frances and Dwaine Plaza. *Carnival is Woman: Feminism and Performance in Caribbean Mas.* Jackson: University Press of Mississippi, 2020.

Hill, Errol. *The Trinidad Carnival: Mandate for a National Theatre.* London: New Beacon Books, 1997.

Liverpool, Hollis. *Rituals of Power and Rebellion: The Carnival Tradition in Trinidad.* Illnois: Research Associate School Times Publications, 2001.

Noel, Samantha. "De Jamette in We: Redefining Performance in Contemporary Trinidad Carnival." *Small Axe 14*(1), 2010: 60–78.

Nurse, Keith. "Trinidad Carnival: Festival Tourism and Cultural Industry." *Events Management 8*(4), 2004: 223–230.

Pantin, Shane. "Water in the City: The Water Riot of 1903." In *In the Fires of Hope Vol. 2*, edited by Debbie McCollin, 61–77. Kingston: UWI Press, 2016.

Pearse, Andrew. "Carnival in Nineteenth Century Trinidad." *Caribbean Quarterly 4*(3/4), 1956: 175–193.

Perkins, Anna. "Carne Vale (Goodbye to Flesh?): Caribbean Carnival, Notions of the Flesh and Christian Ambivalence about the Body." *Sexuality & Culture 15*(4), 2011: 361–374.

Pinto, Samantha. "Why Must All Girls Want to be Flag Women?" Postcolonial Sexualities, National Reception and Caribbean Soca Performance." *Meridians: Feminism, Race, Transnationalism 10*(1), 2009: 137–163.

Riggio, Milla. *Carnival : Culture in Action : The Trinidad Experience.* New York: Routledge, 2004.

Rohlehr, Gordon. *Calypso and Society in Pre-independence Trinidad.* Port of Spain: Gordon Rohlehr, 1990.

Shaw, Andrea. "Big Fat Fish: The Hypersexualization of the Fat Female Body in Calypso and Dancehall." *Anthurium 3*(2), 2005: 1–7.

Trotman, David. "Women and Crime in Late Nineteenth Century Trinidad." *Caribbean Quarterly 30*(3/4), 1984: 60–72.

Allison O. Ramsay

Primary sources

Dennis Mahabir Collection. *Mr. Hamilton's Report on the Causes and Disturbances in Connexion with the Carnival in Trinidad*. London, June 13, 1881.

The Port of Spain Gazette. "The Carnival." February 11, 1888: 5.

The Port of Spain Gazete. "The Carnival." February 15, 1888: 3.

The Port of Spain Gazette. February 17, 1898: 3.

The Port of Spain Gazette. "Police Court News." February 23, 1898: 5.

The Port of Spain Gazette. "The Coming Carnival." February 17, 1898: 3.

The Port of Spain Gazette. "Reflections on the Carnival." February 17, 1899: 7.

The Port of Spain Gazette. March 25, 1903: 4–5.

The Trinidad Chronicle. June 16, 1868: 3.

The Trinidad Chronicle. February 9, 1877.

The Trinidad Chronicle. "The Carnival Disturbances in Port-of-Spain." March 2, 1881.

Trinidad Royal Gazette. February 17, 1892: 221.

Trinidad Royal Gazette. January 16, 1896: 66.

Part IV
Cultural shifts, social change

22

Wives and warriors

The royal women of Dahomey as representatives of the kingdom

Lynne Ellsworth Larsen

In Ryan Coogler's comic-based film *Black Panther* (2018), women play integral roles in the fictional kingdom of Wakanda as queen mother, princess, spy, council members, and warriors. The principal bodyguard of the king, Okoye, leads the elite corps of female warriors known as the Dora Milaje, who wear red armor, have clean shaven heads, and carry spears made of the fictitious potent metal vibranium. At the film's climax, their choreographed attack on the antagonist Killmonger constitutes a display of Black female representation full of courage, grace, and power, anomalous in mainstream media.

While influences for the costumes and weaponry of the Dora Milaje have roots in the Maasai and Turkana peoples of east Africa,[1] the notion of an African female army has a precedent in the precolonial west African kingdom of Dahomey (*c.* 1645–1894). Not unlike those in Wakanda, royal women of Dahomey played significant roles in the kingdom's politics, religion, and military endeavors. Visual and spatial indicators of their importance, in the forms of regalia, uniforms, and palace architecture, functioned as signifiers of the kingdom within and without its borders. Beginning likely in the mid-eighteenth century, every male officer in the royal court had a corresponding female position. Moreover, Dahomey's female military troops were famous for their fierceness in combat. In addition to representing the kingdom on the battlefield, these women became signifiers of Dahomey in French publications and exhibitions abroad. Though the king functioned as Dahomey's political head, royal women played crucial roles in representing the kingdom within the palace, in religious ceremonies, on the battlefield, and in international media.

Royal women in the palace of Dahomey

The kings of Dahomey ruled from a large palace complex located in the precolonial capital of Abomey in the present-day Republic of Benin. Just as the borders of the kingdom expanded with the conquests of various kings, the Palace of Dahomey evolved throughout the kingdom's history. Over the course of the Dahomean dynasty, from King Huegbadja, who settled in Abomey in the early to mid-seventeenth century, to King Behanzin, who was exiled by the French colonists in 1894, the earthen palace complex expanded until it ultimately covered more than 108 acres, was surrounded by a wall approximately two and half miles long, and housed several thousand people, almost all of whom were women. Access into the royal palace was highly restricted. Robert B. Edgerton explains, "Royal palaces helped to symbolize the king's separateness and his greatness. No one could enter any of his palaces without his invitation, and except for eunuchs, no man did so after sunset."[2]

The inner-most courtyards of the palace constituted the residential quarters of the king, royal women, and some slaves and eunuchs. The palace evolved to maintain a female interior/male exterior dichotomy, which provided royal women with a privileged closeness to the monarch but also separated them from the outside population. Royal women had primary access to the king and controlled access to him. They were the first to know when a king died and sometimes had a hand in determining royal succession. As the numbers of royal women within the palace increased, they developed an economy whereby they were able to earn money and spend it in an exclusively female market located within the palace precinct.[3]

The reigns of the nineteenth-century kings Guezo (r. 1818–58) and Glele (r. 1858–89) are remembered as a golden age of Dahomean history. The kingdom was politically stable, facilitating economic growth, diplomatic relations with foreigners, and an increase in the number of wives at court. While exact numbers are difficult to gage, somewhere between 5000 and 8000 *ahosi*, wives or followers of the king, as well as slaves, royal daughters, and female descendants of past kings, resided in the Abomey palace.[4] These *ahosi* included the corps of female warriors, discussed at length later, which became more regimented and notorious during this period.

While the kings' wives and many of the princesses resided in the palace, princes over 10 years of age were forced to leave. King Agadja (r. *circa* 1716–40) established a school for the royal sons, called the Vihondji. A male descendant of the king remained with his mother in the palace until the age of 10, when he was sent to the Vihondji for an education. Here, he learned the qualities of composure, firmness, and resilience.[5] After 10 years of schooling, each prince returned to report to the king on the success of his education, at which time the king, if satisfied, would grant permission for a prince to marry and establish a private home.[6] Generally, only one of each generation of princes would reside in the palace again as king, and not until his predecessor had died.

Dahomean kings maintained sexual control over their wives even when they had occasion to leave the palace walls. Laws forbade anyone to look at these women. Touching one of the *ahosi* was grounds for execution.[7] When leaving the palace, for whatever reason, each wife was accompanied by three or four female servants. One of these former servants, a Yoruba woman, explained in an interview: "If one of the king's wives was going out two female servants would go before and two behind. The two in front would shout, so no one would see them on the way, *A fe su sijaa me dagbe!* A king's wife is coming!" She explained that one of the servants used a hand gong as an additional warning.[8] Upon hearing the call or gong, citizens would evacuate the area. John Duncan, who visited the kingdom of Dahomey in 1845–46, described his experience thus: "The moment this bell is heard all persons, whether male or female, turn their backs, but the males must retire to a certain distance. In passing through the town this is one of the most intolerable nuisances."[9] J. Alfred Skertchly, in his nineteenth-century travel account, made it more vivid when he wrote that with an approaching wife on the road, men and women were forced to "hurry from the path as though a man-eating tiger were approaching."[10] In this way, the king was able to maintain spatial protection of his wives legally to compensate for what he lacked architecturally.

On other occasions, however, royal women were displayed under the king's strict surveillance. In addition to accompanying the king while he received guests in the palace, women took part in processions outside the palace walls. Well-dressed women often ushered the king to ceremonial and political events. In the annual "display of wealth," observed as one of a series of ceremonies and celebrations known as the Annual Customs, women were among those carrying and displaying wealth objects. Using royal wives for this served a two-fold purpose. The king, in this manner, was able to display not only his wealth but also his wives as wealth. Both were indications of the king's power and control, the former showing an economic power and the latter a social and sexual power.

When the larger public was invited to observe such a procession, special precautions were made. In 1772, Robert Norris observed a procession of the royal women during which "a number of men under arms were drawn up at a distance, to prevent the populace from approaching them."[11] As the kings of Dahomey expanded their borders, they often chose wives from every conquered lineage and thus used their wives not only to display their economic, sexual, and military power but also as a symbolic gesture of their political power over the various peoples of the kingdom.

In his nineteenth-century account, Richard Burton describes a procession in which women of rank were carrying sticks of office.[12] Certain *ahosi* also fulfilled administrative duties.[13] For every male office in the royal court, there was a corresponding female position. Even the king had a reign mate, known as the *kpodjito*, who acted as his female counterpart. The establishment of this gender-balanced court likely began with the reign of King Tegbesu (r. 1740–74), whose mother, Hwanjile, aided him in overcoming opposition to the throne.[14] Both male and female officers wore *agbada* robes, traditional men's gowns, with distinct appliquéd patches sewn onto them.[15] Richard Burton, in his report to the Ethnological Society of London, explained, "With regard to the position of women, it must be remembered that the king has two courts, masculine and feminine. The former never enters the inner palace, the latter never quits it except on public occasions."[16] Thus, these gender divisions had spatial manifestations in terms of the palace. Male and female court ministers had corresponding names. Burton explains, "There are, for instance, the female *Mingan* and the man *Mingan*, the she *Meu* and the he *Meu*, and the woman officer is called the '*no*,' or mother of the man."[17] Thus, in title, the feminine positions, through this maternal designation, were granted a slight privilege over the male, just as spatially they were granted access to the privileged palace interior. These women fulfilled administrative duties and functioned as an integral part of the kingdom's government. Gender balance in the kingdom of Dahomey extended beyond the court ministers and into the military.

Royal women as warriors

As Dahomey was an expansionist and slave-trading state, war became a regular part of its political agenda. Unlike many of its neighbors, whose armies disbanded after a conflict's end, Dahomey maintained a standing army. In fact, the kings of Dahomey eventually maintained two armies, one female, who resided in the palace, and the other male, whose quarters were outside the palace complex. Though considered *ahosi*, the king's female soldiers served a unique function. These were warriors, trained to expand the kingdom's borders and provide the king with slaves and sacrificial victims. They often performed dances, songs, and reenactments of battle at ceremonial court functions. On such occasions, they praised the king, declared their loyalty, and demonstrated their desire to fight ruthlessly in his name.

As sources vary, it is difficult to make definite conclusions about the formation of the corps of Dahomean female warriors. Oral sources recount a band of elephant huntresses known as the *gbeto*, who served the court as far back as King Huegbadja (r. *circa* 1645–85).[18] Some sources credit Tassi Hangbé, daughter of Huegbadja and twin sister to Akaba (r. 1685–1708), who likely served as regent for several years after her brother's death. It seems plausible that she would have had an armed female guard to protect her person in the palace during her regency. There is evidence that her successor, Agadja (r. *circa* 1716–40), used armed women in a 1729 battle to march in the back of his army in order to increase its size sufficiently to scare off their opponents, but not necessarily to fight.[19]

King Kpengla (r. 1774–89), in 1781, marched at the head of 800 armed women, whom historian Edna Bay concludes would have been his palace guard, to battle at Agoonah.[20] Some contemporary oral sources credit Guezo (r. 1818–58) with the creation of the corps of female warriors and mention the previous incidents of armed women as merely his inspiration. To be credited with the establishment of a standing female army, Guezo must have developed and strengthened the already armed palace guard and set them apart as their own corps. Their development may have been impelled by the increasingly disproportionate female to male ratios caused by the Trans-Atlantic slave market.[21]

Unlike other West African armies, Dahomean troops wore uniforms. By the mid-nineteenth century, male and female soldiers of Dahomey dressed in distinctive apparel for battle and ceremony. While the battle uniforms went through several iterations, they tended to be somber in color: browns, whites, blues, grays, and blue and white stripes, and for the women, they generally consisted of shorts that extended to just below the knee, a sleeveless tunic that went to the mid-thigh, and a waist sash to hold the tunic close and carry weapons and other items.[22] Female scouts wore an additional grass skirt over their uniform.[23] Several visitors to the kingdom mention that female warriors wore caps or headbands, each appliquéd with a symbol such as a crocodile, shark, cross, or crown to show rank or regiment.[24]

For celebration and ceremony at home, costumes were more colorful, used finer fabrics, and took liberties with the styles, such as the use of knee- or ankle-length skirts to replace the shorts.[25] Uniformed and armed, the Dahomean army acted as an impressive visual indicator of power. As stated by Edgerton, "When Dahomey's large professional army of both men and women paraded, their numbers, flamboyance, and military menace dramatically reaffirmed the king's authority."[26] Unlike other *ahosi*, the female warriors met with men on the battleground without any physical barriers to separate them. However, though they paraded and fought aside men, they were still technically wives of the king, who maintained sexual control over them and executed anyone who sexually defiled one of his female warriors.

This corps of female warriors became known in colonial accounts and abroad as the Amazons of Dahomey. As women who were feared for their military prowess, they upset expectations of nineteenth-century European gender roles, thereby provoking curiosity abroad. They contributed to France's justification for colonization under the dictates of the *Mission Civilisatrice*. French ideology conflated notions of civilization with principles of mastery and restraint: over the body, nature and disease, and social behavior.[27] In both illustrated newspapers and public expositions, Dahomey was presented as desperate for the imperial imposition of this principle of mastery. Notorious among westerners for its human sacrifices, warmongering kings, and Amazon warriors, Dahomey became "an archetype of depraved savagery, its name synonymous with barbarism."[28]

The popular "penny press" papers, the *Petit Journal* and *Petit Parisien*, began to include illustrated supplements in 1889, just in time for the Franco-Dahomean wars.[29] On March 15, 1890, two weeks after the outbreak of fighting in Cotonou, *Le Monde Illustré* published a full-page image of female Dahomean warriors in the thick of battle, claiming the heads of their battle victims and wielding guns. The next day, on March 16, 1890, the *Petit Parisien* published a full-page, six-image montage on Dahomey which included depictions of human sacrifice – skewered heads, a snake-filled "Python Temple" in Ouidah, and the famous Amazon warriors (see Figure 22.1). This largest, centrally placed image portrays three female warriors facing their approaching enemy, one lunging forward aiming her rifle, one running with her gun held high, and one armed with a knife in one hand, a trophy head in the other, and a foot planted on her

Figure 22.1 Illustration published in the *Petit Parisien* on March 16, 1890.

recently decapitated victim. These images, starkly contrasted with the portrayal of the composed, uniformed French colonial administrator Jean Bayol in the page's upper right-hand corner, did more to endorse colonial expansion than to promote accuracy and educate the public on current events. These and other such images of Dahomey enjoyed a wide circulation with the general public, thereby presenting the French "with a vivid picture of the new opponents which colored all subsequent debate on intervention."[30]

Dahomey's infamy was likewise perpetuated in public exhibitions. The "World's Fair" forum, which had been used to demonstrate and promote progress in the scientific and technological realms (including geographic discoveries), by the end of the nineteenth century began incorporating exhibits of colonial acquisitions.[31] Displays of human menagerie and fictive architecture, like the newspaper engravings, were framed through colonial eyes and manipulated to meet political agendas, but in a more immediate and degrading way. For an audience whose opinions of Africans had been tainted by the civilizing cause and by theories of Social Darwinism, witnessing their physical presence in the demeaning state of display and in theatrical reenactments of historic events provided tangible evidence to reinforce those pre-established notions. Dahomey's female army continued to be used as stock signifiers of the kingdom for these events.

Dahomey was one of the cultures that occupied the Chicago Midway during the famous Columbian Exposition of 1893. The Midway Plaisance, interspersed with an animal show, a Ferris wheel, and other fair sensations, consisted of a mile-long series of exhibits displaying different ethnic groups arranged roughly from what was considered savage to civilized by most Americans.[32] Occupying the west end, along with the East Indian and American Indian Villages, and across from "Captive Ballooning," the Dahomey Village featured war dances and battle reenactments.[33] Over the entrance to this exhibit a sign read, "Dahomey Village, Benin French Colony, West Africa Coast" (see Figure 22.2). It was crowned by a French flag and flanked by parallel images of a French colonial officer waving his white pith helmet over his head triumphantly and a female Dahomean warrior holding high a severed head as a war trophy.[34] In addition, two life-size, full-length portraits of bare-breasted female warriors armed with weapons and trophy heads were set down at the viewers' level. Although this exhibition took place in the United States, the billowing tri-color and painted colonial officer, as well as the focus on violence in the depictions and performances of the Dahomeans, indicate a condoning of the colonial cause, while the Midway's general layout and content reveal the pervading racism of the period.

While Dahomey continued to be included in the grand, occasional, international expositions, such as the 1900 Paris World Fair and the colonial exposition held in Marseille in 1922, it also became a subject for the smaller venues. The *Jardin D'Acclimatation* located outside Paris started doing ethnographic exhibits in 1877.[35] For Dahomey, exhibitions in 1891 and 1893 transpired directly following the Dahomean wars and included war dances, mock battles, and military exercises.[36] *Le Casino de Paris* had staged performances by the same group of Amazon

Figure 22.2 Entrance to the Dahomey Village at the Columbian Exposition, 1893, Chicago. Reprinted with permission from the Newberry Library, Chicago, IL.

warriors who performed in the Chicago Columbian Exposition, and those who performed in the spring of 1891 in the Parisian Gardens went on to perform in Prague the next year.[37]

The portrayal of Dahomeans in both the press and the expositions shaped and were shaped by colonial agendas in regards to Dahomey's governance. The same female warriors whose fighting instilled fear in Dahomey's neighbors before colonization became objects of curiosity and justification for colonial endeavors as the French usurped and held power. The French ruled the former kingdom of Dahomey as part of a larger colony, also called Dahomey, from 1894 to 1960. They exiled both King Behanzin (r. 1889–94), the last independent king, who had set fire to the royal palace in 1892 so as not to have it fall into enemy hands, and King Agoli-agbo (r. 1894–1900), who despite being appointed by the French, was not loyal to them. The colony's first governor, Victor Ballot, while working to restore a portion of the Dahomey palace complex, strategically also built several colonial administration buildings within it, from which he initially governed. Ballot's manipulation of the royal architecture was meant to symbolically demonstrate the rise of the new colonial regime and the demise of the old monarchy. Despite colonial efforts to dislodge the power and significance of the precolonial kings, they remain an important part of the cultural and religious landscape of contemporary Abomey, in large part due to the efforts of their female descendants. Throughout the period of colonization and since independence, women have played important religious roles to help preserve the memory and potency of the precolonial kings.

The *dadasi*

Though the last kings of the Dahomean dynastic line had been exiled, the palace was not completely vacated. Designated female descendants of the kings entitled *dadasi* continued, and still continue, to reside in a centrally located section of the palace complex called the Dossoémé. Each of these women is selected through divination to serve as the "wife" of her particular royal ancestor.[38] In accepting this call, each *dadasi* commits to live in the palace, to perform the rituals associated with the altars located in the Dossoémé, and to participate in royal ceremonies.

Historian Bachalou Nondichau claims that the position of *dadasi* was created in the early colonial period as a way to protect the spiritual and physical treasures located in the Dossoémé.[39] In addition to containing important altars associated with the palace and the founding ancestor of the Dahomean line, treasury items which escaped Behanzin's palace fire are said to be buried there. It is therefore forbidden to dig holes within this section of the palace. Whether the *dadasi* existed since the foundation of the Dossoémé, which is believed to date back to the reign of King Agadja in the eighteenth century, or were created to guard the spiritual core of the palace with the onset of colonization, they were firmly established as residents of the palace by the time colonial officer Em. G. Waterlot visited in 1911. He noted, "The palace was no longer inhabited except by some old women" who "devoutly watch over the sacred objects which escaped the fire that took Abomey."[40]

The Dossoémé constitutes a religiously charged, exclusive, female space. While the *dadasi* may marry and have families, their husbands are forbidden to sleep within the Dossoémé, thus maintaining the precolonial restrictions concerning gender and space imposed on the inner portion of the palace. The *dadasi* are permitted to leave the Dossoémé for periods of time on grounds of health and pregnancy but are not allowed to travel a great distance.[41] Once they are set apart in this spiritual calling, their daily clothing consists of no shoes and a *paigne*, or rectangular piece of fabric, wrapped around the body and tied under the armpit.[42] However, for certain ceremonies, they dress in elaborate robes and jewelry, carry canes and parasols, and have their heads bound with white fabric (see Figure 22.3). While for the purposes of ceremonies, it

Figure 22.3 Procession of the *dadasi* during the Gandaxi. Author's photo, 2013.

is only necessary to have one *dadasi* stand in for each royal ancestor (the 12 dynastic kings and the founding ancestors Aligbonon and Agassou), it is possible to have as many as four *dadasi* designated to each king: two assigned to the royal ancestor, one for his *kpodjito*, or reign mate, and one for his *djoto*, or ancestral protector.[43] As of 2013, there were more than 20 women residing in the palace as *dadasi*.

By residing in the palace, the *dadasi* ensure that the palace and royal history remain living and relevant for the people of Abomey. They not only ensure that kings are remembered, but in certain ceremonies, they even facilitate their presence. The culmination of religious activity for the palace and for other royal historic sites is a four-month-long ceremony, which traditionally took place every seven years, known as the Gandaxi. As part of this ceremony, the *dadasi* perform dances in different portions of the palace and at other significant royal sites in Abomey. During some of these dances, a *dadasi* is possessed by the spirit of her ancestor king and performs on his behalf. By enabling the spiritual presence of the precolonial kings, the *dadasi* make immediate the relevance of the kingdom's history to the contemporary population of Abomey. These spirit possessions, as well as the use of royal sites for religious purposes, function to remind the Abomeans of a history, before the imposition of European colonization, that they can claim as their own.

Conclusion

While the historic royal women of Dahomey had substantial political and spiritual influence, the question remains: were they ultimately supporters or even enablers of a patriarchal system? In Coogler's *Black Panther*, there is a moment during the hero T'challa's enthronement ceremony when his sister Shuri raises her hand and thereby appears to challenge him for the throne. After the gasps of those attending subside, she quips, "This corset is really uncomfortable, so can we all just wrap it up and go home?" While the strong female characters in this film have largely been received with feminist approval, this scene inserts female discontent both by referencing corsets, a symbol of feminine restraint, and by making it obvious that Shuri was never earnestly considered for the throne. The fictional women of Wakanda, while they vary in roles, motives, and talents, all arguably serve to support and protect the king. Can the same be said of Dahomey's royal women?

Were the Dahomean women who met in court councils, performed in ceremonies, fought on the battlefield, and had access to the king ultimately subservient to him and thus, to a patriarchal system? Conversely, should we consider that the king did not reign alone? The eventual gender balance that Dahomey maintained in its royal offices and armed forces could also be found in the monarchy. The king reigned with his *kpodjito*, or reign mate, the queen mother, who though not as publicly prominent as the king, held comparable power. The complexity of these issues increases when we consider the diversity in roles and status of women considered wives of the king. Undoubtedly, there were women who increased in power and agency by taking on the title *ahosi* and others, depending on their status and attitude, who endured it as a prison sentence. In our suppositions about Dahomey's women, we must likewise be wary of imposing a western, contemporary version of feminism on another culture, time, and place.

Ultimately, the royal women have been integral in shaping the politics of, opinions about, and memories concerning the kingdom of Dahomey. Throughout history, regalia, uniforms, and palace architecture have visually signified the kingdom at home and abroad. In the kingdom's precolonial history, royal wives represented the king's social, economic, military, and sexual power. The inner courtyard of Dahomey's palace constituted a privileged female space where royal women had access to the king. By the nineteenth century, thousands of wives resided in the palace, many paraded in celebrations, a select few served in the royal court, and others fought in battles.

The representation of Dahomey's female warriors in public expositions and in print media throughout the colonial period exoticized the kingdom and further justified French colonization, a sharp contrast to the contemporary positive portrayal and reception of the Dora Milaje in Coogler's *Black Panther*. Colonizers manipulated the palace and attempted to abolish the kingdom's power and importance. Despite this, women continue to assert the importance of the precolonial kings in the postcolonial moment through ceremonies that revitalize royal architecture and facilitate the spiritual presence of the kings. The *dadasi*, by living in the palace, create a spiritual continuity from the precolonial kings to the postcolonial present. Being female, they resonate the importance and influence of historic royal women while simultaneously emphasizing the potential influence of women in the contemporary moment.

Notes

1 Melena Ryzik, "The Afrofuturistic Designs of 'Black Panther'," *The New York Times*, February 23, 2018, <www.nytimes.com/2018/02/23/movies/black-panther-afrofuturism-costumes-ruth-carter.html>, accessed May 28, 2019.
2 Robert B. Edgerton, *Warrior Women: The Amazons of Dahomey and the Nature of War* (Boulder, Colorado: Westview Press, 2000), 72.
3 Ibid.
4 Edna Bay, "Servitude and Worldly Success in the Palace of Dahomey," in *Women and Slavery in Africa*, ed. Clair C. Robertson and Martin A Klein, 340–67 (Madison: The University of Wisconsin Press, 1983), 341.
5 Bachalou Nondichau (traditional historian), in discussion with author, February 20, 2013, Abomey.

6 Ibid.

7 Richard F. Burton, "The Present State of Dahome," *Transactions of the Ethnological Society of London* 5, no. 3 (July 1932): 405.

8 Peter Morton-Williams, "A Yoruba Woman Remembers Servitude in a Palace of Dahomey, in the Reigns of Kings Glele and Behanzin," *Africa* 63, no. 1 (1993): 106.

9 Melville J. Herskovits and Frances S. Herskovits, *Dahomey, an Ancient West African Kingdom* (New York: J. J. Augustin, 1938), 35.

10 J. Alfred Skertchly, *Dahomey As It Is: Being a Narrative of Eight Months' Residence in That Country with a Full Account of the Notorious Annual Customs, and the Social and Religious Institutions of the Ffons* (London: Chapman and Hall, 1874), 113.

11 Robert Noris, *Memoirs of the Reign of Bossa Ahádee King of Dahomy and Inland Country of Guiney to Which Are Added the Author's Journey to Abomey, the Capital and a Short Account of the African Slave Trade* (London: Frank Cass and Company, 1968), 101–2.

12 Richard F. Burton, *A Mission to Gelele, King of Dahome with Notices of the So Called "Amazons," the Grand Custums, the Yearly Customs, the Human Sacrifices, the Present State of the Slave Trade, and The Negro's Place in Nature* (London: Tinsley Brothers, 1864), vol. 2, 16.

13 Edna G. Bay, "The Royal Women of Abomey" (PhD diss., Boston University, 1977), 128.

14 Edna G. Bay, *Wives of the Leopard: Gender, Politics, and Culture in the Kingdom of Dahomey* (Charlottesville: University of Virginia Press, 1998), 88.

15 Suzanne Preston Blier, *Royal Arts of Africa: The Majesty of Form* (New York: Harry N. Abrams, Inc., Publishers, 1998), 103; Edna G. Bay, *Wives of the Leopard*, 11. Bay explains that just as these women wore traditional men's clothing, the eunuchs who resided in the palace wore traditional women's dress.

16 Burton, "The Present State of Dahome," 405.

17 Ibid.

18 Stanley B. Alpern, *Amazons of Black Sparta: the Women Warriors of Dahomey* (New York University Press, 1998), 20.

19 Bay, *Wives of the Leopard*, 136.

20 Ibid., 137.

21 In places of concentrated slaving, Patrick Manning "calculates an overall average sex ration of seventy adult men for one hundred women in Gbe-speaking areas" (Bay, *Wives of the Leopard*, 146).

22 Alpern, *Amazons of Black Sparta*, 56.

23 Ibid., 56.

24 Ibid., 55.

25 Ibid., 55.

26 Ibid., 72.

27 Alice L. Conklin, "The French Republican Civilizing Mission," in *European Imperialism 1830–1930: Climax and Contradiction*, edited by Alice L. Conklin and Ian C. Fletcher (New York: Houghton Mifflin, 1999), 61.

28 Bay, *Wives of the Leopard*, 278.

29 William H. Schneider, *An Empire for the Masses: The French Popular Image of Africa, 1870–1900* (Westport, Connecticut: Greenwood Press, 1982), 5. Schneider explains that sales for these papers between 1870 and 1900 reached over one million copies daily, and that the illustrations were often in color. Thus, these became powerful tools for shaping public opinion during this period of colonial expansion.

30 Schneider, *An Empire for the Masses*, 103.

31 Ibid, 8–9.

32 Bay, *Wives of the Leopard*, 278–9.

33 Norman Bolotin and Christine Laing, *The World's Columbian Exposition: The Chicago World's Fair of 1893* (Champaign: University of Illinois Press, 2002), 131.

34 This was a mirror-imaged, topless version of the *Petit Parisien*'s March 16th or *Monde Illustré*'s March 15th Amazon published three years earlier.

35 Schneider, *An Empire for the Masses*, 9. The obvious rise in ticket sales in conjunction with ethnographic exhibits and consequent financial benefit motivated the Garden's administration not only to continue them but to look for ways to draw crowds.

36 Schneider, *An Empire for the Masses*, 142.

37 Nicolas Blancel, *Zoos humains: au temps des exhibitions humaines* (Paris: La Decouverte, 2004), 77.

38 Thierry Joffroy, Leonard Ahonon, and Gabin Djimasse, *Palais Royaux d'Abomey: Les Dadassi du quartier Dossoémé* (CRAterre-ENSAG: Grenoble, 2013), 10.

39 Ibid.
40 Em. G. Waterlot, *Les bas-reliefs des bâtiments royaux d'Abomey (Dahomey)* (Paris: Institut d'ethnologie, 1926), 3. He also mentions the residence of women with the title *kpodjito*, which would have represented the deceased queen mothers/reign mates of the precolonial kings.
41 Thierry Joffroy, Leonard Ahonon, and Gabin Djimasse. *Palais Royaux d'Abomey*, 10.
42 Ibid., 12.
43 Ibid., 12.

Works cited

Alpern, Stanley B. *Amazons of Black Sparta: The Women Warriors of Dahomey*. New York: New York University Press, 1998.

Bay, Edna G. *The Royal Women of Abomey*. Ph.D. diss., Boston University, 1977.

Bay, Edna G. "Servitude and Worldly Success in the Palace of Dahomey." In *Women and Slavery in Africa*, edited by Clair C. Robertson and Martin A. Klein, 340–367. Madison: The University of Wisconsin Press, 1983, 341.

Bay, Edna G. *Wives of the Leopard: Gender, Politics, and Culture in the Kingdom of Dahomey*. Charlottesville: University of Virginia Press, 1998.

Blancel, Nicolas. *Zoos humains: au temps des exhibitions humaines*. Paris: La Decouverte, 2004.

Blier, Suzanne Preston. *The Royal Arts of Africa: The Majesty of Form*. New York: Harry N. Abrams, Inc., Publishers, 1998.

Bolotin, Norman and Christine Laing. *The World's Columbian Exposition: The Chicago World's Fair of 1893*. Champaigne: University of Illinois Press, 2002.

Burton, Richard F. *A Mission to Gelele, King of Dahome with Notices of the So Called "Amazons," the Grand Custums, the Yearly Customs, the Human Sacrifices, the Present State of the Slave Trade, and The Negro's Place in Nature*. London: Tinsley Brothers, 1864.

Burton, Richard F. "The Present State of Dahome." *Transactions of the Ethnological Society of London* 5, no. 3 (July 1932), 405.

Conklin, Alice L.. "The French Republican Civilizing Mission." In *European Imperialism 1830–1930 Climax and Contradiction*, edited by Alice L. Conklin and Ian C. Fletcher, 60–66. New York: Houghton Mifflin Company, 1999.

Duncan, John. *Travels in Western Africa in 1845 & 1846 Comprising A Journey from Whydah, Through the Kingdom of Dahomey, to Adofoodia, in the Interior*. London: Frank Cass & Co. Limited, 1968.

Edgerton, Robert B. *Warrior Women: The Amazons of Dahomey and the Nature of War*. Boulder: Westview Press, 2000.

Herskovits, Melville J. and Fances S. Herskovits. *Dahomey, an Ancient West African Kingdom*. New York: J. J. Augustin, 1938.

Joffroy, Thierry, Leonard Ahonon and Gabin Djimasse. *Palais Royaux d'Abomey: Les Dadasi du Quartier Dossoémé*. Grenoble: CRAterre-ENSAG, 2013.

Morton-Williams, Peter. "A Yoruba Woman Remembers Servitude in a Palace of Dahomey, in the Reigns of Kings Glele and Behanzin." *Africa* 63, no. 1 (1993): 102–117.

Noris, Robert. *Memoirs of the Reign of Bossa Ahádee King of Dahomy and Inland Country of Guiney to Which Are Added the Author's Jouney to Abomey, the Capital and a Short Account of the African Slave Trade*. London: Frank Cass and Company Limited, 1968.

Ryzik, Melena. "The Afrofuturistic Designs of 'Black Panther' " *The New York Times*, February 23, 2018, <https://www.nytimes.com/2018/02/23/movies/black-panther-afrofuturism-costumes-ruth-carter.html> accessed May 28, 2019.

Schneider, William H. *An Empire for the Masses: The French Popular Image of Africa, 1870–1900*. Westport, CT: Greenwood Press, 1982.

Skertchly, J. Alfred. *Dahomey As It Is: Being a Narrative of Eight Months' Residence in That Country with a Full Account of the Notorious Annual Customs, and the Social and Religious Institutions of the Ffons*. London: Chapman and Hall, 1874.

Waterlot, Em G. *Les bas-reliefs des bâtiments royaux d'Abomey (Dahomey)*. Paris: Institut d'ethnologie, 1926.

23

Reframing Yaa Asantewaa through the shifting paradigms of African historiography

Naaborko Sackeyfio-Lenoch

This chapter examines how particular lines of inquiry in the literature on African women's history have informed historical analysis of Yaa Asantewaa's remarkable role in the last war against the British at the end of the nineteenth century. The West African heroine is renowned in Ghanaian history and African history more broadly as the woman who led the final Asante war against British colonial rule and has been widely commemorated as such. I trace the nodes of inquiry that have informed existing scholarship on Ghana's past as it relates to the precolonial Asante kingdom, gendered and sexuality dynamics within it, nationalist impulses, and the role of a particular class of women, that of the *ohemaa* or queen mother, in the history of the kingdom. I offer some commentary on the shifts or rather, progression in the paradigms by which Yaa Asantewaa's life history has been understood in the past and more contemporary era. The chapter demonstrates that a broad historical arc has been cast for the (re)positioning of Asantewaa in Asante history, the Ghanaian nation, and the larger African Diaspora. In recent years, alternative geographies and mobility have been mapped onto Asantewaa's life story in powerful and unexpected ways that foster the reframing of the analytic categories used to foreground the diverse histories of African women and for this case, those who went to war.

Early articulations of the state of historical research on women across sub-Saharan Africa demarcated the ways in which historical research on African women shifted from an emphasis on queens and prostitutes, privileged women and heroines, to victims and the exploited.[1] This shift was the result of efforts that brought attention to larger questions around class formation, the development of an urban proletariat, and the existence and experiences of enslaved and other marginalized actors across society.[2] Indeed, African women's history has been concerned about how to balance a gendered approach with class, oppression with agency, and victimization with resistance beyond simplistic binaries.[3] Utilizing gender as a category of analysis and gendered meanings to overcome a singular emphasis on gender roles has been an important facet of the scholarship on women's history.[4]

The emphasis on "queens" or more broadly, on autonomous privileged women was the result of the predominance of political history during the early period of African historiography. The participation of elite African women in nationalist movements underscored the role of individual West African heroines. For instance, scholars centralized the role of Asante queen mothers in the nineteenth century, since they had been marginal in the eyes of British colonial officials and male historians, while others focused on women political leaders in other areas of the region.[5] The result was a body of writing about African heroines in West Africa that aimed to illustrate women's social and economic autonomy in the domestic sphere and the complementary political and economic roles across society.[6]

Considerations of gender and state building in Asante historiography

Iris Berger has underscored the scholarly trajectory of African women's history, noting that it has been shaped by three overarching themes: an interest in women as "forgotten heroines" in the 1970s, a focus on women as "underclass actors" in the 1980s and early 1990s, and "gendered subjects" in the late 1990s into the new millennium.[7] Kate Skinner's recent and excellent overview has examined the ways in which the application and understanding of the categories "women" and gender" in the historiography on African women have informed Ghana-specific literature as it relates to wider trends in the field of African studies, gender history, and women's history.[8] Skinner demonstrates the ways in which scholars have utilized specific categories of women and individual examples of political actors to examine the gendered nature of political power.[9] The centrality of Asante historiography to broader studies of Ghana continues to permeate diverse areas of inquiry. Considerations of the gendering of Ghana's precolonial African history underscore the pre-occupation with state building as manifested in the Asante kingdom and its imperial expansion.[10]

My analysis here is not intended to be a full examination of the vast Asante historiography. Rather, I briefly highlight a few important threads as they relate to Asantewaa's efforts explored later in this chapter. An evolving thread of Asante-centric historiography focused on the theme of matrilineage, among others.[11] An examination of how queen mothers achieved their positions, and the ways in which they exercised their authority and influenced important events, demonstrated the evolution of the Asante state and dynamics of political power. The bureaucratic dynamics and offices that Ivor Wilks had identified in his seminal book in 1975 had largely focused on men.[12] Issues of sexuality later emerged as a point of entry into examining how premenopausal women's disqualification functioned in the Asante kingdom. Agnes Aidoo demonstrated that premenopausal women were prevented from engaging in battle and thus were unable to pursue one of the important avenues for individuals to demonstrate their abilities, accumulate wealth, and elevate their status or proximity to political power. While the office of the *ohemaa* was noteworthy, it did not extend to women beyond the royal lineages, indicating the significance of class and the centrality of elite women.[13] Moreover, queen mothers evidently did not work to advance the interests of women across society or represent them in political matters.[14] They were concerned with lineage affairs, accruing substantial influence through the networks of alliances that could be developed during political contestations.

From the margins to the center: Yaa Asantewaa and the nationalist approach

State and society, patriarchal power and matrilineal kinship, as well as history and memory were central in previous scholarship on the Asante kingdom.[15] Those themes were revisited in the remarkable biography of Asantewaa as an avenue to trace the nature and scope of her agency and resistance to colonization at the turn of the millennium. Much of the literature on Asantewaa is concerned with her role in the last war against British imperial forces in 1900 to 1901. Yet, a lack of precision about her actions in that war has permeated existing scholarship, explored later in this chapter. In McCaskie's summary of the points of inquiry for historians, he notes that scholars have questioned whether she planned, directed, or led the uprising or whether she functioned as a symbol of resistance. They have sought to answer whether she engaged in live battles or oversaw operations from Edweso, the seat of her authority, and the nature of her movements at the end of the war, when it became clear that British troops had won. Moreover, the conditions of her surrender, either voluntary or as the result of betrayal, have been of interest to historians. The circumstances around whether British forces exiled Asantewaa to the Seychelles in 1921 because she was a central player in their last efforts to consolidate rule or because she was deemed to be a figurehead have also captivated historians.[16]

Even in colonial Asante, it seemed that the most powerful authority holder attempted to obscure Asantewaa's role in the war for political reasons. The Asantehene, Osei Agyeman Prempeh II, appointed a committee that labored during the late 1930s and 1940s to produce an authorized history of Asante dedicated to showing the occupant of the Golden Stool to be "king over all." This unpublished *History of Ashanti*, with oral traditions that came from all corners of the former kingdom, formed the core of the text, but their inclusion and interpretation were overseen by the Asantehene. It represented a history from the perspective of the Kumasi dynasty. The section on the war offers scanty treatment of Yaa Asantewaa. Furthermore, the text fails to mention her holding any leadership role, and she receives less attention than several other actors in the resistance.[17] McCaskie posits that considerations of gender and the notion that Asante troops were led by a woman may have played some part in Prempeh II's erasure of Yaa Asantewaa. Notwithstanding, her absence from such a politically fashioned text suggests that the suppression of her role was a calculated one, born of her brother's demands and contesting Kumasi royal power over the Edweso State in the 1880s.[18]

Asantewaa's actions were informed by the widening relationship with the British and their influence on the affairs of the Asante state during the latter decades of the nineteenth century. Between 1874 and 1896, the British presence in the Gold Coast was tentative, in the sense that colonial officials could not decide the extent of territory they wanted to secure. However, relations between the British and Asante took a turn for the worse in 1893 after the Asantehene, Nana Prempeh 1, rejected the offer to Asante by Frederick Hodgson, colonial secretary and acting governor to the Gold Coast Colony, to become a British protectorate. Although the British did not attack Asante that year, Prempeh's rejection of Britain's offer set the stage for the events in January 1896 that led to the arrest of the Asante officials and their subsequent deportation and the declaration of Asante as a British protectorate. This paved the way for the dissolution of the Asante union between Kumasi and constituent states.[19] Asantewaa was present at the meeting in March 1900 where Sir Hodgson, now governor of the Gold Coast, laid out the British policies to a gathering of Asante rulers, who were astonished at the demands but offered no apparent resistance. Asantewaa was reported to have taunted Asante rulers, questioning what she viewed to be their passive response.[20] In any case, a war commenced, with British forces defeating Asante, abolishing the monarchy and disbanding the central government, and annexing it as a British colony on September 26, 1901.

A special issue of *Ghana Studies* was organized by Emmanuel Akyeampong in 2000 to commemorate the state of the field on Yaa Asantewaa and Asante history on the centenary of the Yaa Asantewaa War of 1900. The aim of the special issue was to inspire new modes of inquiry in the history of the period, the war, and Asantewaa's life.[21] The focus on Asante nationalism and statehood, and the distinctive nature of the office of queen mother as an instance of the agency of specific women in resisting colonization, were central in the writings of the various authors. The nationalist dimensions of Asante history are deeply intertwined in the existing historiography, such that it appears impossible to separate Asante nationhood from any analysis of Asantewaa's actions and leadership in the anti-colonial war of 1900–01. Sometimes called the Anglo-Asante War or the Anglo-Kumase war against the impending British colonial onslaught in the Asante region, the events were interpreted in various instances as a "nationalist movement," a "rebellion," and "a resistance."[22] This framework has contributed to the overarching view that Asantewaa committed herself to the restoration of the Asante monarchy and a nationalist cause with the desire for the freedom of the nation from British control after she became sole ruler of Edweso in 1896.

However, in one of the more recent renditions of the debates about Asantewaa's efforts as evidence of an Asante nationalist cause, T.C. McCaskie offers caution about the widespread interpretation of Asantewaa's actions in the literature. He argues that far from a harmonious unity within Asante political and national history, the actions of Yaa Asantewaa between 1894 and 1900 advanced the interests of the Edweso State, which she led, more than those of the Golden Stool that represented Kumasi and Asante monarchical power. McCaskie contends that the events of 1900–01 were not an Asante national war against the British. Although some Asante battled the British, others supported them, and many others stayed neutral.[23] Asantewaa in turn chose to fight and hoped to gain in return concessions that would benefit Edweso. Yet, it is clear that Yaa Asantewaa's stool and the Golden Stool were the ones the British troops sought to acquire in their efforts to overcome Asante.[24] This fact places Asantewaa at the center of Asante politics.[25]

There is evidence that Asantewaa's military involvement was partly inspired by patriotism in the sense that she played a prominent role against British colonial advances for the return of Asantehene Nana Agyeman Prempeh 1. Yet, she did not seek a reinstatement of the Asante past in a nationalist sense but rather, "a restoration of the *status quo ante* of the later 1880s" that would benefit the Edweso State for instrumental reasons.[26] Asantewaa was interested in upholding and ratifying a past religio-political pact between the Asante king, Prempeh 1, and her brother, the Edweso paramount chief, Kwasi Afrane 1, on the one hand, and Afrane's cousin, Ofinsohene Apea Sea, on the other.[27]

She did so because British overrule dissolved the arrangement that a repatriated and independent Asantehene would still be held to the terms of the oaths he had sworn and the promises he had made to Edweso royals. In other words, returning to the dynamics just before 1896 would empower Edweso to recover the status and power that had recently allayed its lengthy history of humiliation and loss at the hands of Kumasi royal power. Moreover, by going to war, Asantewaa could honor the death of her influential brother, reunite with her exiled grandson, and live out her old age in a manner that was likely only a few years before the events of 1896. For McCaskie, these reasons constituted her decision to go to war. It was a high price to pay, for Asantewaa was sent into exile and died, roughly at the age of 90, on the remote Indian Ocean archipelago of Seychelles in 1921.[28]

Establishing precedent or building on traditions of diplomacy

Beyond the question of nationalism and Yaa Asantewaa's political calculations, scholars have focused on whether Asantewaa's role in the war set a precedent or built on established practices of her contemporaries and previous queen mothers. Asantewaa emerged as a figure who followed in the footsteps of Asante women in the nineteenth century, such as Akyaawa Yikwan and Prempeh's mother, Yaa Akyaa, both of whom assisted in shaping Asante politics and foreign relations, especially with the British.[29] For instance, in January 1896, Yaa Asantewaa was in charge of Edweso and engaged in talks and negotiations with the British over mines of interest to Edweso and British speculators.[30] She was part of a long tradition of Asante men and women who distinguished themselves at critical moments in the history of the kingdom.[31] Traditions of opposition to the British were passed on to Yaa Asantewaa of the subordinate state of Edweso. It would seem that the political role of Asante queen mothers was particularly heightened in times of crisis when male leadership was either unavailable or ineffectual.[32] Moreover, Asantewaa followed precedents that connected her to earlier efforts of other fighting queen mothers who had all reached menopause.

Aidoo's survey of some nineteenth-century queen mothers is one of very dynamic women who skillfully blended a sense of history, politics, and responsibility towards the preservation of their communities and societies. Their careers reveal the modalities of their power in local, regional, and national affairs. The careers of Afua Kobi, Yaa Akyaa, and Yaa Asantewaa reveal certain aspects of the queen mother's role in government and politics. The *ohemaa* was most effective when she was free from ritual constraints, when she commanded independent resources, and when there was no available or effective male leadership. The structural definition of her position as a hereditary co-ruler from a royal lineage limited any "representative" features in her position. Her participation in government politics therefore cannot be regarded as a general index to female political activity. Her political goals were defined and generalized from concrete lineage and family interests. Her political fields were the arenas of lineage and state, and she drew her support not from "female power" but from all effective sections of society.[33]

Leading a war and choosing a woman to lead

An important line of inquiry has focused on the military role that Asantewaa played in the 1900–01 war and why Asantewaa's male contemporaries would have chosen a woman to lead it. Kwame Arhin postulates that rivalries between male chiefly authorities or the British military presence in Kumasi, which prevented the city from serving as the center of the uprising, may have encouraged chiefs to select a female war leader. In Arhin's view, Asantewaa "must have had certain outstanding qualities and qualifications for a war leader." Asantewaa was more than a symbolic figure; she surpassed the conventional military and political roles of Asante women. She *achieved* the position of the first female war leader, *sahene*, in planning and leading the War of 1900.[34] Both British colonial and oral and documentary sources confirm that Yaa Asantewaa initiated efforts and carried out the necessary tasks for the rebellion; she was the commander-in-chief and leader.[35]

Yet this interpretation does not appear to take into account the evidence of a tradition in which Asante queen mothers took on crucial political and diplomatic positions in state affairs. There was an established precedent of Akan queen mothers occupying male chieftaincy stools and engaging in war and diplomacy. It seems that what set Asantewaa apart from her predecessors was the military role she played in war. However, perhaps Asantewaa's position was not exceptional in the sense that she was working within the confines of Asante ritual constraints that prevented premenopausal women from going to war, even though that caveat did not apply to her. As a postmenopausal ruler, Yaa Asantewaa was empowered to consult with powerful war deities, prepared medicines for Asante warriors, constructed stockades, and engaged in other war rituals designed specifically for women and men. Asantewaa challenged men and women as they prepared for war with rhetoric about gender differences.[36] She was articulate and provocative as she employed "gender-charged" speeches to incite Asante men and chiefly authorities into action.[37]

Contemporary dynamics in the mapping of Asantewaa at home and abroad

Interpretations of Yaa Asantewaa's position shifted over the course of the twentieth century from political prisoner, dangerous subversive, and anti-colonial leader to having schools named in her honor. In recent years, Asantewaa has emerged in other manifestations and been appropriated as a historical figure to meet the needs of various constituencies.[38] As noted earlier, 2000–1 marked the centenary of the Yaa Asantewaa War (1900–1), and the Asantehene authorized the establishment of a centenary committee to plan the activities. The ways in which the centenary of Asantewaa's efforts was understood to be a preservation of Asante independence was a watershed moment in demarcating Yaa Asantewaa's legacy. The celebrations afforded new opportunities for Asantewaa to be recognized, examined, and placed in the context of Asante history and the country as a whole. The centenary cast Asantewaa as a patriotic Asante heroine who led a national war of resistance.

Commentators who acknowledged the contemporary fascination with her public persona with limited knowledge of her personal life acknowledged that for most of the previous century, scant attention had been paid to her. She represented many things to various communities at home and abroad. Asantewaa was understood to be "an anti-colonial guerilla fighter, role model for black women globally, a conservative royalist who attempted to restore an outmoded imperial system, an African feminist, an antagonist to global capitalist expansion, a Ghanaian heroine, an Asante nationalist par excellence."[39] Lynda Day has traced how Asantewaa's legacy crossed many boundaries by the centenary year and underscores the ways in which the commemoration served as a medium for advancing several agendas that resulted in sites of contested historical discourse. The social construction of historical memory was central to the planning of the commemorative activities in the Asante region.[40] The celebrations utilized historical recreation as a means of reclaiming history's potential for empowering contemporary communities on a local and global stage.[41]

Moreover, the centenary and congress at one of the premier universities in the country, Kwame Nkrumah University of Science and Technology, involved the convening of an international conference to commemorate and honor Yaa Asantewaa in August 2000. McCaskie has documented the ways in which the politics of honoring Asantewaa underscored how political parties and government officials attempted to gain political advantage and international praise by capturing Yaa Asantewaa from Asante and relocating her in the wider Ghanaian, African, and Diasporic consciousness as a transnational, anti-colonial, Black female role model and icon. Asantewaa was recast as an internationally known historical figure, for Asante representations of her have increasingly been shaped by international observations and expectations. Moreover, proclaiming pride in Asante history and culture to a global audience has translated into generating revenue from tourists or investors who identify themselves in one way or another with Asantewaa. Asantewaa has been transformed into a cultural relic, an African heroine who can be (and is) (re)presented on the global Internet in many formations.[42] Others have recently demonstrated the ways in which postcolonial Ghana has immortalized and commemorated Asantewaa's actions through an analysis of museums, monuments, and the memory of Asantewaa. Symbols of nationhood, including money, postage stamps, museum exhibits, monuments, and festivals have been the tools that a range of Ghanaians have utilized to symbolically resurrect Asantewaa in various formulations.[43]

Conclusion

These developments point to the promise of mapping new geographies onto the lives of historical figures such as Asantewaa, which engenders fruitful ways of examining the past in the present. The continued salience and relevance of Yaa Asantewaa's life history for contemporary audiences in continental Africa and its multiple diasporas indicate the multiple directions scholarly analysis can take in studying the West African heroine. Comparative approaches to the questions that have animated historians and contemporary observers would enrich the existing literature and perhaps offer a definitive study of the sources that have enabled scholars to reconstruct Yaa Asantewaa's biography. In turn, establishing Asantewaa's place in the annals of African and global histories of nineteenth-century women at peace and at war would highlight how case studies of African women inform methodology questions of interest to a wide range of historians.

Notes

1 Margaret Jean Hay, "Queens, Prostitutes and Peasants: Historical Perspectives on African Women, 1971–1986," *Canadian Journal of African Studies* 22, no. 3 (1988): 431–47.
2 Hay, "Queens," 434.
3 Nancy Rose Hunt, "Placing African Women's History and Locating Gender," *Social History* Vol. 14, no. 3 (October 1989): 359–79.
4 Hunt, "Placing African Women's History," 371.
5 Agnes Aidoo, "Asante Queen Mothers in Government and Politics in the Nineteenth Century," in *The Black Woman Cross-Culturally*, ed. Filomena Steady (Cambridge, Massachusetts: Schenckman, 1981), 65–77; Simi Afonja, "Women, Power, and Authority in Traditional Yoruba Society," in *Visibility and Power: Essays on Women in Society and Development,* ed. Leela Dube et al. (Delhi: Oxford University Press, 1983); T. Farrar, "The Queenmother, Matriarchy, and the Question of Female Political Authority in Precolonial West African Monarchy," *Journal of Black Studies* 27, no. 5 (1997) 579–597; Kwabena Adu-Boahen, "Female Agency in a Cultural Confluence: Women, Trade and Politics in Seventeenth- and Eighteenth-Century Gold Coast," in *Shadows of Empire in West Africa: African Histories and Modernities* eds. John Osei-Tutu and Victoria Smith (London: Palgrave Macmillan, 2017), 169–199; David Sweetman, *Women Leaders in African History* (Portsmouth, NH: Heinemann, 1986); Judith Van Allen, "'Sitting on a Man': Colonialism and the Lost Political Institutions of Igbo Women," in "The Roles of African Women: Past, Present and Future," Special issue of *Canadian Journal of African Studies* 6 no. 2 (1972): 165–81; Flora Edouwaye and S. Kaplan (eds.), *Queens, Queen Mothers, Priestesses and Power: Case Studies in African Gender* (New York, 1997); Sandra T. Barnes, "Gender and the Politics of Support and Protection in Precolonial West Africa," in *Queens, Queen Mothers, Priestesses and Power: Case Studies in African Gender,* eds. Flora Edouwaye and S. Kaplan (New York, 1997), 1–18; Ronald Cohen, "Oedipus Rex and Regina: the Queen Mother in Africa," *Africa* 5 (1977), 14–30.
6 Hay, "Queens," 433–4. For recent studies, see Nwando Achebe, *The Female King of Colonial Nigeria: Ahebi Ugbabe* (Bloomington, Indiana: University of Indiana Press, 2011) and Achebe, Female Monarchs and Merchant Queens in Africa (Athens: Ohio University Press, 2020); Linda Heywood, *Njinga of Angola: Africa's Warrior Queen* (Cambridge, MA: Harvard University Press, 2017).
7 Iris Berger, "African Women's History: Themes and Perspectives," *Journal of Colonialism and Colonial History* 4, no. 1 (April 2003). doi:10.1353/cch.2003.0005.
8 Kate Skinner, "Women, Gender, and 'Specifically Historical' Research on Ghana: A Retrospective," *Ghana Studies* 21 (2018): 95–120.
9 Skinner, "Women," 108.
10 Skinner, "Women," 105.
11 Ivor Wilks, "Labor, Capital, and the Forest Kingdom of Asante: A Model of Early Change," in *The Evolution of Social Systems*, eds. J. Friedman and M. Rowlands (London, England: Duckworth), 487–534.
12 Ivor Wilks, *Asante in the Nineteenth Century: The Structure and Evolution of a Political Order* (Cambridge: Cambridge University Press, 1975).
13 Agnes Aidoo, "Asante Queen Mothers in Government and Politics in the 19th Century," *Journal of the Historical Society of Nigeria* 9 no. 1 (1977): 1–13.
14 Aidoo, "Asante Queen Mothers," 2–5.
15 Kwame Arhin, "The Asante Praise Poems: The Ideology of Patrimonialism," *Paideuma* 32: 163–97 and Larry Yarak, *Asante and the Dutch* (Oxford: Clarendon Press, 1990); Kwame Arhin, "The Political and Military Roles of Akan Women" in *Female and Male in West Africa*, ed. C. Oppong (London: Allen & Unwin, 1983), 91–8 and Ivor Wilks, "She Who Blazed a Trail: Akyaawa Yikwan of Asante," in *Life Histories of African Women*, ed. P. Romero (Atlantic Highlands, NJ: Ashfield, 1988), 113–39; T.C. McCaskie, "State and Society, Marriage and Adultery: Some Considerations Towards a Social History of Pre-Colonial Asante," *Journal of African History* 22 no.4 (1981): 477–94; E.K. Akyeampong and P. Obeng, "Spirituality, Gender and Power in Asante History," *International Journal of African Historical Studies* 28

no. 3 (1995): 481–508; Isaac Owusu-Mensah, W. Asante, and W.K. Osew, "Queen Mothers: The Unseen Hands in Chieftancy Conflicts Among the Akan in Ghana: Myth or Reality?" *Journal of Pan African Studies* 8, no. 6 (September 2015) 1–16; for queen mothers and succession among colonial and present day Asante in Ghana, see Beverly J. Stoeltje, "Creating Chiefs and Queen Mothers in Ghana: Obstacles and Opportunities," in *The Routledge History of Monarchy*, eds. Elena Woodacre, Lucinda H.S. Dean, Chris Jones, Zita Rohr, and Russell Martin (London: Routledge, 2019), 566–580.

16 T.C. McCaskie, "The Life and Afterlife of Yaa Asantewaa," *Journal of the International African Institute* 77, no. 2 (2007): 151.

17 McCaskie, "The Life," 160. See also Ivor Wilks, "Asante at the End of the Nineteenth Century: Setting the Record Straight," *Ghana Studies* no. 3 (2000): 58.

18 McCaskie, "The Life," 161.

19 Kwame Arhin Brempong, "The Role of Nana Yaa Asantewaa in the 1900 Asante War of Resistance," *Ghana Studies* no. 3 (2000): 98–9.

20 Brempong, "The Role," 99–100.

21 Emmanuel Akyeampong, "Asante at the Turn of the Twentieth Century," *Ghana Studies* no. 3 (2000): 3–12.

22 Boahen, *Yaa Asantewaa*, 4.

23 McCaskie, "The Life," 158-159 and *Asante Identities: History and Modernity in an African Village, 1850-1950* (Bloomington: Indiana University Press, 2000): 76-9.

24 Albert Adu Boahen, "Yaa Asantewaa in the Yaa Asantewaa War of 1900: Military Leader or Symbolic Head?," *Ghana Studies* no. 3 (2000): 111–35.

25 McCaskie, "The Life," 156.

26 McCaskie, "The Life," 159.

27 Pashington Obeng, "Yaa Asantewaa's War of Independence: Honoring and Ratifying an Historic Pledge," *Ghana Studies* no. 3 (2000): 138.

28 McCaskie, "The Life," 159.

29 Obeng, "Yaa Asantewaa's War," 151.

30 McCaskie, "The Life," 157.

31 Obeng, "Yaa Asantewaa's War," 151–2.

32 Aidoo, "Asante Queen Mothers," 12.

33 Aidoo, "Asante Queen Mothers," 5, 13.

34 Arhin, "The Role of Nana Yaa," 110.

35 Boahen, "Yaa Asantewaa," 115–16.

36 Obeng, "Yaa Asantewaa's War," 148.

37 Boahen, "Yaa Asantewaa," 114.

38 See McCaskie, "The Life," 158. See also Asirifi-Danquah, *Yaa Asantewaa: An African Queen Who Led an Army to Fight the British* (Kumasi: Asirifi-Danquah Books Ltd, 2002); Willemina J. Donkoh, "Yaa Asantewaa: A Role Model for Womanhood in the New Millennium," *Jenda: A Journal of Culture and African Women Studies*, 2001.

39 Lynda Day, "Long Live the Queen! The Yaa Asantewaa Centenary and the Politics of History," *Ghana Studies* no. 3 (2000): 153–4.

40 Day, "Long Live," 154.

41 Day, "Long Live," 165.

42 McCaskie, "The Life," 163–71.

43 Harcourt Fuller, "Commemorating an African Queen: Ghanaian Nationalism, the African Diaspora, and the Public Memory of Nana Yaa Asantewaa, 1952–2009," *African Arts* 47 no. 4 (Winter 2014): 58–71 and Nana Pokua Wiafe Mensah, "Nana Yaa Asantewaa, The Queen Mother of Ejisu: The Unsung Heroine of Feminism in Ghana," Master's Thesis, University of Toronto, 2010.

Bibliography

Afonja, Simi. 1983. "Women, Power, and Authority in Traditional Yoruba Society." In *Visibility and Power: Essays on Women in Society and Development*, edited by Leela Dube et al. Delhi: Oxford University Press, 1983.

Aidoo, Agnes. "Asante Queen Mothers in Government and Politics in the 19th Century." *Journal of the Historical Society of Nigeria* 9, no. 1 (Dec. 1977), 1–13.

Aidoo, Agnes. "Asante Queen Mothers in Government and Politics in the Nineteenth Century." In *The Black Woman Cross-Culturally*, edited by Filomena Steady, 65–77. Cambridge, MA: Schenckman, 1981.

Akyeampong, Emmanuel. "Asante at the Turn of the Twentieth Century." *Ghana Studies* 3 (2000): 3–12.

Akyeampong, E.A. and Pashington Obeng. "Spirituality, Gender and Power in Asante History." *International Journal of African Historical Studies* 28, no. 3 (1995): 481–508.

Arhin, Kwame. "The Asante Praise Poems: The Ideology of Patrimonialism." *Paideuma* 32 (1986): 163–197.

Arhin, Kwame. "The Political and Military Roles of Akan Women." In *Female and Male in West Africa*, edited by C. Oppong, 91–98. London: Allen & Unwin, 1983.

Asirifi-Danquah, Asirifi. *Yaa Asantewaa: an African Queen Who Led an Army to Fight the British*. Kumasi: Asirifi-Danquah Books Ltd, 2002.

Barnes, Sandra T. "Gender and the Politics of Support and Protection in Precolonial West Africa." In *Queens, Queen Mothers, Priestesses and Power: Case Studies in African Gender*, edited by Flora Edouwaye and S. Kaplan, 1–18. New York: New York Academy of Sciences, 1997.

Berger, Iris. "African Women's History: Themes and Perspectives." *Journal of Colonialism and Colonial History* 4, no. 1 (April, 2003) doi:10.1353/cch.2003.0005.

Boahen, Albert Adu. "Yaa Asantewaa in the Yaa Asantewaa war of 1900: Military Leader or Symbolic Head?" *Ghana Studies* 3 (2000): 111–135.

Boahen, Albert Adu. *Yaa Asantewaa and the Asante-British War of 1900–1*, edited with an editor's note by E. Akyeampong. Accra: Sub-Saharan Publishers and James Currey, 2003.

Brempong, Arhin. "The Role of Nana Yaa Asantewaa in the 1900 Asante War of Resistance." *Ghana Studies* 3 (2000): 97–110.

Cohen, Ronald. "Oedipus Rex and Regina: The Queen Mother in Africa." *Africa* 5 (1977): 14–30.

Day, Lynda. "Long Live the Queen! The Yaa Asantewaa Centenary and the Politics of History." *Ghana Studies* 3 (2000): 153–154.

Day, Lynda. "What's Tourism Got to Do with It?: The Yaa Asantewaa Legacy and Development in Asanteman." *Africa Today* 51, no. 1 (Autumn, 2004): 99–113.

Donkoh, Willemina J. "Yaa Asantewaa: A Role Model for Womanhood in the New Millennium." Only available online at www.Jendajournal.com in *Jenda: A Journal of Culture and African Women Studies*, no. 1 (2001).

Edouwaye, Flora and S. Kaplan eds. *Queens, Queen Mothers, Priestesses and Power: Case Studies in African Gender*. New York: New York Academy of Sciences, 1997.

Fuller, Harcourt. "Commemorating an African Queen: Ghanaian Nationalism, the African Diaspora, and the Public Memory of Nana Yaa Asantewaa, 1952 – 2009." *African Arts* 47, no. 4 (Winter 2014): 58–71.

Hay, Margaret Jean. "Queens, Prostitutes and Peasants: Historical Perspectives on African Women, 1971–1986." *Canadian Journal of African Studies* 22, no. 3 (1988): 431–447.

Hunt, Nancy Rose. "Placing African Women's History and Locating Gender." *Social History* 14, no. 3 (October 1989): 359–379.

McCaskie, T.C. "State and Society, Marriage and Adultery: Some Considerations Towards a Social History of Pre-Colonial Asante." *Journal of African History* 22 no. 4 (1981): 477–494.

McCaskie, T.C. "The Life and Afterlife of Yaa Asantewaa." *Journal of the International African Institute* 77, no. 2 (2007): 151–179.

Mensah, Nana Pokua Wiafe. *Nana Yaa Asantewaa, The Queen Mother of Ejisu: The Unsung Heroine of Feminism in Ghana*. Master's Thesis, University of Toronto, 2010.

Obeng, Pashington. "Yaa Asantewaa's War of Independence: Honoring and Ratifying an Historic Pledge." *Ghana Studies* 3 (2000): 137–152.

Skinner, Kate. "Women, Gender, and 'Specifically Historical' Research on Ghana: A Retrospective." *Ghana Studies* 21 (2018): 95–120.

Sweetman, David. *Women Leaders in African History*. Portsmouth, NH: Heinemann, 1986.

Van Allen, Judith. "'Sitting on a Man': Colonialism and the Lost Political Institutions of Igbo Women." In *The Roles of African Women: Past, Present and Future. Special Issue of Canadian Journal of African Studies* 6, no. 2 (1972): 165–181.

Wilks, Ivor. "Labor, Capital, and the Forest Kingdom of Asante: A Model of Early Change." In *The Evolution of Social Systems*, edited by J. Friedman and M. Rowlands, 487–534. London: Duckworth, 1977.

Wilks, Ivor. "She Who Blazed A Trail: Akyaawa Yikwan of Asante." In *Life Histories of African Women*, edited by P. Romero, 113–139. Atlantic Highlands, NJ: Ashfield, 1988.

Wilks, Ivor. "Asante at the End of the Nineteenth Century: Setting the Record Straight." *Ghana Studies* 3 (2000): 13–59.

Yarak, Larry. *Asante and the Dutch*. Oxford: Clarendon Press, 1990.

24

The Aba Women's War of 1929 in Eastern Nigeria as anti-colonial protest

Egodi Uchendu and Uche Okonkwo

History reveals that women play significant roles in the development of their society, and this is certainly true of an uprising of women in Nigeria in the early twentieth century. The Aba Women's War of 1929, recorded in British annals as the Aba Women's Riot, portrays a "well organized and successful protest against the imperialist unconstitutional imposition of taxation on women in the Eastern part of Nigeria."[1] The great depression of Europe, which had already manifested in the late 1920s, had severe economic implications for the peasant economy in Eastern Nigeria in particular and Africa in general. This included a register of every male through a 1927 census, followed a year later by direct taxes collected for the first time throughout Eastern Nigeria, then known as the southeastern provinces. The Aba Women's War took place in those areas in the eastern region that can be described as the palm belt region.

Palm oil production in this region had, to a large extent, been within the orbit of women, even though men owned and controlled the land. Mba asserts:

> Most of Igbo and Ibibio land constituted what is known as the "palm belt" area. Until the trade with Europe in palm produce developed in the early 19th century, the production of palm oil was carried out entirely by women and was used principally for immediate household consumption. The women were free to pick palm fruits wherever they found them. However, once palm produce became a major export, it came to be regarded as a man's product since it could now be exchanged for men's goods, such as guns and spirits. The ownership of palm trees was vested in the male landowners and harvesting was strictly regulated. The women still largely carried out the actual extraction of the oil and sold the oil in local markets, but the men took over the long-distance and external trade in palm oil.[2]

The implication is that the taxation of men, which began in 1927, was gradually affecting households that relied on palm oil. This manifested in the gradual decline in palm oil prices beginning from this era. Korieh paints a picture of the development during this era as follows:

> Women termed the existing tax policy unfair considering the effects of the depression on local producers. The discontent began to extend to another major issue of relevance to rural peasants – the price of export produce and increasing inflation. In the late 1920s, the entire

world economy was in a slump due to the great depression. The depression caused a myriad of economic problems, including low prices for palm produce.[3]

Under this economic hardship, women were already resentful. Besides that, they were also involved in the palm kernel business during the colonial period. The economic gains and losses of that season affected them directly and in many ways. On top of this, additional problems emerged following the absence of the district officer of Bende division of Owerri province, A. L. Weir, from his duty post. Weir went on leave and handed his duties over to Captain J. Cook.

After reviewing the 1927 census, which he considered to be inaccurate and incomplete, Cook decided to establish nominal rolls to obtain accurate information on the numbers of men, women, children, and livestock in the Oloko native court area.[4] When the women learned of this, they began to suspect that the colonial government would soon begin to tax women. Sylvia Leith-Ross captured the mood of the women as follows: "they were seriously perturbed. We depend on our husbands, we cannot buy food or clothes ourselves and how shall we get money to pay tax."[5] Notwithstanding these challenges, Captain Cook ordered Chief Okugo (a warrant chief in Oloko) on November 18, 1929, to start counting. Without delay, Chief Okugo employed the services of a schoolteacher, Mark Emeriuwa, who was delighted with the offer.[6] The remainder of this chapter will explore how these incidents unfolded, leading to the Women's War and the post-independence legacy of that war.

Oloko Census

Chief Okugo knew that conducting a census would receive stiff opposition and thus did not want to be directly involved.[7] Before Emeriuwa embarked on the census exercise in Oloko, one Chief Ananaba of Umuala in Oloko had announced to his village that the government had asked for the enumeration of women to tax them. He reminded his community of how the taxation of men had been preceded by a census the year before.[8] Soon, the women had spread rumors of possible taxation of women in Owerri province and beyond. They then waited for an opportunity to make their grievances known to the colonial government.

On November 23, 1929, Mark Emeriuwa went into the compound of Ojim to conduct a census as directed. He met Nwanyeruwa, a woman of Ngwa ancestry and the wife of the late Ojim. Emeriuwa asked Nwanyeruwa the numbers of her sheep and goats as well as people in her household. This led to an exchange of words between them. Thereafter, Nwanyeruwa attended a meeting of women in session in Oloko and informed them that the plan to tax women had come to reality.[9] Immediately, the women moved to Emeriuwa's house to ask why women should be counted. Those notified summoned other women by sending fresh-folded palm leaves to them both in Oloko and beyond, requesting them to show solidarity with their struggle against the taxation of women.[10] Furthermore, the women went to Chief Okugo Okezie to make enquiries and were told by the chief, albeit sarcastically, that women should pay tax. He ordered his servants to drive the women away.[11] These events occurred between November 23 and 24, 1929.

Consequently, by November 25, 1929, women began to "sit on" Okugo, demanding his resignation as warrant chief.[12] "Sitting on a man," as demonstrated by Allen, was a strategy used by women to compel men to give in to the decision of the women.[13] It followed this pattern: scantily clad adult women armed with palm fronds or green leaves, such as cassava leaves, would assemble in the premises of the person they had issues with. Comfortably seated, they would start to sing songs that expressed their grievances and demands, as well as others that ridiculed their target. This continued until their demands were met, sometimes after a day or two or more. Should this exceed one day, the women might disperse late at night and re-converge early the next morning. The sheer number of scantily clad adult women assembled against any man or group of men, as the case might be, was unnerving. For as long as women were sitting on a man, they simultaneously did not continue with their family and marital functions. This would put pressure on other men as well and indirectly force them to wade into the conflict. The men, thus mobilized, would throw in their weight to get the offender to acquiesce to the demands of the women. Once satisfied, the women would disperse to their homes. "Sitting on a man" was women's soft-power diplomacy against patriarchy in precolonial and colonial Igboland.

Thus, the following day, a deputation of women came to Bende, led by Ikonnia and Nwannedia of Umuigwu in Oloko, to demand the immediate removal of Chief Okugo. On November 27, another deputation of women from Oloko came to Bende. These female emissaries from Aba, Owerri, and Ikot Ekpene assembled in Okugo's house. Meanwhile, on November 26, 1929, in an attempt to drive the women away from Okugo's square to the market place, a policeman, Obasi Ogu, was knocked down and received a blow on the arm. Finding himself on the ground, he fired his rifle in the air, supposedly in self-defense.[14] When Captain J. Cook visited Oloko on November 27, 1929, he met about 1000 women in Oloko market place. According to him, the women came from Oloko, Ayaba, and Umuaja court areas. Meanwhile, he visited Ezeala Amongwu and the compound heads, Wolu and Wakama. Cook observed that Chief Okugo had not consulted these authorities before initiating the counting. He thus ordered the arrest of Chief Okugo, who was charged to court accordingly. By November 29, 1929, when he left Oloko, the women had not dispersed.[15]

J. N. Hill took over from Cook as district officer of Bende Division, Owerri province, in the first week of December 1929. He thus inherited the responsibility of controlling the women's group. Indeed, the colonial government blamed Cook for fueling the crisis, which he had triggered through Chief Okugo. The official report reads:

> I think Capt. J. Cook acted very unwisely when he sent a message that nominal rolls should be prepared, giving the names of adult males by families, the number of wives possessed by each male, the number of children, goats and sheep.[16]

Hill gave the leadership of the women's group a fair hearing and encouraged them to articulate their grievances. This they did, listing among other things the illegal collection of money for dowry and building a house as directed by the district officer, extortion in terms of collecting yam seedlings on behalf of the district officer only for him to plant them himself, and other illegalities.[17] The litigation against Chief Okugo lasted for several days. This probably encouraged the spread of the revolt, since the women were generally not sure of the outcome of the court judgment and were not prepared to exercise patience any longer. On December 3, 1929, Okugo was found guilty of two charges: spreading news likely to cause alarm and physical assault on women demonstrators. He was sentenced to two years' imprisonment, while Emeriuwa, on February 27, 1930, was sentenced to three months.[18]

Hill, to a large extent, understood the problems of the women demonstrators from working closely with their leaders – Nwanyeruwa, Ikonnia, Nwannedia, and Nwugo. Without any formal education, these women leaders were intelligent, diplomatic, and brave.[19] Okugo's conviction did not end the protests. In Umuahia, on December 4, 1929, women pressed on against low prices for palm produce. The Oloko women leaders disassociated themselves from this, promising Hill that they would help to stop it. Ikonnia and Nwannedia convinced Umuahia women that protests were not the best solution for controlling prices. Both the police commissioner, Mr. King, and Hill, the district officer, were impressed with the women leaders' efforts.[20] The results these women leaders achieved earned them recognition as apostles of non-violent struggle.[21]

Aba and the battle

Noah argues for the need to dismantle colonial stereotypes because the British-styled "riot" was indeed a war; moreover, he insists that the event should be named after a town, either the town where the event originated or the one that had the highest casualties.[22] In his words:

> The terminology surrounding the events of the Aba riots has been wrongly perpetuated that a revisit is compelling. For it should be stated that the Aba Riot is a misnomer ... The "Aba Women's Riot" was a phenomenon which was neither Aba in origin nor in nature. It was a well-planned uprising by women with known and identifiable goals and leaders. As noted by earlier writers on the subject, a riot suggests an uncontrolled, irrational action, involving violence to property or persons or both. This is why this pejorative term must be changed because it has now become clear that the women's war was better organized and executed beyond the level of a riot.[23]

Umoren agrees, arguing that the incident was not confined to Aba. Indeed, the disturbance was greater in the Annang and Ibibio villages of Utu Etim Ekpo, Ika, Ikot Ekpene, Abak, Itu, Ikono, Okopedi, and Egwanga. These were the real theaters of war, where about 58 women died, with 50 wounded, whereas in Aba, only two died. He puts forward that the event should more appropriately be called "Annang-Ibibio Women's War," as indigenes of those areas called it; they still refer to it as Ekong Iban (Women's War).[24]

Notwithstanding these views, scholars have attempted to justify the use of the nomenclature "Aba Women's War of 1929." Leith-Ross privileged Aba because it was an important trading center on the rail line.[25] To Gailey,

> Aba in 1929 was a moderately large town, remarkably well served by communication links. Four major roads, one each from Owerri, Ikot-Ekpene, Opobo, and Asa led into Aba. Besides, it was on the railroad that connects Port Harcourt with the north. Therefore, Aba acted as a lodestone for rumours and was easily accessible to people from all over Owerri Province.[26]

From December 8, 1929, women began to assemble in Aba. An estimated 10,000 women from Aba township, Ngwa, Ndoki, and Asa villages, scantily dressed, girded with green leaves and carrying sticks, gathered and satirized chiefs, court clerks, and court messengers with songs.[27] Ferguson's eyewitness account shows that the riot in Aba started on December 10, 1929, at about 5:30 p.m. British colonial officials – Messrs F. H. Woodrow, Bullock, and Lendrum – were attacked on their way back from Umuahia. Around 11:00 p.m. that night, women attacked European quarters but were dispersed by four rounds of revolver gunshots.

The following day, December 11, 1929, women resumed their attack on European quarters until Mr. Trovey fired a shot. Ferguson recalls that by December 12, 1929, the number of women demonstrators had increased to about 12,000. According to him, women destroyed government offices and station magistrates and were on the lookout for European women to harm, since they alleged that these women did not pay tax. Continuing his testimony, Ferguson reported that a peaceful protest was scheduled at Ekeopara Square, Aba, on December 13, 1929.[28] However,

Dr. Hunter, a medical officer, was returning to the African Hospital with a nurse, Miss Buist, when he met a crowd of women who threw sticks and stones at them. In trying to avoid them, he knocked down two women. This heightened the fury of the mob, leading to the wounding of Miss Buist.

The crowd broke into Barclays Bank, where they tore all the papers. In the absence of troops, they looted the bank, and efforts by colonial officials to pacify the crowd failed.[29] Nwaguru recorded that the riot proclamation was read first at Aba Bridge to some 4000–5000 women, and after a reasonable interval, the police with the butts of their rifles, assisted by a dozen Europeans, drove the women for about a mile up the Ogbor Hill. The women re-assembled an hour later but were again dispersed by a more determined charge from security officials. Similar action was taken on the Aba and Owerri roads with little resistance from the women. On December 14, 1929, normalcy returned to Aba.[30]

Operations outside Aba

The incident in Aba triggered a series of protests in other locations among women who could not travel to Aba. While the protest occurred at Aba, there were similar revolts in the Imo River, Okpala, Owerrinta, Nguru Ngor, Mbawsi, and Ayaba court areas. Their grievances were similar to those earlier listed by leaders of the revolt: taxation on women, low prices of produce, hatred for court members, abuses by agents of the Eastern Nigeria Marketing Board, and high taxation of the men. On December 13, 1929, Captain Nunns, with a European inspector and 16 police constables, went to Imo River. On their way back, they discovered men looting in Omoba, armed with machetes. They fired at them, wounding one.[31]

From this, it can be deduced that women did not carry out the operations alone but rather, received help from men. However, in an attempt to discredit the women's agency, one of the reports claimed as follows: "An interesting feature of the Owerri District officers report was that the movement was being fostered by men in women's cloth."[32] This development, according to the report, was more pronounced in the Okpala, Nguru, and Ngor areas, where there was heavy looting and destruction of courthouses. There was a report of women who mugged Ihube women on their way to Okigwe market. Meanwhile, in Mbawsi, 19 looters were arrested and relieved of the items they had looted. There was also a report of an attack by women on Chief Oparachekwe of Olakwo for not supporting their protest. After failed attempts, the women recruited armed men to Oparachekwe's house, but two military platoons led by Captain Nunny were already on the ground to defend him. Four men were killed during the attack.[33]

Military patrols were dispatched to turbulent areas: the northern patrol went to Nguru, two platoons to Umukonshe, and the southern patrol to Umuopara, Eberi, and Azumini, among others. The military dimension of the women's war came with the resolution of the Lieutenant-General of the Southern Provinces, Mr. C. W. Alexander, with residents of Owerri and Calabar provinces, and Lieutenant Colonel Currant, the commander of the troops in the disturbed area, to declare a Peace Preservation Ordinance in Owerri province from December 13 and Calabar from December 14, 1929. This was followed by the Collective Punishment Ordinance.[34] Under the Peace Preservation Ordinance, district officers and police officials utilized powers they did not ordinarily possess to deal with individuals and village groups involved in the protest against the British colonial government.[35] The Collective Punishment Ordinance was described as follows:

Under the Collective Punishment Ordinance, levied on village inhabitants who may have had nothing to do with the disturbances, authorities imposed exorbitant fines amounting to six times the annual tax assessment of a given settlement on villages, expecting them to be paid within 24 hours; failure to make the payment might result in the razing of the village. So disproportionate were the punishments meted out that the members of the second commission of inquiry protested that "the amount of burning was excessive." British efforts, which entailed killing and wounding Igbo men and women who persisted in their protests, only brought sufficient peace to the southeastern territories that the British felt they could retract the Peace Preservation Ordinance a year later, on February 1931.[36]

Colonial rule was military rule in the real sense, and thus, the developments concerning women's protests that had spread to the Ibibio and Annang areas invited military solutions. The revolts in Aba between December 14 and 16, 1929, spread like wildfire to Abak, Utu Etim Ekpo, Ikot Ekpene, Uzo Usu, and Opobo.[37] Immediately, the colonial officials began a sensitization of the people, most importantly women, whom they assured that they would not be taxed. Not sure what their fate would be, the colonial government removed valuables, including money, from the native courts at Ika, Utu Etim Ekpo, and Ukanafun. Women succeeded in cutting the telephone lines connecting Itu and Ikot Ekpere, while in Utu Etim Ekpo native court area, they burned the government buildings, houses belonging to court clerks, and the factory of the Nigeria Produce Company Limited.[38] At Abak, police and military detachments, led by Captain Ford, commissioner of police, and the district officer for Abak, asked women not to cross the line drawn by the police. An attempt to do so resulted in the deaths of about six women. It was actually claimed that more than six women died in that confrontation, since about 12 rounds of bullets were fired.[39] Still, in Itu district, on December 15, 1929, about 1000 women blocked the road. After pleading with them to no avail, Reverend James Ballantyne convinced the district officer to send out about 200 leprosy patients to disperse them. In a bid to avoid being infected, the protesting women fled.[40]

On December 16, 1929, women numbering over 2000 converged at Egwanga Beach (also called Opobo and recently, Ikot Abasi) with women leaders from Opobo, Bonny, Andoni, Kwa, Ogoni, and Nkoro present. Lieutenant J. N. Hill had arrived earlier with an army platoon from the 3rd Battalion, a machine gun, and about 32 policemen. Women who were becoming impatient while waiting for documents that would indicate the colonial government's unwillingness to tax women and acquiescence with their other demands started beating their pestles on the bamboo fence of the district officer's residence. Some even attempted to climb it. Enraged, Hill shot one of the leaders, Adiaha Edem, and commanded the troops to open fire. Twenty-six women were killed, 8 drowned, and 31 were wounded.[41]

The actual number of deaths from the Aba Women's War is still subject to intense demographic scrutiny. Isichei gave the official list as 55 women killed, 32 of them at Opobo, and 50 wounded, 31 at Opobo.[42] Crowther suggests 32 people killed and 31 wounded. With respect to Calabar province, Afigbo summarized the casualties as follows: 32 killed in Opobo and 31 wounded; 3 killed in Abak, none wounded; 18 killed in Utu Etim Ekpo and 19 wounded.[43]

The colonial government's record of casualties, presented by Orugbani, claims that 32 women died: 12 from Opobo, 9 from Nkoro, 5 from Ogoni, and 2 from Andoni. Additional casualties were from Lagos (1) and Annang (2).[44] To Orugbani, this means that all but three women on the official casualty list were from the coastal section of Eastern Nigeria. No other area suffered so much, yet the incident is popularly called the Aba Women's War. It was argued that with a casualty list of 31 wounded – Opobo (13), Andoni (1), Bonny (1), Nkoro (8), and Ogoni (5) – it is most likely that the number of women killed in the entire struggle that occurred in the palm belt region of Eastern Nigeria would have comprised a far higher casualty figure than reported, perhaps in the hundreds.[45] Even by this period in Nigeria's history, usage of official casualty records was politicized because of its strong impact on shaping public opinion.

Whatever else, the women's protest that turned into a war against the colonial institution attracted inquiry into the obnoxious practices inherent in the warrant chief system in colonial Eastern Nigeria. Incidentally, the first commission of inquiry to investigate the loss of lives was led by the administrator of the Colony of Lagos, Mr. Gray, and the crown counsel, Mr. Birrel. This commission exonerated those responsible for the fatalities recorded among protesting women.[46] Dissatisfaction with the outcome of the work of this commission led to the setting up of another committee in February 1930. Members of the committee included the Chief Justice, Sir Donald Kingdom (as chairman), Mr. W. E. Hunt, a senior resident, Mr. Graham Paul, an unofficial European lawyer, Sir Kitoyi Ajaka, and Mr. Eric Moore – both African barristers – and Mr. Osborne. Messrs A. E. F. Murray and F. B. Carr were the secretaries.[47] The outcome of their report led to the reforms that brought about the native administration to replace the village assemblies. This incapacitated women, because it encouraged excessive masculine domination. An estimated £60,000 worth of property was reportedly destroyed, and this was repaid through taxation.[48] In effect, in conceding to the demands of women, the colonial administration did not abandon their original plan to tax their subjects but found a convenient way to implement it in the short term. Eventually, formal taxation of women commenced in 1956.[49]

Conclusion

The Aba Women's War, one of a series of anti-colonial demonstrations by women in Southern Nigeria, was among the early manifestations of twentieth-century proto-feminist movements in Africa. It demonstrated women's indirect but active participation in the colonial experiment. Women's agency, until then ignored by British colonial officials, was thereafter acknowledged. And in spite of the punitive measures enacted to moderate women, their efforts in that struggle forced open the doors of local administration to female colonial citizens of Eastern Nigeria. Some were admitted as members of the new native courts. In Umuakpo native court, for instance, 3 women were incorporated amidst 27 male members; while in Nguru Mbaise native court, 1 woman joined 13 men. Similar concessionary appointments were made across the region. Not ending there, the Aba Women's War became a reference point used to rally women in Southern Nigeria during the anti-colonial struggle of the 1940s and 1950s as well as in the struggles for women's rights in post-independence Nigeria.[50] In all, the Women's War remains a significant landmark event in the fight against masculine oppression in Nigeria. It cleared the path for a post-independent feminist movement in the country.

Notes

1 Emily Oghale God's Presence, "Women Leadership and its Relevance to National Development in the 21st Century," in *UJAH: Unizik Journal of Arts and Humanities* (2014): 158–73.
2 N. E. Mba, "Heroines of the Women's War," in *Nigerian Women: A Historical Perspective*, ed. Bolanle Awe (Ibadan: Bookcraft Ltd, 1992), 87.
3 C. J. Korieh, "Women and Peasant Movement in Colonial Eastern Nigeria," in *Shaping Our Struggles: Nigerian Women in History, Culture and Social Change*, eds. Obioma Nnaemeka and C. J. Korieh (Trenton: Africa World Press, 2010), 66.
4 A. H. Gailey, *The Road to Aba: A Study of British Administration Policy in Nigeria* (London: London University Press, 1971), 107.
5 Silvia Leith-Ross, *African Women: A Study of the Ibo of Nigeria* (London: Routledge and Kegan Paul, 1939), 24.
6 Gailey, *The Road to Aba,* 107–8.

7 E. O. Akpan and Violetta I. Ekpo, *The Women's War of 1929: A Popular Uprising of Southeastern Nigeria Preliminary Study* (Calabar: Government Printers, 1988), 26.

8 U. K. Umoren, "The Symbolism of the Nigerian Women's War of 1929: An Anthropological Study of an Anti-Colonial Struggle," *Africa Study Monographs* 16, no. 2 (1995): 64.

9 Judith van Allen, "Aba Riots or the Igbo Women's War: Ideology, Stratification and the Invisibility of Women," *Ufahamu: Journal of African Studies* 6, no. 1 (1975): 22.

10 A. E. Afigbo, *The Warrant Chiefs: Indirect Rule in Southeastern Nigeria, 1891–1929* (London: Longman Group Limited, 1972), 238.

11 National Archives Enugu (hereafter NAE), J. N. Hill, "Disturbances by Females in Bende Division," November 24 to December 9, 1929, C. 53/1929, Umprof 1/5/5.

12 Judith van Allen, "'Sitting on a man': Colonialism and the Lost Political Institution of Igbo Women," *Canadian Journal of African Studies* 6, no. 2 (1972): 169.

13 C. J. Korieh and N. L. Njoku, "Culture, Gender, and Peasant Intellectual Protest in Colonial Eastern Nigeria," *Mbari: The International Journal of Igbo Studies* 1, no.1 (2008): 123.

14 NAE, J. Cook, Ag. District Officer Bende, to Resident Owerri Province, Port Harcourt, "Women's Movement in Oloko," November 28, 1929.

15 NAE, "Women's Movement in Oloko."

16 NAE, "Disturbances by Females in Bende Division."

17 NAE, "Disturbances by Females in Bende Division."

18 Gailey, *The Road to Aba*, 111.

19 U. U. Okonkwo, "Nwanyeruwa, Ikonnia, Nwannedia, and Nwugo as Heroines of the Aba Women's War of 1929 in Eastern Nigeria," *Journal of Humanities* 3, no.2 (2007): 70–7.

20 NAE, The District Officer Bende to the Resident Aba "Women's Movement Owerri Province" 20 December 1929, C./53/1929, Umprof 1/5/5.

21 J. N. Oriji, "Igbo Women from 1929–1960," *West Africa Review* 2, no. 1 (2000): www.africaknowledgep roject.org/index.php/war/article/view/430, accessed August 14, 2019.

22 M. E. Noah, "Aba Women's Riot: The Need for a Redefinition," in P. Chike Dike, ed. *The Women's Revolt of 1929: Proceedings of a National Symposium to Mark the 60th Anniversary of the Women's Uprising in South-Eastern Nigeria* (Lagos: Nelag, 1995), 113.

23 Noah, "Aba Women's Riot: The Need for a Redefinition," 105.

24 Umoren, "The Symbolism of the Nigerian Women's War," 65.

25 Leith-Ross, *African Women*, 26.

26 Gailey, *The Road to Aba*, 117.

27 J. E. N. Nwaguru, *Aba and British Rule 1896–1960* (Enugu: Santana Publishers, 1973), 102.

28 NAE, Memorandum from R.E.G. Ferguson, District Engineer Public Works Department Aba to the Resident Owerri Province, "Riots in Aba" cont., No.13/1930, C53/1929, Vol. 1 part 2, Women Movement Aba Patrol SS.P Bende Division, January 9, 1930.

29 NAE, F. H. Ingles, "Report on Events and Happenings during the Women's Movements, 1929," Umprof 1/5/2.

30 Nwaguru, *Aba and British Rule 1896–1960*, 103.

31 NAE, "Report on Events and Happenings."

32 NAE, "Report on Events and Happenings."

33 NAE, "Report on Events and Happenings."

34 Nwaguru, *Aba and British Rule 1896–1960*, 104.

35 M. B. L. Matera and S. K. Kent, *The Women's War of 1929: Gender and Violence in Colonial Nigeria* (Basingstoke: Palgrave Macmillan, 2012), 145.

36 Matera and Kent, *The Women's War of 1929*.

37 Akpan and Ekpo, *The Women's War of 1929: A Popular Uprising of Southeastern Nigeria*, 39.

38 Akpan and Ekpo, *The Women's War of 1929*, 34.

39 Akpan and Ekpo, *The Women's War of 1929*, 35.

40 Akpan and Ekpo, *The Women's War of 1929*, 35.

41 Udo Udoma, *The Story of the Ibibio Union* (Lagos: Spectrum Books, 1987), iii. See also Akpan and Ekpo, *The Women's War of 1929*, 42.

42 Elizabeth Isichei, *A History of the Igbo People* (London: Macmillan, 1976), 155.

43 Afigbo, *The Warrant Chiefs*, 241.

44 A. Orugbani, "Sacrificial Lambs of Heroines: Rivers Women's Place in the Events of 1929," in *The Women's Revolt of 1929*, ed. P. C. Dike (Lagos: Nelag, 1995), 127.

45 J. S. Coleman, *Nigeria: Background to Nationalism* (Berkeley: University of California Press, 1965), 174.
46 Allen, "Sitting on a Man," 174.
47 O. E. Ekelaka, "Gender Ideology and the 1929 Women's Revolt in Eastern Nigeria," in *Gender, Culture and Development: Essays in Honor of Dame Victoria N. Akanwa*, eds. R. C. Iwuchukwu and U. U. Okonkwo (Lagos: Grace Anasiudu Press, 2006), 124.
48 Oriji, "Igbo Women from 1929–1960."
49 N. E. Mba, *Nigerian Women Mobilized: Women's Political Activity in Southern Nigeria, 1900–1965* (California: University of California, 1982), 102.
50 Stella Effah-Attoe's interview with Chief Mrs. Margaret Ekpo in December 1991 in Stella Effah-Attoe, *Women Empowerment and Nation Building in Nigeria* (Calabar: University of Calabar Press, 2004), 80–1.

Bibliography

Afigbo, A.E. *The Warrant Chiefs: Indirect Rule in Southeastern Nigeria, 1891–1929* (London: Longman Group Limited, 1972).

Akpan, E.O. and Violetta I. Ekpo, *The Women's War of 1929: A Popular Uprising of Southeastern Nigeria Preliminary Study* (Calabar: Government Printers, 1988).

Coleman, J.S. *Nigeria: Background to Nationalism* (Berkeley: University of California Press, 1965).

Effah-Attoe, S. *Women Empowerment and Nation Building in Nigeria* (Calabar: University of Calabar Press, 2004).

Ekelaka, O.E. "Gender Ideology and The 1929 Women's Revolt in Eastern Nigeria," in *Gender, Culture and Development: Essays in Honor of Dame Victoria N. Akanwa*, eds. R.C. Iwuchukwu and U.U. Okonkwo (Lagos: Grace Anasiudu Press, 2006).

Gailey, A.H. *The Road to Aba: A Study of British Administration Policy in Nigeria* (London: London University Press, 1971).

God's Presence, E.O. "Women Leadership and its Relevance to National Development in the 21st Century," *UJAH: Unizik Journal of Arts and Humanities* 15, no. 2 (2014): 158–173.

Isichei, E. *A History of the Igbo People* (London: Macmillan, 1976).

Korieh, C.J. "Women and Peasant Movement in Colonial Eastern Nigeria," in *Shaping Our Struggles: Nigerian Women in History, Culture and Social Change*, eds. Obioma Nnaemeka and C.J. Korieh (Trenton: Africa World Press, 2010).

Korieh, C.J. and N.L. Njoku, "Culture, Gender, and Peasant Intellectual Protest in Colonial Eastern Nigeria," *Mbari: The International Journal of Igbo Studies* 1, no.1 (2008): 114–146.

Leith-Ross, S. *African Women: A Study of the Ibo of Nigeria* (London: Routledge and Kegan Paul, 1939).

Matera, M.B.L. and S.K. Kent. *The Women's War of 1929: Gender and Violence in Colonial Nigeria* (Basingstoke: Palgrave Macmillan, 2012).

Mba, N.E. *Nigerian Women Mobilized: Women's Political Activity in Southern Nigeria, 1900–1965* (California: University of California, 1982).

Mba, N.E. "Heroines of the Women's War," in *Nigerian Women: A Historical Perspective*, ed. Bolanle Awe (Ibadan: Bookcraft Ltd, 1992).

NAE, *The District Officer Bende to The Resident Aba "Women's Movement Owerri Province*, 20 December 1929, C./53/1929, Umprof 1/5/5.

NAE, F.H. Ingles, "Report on Events and Happenings during the Women's Movements, 1929," Umprof 1/5/2.

NAE, J. Cook, Ag. *District Officer Bende, to Resident Owerri Province, Port Harcourt, 'Women's Movement in Oloko'*, November 28, 1929.

NAE, *Memorandum from R.E.G. Ferguson, District Engineer Public Works Department Aba to the Resident Owerri Province, 'Riots in Aba' Cont., No.13/1930, C53/1929, Vol. 1 Part 2, Women Movement Aba Patrol SS.P Bende Division*, January 9, 1930.

National Archives Enugu (hereafter NAE), *J. N Hill, Disturbances by Female in Bende Division*, November 24 to December 9, 1929, C. 53/1929, Umprof 1/5/5.

Noah, M.E. "Aba Women's Riot: The Need for A Redefinition," in P. Chike Dike, ed. *The Women's Revolt of 1929: Proceedings of a National Symposium to Mark the 60th Anniversary of the Women's Uprising in South-Eastern Nigeria* (Lagos: Nelag, 1995).

Nwaguru, J.E.N. *Aba and British Rule 1896–1960* (Enugu: Santana Publishers, 1973).

Okonkwo, U.U. "Nwanyeruwa, Ikonnia, Nwannedia, and Nwugo as Heroines of the Aba Women's War of 1929 in Eastern Nigeria," *Journal of Humanities* 3, no. 2 (2007): 70–77.

Oriji, J.N. "Igbo Women from 1929–1960," *West Africa Review* 2, no. 1 (2000): https://www.africaknowled geproject.org/index.php/war/article/view/430, accessed August 14, 2019.

Orugbani, A. "Sacrificial Lambs of Heroines: Rivers Women's Place in the Events of 1929," in *The Women's Revolt of 1929*, ed. P.C. Dike (Lagos: Nelag, 1995).

Perham, M. *Native Administration in Nigeria* (London: Oxford University Press, 1937).

Udoma, U. *The Story of the Ibibio Union* (Lagos: Spectrum Books, 1987).

Umoren, U.K. "The Symbolism of the Nigerian Women's War of 1929: An Anthropological Study of an Anti-colonial Struggle," *Africa Study Monographs* 16, no. 2 (1995): 61–72.

United Nations, *Gender Equality: The Unfinished Business of Our Time*, https://www.un.org/en/section/issues-depth/gender-equality, accessed 09 August 2019.

Van Allen, J. "'Sitting on a Man': Colonialism and the Lost Political Institution of Igbo Women," *Canadian Journal of African Studies* 6, no. 2 (1972): 165–181.

Van Allen, J. "Aba Riots or the Igbo Women's War: Ideology, Stratification and the Invisibility of Women," *Ufahamu: Journal of African Studies* 6, no. 1 (1975): 11–39.

25

Black women writers in early twentieth-century Paris

Claire Oberon Garcia

There is much to discover and ponder in Black women's contributions to African diasporic intellectual and literary history in Paris, France, a major crossroads of the Black Atlantic. Paris in the early decades of the twentieth century was a dynamic center of artistic, intellectual, and financial activity that attracted people from all classes and many nations. Political and economic refugees, from dislodged aristocrats to persecuted Jewish musicians, laborers from throughout France's colonies, aspiring artists, restless intellectuals, and students seeking the prestige of a French university degree converged upon the city, particularly in the years between the First and Second World Wars.

Women from throughout the African diaspora were among those who were drawn to Paris, particularly for the educational and performing opportunities the city offered. Several Black women writers had meaningful sojourns in Paris that influenced their aesthetics and politics as they discovered that the French imperial capital was also a major nodal point of the global African diaspora. The questions that the work of these women writers, who came from various backgrounds, raise about the intersections of race, class, gender, and citizenship status demonstrate that each of these writers in her own way theorized intersectionality *avant la lettre*. Their writing engaged questions of race, class, gender, religious, national, cultural, linguistic, and other identities.

French Antillean women writers

A handful of bright young men from the relatively privileged class of "gens de couleur" (mixed-race people) of Martinique, Guadeloupe, and Saint-Pierre had been leaving their islands to pursue an education in the metropole since the eighteenth century. Toward the end of the nineteenth century, public education opened educational possibilities for less privileged young people: "Le développement de l'école laïque à partir de la fin de XIXème siècle permet l'éclosion dans la sphère intellectuelle, de personnalités masculines et féminines, issues de la bourgeoisie mulâtre ou noire"[1]/("The development of secular schools at the end of the nineteenth century spurred a sudden transformation in the intellectual sphere of both masculine and feminine identities among the *mulâtre* and Black bourgeoisie.")[2] It was not until after the First World War, however, that French Antillean women began to arrive in significant numbers to earn university degrees and professional certificates in France. At a time when the vast majority of people of African descent in the French Antilles labored in the fields and lived in abject poverty, the presence of these young women in the city that epitomized modernity was unprecedented. The Martinican actress and singer Jenny Alpha was among them. In her autobiography, *Paris Créole Blues*, Alpha describes the expectation that young women like herself from the *petite bourgeoisie* of the island would earn a degree and return to take a comfortable place in the colonial economy:

> Mes parents voulaient que je quitte la Martinique, pour continuer mes études … [M]es parents voulaient que j'aille à l'université pour devenir professeur, ou à la rigueur que je travaille à la douane ou à la poste comme eux.

> (My parents wanted me to leave Martinique to continue my studies … My parents wished that I go to university to become a teacher, or if need be, to work in the customs or post office, as they did.)[3]

Although according to Alpha's compatriot, the journalist, editor, and activist Paulette Nardal, earning degrees through correspondence courses was "*très en vogue*" in Martinique at the time, a young Antillaise who was serious about her education "va passer quelques années en France, de préférence à Paris"/("was going to spend a few years in France, preferably in Paris").[4] These years, however, were not easy for young Black Frenchwomen as they navigated French gender and racial biases.

Paulette Nardal credited deracinated and marginalized young Black Frenchwomen for catalyzing what she called the "éveil de la conscience de race"/("the awakening of race consciousness") that undergirded the Black diasporic cultural and political activism of the twentieth century. In this essay, Nardal alludes to her friend and colleague Roberte Horth's short story "Une histoire sans importance"/"A Story of no Importance" as epitomizing the social and psychological condition of young Black women students in Paris. The story draws upon Horth's own personal experiences. Horth, who was originally from French Guyana, was the first female student to study at the College de Cayenne and came to Paris to achieve a degree in philosophy. The story describes the racism that confronts Léa, a smart, idealistic, young Black woman, when she comes to the metropole to pursue her studies. The story, written in the manner of a fairytale, describes Léa as a smart and imaginative child who had long dreamed of the metropolis, "une ville de cristal et de rêve, un visage énorme, brillant et doux auquel elle donne un nom chantant … ce pays lointain est policé, courtois et que le people qui l'habite accueille tous les bons esprits/(a phantom city, a cristal [*sic*] dream to which she gave a musical name … people were polished, courteous, and friendly to all intelligent strangers)."[5] Yet the very first paragraph situates her as someone who will never be a full citizen of that city because she cannot express her true identity there. The story opens with her name in a one-word sentence. It is "[u]n nom comme un autre/([j]ust a name like any other)," but it is not the name that she goes by when she eventually sojourns in the city: her white French friends believe that the name does not do justice to the exotic identity that they impose upon her:

> Ils la baptisent de quelques onomatopée, évocatrice de fruits étranges, de senteurs inconnues, de danses bizarres et de pays ignorés./(They christened her with some queer nickname full of the aroma of strange fruits, of unknown fragrance, of weird dances and far-off lands.)[6]

By changing her name, they strip her of her identity as her mother's well-loved daughter as well as "une femme comme toutes les autres/(a woman like all the others)."[7] They replicate the rhetorical violence of enslavement by substituting a Black person's given name with a new name. Thus, she acquires a new identity as a subordinate subject in a colonial and racist caste system. Black women of Horth's generation who arrived in Paris brought with them many of the idealizations of the city that other young intellectuals shared, but Black women's presence as intellectual compatriots was new and unprecedented. Thus, Paris plays a significant role in the Black Frenchwoman's imaginary and intellectual formation.

Paulette Nardal is one of the major figures in the literary history of Black Paris. Born on October 12, 1896, to a family that included seven sisters, she arrived in Paris in 1920 to study American literature. She hoped to complete a dissertation on Harriet Beecher Stowe's *Uncle Tom's Cabin*, but there is no evidence that she achieved this. In a series of articles on Antillean women that she wrote for the Parisian newspaper *Le Soir*, Nardal asserts that most Antillaises were drawn to studies in the humanities, but the fields in which Antillean women were found were expanding:

> Elle semble jusqu'au ici préférer les lettres et les arts aux sciences. Il y a, parmi les Antillaises, de nombreuses licenciées en philosophie. Les langues étrangères, les lettres pures, l'histoire et la géographie ont aussi beaucoup d'attrait pour elles. Elles commencent à s'intéresser aux sciences sociales et au journalisme. On compte déjà quelque doctoresses en médecine, mais beaucoup plus d'ingénieurs-chimistes, de dentistes et de pharmaciennes.

> She seems up until this point to prefer letters and arts to the sciences. There are, among the Antillean women, many who are licensed in philosophy. Foreign languages, pure letters, history, and geography also hold a lot of attraction for them. They are developing an interest in the social sciences and in journalism. One counts already a few doctors in medicine, but many more chemical engineers, dentists, and pharmacists.[8]

Nardal came to Paris to earn a degree but soon got caught up in journalistic and cultural activities. She was joined by her younger sisters: Jane, who had a fierce interest in Africa and Black internationalism and was studying classical literature at the Sorbonne; Andrée, who studied and wrote about Martinican folk music; and Alice, also musical, who later developed a solid career as an opera singer. All the sisters were fluent in English and had a special interest in the ideas of the American New Negro movement. They were committed to fostering dialogue and cultural exchange among the members of the African diaspora who crossed paths in Paris. They held salons every Sunday afternoon at their apartment just outside Paris, in Clamart, where Black artists, students, writers, and intellectuals met for lively conversations and impromptu concerts.

It was in the Nardal sisters' salon that Langston Hughes and Claude McKay met Aimé Césaire, Léopold Senghor, and Etienne Léro, among others. The relationships nurtured in the salon led to a myriad of collaborations and cultural exchanges. The Howard University professor Clara Shepherd met Louis Th. Achille, who later taught in Howard's French Department. Clara Shepherd also became a regular contributor to *La Revue du Monde Noir*, a bilingual journal that Paulette Nardal co-founded with the Haitian scholar Léo Sajous. It was in these rooms that Aimé Césaire and Léopold Senghor encountered the young artists and writers on the frontiers of the New Negro movement, and honed the political and cultural ideas that underpinned the Negritude movement. According to Achille,

> Les sœurs Nardal rassemblèrent, à Clamart, près de Paris, des descendants des Africains déportés au nouveau Monde et dispersés sous une demi-douzaine de bannières nationales européennes ; elles les présentaient à de vrais Africains, plus récemment colonisés. Au cours de réunions récréatives ou laborieuses, ces Noirs se sentaient habités par un formidable et pacifique défi aux caprices de la géographie et de l'histoire, de la politique et de l'économie. Ils se découvraient une commune manière d'être, de sentir, d'espérer et bientôt, d'agir ! Incapables pour la plupart de retrouver de communes racines africaines, ils se dirent tout simplement « Noirs. »

> The Nardal sisters gathered, at Clamart, close to Paris, the descendants of Africans deported to the new world and dispersed under a half dozen European national flags; they introduced them to true Africans, more recently colonized. Through these recreational or task-oriented meetings, these Black people felt themselves inhabited by a formidable and peaceful defiance of the caprices of geography and history, of politics and economics. They discovered in themselves a communal manner of being, of feeling, of hoping, and shortly, acting! Incapable for the most part of finding again common African roots, they said to themselves simply, "Black."[9]

Paulette Nardal also contributed to Black international conversations in Paris's lively print culture. Thanks to an introduction by her sister Jane,[10] Nardal was a regular contributor to *La Dépêche Africaine*, a newspaper that covered current events in the colonies and incidents of racial injustice throughout the African diaspora. *La Dépêche* followed the Scottsboro case in the United States, the outrages of the Belgians in the Congo, as well as "erreurs et brutalités coloniales" in Madagascar and elsewhere in French colonies and territories. While *La Revue* was bilingual in French and English, *La Dépêche* published occasional whole pages of stories in English. Though she preferred living in Paris, Nardal returned to Martinique at the outbreak of the Second World War, where she became active in early childhood education efforts. When French women earned the right to vote after the war, Nardal spearheaded the effort to maximize Martinican women's civic engagement by founding the newsletter *La Femme dans la Cité*, which was associated with a Catholic women's group.

Paulette Nardal was a Catholic humanist who was skeptical of the Marxist politics that other feminist leaders on the island espoused. Her sister, Jane, was more radical in her politics than her older sibling. In a photograph found by the historian Emily Musil of the two sisters en route to France on an ocean liner, Paulette is in a suit and pearls, and Jane is in African-inspired garb. Jane was a classics teacher but had a life-long interest in Africa, and made several efforts to find a way to work and live there. Although she was denied a visa when she applied to travel to Africa in 1930,[11] she did spend two years working in Chad later in life. In articles that she wrote for *La Dépêche Africaine*, she attacked the exoticization of Black women ("Pantins Exotiques" ("Exotic Puppets" [1928]) and advocated for Black internationalism ("Internationalisme Noir" [1928]).

Nardal saw that the various white constructions of blackness – be they the idealized creations of Bernadin and Harriet Beecher Stowe or the "realistic" vile and violent portrayals in works by Soupault and Carl van Vechten – served white interests and perpetuated white supremacy. Nardal notes that Josephine Baker, with her "shellacked hair" and banana skirt, unites white fantasies of the primitive jungle with the allure of urban modernism, and once more presents an opportunity for a Black woman's body to serve white economic, political, and psychological interests: "la vogue des nègres en ces dernières années les a surtout faire à considérer comme des gens destinés à servir à l'amusement, voir au plaisir artistique ou sensuel du blanc"/"the vogue for negroes during these last years have above all made them considered a people destined to serve the amusement and artistic or sensual pleasures of the white."[12] Jane had no patience with that.

Another notable Martinican woman writer in Paris during the interwar years was Suzanne Roussy (also spelled Roussi). Suzanne Roussy was born in the same village as Napoleon's wife Josephine, Les-Trois-Ilêts, in 1915 and came to France to study literature at the University of Toulouse. There she met the student Aimé Césaire through her sister, married him, and moved to Paris in 1937. She was very involved in the editorial work of the militant student newspaper that her husband co-founded, *L'étudiant noir*, and after her return to Martinique during the Second World War, she co-founded with Césaire and Réné Ménil the influential surrealist cultural journal *Tropiques*. Although her published body of work is small, consisting of only seven essays, all originally published in *Tropiques*, and a play, *Youma: Aurore de la liberté*, whose manuscript has been lost, her literary legacy is significant, as it forged new ground for thinking about Antillean identity that rejected the predominant tendency to valorize assimilation to French mores. Powerful and prescient, her writing diverges from the basic premises of Negritude in that it highlights the multicultural aspects of Caribbean identity, leading some critics, such as the novelist Maryse Condé and the literary scholar Kara Rabbitt, to see her as a mother of theories of créolité and hybridity as later expounded by Edouard Glissant and others.

As is frequently the case with earlier women writers, Suzanne Césaire's literary productivity tapered off once she started mothering; she and Aimé had six children. Roussy Césaire sought a divorce when their youngest child was 12 and returned from Paris to Martinique, where she wrote a play that apparently was staged by a youth group in Fort-de-France. Sadly, 3 years after her divorce, she died at age 50 from a brain tumor.

Tempting though it may be to mourn the paucity of literary output from what was clearly a woman with a critical and creative mind as sharp and original as her more famous husband's, we can only imagine "what might have been" if the traditional constraints of gender – the expectations of mothers and wives – had not shaped her literary career.

However, the Guadeloupean novelist Daniel Maximin, who edited and provided a foreword to the collection of Césaire's work, *Le grand camouflage: Ecrits de dissidence 1941–1945* (2009), cautions readers against drawing such easy conclusions about the limitations of her literary output:

> En cela sûrement réside la fascinante leçon de vie de Suzanne Césaire, car malgré son absolu silence après *Tropiques*, en dehors d'une pièce de théâtre … malgré tous les malgré que font taire scandaleusement l'écriture des femmes, malgré tant de place laissée à l'homme dans sa vie comme dans ses textes, malgré la réticence des poètes à libérer les muses, elle a, dans tous ses articles … enracinés sa pensé non sur un territoire littéraire balisé, une propriété privée d'altérité, mais dans une terre fertilisée par tous les possibles de l'écriture et de la mémoire vive. [13]

> (Therein lies the fascinating life-lesson of Suzanne Césaire, for in spite of her absolute silence after *Tropiques* – outside of a play … despite all of the "in spite ofs" that scandalously silence women's writing, in spite of so much space left to man in her life as well as in her texts, in spite of the reticence of poets to liberate their muses, she has in all her articles … rooted her thought not in a marked-out literary territory, a private property of otherness, but in a land made fertile by all the possibilities of writing and a sharp memory).[14]

Roussy Césaire's writing is notable for its appropriation and transformation of the tenets of surrealism – particularly as understood by her friend and colleague André Breton – to express specifically Martinican subjectivity: a subjectivity formed by the particular social, cultural, and physical environment of Martinique and a frank confrontation with the legacy of slavery: "La poésie martiniquaise sera cannibal ou ne sera pas"/"Martinican poetry will be cannibalistic or it will not be").[15] Surrealism, for Roussy Césaire, could bypass the dangerous and delusional adherence to and imitation of the colonizer's ways by the colonized, by connecting directly with the Martinican self and thus allowing an authentic and critical freedom.

African American women writers

Paris during the interwar years was a lively crossroads for African Americans from all walks of life, from itinerant jazz musicians and stage performers to diplomats and, of course, artists and intellectuals, as well as bourgeois tourists such as teachers and ministers who found postwar Paris affordable. Many educated African Americans harbored a keen interest in France and the French language, which was the primary foreign language taught in the segregated Black schools in the United States. The interest in French was augmented by the experiences of African American soldiers during the First World War, when France, and Paris in particular, gained a reputation as a space free from the daily indignities of Jim Crow.

In Paris, Black people could sit in cafés, buy theatre tickets and sit wherever they pleased, and even socialize with white people. Of course, France also represented the sacred font of the best that European civilization had to offer, from its Enlightenment values to its storied art history. But African Americans who spent time there had a nuanced and complicated view of the city and the French history and culture that it represented. The American activist and educator Anna Julia Cooper was the first Black woman to defend a doctoral dissertation at the Sorbonne in 1926, but her dissertation topic, a new reading of the Haitian Revolution in relationship to French narratives of liberty, was from a Black and thus unconventional perspective.

Jessie Redmond Fauset, one of the most prolific writers of the Harlem Renaissance, visited France several times, at least twice for extended stays. A French major with a degree from Cornell University who later taught French in Black public schools, she helped W.E.B. DuBois organize both the First and Second Pan African conferences, which were held in Paris in 1919 and London in 1921. She lived for a year in Paris, earning a certificate in French language and cultural studies. Fauset, who served as literary editor for the National Association for the Advancement of Colored People (NAACP)'s *The Crisis Magazine: A Record of the Darker Races* from 1919 to 1927, was a frequent contributor to both the magazine and its offshoot for children, *The Brownies Book*. Her fiction and poetry often included allusions to France and French culture, and she published a handful of nonfiction articles on her experiences in France, from her reminiscence of France on the eve of the First World War, "Tracing Shadows," to her report on her trip to French colonized Algeria in 1926, "Dark Algiers the White." Although she was sometimes mischaracterized as a "genteel Francophile" by scholars such as Michel Fabre, her view and use of France in her life and work was critical and complex. Like many well-read African Americans of her time, including Langston Hughes, she often employed France and French society as a lens through which to compare and contrast American racial attitudes and possibilities, as both nations professed to be founded on liberty and equality.

Though Fauset enjoyed her sojourns in France and the respite it offered her from segregation and discrimination in the United States, she was adamant that she had no interest in permanently expatriating herself to France. In an interview with Pierre Loving, a writer for the American newspaper based in Paris, the *Herald Tribune*, Fauset stated that while she enjoyed the freedom Paris offered her, she had no desire to leave her native country:

I am colored and wish to be known as colored, but sometimes I have felt that my growth as a writer has been hampered in my own country. And so – but only temporarily – I have fled from it. I love my own people and love to be among them, despite the race issue in America.[16]

In her early short stories, "Emmy" (1912) and "There Was One Time!: A Story of Spring" (1917), both published in *The Crisis*, the French language connects Black characters from across the African diaspora whose shared past was forged by the experience of enslavement and colonialism. The eponymous protagonist of the former story is the daughter of a woman who makes her living doing French translations from her home in a period when few professions were open to educated Black women. However, the reasons why Emmy's mother is fluent in French are a product of a painful history of enslavement, the psychological remnants that destroyed a Black marriage a generation after abolition.[17] "There Was One Time!: A Story of Spring" features a young Black woman, like Fauset, a reluctant and resentful teacher of French in a segregated school where French fairy tales have little relevance to the pupils' constrained and impoverished lives.

Fauset's story depicts a relationship – initiated, then obscured, then revealed –between the teacher and a colonial nomad that offers a new paradigm of Black love by, to use Roussy Césaire's term, "cannibalizing" the French fairytale form.[18] In her writing, Fauset often made claims for a Black woman's place in spaces thought to be properly and purely white,[19] as she does in "The Enigma of the Sorbonne" (1925), at the time one of the most renowned universities in the world. She ends the historical overview of the fabled university with a description of its current place in the French university system, and concludes the article with a description of Black women students striding confidently across its iconic square:

> Across the courtyard they file, loitering, rushing, gesticulating, exclaiming, living, being, – being simply what they are; unhampered by externals, impervious to criticism. No criticism exists. Two absolutely black girls swing through the rectangle, Haitian, I judge from their accent, pure African I am sure from their coloring. Their hair, stiff, black, and fuzzy frames cloudily the soft darkness of their faces; their voices ring clear and staccato; their movements free and unrestrained striding beneath the indifferent and tolerant gazes of the statues of Louis Pasteur and Victor Hugo. [20]

Like Paulette Nardal, Fauset makes an argument for a space for Black women to exist and belong on their own terms in Western intellectual, artistic, and political discourses that are symbolized by literal and metaphorical spaces in Paris. Fauset recognized that Parisian spaces were polyglot and multicultural, and raised issues of class and migration. In "This Way to the Flea Market" (1926), an essay that recounts Fauset's excursion to the *marché aux puces* at the Porte de Clignacourt, she notes that "the poor of Europe are very poor" and the market was

> full of the poorer groups of all those nationalities with which Paris teems. Many of the merchants were Poles and Russians, but among the changing crowds of customers were Greeks, Italians, Spanish, Tunisians, Algerians, Annamites, Chinese, Kabyles. These last formed a striking and easily detected group ... Hardy sons of the desert they might be, yet not the least of such nostalgia as they felt could be traced back to an unvoiced sense of contrast between the dampness of a French winter and the baking sun of Africa.[21]

Here, as elsewhere in her writing, Fauset is particularly interested in the condition and activities of women: "the women merchants are the hardest bargainers, seldom if ever yielding."[22] In an excursion to Algiers, then a French colonized city, Fauset focuses her attention on learning more about the women of the city, who for cultural reasons are not easily encountered by tourists such as Fauset and her traveling companion, the artist Laura Wheeler Waring. Fauset enlists the help of a white French woman to arrange a visit over tea with some local women, and the two-episode essay becomes a meditation on the possible interactions between women across class, race, national, cultural, and linguistic barriers.[23] Being in France afforded Fauset more mobility in exploring spaces and places that were not policed by formal and informal Jim Crow laws and practices, but her commitment to her communities in her native country kept her from romanticizing French society in both her life and her work.

Fauset's compatriot, Gwendolyn Bennett, was far more ambivalent about her experiences in Paris than Fauset was. Bennett was a poet, painter, and professor in the Fine Arts Department of Howard University when she took a leave of absence in June 1925 to study at a variety of well-known art schools in Paris. Funded by a $1000 scholarship from the Black sorority Delta Sigma Theta, Bennett was able to live over the course of the year in comfortable lodgings both in Paris and in the bucolic commune of Pointoise, 17 miles from the city.[24] Despite pursuing an active social life between her hours in studios, Bennett often felt lonely and disconnected, as recounted in her diary entry describing her first Fourth of July abroad:

> To have one's National Holiday roll around when one is in a strange land and can't speak the language is an experience never to be forgotten. A homesickness more poignant and aching than anything I can ever imagine held me in its grip. All day long I did not see or speak to a single one of my compatriots nor did I even hear a word of English spoken. There is this marvelous thing about being here in France. A strange new patriotism has sprung up in me since I've been here in France … there are times that I'd give half my remaining years to hear "The Star Spangled Banner" played. And yet even as I feel that way I know that it has nothing to do with the same "home" feeling I have when I see crowds of American white people jostling each other about the American express [sic].[25]

Bennett's two short stories that are set in France are frank about how in France, the American racism that shapes Black life does not disappear on the other side of the Atlantic. The protagonists in both "Wedding Day" (1926)[26] and "Tokens" (1927)[27] are Black American men who at the time of the stories are drifting and disconnected, having suffered traumatic love affairs that leave them with little to live for. In "Wedding Day," Paul Watson, an embittered former boxer with a virulent hatred of white people, finds himself falling in love with a desperate white American performer, stranded penniless in Paris. They get engaged, but then she abandons him on the morning of their wedding when she realizes that love between individuals in a foreign country cannot overcome the United States' history of visceral racial animus.

Jenks Barnett, the protagonist of "Tokens," an alcoholic former jazz musician who finds himself dying in a tuberculosis clinic outside Paris, is the victim of a "madness" he felt for a singer who eventually left him after his obsession with her caused him to be unable to work, and his subsequent alcoholism sent him on a downward spiral of poverty and violence. He meets a young French girl in the clinic, whose perseverance and kindness give him hope for humanity; the story closes with his asking his last friend from the past to make sure that the girl inherits his most valuable possession: a clock. His visitor doesn't have the heart to tell Jenks that the girl had passed away several months ago:

> Bill sighed as he placed the little clock on the mantle-piece. Funny world, this! The French girl had died in late May. He had better not tell Jenks … it might upset him. No-o-ope

better just keep the clock here. Funny how the first kind thing Jenks had done for anybody since Tollie left him should be done for a person who was dead.[28]

Just as the close of "Wedding Day" depicts Paul Watson discovering that he possesses "a first-class ticket in a second-class coach," the close of "Tokens" shows that any French respite from the loss and suffering that has shaped both African American men's lives is purely illusory. It was daring of Bennett to take on the highly charged topic of sexual or emotional relationships between Black men and white women and to portray the Black male partners in the relationship as emotionally complex and damaged, rather than damaging.

Both these stories were first published in "radical" publications. "Wedding Day" was included in *FIRE!!*, a very short-lived little magazine co-edited by Langston Hughes, Wallace Thurman, and others, dedicated to the work of "younger Negro artists" who were rejecting the politics and aesthetics of the Black bourgeoisie; "Tokens" was originally published in *Ebony and Topaz: A Collecteanea*, edited by Charles S. Johnson, whose editorial philosophy was to show how the range and richness of Black life challenged stereotypes and familiar narratives. Bennett's own sojourn in France was a very mixed experience, and after her one year living there, she never returned.

Conclusion

These writers came from different backgrounds, but their writing enterprises share particular characteristics. Each in her own way was inscribing the experiences and perspectives of Black women in the overdetermined literal and metaphorical spaces of Paris, which in the early decades of the twentieth century was the intellectual and artistic capital of the Western world, as well as a powerful empire. In their own particular ways – as activists, as creative writers, as journalists committed to exploring, valuing, and sharing conversations throughout the global African diaspora – these women were both making a claim for a space for Black women in already established cultural and political discourses and creating new narratives born of their own intersectional experiences of class, gender, race, nationality, and other markers of difference. Their intelligence and efforts were at the heart of, not peripheral to, the Black liberation project in the early decades of the twentieth century. Black women's intellectual history is a relatively new field, and only recently have scholars begun to acknowledge and analyze the contributions of Black women to the political and cultural projects that undergirded modern civil rights and anti-colonial movements. These women raised questions that we are still struggling with today: what does freedom look like if we decenter whiteness and maleness? What is the relationship between civil rights, citizenship rights, and human rights? When the colonizer's language is your mother tongue, how do you express yourself in words? The body of these women's work provides a variety of intriguing responses that are relevant to us today.

Notes

1 All translations, with the exception of those from *La Revue du Monde Noir*, which was a bilingual French/English periodical, and the excerpt from *La Grande Camouflage*, are my own.
    Muriel Descas-Ravoteur, Micheline Marlin-Godier, and Dominique Taffin, *Femmes de la Martinique: Quelle Histoire?* (Fort-de-France: Archives départementales de la Martinique, 2008), 60.
2 Jenny Alpha, *Paris Créole Blues* (Paris: Éditions Toucan, 2011), 51.
3 Paulette Nardal, "L'Antillaise étudiante à Paris," *Le Soir* 30 (Juin 1930): n.p.
4 Roberte Horth, "Histoire sans importance/A Thing of No Importance," *La Revue du Monde Noir* 2 (1931): 48.

5 Ibid., 48.

6 Ibid., 49.

7 Nardal, "L'Antillaise étudiante à Paris."

8 Louis-Thomas Achille, Preface to *La Revue du Monde Noir/The Review of the Black World* (Paris: Jean Michel Place, 1992).

9 Jennifer Boittin, *Colonial Metropolis: The Urban Grounds of Anti-Imperialism and Feminism in Interwar Paris* (Omaha: The University of Nebraska Press, 2010).

10 Robert P. Smith, "Black Like That: Paulette Nardal and the Negritude Salon," *CLA Journal* XLV (2001) : 61.

11 Jane Nardal, "Pantins Exotiques," *La Dépêche Africaine*, October 15, 1928, 1.

12 Suzanne Césaire, *Le grand camouflage : Essais de dissidence (1941–1945)*. Daniel Maximin, ed. Paris : 2209. Editions de Seuil.22.2.

13 Suzanne Césaire, *The Great Camouflage: Writings of Dissent (1941–1945)*. Daniel Maximin, ed. Translated by Keith L. Walker (Middletown: Wesleyan University Press, 2012).

14 Suzanne Césaire, "Misère d'une poésie John-Antoine Nau," *Le Grand Camouflage : Écrits de dissidence (1941–1945)*. Daniel Maximin, ed. Paris : 2209. Editions de Seuil.22.

15 Hugh Ford, ed. *The Left Bank Revisited: Selections from the Paris Tribune 1917–1934* (University Park: Pennsylvania State University Press, 1973).

16 Jessie Fauset, "Emmy," *The Crisis*, December 1912: 79–87; January 1913: 134–42.

17 "There Was One Time!': A Story of Spring," *The Crisis: A Record of the Darker Races*, April 1917: 14–1?; May 1917: 11–15.

18 Cord, J. Whitaker, "B(l)ack Like That: Medievalism in Jessie Fauset's 'My House and a Glimpse of my Life Therein.'" *postmedieval: a journal of medieval cultural studies* 10, no. 2: 164.

19 Jessie Fauset, "The Enigma of the Sorbonne," *The Crisis: A Record of the Darker Races*, March 1925: 219.

20 Jessie Fauset, "This Way to the Flea Market," *The Crisis: A Record of the Darker Races* 29 (February 1926): 162.

21 Ibid., 162.

22 Jessie Fauset, "Dark Algiers the White," *The Crisis. A Record of the Darker Races*. April 1925: 255–58; May 1925: 16–22.

23 T. Denean Sharpley-Whiting, *Bricktop's Paris: African American Women in Paris Between the Two World Wars* (Albany: The State University of New York, 2015), 98.

24 Gwendolyn Bennett, *A Stranger in the Village: Two Centuries of African American Travel Writing*, Farah J. Griffin and Cheryl Fish, eds. (Boston: Beacon Press, 1999), 177.

25 Gwendolyn Bennett, "Wedding Day," *Fire!!* Walter Thurman, ed., November 1926, v.1, no. 1: 25–8.

26 Gwendolyn Bennett, "Tokens," in *Ebony and Topaz: A Collectanea*, ed. Charles S. Johnson (Manchester, NH: Ayer Co. Publishing, 1927), 149–50.

27 Ibid., 150.

28 Ibid., 150.

Primary sources

Alpha, Jenny. *Paris Créole Blues*. Paris: Editions Toucan, 2011.

Bennett, Gwendolyn. "Wedding Day." Fire!! Ed. Walter Thurman. 1, no. 1 (November 1926): 25–28.

Bennett, Gwendolyn. "Tokens." *Ebony and Topaz: A Collectanea*. Ed. Charles S. Johnson. Manchester, NH: Ayer Co. Publishing, 1927, 149–150.

Bennett, Gwendolyn. "Excerpts from the Diaries of Gwendolyn Bennett." *A Stranger in the Village: Two Centuries of African American Travel Writing*. Eds. Farah J. Griffin and Cheryl Fish. Boston: Beacon Press, 1999, 176–179.

Césaire, Suzanne. *Le grand camouflage: Essais de dissidence (1941–1945)*. Ed. Daniel Maximin. Paris: Editions de Seuil, 2009.

Césaire, Suzanne. *The Great Camouflage: Writings of Dissent (1941–1945)*. Ed. Daniel Maximim, Trans. Keith L. Walker. Middletown: Wesleyan University Press, 2012.

"Éveil de la conscience de Race/Awakening of Race Conciousness." *La Revue du Monde Noire* 6 (1932): 25–31.

Fauset, Jessie. "Emmy." *The Crisis*. December 1912: 79–87; January 1913: 134–142.

Fauset, Jessie. "There Was One Time!': A Story of Spring." *The Crisis: A Record of the Darker Races*. April 1917: 14–1; May 1917: 11–15.

Fauset, Jessie. "Dark Algiers the White." *The Crisis. A Record of the Darker Races*. April 1925: 255–258; May 1925: 16–19.

Fauset, Jessie. "The Enigma of the Sorbonne." *The Crisis: A Record of the Darker Races*. March 1925: 216–219.

Fauset, Jessie. "This Way to the Flea Market." *The Crisis: A Record of the Darker Races*. February 1926: 161–163.

Horth, Roberte. "Histoire sans Importance/A Thing of No Importance." *La Revue du Monde Noir* 2 (1931): 48–50.

Nardal, Paulette. "L'Antillaise étudiante à Paris." *Le Soir* 30 (June 1930).

Secondary sources

Achille, Louis-Thomas. *Preface to La Revue du Monde Noir/The Review of the Black World*. Paris: Jean Michel Place, 1992.

Boittin, Jennifer. *Colonial Metropolis: The Urban Grounds of Anti-Imperialism and Feminism in Interwar Paris*. Omaha: The University of Nebraska Press, 2010.

Descas-Ravoteur, Muriel and Marlin-Godier, Micheline and Taffin, Dominique. *Femmes de la Martinique: Quelle Histoire?* Fort-de-France: Archives départementales de la Martinique, 2008.

Ford, Hugh, ed. *The Left Bank Revisited: Selections from the Paris Tribune 1917–1934*. University Park: Pennsylvania State UP, 1973.

Sharpley-Whiting, T. Denean. *Bricktop's Paris: African American Women in Paris Between the Two World Wars*. Albany: The State University of New York, 2015, 98.

Smith, Robert P. "Black Like That: Paulette Nardal and the Negritude Salon." *CLA Journal* XLV (2001): 61.

Whitaker, Cord. "B(l)ack Home in the Middle Ages: Medievalism in Jessie Fauset's "My House and a Glimpse of my Life Therein." *Journal of Postmedieval: A Journal of Medieval Cultural Studies* 10, no. 2 (2019): 164.

26

The transnational Black feminist politics of Claudia Jones

Carole Boyce-Davies

There are several entry points for examining the activist/intellectual who became Claudia Jones. Among these, her Caribbean American identity remains prominent. But in her later years, she would be central to the development of a Black British political identity after choosing exile in the then English colonial center of London. There, her Panfricanism and transnational activism were honed and practiced. Consistently though, she is readable cumulatively through her transnational Black left feminist activism. In other words, what we can define now as transnational Black feminism was retrospectively for Jones not only the art of navigating a variety of complex positions around race, gender, class, and nation through the generative experiences of migration across three geographical locations. An interesting blend of theoretical and practical positions created a life that preceded discourses of intersectionality, finding a place for art and culture as well; finding also a sense of personal political style that captured these identities.

Claudia Vera Cumberbatch was born in Belmont, Port-of-Spain, Trinidad, in 1915 and migrated with her siblings to join her parents in Harlem, New York City, in 1924. In that same year, another Trinidadian of note, pianist Hazel Scott, who would later marry Adam Clayton Powell, Jr., would have a similar trajectory, migrating to New York also in 1924 and similarly being targeted by the House Un-American Activities Committee (HUAC) during the McCarthy era. In her case, because she refused to perform before segregated audiences and was an outspoken advocate for Black Civil Rights, the political harassment she received led to her migrating to Paris, where she lived throughout the 1950s. Dancer Pearl Primus, also from Trinidad, would also migrate with family to New York City in 1923 at the age of four and begin the development of her international African dance career there.

Clearly, the post–Panama Canal migratory period from the Caribbean to the United States produced one of the formative demographic movements that created the New York Caribbean American creative-political communities to which they belonged (Watkins-Owens, 1996). Claudia Jones, for her part, would attend elementary and secondary schools in New York but followed a more distinct political trajectory as she joined the Young Communist League of the CPUSA (Communist Party USA) at the age of 18, which defined her life of activism. Here, she developed oratory, community organizing, and journalistic skills, which were usable throughout her life professionally and economically. Claudia Vera Cumberbatch, who would take the name Claudia Jones as her activist name, a protective shield after she joined the CPUSA, is known for advancing the "super-exploitation of the Black woman" as a concept which identifies the ways that Black women's labor is multiply exploited by a variety of other "class fractions" – Black men, white women, white men – rendering her multiply and super-exploited in her relations with the rest of society. But beyond that formation, her activist and intellectual understandings of the Black woman as a political and economic subject meant that she understood the Black woman in a transnational context borne of not only her own experiences as a young Afro-Caribbean woman, living and working in cosmopolitan centers like New York and London, but also her study of and encounter with other Black women from a variety of locations.

Transnational Black feminist politics

According to Julia Sudbury in "Feminist Critiques, Transnational Landscapes, Abolitionist Visions," the introduction to *Global Lockdown: Race, Gender, and the Prison-Industrial Complex*, transnational feminism is part of a "wider anti-imperialist, anticapitalist endeavor." As she further explains:

> Unlike global feminism, transnational feminist practices do not depict "women's oppression" as unitary or universal. Nor do they subscribe to the vision of women's experience as a fragmented mosaic of cultural and national difference. Rather this approach focuses on the linkages that emerge out of transnational networks of economic and social relations.
>
> *(xiii)*

The actual position of the Claudia Jones gravestone marker, to the left of Karl Marx in Highgate Cemetery, London, as one confronts the Marx bust, is the generative image for the titling of my work, *Left of Karl Marx. The Political Life of Black Communist Claudia Jones* (2008), where I assert that in many ways, Claudia Jones's work pre-dates what is defined today as transnational Black feminism or anti-imperialist Black feminism. Jacqui Alexander, in her chapter "Transnationalism, Sexuality, and the State: Modernity's Traditions at the Height of Empire," from her book *Pedagogies of Crossing* (Alexander, 2006), has perhaps one of the most detailed articulations of some of the discursive positions that transnational Black feminism advances. She sees it as a response, for example, to a great deal of "entanglement between state and corporate power" (182). She raises a series of questions aimed at unpacking the nature of state's "heterosexualizing of the nation … a way of looking at how feminist praxis can address state's investments in sexuality within formulations of transnationalism" (182). Her conclusion is that:

> As we recognize that the nation-state matters more to some than to others, we also need to recognize that the borders of the nation-state cannot be positioned as hermetically sealed or epistemically partial. Our knowledge-making projects must therefore move across state-constructed borders to develop frameworks that are simultaneously intersubjective, comparative and relational, yet historically specific and grounded.
>
> *(Alexander, 2006, 253–4)*

Along the way, Alexander sees "modernity" as a more polite wording of neo-imperial projects. Thus, she does not want to see transnational time as linear but rather, palimpsestic, a series of traces on which are inscribed new formations of the same.

Examining the literature on transnational Black feminism, I was able to conclude that transnational Black feminist work recognizes that our current geographical locations are products of multiple historical processes, many of which we had no control over, which have produced us, as subjects, in various "nation-states" of the world, having to interact with other similarly or differently produced individuals. These displacements are the end-product of some very hateful processes: wars of domination, colonialisms, enslavements, holocausts, encampments, dispossession, and genocide. Thus, preliminarily, transnational or cross-cultural feminist work has to assess how we were produced as subjects in the wake of European Enlightenment and modernism, colonialism, and their various enterprises. More recent structural adjustments, economic globalization and the transnational movement of capital in its search for cheap labor sources worldwide, are re-produced under various nationalist/regional and global imperatives.

Minimally, then, we are accounting for a large international community, which continues to engage feminism from a variety of ethnic locations other than U.S. Black feminist positions. Transnational feminism would arise preliminarily from one larger assumption: working cross-culturally is an essential feature of our contemporary world, and our own specific locations and identities must be part of the basis of our analyses. With this in mind, then, any contemporary cultural and political work that wants to move out of fixity and specific imperialistic interpellations has to account for its particular location, articulate its own specificity, and move towards the recognition of the existence of other cultures and political realities in some cross-cultural/trans-locational way. The category "Black woman" or "Black feminism" deployed in a limited nation-state way is thereby re-defined, based on the experiences of a number of Black women internationally.

My earlier formulation of "migratory subjectivity" (Boyce Davies, 1994) accounted for the ways our identities are formulated in movement. And in some ways, its meaning may be considered here as generative, as it is through migration of bodies, ideas, and perspectives that one gets to the transnational. Perhaps the most critical recognition, in doing transnational feminist work, is understanding that the nation-states in which we live as subjects have been produced out of specific political imperatives and histories and therefore seek to contain, arbitrarily, a variety of peoples subject to the whims of these same nation-state enterprises. Thus, African Americans/Caribbean Americans in the United States end up carrying some of the weight of U.S. imperialism and its manifestations in war efforts and capitalist expansion. The series of persons displaced via global economic processes, who must constantly reconcile themselves to existing emotionally and physically in different spaces, may enter what is popularly referred to now as diaspora, a space that resists centering even as it identifies longing, homelands, and a myth of origin. Still, there are those who remain outside diaspora or live in intersecting diasporas. "Migrating subjects," as I have argued, already consistently negotiate borders in assertive ways, challenging the entrenched meanings of those in intact locations, crossing and re-crossing them, making them sites of transformation.

A growing body of scholarship, produced by Black women/women of color themselves, is systematically addressing the specificities of women's lives in myriad locations, identifying what the particularities of gender, sex, sexuality, race, class, and so on mean when looked at with different lenses or at least when removed from the fixed location of "under western eyes" (Talpade Mohanty (1991). Beverly Guy-Sheftall's overview, "Speaking For Ourselves: Feminisms in the African Diaspora" (2003: 27–43), offers a range of Black feminist contributors and positions across the African diaspora, beginning with Anna Julia Cooper and ranging through the Casely-Hayfords to Funmilayo Ransome-Kuti to the contemporary contributors to black feminist production internationally. Transnational Black feminist work, which accounts for some of these movements and migratory journeys as they also attempt to make connections, makes meaning based on a variety of these experiences and is reflected as well in the kind of gender work that Jones did from a variety of political positions and geographical locations. And there is sufficient evidence, as Guy-Sheftall reveals, that these women often worked collaboratively across continents. Amy Ashwood Garvey, Eslanda Goode Robeson, Charlene Mitchell, Anna Davin, and Jones maintained an international friendship and communication and were supportive of each other's projects, crossing oceans at times. Jones is identified as attending the same meeting as Funmilayo Ransome Kuti at the World Congress of Women in the USSR in 1963 (Sherwood et al., 1999, 110).

With the various trajectories accounted for, it is not difficult to begin a process of recognition of the various positionalities we occupy/have occupied historically. This is the process that for me, offers the possibilities for the transformation of the unequal bases of our arrangements. The context in which I want to locate this particular work on Jones is one that recognizes the transnational as it relates to the local. For Jones herself was able to link the specific struggles of women from a variety of locations to those of women in world hegemonic powers like the United States.

As cultural critic Stuart Hall (1991) appropriately asserted well before the popular discourses of globalization, the global has now become the local; indeed, they (the global and the local) are imbricated, one in the other. Separating them masks the ways in which capital traffics in global ways. Media, markets, and communications of various sorts produce a multiplicity of possibilities. At the same time, they continue to exact a toll on those left out or exploited by these same processes. Inderpal Grewal and Caren Kaplan, in their introduction to *Scattered Hegemonies. Postmodernity and Transnational Feminist Practices* (1994), see the transnational as problematizing purely locational politics of global–local or center–periphery. They would assert that "transnational linkages influence every level of social existence. Thus the effects of configurations of practices at those levels are varied and historically specific" (13). Caren Kaplan in "The Politics of Location as Transnational Feminist Critical Practice" sees this formulation by Adrienne Rich as attempting the "dewesternization of the feminist movement."

Feminist thinking in the presence of globalization, in my view, cannot help but be minimally transnational. A more fully relational scholarship and activism allows us to find models of this kind of work that already existed in prior and current activist/intellectual work (Eisenstein, 2019). Claudia Jones had clearly already gestured to this interconnection as early as the 1940s. Thus, we can more definitively embrace a history of transnational Black feminist *work*, making a distinction between *work as activism* and Black feminist theory as *ideas* solely. The Claudia Jones model reveals a labor-intensive set of activities that link activist work with intellectual work. For those of us working in this phase of capitalist globalization, and in the presence of a phenomenal rise in the distinctions between those with and without access to power and resources, a refined critique of imperialism in its many forms has to be redesigned. A feminism that sees the other only as subject of research and not as creator of meaning, or cannot make the fine class distinctions or take the kind of political risks that earlier generations took, would have little relevance.

Jones was a ground-up activist who not only lived her life as a transnational Black feminist subject but also articulated these positions conceptually in her practice as in her ideas. For her, the transnational was a fundamental feature of understanding the local. Her clarity about the nature of Euro-American imperialism, honed in her Marxism-Leninism, afforded her an ability to assert resisting positions, not only to capitalism and imperialism but also to patriarchal dominance. Jones lived and organized at the intersection of a variety of positionalities – anti-imperialism and decolonization struggles, activism for workers' rights, the critique of appropriation of Black women's labor, and the challenge to domestic and international racisms and their links to colonialism – and therefore, was able to articulate them in ways that preceded many contemporary articulations of transnational African diaspora/feminist politics.

Angela Davis, in an interview in *Abolition and Democracy: Beyond Empire, Prisons, and Torture* (2005), sees a link "between the internationalism of Karl Marx's era and the new globalisms we are seeking to build today." Davis makes further links with the global assembly line that has already been well documented in her discussion of the commodity that Marx identified in *Capital*, which "penetrated every aspect of people's lives all over the world in ways that have no historical precedent" (25). She also identifies her affinity with the Pan-Africanism of W.E.B. DuBois, which made links with people in Africa, Asia, the Caribbean, and Latin America.

This is what in my viewpoint, puts Claudia Jones and a range of left individuals like her on the other side of Marx. Jones would also do the same in her journalism in *The Daily Worker* and eventually in her work on the *West Indian Gazette and Afro-Asian Caribbean News* (Boyce Davies, 2008, Chapters 2 and 5). In the former, she spends a great deal of her time identifying the "half the world" logic in terms of accounting for women's lives globally located in struggle, and Black women in particular, and then in the *West Indian Gazette and Afro-Asian Caribbean News*, she gives space and voice to the articulation of political movements across the African world.

Feminists' ongoing repudiation, engagement, and critique of Marxism is well documented, requiring all sorts of qualifiers – red feminism, Marxist-feminism – and so on in order to relocate the gender issue at the same level as class and not solely in bourgeois family operations. Sylvia Wynter, for her part, in "Beyond Liberal and Marxist Feminisms: Toward an Autonomous Frame of Reference" (1982), argues that all these models are still limited frames of reference that operate within Western conceptions of the human.

A radical life

Entering the United States at the age of eight, Claudia experienced the effects of U.S. racial capitalism directly and as a result, saw her family's condition as linked to that of other struggling Black people, many of whom had also moved from the rural Jim Crow South to urban poverty in the North. Indeed, her educational and political formations were cultivated in New York. Her political affiliations and positions are reflected in the range of descriptors with which she is identified: advocate for Black rights, political activist, feminist, communist, anti-imperialist, journalist, community organizer. Her professional training as a journalist gave her the skills to work in that field, moving from early articles in Black newspapers to her work in the Young Communist League's *Weekly Review* and a steady movement through the editorial ranks. In each of these cases, her work as a journalist paralleled other political positions and served as a means of public education and organizing. Her work on the *Weekly Review* accompanied her service as education director for New York State of the Young Communist League. Her subsequent work on *The Worker* and *Daily Worker* paralleled her position as secretary of the National Women's Commission of the CPUSA.

Because of her activity in organizing working-class communities for the Communist Party, Claudia Jones became targeted for surveillance by the FBI, was imprisoned three times by the U.S. government, and was finally sentenced to a year at the Federal Women's Prison in Alderson, West Virginia before being deported in 1955 under the notorious Smith Act and McCarran-Walter Act of 1952, also known as the Immigration and Nationality Act. She is identified as one of 13 communists tried and imprisoned for having communist ideas in the United States and thus also became a political prisoner. Still a British subject then, she spent the years from 1955 to 1964 doing political and cultural organizing among the Black London community, and is known particularly for founding and editing *The West Indian Gazette and Afro-Asian Caribbean News* and for organizing the first Caribbean Carnival in 1958, which has now become known in its outdoor street carnival version as the famous Notting Hill Carnival. A number of community organizations in London have been named after Jones, but for years she was dis-remembered in the United States and the Caribbean. Jones died in her sleep on Christmas Eve, 1964, and following an almost state-level funeral of left activists, she was interred to the left of Karl Marx in Highgate Cemetery, London.

Deported from the United States during the McCarthy period, she was meant to be erased. Making her way to London, doubly and then triply "diasporized," as Stuart Hall describes the London diaspora experience, Jones arrived in London just after the *Windrush* (1948), the first ocean liner to begin the massive influx of Caribbeans into London and which has given its name to an entire generation of "West Indian" migrants. She was able, therefore, to have a role in providing institutions for the burgeoning Black community in London. Far from ever abandoning her Marxist politics, she found ways to re-shape it, as I argue in *Left of Karl Marx* (2008), which expanded Marxism to account for Black women, people of color, and African Caribbean migrants to Europe. She so impacted that society that her burial left of Karl Marx is a fitting statement of the nature of her politics, as of her life.

Claudia Jones's art of Black left feminism is marked by the practice of a radical transnational poetics marked by insightful political analysis and action. Her entire range of theoretical and creative articulations describes a transnational Black feminism, informed by her communist identification – articulated in space, place, and time, and using a variety of images (in both poetry and prose) to articulate self as well as a range of theoretical positions. It is a movement outside what Glissant called "forced poetics" to "natural poetics" (*Caribbean Discourse*, 120). For him in "natural poetics,"

[E]ven if the destiny of a community should be a miserable one, or its existence threatened, these poetics are the result of activity with the social body … The most violent challenge to an established order can emerge from a natural poetics when there is a continuity between the challenged order and the order that negates it.

(Glissant, 1989, 120)

In the work of Jones, we can observe a radical poetics operating in her poetic contributions, written mostly during incarceration, and in her political essays. Jones would herself own the idea of Black radicalism conceptually in *Ben Davis, Fighter for Freedom*, which was a spirited defense of communist Congressman Ben Davis, who was tried and also incarcerated for communism in the group of communist leaders before Claudia's, by stating that:

The very core of *all* Negro history is then, there are those who tell us that to be radical and black means three strikes against us, or to be black and red is even worse … The very core of all Negro history is radicalism against conformity to chattel slavery, radicalism against the betrayal of the demands of Reconstruction, radicalism in relation to non-acceptance of the status quo.

(Jones, 1954, 36–7)

Indeed, all scholars who did any Black activism at that time, according to Gerald Horne in *Black and Red* (1985), were considered communist; intellectual work and activist work of all Black people was assigned to communism. Witch hunts, deportation, arrests, and detention were common. The FBI became the machinery used to document and target Black entertainers – poets like Langston Hughes, dancers like Pearl Primus, singers like Paul Robeson, and activists of all kinds. This would be continued in the deadly assault on Black leadership and subsequent organizations like the Black Panther Party and a range of activists and intellectuals who were not communist (Boyce Davies, 2008, chapter 6).

The result is the strategic conflation today of "left" as anything that critiques conservatism. People who were actually leftists, like Jones, would be the object of the most intense reprisal, including imprisonment as political prisoners and finally, deportation. But, as we shall see, she was able to turn this towards creating something even more beautiful for the Caribbean diaspora in London: a Caribbean diaspora–focused newspaper and the London Carnival.

Still, one has to identify a black radical intellectual tradition to which many scholars would consciously belong. Several Caribbean scholars are indicated as representatives of this tradition: Eric Williams, Lloyd Best, Sylvia Wynter, C.L.R. James, and Amy Ashwood Garvey are exemplars. As Robin D.G. Kelley described the Black radical tradition, there were several scholars and activists trying to figure out the "global implications of black revolt." Significantly in this process, they tended to embrace "some kind of diasporic sensibility, shaped by anti-racist and anti-imperialist politics of the nineteenth and twentieth centuries." Thus he was able to conclude that "black intellectual and historical traditions, profoundly shaped historical scholarship on Black people in the New World" (Kelley, 1999, 1047).

It is important to say as well that much of the intellectual activity of the time of Jones remained outside the university. Most major institutions of higher learning were closed to Black people... There were few PhDs at the time, and often the intellectuals of the stature of a John Henrik Clarke (1915–98), an organic intellectual and pioneer of the field of Black Studies, were more respected than those in the academy. Not only that, but scholars like poet Melvin Tolson (1898–1966), memorialized in the film *The Great Debaters* (2007), saw the care, nurturing, and advancement of students as a sacred mission to make them be the best they could be; his role as a community activist was just as important.

It is in these pioneering actions that the field of Black Studies got its founding energies and logic of transformation. Carter G. Woodson (1875–1950) founded the Association for the Study of African American Life and History (ASALAH) to promote historical research and to publish books on black life and history. He, too, would be considered by the FBI to be a subversive. It is in that context of the struggles for Black political and intellectual recognition and the legacy of Black women's self-assertion that Claudia Jones had pronounced at her trial:"you do not assume that black women can think, and speak and write" (Jones, 1953).

Conclusion

Claudia Jones's "why are they afraid of the words of one black woman?" resonates. In the speech for which she was eventually arrested, "International Women's Day and the Struggle for Peace" (1950), she asserts that as far as the question of Black and white women workers are concerned, "left progressives in unions and elsewhere have contributed to the gross lack of awareness of the need to struggle for women's demands." This is a point she would reaffirm consistently and appears more firmly in her classic 1949 essay, "An End to the Neglect of the Problems of the Negro Woman."

Jones, definitely a transatlantic activist, a Black radical intellectual from the Caribbean, and a Black left transnational feminist, moved Marxism-Leninism to another place and re-opened it for different utility, particularly because she addressed in her time those issues that Marx and Lenin left unarticulated. Indeed, it is my assertion that Claudia Jones, who had already provided superb analyses of the issue of Black women's "super-exploitation" and an understanding and articulation of the role of the "third world" in left politics, is part of the ongoing process of recuperation. Her anti-imperialism, truly international in nature, allowed her to make decided links with other women struggling for liberation in a variety of locations, even as her own personal autobiography is implicated in her transnational approach.

Bibliography

Alexander, M. Jacqui. 2006. *Pedagogies of Crossing. Meditations on Feminism, Sexual Politics, Memory, and the Sacred*. Durham, NC: Duke University Press.
Alexander, M. Jacqui and Chandra Talpade Mohanty, eds. 1996a. *Feminist Geneaologies, Colonial Legacies, Democratic Futures*. London: Routledge.

Alexander, M. Jacqui and Chandra Talpade Mohanty. 1996b. *Feminism Without Borders: Decolonizing Theory, Practicing Solidarity*. London: Routledge.

Baker, Houston A. 1989. "There is No More Beautiful Way. Theory and the Poetics of Afro-American Women's Writing," in Houston Baker and Patricia Redmond, eds. *Afro-American Literary Study in the 1990's*. Chicago, IL: University of Chicago Press: 135-153.

Boyce Davies, Carole. 1994. *Black Women, Writing and Identity: Migrations of the Subject*. London: Routledge.

Boyce Davies, Carole. 2001. "Deportable Subjects: U.S. Immigration Laws and the Criminalizing of Communism," *The South Atlantic Quarterly*, 100:4 (Fall, 2001): 949–966.

Boyce Davies, Carole. 2008. *Left of Karl Marx. The Politics and Poetics of a Black Communist Woman*. Durham, NC: Duke University Press.

Boyce Davies, Carole and Monica Jardine. 2003. "Imperial Penetrations and Caribbean Nationalism: Between 'A Dying Colonialism' and Rising American Hegemony," *New Centennial Review*, 3:3 (Fall): 131–149.

Camara, Fatou Kine. 2015. "African Women and the Gender Equality Regime in Africa: From Patriarchy to Parity," in *Black Women and International Law. Deliberate Interactions, Movements, and Actions*. Ed. Jeremy I. Levitt. Cambridge: Cambridge University Press: 61–87.

Davis, Angela. 2005. *Abolition and Democracy. Beyond Empire, Prisons, and Torture*. New York: Seven Stories Press: 88–119.

Eistenstein, Zillah. *Abolitionist Socialist Feminism: Radicalizing the Next Revolution*. New York: Monthly Review Press, 2019.

Glissant, Edouard. 1989. *Caribbean Discourse. Selected Essays*. Charlottesville: University of Virginia Press.

Grewal, Inderpal and Caren Kaplan. 1994. *Scattered Hegemonies. Postmodernity and Transnational Feminist Practices*. Minneapolis, MN: University of Minnesota Press.

Guy-Sheftall, Beverly. 2003. "Speaking for Ourselves. Feminisms in the African Diaspora," in *Decolonizing the Academy: African Diaspora Studies*. Ed. Carole Boyce Davies, Meredith Gadsby and Henrietta Williams. Trenton, NJ: Africa World Press: 27-43.

Hall, Stuart. 1991. "The Local and the Global: Globalization and Ethnicity" and Old and New Identitied, Old and New Ethnicities," in *Culture, Globalization and the World System*. Ed. Anthony King. London: Macmillan: 19–39, 41–68.

Horne, Gerald. 1985. *Black and Red, W. E. B. Du Bois and the Afro-American Response to the Cold War, 1944–1963*. Albany: SUNY Press.

Jones, Claudia. 1949. "An End to the Neglect of the Problems of the Negro Woman," in *Claudia Jones. Beyond Containment*. Ed. Carole Boyce Davies. Banbury: Ayebia, 2011, 74–86.

Jones, Claudia. 1950. "International Women's Day and the Struggle for Peace," in *Claudia Jones. Beyond Containment*. Ed. Carole Boyce Davies Banbury: Ayebia, 2011: 90–103.

Jones, Claudia. 1953. *Speech to the Court' in Thirteen Communists Speak*. New York: New Century Publishers, 1955. Reprinted as "Back Women Can Think and Speak and Write. 'Statement before Being Sentenced' in *Claudia Jones. Beyond Containment*. Banbury: Ayebia, 2011: 6–10.

Jones, Claudia. 1954. *Ben Davis – Fighter for Freedom*. New York: National Committee to Defend Negro Leadership. (Reprinted in Claudia Jones. Beyond Containment. Ed. Carole Boyce Davies. Banbury: Ayebia, 2011: 123-153.

Kelley, Robin D.G. 1999. "But a Local Phase of a World Problem': Black History's Global Vision, 1883–1950," *Journal of American History* 86:3 (December): 1045–1077.

Mohanty, Chandra. 1991. "Under Western Eyes: Feminist Scholarship and Colonial Discourses." In *Third World Women and the Politics of Feminism*. Ed. Chandra Talpade Mohanty, Anna Russo and Lourdes Torres. Bloomington: Indiana University Press: 51–80.

Noh, Eliza. 2003. "Problematics of Transnational Feminism and Asian American Women." *New Centennial Review* 3:3 (Fall): 131–149.

Sherwood, Marika, Donald Hinds and Colin Prescod. Eds. 1999. *Claudia Jones. A Life in Exile*. London: Lawrence and Wishart.

Sudbury, Julia. 2005. "Feminist Critiques, Transnational Landscapes, Abolitionist Visions," Introduction to *Global Lockdown. Race, Gender, and the Prison-Industrial Complex*. London: Routledge, xi–xxvii.

Watkins-Owens, Irma. 1996. *Blood Relations: Caribbean Immigrants and the Harlem Community, 1900–1930*. Bloomington: Indiana University Press.

Wynter, Sylvia. 1982. *Beyond Liberal and Marxist Feminisms: Toward an Autonomous Frame of Reference*. San Francisco: Annual Conference of the American Sociological Association, September.

27

Confronting apartheid

Black women's internationalism in South Africa and the United States

Nicholas Grant

Eslanda Goode Robeson was thinking about South Africa. It was March 1952, and the noted journalist, anthropologist, and activist was writing to Black newspaper editors about the forthcoming April 6 mass meetings called to protest the introduction of new apartheid laws by the country's white Afrikaner government. Organized by the African National Congress (ANC) and South African Indian Congress (SAIC), the day of action represented a landmark moment in the nascent anti-apartheid struggle, marking a shift to nonviolent mass civil disobedience and inaugurating the Campaign for the Defiance of Unjust Laws, which over the following months, would result in more than 8000 arrests.

In her letter to the Black press, Eslanda commented, "It seems to me that we here in America should not only read about and be thrilled by the heroism of our brothers and sisters in South Africa, but should DO something about it, too." She implored African Americans to write messages of support to the leaders of the Defiance Campaign and called for "Negro churches and Negro communities throughout the country [to] observe two minutes of silence at the stroke of noon on Sunday, April 6, in commemoration and support of the desperate struggle of our South African brothers and sisters." Finally, while noting the need for a similar protest movement in the United States, she asserted:

> Here is a splendid opportunity, I think, for the Negro people to act together on a simple, common objective and strike a telling blow against Jim-Crow and for the rights of black people at home and abroad.[1]

Eslanda Robeson's insistence that the struggle against apartheid and Jim Crow were interconnected had deep roots. Her Black international consciousness was informed by encounters and networks that she had forged on the African continent.[2] She first visited South Africa in 1936, meeting ANC leaders and attending the All-African National Convention in Bloemfontein, held as a response to the prospect of new segregation laws.[3] Indeed, it was on this trip that Eslanda met Max Yergan, an African American missionary and activist living in South Africa, whom she then worked with the following year in London to help set up the International Committee on African Affairs (ICAA).[4] The ICAA ultimately migrated to New York and morphed into the radical anti-imperialist lobby the Council on African Affairs (CAA), which for most of its existence was chaired by Eslanda's husband – the famous actor, singer, and activist Paul Robeson.[5]

Eslanda remained a staunch critic of the apartheid state up until her death in 1965. She worked as a correspondent and editorial consultant for the leftist newspaper the *New World Review* and wrote prolifically on anti-colonial movements in the African American press (Ransby, 2013, 206).[6] Significantly, her writing regularly focused on the lives and activism of women, emphasizing the gender dynamics of colonialism and white supremacy that placed them at the center of the global struggle for Black liberation. Indeed, when asked by an interviewer about her thoughts on the "African woman" in the early 1960s, she insisted that women were at the forefront of freedom movements in Africa, returning to South Africa to note that during the protests of the 1950s, women "offered resistance everywhere," stating:

> In fact, the women of Africa have always taken an active part in protests and demonstrations for independence, and against repression. They have come out, with their children, some of them with babies on their backs, to join the men in protest.[7]

Eslanda's engagements with South Africa were shaped by the thoughts, actions, and collective fate of women who confronted segregation and apartheid. As the historian Erik McDuffie has argued, Eslanda and her radical comrades forged a "black women's international," a gendered articulation of Black internationalism insisting that the interrelated struggles against racism, sexism, and economic inequality placed women at the vanguard of the global struggle for Black liberation.[8]

This chapter demonstrates how Black women, working in and in-between the United States and South Africa, played an important role in the development of the global anti-apartheid movement in the 1950s. Focusing in on the activism of Robeson, Frieda Matthews, and the Sojourners for Truth and Justice (STJ), it traces how radical Black women insisted that the fate of both nations were bound up with one another. These individuals defied the power of the state in order to travel, foster personal relationships, write, and organize against race, gender, and class exploitation in both countries.[9] Shedding light on the "gendered contours of Black internationalism," they drew inspiration from one another's struggles, engaging in transnational exchanges that challenged race and gender oppression.[10]

"The other U.S.A."

It's hard to separate white supremacist histories of the United States and South Africa.[11] State racisms are produced in exchange, and both countries have played a central role in shaping the transnational politics of white domination.[12] Speaking in New York City in 1949, the South African ambassador to the United States reflected on these shared histories of settler colonialism and racist oppression. Referring to the Union of South Africa as "the other U.S.A.," Harry T. Andrews stated in front of his predominantly white audience:

> We are indeed both *pioneering peoples*, and the problems, experiences and perils of the early settlement of our forefathers in what were then uncivilized lands, among wild and warlike savages, were very similar in their nature. Perhaps in that very fact lies the fundamental reason why Americans and South Africans have so many characteristics in common, and why the South African way of life is today so comparable in so many respects to your own American way of life.[13]

African Americans and Black South Africans were all too aware of these racist connections. Encountering one another through religious missionary work, educational institutions, Marcus Garvey's United Negro Improvement Association (UNIA), international Communism, trade unions, and other networks throughout the nineteenth and early twentieth centuries, people of African descent identified the United States and South Africa as a key nexus of what W.E.B. Du Bois referred to as the global "color line."[14] The racial politics of both nations became even more tightly bound together following the election of the National Party in 1948 and the subsequent establishment of the apartheid state. Coinciding with the advance of the civil rights movement in the United States, the era of decolonization, and the escalation of the Cold War, it became virtually impossible to think about the Black liberation struggle in either country through a solely national lens.

The late 1940s and 1950s ushered in a new era of activism in South Africa. Following the rise to power of the National Party, the ANC moved towards a political strategy of mass-action. Galvanized by the militancy of events such as the 1946 African Mine Workers Strike, members of the ANC's Youth League (ANC-YL) established a Programme of Action in 1949 that committed the organization to a strategy of active boycott, strikes, and civil disobedience. This political shift culminated in the 1952 Defiance Campaign, which saw the ANC and SAIC resist the introduction of apartheid laws that made the residential separation of racial groups compulsory, placed severe restrictions on the right to protest, and insisted that Africans belonged in "tribal reserves."[15] The acts of civil disobedience that followed in 1952 would reverberate around the world, especially in the United States, as African Americans watched and were inspired by this large-scale challenge to white supremacist rule.[16]

Women were at the forefront of these protests, often spending weeks in prison after breaking pass laws and entering "whites only" spaces.[17] Despite a long and varied history of women's activism in South Africa, it wasn't until 1943 that African women were permitted to become full members of the ANC. The ANC Women's League (ANC-WL) was formally established at this time, eventually expanding to develop regional chapters and engaging in the politics of non-violent resistance.[18] Later, in 1954, a multiracial national organization, the Federation of South African Women (FSAW), was founded

> [t]o bring the women of South Africa together, to secure full equality of opportunity for all women, regardless of race, colour or creed: to remove social and legal and economic disabilities; to work for the protection of the women and children of our land.[19]

Working across the ANC-WL and FSAW, African women such as Ida Mtwana, Bertha Mkhize, Lilian Ngoyi, Dora Tamana, and Florence Matomela confronted white settler rule – repeatedly exposing apartheid as a gendered system of racial control.[20] As Mtwana asserted in her address to FSAW's inaugural conference in 1954:

> Gone are the days when the place of women was in the kitchen and looking after the children. Today women are marching side by side with the men on the road to freedom. They are beginning to break the chains which have been created by the oppressors to retard the progress of women. Today we have come together to build up one big family.[21]

Central to this political mobilization was the National Party's 1952 announcement that African women would soon be required to carry passes. After challenges to earlier efforts to extend the pass laws (which had long applied to African men), this renewed effort to control women's movement and labor was met with fierce resistance.[22] In October 1955, a crowd of 2000 demonstrated outside the Union buildings in Pretoria against the new laws. The following year, on August 9, over 20,000 women returned to Pretoria – standing in silence outside the government buildings for 30 minutes after delivering a petition to the prime minister's office. The anti-pass protests continued throughout the 1950s, long after the Defiance Campaign had fizzled out, as women set the agenda for the liberation struggle during the decade. Working through FSAW, the ANC-WL, and the broader Congress Alliance, African women organized demonstrations, ran campaigns, went to jail, held conferences, published materials, and forged international connections as they targeted race, gender, and class oppression in apartheid South Africa.[23]

Transatlantic connections: Frieda Matthews and the Sojourners for Truth and Justice

Frieda Bokwe Matthews arrived in New York City in September 1952 as the Defiance Campaign was in full swing. She had ostensibly made this transatlantic journey to join her husband Z.K. Matthews, a renowned Fort Hare professor and president of the Cape branch of the ANC, who had taken up a visiting position at the Union Theological Seminary. However, as the racial situation in South Africa made headlines around the world, Frieda seized upon the politically opportune timing of her trip to become a key overseas spokesperson for the anti-apartheid movement. As Z.K. recalled in his autobiography,

> People – especially the Negro sections of the community – were anxious to know what was happening … the word apartheid was being bandied about and people wanted to know what it meant, and what its implications were for the black folks of South Africa.[24]

Faced with a captive audience eager to learn about the explosive political situation back home, Frieda and her husband made a significant contribution to increasing awareness of and support for the anti-apartheid movement overseas.

A talented writer and musician, Frieda Matthews was an outspoken critic of South African racism, particularly in relation to the issue of "Bantu" education.[25] She traveled widely and in 1935 moved to London with Z.K. while he studied at the LSE, meeting anti-colonial activists including Jomo Kenyatta as well as Eslanda and Paul Robeson.[26] The following year, they hosted Eslanda and her son Paul Jr. at their home in Alice in the Eastern Cape. The visit coincided with the marriage of Frieda's brother Rosebery Bokwe, a physician who had also been an acquaintance of the Robesons in Britain. Reflecting on this time, she commented:

> The fortnight they spent with us was exciting as Mrs. Robeson was a brilliant conversationalist, and our house was inundated with visitors curious to see the wife of the great baritone of whom all Black people were proud, and to discuss with her "the problems of our people here in Africa and America."
>
> *(Matthews, 1995, 24, 27–28)*

Frieda would develop these Black international conversations in the United States years later. While initially apprehensive about leaving South Africa at such an explosive time, she embraced the opportunity to challenge apartheid on the international stage. The Matthews were inundated with invitations to address the political situation in South Africa, with Frieda being as much in demand as her husband, speaking at meetings "at least four times a week" (Matthews, 1995, 50; Matthews, 1981, 160). Frieda and Z.K. also engaged in lobbying work for ANC in the United States, collaborating with diverse groups interested in African affairs, such as the

National Association for the Advancement of Colored People (NAACP), Americans for South African Resistance (AFSAR), and the CAA.[27]

Their activities provoked the ire of the National Party while also arousing the suspicions of the FBI.[28] Commenting on her advocacy on behalf of the Defiance Campaign, Frieda noted, "Little did we realise that our government was keeping a close watch on us," adding defiantly, "Not that this knowledge would have made any difference to what we told our audiences" (Matthews, 1995, 51). The South African government refused to issue the couple passports so they could extend their visit, while on their return home they were met at the airport by the police, who subjected them to humiliating searches and confiscated their private documents before launching an official investigation into their activities abroad.[29]

Significantly, Frieda Matthews' time in the United States also coincided with the emergence of a short-lived but pioneering African American women's organization – the Harlem-based STJ. Founded in September 1951, the Sojourners were a who's who of progressive Black women, including Eslanda Robeson, Louise Thompson Patterson, Beulah Richardson, Shirley Graham Du Bois, Claudia Jones, Dorothy Hunton, Charlotta Bas, and Alice Childress.[30] Noting the gender and class politics of Jim Crow, the STJ insisted that "Negro Women, whose physical and economic security are always threatened by UnAmerican practices and violence … are especially fitted to challenge our Government, and to point out that DEMOCRACY BEGINS AT HOME."[31]

The Sojourners not only argued that these interlocking oppressions meant that African American women were at the center of the struggle against white supremacy in the United States but also stressed the need for a global analysis of racism and a clear commitment to the anti-colonial struggle. While the STJ was already fragmenting due to the repressive politics of the Second Red Scare as Frieda arrived in the United States, her visit coincided with the organization's efforts to forge links with anti-apartheid activists (McDuffie, 2011, 182). Working in tandem with the CAA, the Sojourner leadership wrote to Black South African women, including Mina T. Soga of the National Council of African Women (NCAW) and Bertha Mkhize of the ANC-WL, stressing the need for solidarity between women of color in Asia, Africa, and the United States, while also insisting on the need for "complete emancipation of women throughout the world" (Castledine, 2008, 58; McDuffie, 2012, 16–18).

At the same time, Louise Thompson Patterson and Charlotta Bass contacted Ray Alexander, a white South African Communist Party and labor organizer who would later play a key role in the founding of FSAW, noting that:

> We have been inspired by the example of militant action on the part of African women. We realize that our fight for freedom in the United States is inextricably linked to the struggle against the tyranny of the white supremacists not only in South Africa but throughout the entire Continent.
>
> *(McDuffie, 2012, 17)*

The refusal of Black South African women to accept apartheid laws, to surrender control of their mobility, employment, bodies, and families to the white settler state, clearly resonated with the Sojourners. While it is unclear whether Frieda Matthews had any direct dealings with the group, her visibility in the United States during the Defiance Campaign would have undoubtedly reinforced these links, further establishing apartheid and Jim Crow as interrelated systems of racial control, while also providing a visible reminder of the centrality of Black women in the struggle against colonialism and white supremacy in Africa.

Disrupting Black international solidarities

The state-sponsored hounding of the Matthews and the Sojourners is testament to the radical potential of these connections. Concerned about negative publicity and fearful of jeopardizing what was a mutually profitable political, economic, and strategic Cold War relationship, both the U.S. and South African governments deployed the language of anti-communism to try to marginalize dissenting Black voices and bolster white supremacist power.[32] Indeed, the apparent lack of engagement of African American women with FSAW upon its founding in 1954 was a direct consequence of this harassment.

FSAW had a global outlook, working with the Women's International Democratic Federation (WIDF) to forge transnational solidarities with women overseas. Made up of affiliate organizations in over 60 countries, the WIDF was a progressive feminist and anti-colonial organization committed to fighting for women's rights.[33] FSAW's desire to challenge racism and sexism internationally was most vividly demonstrated by their decision to send Lilian Ngoyi and Dora Tamana to the WIDF's World Congress of Mothers held in Lausanne, Switzerland in July 1955 (Healy-Clancy, 2017, 856–60).[34] Ngoyi and Tamana's travels were both audacious and illegal. In attempting to escape the country, both women tried to stow away, under "white names," on a boat leaving Cape Town, defied segregated seating on a plane bound for London with the help of a sympathetic pilot, and finally gained entry to Britain – before traveling to Switzerland – under the pretext that they were enrolled in a bible studies course.[35] At Lausanne, Ngoyi presided over the second session of the conference, giving its opening address, while Tamana stood in front of assembled women and mothers from almost every continent and declared: "The Federation of South African Women … has joined hands with all organisations fighting for democratic rights, for full equality, irrespective of race or sex."[36]

Ngoyi and Tamana were two of 1063 delegates who attended the World Congress of Mothers. Participants from 66 countries made the journey, united in their insistence on women's rights and readiness to agitate for democracy and peace in the second half of the twentieth century. African American women, however, were not involved in these discussions. In fact, there is no evidence that any delegates from the United States attended the gathering. Key members of the Sojourners had been in the WIDF's orbit, with Eslanda Robeson attending the federation's 1949 Moscow conference and subsequently becoming a member of the organization's U.S. affiliate, the Congress of American Women (CAW) (Ransby, 2013, 197–98). The Sojourners' efforts to engage with Black South African women had also brought them into direct contact with FSAW leaders. It is therefore not difficult to imagine an alternative history where progressive African American activists were among the delegates who heard Ngoyi and Tamana condemn apartheid in Lausanne. However, by the time of this gathering, the Sojourners had been defunct for two years, while the CAW had been declared a subversive organization in the United States, and the WIDF had lost its official consultative status at the United Nations in 1954 at the behest of the American delegation.

Individual Sojourners were also persecuted. Eslanda Robeson, Shirley Graham Du Bois, and Charlotta Bass were all refused passports by the State Department, which had concluded that their travel abroad would "not [be] in the best interests of the United States." Claudia Jones, meanwhile, was prosecuted under the Smith Act, imprisoned, and eventually deported from the United States in 1955.[37] The National Party also fervently embraced anti-communism, using the threat of "foreign subversion" to limit opportunities to protest and placing 156 activists – including Mkhize and Ngoyi – on trial for treason in 1956. State repression and harassment therefore severely limited the opportunity for African American and South African women to engage in transnational exchanges and develop Black international solidarities.

Conclusion

The 1950s were a transformative moment in the struggle against white supremacy in South Africa. While unsuccessful in their immediate aim to overturn new discriminatory laws, the mass protests and civil disobedience campaigns of this era produced strategies, alliances, and landmark events that would continue to resonate during the long struggle against apartheid. It is impossible to account for the scale, militancy, and vibrancy of these protests without acknowledging the role of women. Furthermore, the staunch refusal of African women to accept passes and their opposition to apartheid more broadly inspired likeminded activists around the world.

Indeed, these acts of resistance clearly resonated with African American women in the United States. Eslanda Robeson, STJ, and Frieda Matthews all had a deep-seated belief that they could learn from one another's struggles. Engaging with one another's struggles across national borders, they challenged state efforts to contain their activism by insisting on the need for a global response to institutionalized white supremacy.

Centering the experiences and contributions of women sheds light on how broad and multifaceted the global anti-apartheid movement really was. Through their travels, exchanges, and organizing efforts, these activists defied the repressive power of the state to play a vital role in fostering international opposition to apartheid. They made sure that African women were visible on the international stage and in the process, challenged Black activists to expand their political vision beyond the boundaries of the nation and to foster a global community committed to eradicating race and gender oppression.

Notes

1 Eslanda Goode Robeson, "Letter to the Editor," c. March, 1952, Eslanda G. Robeson Papers, Moorland-Spingarn Research Center, Howard University. Box. 12; "Urges Silent Campaigns To Aid S. Africa," *New York Amsterdam News*, March 22, 1952, 2.

2 Imaobong D. Umoren, *Race Women Internationalists: Activist-Intellectuals and Global Freedom Struggles* (Berkeley: University of California Press, 2018), 46–52.

3 Eslanda Goode Robeson, *African Journey* (New York: John Day Company, 1945).

4 Jacqueline Castledine, "'In a Solid Bond of Unity': Anticolonial Feminism in the Cold War Era," *Journal of Women's History* 20, no. 4 (2008), 68–9.

5 Charles Denton Johnson, "Re-Thinking the Emergence of the Struggle for South African Liberation in the United States: Max Yergan and the Council on African Affairs, 1922–1946," *Journal of Southern African Studies* 39, no. 1 (2013), 171–92.

6 Barbara Ransby, *Eslanda: The Large and Unconventional Life of Mrs. Paul Robeson* (New Haven: Yale University Press, 2013), 206; Imaobong Umoren, "'We Americans Are Not Just American Citizens Any Longer': Eslanda Robeson, World Citizenship, and the New World Review in the 1950s," *Journal of Women's History* 30, no. 4 (December, 2018), 134–58.

7 Eslanda Goode Robeson, "Interview: African Women," n.d., EGRP. Box. 9, 4.

8 Erik S. McDuffie, *Sojourning for Freedom: Black Women, American Communism, and the Making of Black Left Feminism* (Durham: Duke University Press, 2011), 3–6.

9 Claire Cooke and Ana Stevenson, "Defying Borders: Transnational Networks of Gender and Race in South Africa and the United States," *Safundi* 19, no. 1 (January, 2018).

10 Keisha Blain and Tiffany Gill, *To Turn the Whole World Over: Black Women and Internationalism* (Champaign: University of Illinois Press, 2019), 9; Pamela E. Brooks, *Boycotts, Buses, and Passes: Black Women's Resistance in the U.S. South and South Africa* (Amherst: University of Massachusetts Press, 2008).

11 George M Fredrickson, *White Supremacy: A Comparative Study in American and South African History* (New York: Oxford University Press, 1981).

12 Marilyn Lake and Henry Reynolds, *Drawing the Global Colour Line: White Men's Countries and the International Challenge of Racial Equality* (Cambridge: Cambridge University Press, 2008).

13 Harry T. Andrews, "Address Delivered to the English-Speaking Union," April 7, 1949, South African National Archives, Pretoria, BWA, vol. 1, 1/1/1, 1–2.

14 W.E.B. Du Bois, *The Souls of Black Folk* (Chicago: McClurg, 1903). For recent scholarship on these connections in this era, see Claire Cooke, "Forlorn Daughters? The Role of Social Motherhood in Transnational African Methodist Episcopal Missionary Women Networks, 1900–1940s," *Safundi* 19, no. 1 (January, 2018), 36–54; Laura Chrisman, "American Jubilee Choirs, Industrial Capitalism, and Black South Africa," *Journal of American Studies* 52, no. 2 (May 2018), 274–96; Dawne Y. Curry, "'What Is It That We Call the Nation': Cecilia Lillian Tshabalala's Definition, Diagnosis, and Prognosis of the Nation in a Segregated South Africa," *Safundi* 19, no. 1 (January, 2018), 55–76; Elisabeth Engel, *Encountering Empire: African American Missionaries in Colonial Africa, 1900–1939* (Franz Steiner Verlag Wiesbaden GmbH, 2015); Meghan Healy-Clancy, "The Daughters of Africa and Transatlantic Racial Kinship: Cecilia Lilian Tshabalala and the Women's Club Movement, 1912–1943," *Amerikastudien / American Studies* 59, no. 4 (2014), 481–99; Holly Y. McGee, "Before the Window Closed: Internationalism, Crossing Borders, and Reaching out to Sisters across the Seas," *Safundi* 19, no. 1 (January, 2018): 77–92; Robert Trent Vinson, *The Americans Are Coming!: Dreams of African American Liberation in Segregationist South Africa* (Athens: Ohio University Press, 2012).
15 Tom Lodge, *Black Politics in South Africa since 1945* (London: Longman, 1983).
16 Peter Cole, *Dockworker Power: Race and Activism in Durban and the San Francisco Bay Area* (Urbana: University of Illinois Press, 2018), chapter 2; James Meriwether, *Proudly We Can Be Africans: Black Americans and Africa, 1935–1961* (Chapel Hill: University of North Carolina Press, 2002), chapter 3; Francis Njubi Nesbitt, *Race for Sanctions: African Americans against Apartheid, 1946–1994* (Bloomington: Indiana University Press, 2004), chapter 1.
17 Cherryl Walker, *Women and Resistance in South Africa*, 2nd edition (New York: David Philip Publishers, 1991), 131–2.
18 Shireen Hassim, *Women's Organizations and Democracy in South Africa: Contesting Authority* (Madison: University of Wisconsin Press, 2006), 22–3.
19 Hilda Bernstein and Ray Alexander, "Draft Constitution: Federation of South African Women," 1954, Federation of South African Women Records, Historical Papers, William Cullen Library, University of Witwatersrand, Aa1, 1.
20 Meghan Healy-Clancy, "Women and Apartheid," *Oxford Research Encyclopedia of African History*, June 28, 2017.
21 Ida Mtwana, "FSAW: Inaugural Conference 1954, Addresses," April 1954, FSAW Records, Historical Papers, William Cullen Library, University of Witwatersrand, AC1.5.1.
22 Judy Kimble and Elaine Unterhalter, "'We Opened the Road for You, You Must Go Forward' ANC Women's Struggles, 1912–1982," *Feminist Review* 12, no. 1 (November, 1982), 18–20, 25–8; Bahati Kuumba, "'You've Struck a Rock': Comparing Gender, Social Movements, and Transformation in the United States and South Africa," *Gender & Society* 16, no. 4 (August, 2002), 508.
23 Nomboniso Gasa, "Feminisms, Motherisms, Patriarchies and Women's Voices in the 1950s," in Gasa, ed., *Women in South African History: They Remove Boulders and Cross Rivers* (Cape Town: HSRC Press, 2007); Meghan Healy-Clancy, "The Family Politics of the Federation of South African Women: A History of Public Motherhood in Women's Antiracist Activism," *Signs: Journal of Women in Culture and Society* 42, no. 4 (May, 2017), 843–66; Zine Magubane, "Attitudes towards Feminism among Women in the ANC, 1950–1990: A Theoretical Re-Interpretation," *The Road to Democracy in South Africa* 4 (2010), 976–1015.
24 Z.K. Matthews, *Freedom for My People: the Autobiography of Z.K. Matthews, Southern Africa 1901 to 1968* (London: R. Collings, 1981), 160.
25 Frieda Matthews Interview, November 26, 1981, Gaborone, Botswana. SAIRR Oral History – AD1722, Historical Papers, University of Witwatersrand.
26 Frieda Bokwe Matthews, *Remembrances* (Bellville: Mayibuye Books, 1995), 23–4.
27 Nicholas Grant, "Crossing the Black Atlantic: The Global Antiapartheid Movement and the Racial Politics of the Cold War," *Radical History Review* 2014, no. 119 (Spring, 2014): 83–4.
28 A Special Correspondent, "S.A. and US Govts. Tried to Bully Prof. Matthews: Frightened of Revelations before United Nations," *Advance*, December 4, 1952.
29 "No 'Welcome Home' for Prof. Matthews," *Advance*, May 28, 1953.
30 Dayo F. Gore, *Radicalism at the Crossroads: African American Women Activists in the Cold War* (New York: New York University Press, 2011), 85–9; Erik S. McDuffie, "A 'New Freedom Movement of Negro Women': Sojourning for Truth, Justice, and Human Rights during the Early Cold War," *Radical History Review*, no. 101 (Spring, 2008), 81–106.
31 "Call to Negro Women," 1951, EGRP, Box. 13.

32 Gerald Horne, *White Supremacy Confronted: U.S. Imperialism and Anti-Communism vs. the Liberation of Southern Africa, from Rhodes to Mandela* (New York: International Publishers, 2019); Thomas J. Noer, *Cold War and Black Liberation: United States and White Rule in Africa, 1948–68* (Columbia: University of Missouri Press, 1985).

33 Francisca de Haan, "Continuing Cold War Paradigms in Western Historiography of Transnational Women's Organisations: The Case of the Women's International Democratic Federation (WIDF)," *Women's History Review* 19, no. 4 (September 1, 2010): 547–73.

34 See also Nicholas Grant, *Winning Our Freedoms Together: African Americans and Apartheid, 1945–1960* (Chapel Hill: The University of North Carolina Press, 2017), 180–5.

35 "Lilian Ngoyi Biographical writing," 1972. Lilian Masediba Ngoyi Collection, Historical Papers, William Cullen Library, University of Witwatersrand, A2551. 7–10.

36 Dora Tamana, "Speech: WIDF Conference Geneva," February 1955, The Simons Papers, Manuscripts and Archives Department, University of Cape Town Library, Folder R9.3.2.

37 Carole Boyce Davies, *Left of Karl Marx: The Political Life of Black Communist Claudia Jones* (Duke University Press, 2008), chapter 4.

Bibliography

Blain, Keisha, and Tiffany Gill. *To Turn the Whole World Over: Black Women and Internationalism.* Champaign: University of Illinois Press, 2019.

Brooks, Pamela E. *Boycotts, Buses, and Passes: Black Women's Resistance in the U.S. South and South Africa.* Amherst: University of Massachusetts Press, 2008.

Castledine, Jacqueline. "'In a Solid Bond of Unity': Anticolonial Feminism in the Cold War Era." *Journal of Women's History* 20, no. 4 (2008): 57–81.

Chrisman, Laura. "American Jubilee Choirs, Industrial Capitalism, and Black South Africa." *Journal of American Studies* 52, no. 2 (May 2018): 274–96.

Cole, Peter. *Dockworker Power: Race and Activism in Durban and the San Francisco Bay Area* Urbana: University of Illinois Press, 2018.

Cooke, Claire. "Forlorn Daughters? The Role of Social Motherhood in Transnational African Methodist Episcopal Missionary Women Networks, 1900–1940s." *Safundi* 19, no. 1 (January 2, 2018): 36–54.

Cooke, Claire, and Ana Stevenson. "Breaking Boundaries, Defying Borders: Transnational Networks of Gender and Race in South Africa and the United States." *Safundi* 19, no. 1 (January 2, 2018): 1–8.

Curry, Dawne Y. "'What Is It That We Call the Nation': Cecilia Lillian Tshabalala's Definition, Diagnosis, and Prognosis of the Nation in a Segregated South Africa," *Safundi* 19, no. 1 (January, 2018): 55–76.

Davies, Carole Boyce. *Left of Karl Marx: The Political Life of Black Communist Claudia Jones.* Durham: Duke University Press, 2008.

de Haan, Francisca. "Continuing Cold War Paradigms in Western Historiography of Transnational Women's Organisations: The Case of the Women's International Democratic Federation (WIDF)," *Women's History Review* 19, no. 4 (September 1, 2010): 547–73.

Du Bois, W.E.B. *The Souls of Black Folk.* Chicago: McClurg, 1903.

Engel, Elisabeth. *Encountering Empire: African American Missionaries in Colonial Africa, 1900–1939.* Stuttgart: Franz Steiner Verlag, 2015.

Fredrickson, George M. *White Supremacy: A Comparative Study in American and South African History.* New York: Oxford University Press, 1981.

Gasa, Nomboniso. "Feminisms, Motherisms, Patriarchies and Women's Voices in the 1950s." In Gasa ed, *Women in South African History: They Remove Boulders and Cross Rivers.* Cape Town: HSRC Press, 2007.

Gore, Dayo F. *Radicalism at the Crossroads: African American Women Activists in the Cold War* New York: New York University Press, 2011.

Grant, Nicholas. "Crossing the Black Atlantic: The Global Antiapartheid Movement and the Racial Politics of the Cold War." *Radical History Review* 119 (March 20, 2014): 72–93.

Grant, Nicholas. *Winning Our Freedoms Together: African Americans and Apartheid, 1945–1960.* Chapel Hill: The University of North Carolina Press, 2017.

Hassim, Shireen. *Women's Organizations and Democracy in South Africa: Contesting Authority* Madison: University of Wisconsin Press, 2006.

Healy-Clancy, Meghan. "The Daughters of Africa and Transatlantic Racial Kinship: Cecilia Lilian Tshabalala and the Women's Club Movement, 1912–1943." *Amerikastudien / American Studies* 59, no. 4 (2014), 481–99.

Healy-Clancy, Meghan. "The Family Politics of the Federation of South African Women: A History of Public Motherhood in Women's Antiracist Activism." *Signs: Journal of Women in Culture and Society* 42, no. 4 (May, 2017): 843–66.

Healy-Clancy, Meghan. "Women and Apartheid." *Oxford Research Encyclopedia of African History*, June 28, 2017.

Horne, Gerald. *White Supremacy Confronted: U.S. Imperialism and Anti-Communism vs. the Liberation of Southern Africa, from Rhodes to Mandela.* New York: International Publishers, 2019.

Johnson, Charles Denton. "Re-Thinking the Emergence of the Struggle for South African Liberation in the United States: Max Yergan and the Council on African Affairs, 1922–1946." *Journal of Southern African Studies* 39, no. 1 (2013): 171–92.

Kimble, Judy, and Elaine Unterhalter. "'We Opened the Road for You, You Must Go Forward' ANC Women's Struggles, 1912–1982." *Feminist Review* 12, no. 1 (November 1, 1982): 11–35.

Kuumba, M. Bahati. "'You've Struck a Rock': Comparing Gender, Social Movements, and Transformation in the United States and South Africa." *Gender & Society* 16, no. 4 (August 1, 2002): 504–23.

Lake, Marilyn and Henry Reynolds. *Drawing the Global Colour Line: White Men's Countries and the International Challenge of Racial Equality.* Cambridge: Cambridge University Press, 2008.

Lodge, Tom. *Black Politics in South Africa Since 1945.* London: Longman, 1983.

Magubane, Zine, "Attitudes Towards Feminism among Women in the ANC, 1950–1990: A Theoretical Re-Interpretation." *The Road to Democracy in South Africa* 4 (2010): 976–1015.

Matthews, Frieda Bokwe. *Remembrances.* Bellville: Mayibuye Books, 1995.

Matthews, Z.K. *Freedom for My People: the Autobiography of Z.K. Matthews, Southern Africa 1901 to 1968.* London: R. Collings, 1981.

McDuffie, Erik S. "A 'New Freedom Movement of Negro Women': Sojourning for Truth, Justice, and Human Rights during the Early Cold War." *Radical History Review* 101 (Spring, 2008): 81–106.

McDuffie, Erik S. "'For Full Freedom of . . . Colored Women in Africa, Asia, and in These United States . . .': Black Women Radicals and the Practice of a Black Women's International." *Palimpsest: A Journal on Women, Gender, and the Black International* 1, no. 1 (2012): 1–30.

McDuffie, Erik S. *Sojourning for Freedom: Black Women, American Communism, and the Making of Black Left Feminism.* Durham: Duke University Press, 2011.

McGee, Holly Y. "Before the Window Closed: Internationalism, Crossing Borders, and Reaching out to Sisters Across the Seas." *Safundi* 19, no. 1 (January, 2018): 77–92.

Meriwether, James. *Proudly We Can Be Africans: Black Americans and Africa, 1935–1961.* Chapel Hill: University of North Carolina Press, 2002.

Nesbitt, Francis Njubi. *Race for Sanctions: African Americans Against Apartheid, 1946–1994.* Bloomington: Indiana University Press, 2004.

Noer, Thomas J. *Cold War and Black Liberation: United States and White Rule in Africa, 1948–68.* Columbia: University of Missouri Press, 1985.

Ransby, Barbara. *Eslanda: The Large and Unconventional Life of Mrs. Paul Robeson.* New Haven: Yale University Press, 2013.

Robeson, Eslanda Goode African. *Journey.* New York: John Day Company, 1945.

Umoren, Imaobong. *Race Women Internationalists: Activist-Intellectuals and Global Freedom Struggles* Berkeley: University of California Press, 2018.

Umoren, Imaobong. "'We Americans Are Not Just American Citizens Any Longer': Eslanda Robeson, World Citizenship, and the New World Review in the 1950s." *Journal of Women's History* 30, no. 4 (December 8, 2018): 134–58.

Vinson, Robert Trent. *The Americans Are Coming!: Dreams of African American Liberation in Segregationist South Africa.* Athens: Ohio University Press, 2012.

Walker, Cherryl. *Women and Resistance in South Africa*, 2nd edition. New York: David Philip Publishers, 1991.

28

Black feminisms, queer feminisms, trans feminisms

Meditating on Pauli Murray, Shirley Chisholm, and Marsha P. Johnson against the erasure of history

Jenn M. Jackson

Since the era of slavery and post-emancipation, Black civil rights figures of all stripes have emerged from communities around the United States to organize around social issues facing African Americans. While many of the most recognizable figures were cisgender, heterosexual men, many others were not. In particular, gender nonconforming legal scholar and activist Pauli Murray, presidential candidate Shirley Chisholm, and trans rights activist Marsha P. Johnson were integral in radically rethinking justice in the United States. However, they are rarely acknowledged as such, despite their pivotal roles in landmark events. Murray's legal strategies helped to end school segregation in the 1954 Supreme Court case *Brown v. Board of Education*; Chisholm became the first woman and African American to make a major-party run for the U.S. presidency in 1972; and Johnson helped to ignite the Stonewall uprising in 1969 that ushered in the modern gay and lesbian liberation movement.

In this chapter, I ask: how does the erasure of unrespectable, queer, gender nonconforming, and trans women and non-men shape our notion of feminism, rights, and activism? Moreover, what does their erasure imply about the role of the archive? I argue that important figures, like Murray, Chisholm, and Johnson, are frequently excluded from the archives of Black civil rights history primarily because of their non-traditional, anti-establishment methods. These characteristics are coupled with their gender, sexuality, and physical embodiment, which do not comport with the class-based and gender-based expectations of mainstream social justice and political leaders. A case in point is the historical erasure of unwed pregnant teenager Claudette Colvin, who refused to give up her seat on a segregated bus in Montgomery, Alabama nine months before Rosa Parks did the same on December 1, 1955. The archive thus not only functions as an artifact of historical time; it is also a site of contestation. As evidence, I rely on first-hand narratives and biography, and Black feminist and queer theory, as I meditate on Murray's, Chisholm's, and Johnson's movements in, out, and through the annals of history.

In her 1999 book *Gender Trouble*, Judith Butler writes that "'[i]ntelligible' genders are those which in some sense institute and maintain relations of coherence and continuity among sex, gender, sexual practice, and desire" (1999, 23). She elaborates that these forms of gender and sexuality are reinforced and reproduced through public law, expectation, and norm making, which essentially codify gender through pre-modeled forms of sexual and bodily practice (1999). What, then, becomes of genders and sexualities that fall outside designated norms? For cisgender heterosexual women whose race, class, and embodiment breach norms of feminine identity, how do their political actions shape our knowledge of feminism and activism? Moreover, for queer, gender nonconforming, and trans individuals whose struggles for liberation do not align with mainstream movements, how does history remember them, their work, and their contributions? Does it remember them at all? These inquiries animate this chapter.

Black queer and straight women, trans women, and nonbinary people: they all occupy a liminal space both in Black communities and in the subsequent movements for social and racial justice which form within them. Black feminist and queer scholars have articulated the complexity of this nuanced position. For example, Boston-based activists and scholars of the Combahee River Collective explained in their collective statement in 1977:

> The most general statement of our politics at the present time would be that we are actively committed to struggling against racial, sexual, heterosexual, and class oppression, and see as our particular task the development of integrated analysis and practice based upon the fact that the major systems of oppression are interlocking. The synthesis of these oppressions creates the conditions of our lives.
>
> *([1977]1981, 210)*

Likewise, Kimberlé Crenshaw illustrated the multiplicity of these myriad, simultaneously interlocking positions of oppression in her critical legal essays on intersectionality (1989; 1991). These philosophical contributions and interventions shape both the analyses in this chapter and the larger frameworks that it critiques.

Before the term "intersectionality" had entered the mainstream lexicon, freedom fighters like Pauli Murray, Shirley Chisholm, and Marsha P. Johnson were forging new pathways for a Black and queer feminism that would, one day, seek to contain the fullness of blackness. Though their work and struggles were not fully appreciated in their lifetimes, new attention to Murray's, Chisholm's, and Johnson's legacies highlights how prescient their visions of Black liberation truly were. While the archives of Murray's, Chisholm's, and Johnson's deep contributions to liberatory politics in their generations remain scant, I suggest that this is no indication of the impact or magnitude of their work. Rather, I argue, it is significant that the mainstream archivists of their eras failed to fully record Murray's, Chisholm's, and Johnson's activism and ideological interventions; yet their ideas and actions still seeded today's movements. Thus, these three forestrugglers show that the archive does not, in fact, have the final word when it comes to the liberation and memory of all Black people.

Murray's posthumously published memoir *Song in a Weary Throat: Memoir of an American Pilgrimage* and Chisholm's autobiographical work *Unbought and Unbossed* are central entry points into analyzing how their experiences at the intersections of race, gender, class, sexual orientation, and physical embodiments influenced their social and political lives. For Johnson, much of the contemporary work on her life and legacy have been exercises in reclamation; thus, the archive remains quite thin. I ruminate on this in what remains of this chapter. I start by providing three theoretical frameworks, which anchor this analysis. Then, I articulate how Murray's, Chisholm's, and Johnson's lives and work show the fissures and discontinuities of Black activist struggles for justice. Finally, I close the chapter by providing a vision for the future of queer, trans, and gender nonconforming–centered movement work.

Queering gender and politics

In this chapter, I rely on Cathy Cohen's notion of queerness as a site of resistance and coalition building that pertains to not only the sexual practices of individual queer group members but also the political agendas, ideas, and actions those individuals espouse with respect to social organizing and political change. For instance, some heteronormative African Americans' lives, while not sexually queer, are indeed politically queer with respect to singular narratives of sexual identity. By highlighting myriad forms of "nonnormative heterosexuality," Cohen underscores how various marginalized people (like poor women, "welfare queens," and other deviant African Americans) have long been demonized for their sexual and political choices (1997). Underlying this framework of queerness, and social organizing, is an effort to destabilize both queer politics and heteronormativity. As Cohen states,

> Thus, if there is any truly radical potential to be found in the idea of queerness and the practice of queer politics, it would seem to be located in its ability to create a space in opposition to dominant norms, a space where transformational political work can begin.
>
> *(1997, 438)*

It is this site of transformation that, I argue, Murray, Chisholm, and Johnson leveraged in their enduring struggle for Black liberation.

In this way, by examining how Black queer, trans, and gender nonconforming individuals recognize and organize around their multiple deviations from normative identity, this chapter elucidates how the queer sexual and/or political identities of activists like Murray, Chisholm, and Johnson intervened in the existing social movement regime. Furthermore, their mobilization around these queer identities undermined the status quo, making their work and political actions particularly salient among multiply marginalized[1] populations.

Respectability

In 1993, Evelyn Brooks Higginbotham coined the term "politics of respectability" in her book *Righteous Discontent: The Women's Movement in the Black Baptist Church, 1880–1920*. Higginbotham writes that "[t]he politics of respectability emphasized reform of individual behavior and attitudes both as a goal in itself and as a strategy for reform of the entire structural system of American race relations" (1993, 187). These efforts toward individual behavior reform fell hardest on African Americans who were deemed furthest from the mainstream norms of white Americans, like poor, queer, and sexually "deviant" individuals. According to Higginbotham, during this post-bellum era, it was believed in religiously conservative, Black Baptist circles that adhering to a politics of respectability would subvert societal subordination of African Americans and ideally, shift the racial order (1993). Artifacts of class and access like clothing, hair style, and even odor were judged in this set of politics. And, just as today, "respectable Negros" were clearly set apart from their unrespectable social group members.

In the vein of Higginbotham and building upon her claims about the role of queerness in creating sites of transformation for marginalized Black people, Cathy Cohen articulates how deviations from societal norms of gender and sexuality become pivot points for larger social judgements about who is and who is not a respectable subject. Cohen explains:

> For me this is the process of the queering of Black studies: making visible all those who in the past have been silenced and excluded as full members of Black communities—the poor,

women, lesbians and gays—those people on the margins of society and excluded from the middle-class march toward respectability.

(2004, 42)

Here, Cohen makes clear that queer identities and politics, which frequently fall outside normative ideas of gender and sexuality, must be incorporated into full membership in Black communities. What's more, this incorporation must include a reckoning with how these deviations have been used to justify exclusion and isolation of nonnormative group members due to ideas of respectability (Cohen 2004). For Murray, Chisholm, and Johnson, their nonnormative personal identities, coupled with their nonnormative political struggles, make them all unrespectable subjects. Therefore, their contributions to social and political history require deeper investigation and analysis.

Erasure in the archive

For all intents and purposes, the archive is assumed to be chronologically accurate and all-encompassing. However, it does not account for ruptures that occurred prior to the point of archiving. Hortense Spillers' 1987 essay "Mama's Baby, Papa's Maybe" elucidates how, because African Americans' lives are defined by the disjuncture of forced migration from the African continent to the Americas, the manners in which they live, experience gender and sexuality, and function as political subjects is rooted in a phenomenon called "American Grammar." Spillers writes:

> The symbolic order that I wish to trace in this writing, calling it an "American Grammar," begins at the "beginning," which is really a rupture and a radically different kind of cultural continuation. The massive demographic shifts, the violent formation of a modern African consciousness, that take place on the subsaharan Continent during the initiative strikes which open that Atlantic Slave Trade in the fifteenth century of our Christ, interrupted hundreds of years of black African culture.

(1987, 68)

Here, Spillers underscores the contradiction of Americanness as something that begins at the "beginning," when in fact, for African Americans, Americanness is necessarily rooted in a restarting of identity. Thus, while this "American Grammar" becomes the typesetting for the archive of Black experiences, it is fundamentally rooted in the absence of true history, the overlooking of pasts not associated with the desired "American" future, and the loss of critical linkages to an African tradition and history that might more expansively depict the genders, bodies, and identities of Black Diasporic peoples.

As Spillers explains, the archive is not one thing but many. And for those individuals whose identities lie at multiple intersections, the archive rarely provides a full or complete picture of the attenuated circumstances and constrained agency that typically mark the lives of marginalized people. Marisa Fuentes illustrates this contention in her deep analysis of the life of Rachael Pringle Polgreen, a freed woman in Barbados in the late nineteenth century who is recorded as having used her position as a brothel owner to enslave and sexually exploit other Afro-descendant and Black Diasporic women (2010). What Fuentes brings to the fore is that white colonialists and enslavers were the primary recorders of Polgreen's life, actions, choices, and utterings. Instances of violence that Polgreen exhibited in the presence of colonial officers were more likely to enter the archive than any benevolence or quotidian, day-to-day tasks in which she may have engaged (2010). In this way, the management and facilitation of the archive reflect the power dynamics, narratives, and societal constructs that organize life at the time the archival image is recorded (Sekula 1986). For unrespectable, queer, trans, and gender nonconforming individuals, these constraints on history-making and history-remembering are deeply erasive and limiting.

While both the logics of "American Grammar" and the power embedded in the archive vastly delimit the recorded range and depth of Black history, gender and sexuality, and lived experiences, they do not completely erase African Americans' capacity to write their own archives, tell their own stories, and record their own narratives. The Combahee River Collective highlights this point when they write:

> [t]he fact that individual Black feminists are living in isolation all over the country, that our own numbers are small, and that we have some skills in writing, printing, and publishing makes us want to carry out these kinds of projects as a means of organizing Black feminists as we continue to do political work in coalition with other groups.
>
> *(Combahee River Collective [1977] 1981, 217)*

For these lesbian activists, entering and controlling the archive was not just a facile or performative element of transcribing history. Rather, their work to write, print, and publish was directly linked to collective movement and Black liberation.

Pauli Murray and the trouble with gender

Anna Pauline Murray was born to a "colored," mixed race high school principal and nurse in Baltimore, Maryland, in 1910. After her[2] mother passed away, her father entered a mental facility and was unable to care for Murray and her five siblings. As detailed in her posthumously published 1987 memoir, *Pauli Murray: Song in a Weary Throat*, Murray describes being raised by her maternal aunts and grandparents in Durham, North Carolina. Her early years were riddled with racial and gender contestation and confrontation in her neighborhood and school. While Murray had found solace during adolescence in her Aunt Pauline, her mother's sister who raised her after she was orphaned, she struggled to find the same home among family when she left for college. After attempting to enroll at Columbia (which didn't enroll women) and Barnard (which she was not qualified for and could not afford), Aunt Pauline and Murray arrived at Hunter College, the school where she would later matriculate. Murray moved in with Cousin Maude, a fair-skinned woman who lived among white neighbors. Murray describes her experiences with Cousin Maude, saying, "I was being made to feel ashamed of my color, a message conveyed not by the outside world, as in the South, but by the members of my own family" (2010, 89). Because of the gaze of white neighbors and societal judgements about the abilities of African Americans, Murray's experiences with Cousin Maude were tense and strained. Specifically, Murray's presentation as "colored" disrupted Cousin Maude's white assimilative, heteronormative presence in the well-to-do Richmond Hill community in which she lived. What's more, Murray's analysis of these experiences was rooted in her knowledge of the otherness of her own blackness. For Murray, her status as both a race and a class outsider shaped her analysis and approximation of power and respectability across racial groups.

Later, after having worked through an all-male environment at Howard Law School and deciphering the D.C. Code of 1901 that eventually dealt the "death blow" to *Plessy v. Ferguson*, Murray established herself as a fixture in American civil rights (Murray [1987]2010, 286, 298). She had also coined the term "Jane Crow" to denote her experiences with racial and gender discrimination, including her denial by Harvard Law School, which didn't admit women

(Murray [1987]2010). In the 1950s and 1960s, on the heels of having published her 1956 autobiography *Proud Shoes: The Story of an American Family*, Pauli Murray began working as an attorney at Lloyd Garrison's New York law firm, an opportunity that had eluded her prior to the publication of *Proud Shoes*. In this position, Murray began as one of three women and the only African American at the firm. In time, as the other women quit the firm, Murray became the only woman and the only Black person, leaving her in an "indeterminate position," which "sometimes created an awkwardness in office relations" ([1987]2010, 206). These experiences included her inability to build communal relationships with male co-workers and her general exclusion from corporate life. At times when she was acknowledged as an equal, Murray recalls feeling gratified that she had been accepted "as a person and a colleague" ([1987]2010, 406). As Murray recounts her struggles with white male–dominated legal institutions, she situates them as inherently linked to her race and gender. However, in *Song in a Weary Throat*, Murray provides nary a mention of her sexual identity. It is in the historical archive of her personal affairs and correspondence that these details reside.

In her analysis of Pauli Murray's archival documents, Brittney C. Cooper notes how, during her long struggle for civil rights and justice for African Americans, Murray was also combating mental distress related to her sexual identity. Cooper writes that Murray "lamented that she could not publicly fall in love, or date, or share expressions of affection with members of the same sex" (2017, 90). Seeking assistance from medical doctors, Murray questioned whether she might actually be an intersex person who was experiencing conflict due to hormonal imbalances (Cooper 2017). Over the years, Murray experienced repeated in-patient hospitalizations related to her concerns. These struggles with Murray's public and private identity are critical in this analysis because they were so intentionally hidden from public sight and consumption.

In Murray's archiving of her own life in *Song in a Weary Throat*, she omits her own experiences with a desire to exhibit maleness and her performance of transgressive gender. In fact, Murray exhibited masculine-of-center, nonbinary gender performance when arrested during a protest against segregation in 1940. Cooper highlights this when she writes, "[t]he complicated gender performances that underlie Murray's 'respectable' autobiographical narration of this incident evince some tensions concerning how dissemblance operates within Black women's leadership memoirs versus how it operates in public space" (2017, 93). The absence of Murray's personal life from *Song in a Weary Throat* begs questions about the centrality of her personal sexual identity to her organizing and movement efforts. Moreover, it illustrates that when Black women at multiple margins enter the archive, they often do so under the auspices of assimilation, legibility, and comportment to mainstream norms of identity.

Shirley Chisholm's fearless body politic

Shirley Anita St. Hill (later Chisholm) was born in Brooklyn, New York in 1924 to Charles St. Hill, a native of British-Guiana, and Ruby Seale, a Barbadian. Chisholm was the oldest of three girls. As detailed in her 1970 autobiography *Unbought and Unbossed*, the St. Hills were plagued by financial insecurity. Facing the Great Depression, Chisholm's parents decided that she and her sisters should live with their maternal grandmother, Emily Seales, back on the farm in Barbados until the St. Hills could save enough money to keep them in the States. Chisholm and her sisters were educated in predominantly white, mostly Jewish schools. It was in college that Chisholm began to see stark differences in the treatment African Americans faced as she encountered whites who "looked at [her] people as another breed, less human than they" (Chisholm [1970] 2009, 42).

In those experiences, Chisholm also noted that other Black people would often comport themselves to the expectations and behaviors associated with respectability by whites. She writes,

"Blacks played by those rules; if a white man walked in, they came subtly to attention" ([1970] 2009, 42). As Chisholm encountered these experiences, she began to develop anger and frustration at the status quo, which relegated African Americans to a place of subservience to whites. Furthermore, she became keenly aware of how her deviant positions as Black, poor, perceived as an immigrant, and a woman simultaneously regulated her ability to navigate public spaces and to fully articulate her vision for Black political outcomes. Chisholm was an intersectional subject whose interlocking identities and oppressions shaped both her political work and how the world received her.

Likewise, as the first Black woman elected to Congress, Chisholm's agenda for Black liberation was unequivocally connected to her concerns about women's rights. She writes, "Women should perceive that the negative attitudes they hold toward their own femaleness are the creation of antifeminist society, just as the black shame at being black was the product of racism" ([1970] 2009, 178). But Chisholm's concerns about the plight of women extended beyond combating stereotypes and sexist ideas. In 1969, Chisholm became deeply concerned with abortion rights in Congress when she became honorary president of the National Association for the Repeal of Abortion Laws (NARAL). Based on her experiences in Brooklyn with Black, Puerto Rican, and other Afro-Latinx persons, she saw the predominant narratives about legal abortion clinics as "male rhetoric, for male ears" ([1970] 2009, 130). Understanding that reproductive justice was not just about race and gender but also about class, Chisholm advocated for equal access to abortion and family planning resources regardless of one's economic status at a time when the costs for such an argument were steep. For Chisholm, her own background informed her politics. Her identities and experiences were central to her activism and political work. For her, the struggles for race and gender justice were interconnected.

For Chisholm, reactions to her presence in predominantly white spaces became more critical and ad hominem when she decided to enter presidential politics, becoming the first woman to make a viable bid for the highest office in the land. In a 1972 *New York Times* article, Stephan Lesher wrote:

> [t]hough her quickness and animation leave an impression of bright femininity, she is not beautiful. Her face is bony and angular, her nose wide and flat, her eyes small almost to beadiness, her neck and limbs scrawny. Her protruding teeth probably account in part for her noticeable lisp.

Lesher then critiques Chisholm's own accounting of herself in her autobiography when she writes, "after a skinny adolescence I had blossomed into an attractive enough quiet little girl with long hair" ([1970] 2009, 62). Lesher's fixation on Chisholm's speech patterns and physical appearance in such a high-profile publication represent the mainstream archival history of the times. The juxtaposition of Lesher's editorializing of Chisholm's physical features against Chisholm's own understanding of her personal characteristics underscores how the facilitation of the archive frequently misnames, misrecognizes, and excludes the fullness of Black, queer, and trans individuals. Likewise, it wasn't just Chisholm's appearance that drew ire from critics during her run for the presidency. Just the mere fact that she was in the race at all transgressed traditional notions of respectability, femininity, and the role of women in society.

Reclamation and memorializing Marsha P. Johnson

Marsha "Pay It No Mind" Johnson was a prostitute, transgender activist, and drag queen whose adult life was centered in New York City in the 1960s and 1970s. She was born on August 24,

1945, in Elizabeth, New Jersey. While not much is known about Johnson's early life, according to the film *The Death and Life of Marsha P. Johnson* (2017), Sylvia Rivera and Marsha P. Johnson started "STAR House" or the Street Transvestite Action Revolutionaries in 1970 to provide a place for queer and trans people to find solace and protection instead of remaining on the streets. In the film, trans activist Victoria Cruz works with the Anti-Violence Project (AVP) to reopen the case of Johnson's unsolved death while highlighting the ways Johnson's life fundamentally changed the gay rights movement in New York City. In the film, friends of Johnson described her clothing and makeup as at once elaborate and messy (France 2017). They also reflected on the ways she walked New York City streets in support of other queer and trans people, becoming a symbol of a growing movement (France 2017). Johnson died in 1992 under unclear circumstances when her body was found floating in the Hudson River from an apparent drowning. Her case was reopened for investigation in 2012. In *Death and Life*, while reflecting on Johnson's life, Johnson's long-time friend Kitty Rotolo asks Cruz, "What happens when a flower gets wilted? Does it just die away and is forgotten?" Cruz replies that hopefully that flower has "shed some seeds that will grow [into] a movement. That's what I hope." Now, Riviera and Johnson are both slated to be honored with monuments near Stonewall Inn (Jacobs 2019).

Directors Tourmaline and Sasha Wortzel elucidate Johnson's gender transgressing presence and performance in the fictional film *Happy Birthday, Marsha!* (2017). In the short film, they recreate the hours before Johnson ignited the 1969 Stonewall Riots at the historic Stonewall Inn in Greenwich Village. Using both scripted footage and Johnson's interviews, the directors highlight the small joys of Johnson's life and community juxtaposed against the constant surveillance and harassment from police. C. Riley Snorton theorizes these types of gender performances as inherently liberatory. He says, "ungendered blackness provide[s] the grounds for (trans) performances of freedom" (2017, 58). These performances, of openly existing while Black and transgender, are embodiments of gender and identity that expand the ways marginalized people imagine liberation. Thus, Johnson's freedom struggle was inherently threatening to the status quo, because her mere being transgressed all boundaries of normative identity.

The struggle to fully understand the conditions shaping the end of Johnson's life parallels the struggle over telling Johnson's story. According to Tourmaline, a trans activist and filmmaker, France's film plagiarized her intellectual work, only further contributing to the erasure of Black trans women's narratives in the archive (Ennis 2018). The ongoing struggle over the archive of Johnson's life and story represents the persistent struggle many trans people face when seeking to control their own narratives and archives. In writing of the invisibility and erasure Johnson's movement work faced, Tourmaline et al. write:

> although their life, fashion, and labor shared the same constitutional ground on which the entire early gay rights movement was built, poor people, mostly of color, as well as trans people who were sex workers did not find their own issues addressed or accommodated by the larger movement.
>
> *(2017, xvii)*

Unfortunately, as *Death and Life* shows, Johnson's death remains cloaked in secret, as the murders and deaths of trans women in the 1990s, much like now, were usually overlooked, underdocumented, and rarely covered by mainstream media (France 2017). The film illustrates how the effects of age, and the ravages of the HIV/AIDS crisis, have severely limited the numbers of first-hand narratives available to reclaim and archive Johnson's movement work or the conditions of her death. Here, the significance of who controls the archive cannot be overstated.

Conclusion

In analyzing the lives of Pauli Murray, Shirley Chisholm, and Marsha P. Johnson, I have set out to spotlight how many Black women's identities are fundamentally linked to the forms of political work and activism they often take up. Specifically, through the lenses of queerness and respectability, we see how these individuals, though struggling against different forms of structural racism, sexism, transphobia, and anti-blackness, leverage their identities for the liberation of others. Moreover, we see how their deviations from normative identity characteristics (like whiteness, maleness, wealth, and cisgender identity) shape their entrance to and exit from the archive.

In the case of Murray, her upbringing at the margins of race and class situated her at odds with a law career committed to ending segregation. Even amidst this monumental contribution to civil rights, her archival footprint remains incomplete, partially by her own doing. As it pertains to Chisholm, her upbringing in a Black immigrant household during the Depression animated her orientation not only to white Americans but also to other African Americans for whom respectability was a necessary coping mechanism to deal with racism and exclusion. As she entered politics, the fixation on her physical body in the archive highlighted her deviation and queerness with respect to mainstream femininity, although she was both cisgender and wed in a heteronormative marriage. And in the case of Johnson, her embodiment of transgressive gender, gender without boundaries, in a moment marked by the hyperpolicing of Black, brown, poor, queer, trans, and disabled bodies, made her vulnerable to all manner of harassment and persecution, and likely led to her unfortunate death at just 46 years old. For each of these forestrugglers, their political work and social positions were deeply entangled. Without their unrespectable, anti-establishment lives and praxes, Black movements of today might look wholly different.

A contemporary theoretical framework that indirectly takes up the charge of Murray, Chisholm, and Johnson is the Black queer feminist lens as articulated in the book *Unapologetic: A Black, Queer, and Feminist Mandate for Radical Movements*. Charlene Carruthers explains that

> the Black queer feminist (BQF) lens is a political praxis (practice and theory) based in Black feminist and LGBTQIA+ traditions and knowledge, through which people and groups seek to bring their full selves into the process of dismantling all systems of oppression.
>
> *(2018, 10)*

This extension of intersectionality is rooted in the long tradition of leveraging identity as a unifying and coalition building force within marginalized communities. It underscores that fights against oppression must be community- and group-based rather than the work of individuals alone. Murray, Chisholm, and Johnson understood this implicitly. While Murray's, Chisholm's, and Johnson's work for black liberation began long before intersectionality and the BQF lens existed, their entrances into the archive of Black feminist, queer, and trans struggles for Black freedom were critical in seeding today's language, agenda-setting, and orientation to collective struggle. However, as this analysis shows, these entrances and exits remain constrained by time, power dynamics, and political fractures through which they struggle.

Notes

1 This is a term coined by Jennifer C. Nash to describe those individuals who are "multiply burdened" or who represent intersectional subjectivity ("Re-Thinking Intersectionality," *Feminist Review*, pp. 1–15).

2 In this chapter, I use she/her pronouns when discussing Murray, as in her formal memoirs and autobiographical accounts of her life, she refers to herself as a woman, and her gender group membership remains consistent in her own archiving of her life.

Bibliography

Butler, Judith. 1999. *Gender Trouble: Feminism and the Subversion of Identity*. New York: Routledge.

Carruthers, Charlene A. 2018. *Unapologetic: A Black, Queer, and Feminist Mandate for Radical Movements*. Boston: Beacon Press.

Chisholm, Shirley. [1970] 2009. *Unbought and Unbossed*. Washington, DC: Take Root Media.

Cohen, Cathy. 1997. "Punks, Bulldaggers, and Welfare Queens: The Radical Potential of Queer Politics?" *GLQ*, 3, pp. 437–465.

Cohen, Cathy. 2004. "Deviance as Resistance: A New Research Agenda for the Study of Black Politics." *Du Bois Review*, 1(1), pp. 27–45.

Combahee River Collective. [1977] 1981. "A Black Feminist Statement." In *This Bridge Called My Back: Writings by Radical Women of Color* (eds Cherríe Moraga and Gloria Anzaldúa). Watertown, MA: Persephone Press.

Cooper, Brittney C. 2017. *Beyond Respectability: The Intellectual Thought of Race Women*. Urbana: University of Illinois Press.

Crenshaw, Kimberlé. 1989. "Demarginalizing the Intersection of Race and Sex: A Black Feminist Critique of Antidiscrimination Doctrine, Feminist Theory and Antiracist Politics." *The University of Chicago Legal Forum* p. 139.

Crenshaw, Kimberlé. 1991. "Mapping the Margins: Intersectionality, Identity Politics, and Violence against Women of Color." *Stanford Law Review*, 43(6), p. 124.

Ennis, Dawn. 2018. "Inside the Fight for Marsha P. Johnson's Legacy." *The Advocate*, January 23. Retrieved from https://www.advocate.com/arts-entertainment/2018/1/23/inside-fight-marsha-p-johnsons-legacy, February 12, 2020.

France, David. 2017. *The Death and Life of Marsha P. Johnson*. Los Gatos, CA: Netflix.

Fuentes, Marisa J. 2010. "Power and Historical Figuring: Rachael Pringle Polgreen's Troubled Archive." *Gender & History*, 22(3), pp. 564–584.

Higginbotham, Evelyn Brooks. 1993. *Righteous Discontent: The Women's Movement in the Black Baptist Church, 1880–1920*. Cambridge, MA: Harvard University Press.

hooks, bell. 2000. *Feminist Theory: From Margin to Center*. Cambridge, MA: South End Press.

Jacobs, Julia. 2019. "Two Transgender Activists Are Getting a Monument in New York." *New York Times*, May 29. Retrieved from https://www.nytimes.com/2019/05/29/arts/transgender-monument-ston ewall.html, February 12, 2020.

Lesher, Stephan. 1972. "The Short, Unhappy Life of the Black Presidential Politics, 1972." *New York Times*, June 25. Retrieved from: https://www.nytimes.com/1972/06/25/archives/the-short-unhappy-life-of-black-presidential-politics-1972-black.html, September 4, 2019.

Murray, Pauli. [1987] 2010. *Song in a Weary Throat*. New York: Liveright Publishing.

Nash, Jennifer C. 2008. "Re-Thinking Intersectionality." *Feminist Review*, pp. 1–15.

Sekula, Allan. 1986. "The Body and the Archive." *October*, 39, pp. 3–64.

Snorton, C. Riley. 2017. *Black on Both Sides: A Racial History of Trans Identity*. Minneapolis: London University of Minnesota Press.

Spillers, Hortense J. 1987. "Mama's Baby, Papa's Maybe: An American Grammar Book." *Diacritics*, 17(2), Culture and Countermemory: The "American" Connection. pp. 64–81.

Tourmaline (fka Reina Gossett), Eric A. Stanley, and Johanna Burton. 2017. *Trap Door: Trans Cultural Production and the Politics of Visibility*. Cambridge, MA: The MIT Press.

Tourmaline (fka Reina Gossett) and Sasha Wortzel. 2017. *Happy Birthday, Marsha! Directed by Tourmaline (fka Reina Gossett) and Sasha Wortzel*. San Francisco: Frameline. Retrieved from https://www.frameline.org/distribution/distribution-catalog/distribution-film-index/happy-birthday-marsha.

Part V

Black identities, feminist formations

29

Traces of race, roots of gender
A genetic history

Amade M'charek

In this chapter, I use the metaphor of the triptych to tell a story about race, gender, and science. The triptych is a threefold, and it is a work of art to narrate stories that do not hang together in a straightforward way, in which time and place relate in nonlinear ways: the three panels of the triptych can be folded and unfolded, superimposing historically remote moments in time or setting them apart. Taking the folding-effect of the triptych seriously, the stories in this chapter are not written in chronological order but jump back and forth in time.

Each of the panels in this chapter focuses on DNA and its relation to race and the female body, which has repercussions for how we conceptualize and de-essentialize Black women's histories. The first panel sketches the use of DNA in "root-seeking practices" (Nelson 2008) to restore genealogies, which often comes with the price of fixating African-ness and representing an archaic image thereof. The second panel takes us to the field of population genetics and drafts the genetic out-of-Africa story, also called the Mitochondrial Eve theory. Starting with a seminal paper published in 1987, I examine how it un/does race by situating it in a longer history of racial science and attend to the crucial role of gender therein. The third panel focuses on genetics, exploring one key technology: a DNA reference sequence on which all research discussed here is based. Unraveling the history of the sequence shows how it folds into itself histories of race, racism, and misogyny as they relate to Henrietta Lacks.

Genetic genealogy and DNA as a technology of belonging

It is January 17, 2008. A gathering in the Magic Johnson Theater at Crenshaw. On stage, we see a number of well-known African Americans, such as the actors Isaiah Washington and Vanessa A. Williams. Speaking to them, and in this instance addressing Williams in particular, is Rick Kittles, a geneticist who is also African American. Kittles is the co-founder of African Ancestry, a company that offers DNA tests to trace one's African lineage. As Kittles speaks to Williams and is about to reveal the results of her DNA tests, we can feel her growing tension. Finally, the redeeming words fill the room: "the Tikar and Bamileke people in Cameroon." Williams is overtly emotional and describes these results as her homecoming: "I am home. I am finally home."[1]

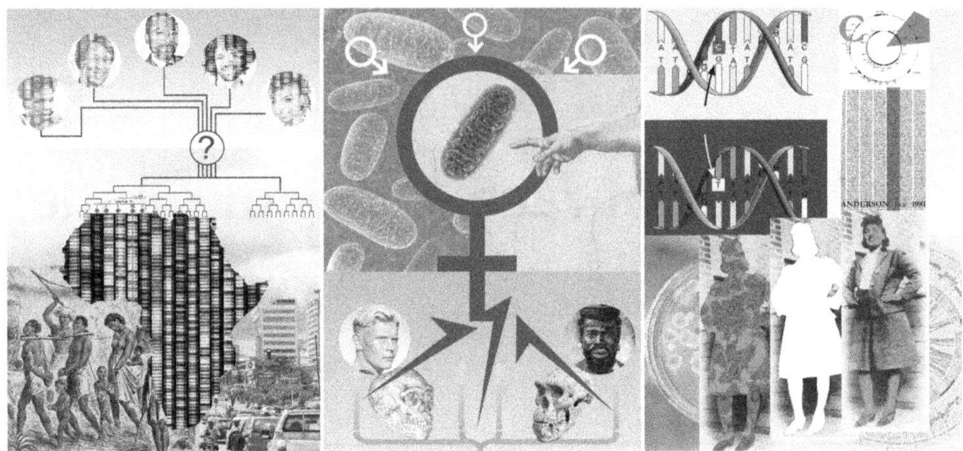

Figure 29.1 Triptych, mixed media collage. © Olaf Posselt.

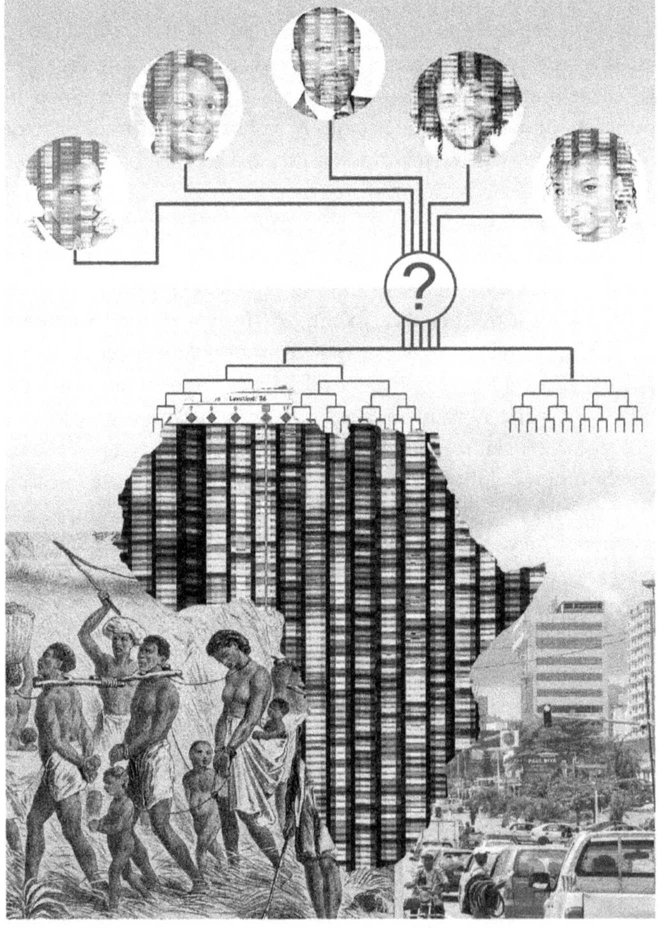

Figure 29.2 Genetic belonging panel, mixed media collage. © Olaf Posselt.

The ABC News segment covering this event situates the DNA tests, visually, in the context of the transatlantic slave trade. The revelation of the test results is flanked by historical images of slavery, such as shackles, ships, and economically busy coastlines and harbors. Images that index the genealogical repair work that DNA is doing. This work pertains to overcoming what I call "the violent genealogical cuts" between people and place.

DNA, in the moment of installing a connection between a person here and ancestors there, does not only present a repair of lineage but also helps to make the violence concrete and tangible. Various DNA tests are available that allow people to bridge the genealogical cuts produced by the history of slavery. Through such tests, it has become possible to trace descendants in Africa and even suggest a link to specific people living in Africa today. To be sure, such test results do not provide certainty. The outcomes are based on comparisons between the "DNA profile" of the root-seeker and the DNA in the database of the company. Comparisons with another database might lead to different outcomes. For example, when Oprah Winfrey did a DNA test in 2005, her genealogical ancestry seemed to be in Zulu Nation, South Africa.[2] When her DNA was tested again in 2010, her ancestry "shifted" and was found to be in Liberia and Cameroon.

However important this work of repair is, descendants of enslaved people have multiple biological and cultural origins. Yet DNA, with all its power and prestige, might be contributing to what Chimamanda Ngozi Adichie has aptly called "the danger of a single story."[3] As many have argued, imaginations of Africa as homeland can be essentialist and homogenizing (Appiah 1992; Gilroy 2000; Nelson 2008). While DNA testing might provide root-seekers with a genetic genealogical origin, it also contributes to a rigid and Eurocentric vision of Africa.

The other side of "imagining Africa as the origin" is indeed a pre-lapsarian past (Gilroy 2000). For example, right after the revelation of the DNA tests, the news segment that covers Vanessa A. Williams's story takes us to Africa. According to the test results, her roots are to be found in Cameroon among the Tikar and Bamileke people. However, rather than explore, say, Yaoundé, the mundane capital of Cameroon that resembles many Western cities, we are instead taken to a rural village. A woman is preparing *fufu* in a huge pot on an open fire as children gather around her; we also see camels. Africa is thus idealized and made into an archaic site for root-seeking (Gilroy 2000). Nevertheless, as we will see later, such DNA tests also offer possibilities to connect bodies and lives to a history that is more complex and for many, probably too large to apprehend in concrete ways.

It is important to note that root-seekers do not always take the results at face value. Those who are aware of the imprecise nature of DNA results – for example, their probabilistic nature and the limitations of the database used – tend to reconfigure DNA testing results according to their personal biographies. This is precisely because results do not provide an ultimate answer but rather, contribute to what Alondra Nelson has called spaces of indeterminacy. Drawing on Janet Carsten's concept of "cultures of relatedness," Nelson argues that root-seekers configure relationships, experiences, and narratives with the help of DNA as well as other modes of knowing (Nelson 2008, 260).

While genealogical DNA testing can produce surprises, it might also produce new insights about the social aspects of slavery. Take the example of Mark Anderson, a young Black Londoner interested in his roots. In the early 2000s, Mark was enrolled in a genetic study in the United Kingdom that was focused on persons of African Caribbean descent. In this study, 229 volunteers (109 men and 120 women) with an interest in their genetic genealogy were enrolled, but only three figured in the BBC documentary that was later produced about this study.

Mark was expecting to find his roots unequivocally in Africa, probably in Cameroon, and the results of his first test disturbed him. This test was a so-called Y-chromosomal DNA test. The Y-chromosome is the male sex chromosome, inherited only by males from their fathers, and it thereby provides insights into paternal lineage. In Mark's case, the Y-chromosome led not to Africa but to Europe. Completely baffled, we hear him say: "So, all those white men are my brothers." A geneticist explains to Mark that this result is more common and even understandable in light of history. It attests to the legacy of the transatlantic slave trade and demonstrates the fact that many European men fathered children with enslaved African women. Doing so, these men passed on their European Y-chromosomes to all male descendants. Since this male sex chromosome is passed on unchanged from father to son, many Black men carry European Y-chromosomes.[4]

Visibly confused by his genetic European-ness, Mark turned to his maternal DNA lineage. Hoping that his maternal lineage would confirm his African soul, Mark was overtly pleased with the results, which stated that he is a descendant of the Kanuri people in present-day Niger. We follow him on his journey to Niger, where he is taken to visit a Kanuri tribe. The interaction is far from smooth, and while Mark is hoping to learn about noble predecessors and his history of slavery, an anthropologist in Niger studying the Kanuri people explains that the Kanuri were not so much victims as perpetrators in the slave trade. Mark's journey thus slowly unpacks the complexity of Africa and its history, as well as that of slavery, race, and roots.

This work is, however, not univocal. While it provides genealogical belongings and identities for root-seekers, DNA may also contribute to the simplification and essentialization of Africa as homeland or produce a more complex, and perhaps more confusing, account of history and relatedness. Yet, as Nadia Abu El-Haj has long cautioned about genomics in general, the DNA tests discussed earlier tend to "reauthorize race as a biological category" (2007, 284). And it is this concern, as well as the naturalization of gender differences, to which we turn in the next panel of the triptych (Figure 29.3).

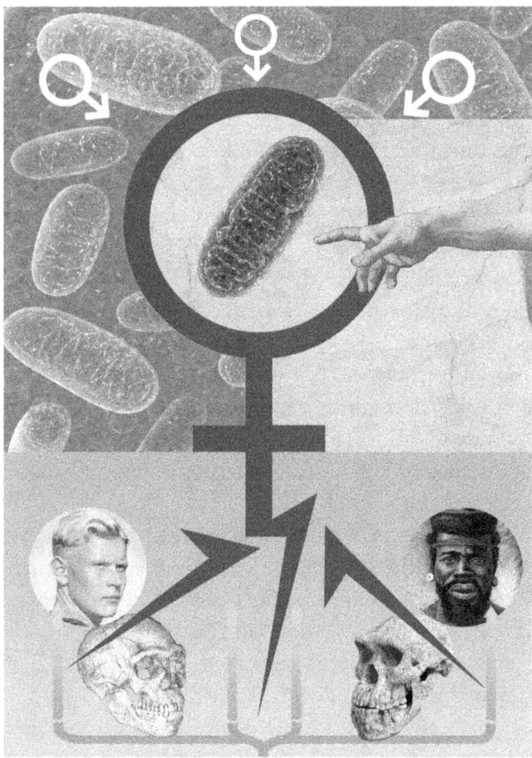

Figure 29.3 Genealogical mother panel, mixed media collage. © Olaf Posselt.

Everyone's genealogical mother: the legacy of Mitochondrial Eve

The journal *Nature* had decided to call her Eve. It is 1987, and the journal features a sensational paper in which geneticists have demonstrated the out-of-Africa theory through the analysis of the mitochondrial DNA of 147 individuals (Cann et al. 1987). They show that genetic diversity is much higher in Africa than in other regions of the world and thus conclude that the origin of modern humans began in Africa. Based on this conclusion and an analysis of the accumulated mutations (random changes in the DNA), they argued that all mitochondrial DNA that humans carry must have been passed on by one ancestral mother. A mother who must have lived in Africa some 200,000 years ago. Eve was thus the name given to this common ancestor of all human beings.

The importance of this paper for science and society cannot be overestimated. For example, most of the genealogical research addressed earlier in this chapter could not have been conceived without the work laid out in this paper. The paper received wide public attention, as it underlined that all human beings are part of one human family. This was at a time when biological and evolutionary explanations of human behavior and human differences were *en vogue* again. A time when the so-called *sociobiological* rendition of who we are was revisited (see, e.g., Lewontin 1979). The Mitochondrial Eve theory intervened precisely in that debate and was a major argument for the nonexistence of races.

Based on genetic research, it could be claimed, "race is a variation on one common theme." In an interview sparked by the *Nature* publication, the eminent paleontologist Stephen Jay Gould states:

> If it's correct, and I'd put money on it, this idea is tremendously important. [...] It makes us realize that all human beings, despite differences in external appearance, are really members of a single entity that's had a very recent origin in one place. There is a kind of biological brotherhood that's much more profound than we ever realized.

Note the "biological *brotherhood*" in research that is based on particles that are *maternally* inherited and that have led to our ancestral mother. I will come back to the issue of gender shortly, but it is significant to note here that Gould's message is also a political intervention in an ongoing debate between geneticists and paleontologists. This debate revolves around two major issues: the age of modern humans and the origin of the human species. First, whereas the mitochondrial DNA study claims that modern humans are quite young and made their entrance around 200,000 years ago, paleontologists, based on their artifacts, assume that we are a much older species that appeared on the scene some two million years ago. Second, whereas the DNA study suggests one origin of all humans in Africa – the so-called African-origin theory – paleontologists instead contend that anatomically modern humans originated in several locations: Africa, Europe, Asia, and Indonesia, a hypothesis called the multi-regional theory (Wolpoff et al. 1988).

The paleoanthropologist Milford Wolpoff, one of the most ardent critics of the mitochondrial DNA paper, alongside two colleagues put forward their view as follows:

> By stark contrast [to the out-of-Africa theory], if modern people evolved locally in many different places, then each population ought to resemble its own antecedents. In this case regional continuity in the features of human fossils should be the norm. [...] In conflict with the Eve theory, our measurements show that modern Chinese, Australasians and Europeans each resemble their local predecessors much more than they resemble archaic Africans.
>
> *(Wolpoff 1991)*

Based on studies of various skulls collected in different parts of the world, Wolpoff and colleagues thus argue for the existence of different and historically distinct biological human races. More broadly, the multi-regional theory has configured races as different species altogether (Gould 1981).[5]

In a conversation I had with one of the authors of the Mitochondrial Eve paper, Mark Stoneking, I asked him about this controversy. He was very clear about who the winners of this controversy were and about the scientific validity of genetic research: "We geneticists know that our genes must have had ancestors, but paleontologists can only hope that their fossils had descendants" (interview with author, March 11, 1997). This was precisely the bomb that the mitochondrial DNA study had placed under the multi-regional theory of paleontologists and others. As such, this genetic approach broke with a longstanding tradition of racial science in the field of biological anthropology.[6]

However, Mitochondrial Eve did not only interfere in a debate on race. Eve was also about gender. As said, a crucial fact about mitochondrial DNA is that this DNA is solely passed on via the mother.[7] Men inherit this DNA from their mothers but cannot pass it on. This is what is called a maternal line of inheritance, a pattern of inheritance that makes it possible to reconstruct a maternal lineage. To be sure, Eve has caused a bit of "gender trouble." And it is to this gender trouble that the final part of this second panel will turn.

The trouble with Eve

Calling her Eve helped to bring the contribution of this scientific paper to the attention of a wider public. Because it invoked a commonly known origin story, it was easy to communicate the facts of science. But the Eve metaphor was also problematic. It obviously interfered with the Christian origin story and its timing, say 5000 years ago, of the origin of humankind. Mitochondrial Eve puts our origin at 200,000 years ago. More importantly, the fact that Mitochondrial Eve was our most recent common ancestor does not mean that she was the only woman from whom we descended. She passed on her mitochondrial DNA to us, but other women (and men) were responsible for the rest of our DNA. These women and men might have lived in the same part of Africa or elsewhere in Africa, and they might have lived a bit earlier or later in time. So to be clear, also genetically speaking, there is not one single origin story, but multiple ones. Moreover, as a long article dedicated to Mitochondrial Eve in the magazine *Newsweek* indicates, we need to picture Eve differently. Not

> the weakwilled figure in Genesis, the milk-skinned beauty in Renaissance art, the voluptuary gardener in "Paradise Lost" who was all "softness" and "meek surrender" and waist-length "gold tresses." The scientists' Eve […] was more likely a dark-haired, black-skinned woman, roaming a hot savanna in search of food. She was as muscular as Martina Navratilova, maybe stronger; she might have torn animals apart with her hands, although she probably preferred to use stone tools.
>
> *(Tierney 1988, 46)*

Much can be said about the entwinement between race and gender in this quotation, such as the reification of differences, here between the fragile beauty of the white woman in theology and that of a brutal Black woman in biology (see also Oikkonen 2015). Yet by comparing Mitochondrial Eve to the muscular Martina Navratilova, the star tennis champion of the 1980s and 1990s, rather than the frail figure of Genesis, we see that something else happens as well. Precisely by comparing her to Navratilova, a blond white woman from Czechoslovakia, the analogy foregrounds power and strength rather than color. For while assuming the black color of Eve, the major intervention of Mitochondrial Eve is that she undermines racial difference.

However, in the controversy between the geneticists and the paleontologists, Eve's gender was mobilized to weaken the theoretical claims of the geneticists, to weaken their intervention in race science. While the preceding quotation presented Eve as a strong woman, critiquing the African-origin theory and the descending of modern humans from an African woman, in a well-known gender politics gesture, the paleontologists Wolpoff, Thorne, and Lawn (1991, italics added) state that Eve "on the face of it, seemed like a *fantastic* claim" and that she "was suddenly a newspaper *celebrity*" and a "*brain child* of Allan Wilson." In the words of Venla Oikkonen (2015, 755), Eve was thus turned into "a fashionable but unsubstantiated idea and thus as purely imaginary." Oikkonen continues that "[i]nstead of the prehistoric hunter with the strength of a female tennis champion, we encounter here a fragile figure associated with the fickleness of popular stardom and, by implication, idealized femininity" (2015, 755–6).

This gender politics as a mode of disqualifying the theory did not pertain only to the figure of Eve but also to the main author of the paper, the geneticist Rebecca Cann. While she was encouraged and supported to pursue her research by the head of the laboratory, Allan Wilson,[8] once the paper was published, she received backlash:

> I got a lot of hate mail, crank mail, some with strange scrawling notes […] I was unprepared for this role as the molecular person questioning the fossils – and for people like Wolpoff saying these archaic people evolved into modern people.
>
> *(Gitschier 2010)*

In a personal account on the Mitochondrial Eve, racism, and misogyny, Cann writes that

> when the discussion of diversity gets too close to us, taking on a female face and black skin, the intensity increases dramatically. […] For example, as a result of speaking about women's genes and human origins for public television, I became bombarded with hate mail from both creationists and various political groups. One family member admonished my parents for my behavior, asking them why I would tell perfect strangers that my ancestors were black when all the family picture albums show the real truth! After participating in a heated forum on human evolution at a large museum, I was taken aside by a trustee and told that I should learn to respond to hostile questions in a more feminine manner, in order to make my message easier for audiences to digest.
>
> *(Cann 1997, 78)*

This hostility and lack of appreciation were also to be encountered within the field of population genetics itself. The population geneticist Lucca Cavalli-Sforza had at that time just co-published a paper in which he and his colleague argued that human origin was likely to be in Asia "and that Africans just had this wild mutation rate because their environment was so bizarre" (Cann in Gitschier 2010). Moreover, as Cann recounts in an interview with Jane Gitschier, many, including Milford Wolpoff, were eager to voice that Rebecca "in particular could never be right" (Gitschier 2010). Although in the end, Cavalli-Sforza had to accept the evidence of the out-of-Africa theory, he could not but disqualify the work of Cann: "Well they got the right answer, but they didn't know why they got it" (Gitschier 2010). The "they" here is typically directed at the first author who actually conducts the research.

Nonetheless, the seminal out-of-Africa paper became an important intervention in a long history of race and scientific racism. It was therefore immediately caught up in a controversy

Figure 29.4 HeLa panel, mixed media collage. © Olaf Posselt.

about race and human origin. The figure of Mitochondrial Eve had become both a vehicle to disseminate the novel insight about our common human origin in Africa and a gendered site for fierce critique and disqualifiers of the out-of-Africa theory. In the final panel, we will see how race and gender sometimes hide in seemingly unproblematic genetic technologies (Figure 29.4).

The ghost of HeLa: race and misogyny in scientific practice

In 1981, the scientific magazine *Nature* featured another landmark paper on mitochondrial DNA. It was the presentation of the first complete genetic map of this DNA molecule (Anderson et al. 1981). It came to be called the Anderson sequence, after the first author of the paper. A short introductory paper pointing the readers to this major achievement and to its import for genetic research was entitled "Small Is Beautiful: Portrait of a Mitochondrial Genome" (Borst and Grivell 1981).[9] "Small" refers to the size of the mitochondrial DNA genome. Compared with the nuclear DNA (located on the 46 chromosomes), which consists of three billion base-pairs (DNA building blocks), mitochondrial DNA is fairly small and has only 16,500 base-pairs. The beauty of this genome, Borst and Grivell (1981) tell us, relates not only to its classical form – it is not a chaotic stretch but a circular genome – but also to its efficient organization. But it

304

is especially the use of the word "portrait" that is puzzling. For whereas "portrait" suggests that it represents and captures the essence of an individual, the Anderson sequence is based on the DNA of not one but three individuals. It is a composite sequence based on DNA from a placenta collected in a British hospital, HeLa cell DNA, and the DNA of a cow.

The peculiar collection of DNA that went into the Anderson sequence indicates the challenges of producing such a sequence in the early 1980s. Whereas today it would take only a few hours to sequence the full mitochondrial DNA genome, doing so was a huge achievement then. The scientists were pragmatic about using already available parts of the genome. The lab in Cambridge had just produced the complete sequence of bovine mitochondrial DNA. So part of that sequence was simply added to the human version of it, assuming that humans and cows looked alike in those stretches of DNA. Other parts that came from HeLa were added because the lab had just received a gift of sequenced HeLa DNA.

It was in a laboratory that I first encountered the Anderson sequence. As an ethnographer and a trainee who was trying in the late 1990s to learn to conduct genetic research, I had to work with the reference sequence on a daily basis.[10] The reference sequence intrigued me, and I became interested in where it came from, how it was produced, and where it was produced.

HeLa is an acronym given to the first human cell line ever produced. Although it took me some time and effort to find out what HeLa was – for example, I first encountered her as Helen Lane – this does not compare to the effort it took me to learn about the source of the cell line.[11] During my search, I learned that the HeLa cell line was extensively used in cancer research. So I contacted the already mentioned Piet Borst, who at that time was the head of the Dutch Cancer Institute. Borst sent me an interesting paper by Howard Jones, a physician who had examined a patient named Henrietta Lacks.

In this paper, Jones recounts the difficulties that cell biologists met when trying to grow a cell line successfully in the early 1950s: "The project [of making a cell line] appeared to be a failure until Henrietta Lacks walked onto the stage" (Jones 1997, 227). Mrs. Lacks suffered from a cervical carcinoma that grew fast enough to facilitate the cell line, Jones explains. The paper provides information about the age of Henrietta Lacks, the number of children she had had, and her clinical diagnosis, but interestingly enough, it omits one bit of information that has haunted the cell line since the 1960s: Henrietta Lack's color. The Mitochondrial Eve paper provided more information. There, the HeLa cells were labeled as "derived from a Black American" (Cann et al. 197, 32). Interestingly enough, in the Mitochondrial Eve study, both HeLa and the Anderson sequence figured as individuals, as part of the 148 samples analyzed. While Anderson remained indeterminate in terms of descent or race, Henrietta Lacks' and 17 other samples were qualified as Black Americans and a "reliable source of African mtDNA" (Cann et al. 197, 32).

The HeLa cell line was produced in 1951. While it started out as a major achievement of science, an achievement through which life could be studied *in vitro*, in the 1960s the origin of the cell line, a Black woman, became a pivot in a grim racist debate (Landacker 2000; Weasel 2004; M'charek 2014). The racialization of an initially unmarked cell line went hand-in-hand with its becoming a problem in scientific practice. HeLa cells grew so rapidly that they started to contaminate laboratory spaces. The origin of the cell line became an issue and was first disclosed by Howard Jones and colleagues in 1970 in an obituary of the maker of the cell line, George Otto Gey.

The origin in a Black woman was soon placed center stage, and the reproductive capacity of the cells in laboratory spaces was linked to a discourse on promiscuity, pollution, and race, which conveniently equated alleged (promiscuous and polluting) characteristics with the Black other. Problems with HeLa cells in research became part of the "one drop of blood/HeLa" discourse among geneticists. As science journalist Barbara J. Culliton wrote: "If a non-HeLa culture is contaminated by even a single HeLa cell, […] that cell culture is doomed. In no time at all, usually unnoticed, HeLa cells will proliferate and take over the culture" (quoted in Landecker 2000, 65). The language of threat to the self by the other is obvious. The enemy is among us. As Landecker shows, discussions about this cell line took place both in scientific journals and in the popular media, fueling racist debates. As part of the Anderson sequence, however, the HeLa cell line went unmarked to become part of a standardized, naturalized technology. But not for all geneticists!

The original Anderson sequence was revised in 1999 (Andrews et al. 1999). Over the years, practitioners in the field of medical genetics had reported possible mistakes in the reference sequence. In 1999, the placental DNA used to produce the Anderson sequence in 1981 was resequenced. This resulted in a remarkable revision, one that could be called whitewashing. The new reference sequence, now called the Revised Cambridge Reference Sequence (rCRS), consists only of the DNA of the placenta. It appeared that the bovine DNA stretch did not match human DNA at those parts of the genome. But Andrews and his colleagues had also decided to remove the DNA stemming from the HeLa cells. In fact, the DNA stretch derived from HeLa cells hardly differed from placental DNA. The authors put it as follows:

> The only *error* that we were able to explain using the HeLa sequence was that at nt [nucleotide] 14,766 (T versus C, respectively). The revised CRS mtDNA belongs to the *European* haplogroup H.
>
> *(Andrews et al. 1999, 147, emphasis added)*

One "T" in the HeLa sequence had to be "corrected," replaced by a "C" in accord with the placental DNA. Almost an innocent gesture. But the goal of this intervention is race and the racial identity of the reference sequence, a scientific standard. The problem was not that HeLa DNA constituted an error. For example, as I show elsewhere (M'charek 2014), a true and technical error, which assumed that the reference sequence had an extra "C" that was lacking in all humans, was not corrected. Moreover, HeLa DNA is common DNA, and there was no reason to "correct" it. Yet labeling the "T" derived from HeLa an *error*, and replacing it by a "C," turned the revised sequence into a *European* standard.

Initially an unmarked cell line and valued for the work it made possible, when HeLa started to contaminate other research, the origin of the cell line became a matter of concern. The scientific challenges met in practice provoked a discourse of racism and misogyny the moment it became clear that the cells originated from an African American woman. This constant racism finally figured in the "error" that needed correction to make the mitochondrial DNA reference into a European one.

Conclusion

As we moved from one panel to the next, an increasingly complex story about genetics, race, and gender unfolded. We began with genetic genealogy and the possibilities of repairing the violent cuts of the transatlantic slave trade with DNA research. While DNA might function here as a "technology of belonging" (M'charek et al. 2014), it also relies on and reinforces a simplistic idea of Africa as an archaic place of origin. Interesting to observe, however, is how gender intersects with race, as the maternal line is the link that traces back to Africa.

Moving on to the second panel, the centerpiece of the triptych, we encountered the important contribution of DNA research in the 1980s in debunking racist ideas about human differences. The genetic out-of-Africa theory relied on the figure of Mitochondrial Eve, an ancestor who passed on her mitochondrial DNA to all subsequent human beings. While Eve was an important vehicle to disseminate these scientific results, she became a site of misogyny and race and was mobilized in a gendered politics to disqualify the theory. In the final panel, race and gender move in and out of focus. While they never fully disappear and are folded into the tools and technologies of science, they are also hard to grasp. Yet opening the box of Pandora showed a grim politics of sexism and racism, first against Henrietta Lacks herself and later through the exclusion of DNA stemming from the HeLa cell line.

The triptych as a whole demonstrates how genetics is dependent on presumably Black female bodies, from matrilineal links in DNA, to Mitochondrial Eve, to Henrietta Lacks, from whose body the HeLa cell line was extracted, upon which much of the research in the field of genetics has emerged. Genetics, however, is neither an enemy to be defeated nor a savior to be embraced to repair racism or sexism in society. While genetic knowledge is powerful and can be mobilized to destabilize rigid differences, doing so requires careful attention and a situated approach that takes into account colonial legacies of race and gender in science and their novel iterations. It is thus, to paraphrase Donna Haraway, that race and gender require that we stay with the trouble.

Acknowledgments

I thank Janell Hobson for her enthusiasm, guidance, and feedback on earlier versions. Sanne Boersma has provided me with valuable feedback and suggestions, for which I am very grateful. The wonderful triptych was produced by Olaf Posselt. I cannot even begin to thank him for his creative work and for thinking along with my text. Finally, I am grateful to the European Research Council for supporting my research through an ERC Consolidator Grant (FP7-617451-RaceFaceID-Race Matter: On the Absent Presence of Race in Forensic Identification).

Notes

1 www.youtube.com/watch?v=WBPtOlFX_as
2 www.youtube.com/watch?v=nw43kWEKjn8
3 www.youtube.com/watch?v=D9Ihs241zeg
4 In 2003, studies showed that "27% of British African-Caribbean men have a Y chromosome (passed directly from father to son) that traces back to Europe not Africa." www.bbc.co.uk/pressoffice/pressreleases/stories/2003/02_february/05/motherland.shtml
5 Paleontologists' multi-regional theory has a version in physical anthropology, the so-called polygenism. Georges Cuvier, an eighteenth-century French naturalist, also referred to as the founding father of paleontology and the anatomist who was determined to claim and study the body of Sara Bartman (Fausto-Sterling 1995; Scully and Crais 2008), was instrumental in this polygenist thinking. Although as a religious man he believed in one origin for all humans, his scientific work fed into the idea that different races have different origins (Stocking 1982: 39).
6 Another classical contribution, long before the out-of-Africa paper, is the UNESCO statement on race. Based on population genetic approaches, it argued that race does not exist and that the differences between populations are statistically distributed rather than rigid.
7 Mitochondrial DNA is located not in the nucleus of the cell (like the 46 chromosomes) but outside the nucleus, in the cytoplasm. During fertilization, only the nucleus of the sperm enters the egg cell, where the mitochondrial DNA of the mother is located. It is for this reason that the mitochondrial DNA of the father is not passed on.
8 Allan Wilson was apparently a coach to many women who faced a hostile atmosphere in other labs. In an interview with Cann, she recounts:

> He knew how hard it was for women to get going in science … his lab was a haven for the women in the program and the male professors from other labs would joke that Allan had all the women … He was gender blind. If you had a good idea, it was a good idea.
>
> (Gitschier 2010)

9 As I argue elsewhere, it is remarkable that the metaphor of a portrait is used here (M'charek 2014). In the context of the Human Genome Project, which was aimed at nuclear DNA (the 46 chromosomes), the metaphors used are, rather, "book" or "map."

10 See for an account of that ethnographic study M'charek (2005).

11 For this quest, see M'charek (2014). The final part of this chapter draws on my analysis in that paper.

References

Abu El-Haj, Nadia. "The Genetic Reinscription of Race." *Annual Review of Anthropology* 36 (2007): 238–300.

Anderson, Stephen, et al. "Sequence and Organization of the Human Mitochondrial Genome." *Nature* 290, no. 5806 (1981): 457–465.

Andrews, Richard M., et al. "Reanalysis and Revision of the Cambridge Reference Sequence for Human Mitochondrial DNA." *Nature Genetics* 23, no. 2 (1999): 147.

Appiah, Kwame Anthony. *In My Father's House: Africa in the Philosophy of Culture.* Oxford: Oxford University Press, 1992.

BBC Two. "Motherland: A Genetic Journey." *Directed by Archie Baron and Produced by Tabitha Jackson,* 2003.

Borst, Piet, and Leslie A. Grivell. "Small Is Beautiful: Portrait of a Mitochondrial Genome." *Nature* 290, no. 5806 (1981): 443–444.

Cann, Rebecca L. "Mothers, Label, and Misogyny." In *Women in Human Evolution,* edited by Lori D. Hager, 75–91. London: Routledge, 1997.

Cann, Rebecca L., Mark Stoneking, and Allan C. Wilson. "Mitochondrial DNA and Human Evolution." *Nature* 325, no. 6099 (1987): 31–36.

Carsten, Janet, ed. *Cultures of Relatedness: New Approaches to the Study of Kinship.* Cambridge: Cambridge University Press, 2000.

Fausto-Sterling, Anne. "Gender, Race and Nation: The Comparative Anatomy of "Hottentot" Women in Europe, 1815–1817." In *Deviant Bodies: Critical Perspectives on Difference in Science and Popular Culture,* edited by Jennifer Terry and Jacqueline Urla, 19–49. Bloomington: Indiana University Press, 1995.

Gilroy, Paul. *Against Race: Imagining Political Culture beyond the Color Line.* Cambridge: Harvard University Press, 2000.

Gitschier, Jane. "All about Mitochondrial Eve: An Interview with Rebecca Cann." *PLoS Genetics* 6, no. 5 (2010): e1000959.

Gould, Stephen J. *The Mismeasure of Man.* New York: Norton, 1981.

Jones, Howard W., Jr. "Record of the First Physician to See Henrietta Lacks at the Johns Hopkins Hospital: History of the Beginning of the HeLa Cell Line." *American Journal of Obstetrics and Gynecology* 176, no. 6 (1997): s227–s228.

Keller, Evelyn Fox. *A Feeling for the Organism: The Life and Work of Barbara McClintock.* New York: Macmillan, 1984.

Landecker, Hannah. "Immortality, in Vitro: A History of the HeLa Cell Line." In *Biotechnology and Culture: Bodies, Anxieties, Ethics,* edited by Paul Brodwin, 53–72. Bloomington: Indiana University Press, 2000.

Lederman, Muriel, and Ingrid Bartsch, eds. *The Gender and Science Reader.* New York: Routledge, 2001.

Lewontin, Richard C. "Sociobiology as an Adaptationist Program." *Behavioral Sciences* 24, no. 1 (1979): 5–14.

M'charek, Amade. *The Human Genome Diversity Project: An Ethnography of Scientific Practice.* Cambridge: Cambridge University Press, 2005.

M'charek, Amade. "Race, Time, and Folded Objects: The HeLa Error." *Theory, Culture and Society* 31, no. 6 (2014): 29–56.

M'charek, Amade, Katharina Schramm, and David Skinner. "Technologies of Belonging: The Absent Presence of Race in Europe." *Science, Technology, & Human Values* 39, no. 4 (2014): 459–467.

Nelson, Alondra. "Bio Science: Genetic Genealogy Testing and the Pursuit of African Ancestry." *Social Studies of Science* 38 (2008): 759–783.

Oikkonen, Venla. "Mitochondrial Eve and the Affective Politics of Human Ancestry." *Signs* 40, no. 3 (2015): 747–772.

Scully, Pamela, and Clifton Crais. "Race and Erasure: Sara Baartman and Hendrik Cesars in Cape Town and London." *Journal of British Studies* 47, no. 2 (2008): 301–323.

Stocking, George W. *Race, Culture, and Evolution: Essays in the History of Anthropology.* Chicago: University of Chicago Press, 1982.

Tierney, John. "The Search for Adam and Eve." *Newsweek* 111 (January 11, 1988): 46–52. https://i.b5z.net/i/u/736324/i/IN_SEARCH_FOR_ADAM___EVE.pdf.
Weasel, Lisa H. "Feminist Intersections in Science: Race, Gender and Sexuality Through the Microscope." *Hypatia* 19, no. 1(2004): 183–193.
Wolpoff, Milford H., et al. "Modern Human Origins." *Science* 241, no. 4867 (1988): 772–773.
Wolpoff, Milford H., Alan Thorne, and Roger Lawn. "The Case Against Eve." *New Scientist*, June 22, 1991. http://www.newscientist.com/article/mg13017745.700-the-case-against-eve-where-did-we-originate-some-researchers-think-that-all-modern-humans-evolved-from-a-single-african-women-the-testimony-of-fossils-suggests-otherwise.html.

30

Is twerking African?
Dancing and diaspora as embodied knowledge on YouTube

Kyra D. Gaunt

The dancing body is an environment where sounds and ethnic worlds become landscapes that speak to us and through us. Ethnicity offers various concepts through which to discuss the shared and shareable culture gained from witnessing and deliberately practicing Black forms of sensational knowledge across generations for girls and women. Knowledge can appear or disappear, arise and surprise us in sacred or secular contexts of dance. How we learn to interpret their meanings depends on our ecological awareness, our social location, the structuring elements of kin and kith, that situate our local knowledge about our Selves as people of African descent as well as individual and collective dancing. Things get complicated on YouTube.

What we see and feel when dancing – the expression of something that gets turned on, shaped by a particular linguistic, social, and ecological situation or musical circumstance – may not be linked to genetics. Sound and acoustics are, after all, environments that speak to us as biological and socio-cultural beings. Music is our sonic world, and the dancing body is one of its settings. The *situational negotiation of identity* (individual's self-identification with a particular group that can shift according to social location) is a crucial aspect of African and African American ethnicity (Guest 2014). The notion of DNA or "blood memory" is often used as a misnomer for what comes to mind as ancestral connection for African Americans. But, far too much blood has been spilt dehumanizing or essentializing Blacks and Africans in the name of biological determinism and eugenics.

Twerking is African?: origin myths

"See that girl shake that thang? Everybody can't be Martin Luther King."

~ Julian Bond.

Whatever we are inclined to think about Black girls comes automatically. We never question it as hindsight bias. We hold on to conventional wisdom that is mostly myths, stigmas, and stereotypes (what we might think about Black girls twerking on YouTube versus what Black girls – if ever asked or heard instead of merely seen – actually think or feel about the meaning behind twerking).

In 2017, while searching for twerking videos for my next book *Played: Twerking at the Intersection of Music, Technology, and Violence Against Black Girls on YouTube*, I stumbled upon a thumbnail that read "THE ORIGIN OF THE TWERK." The video had been uploaded by hair vlogger CHIME (Hair Crush) on May 16, 2017, with the title "AMERICAN DANCES THAT ORIGINATED IN AFRICA." Its description read:

> Ever wonder where twerking began? It all started in Africa. There are many dances within the Black community that can be linked back to the motherland besides twerking like crumping and stepping. Sometimes, we just have to explore to find those connections. The next time you see someone twerking or wanting to learn how to twerk, remember where it all began:) [smiley emoticon closes the sentence]
>
> *(Chime 2017)*

Chime's YouTube video essay is an attempt to historicize twerking and establish a respectable *origin myth* for a dance constantly under attack. An origin myth is a story told about the history of a particular group or group activity that reinforces a sense of common identity or ethnicity. Chime's claim that twerking is African is an example of an aspect of ethnicity that sociologists call a "social fact": a belief that positively or negatively coerces ways of thinking, feeling, believing, and behaving (Durkheim 1982). She opens the video with this scripted narration:

> African Americans are deeply connected to Africa and many of us don't even realize it. Many of us are attracted to certain music … because of our genetics. It's deeply embedded in our psyche even though we've never been to the motherland. Many of the dances that African Americans do are *exactly* like the dances they've been doing in Africa for hundreds of years. Mapouka is a traditional dance that those in the States call twerking. [emphasis added]

It may be satisfying to equate twerking with *mapouka* – a dance practiced by young Ivoirian women that was "banned from television, judged too vulgar by the government" (Onishi 2000) – but it may perpetuate superstitious and abstract thinking about Africa, a continent of over 54 nations, and its diaspora: the World Bank estimates that there are "39 million from the African Diaspora [in North America]; 113 million in Latin America; 13.6 million in the Caribbean; and 3.5 million in Europe" (Kajunju 2013).

The *video essay* became a popular form of storytelling among YouTube vloggers in 2010. Creators apply video editing by giving proportional weight to the moving image, the language, as well as the sound to capture some deeper truth from the creator's perspective (Bresland 2010).

Figure 30.1 Screen capture of the YouTube thumbnail for Chime's 2017 video essay by author.

The form blurs documentary narrative with partial truths and even "fake" news. Commenters reinforce Chime's claim, creating filter bubbles. Users often select videos and follow subscribers who affirm what they are already inclined to think. Comments like the following add weight to Chime's influence on other users who will like or react to the same ideas together, joining the bandwagon:

> I wish everyone could watch this video AND really understand … Twerking actually originates from Africa!! Not African Americans. I noticed when I recently watched traditional west African dance.
>
> *(Chime 2017)*

Chime's description and the comment cited are examples of "social fact." Social facts are coercive; they are thoughts and feelings shared by a group that reflect norms or values that can function to control or maintain groupthink (or the status quo). The long-held belief that the nappier your hair is, the closer you are to "Africa" suggests that less nappy hair is closer in proximity to some superior notion of beauty defined by whiteness. *Xenocentrism* is the belief that another culture is superior to one's own. Like xenophobia, it can negatively affect the behavior and attitudes of people within the African diaspora, which is why name-calling like "African booty scratcher" or "A-meh-ri-can niggerrr" continues. "Twerking is African" is a social fact that demands further inquiry.

The intention of this chapter is to help readers parse, prune, and play with the question: "Is twerking African?" In so doing, we might begin to deconstruct the deeply ingrained structures that govern the notion of a single Black or African identification; a notion that is continually mapped onto Black girls' bodies when they twerk on YouTube, reproducing binary-thinking about a rich, nuanced, and complex spectrum of embodied performativity and expression too easily likened to twerking. When we are inclined to ask if twerking is "African," how do we complicate the question itself?

Dancing diaspora, dancing ancestry

Twerking on YouTube or watching twerking on YouTube is not situated in the same local settings where one may experience popping, locking, or bouncing the booty to the beats and rhymes of a song as a dancer of *bounce* in New Orleans, popular and traditional forms of *mapouka* in Côte d'Ivoire (Ivory Coast), *perreo* in Puerto Rico or *sandungueo* in the Dominican Republic, or *funk carioca* in Brazil. In fact, on YouTube, there are dozens of dances, like disjointed limbs across the African diaspora, that may or may not connect Black Americans to specific populations of African people or the African, Caribbean, and Afro-Latinx diaspora. Just as twerking isn't one thing, neither are people of African descent.

Given this complexity, cultural memory about Africa is easily distorted because memory is malleable, as anyone has witnessed in the game of *telephone* among kids, the misreading of an instant replay, or misidentifications from eyewitness testimony:

> [T]he assumption that memory provides an accurate recording of experience, much like a video camera, is incorrect. Memory evolved to give us a personal sense of identity and to guide our actions. We are biased to notice and exaggerate some experiences and to minimize or overlook others.
>
> *(Chew 2018)*

Our cultural memory about Africa is complicated not only by physical and social distancing between groups, but also by the dissonance created by disinformation about Africa by African Americans themselves. But there's something about dance that seems different.

In 1996, I spent seven weeks studying Ewe music-making in a student ensemble run by a colleague. The drum-and-dance ensemble was co-led by a visiting lecturer, a traditional African master drummer named Fred Dunyo. Even though it was a predominately white classroom setting (and I was raised Catholic, not Pentecostal or Baptist), in the middle of a rehearsal, I inexplicably went into a trance. In 2002, I published an article about the experience: "Though I had participated in a few other West African traditions, the Ewe performance practice spoke to me as if a kindred spirit; [it] resonated with my [personal] identifications with African American musical and communal ideals" (Gaunt 2002, 122). For a fleeting moment, I thought my African ancestry was speaking through me or speaking to me.

When I finally traveled to the continent and stood before the "door of no return" (a sliver no wider than one of my thick legs), the fact that over 10 million enslaved Africans disembarked from slave forts like El Mina Castle in the former Gold Coast colony that is now Ghana struck me dumb. African women, children, and men were captured and starved for months so they could pack as much "cargo" as possible in the belly of thousands of ships that sailed between 1514 and 1866.

The immensity of the Trans-Atlantic Slave Trade, like the true size of the continent on Mercator maps, has been an ongoing project and "product" of disinformation since then. As Nigerian novelist Chimamanda Ngozi Adichie stated in a 2009 TED talk titled "*The danger of a single story*," as early as 1561, Western literature portrayed Sub-Saharan Africa as "a place of negatives, of difference, of darkness" in stories that are embedded in the psyche of white supremacist thinking (Adichie 2009).

Furthermore, Black Americans' repeated exposure to fabricated or deliberately manipulated information about our African ancestors (not to mention the disinformation mediated about us through the media) has distorted our relationship not only to African geography and populations, but also to the modern waves of Black immigration that have arrived in the United States since the passing of the Immigration and Nationality Act of 1965 or the United States Refugee Act of 1980.

Black Americans like me – my family goes back nine generations to Portsmouth, Virginia – live in an assumptive world about the African past, our ancestry, or even what they think is happening when search results and recommendations feed us videos of African dancing that resemble twerking on YouTube's platform (Gaunt 2006, 2015).

The act of twerking on YouTube, of shaking your booty to the beats and rhymes of rap lyrics that often feature what Moya Bailey coined as *misogynoir* (anti-Black sexism) on a general-audience mobile platform, also recalls the historical misogynoir that undergirded the degradation and dehumanization of Saartjie [Sarah] Baartman. In 1810, an indigenous Khoisan woman from Southern Africa was trafficked into a European traveling freak show. She was sold like an animal, equated with an orangutan; upon her early death, her skull, skeleton, and female anatomy were dissected and displayed in a museum in Paris until 1974. Her remains would not be returned to her homeland for burial until 2002 (Parkinson 2016). Her life is often remembered by the derogatory Dutch word for Khoisan people (Hottentot), and the disinformation was perpetuated by anatomical illustrations that represented her buttocks and vulva as grotesquely oversized, as a deviation from some European norm of anatomy and sexuality (see Hobson 2003; Gilman 1985).

As an artful and sophisticated aspect of "kinetic orality," twerking can be and likely is an antidote to the structures of dehumanization that surround Black girls and their adult counterparts.

It can re-situate even the abused girl deeply in her body, expressing a kind of freedom of expression not allowed from her voice. As Mae Henderson reminds us, "It is not that Black womxn have had nothing to say, but rather that they have had 'no say'" (Henderson 2013, 24). I would assert that the body has been doing all the talking for Black women, and it is time we read the messages behind their kinetic orality.

Handclapping game-songs and double-dutch rope jumping, like twerking, are examples of oral-kinetic lessons or *études* (short musical compositions) in musical Blackness. Through the repeated practice of kinetic orality, we transmit intra- and inter-generational knowledge by word of mouth (orality) and the motion of the body (kinetics). Twerking is an *oral-kinetic étude* that is part of a larger network of danced diasporic expressions often practiced by womxn and girls (Gaunt 2006).

The word twerk is a contraction of "*to work.*" It refers to the intentional undertaking of a mentally and/or physically engaging task. In Black social dancing, it may be articulated as the ability to "work the middle" or in patois, to "werk di batty"; in other words, to control in musical ways the hips and fleshy excess that define the figure of a significant number of womxn and girls of African descent.

As you learn to twerk, you embody the *roux* of a music that originated in New Orleans. Just like making gumbo, the mix of flour (the percussive music-making) and fat (the fleshy parts) thickens the feel of a danced performance. Black girls' musical games, like the cheer *Jig-a-low* and *Down, down, baby* with their calls to "*do your thing,*" and tween twerking videos where girls dance their behinds off to Huey's "Pop Lock and Drop it" or Kstylis' "Hands up, Get Low," are Black expressions of kinetic orality among girls and womxn who broadcast themselves on YouTube.

As twerk scholar Kimari Brand states in the documentary film *Twerk it Girl*, "We enjoyed ourselves … exploring our body and our erotic autonomy and moving in ways that, you know, sometimes we might be afraid to expose or explore" (Garcia 2014, cue: 4:10″). Twerking is arguably a form of political speech, and videos of twerking are girls' *abolitionist steganography*: the practice of concealing messages and information in plain sight through dance. It is their version of YouTube vlogging expressed by word of body through a kinship with movement and the drums of ancestral knowledge.

Throw it back: how NOLA and Nipplegate made YouTube

Many non-Black folks think twerking began with Miley Cyrus, since she was a finalist for Time's *Person of the Year* after her white wonderland appropriation of the dance at the MTV Video Music Awards in August 2013. Yet, the music and dance that inspired twerking began at least a decade before. In fact, the same year Miley was born (1992), the word "twerk" was first heard on a New Orleans mix-tape recorded by a popular bounce music pioneer, DJ Jubilee (born Jerome Temple), on the track "Do the Jubilee All" (Fensterstock 2013).

The music and dance can be traced back to the late 1980s' social club culture, to dancing that resembles bounce practiced throughout the 100-year history of Mardi Gras' Treme Million Dollar Baby Dolls. The Baby Dolls marchers dressed as "innocents" done up in satin bonnets, toting booze-filled baby bottles to express their "independence and self-fulfillment," according to Xavier University professor Kim Marie Vaz-Deville (Reckdahl 2017). Moreover, Big Freedia, the queen of bounce music in New Orleans, explains the local knowledge of the music and dance in a 2013 NPR interview a month before Miley Cyrus dropped her first twerking video on Facebook:

> Bounce is based in hip-hop. It favors punchy tempos, heavy bass and call-and-response vocals. Many of the songs are structured around a handful of samples, most notably a snippet from

"Drag Rap," a 1986 track by the New York rap group The Showboys [aka the "Triggaman" beat]. Bounce is party music, hypersexual and made to be danced to. The more your butt is moving, the better. You've gotta leave room for the bass and the boom and the knock and for people to be able to just free themselves and express themselves through dance.

(NPR Staff 2013)

So how did twerking go from Mardi Gras to YouTube? In 2005, the intersection of two cataclysmic events occurred. Three former PayPal employees launched a free video-sharing platform in April, and Hurricane Katrina hit the homeland of bounce music and dance in late August. The damage from the levees breaking left thousands dead and over 400,000 people displaced: scattered throughout all 50 states, DC, and Puerto Rico (Ericson et al. 2005).

When I first heard about Katrina's diaspora, the ethnomusicologist in me thought *we are gonna have Mardi Gras everywhere* – because the people who came from the cultural hotbed that is the birthplace of Congo Square, jazz, Dixieland, Zydeco music, and Cajun cuisine like gumbo will take that culture wherever they land.

We didn't get Mardi Gras.

Instead, we got twerking, as hundreds of displaced youth and newly mobile music producers began reconnecting and uploading audio and video recordings through YouTube. In 2014, a collection of over 1000 bedroom twerking videos featuring Black girls' online play offered evidence of twerking to bounce music. As early as 2006, cis- and transgender girls uploaded videos of themselves dancing to local mix-tapes with a distinct soundmark of a one-bar drum loop called the Triggaman beat.

In 2011, the bedroom culture of twerking videos, primarily of girls and womxn, began to register as a tiny trend in Google search results (search "twerking" on the Google Trends site). By 2013, twerking reached a dramatic peak on the night Miley Cyrus performed at the MTV Video Music Awards. In my dataset of over 1000 videos, tween and teen girls, Black and Brown, were already uploading content tagged as "twerking" from the United States and Puerto Rico, the Afro- and Afro-Latinx Caribbean, from Francophone Africans in Europe and "African Americans" in Brazil, the largest population of people of African descent outside the continent.

Most YouTube users do not know that founders Chad Hurley, Steven Cehn, and Jawed Karim registered a domain name on Valentine's Day and that their first venture was a dating site. They placed an ad on Craigslist offering $100 for female users to upload 10 videos, but they claim no one took the bait (Entis 2016).

Within the first year of their launch, teen girls began broadcasting their bedroom play for free, and the MTV marketing model of selling music with female sexuality was perpetuated by young girls with a smartphone but without a parent's permission. YouTube has become the number one music discovery channel and archive for new and existing music around the world after 15 years as a platform.

While the presence of young girls contributed to YouTube's new attention economy, it was actually the search for videos of the wardrobe malfunction that took place at the 2004 Super Bowl known as Nipplegate. In the 2020 *Rolling Stone* issue devoted to the 15th anniversary of YouTube, journalist Rob Sheffield referred to the nine-sixteenths-of-a-second moment when Janet's breast was fully exposed to the world at the biggest event in national television by using a cringe-worthy, titillating term, "Nipple bounce," to spark attention to what is always in fashion and never considered poor taste: misogynoir's anti-Black sexism against women of African descent. One question still lingers: How did the brief and spectacular moment in 2004 (a whole year before YouTube launched) kickstart the platform into a meteoric rise? If we recall, in 2006, Google acquired YouTube for $1.65 billion.

The idea of a video-sharing platform instead of a dating site came during a conversation at a dinner party. The tech founders lamented how tough it was to find any footage of Nipplegate, and at the time, there was no way to store or share videos, and definitely not for free. But once they launched the beta site on April 23, 2005, YouTube's interface had been designed to allow anyone to upload, store, and more importantly, share videos via any other platform.

Janet Jackson was shamed by the national media and lost millions of dollars in a rip off, supposedly, of family values and the massive loss of advertisers for the Super Bowl that year. She didn't expose her own nipple. Pop singer Justin Timberlake ripped off the front of her bodice. Still, a Black woman was blamed for the spectacle-turned-freak-show within its treatment that clearly recalls the body of Sarah Baartman. Janet's performance was dissected to the degree that she was banned from the Grammys the following month (Sheffield 2020).

On August 24, 2005, four days before levees broke during Hurricane Katrina, YouTube learned the power of outsourcing its labor where "broadcast yourself" could be done for free. Israeli YouTubers Lital Maizel and Adi Frimmerman lip-synced a cover of "Hey" by the Pixies, an alternative rock group out of Boston, uploaded directly from their bedroom in Israel. Their 2005 "Hey clip" was probably the first uploaded music content to reach a million views on the beta platform. In its first year, YouTube learned the need to find user-generated videos from a spectacle associated with a Black woman's breast, and they also learned about the virality of women's unpaid, affective labor. Lital and Adi made the video for a boyfriend's birthday.

MTV washed its hands of music videos following Nipplegate, immediately programming cheaper reality TV shows. YouTube's Content ID system was implemented within a year to track, block, and monetize music streams for copyright holders and major media conglomerates, solving the piracy problem that had begun with the rise of Napster. In 2013, Billboard and Nielsen struck a deal with Google/YouTube; music streams would partially count towards gold and platinum records in the recording industry. Lastly, Sheffield pointed out that we have Nipplegate and YouTube to thank for "Netflix and the whole stream-and-binge economy" (Sheffield 2020).

Perhaps all these innovations owe their success in music, entertainment, and technology to the shaming of a Black woman and the need to dissect the instant replay of a Super Bowl halftime show gone wrong. Thus, it is befitting to quote the words of a Black woman here: On the internet, "[w]e all drink from the well poisoned by the anti-blackness that wants everyone to forget when blackness [particularly female blackness] goes viral" (Jackson 2019). The burden of misogynoir wrought upon Black girls who twerk on YouTube, like the unintended consequences of Nipplegate and Hurricane Katrina, always feel intentional and are always more profitable for everyone but womxn and girls of African descent, online or off.

False cognates + unfinished migrations

Information about Black expressive dances must become a *situated knowledge*. It need not call on African memory to be expressed. Black people often shift or negotiate their bodies to the situations of music they are in. A *transactional* philosophy is steeped in the notion that human behavior is shaped by its ecological fitness or situatedness. When we dance to reggae or dancehall, we *two-step* or *wine di batty*. When the rhythm and blues of a Ruth Brown or Shimmy Shimmy Ko-Ko Bop of Harlem doo-wop plays, we do *bop* as apart-dancing or the *Lindy* with a partner. When funk or go-go is heard, we do *The Bump* or start *doin' the Butt*, accordingly. *Gizomba* and *samba*, and we work the middle of the belly or shuffle the feet and hips.

The *situational negotiation of dance* means that Black people shift forms of dance to different occasions of music. Dozens of dances feature hip gyrations that resemble twerking. On some level, they may be "false friends" or what language teachers call "false cognates" in translating an idea from one language to another. Just because they look alike doesn't automatically mean they are the same.

The same elements – hip gyrations and popping gestures that punctuate a musical phrase – do not always reflect the same conditions or contexts of meaning. Diasporic dances are not always oriented to the same metric pulse. Beats 1 and 3 may be emphasized in a Trinidadian road march, while beats 2 and 4 are syncopated to emphasize the backbeat in much of R&B, funk, and soul. Composers in Caribbean and African settings may choose major scales, especially in festival music, while composers in Mississippi Delta, Francophone musicians from the Niger-Delta basin in Mali and Niger, or hip-hop producers use pentatonic scales. The cultural contexts of our performances of dance are allowed to be different, though we share ethnic boundary markers or some sense of ancestral belonging that is not about DNA but has everything to do with spirit(s) and sensibilities. #thatsafrican

When African dances are subsumed under the label of "twerking," it flattens possibilities for nuance. When our conversations follow YouTube's search results, this drives algorithms to flatten what we mean by "twerking" or "bounce," not to mention what being "African" means to general and often miseducated audiences. It also flattens how we make sense of Black womxn's identifications and expressions on YouTube; not just to non-Black people, but more importantly, among diverse groups of Black people here in the United States and around the world.

To return to Chime's video essay, while I found it enjoyable, what concerned me as a pragmatist was the collapse of different dances; turning them into abstractions unmoored from their rich and significant situational settings just to seemingly argue for dignity or self-empowerment. I worry that the social fact that twerking is African is actually a form of American exceptionalism that defies an Africanist philosophy of what is real, true, and/or beautiful.

African Americans have been exposed to so little concrete knowledge or experience of the communal life of being African, including little interest in attending local parties where first- or second-generation migrants from cities like Accra, Lagos, Freetown, Port of Spain, the *banlieues* of Paris, or the *favelas* of Salvador are the norm. Speaking for myself, I have felt out of place in my own country at parties where Black Americans or expected forms of Black music are not dominant in public settings (and not all the time … but it still can happen).

We far too easily take these circumstances (and their dances) for granted. We'd rather subsume their dances under what is already an abstraction of bounce. Calling *mapouka, baikoko, kwassa kwassa* "twerking" reveals Black Americans' naiveté about Africans and their lived experience. This is not to shame or blame us, but to invite us to explore more than what we are inclined to think without any further study.

The plethora of dances tagged as twerking bind and unbind Black ethnicities on YouTube's platform, which are rarely understood as complex and meaningful in ways that are sophisticated, unique, and often unknown to many Black Americans in the States. Thus, the medium of YouTube, with its collapsing and colliding contexts, blocks the path of any serious inquiry. It leaves us with what Toni Morrison called the "symbolic looting of language" that lives in the "tendency of its users to forgo its nuanced, complex, mid-wifery properties, replacing them with menace and subjugation" (Morrison 1994). We must ask why twerking needs to be African without questioning inaccurate knowledge. Ultimately, we must ask ourselves: Which Africa is it we wish to see, hear, or feel?

Conclusion: situating ourselves and our bodies in the world

People around the world broadcast themselves mechanically repeating, lip syncing, remixing, and parodying songs like Sir Mix-a-lot's 1992 hit "Baby Got Back" or Nicki Minaj's 2014 mega-version "Anaconda." Both versions have millions of offspring on YouTube that repeat the "Valley girls" speak of the opening montage that is as iconic as the actual song. Before the beat drops, we always hear: "Oh, my, God Becky, look at her butt. … she looks like a total prostitute … I mean GROSS! Look! She's just so (pregnant pause) BLACK!" The virgin/whore trope in the Valley-girl speak of two ordinary white girls spewing oppressive lyrics usually comes from the mouths of 1990s gangsta rappers. Since the only Black women on screen are background dancers silenced by the stereotype of video vixen, the intro – where two white women speak to each other, not about men directly, but instead teaching billions of women of every color to mimic and self-objectify misogynoir – fails the minimum standard of a Bechdel-Wallace test. With YouTube streaming, the beating goes on ad infinitum. Readers may find it ironic that the woman whose voice mimicked the Valley-girl speak was Amylia Rivas, an Afro-Latina musician and voice actor (USA TODAY 2015).

I get trapped into those misogynoir lyrics by the Spotify playlists at my gym. I was even tormented by two seven-year-old white-adjacent twins singing to Becky at the breakfast table during an extended stay with friends after seeking freedom from an emotionally and financially abusive relationship. These lyrics have never introduced me to love of self. Instead, they function as a kind of gaslighting rooted in structural and intersectional inequalities. Gaslighting, according to sociologist Paige Sweet, is a type of "psychological abuse aimed at making victims seem or feel 'crazy,' creating a 'surreal' interpersonal environment" (Sweet 2019). Repeatedly hearing others voice a mis-interpretation and abstraction of a Black female body, as if YouTubers talking about our bodies were a reward, as if rappers' lyrics fetishizing one aspect of our Self spoke for us, is crazy. They – white women and Black men – might like big butts, but they still deny us equal access to remuneration for it and rob us of a voice situated as an authority, not as a side show.

Popular songs teach us how to perform racialized gender roles. YouTube teaches us to manipulate our bodies for attention that ain't free. Dances like twerking, bounce, *mapouka*, or *baikoko* drive attention to the patriarchal business of music at the strip club, the night club, and in viral videos, but here's the thing. If ladies get in free, they're the product!

Those who portray and respond to the erotic autonomy, kinetic orality, and the sensational knowledge of Black womxn and girls often misrecognize and misrepresent twerking and its false cognates as if solely a pornographic performance, even when the dancer is five to seven years old. It's as if the sole purpose of their culturally appropriated aspirational play is a for-profit operation that discloses children's personal information and sexually grooms and exploits very young girls and their "virginal" user-generated content with a few dollar bills of attention thrown their way on YouTube (Gaunt 2018). And don't get it twisted: *making it rain* is not culturally equivalent to the tradition of spraying local money, such as *nairas* at a Lagos wedding or *cedis* at a local club in Accra.

How sustainable has it been, and will it be in 2020 and beyond, to express "empowerment twerking" in the lion's den of a corporate-controlled platform that exploits Black girls and their adult counterparts? YouTube cannot be the end-all of our aspirational pursuits, and twerking is only the beginning of reclaiming our voice and our time.

Let me end with the words of activist Makalya Gilliam-Price, a 17-year-old Black Lives Matter movement activist, who situates her reading of twerking at a 2015 Baltimore BLM protest to her locality rather than to Africa:

> In Baltimore, Black womxn and Black girls have been reclaiming their femininity, … making spaces for themselves, making transient zones of freedom … for themselves. [They have been] inserting their sexuality, inserting their intersectional identities, inserting their

fluidity, creating space for ourselves to be embraced and that's what being a movement baby looks like for me in Baltimore. [Twerking] is just … a way to reclaim my identity.

(Gilliam-Price 2015)

This may not be the same meaning shared by dancers of *mapouka* in Ivory Coast, *perreo* in Puerto Rico, *funk carioca* in Brazil, or even twerking in different settings. But it resists essentializing who and what twerking is, it doesn't perpetuate disinformation about Africa or the diaspora, and it is situated in a specific time and place that does not deny anyone else's truth. Situated knowledge matters.

Bibliography

Adichie, Chimamanda Ngozi. "The Danger of a Single Story." *TED Conferences*, 2009.

Bresland, John. "On the Origin of the Video Essay." *Blackbird Archive - an Online Journal of Literature and Arts* 9, no. 1 (Spring 2010). https://blackbird.vcu.edu/v9n1/gallery/ve-bresland_j/ve-origin_page.shtml.

Chew, Stephen L. "Myth: Eyewitness Testimony Is the Best Kind of Evidence," *Association for Psychological Science* (August 20, 2018). Available: https://www.psychologicalscience.org/teaching/myth-eyewitness-testimony-is-the-best-kind-of-evidence.html (accessed November 15, 2020).

Chime (Hair Crush). "American Dances That Originated in Africa." *YouTube*. 2017. https://www.youtube.com/watch?v=iO433P17g3U.

Durkheim, Emile. "What Is a Social Fact?" In *The Rules of Sociological Method: And Selected Texts on Sociology and Its Method*, edited by Steven Lukes, 50–59. Contemporary Social Theory. London: Macmillan Education UK, 1982.

Entis, Laura. "YouTube's Co-Founder Just Made a $1.65 Billion Case for the Early Pivot." *Entrepreneur*, March 17, 2016.

Ericson, Matthew, Andrew Tse, and Jodi WIlgoren. "Katrina's Diaspora. (map)." *The New York Times*, October 2, 2005. https://archive.nytimes.com/www.nytimes.com/imagepages/2005/10/02/national/nationalspecial/20051002diaspora_graphic.html.

Fensterstock, Alison. "DJ Jubilee Had Preservation Hall Backing That Thing up, Right into the History Books." *NOLA.com/The Times-Picayune*, November 23, 2013.

Garcia, Irma L. "Documentary: Twerk It Girl (f/ Kimari Brand)." *Vimeo*, April 25, 2014. https://vimeo.com/92922772.

Gaunt, Kyra D. "Got Rhythm?: Difficult Encounters in Theory and Practice and Other Participatory Discrepancies in Music." *City & Society* 14, no. 1 (2002): 119–40.

Gaunt, Kyra D. *The Games Black Girls Play: Learning the Ropes from Double-Dutch to Hip-Hop*. New York: NYU Press, 2006.

Gaunt, Kyra D. "YouTube, Twerking & You: Context Collapse and the Handheld Co-Presence of Black Girls and Miley Cyrus." *Journal of Popular Music Studies* 27, no. 3 (September 21, 2015): 244–73.

Gaunt, Kyra D. "The Disclosure, Disconnect, and Digital Sexploitation of Tween Girls' Aspirational YouTube Videos." *Journal of Black Sexuality and Relationships* 5, no. 1 (2018): 91–132.

Gilliam-Price, Makayla. "Makayla Gilliam-Price [at Black Girl Movement Conference, Columbia University, April 7–9. 2015]." *YouTube*, June 23, 2016. https://www.youtube.com/watch?v=n2H-sKqYBlc.

Gilman, Sidney. "Black Bodies, White Bodies: Toward an Iconography of Female Sexuality in Late 19th-Century Art, Medicine, and Literature." *Critical Inquiry* 12, no. 1 (1985): 204–242.

Guest, Kenneth J. *Cultural Anthropology: A Toolkit for a Global Age*. 1st ed. New York: W. W. Norton & Company, 2014.

Henderson, Mae G. "About Face, or, What Is This 'Back' in B(l)Ack Popular Culture? From Venus Hottentot to Video Hottie." In *Understanding Blackness Through Performance: Contemporary Arts and the Representation of Identity*, edited by Anne Crémieux, Xavier Lemoine, and Jean-Paul Rocchi, 159–79. New York: Palgrave Macmillan US, 2013.

Hobson, Janell. "The 'Batty' Politic: Toward an Aesthetic of the Black Female Body." *Hypatia* 18, no. 4 (2003): 87–105.

Jackson, Lauren Michele. "The Undeniable Blackness of Vine (RIP)." *Wired*, November 12, 2019.

Kajunju, Amini. "Africa's Secret Weapon: The Diaspora." *CNN*, November 1, 2013.

Morrison, Toni. *The Nobel Lecture in Literature, 1993*. New York: Knopf, 1994.

NPR Staff. "Big Freedia Lays Out The Basics Of Bounce." *NPR.org*, January 27, 2013.

Onishi, Norimitsu. "Dance Has Africans Shaking Behinds, and Heads." *The New York Times*, May 28, 2000, sec. World.

Parkinson, Justin. "The Significance of Sarah Baartman." *BBC News*, January 7, 2016, sec. Magazine.

Reckdahl, Katy. "All Dolled up for Mardi Gras: A Carnival Tradition Evolves with the Times." *NOLA.com*, February 27, 2017.

Sheffield, Rob. "YouTube Origins: How Nipplegate Created Streaming Site." *Rolling Stone*. Accessed July 20, 2020.

Sweet, Paige L. "The Sociology of Gaslighting." *American Sociological Review* 84, no. 5 (October 2019): 851–75.

Tasha. "Hey Clip [Pixies Cover by Lital Maizel and Adi Frimmerman]." *YouTube*, 2016. https://www.youtube.com/watch?v=-_CSo1gOd48.

Touch, Hanex. *Kabulengane - Bebe Cool 'OFFICIAL HD VIDEO' '2016–2017'*. 2016. https://www.youtube.com/watch?v=ksQUDsKb6Nk&feature=emb_title.

USA TODAY. *(48) OMG, Meet the Real 'Becky' from 'Baby Got Back' - YouTube*. June 2, 2015. https://www.youtube.com/watch?v=ehA02-_sah8.

31

Sites of resistance

Black women and beauty in Black Brazilian communities of São Paulo and Bahia

Valquíria Pereira Tenório and Flávia Alessandra de Souza

The year 2019 marked an unprecedented moment to ponder beauty in the context of gender and race relations. Four top beauty pageants – Miss USA, Miss America, Miss World, and Miss Universe – had crowned Black women. Brazil, the largest Black country outside Africa and the center of the African diaspora, featured a white contestant, Júlia do Vale Horta, at the Miss World pageant, positioned in opposition to Nigeria's Nyekachi Douglas and Jamaica's Toni-Ann Singh, both of whom were Black. Miss Jamaica was declared the winner of the 2019 Miss World, with the heart-warming support of Miss Nigeria during the crowning ceremony.

Miss Brazil's white skin at the 2019 Miss World is emblematic of a racial pattern embodied in the structure of Brazilian society, which further stands out in a moment of the twenty-first century when positive representations of Black beauty assumed global status. In Brazil, where most women resemble the Black Miss Jamaica and Miss Nigeria, the paradigm of beauty positivity for Black women has faced deep resistance in the social imaginary. In such an oppressive context, the emergence of Black spaces for celebration and the crowning of the beauty of Black women historically function as sites of resistance in Brazil – as we present in this chapter through the analysis of this phenomenon in the states of São Paulo and Bahia.

Brazil underwent significant changes in its demographics in the twentieth century, and this has implied the "transformation of racial dynamics in different parts of the country" (Hanchard, 2001, p. 44). In addition, there had been an increase in the industrialization and urbanization process, highlighting São Paulo as one of the states most affected by this movement and the immigration of Italians who came to replace slave labor post-abolition, which facilitated the racial whitening project of the nation (Andrews, 1998). São Paulo, according to the 2010 census record, includes 63.9 percent of inhabitants who declared themselves white and 34.6 percent who declared themselves Black, unlike the state of Bahia, where the population is mostly Black at 76.3 percent. This demographic difference represents multiple racial interaction patterns (Hanchard, 2001, p. 44), and for the purposes of this chapter can provide us with differentiated data on how people understand, learn, and experience Black beauty.

The debate about Black identity in Brazil brings with it the plurality of the concept of "being Black" and what would be "Black identity," something that can only be thought of plurally, as we speak about a country of continental proportions in which history, space, and culture play a fundamental role in identity construction. It is possible to assume the existence of plural and differentiated experiences of being Black in Brazil, but as they started from a common point – the forced arrival of millions of Africans for slave labor – they share points of convergence.

Forms of Black organization in the state of São Paulo

The existence of Black recreational associations, clubs, and balls in the countryside of the state of São Paulo is of central importance to thinking about Black population, forms of mobilization, resistance, and structure inside cities and mostly, comprehending Black identity at the beginning of the twentieth century and today. We can point to a Black celebration movement in the state of São Paulo through many clubs, balls, and sociocultural events in places such as Araraquara (170 miles from São Paulo's capital) and Rio Claro (110 miles from São Paulo's capital), which we will address more accurately, as our previous studies approached the reconstruction of the Black community's history in both cities. Our work highlights the relevance of Black associations and sociability sites for the construction of Black identity (Souza, 2004, 2008; Tenório, 2010, 2013).

The large quantity of Black sociocultural events in many countryside cities of the state of São Paulo is also a form of opposing the discriminatory practices that produced racial segregation in leisure spaces, which include "the samba schools, the soccer teams, the dance courts and the religious temples [that] are architectonical and spatial coordinates of the physical existence of black communities" (Hanchard, 2001, p. 44). Brazil did not have racial segregation laws as we find in the United States or South Africa, but the nation built an efficient system of non-formal segregation, keeping Black people in subordinate roles, producing and sustaining inequalities in the context of the myth of Brazilian racial democracy.

> Such inequality is not only material, but promotes uneven power relations, subjective impressions of inferiority of a citizen or their treatment as inferior, and their inability to effectively take part in social life, regarding their access to work, education, healthcare, housing, as well as their political and civil rights.
>
> *(Telles, 2003, p. 137)*

In our research on Black history in Araraquara and Rio Claro, many Black people addressed the impossibility of participating in parties and balls and joining white recreational clubs. We were able to interview people from both cities who were there in the first half of the twentieth century (Souza, 2004, 2008; Tenório, 2010, 2013) and expressed their visions of the interdictions they suffered or witnessed with Black friends and relatives when they tried to attend white spaces.

Black clubs and associations in the state of São Paulo established themselves as sites where the Black community shared similar world conceptions and built their means and interpretations on how to advance Black beauty and identity.

> Race, associated to physical characteristics, social condition and expected behavior, has attributed the black body with a meaning in society. This prejudice "surrounded" sense has in the Brazilian black body the incarnation of stereotypes defended since colonial times. Since then the black body has been imputed with the notion of inferior intellectuality,

322

propensity to extenuating manual labor, displeasure with formal work, exacerbated sexuality, unclean skin, careless hair and ugliness. These stereotypes attributed to the black population have deeply marked their corporeality.

(Souza, 2015, p. 30)

It was necessary to oppose these ingrained stereotypes in the São Paulo cities – spaces that had European ideals of beauty especially due to European immigration to that State – constructing sites where the Black community, mainly Black women, could have their beauty reverenced, thus strengthening their bonds.

Black manifestations resisted and continued to develop in twentieth-century Brazil in the shape of social clubs, carnival groups, and religious brotherhoods, among others. In Rio Claro and Araraquara, the Black organizations undertook a series of specific collective strategies to abandon what we call racial intermittent spaces and thus occupy their own spaces of race – which would only happen at the end of the 1960s, specifically in Rio Claro (Souza, 2004, 2008).

It is worth mentioning that Rio Claro and Araraquara had a majority white population at the beginning of the twentieth century. What did it mean for Black men and women to live in cities where the population was overwhelmingly white? In other words, to what kind of racial embarrassment would the Black portion be subjected as a political and quantitative minority in these cities? Both the testimonies from our research and the newspapers analyzed show the ongoing pressure and racial humiliations that Black people suffered in local contexts without any legal means to solve the problem.

Newspapers from Rio Claro and Araraquara from the first half part of the twentieth century openly expressed the depreciative and prejudiced views on Black people that the white population had held also in the Brazilian republican regime. Such attitudes were not restricted to the cities in the countryside of São Paulo but were aligned to scientific racial doctrines from the end of the nineteenth century, which affirmed the superiority of the white race and the innate and permanent inferiority of non-white races. At the end of slavery, society valued European immigrants, which maintained and increased the inequality between Blacks and whites in Brazil (Guimarães, 1999; Monsma, 2010; Souza, 2004, 2008; Tenório, 2010).

Between 1880 and 1930, according to Andrews, whitening via European immigration was an ideal of all American countries colonized by Spain or Portugal between the sixteenth and nineteenth centuries. The objective was to whiten what the author defines as Afro-Latin America, that is, a whole set of countries deeply shaped by the African presence and the historical experience of plantation agriculture. Only between the decades of 1940 and 1960 did the federal governments pass anti-discrimination laws in Brazil (1951), Venezuela (1951), Panama (1956), and Costa Rica, even if they were never effectively applied (Andrews, 2004).

It was definitely not easy to maintain such an Africanized tradition in Araraquara and Rio Claro, where the strong presence of immigrants and their descendants, especially from Italy and Germany, produced a collective identity that pushed their racism against the Blacks of the city as a form to extend the celebration of fascism and Nazism locally. Despite the efforts of the state and sectors of the national intellectual elite to build the race of Brazilians, in Rio Claro, in practice, throughout the twentieth century, Black was still Black, and white was still white, each with their own symbols, sociability and spatiality around the respective race. Moreover, the Black woman (and Blacks in general) still faced wide-open racism by white people in the local context (Souza, 2004, 2008).

According to Andrews (1998), "it is through social clubs that middle-class Brazilians build their bonds and strengthen ties with people who can do 'favors' to each other" (Andrews,

1998, p. 267). For the author, social clubs for the white middle class are a form of integration and social progress for whites, becoming a difficult barrier for Blacks, who were not admitted to these clubs and were excluded from interpersonal contact and social networks that could enable them to get, among other things, better jobs and income. In addition to this economic aspect, non-admission to white clubs also had a psychological effect and negatively affected the self-esteem of Black people, as many were barred or expelled from these white places (Andrews, 1998, p. 269). This situation led to the formation of several essential Black clubs in the state of São Paulo.

Under this context of prejudice, we think of São Paulo's Black identity through the concrete experiences of discrimination against Blacks that led to the creation of Black associations and the realization of cultural gatherings. Such events offered Black people the possibility of experiencing the feeling of being Black without any interdiction or discrimination, being among their racial group in structured environments designed to recognize beauty and raise Black self-esteem.

Black women's beauty in the racial sites of Araraquara and Rio Claro

The Black presence in Araraquara and Rio Claro is directly connected to the slave labor that sustained the coffee farms in the west of the state of São Paulo. The medium-size cities in the countryside of the state had railroads as a form of social mobility for immigrants (mostly Italians) and the local small "Black middle class," who constructed organizations that congregated Black people at municipal and neighboring events, especially those dedicated to strengthening Black women's self-esteem.

Araraquara has a traditional and widely known event called "Baile do Carmo" ("Carmo's ball," named after the neighborhood where it takes place and also because of the celebration in honor of "Nossa Senhora do Carmo"), which is a resource for thinking, event directly linked to Black women's identity and self-esteem. Between 1930 and 1987, Black recreational associations in Araraquara, mostly founded by Black railroad workers and public employees, held the balls at rented white club saloons, reuniting hundreds of people from different families of the city and region, including Rio Claro. Accompanied by the big orchestras of that time, Black community members gathered at these balls, creating a space for Black sociability, memory and identity (Tenório, 2010, 2013).

When interviewed about the ball, people largely used such Portuguese words as "elegância" or "chique" to describe the "Baile do Carmo", especially women of different ages, who thus characterized the gala night of the event, which currently holds festivities that last several days. In Portuguese, "elegância" means "grace, dress, manner and forms [of] distinction," whereas "chique" stands for "beautiful, elegant, good taste". These words convey the idea of distinction and refinement, which for a population used to having a deprecated image, represents the way they want to be known and how they want to demonstrate knowledge and mastery of social behavior (Tenório, 2010, 2013).

According to Gomes, "by establishing leisure territories similar to those of whites – regarding the codes of conduct and conquered status symbols (in clothing and language, above all) – but exclusively frequented by blacks, the distance to 'equality' was shortened" (Gomes, 2005, pp. 38–9). In other words, Black recreational associations sought to reduce the inequality between whites and Blacks, even in their forms of leisure. If whites perform their balls, Blacks also perform their own; more than that, Black dances, like the "Baile do Carmo", occurred in white spaces as a form of occupation and protagonism in the space of

Figure 31.1 Photograph from a 1960s edition of "Top Ten Ball." (Tenório, 2013, 104)

the other. It is worth mentioning that these sites are best suited for the gala evening of "Baile do Carmo" as they can accommodate a large number of people, but also due to their location, architecture, status, and what they had represented in the past: forbidden spaces for this population (Figure 31.1).

During the 1950s, the Black community of Araraquara held beauty pageants for the most elegant Black women, who anxiously waited the whole year for the moment of doing their hair and choosing their outfit in order to feel pretty and elegant within their community. According to former directors of the Black clubs of Araraquara, there was a "Top Ten Ball" during the 1960s, when associates elected the top 10 most elegant Black women (Figure 31.2).

The "Baile do Carmo" is still held nowadays and, since the 1990s, has elected a Ball Muse – a young Black woman chosen for her beauty and resourcefulness – a reminder of the Black beauty pageants promoted by many Brazilian Black associations at least since the beginning of the twentieth century. According to one of the elected muses, Doralice, the event gives visibility to Black beauty and the ball:

> It was really good! People treat you well wherever you go; everyone says "she was the muse of the Baile do Carmo". We are well known. As the ball is very famous, we become kind of famous too, so most people know me because of it, and they say "Dora was the muse of the Baile do Carmo". So that's it. It was good for me.
>
> *(Tenório, 2010, p. 98).*

The election of the muse is also a site where the contestants do not suffer any discrimination. When questioned on whether she had already gone through any prejudice or difficulty at fashion shows, Doralice affirmed:

Figure 31.2 Photograph from a 1960s edition of "Top Ten Ball." (Tenório, 2013, 105)

> Always! Mostly when I used to walk the runways, there was always prejudice! But not at the Baile do Carmo, because the event is for us, so no one feels different, people treat each other well. But I did suffer in many places.
>
> *(Tenório, 2010, pp. 98–9)*

Through Doralice's speech, we are able to see the identification with the event when she says that there is no prejudice because the ball is "for us," and hence, she feels protected in the "Baile do Carmo" environment. To Doralice, there is no difference between the participants, a distinct situation from what she has seen doing other jobs as a model. The election of the muse and the existence of the Black balls that value the beauty of Black women have been crucial sites of resistance and strengthening, in the past and in the present. In Rio Claro, the Black population spent the majority of the twentieth century holding their dancing and civic activities in rented or lent spaces, wishing to build their own physical space as the Italians, Germans and Japanese had done in the city. For the Rio Claro Black community, the dream of their own house would only become real in the late 1960s and the beginning of the 1970s.

Parallel to the development of Nazi and fascist communities, the identification mechanism continued to be present at the Black associations of Rio Claro. The 1936 carnival, for instance, had the participation of the following Black societies: "Sociedade Dançante 28 de Setembro" ("September 28th Dancing Society"), "Sociedade Dançante Progresso da Mocidade" ("Youth Progress Dancing Society") and "Sociedade Dançante Uma Noite de Alegria" ("A Night of Joy

Figure 31.2 Continued

Dancing Society"). The newspaper *Cidade de Rio Claro* covered the preparations for the parades and radically innovated the reports by printing in its pages a few clichés (the equivalent to photography at that time) of members from the city's "color societies":

> After the three-day carnival, the Black champion "Progresso da Mocidade" held a ball where they named their two carnival cups (won at the 1935 and 1936 carnivals), at a ceremony with the presence of the Black queens Sebastiana Pedro and Lourdes Calixto, both symbols of Black women's beauty. A caravan of Black women came from São Carlos, a nearby city, to honor the solemnity.
>
> *(Souza, 2008)*

Between the 1950s and the 1960s, the movement of the Rio Claro Black collective was intense around the election of the race queens. Such movement meant three things: (1) the valuation of self-image and the revitalization of race identity through the mirroring of one another; (2) an answer to the other beauty queen pageants of the city, which mostly did not offer space for Black representation; (3) an answer to the racial discrimination that particularly hit Black women, such as newspaper ads for white-only maids and white-only wet nurse, for instance. In this period, the Black organizations of Rio Claro (and of the state of São Paulo) aimed at pairing race and beauty, especially for the eyes of a larger society. Black people fostered their own dignity as they valued and crowned Black women – the triple discriminated element of the race (Souza, 2008) (Figure 31.3).

In Rio Claro, there was a Black soccer team named Tamoio, famous among Black and white people in the city. In 1955, when a contest for the Sports Queen of Rio Claro was held, Tamoio

Figure 31.3 First Black queen of Rio Claro city, 1951. *Diário do Rio Claro* newspaper, December 22, 1951 (Souza, 2008, 172)

Figure 31.4 The candidate of Tamoio Futebol Clube as the queen of sports in Rio Claro city. *Diário do Rio Claro* newspaper, December 8, 1955 (Souza, 2008, 175)

was the only sports club to present a Black contestant for the title — a direct reflection of the club's racial composition. Five sports clubs took part in the pageant, and votes from supporters determined the results. The Black competitor from Tamoio reached third place, not so far from the first two white misses in terms of voting (Souza, 2008) (Figure 31.4).

The participation of the Tamoio club in a universal pageant (that is, one that was not held exclusively for Black people) was deeply connected to race dignity and representation. The associates and supporters of Tamoio were aware that in a majority white city, filled with discrimination and racism, a Black queen had no chance of winning. However, that was precisely what motivated Tamoio: as a Black club, they wanted to rebel against the racial status given by the majority of the population. Thus, presenting a "unique" contestant at a "universal" pageant required Tamoio (1) to have enough racial self-esteem to refuse to select a pattern candidate (in terms of race) and (2) to mobilize their members to support their Black queen, especially through voting (which partially worked, as the Tamoio queen was not far behind the winners). In other words, the participation of Tamoio meant a racial struggle for dignity, value and representation of Blacks in a majority white space (Souza, 2008).

However, both the Tamoio club and the José do Patrocínio club (named after the Brazilian Black doctor and journalist José do Patrocínio, a key figure for the abolition movement in Brazil) held internal contests for the election of race queens instead of taking part at "universal" pageants in Rio Claro. This happened not only because there was no real chance of a Black victory at the majority white beauty pageants in the city but also because these institutions were resistant sites of production and propagation of Black racial identity, which guaranteed their own collective existence in a white world (Souza, 2008).

The beauty queens had pivotal roles in the construction of these permanent sites in Rio Claro as the main figures of balls, lunches, cocktail parties and festivals. During the 1960s, while the Black is Beautiful movement was rising around the world, the Black beauty queens of Rio Claro were central for the establishment of the Black clubs and associations (Souza, 2008).

The beauty of the Black woman in the context of the Ilê Aiyê African block in the city of Salvador (Bahia, Brazil)

Unlike the state of São Paulo, Bahia was the first place in Brazil to receive African men and women in the sixteenth century for slave work at the sugar cane plantations. Currently, Bahia has a majority Black population and has become some sort of "Africa" in Brazil because of both the number of Blacks and the lasting African cultural traditions. It is described as "Black Rome" by travelers due to its central location of African-based religions, much like Rome's central location for Catholicism. In the twentieth century, Bahia has taken an important role in the constitution of African-American anthropology, which has considered Salvador, the capital of Bahia, as a place where the black culture has kept African traits at larger degrees than any other location. While in Araraquara and Rio Claro, in the state of São Paulo, the Black associations of the twentieth century fought racism by demonstrating to white society that Black people had equal abilities to dress and behave elegantly, in Salvador, the cultural Black associations arose during the 1970s with a Black beauty ideal directly connected to the ethnic and racial affirmation process linked to traditions from Candomblé, a religion of African origins.

> The intention was to affirm blackness as something positive; "The most beautiful of all", "black beauty"; to contest the myth of racial democracy; to denounce the innumerous racist practices and, most of all, the lack of reparation public policies. The expression "Black Rome" gains a political meaning, that is, a site of blackness and resistance.
>
> *(Silva, 2018, pp. 9–10)*

According to Chagas (2001, 2004), the bonds with Africa were vehemently affirmed in Bahia during the 1970s. The Afro blocs, the Black organizations of Bahia during carnival season, produced new ideas about Black pride based in African traditions that were rebuilt in Brazil, along with the Black is Beautiful movement from the United States and the Ubuntu principle against apartheid in South Africa. One of the most traditional Afro blocs of Salvador is "Ilê Aiyê" (recognized as "O mais belo dos belos", meaning "The most beautiful of all"). Founded with female protagonism in 1974, its trajectory is aligned to "the history of black organizations in Brazil and their attempt to promote blacks in a society marked by racial inequality" (Chagas, 2001, p. 93).

Ilê Aiyê was established through the ideals of the Black religious leader Hilda Dias dos Santos. Known as Mãe Hilda Jitolu, the ialorixá (priestess) became famous for her social actions and the struggle for the expansion of bonds between Brazilians and Africans, which was decisive for the formation of the block.

> She was responsible for the creation of the Literacy School in 1988, encouraging candom-blé followers to study. The actions of Mãe Hilda served as a stimulus to the execution of the Pedagogical Extension Project of Ilê Aiyê in 1995, that acted [like a] public school in the Liberdade neighborhood, in Salvador.
>
> *(Vieira, 2018)*

The Ilê Aiyê block annually holds the "Noite da Beleza Negra" ("Night of Black Beauty") in order to elect the queen of the block, the "Deusa de Ébano" ("Ebony Goddess") for the carnival – a similar event to the ones from Araraquara and Rio Claro described earlier in this chapter. The "Noite da Beleza Negra" happens in January and is one of the most important moments for the Ilê Aiyê block, which has promoted the event since the 1980s, and is one of the biggest events of this nature in the country. The contestants must present themselves with outfits and hairstyles of strong African inspiration, accompanied by the block percussion music. "It is essential to have dark skin to participate. The blacker, the better. The winner will be the queen of the block through the whole carnival" (Chagas, 2001, p. 152).

The "Noite da Beleza Negra" is intended to promote the self-esteem of Black women. Unlike many other beauty pageants in the country, at this contest, women do not present themselves in swimsuits but in clothes made of African fabric, with elaborated hairstyles and outfits of symbolic colors based on Candomblé religion. "The competition is based on African notions of beauty, instead of the beauty patterns in Brazil. The one who best dances and represents African-Brazilian culture, wins" (Dias, 2019, s/p) (Figure 31.5).

The words of Daniela Nobre, Ilê "Ebony Goddess" of 2019, deeply express the meaning of Black beauty:

> Black beauty is not a fight for the first position; it is about female empowerment. We are all pretty, but this title values the woman. It is not financially rewarding or anything. It is just the recognition of winning a competition where my beauty is accepted. I do not need to have a sharp nose, or white skin, or big buttocks, neither expose my body. I became a Goddess due to all of me, my dance, my beauty, my wrinkled nose. It is surreal.
>
> *(Dias, 2019)*

Final considerations

In Brazil, the heart of the African diaspora, marked by racism and slavery perpetrated by Europe, there has always been the idea that white people represent what is beautiful, sublime and aesthetically positive, while Black people represent what is ugly and aesthetically negative. In such contexts, Black women from Araraquara and Rio Claro, in the state of São Paulo, and Salvador, in the state of Bahia, have challenged these representations by entering competitions that affirm them as symbols of beauty, royalty and positive identity among Black communities.

Figure 31.5 "41st Night of the Black Beauty of Ilê Aiyê, 2020." Image credit: Josafá Araújo – Fafá Ancestral Rescue Photography.

Naturally, female beauty events created inside a male chauvinist, patriarchal, capitalist and Eurocentric society will raise many sociological questions about the absence of autonomy of women as decision and power agents. At the same time, the mirroring of identity and positive representation matter to Black women, historically affected by structural disadvantages of combined race, gender and class categories, which will influence them from early childhood to elder age. The exaltation of Black women then assumes a character of protest and contestation.

At the close of the second decade of the twenty-first century, Brazil is governed by right-wing conservatives who consistently diminish the fight against racism and discrimination under false claims that these problems are exaggerated and that political minorities such as Blacks and LGBT are seeking advantages over the rest of the population. The deaths of cleaning assistant Claudia Silva Ferreira in 2014 (killed by white policeman and dragged for over 300 meters by a police car in Rio de Janeiro) and of councilwoman Marielle Franco in 2018 (assassinated in Rio de Janeiro by white policemen with the apparent involvement of white male politicians) are terrible and fatal examples of so many Black women whose lives are daily ripped away in Brazil. In such a context, celebrating the life and crowning the beauty of Black women constitutes a challenging, pedagogical and political manifest that definitely matters.

References

Andrews, Georg Reid. *Negros e brancos em São Paulo (1888–1988)*. Tradução Magda Lopes, Bauru: Edusc, 1998.
Andrews, George Reid. *Afro-Latin America (1800-2000)*. New York: Oxford University Press, 2004.

Chagas, Patrícia de S.P. *Em busca da mama África: identidade africana, cultura negra e política branca na Bahia.* *2001, 316f. Tese (Doutorado em Ciências Sociais) – IFCH.* Campinas: Unicamp, 2001.

Chagas, Patrícia de S. P. *Reinvenções da África na Bahia.* São Paulo: Annablume, 2004.

Dias, Guilherme Soares. *Beleza Negra: a noite em que todos somos deuses do ébano.* 29 fev. 2019, Disponível em: <https://www.geledes.org.br/beleza-negra-a-noite-em-que-todos-somos-deuses-do-ebano/> Acesso em: 15 out. 2019.

Gomes, Flávio. *Negros e política (1888 – 1937).* Rio de Janeiro: Zahar, 2005.

Gonçalves, Gabriela da Costa. *Bloco Afro Ilê Aiyê elege a 'Deusa do Ébano' 2019.* 19 fev. 2019, Disponível em: <http://www.palmares.gov.br/?p=53443>Acesso em: 10 jan. 2019.

Guimarães, Antonio Sérgio Alfredo. *Racismo e Anti-Racismo no Brasil.* São Paulo: Editora 34, 1999.

Hanchard, Michael. *Orfeu e o Poder: Movimento Negro no Rio e São Paulo (1945-1988).* Rio de Janeiro: EdUERJ, 2001.

Monsma, Karl. Vantagens de imigrantes e desvantagens de negros: emprego, propriedade, estrutura familiar e alfabetização depois da abolição no oeste paulista. *Dados* [online]. 2010, vol.53, n.3 [cited 2020-11-13], pp.509-543. HYPERLINK "https://doi.org/10.1590/S0011-52582010000300001" doi: 10.1590/S0011-52582010000300001

Silva, Maria Alice P. da. Salvador-Roma Negra: cidade diaspórica. In: *Congresso Brasileiro de Pesquisadores Negros, 18,* 2018, Uberlândia. Disponível em: <https://www.copene2018.eventos.dype.com.br/resources/anais/8/1530393388_ARQUIVO_Salvador-RomaNegra.pdf> Acesso em: 15 out.2019.

Souza, Flávia Alessandra de. *Poder Local e Representação Política: Negros e Imigrantes no Interior Paulista (Um estudo sobre o Município de Rio Claro-SP).* Dissertação, Departamento de Pós-graduação em Ciências Sociais, Universidade Federal de São Carlos, 2004.

Souza, Flávia Alessandra de. *Organizações e Espaços da Raça no Oeste Paulista: Movimento Negro e Poder Local em Rio Claro (dos anos 1930 aos anos 1960).* 2008. 231f. Tese (Doutorado em Sociologia) – Universidade Federal de São Carlos. 2008.

Souza, Joyce Gonçalves Restier da Costa. *"Nós também somos belas" A Construção Social do Corpo e Da Beleza em Mulheres Negras.* Dissertação De Mestrado Do Programa De Pós-Graduação Em Relações Étnico-Raciais-CEFET/RJ., 2015. Disponível em: doi:I10.13140/RG.2.2.33536.94724.

Telles, Edward. Repensando as relações de raça no Brasil. In: *Teoria e Pesquisa,* 42–43, 2003, 131–160, Departamento de Ciências Sociais, Universidade Federal de São Carlos.

TENÓRIO, *Valquíria Pereira. Baile do Carmo: festa, movimento negro e política das identidades negras em Araraquara-SP.* Tese de Doutorado em Sociologia. São Carlos: Programa de Pós-Graduação em Sociologia, UFSCar, 2010.

TENÓRIO, *Valquíria Pereira. Baile do Carmo: memória, sociabilidade e identidade étnico-racial em Araraquara.* Belo Horizonte: Nandyala, 2013.

Vieira, Kauê. *Você não pode fechar 2018 sem ver a 'Ocupação Ilê Aiyê', primeiro bloco afro do Brasil.* 16 dez. 2018, Disponível em: <https://www.geledes.org.br/voce-nao-pode-fechar-2018-sem-ver-a-ocupacao-ile-aiye-primeiro-bloco-afro-do-brasil/>. Acesso em: 15 out. 2019.

32

Hail to the chefs

Black women's pedagogy, sacred kitchenspaces, and Afro-Diasporic religions

Elizabeth Pérez

For well over a century, Afro-Diasporic religions have been depicted as synonymous with sacrifice. Although the etymology of the word stems from the Latin term for "holy" (*sacer*), popular representations have cast life offerings to Black deities as anything but. Along with spirit possession and zombies, "voodoo" sacrifice became spectacularized when Hollywood was in its infancy. Scenes of frenzied carnage in films, travelogues, and other literary texts sought to justify repeated military occupations of Haiti by the United States and its other "interventions" throughout the Caribbean. Such tableaux exploited earlier European renderings of the 1791 Haitian Revolution not as an "unthinkably" coordinated war of decolonization but as an orgy of violence.[1] Generations of historians rehearsed nineteenth-century reports that the uprising commenced among maroons and enslaved participants in a Vodou ceremony at Bois Caïman, culminating in the killing of a black pig by the *mambo* Cécile Fatiman.[2] The nation of Haiti later reappropriated *Bwa Kayiman* as its origin myth, yet elevating this narrative had the unintended effect of reinscribing sacrifice as the focal point – the veritable *poto mitan* – of Afro-Diasporic ritual.[3]

Cécile Fatiman purportedly ordered those assembled before her to seal their insurrectionary pact by drinking the slain pig's blood. Captured by innumerable visual artists and writers, this parody of the Roman Catholic Eucharistic meal featured the ultimate non-kosher and non-halal substance, thus inverting the three major patriarchal religions at once. The story of *Bwa Kayiman* also enlarged existing stereotypes of Caribbean religions that are still with us today. For instance, in the United States, the criminalization of Afro-Cuban traditions such as Yorùbá-inspired Lucumí/Santería has focused on allegations of animal abuse and improper disposal of sacrificial waste. Even the 1993 Supreme Court case that established practitioners' right to perform sacrifice served to buttress its discursive placement as the axis around which Afro-Diasporic religions revolve.[4] Having internalized this conceptual schema, detractors as well as neophytes tend to overemphasize the frequency and centrality of ritual slaughter. A case in point: the Harlem-born rapper/singer Azealia Banks caused an uproar in late 2016 when she shared an Instagram video of a closet encrusted with the residue of dead poultry. A novice initiate in the Kongo-inspired Afro-Cuban tradition of Palo Mayombe, Banks said she was about to clean up "three years' worth of *brujería* [witchcraft]." At the end of the clip, Banks quipped, "Real witches do real things," inadvertently reinforcing the notion of bloodshed as the authentic core of Black Atlantic traditions.[5]

No accounts to date have asked what became of the pig at Bois Caïman. Had it been a Vodou rite according to contemporary precedent, the pig would have become pork. Women would have cooked it after seeing to its meticulous washing, skinning, and butchering. (By "women," here and throughout, I mean both cisgender and transgender women – except when otherwise specified – and include all sexual orientations.) The deities (or *lwa*) would have accepted their share of the fried or roasted meat, and then, their human co-conspirators would have feasted on their favorite morsels. Sacrifice does feature in Afro-Diasporic religions, but an accurate understanding of them involves much greater attention to food preparation and the practitioners placed in charge of their kitchens. While sacrifice transpires in a matter of minutes, historians of religions have privileged its analysis due to its theological currency and normative performance by men. Cooking, on the other hand, often lasts hours, but it awaits comparable scholarly interest due principally to its association with women's work. To inquire into what happens after the moment of slaughter, then, is to open up a scandalously delayed investigation into one obscured aspect of Black women's religious histories.

The "real things" that Black women do in Afro-Diasporic religions are the subject of the present chapter. Women and gay men of African descent have historically governed kitchen-spaces in initiatory Black Atlantic traditions. In what follows, I concentrate on their cooking to highlight an undervalued modality of racialized and gendered religious labor. I argue that in kitchenspaces, elders have disabused newcomers of their misconceptions about sacrifice and inaugurated the embodiment of sacred knowledges. Drawing on ethnographic fieldwork in a predominantly African American community devoted to Afro-Cuban traditions, I underscore the corporeal enskillment that occurs as practices of care and deference dovetail with educational processes. I then outline the Afro-Diasporic religious pedagogy elaborated by (and largely for) Black women that has supported the worship of African deities in the twentieth century. I close by problematizing the kitchen as a site fraught with tensions, the reclamation of which must be approached with caution and several grains of salt.

Stirring the pot: portrayal vs. praxis

By the dawn of the twentieth century, Black Atlantic traditions that had crystallized during the transatlantic slave trade were beset on all sides. Religious practitioners fell victim to incarceration, mob violence, and other forms of white supremacist terror. Tabloids and prestigious journals alike helped to circulate rumors of child abduction and murder that endangered formerly enslaved peoples' lives and imperiled their livelihoods. In the United States, regional varieties of conjure and rootwork endured in the South and spread North and West through the Great Migration, but the last "voodoo" communities in New Orleans had vanished in the wake of dogged legal prosecution in the 1850s and 1860s.[6] In the Anglophone Caribbean, so-called obeah and "high science" continued to be outlawed. "Witch crazes" in Cuba saw to the arrest, lynching, and garroting of Black men and women called *brujos*. In Brazil, Candomblé temples (*terreiros*) fought to be decriminalized. The ban on Winti in Suriname held fast until 1971.

Genealogies of West and Central African religions in the Americas tend to stress their centuries-old provenance. Their roots are undoubtedly profound, some stretching into the late fifteenth century. However, the early 1900s was a crucial period of consolidation and efflorescence that would determine their future in a post-emancipatory world. In Cuba, the railroad facilitated the expansion of Lucumí beyond Havana, Regla, and Matanzas into the far hinterlands, as priests journeyed to initiate protégés in provinces dominated by Kongo-inspired religious formations and Espiritismo; train travel increased the uniformity of these and Yorùbá-inspired practices.[7] In Candomblé, terreiros contended with the rise of Umbanda as a rival tradition and confronted concerns over the initiation of white Brazilians and foreigners. Vodou in Haiti – post-emancipatory since 1804 – faced the outrages of U.S. Marines and those of local Christian "antisuperstition" campaigners. Mail-order catalogs from such enterprises as Chicago's De Laurence, Scott, and Company distributed obscure esoteric tracts and "magical" merchandise that would find ready niches in Black Atlantic traditions.

In this period, practitioners made common cause with scholars to collaborate in their documentation, creating a textual "ethnographic interface" that redounded to the benefit of both parties.[8] Scholars such as Black anthropologists Zora Neale Hurston and Katherine Dunham obtained access to coveted information, while practitioners gained some degree of advocacy. To counter the hegemonic emphasis on sacrifice, informants accentuated the facets of their traditions that aligned them with those recognized as "world religions," unanimously characterized by the leadership of literate male clerics. Although scholars consulted informants with a veritable Whitman's Sampler of racialized genders and sexual identities, heteronormative analyses based on the testimony of straight, cisgender men held sway. The politics of respectability demanded that these traditions be distanced from misrepresentations dripping with misogynoir.[9] Unfavorable portrayals of Black women at the stove equated them with medieval witches, Caribbean witch doctors, African cannibals at their cauldrons, and hoodoo doctors "laying tricks." The flip side of these visual and literary tropes was the aproned figure of the pathetically acquiescent mammy.[10]

None of these caricatures projected legitimate religious authority or sacred power to the publics addressed by them. Consequently, cooking did not go unobserved, but it was not thematized. The exceptions prove the rule; for example, the ubiquity of food and cooking in Ruth Landes' 1947 *The City of Women* was undoubtedly a factor in its reception as unserious and steeped in petty minutiae, despite the anthropological evidence it tendered for her thesis that Bahian Candomblé was a matriarchate.[11] Similarly, the hunger of Afro-Diasporic gods was reduced to a thin metaphor and held at arms' length so as to attenuate their association with bloodlust and other crude appetites. In reality, these deities require feeding in rituals of consecration and ordination to abide within objects that function as material instantiations of their sovereignty. The gods also request animals (differentiated by age, size, sex, and color) through divination and in the oracular speech of initiates possessed by them. Yet their sacrificial remains must be cooked according to tradition-specific protocols, unless the deities explicitly dictate otherwise.

Although Black women have occupied prominent positions as diviners, dancers, praise singers, and other types of religious virtuosi, their careers as executive chefs and kitchenhands have been erased. This restaurant industry terminology may be anachronistic, but as trailblazing culinary historian Jessica B. Harris once said, "I work in a cuisine that (falsely) only has cooks, very few chefs."[12] How much of their labor has been expunged from the record simply through an author's choice of the passive voice ("meat was cooked," "dishes were made," "meals were prepared")? A handful of Black Atlantic traditions have deemed kitchen managers valuable enough to bestow titles on them: in Lucumí, *alashé* or *cocinera/o*; in Vodou, *hounsi cuisinièr/e*; in Candomblé, *iya bassê, iabassé, ayabasè,* or *abassê*; and among Spiritual Baptists in Trinidad, *husie,* a locution that may be etymologically related to *hounsi.*[13] Not all such positions have been held by women; in the Afro-Cuban initiatory brotherhood of Abakuá, the *nkandembo* has been a cisgender man (presumably heterosexual, given the tradition's defining patriarchal masculinity). Yet we may confidently extrapolate that, by and large, it is women who have preserved time-tested recipes and introduced inestimable innovations.

Letting it percolate and getting it right

Kitchenspace refers to the domestic zone of food preparation and consumption customarily demarcated by women.[14] Michael W. Twitty writes lyrically of ancestral African kitchenspaces:

> The little hearth – located under heaven or a thatch structure or building used during the rainy season – was itself a ritual space, an altar, a face of spirits, usually a female entity representing motherhood and nurture, the pot itself a kind of womb. To be certain, many of us cooked this way in the slave quarters in our swept yards and at the edges of the fields.[15]

The mythologies of Afro-Diasporic religions describe the gods themselves as fixing meals, magic, and medicine in open-air kitchenspaces. Although practitioners envision most of those doing so as female, it is imperative not to essentialize the customary. Traditions of Yorùbá-inspired orisha/orixá worship cast the hypermasculine blacksmith Ogún – master of the forge, railroad track, and knife-edge – as fixing meals for himself; his erratic relations with women mean that he must know how to cook. The Lucumí Ogún's consecrated objects dwell inside a small three-legged cauldron, symbolic of the life-kindling transformation wrought by his primordial heat.

For several years, the kitchenspace at the heart of my research was to be found in Ilé Laroye, a Chicago-based Lucumí, Palo Monte, and Espiritismo community. Led since 1986 by African American diviner and praise-singer Ashabi Moseley, Ilé Laroye has a sizeable contingent of non-Black Latinx, white American, and LGBTQ "godchildren."[16] It differs from Black separatist Ifá communities in maintaining and cultivating ties with Cuban elders – initiates with seniority – embraced as the inheritors of a precolonial Yorùbá tradition passed down through oral tradition. For the most part, my interlocutors had embarked on the worship of African deities after the Mariel boatlift of 1980 brought unprecedented numbers of Afro-Cuban religious practitioners to the United States. Many members of Ilé Laroye had been brought up as Roman Catholics. Some had been adherents of the Black Spiritual Church or the Black Nationalist Pan African Orthodox Christian Church, launched by theologian Albert Cleage as Detroit's Shrine of the Black Madonna in 1967.

One of my main interlocutors was the alashé Arlene Stevens when she ran the kitchenspace of Asabi's South Side bungalow. Arlene called herself "American African," although she hastened to acknowledge, "the world isn't ready for that yet."[17] Anthropologist Akissi Britton writes of her ethnographic site, a Brooklyn-based house of orisha worship,

> As people worked feverishly, exhaustively, yet lovingly in the kitchen they followed the lead of women who had "come up in the movement" and who approached ocha work with the same diligence and devotion as they did with nation-building in Black Nationalist organizations ... The women leading this kitchen were/are fierce, loving, protective and very much about their business.[18]

Britton's description fits elders like Arlene remarkably well. On one occasion, she told me that she nearly broke down crying when she saw one of her son's new textbooks, filled with pages and pages of "positive, beautiful" images of Black folks, "and that was the *math book.*" She said she was one of those who had fought hard to get any representation of people of color in school books, that "we" had "sat on a cold stone bed in jail" to get there, and it made her choke up to see how far "we" had come.

Arlene added that she had been riding the bus recently and overheard two young women dismiss the Black Panthers as a street gang. She let them go back and forth, then interrupted them and delivered a brief history lesson before exiting the bus. In the same discussion, Arlene excoriated "snooty," "Blacker-than-thou," "*Black*," ostentatiously Afrocentric "upper middle class" types at her son's elementary school whose "mixed metaphor" idea of Black nationalism had them reciting libations that started in Swahili and ended in Yorùbá. She blasted the laminated posters of Kemetic gods at her son's school as promoting a "blended, homogenous-*ized*" view of Africa without regard to "structure or tradition," an anachronistic pastiche rooted in an ideology that inculcates pride at the expense of history and geography. Sporting twisted silver locs, spiral-carved bone earrings, and elegant bogolan caftans, she bemoaned the fact that her acquaintances could embrace Africa culturally but not religiously thanks to everything that the phrase "Dark Continent" connoted.

Arlene availed herself of these critical registers to verbalize her relationship with Africanity, yet her bond with it materialized most vibrantly in kitchenspaces. She and other elders approached food preparation as one of the most tangible connections with the Afro-Cuban past that engendered Lucumí and considered Yorùbá recipes tailored to the deities' tastes a sociocultural archive. They spared no pains in schooling their juniors on the obligation to handle sacred cuisine with fidelity to hallowed convention. Their education to this effect socialized outsiders into the community once they proceeded to offer assistance for ceremonies instead of simply turning up for scheduled divination sessions and celebratory drum rituals. Arlene put newcomers to work on such "inglorious and unglamorous" tasks as chopping onions, steaming banana leaves, boiling grits, cracking coconuts, and plucking poultry.[19] Her apprentices acquired the expertise to systematically butcher birds and, occasionally, to quarter ram and goat.[20] Dependable regulars attained proficiency in the intricacies of braising.

Elders defined practitioners' moral and material nourishment as dependent upon the alimentation of their spiritual patrons. They classified portions of the blood, sacred viscera, and extremities of sacrifices as *iñalés* or *ashés* (plural), meaning "food for the gods." Sensorily and affectively demanding, the rigors of "taking out" or "pulling" *ashés* furnished the opportunity to learn Lucumí from the inside out – beginning with the fact that blood sacrifice (*ebó eyé* or *ebó woní*) belongs to a much larger category of cleansing and curative ritual endeavor called *ebó*. Practitioners understand more than a few ebó to be a feeding of different entities, from the orishas to the ancestral dead (*egún*) to the deity of one's own head (*Orí*). Most often, they receive fruit, honey, desserts, and savory dishes heavy on vegetables, legumes, and grains. Elders validated newcomers' squeamishness toward ashés but insisted that involuntary emotions like disgust arise from sociocultural conditioning. Such reflexes had to be un-learned in order for the orishas to get fed. Elders taught that orishas need ashés to render their own primordial substance and vital energy (*aché*) communally accessible for the purposes of individual healing and institutional reproduction.

Yet the gastronomic pleasure of the gods was not merely about good intentions or surface appeal. Food had to be right: correctly cleaned, cut, and cooked. Elders coached newcomers to remove feathers from fowl and excise excess flesh from ashés as if an orisha might possess an initiate's body at any moment and wish to consume the immolated offerings. For elders, the health, safety, and satisfaction of a real person was at stake. This stringent standard of care entailed submission to the religious hierarchy as well as the performance of deference, conceptualized as "a set of practices that has ceremonialized elders' privilege as teachers."[21] Ideally, the anticipation of elders' judgments would lead to discernment of the orishas' desires. If newcomers internalized this ethos of care, they would graduate from clients of Ilé Laroye's ritual specialists to servants of the orishas (who would have become "real persons" in their own right). Such practitioners would eventually become initiates.

A pedagogy of kitchenspace

> Pedagogies of the Sacred are pedagogies of Crossing.
>
> —M. Jacqui Alexander[22]

Within kitchenspaces, elders have not only wedded the aesthetics of sacred cuisine to a code of ethics. They have deconstructed and reassembled the corporeal sensoria of the uninitiated. By teaching cooking, elders have ingrained the proper postures of action to assume in engaging with deities, ancestors, and other entities. In so doing, they have equipped practitioners with synaesthetic training integral to the survival of Black Atlantic traditions in the midst of extraordinary external pressures. For these reasons, I submit that many of the mundane micropractices sustaining African deities in Diaspora have been culinary. This may sound like a bold claim, but I would go further and state that the religious pedagogy of Afro-Diasporic kitchenspaces has prioritized Black women as both teachers and students. Their methodologies have emphasized embodied memorization; scaffolding and sensorimotor emulation (learning-by-doing); dialogic learning among peers; somatic and emotional discipline; and the translation of "Diaspora Literacy" (as coined by VèVè Amasasa Clark) into what Joyce E. King calls "Heritage Knowledge (group memory)."[23]

Black women's pedagogy enabled Afro-Diasporic religions to emerge from the Middle Passage and cross over the borders of nation-states and other artificial boundaries into the twenty-first century. Key to their "teaching *through* culture" has been a reliance on Black Atlantic idioms and allusions to interpret religious experience.[24] For example, Ashabi's godchild Oshunleye once said that it was hypocritical for Christians to brand orisha worship "black magic" when as soon as Pope John Paul II died, she heard a woman on television saying that she'd lit a candle and was already praying to him. "He's gonna be workin'!" Oshunleye exclaimed, using the word *work* in the sense of achieving transformative results, especially through liturgical action. "Straight up *egún* [ancestor] worship," she shrugged.[25] While globalizing and transnational Afro-Diasporic religions have admitted racially and ethnically diverse practitioners, Black women have instructed them using verbal locutions and physical gestures that speak to those endowed with either Diaspora Literacy or Heritage Knowledge. Others have gotten it, or they haven't.

Oshunleye's words may seem like idle conversation, yet such undertheorized activities as cracking jokes and swapping anecdotes have effectively seasoned individuals into gendered and racialized forms of religious subjectivity.[26] "Chewing the fat" while cooking has tutored greenhorns and old heads alike on the deities' routine manifestation in everyday life. To cite perhaps the most consequential example, elders have tended to talk about their initiations in kitchenspaces. They have almost invariably narrated entry into the priesthood as an "unchosen choice," made solely to save their lives or those of family members, in the absence of any desire whatsoever to affiliate with the religion(s) in question. In Black Atlantic traditions, this speech genre has not just reported on experience; it has persuaded participants of the deities' phenomenal reality and their power over affliction.[27] Initiation stories have conveyed intersubjective frames of reference that interpellate (or "hail") listeners, sparking responses that herald the realization of themselves as religious subjects.

Among these subjects have been countless LGBTQ people. After her "retirement" from the kitchen, Arlene was succeeded as alashé by a tall, white, multiply tattooed and pierced gay man in his twenties with a slight Southern drawl and a Master of Fine Arts. It is beyond the scope of this chapter to do more than suggest the contributions of LGBTQ people in transmitting Black Atlantic traditions, but my archival and ethnographic research reveals that the sacred kitchen has been a queer space in which embattled religious formations have been re-membered and reproduced. The rapport between older women and more youthful gay men has flourished in the intensity and intimacy of kitchenspaces. The familial atmosphere of those far beyond Ilé Laroye's has recalled the "queer world-making" of urban "house culture" with adoptive mothers who feed, shelter, and perform publicly alongside their LGBTQ children.[28] This analogy is particularly apt given gay men's renown as possession mounts in drumming rituals and the importance of dance as a mode of worship, which lends itself to comparison with the sacred kitchen's complex choreographies.

Kindred kitchenspaces

In her kitchenspace ministry, Arlene followed in the footsteps of her Mississippi-born "she-ro" grandmother M'dear, the assistant pastor of a Black Spiritual Church and cook for the wealthy scion of a Chicago business dynasty. Arlene relished the parallels between their religious trajectories, replete with Diasporic linkages worthy of Ntozake Shange's 1998 gastronomic memoir *If I Can Cook/You Know God Can*. The sacred cuisines of Black Atlantic traditions share signature elements with those prized within Afro-Protestant denominations, from culinary techniques to table manners. Instead of measuring ingredients exactly, for example, elders "cook by 'vibration,'" as Vertamae Smart-Grosvenor puts it.[29] In Christian churches, as in Afro-Diasporic religions, Black women have been the chief organizers and unpaid caterers for the overwhelming majority of potlucks, cookouts, after-service repasts, and funeral "repasses"; similar statements may be made about food provisioning in the Nation of Islam and other Muslim groups.[30] Converting basements and backyards into kitchenspaces, Black women have made fellowship flavorful.

In seeking to honor their labor, caution must be exercised so as not to romanticize it. Even in Afro-Diasporic religions labeled "female normative," negative stereotypes cling to cooking, and gendered divisions of labor pose obstacles to equitable participation in disparate arenas.[31] Within houses of worship that restrict plucking poultry and cooking to cisgender women, their sequestration in kitchenspaces has blocked access to roles requiring apprenticeships to male elders. Tracey E. Hucks quoted one "senior priestess" in an African American house of worship as saying,

> I've been trying to get the odus [Ifá divination verses] and get the women to study the odus, but the men keep us busy cooking goat and STUFF and STUFF and STUFF. Women doing anything beyond the menial jobs is not encouraged in Ifa [the African American practice of Yorùbá traditional religion, also known as *Isese*]. Just sit up and look good, look cute.[32]

While I have argued here and elsewhere that this toil is hardly menial, its back-breaking quality cannot be denied, either now or in previous eras. Born in 1908, the Lucumí elder Pampa Patrocinia Reyes remembered her religious mentor's requests when he would incorporate Ogún in possession during multi-day drum feasts: "Ogún would come and say, 'Make food, make food, the party isn't over' … And we were tired, tired of plucking chicken and cooking those huge cauldrons of food, and cooking, and cooking, and serving food."[33]

Neither feminist nor Womanist approaches to Black women's identities in Afro-Diasporic religions can ignore the injustice of unwilling self-sacrifice. Not everyone who can take the heat in the kitchen will thrive in it. Bearing in mind the intersectionality of Black women's oppressions, we can deduce that even sacred kitchenspaces have harbored abuse and sexual harassment as well as "microaggressions" ranging from subtle denigration to the misgendering of nonbinary or transgender practitioners. Despite the argument advanced here concerning the indispensability of sensorimotor enskillment through cooking, Black Atlantic traditions hold out myriad paths to serving the spirits, gods, and ancestors. In every religious office Black women have held, they have found means of instilling content ("the knowledge tradition and alternative vision of society that Diaspora Literacy reveals as Heritage Knowledge") and method (an epistemology, nothing less than a way of knowing).[34]

Scholars understand too little about the contributions of Black women to the sacred cuisines of the African Diaspora. We remain ignorant about their precise impact on rituals characterized by multitudinous plates of food, such as Afro-Cuban *agban* (or *awán*) for the orishas Olokún and Babalú Ayé. We are acquainted with too few of the women who have commanded religious kitchenspaces, like Luz Barroso, who cooked in the ceremonies mounted by lineage founder Edmunda "Munda la grande" Rivero, initiated into Lucumí in 1896.[35] We know even less about the nonbinary people and gay men whose perceived proximity to women – due to gender presentation or sexual orientation alone – afforded them not only admission to kitchenspaces, but stewardship of them. While accolades during their lifetimes brought them no lasting fame, their names are embedded within lineages that practitioners may yet discover, excavate, and revitalize. The next generation stands ready to step into the fire.

Notes

1 Michel-Rolph Trouillot, *Silencing the Past: Power and the Production of History* (Boston: Beacon, 1995).
2 See Mintz and Trouillot 1995.
3 A *poto mitan* is the tall vertical post at the center of a *peristil* (a large ceremonial space adjacent to or inside a Vodou temple) around which practitioners dance and perform rituals.
4 Church of the Lukumi Babalu Aye, Inc. v. City of Hialeah, 508 U.S. 520 (1993).
5 Colin Stutz, "Has Azealia Banks been sacrificing chickens in her closet?" *Billboard*, December 30. www .billboard.com/articles/columns/hip-hop/7640587/azealia-banks-sacrificing-chickens-in-closet-vide o (accessed June 26, 2019).
6 Ina Johanna Fandrich, "Defiant African Sisterhoods: The Voodoo Arrests of the 1850s and 1860s in New Orleans," in Patrick Bellegarde-Smith, ed., *Fragments of Bone: Neo-African Religions in a New World* (Urbana: University of Illinois Press), 187–207. This is the era of "voodoo queen" Marie Laveau (ca. 1801–81), who appears to have escaped prosecution entirely, perhaps due to her close relationships with Roman Catholic clergy and members of the New Orleans elite. Laveau seems to have retired from her duties as a Vodou ritual specialist in 1869 and spent the rest of her life performing acts of charity among condemned prisoners and the infirm. See Carolyn Morrow Long, "New Orleans Voodoo" in *Spiritual Merchants: Religion, Magic, and Commerce* (Knoxville: University of Tennessee, 2001), 37–62; 270–9.
7 Jorge Luís Sánchez, *Los Alagbas* (unpublished manuscript, ca. 2004), 45–6.
8 See Stephan Palmié, *The Cooking of History: How Not to Study Afro-Cuban Religion* (Chicago: University of Chicago Press, 2013).
9 Evelyn Brooks Higginbotham, *Righteous Discontent: The Women's Movement in the Black Baptist Church, 1880–1920* (Cambridge: Harvard University Press, 1993); Moya Bailey, "They aren't talking about me …" *Crunk Feminist Collective*, March 14, 2010, www.crunkfeministcollective.com/2010/03/14/ they-arent-talking-about-me/ (accessed October 15, 2013); Moya Bailey and Trudy, "On Misogynoir: Citation, Erasure, and Plagiarism," *Feminist Media Studies* 18, no. 4 (2018): 762–8.
10 This is not to deny subversive literary, artistic, and scholarly reappropriations of the mammy figure, especially by African American women. In North American versions, she is desexualized, while Caribbean and Latin American instantiations endow the mammy with a ribald sense of humor and depict her smoking a cigar (as shown in different genres of blackface minstrelsy); in both contexts, it has been up to women of African descent to invest the mammy figure with dignity, power, and even Afro-Diasporic divinity. See Elizabeth Pérez, "Nobody's Mammy: Yemayá as Fierce Foremother in Afro-Cuban Religions," in Solimar Otero and Toyin Falola, eds., *Yemoja: Gender, Sexuality, and Creativity in the Latina/o and Afro-Atlantic Diasporas* (Albany: State University of New York Press), 1–20.
11 J. Lorand Matory, "Gendered Agendas: The Secrets Scholars Keep about Yoruba Atlantic Religion," *Gender and History* 15, no. 3 (2003): 409–39.

12 Baltasar Fra Molinero, Charles Isidore Nero, and Jessica B. Harris, "When Food Tastes Cosmopolitan: The Creole Fusion of Diaspora Cuisine: An Interview with Jessica B. Harris," *Callaloo* 30, no. 1 (2007): 293.

13 Kenneth Anthony Lum, *Praising His Name in the Dance: Spirit Possession in the Spiritual Baptist Faith and Orisha Work in Trinidad, West Indies* (Amsterdam: Harwood Academic Publishers, 2000), 119.

14 Maria Elisa Christie, "Kitchenspace: Gendered Territory in Central Mexico," *Gender, Place and Culture: A Journal of Feminist Geography* 13, no. 6 (2006): 653–61.

15 *The Cooking Gene: A Journey through African American Culinary History in the Old South* (New York: Harper Collins, 2017), 13.

16 These names and that of Arlene Stevens are pseudonyms.

17 Personal communication, February 5, 2005.

18 "Lucumi and the Children of Cotton: Gender, Race, and Ethnicity in the Mapping of a Black Atlantic Politics of Religion" (PhD diss., City University of New York, 2016), 6.

19 Frances Short, *Kitchen Secrets: The Meaning of Cooking in Everyday Life* (Oxford: Berg, 2006), 69.

20 In this community, men and women initiated to male orishas generally assumed the responsibility of removing *iñalés* from four-legged animals, reflecting gendered constructions of both animals and butchering.

21 Michael D. McNally, "Honoring Elders: Practices of Sagacity and Deference in Ojibwe Christianity," in Laurie F. Maffly-Kipp, Leigh E. Schmidt, and Mark Valeri, eds., *Practicing Protestants: Histories of Christian Life in America, 1630–1965* (Baltimore: Johns Hopkins University Press, 2006), 80.

22 M. Jacqui Alexander, *Pedagogies of Crossing: Meditations on Feminism, Sexual Politics, Memory, and the Sacred* (Durham: Duke University Press, 2006), 329.

23 "Developing Diaspora Literacy and Marasa Consciousness," in Hortense Spillers, ed., *Comparative American Identities: Race, Sex, and Nationality in the Modern Text* (New York: Routledge, 1991), 40–60; Joyce E. King, "'If Justice Is Our Objective': Diaspora Literacy, Heritage Knowledge, and the Praxis of Critical Studyin' for Human Freedom," *Yearbook of the National Society for the Study of Education* 105, no. 2 (2006): 337–60.

24 Ibid., 344.

25 Personal communication, May 7, 2005.

26 The resonance of "seasoning" is discussed at length in Pérez (2016).

27 The initiation story "is rhetorical in the sense that it is an *argument* about the transformation of self that lost souls must undergo, and a *method* of bringing about change in those who listen to it" (emphasis in the original). Susan F. Harding, "Convicted by the Holy Spirit: The Rhetoric of Fundamental Baptist Conversion," *American Ethnologist* 4 (1987): 167.

28 I am indebted to Janell Hobson for insightful prompting on this point and many others throughout this chapter.

29 *Vibration Cooking: Or, the Travel Notes of a Geechee Girl* (New York: Doubleday, 1970), xxxvii.

30 See Jualynne E. Dodson and Cheryl Townsend Gilkes, "'There Is Nothing Like Church Food': Food and the US Afro-Christian Tradition: Re-membering Community and Feeding the Embodied S/spirit(s)," *Journal of the American Academy of Religion* 63, no. 3 (1995): 519–38; Jessica B. Harris, *High on the Hog: A Culinary Journey from Africa to America* (New York: Bloomsbury, 2011); and Rafia Zafar, *Recipes for Respect: African American Meals and Meaning* (Athens: University of Georgia Press, 2019).

31 Mary Ann Clark, *Where Men Are Wives and Mothers Rule: Santería Ritual Practices and Their Gender Implications* (Gainesville: University Press of Florida, 2005).

32 *Yoruba Traditions and African American Religious Nationalism* (Albuquerque: University of New Mexico Press, 2012), 315.

33 The translation is mine. Silvia Testa, *Como una memoria que dura: cabildos, sociedades y religiones afrocubanas de Sagua la Grande* (La Habana: Ediciones La Memoria, Centro Cultural Pablo de la Torriente Brau, 2004), 104.

34 Ibid., 348.

35 Sánchez, *Los Alagbas*, 94.

References

Mintz, Sidney, and Michel-Rolph Trouillot. "The Social History of Haitian Vodou." In *Sacred Arts of Haitian Vodou*, ed. Donald J. Cosentino, 123–47. Los Angeles: UCLA Fowler Museum, 1995.

Pérez, Elizabeth. 2016. *Religion in the Kitchen: Cooking, Talking, & the Making of Black Atlantic Traditions*. New York: New York University Press.

33

Black women's feminist literary renaissance of the late twentieth century

Carmen R. Gillespie

Although this chapter focuses on the African American women's literary renaissance of the 1970s and 1980s, that flourishing of Black literature requires some historical context. The date of the arrival of Black people in what is now the United States is an issue of debate and contention, which was highlighted by the 400th anniversary in 2019 of the documentation noting the arrival at the Virginia coast in 1619 of 20 Africans, who were sold into slavery and/or indenture. Scholars have noted that this date ignores other historical evidence of the arrival of Blacks in what is now America.[1] Most notably, the arrival of Africans with Spanish colonists and explorers in the 1500s is a particular area of speculation regarding accurate dates. What is indisputable, however, is that the arrival of Blacks into what would become the United States also marked the beginning of Black female creativity in the new world. Unfortunately, much of this creative production was neither documented nor recoverable in the historical record. Nonetheless, Black women, from the time of their arrival in the still-to-be-formed United States, were the source of oral narratives, communal histories, and artistic production.

Early Black women writers

As this chapter focuses on print culture, in spite of the other iterations of creative and artistic expression, it is important to begin the discussion with the first African American women to *publish* works of literature. In 1746, Lucy Terry Prince wrote the first-known poem by a Black woman in what would soon become the United States. Prince's poem "Bars Fight" is a chronicle of a raid by Abenakis upon the community in which Prince resided in Deerfield, Massachusetts. Prince's poem borrows from the traditions of oral literatures in that it is a ballad-like recitation of the events of the raid and may mark a transition between oral creation by Black women and written texts that were validated by publication. Although composed and publicized in the 1740s, Prince's poem was published in the text of a lecture in 1819.[2]

Subsequently, the controversy over recognition of the first publication is complex and no doubt, will remain so with future discoveries of previously unknown works. Most literary histories still note that Phillis Wheatley's book *Poems on Various Subjects, Religious and Moral*, published first in England in 1773, remains the first-known publication by an African American woman. Wheatley's struggle to become a published writer is emblematic of the erasure that

Black women writers/artists have undergone to be recognized as contributors to the body of American literature. As scholars such as Henry Louis Gates have noted, Wheatley's publication endeavors are not merely literary history but are metaphoric for the struggle of Black women *and* men for recognition as citizens and more fundamentally, as human beings in a country that from its founding, refused to acknowledge that reality.

When Wheatley presented her book of poetry for publication, she and her work were suspect. The community in which she lived did not believe that as a Black woman, she could have written her book; however, there was much more at stake. If Wheatley was capable of writing poetry, then her accomplishments would stand as evidence against the presumptions about Black people that provided justification for slavery and for their lack of citizenship and inclusion in the basic precepts of the new nation. From its inception, Black women's writing has been held accountable not only for its literary and aesthetic qualities but for the standing and consideration of the race as a whole.[3]

Wheatley successfully completed her trial and substantiated to 18 white Bostonian men, who were held in regard by their community, that she had in fact written her collection. Not finding a publisher willing to publish her volume, her owner helped Wheatley to have it published in England in 1773. George Washington expressed admiration for Wheatley's talents in a 1776 letter. In his praise of the young poet, Washington noted her "elegant Lines" and "her great poetical Talents."[4] Contrary to this, however, was Thomas Jefferson's assessment of Wheatley as articulated in his profoundly influential *Notes on the State of Virginia*. In the book, Jefferson notes his opinion that "Religion indeed has produced a Phyllis Wheatley; but it could not produce a poet. The compositions published under her name are below the dignity of criticism."[5] This condemnation by Jefferson held sway with a majority of Americans well into the current era and in part, accounts for the erasure and invisibility of Black women writers from the American literary canon, as well as the necessity and significance of the African American women's literary renaissance of the late twentieth century. It is also significant to note that Wheatley's work was criticized and rejected by many Black writers and critics during the 1960s and 1970s for the opposite reason – her work was frequently regarded as too apologetic regarding slavery and not critical enough of the abject oppressions that Blacks in the newly formed nation were subject to withstanding.[6]

Of course, Black women did not stop writing or creating as a consequence of this lack of recognition and acknowledgment. One of the consequences of the African American women's literary renaissance was the recovery of many Black women writers' voices and narratives that had remained obscured and excluded from the literary record. One of the tremendous consequences of the renaissance was the birth of a vibrant and expansive field of African American women's literary history and criticism.

Following Wheatley's essential publication are the nineteenth-century works of writers such as Jarena Lee, whose 1831 publication, *The Life and Religious Experience of Jarena Lee*, was the first autobiography published in the United States by an African American woman. Lee was the first woman authorized by Richard Allen, leader of the African Methodist Episcopal Church, to preach. Activist Maria Stewart was an important voice in this period, publishing two treatises in 1831 and 1832, *Religion and the Pure Principles of Morality, the Sure Foundation on Which We Must Build* and *Meditations from the Pen of Mrs. Maria Stewart*. Another significant publication during the period was one of the first African American novels published in the United States: Harriet E. Wilson's 1859 text, *Our Nig; or, Sketches from the Life of a Free Black, in a Two-Story White House, North. Showing That Slavery's Shadows Fall Even There. By "Our Nig."* Wilson's semi-autobiographical text reveals the complexities of Black female experience in the North. In 1868, Elizabeth Keckley published a memoir based on her work as a seamstress to First Lady Mary

Todd Lincoln, *Behind the Scenes; or, Thirty Years a Slave and Four Years in the White House*. One of the most popular and important slave narratives written by a woman was Harriet Jacobs's 1861 *Incidents in the Life of a Slave Girl*. Jacobs's narrative was one of the few to focus on the sexually abusive and eviscerating realities of enslavement. Other major literary figures of the nineteenth century include Francis Ellen Watkins Harper, Charlotte and Angelina Grimke, Mary Church Terrell, Ida B. Wells-Barnett, and Anna Julia Cooper.[7]

The turn of the century was a particularly difficult and dangerous time for African Americans. The early years of the twentieth century are often referred to as a nadir. Lynchings, riots, and economic and political discrimination spurred the Great Migration, the mass movement of African Americans out of the rural South to the urban North. Women writers were a potent source of expression during this time of travail and transition. During this time, the Harlem Renaissance produced several important Black women writers, including Georgia Douglass Johnson, Jessie Redmond Fauset, Zora Neale Hurston, Shirley Graham DuBois, Maria Bonner, Nella Larson, and Regina Anderson, among others. In spite of their significant and primary contributions to the Harlem Renaissance, these women were largely overlooked and neglected in the literary record and in the scholarship until the contemporary Black women's literary renaissance of the 1970s and 1980s.[8]

In the years between the end of the Harlem Renaissance and the beginning of the contemporary African American women's literary renaissance, African American literature began a slow ascendancy and recognition in the form of anthologies, critical attention, and establishment of professional organizations. Largely excluded from that project of recuperation were Black women writers. Some of the most important women writers of this period were Dorothy West, Lorraine Hansberry, Paule Marshall, and Ann Petry. An exception in terms of recognition is poet Gwendolyn Brooks, who won the Pulitzer Prize in 1950 for her collection *Annie Allen*. She became the first African American to win the prize.

The Black Arts Movement has its origins in the 1965 assassination of Malcolm X and reaction to that tragedy by writers and other artists. Most specifically, Amiri Baraka (LeRoi Jones) coined the movement and, along with other artists such as Larry Neal, Ishmael Reed, and others, defined the precepts of the movement as grounded in the production of art that was aesthetically linked to the uplift and progressive movement of Black people. The platform of the Black Arts Movement is closely aligned with the political goals of the Black Power movement. The role of women writers in the movement is complicated. In Black Arts Movement poetry, which was its predominant genre, Black women were often stereotyped on the virgin–whore spectrum. On the other hand, women writers involved in the movement were able to gain some agency by establishing publication entities that they were able to control and to make the decisions about what texts were to be published. An example of one of these presses is Naomi Madgett Long's Detroit-based Lotus Press, which is still in operation.

Despite the often overtly sexist articulations of the movement, many women writers whose works mark significant milestones in the contemporary renaissance had their literary origins in the Black Arts Movement. Women writers such as Nikki Giovanni, Maya Angelou, Sonia Sanchez, Adrienne Kennedy, Jayne Cortez, Carolyn Rogers, June Jordan, Mari Evans, and Audre Lorde became well-known and acclaimed writers during the movement. The writings of these artists were a direct contradiction to the often masculinist stances of the movement, which, like Black Power, often made an equivalency between the rehabilitation of the Black man as head of the Black family and community with the aims of equal and civil rights. Out of some Black Arts Movement rhetoric comes an awareness of the necessity for a specific articulation of the subjective realities and needs of Black women. During this time, there was a concerted effort to organize by Black women and a particular articulation of a Black feminist consciousness.

Although, as demonstrated, Black women have been creating and writing since the constitution of the nation, the particular congruencies of the late 1960s – politically, socially, and artistically – set the stage for what would come to be called the contemporary Black women's feminist literary renaissance.[9]

1970: milestone year

The year 1970 is most often noted as the beginning of the renaissance, and there is a plethora of evidence to support that the year marked a zeitgeist in African American women's history. As previously stated, one of the critical roles of the renaissance was the recovery of texts by African American women writers whose works had been forgotten and obscured in the literary record. One essential text to both writers and literary critics, who were the major figures of the renaissance, was Zora Neale Hurston's novel *Their Eyes Were Watching God*. Originally published in 1937, Hurston's novel was controversial from its introduction. Writers such as Richard Wright criticized the work as not political enough and felt that its use of Black vernacular would be indicative of a kind of racial blemish and inferiority. At the time of Hurston's death in 1960, *Their Eyes Were Watching God* was out of print. The novel was reissued in 1965, although it was again out of print by 1970. Its 1965 republication was important in that it provided access to the novel for a new generation of women, such as Alice Walker and Mary Helen Washington, for whom the novel would be a watershed. *Their Eyes Were Watching God* is the narrative of its protagonist Janie Crawford's quest for selfhood, voice, and autonomy as a Black woman inhabiting various patriarchal communities. Whether Crawford achieves that autonomy or not is a matter of critical debate, but the novel was a unique and original take on the possibilities of Black female autonomy. The role that the novel played as a source of inspiration for contemporary Black women writers cannot be overstated.

The first republication of *Their Eyes Were Watching God* in 1965 was not only a textual counterpoint to the foundational articulations of the Black Arts Movement but also coincided with the emergence of Black Studies as an institution within the academy. The emergence of Black Studies as a formal academic entity in the 1960s is usually situated in relation to three events: the rise of the Black Power movement phase of the Civil Rights movement, the assassination of Rev. Dr. Martin Luther King on April 4, 1968, and Black student activism, largely on predominately white campuses. The development of Black Studies as an academic enterprise, coupled with the demands of a new generation of students, made plain and urgent the need for African American women's literature. Alice Walker taught Hurston's *Their Eyes Were Watching God* in what has been noted as the first African American literature course in the United States in 1972. However, distressed that the novel had gone out of print in 1975, Walker was a major force in the novel's 1978 second republication and in its centrality to the renaissance.

In addition to the imperatives created by the development of Black Studies, and central to the emergence of the renaissance, is the response of Black women writers and critics to both the Civil Rights/Black Power movements and the feminist movements of the 1950s and 1960s. In the articulation of the struggle for Black equality, Black women often found themselves subordinated by questions exclusive to race that did not consider issues of gender discrimination. Likewise, Black women's specific experiences of gender discrimination were largely ignored and disregarded by white feminists. This dilemma was perfectly articulated by the title of the 1982 renaissance publication *All the Women Are White, All the Blacks Are Men, But Some of Us Are Brave: Black Women's Studies.* Important to note is the fact that Black lesbian women frequently articulated a kind of invisibility in both movements and also to cis-gender Black women.[10]

Due to the conflation of all these social and political currents, the exact date of the beginning of the renaissance may be impossible to pinpoint; however, 1970 remains a particularly salient moment for Black women's publication history and for the origins of the renaissance. As one of the primary progenitors of the contemporary African American women's renaissance in terms of her role as editor at a major publishing house, as a mentor, and, it goes without saying, as a writer, Toni Morrison articulated her perspective on some of the reasons why the subjective articulations of African American women writers were so essential in 1970, particularly as a counterpoint to the messages that were expressed by some of the artists and activists associated with the Black Arts Movement. In 2012, Morrison reflected on the necessity for her first book, *The Bluest Eye*, which was published in 1970.

> All the books that were being published by African American guys were saying "screw whitey," or some variation of that. Not the scholars but the pop books. And the other thing they said was, "You have to confront the oppressor." I understand that. But you don't have to look at the world through his eyes. I'm not a stereotype; I'm not somebody else's version of who I am. And so when people said at that time black is beautiful – yeah? Of course. Who said it wasn't? So I was trying to say, in *The Bluest Eye*, wait a minute. Guys. There was a time when black wasn't beautiful. And you hurt.[11]

As I have written elsewhere, an important contextualization of the contemporary Black women's literary renaissance can be found in American popular culture. Popular musical hits for 1970 included top 100 best-selling songs from Diana Ross, Freda Payne, Aretha Franklin, and Dionne Warwick. That same year, Cheryl Adrienne Brown won the Miss Iowa pageant and went on to become the first Black Miss America Beauty Pageant contestant. Jayne Kennedy, who would later become a well-known African American actress, won the Miss Ohio beauty pageant and became the first Black woman to compete in the Miss USA Beauty Pageant. In 1970, *Essence* magazine began publication with the slogan "for today's black woman." Actress Gail Fisher became the first Black woman to receive an Emmy Award for her portrayal of Peggy Fair, a character on the television show *Mannix*. Director Madeline Anderson's short, *I Am Somebody*, cataloged the struggles of a strike by Black women workers and was among the first documentaries created by Black women.

In spite of their visibility and presence in popular culture, the 1970s began with African American men and women facing an unemployment rate nearly double that of their white counterparts. Rates of unemployment for Black women were at 8 percent compared with nearly 5 percent for white women.[12] Stating economic inequity as one of its primary concerns, the New York Coalition, later called the National Coalition of 100 Black Women, was formed in 1970 in New York City.

In 1970, Angela Davis was fired from her position at the University of California, Los Angeles, for her involvement in the defense of the Soledad Brothers, including George Jackson. After being placed on the FBI's most-wanted list and evading her pursuers for two months, Davis was captured. She was eventually acquitted and would later write an autobiography about her experience, edited by Toni Morrison. Also in 1970, Shirley Chisholm began her second year of service as the first Black woman elected to the United States Congress. Later, Chisholm would become the first Black person to become a candidate for the United States Presidency.

In addition to this new public and political visibility and arguably, viability for Black women, writings by African American women entered a period of astounding productivity. This proliferation, termed the "Afra-American renaissance" by literary critic Joanne Braxton, ushered in early publications by the major figures in contemporary American and African American literature.[13] In addition to *The Bluest Eye*, 1970 saw the publication of a critical and ground-breaking compilation of writings by Black women: Toni Cade Bambara's *The Black Woman: An Anthology*, which included poems, short stories, and essays by a wide-range of Black women writers, among them Alice Walker, Audre Lorde, Nikki Giovanni, Paule Marshall, and Abbey Lincoln. Other works published by Black women that same year include, among others, Maya Angelou's *I Know Why the Caged Bird Sings*, Mari Evans' *I Am a Black Woman*, Nikki Giovanni's *Black Feeling, Black Talk/Black Judgement*, Lorraine Hansberry's posthumous *To Be Young, Gifted and Black: An Informal Autobiography*, Gwendolyn Brooks's *Family Pictures*, Sonia Sanchez's *We a Baddddd People*, and the first of Alice Walker's novels, *The Third Life of Grange Copeland*. Further indication of the import of the renaissance was the double reprinting of Paule Marshall's *Brown Girl, Brown Stones*, originally published in 1959.

Literary outpourings

What may have been the common denominator for these Black women writers was the recognition that their accomplishments were made possible by their literary foremothers. The texts listed earlier, largely manifesting in 1970 and the early 1970s, can loosely be defined as representing a deliberate acknowledgment of that connection with the past, and with the women who lived and wrote earlier, through an articulation of a particular and specific Black woman's experience. Although these texts are diverse and varied in their content, they share an imperative to translate into literature some of the multiple experiences and expressions of Black womanhood.

The primary publications of the renaissance that followed this early outpouring vary in genre and consist of novels, short stories, poetry, plays, autobiography, and literary criticism, including, but not limited to, Gayl Jones's *Corregidora* (1975); Ntozake Shange's *For Colored Girls Who Have Considered Suicide, When the Rainbow Is Enuf : A Choreopoem* (1975); Lucille Clifton's *Generations* (1976); Toni Morrison's *Song of Solomon* (1977), chosen as a Book-of-the-Month Club selection; Barbara Smith's *Towards a Black Feminist Criticism* (1977); Michele Wallace's *Black Macho & the Myth of the Superwoman* (1979); Octavia Butler's *Kindred* (1979); June Jordan's *Passion: New Poems* (1980); Toni Cade Bambara's *The Salt Eaters* (1980); Audre Lorde's *The Cancer Journals* (1980); bell hooks's *Ain't I a Woman?: Black Women and Feminism* (1981); Alice Walker's *The Color Purple* (1982), which won the Pulitzer Prize for Fiction and in 1985, was made into a hit film directed and produced by Steven Spielberg; and Gloria Naylor's *The Women of Brewster Place* (1982), which was made into a television mini-series in 1989, produced by and starring popular television show host Oprah Winfrey. It is worth noting that Winfrey is a key figure in the promotion and popularization of several Black women writers of the renaissance, due not least to her acting debut in the film adaptation of *The Color Purple* and her subsequent adaptation of the novel into a hit Broadway musical in the twenty-first century.

As a consequence of this literary outpouring, the fields of Black women's studies and Black feminist studies became a fixture in academic institutions and scholarship. Positions were established in colleges and universities across the country and the world in Black women's literary and feminist studies. Black feminism flourished, not only as a field of study but as an activist endeavor related to and catalyzed by the work of the renaissance. As a tangible example, the 1970s and 1980s saw the birth of the organizations the National Black Feminist Organization (1973), Black Women Organized for Action (1973), the Combahee River Collective (1974), the National Alliance of Black Feminists (1976), and the Black Women's Health Imperative, formerly the Black Women's Health Project (1983).[14]

In addition to Black feminist critics such as Barbara Christian, Barbara Smith, Hazel Carby, and many others, renaissance luminary Alice Walker contributed to the conversations and definitions of Black feminism with her 1979 articulation of the theoretical construct of *womanism* as an alternative to Black feminism in her short story "Coming Apart." The renaissance also occurred conterminously with an exponential increase in the number of Black women elected to various public offices. Although a full-throated conversation about commercial fiction by Black women is beyond the scope of this chapter, it is important to note that the renaissance helped to impact the profound success of that genre. Beginning with the unprecedented success of Terry McMillan's *Waiting to Exhale* in 1992, Black commercial fiction written by both women and men enjoyed newfound proliferation.[15]

An additional, previously mentioned activity of the renaissance was the recovery of forgotten African American women writers, resulting in the reformation of both the African American and American literary canons. Alice Walker was pivotal in the reemergence of Zora Neale Hurston as a major literary figure. Other important recovered writers were Lucy Terry, Harriet Wilson, Linda Brent/Harriet Jacobs, and Nella Larson, among many others. In addition to Mary Helen Washington, Barbara Christian, Deborah McDowell and others, Henry Louis Gates and Nellie McKay edited and published the essential collection *The Schomburg Library of 19th Century Black Women Writers.*

Of particular significance to the renaissance is the role of Toni Morrison, one of the most acclaimed figures of the period, not only in her role as writer and critic but especially in her role as editor. Just before her death in the summer of 2019, Toni Morrison's life and career were the subject of the documentary *The Pieces I Am*, directed by Timothy Greenfield Sanders. As she recounts in the documentary, she applied for a job as an editor in Syracuse, New York, after finding herself back at home, divorced, and the mother of two sons.

In the midst of a buyout by Random House of the Syracuse publishing house L. W. Singer, Morrison was transferred to the scholastic division of Random House and later worked for the company as a trade editor. In that capacity, she published one of the first critical studies of lesbianism, as well as anthologies of African and Third World literatures. She also published works by Muhammed Ali, Toni Cade Bambara, Angela Davis, Gayle Jones, Quincy Troupe, Barbara Chase Riboud, Lucille Clifton, Jane McCloskey, Huey P. Newton, Soledad Brothers, Betty Wilson, and many others. She was also responsible for the publication of the landmark *The Black Book* (1974). Morrison's influence was a major factor not only in the proliferation of the renaissance but in Black literature in general.[16]

Black women writers and their work received significant recognition by the literary establishment, which helped to fuel the renaissance. In 1989, Gwendolyn Brooks was awarded the Robert Frost Medal. The year 1993 was especially a landmark year for public acknowledgment of the achievements of Black women writers. Maya Angelou read her poem "On the Pulse of Morning" at Bill Clinton's presidential inauguration, Rita Dove was appointed Poet Laureate of the United States, and Toni Morrison won the Nobel Prize for literature, the first African American writer to do so. These illustrious triumphs were followed in 1995 by the selection of science fiction writer Octavia Butler for the prestigious MacArthur Foundation Grant.

Conclusion

It is not possible to conclude this overview of the Black women's feminist literary renaissance without some conversation about the backlash that the renaissance received. The earliest publications of the renaissance were often negatively reviewed by white critics, whose evaluations were often steeped in racism. Another form of disparagement came from some Black male critics, who often voiced the criticism that Black women writers, particularly Ntozake Shange,

Toni Morrison, and Alice Walker, articulated an unfair representation of Black men as abusive, violent, and destructive. This backlash was articulated publicly and became a source of much contention between Black men and women that manifested in many forms – the controversies over *for colored girls*, *The Color Purple* (novel and film), and Morrison's Nobel Prize are notable examples.[17]

Although the assumed 1995 end date of the renaissance used here is somewhat arbitrary, the year marks a diffusion in the renaissance and a resurgence in publications by Black men. The proliferation of African American women's writings had reached a kind of apex, or perhaps pendulum swing, that would continue into the new century. By 2018, for example, the *New York Times* featured the article "Black Male Writers for Our Time."[18] Nonetheless, the renaissance was a major factor in the development of Black women's studies and Black feminist studies and changed the face of the academy as well as the conception of what great literature looks like. It is not the least bit insignificant, and speaks to the long-term resonance of the renaissance, that as of this writing, Toni Morrison is the only African American Nobel Laureate in Literature.

Notes

1 Michael Guasco, "The Misguided Focus on 1619 as the Beginning of Slavery in the U.S. Damages Our Understanding of American History," www.smithsonianmag.com/history/misguided-focus-1619-beg inning-slavery-us-damages-our-understanding-american-history-180964873/#OO8jUKrpEo7w6 AjK.99.

2 Gretchen Holbrook Gerzina, *Mr. and Mrs. Prince: How an Extraordinary Eighteenth-Century Family Moved out of Slavery and into Legend* (New York: Harper Collins, 2008).

3 Henry Louis Gates, Jr., *The Trials of Phillis Wheatley: America's First Black Poet and Her Encounters with the Founding Father,* (New York: Basic Books, 2003).

4 "From George Washington to Phillis Wheatley, 28 February 1776," Founders Online, National Archives, accessed April 11, 2019, https://founders.archives.gov/documents/Washington/03-03 -02-0281. [Original source: The Papers of George Washington, Revolutionary War Series, vol. 3, 1 January 1776–31 March 1776, ed. Philander D. Chase (Charlottesville: University Press of Virginia, 1988), p. 387.]

5 Thomas Jefferson, *Notes on the State of Virginia* (Philadelphia: Prichard and Hall, 1787), 267.

6 For example, see Eleanor Smith, "Phillis Wheatley: a Black Perspective," *The Journal of Negro Education* 43 (1974): 405.

7 Hollis Robbins and Henry Louis Gates, eds., *The Portable Nineteenth-Century African American Women Writers* (New York: Penguin Classics, 2017).

8 Cheryl A. Wall, *Women of the Harlem Renaissance* (Bloomington: Indiana University Press, 1995).

9 John H. Bracey, Sonia Sanchez, and James Smethurst, eds., *SOS – Calling All Black People: A Black Arts Movement Reader* (Amherst: University of Massachusetts Press, 2014).

10 Gloria Hull, et al., eds., *All the Women Are White, All the Blacks Are Men, But Some of Us Are Brave: Black Women's Studies* (New York: Feminist Press, 1981).

11 Emma Brockes, "Toni Morrison: 'I Want to Feel What I Feel. Even If It's Not Happiness,'" *The Guardian*. April 13, 2012, http://guardian.co.uk.

12 Susan Carter, et al., eds., *Historical Statistics of the United States*, Millennial Edition (New York: Cambridge University Press, 2001), www.hks.harvard.edu/fs/phall/HSUS.pdf.

13 Joanne Braxton and Andree Nicola McLaughlin, eds., *Wild Women in the Whirlwind: Afra-American Culture and the Contemporary Literary Renaissance* (New Brunswick, NJ: Rutgers University Press, 1990).

14 Kimberly Springer, "The Interstitial Politics of Black Feminist Organizations," *Meridians*, 1, no. 2 (Spring, 2001): 155–91.

15 Daniel Max, "McMillan's Millions," *New York Times Magazine*. August 9, 1992.

16 *The Pieces I Am*. Dir. Timothy Greenfield-Sanders. New York: Magnolia Pictures, 2019.

17 Mel Watkins, "Sexism, Racism and Black Women Writers," *New York Times*, June 15, 1986, 58 , 92 , 93, 609.

18 Ayana Mathis, "Black Male Writers for Our Time," *New York Times*, November 30, 2018.

Select bibliography of Black feminist renaissance creative and critical texts

Andrews, William L., ed. *Sisters of the Spirit: Three Black Women's Autobiographies of the Nineteenth Century*. Bloomington: Indiana University Press, 1986.

Angelou, Maya. *I Know Why the Caged Bird Sings*. New York: Random House, 1970.

Bambara, Toni Cade, ed. *The Black Woman*. New York: New American Library, 1970.

Bambara, Toni Cade. *Gorilla My Love*. New York: Random House, 1972; London: Women's Press, 1984.

Bambara, Toni Cade. *The Salt Eaters*. New York: Random House, 1980: London: Women's Press, 1982.

Bell, Roseann Pope, Bettye J. Parker, and Beverly Sheftall, eds. *Sturdy Black Bridges: Visions of Black Women in Literature*. New York: Anchor Press, 1979.

Braxton, Joanne M. and Andrée Nicola McLaughlin. *Wild Women in the Whirlwind: Afra-American Culture and the Contemporary Literary Renaissance*. New Brunswich: Rutgers University Press, 1990.

Brooks, Gwendolyn. *Report from Part One*. Detroit: Broadside Press, 1972.

Butler, Octavia E. *Kindred*. Garden City, NY: Doubleday, 1979.

Chisholm, Shirley. *Unbought and Unbossed*. Boston: Houghton Mifflin, 1970.

Christian, Barbara. *Black Women Novelists: The Development of a Tradition, 1892–1976*. Contributions in Afro-American and African Studies, No. 52. Westport, CT: Greenwood Press, 1980.

Christian, Barbara. *Black Feminist Criticism: Perspectives on Black Women Writers*. New York: Pergamon, 1985.

Cornwell, Anita. *Black Lesbian in White America*. Tallahassee, FL: Naiad Press, 1983.

Cortez, Jane. *Coagulations: New and Selected Poems*. New York: Thunder's Mouth Press, 1984; London: Pluto, 1986.

Davis, Angela. *Angela Davis: An Autobiography*. New York: Random House, 1974.

Douglas, Christopher. *A Genealogy of Literary Multiculturalism*. Ithaca: Cornell University Press, 2009.

Dove, Rita. *Thomas and Beulah*. Pittsburgh: Carnegie-Mellon University Press, 1986.

Dunnigan, Alice. *A Black Woman's Experience from Schoolhouse to White House*. Philadelphia: Dorrance, 1974.

Evans, Mari. *Black Women Writers (1950–1980): A Critical Evaluation*. New York: Anchor Press; London: Pluto, 1984.

Exum, Pat. Contemporary. *Black Women Writers*. Deland, FL: Everett/Edwards, 1976.

Franklin, J. E. *Black Girl*. New York: Dramatist Play Service, 1971.

Giovanni, Nikki. *Black Feeling Black Talk Black Judgement*. New York: William Morrow, 1970.

Harley, Sharon, and Rosalyn Terborg-Penn, eds. *Afro-American Women: Struggles and Images*. New York: Kennikat Press, 1978.

Hooks, Bell. *Ain't I a Woman?: Black Women and Feminism*. Boston: South End, 1981; London: Pluto, 1983.

Hull, Gloria T. et al., eds. *All the Women are White All the Blacks are Men but Some of Us are Brave: Black Women's Studies*. New York: Feminist Press, 1981.

Hull, Gloria T. *Color, Sex, and Poetry: Three Women Writers of the Harlem Renaissance*. Bloomington: Indiana University Press, 1987.

Ikard, David. *Breaking the Silence: Toward a Black Male Feminist Criticism*. Baton Rouge: Louisiana State University Press, 2007.

Jackson, Jaquelyne J. *Black Women: Their Problems and Power*. New York: Barrons, 1974.

Jones, Gayl. *Corregidora*. New York: Bantam Books, 1975; London: Camden Press, 1988.

Lader, Joyce. *Tomorrow's Tomorrow: The Black Woman*. New York: Doubleday, 1971.

Leak, Jeffrey B. *Racial Myths and Masculinity in African American Literature*. Knoxville: University of Tennessee Press, 2005.

Lerner, Gerda, ed. *Black Women in White America: A Documentary History*. New York: Pantheon, 1972.

Loewenberg, B., and Ruth Bogin, eds. *Black Women in Nineteenth-Century American Life: Their Words, Their Thoughts, Their Feelings*. University Park: Pennsylvania State University Press, 1976.

Lorde, Audre. *Coal*. New York: W. W. Norton, 1978.

Lorde, Audre. *The Cancer Journals*. San Francisco, Calif.: Spinster Aunt Lute, 1980.

Marshall, Paule. *Praisesong for the Widow*. New York: Putnam; London: Virago, 1983.

Morrison, Toni. *The Bluest Eye*. New York: Holt, Rinehart & Winston, 1970.

Morrison, Toni. *Sula*. New York: Alfred A. Knopf, 1974; London: Chatto, 1980.

Morrison, Toni. *Song of Solomon*. New York: Alfred A. Knopf, 1977; London: Chatto, 1978.

Morrison, Toni. *Tar Baby*. New York: Alfred A. Knopf; London: Chatto, 1981.

Morrison, Toni. *Beloved*. New York: Alfred A. Knopf; London: Chatto, 1987.

Morrison, Toni. "Unspeakable Things Unspoken: The Afro-American Presence in American Literature." *Michigan Quarterly Review* 28, no. 1 (Winter 1989): 1–34.

Noble, Jeanne. *Beautiful Also Are the Souls of My Black Sisters: A History of the Black Women in America.* Englewood Cliffs, NJ: Prentice-Hall, 1978.

Pryse, Marjorie, and Hortense J. Spillers, eds. *Conjuring: Black Women. Fiction, and Literary Tradition.* Bloomington: Indiana University Press, 1985.

Rodgers-Rose, La Frances, ed. *The Black Women.* Beverly Hills, CA: Sage, 1980.

Shakur, Assata. *Assata: An Autobiography.* Westport, CT: Lawrence Hill, 1987.

Shange, Ntozake. *For Colored Girls Who Have Considered Suicide When the Rainbow Is Enuf.* New York: Macmillan, 1975.

Shockley, Ann Allen. *The Black and White of It.* Tallahassee, FL: Naiad Press, 1980.

Smith, Barbara. "Toward a Black Feminist Criticism." In *The Memory and Spirit of Frances, Zora, and Lorraine: Essays and Interviews on Black Women and Writing,* edited by Juliette Bowles, 32–40. Washington, DC: Howard University, 1979.

Smith, Barbara, ed. *Home Girls: A Black Feminist Anthology.* Latham, NY: Kitchen Table Press, 1983.

Sterling, Dorthy. *Black Foremothers: Three Lives.* New York: Feminist Press, 1979.

Stetson, Erlene, ed. *Black Sister: Poetry by Black American Women, 1746–1980.* Bloomington: Indiana University Press, 1981.

Tate, Claudia, ed. *Black Women Writers at Work.* New York: Continuum, 1983.

Walker, Alice, ed. *I Love Myself When I Am Laughing . . . and Then Again When I Am Looking Mean and Impressive: A Zora Neale Hurston Reader.* New York: Feminist Press, 1979.

Walker, Alice. *The Color Purple.* New York: Harcourt Brace Jovanovich, 1982; London: Women's Press, 1983.

Wall, Cheryl A. "Toni Morrison, Editor and Teacher." In *The Cambridge Companion to Toni Morrison,* edited by Justine Tally, 139–48. Cambridge: Cambridge University Press, 2007.

Wallace, Michele. *Black Macho and the Myth of the Superwoman.* New York: Dial; London: John Calder, 1979.

Walters, Tracey L. *African American Literature and the Classicist Tradition: Black Women Writers from Wheatley to Morrison.* New York: Palgrave Macmillan, 2007.

Washington, Mary Helen, ed. *Black-Eyed Susans: Classic Stories by and about Black Women.* New York: Anchor/Doubleday, 1975.

Washington, Mary Helen. *Midnight Birds: Stories of Contemporary Black Women Writers.* New York: Anchor/Doubleday, 1980.

Washington, Mary Helen. *Invented Lives: Narratives of Black Women 1860–1960.* New York: Anchor Press, 1987.

Watson, Carole M. *Prologue: The Novels of Black American Women 1891–1965.* Westport, CT: Greenwood Press, 1985.

Wheatley, Phillis. *The Collected Works of Phillis Wheatley.* New York: Oxford University Press, 1988.

Wilkerson, Margaret B., ed. *9 Plays by Black Women.* New York: Mentor, 1986.

Willis, Susan. *Specifying: Black Women Writing the American Experience.* Madison: University of Wisconsin Press, 1986.

Young, John K. *Black Writers, White Publishers: Marketplace Politics in Twentieth-Century African American Literature.* Jackson: University Press of Mississippi, 2006.

34

Black women, sexual violence, and resistance in the United States

Janell Hobson and Donna E. Young

In October 2017, in the wake of sexual assault allegations against Hollywood mogul Harvey Weinstein, the white American actor Alyssa Milano took to Twitter and encouraged women everywhere to tweet #MeToo if they had similar experiences. The hashtag quickly went viral and spawned a global movement against sexual violence. However, as is often the case on Twitter, several Black feminists reminded the public that "Me Too" had a longer history, having been founded by African American anti-rape activist Tarana Burke, who had coined "Me Too" back in 2006 – the year Twitter came into existence – after encountering a young adolescent survivor of sexual assault whom she wished she had supported by saying "me too" due to her own history as a survivor. Burke has since taken on a leadership role in the Me Too movement, not just being acknowledged by Milano herself but also appearing with other movement leaders on Time's 2017 "Silence Breakers" Person of the Year cover and being paired with Hollywood actor Michelle Williams at the 2018 Golden Globes Awards Show, where women entertainers joined activists – in response to a solidarity letter from the female farmworkers of Alianza Nacional de Campesinas – and unveiled the next phase of the movement, called *Time's Up*. This phase would advance equality for women in the workplace and create a commission on sexual harassment in the movie industry, to be headed by Anita Hill, renowned for her role in the 1991 Congressional hearings on the sexual harassment charge she made against then Supreme Court Justice nominee Clarence Thomas.

That Burke and Hill have become the visible faces of a movement against sexual violence is a reminder of Black women's experiences in the United States at the intersection of sexual violence and racism. Indeed, at the 2018 Golden Globes show, celebrated Black media mogul and entertainer Oprah Winfrey issued remarks that doubled both as an acceptance speech for her Cecil B. deMille Lifetime Achievement Award and as a rallying cry for the Me Too/ Time's Up movement. In her commentary, Winfrey honored the recent passing of Recy Taylor (1919–2017), a Black survivor of a vicious interracial gang rape during the Jim Crow era in 1944 in Abbeville, Alabama, who never received justice but whose case was investigated by civil rights pioneer Rosa Parks (1913–2005), who had served as secretary to a local National Association for the Advancement of Colored People (NAACP) chapter. As Winfrey described Taylor,

> She lived, as we all have lived, for too many years in a culture broken by brutally powerful men. For too long, women have not been heard or believed if they dared to speak their truth to the power of those men. But their time is up. *Their time is up!*[1]

Winfrey, who has spoken candidly about her own experiences of intraracial sexual assault, discursively shaped her remarks to link sexual violence with the history of white supremacy, which gestured toward the systemic prevalence of these issues rather than to the interpersonal level of women's experiences.

This is worth considering, given that two legal and political cases of sexual harassment in the Supreme Court and in Congress – *Vinson v. Meritor Savings Bank* (1986) and the Anita Hill/Clarence Thomas hearings (1991) – have become landmark events in the trajectory of the anti–sexual violence movement. Both cases involved assault on Black women by Black men, even though their experiences bear the legacies of intersectional oppressions. Indeed, Kimberlé Crenshaw, who assisted Anita Hill's legal team, coined the term "intersectionality" to illustrate Black women's complex positioning between race and gender. As she argues about Hill's experience in Congress: "Caught between the competing narratives of rape (advanced by feminists) on the one hand and lynching (advanced by Thomas and his anti-racist supporters) on the other, the race and gender dimensions of her position could not be told" (Crenshaw 1993, 1298). This chapter, therefore, explores how Black women, through their intersectional positionality, are caught in the middle between struggles against racism and sexism while simultaneously serving as the catalyst for change to systemic violence. In the pages that follow, we trace the history of Black women at the nexus between racism and sexual violence, and how they resisted these forces, and then investigate the continued legacies of both Mechelle Vinson and Anita Hill, who broke the silence on sexual harassment when they elected to bring charges against their violators in a legal and political context.

A history of racialized sexual violence

Sexual violence had already marked the "Middle Passage" experience of captive Africans journeying from the West African coast to the Americas. Women and girls were segregated aboard slave ships and placed in close proximity to the ship's crew.[2] And despite laws against rape, which were essentially laws that guarded against women as patriarchal property, the United States in its infancy institutionalized sexual violence, which in turn constituted race, as represented by a 1662 slave law in Virginia stipulating that children born of enslaved women would follow the status of their mother. The Virginia law explicitly stated that children would inherit the "condition of the mother," whether she be free or enslaved. As historian Paula J. Giddings notes, "Such legislation laid women open to the most vicious exploitation. For a master could save the cost of buying new slaves by impregnating his own slave, or for that matter having anyone impregnate her" (1984, 37).

Despite the reproductive exploitation of enslaved women being enabled by law, Black women resisted their conditions. From what Stephanie M. H. Camp calls the "everyday resistance" of enslaved women – "foot dragging, short-term flight, and feigning illness" (Camp, 2) – to outright rebellion, these women found ways to curtail the legal and societal strangleholds on their bodies and transgressed the spaces allotted to them. They ran away from enslavers. They used contraceptives and abortive medicines to control the number of children they bore. They resisted partners chosen for them while making choices based on their own desires.

With regard to outright rebellion, we have examples throughout the Americas, from Nanny (ca. 1688–1733) on the Caribbean island of Jamaica, who formed maroon communities of ex-slaves in the mountainous terrain away from the plantations owned by British colonizers (Sharpe 2003, 2), to Marie-Joseph Angélique (1710–34) who was convicted and hanged for burning down the city of Montreal in Canada in 1734.[3] Women like Nancy Prosser, with her husband Gabriel (1776–1800), led a rebellion of a thousand slaves in Richmond, Virginia in 1800 (Giddings 1984, 40), which struck fear into slaveholding communities, coupled with the successful slave insurrection on the Caribbean island of Haiti, which won its independence as the first Black republic in the world a few years later in 1804.

Afterwards, in 1807, the transatlantic slave trade was legally banned, partly due to the international abolitionist movement, and England – which did not abolish slavery in its colonies until 1834 – would boast of being a nation where the formerly enslaved could "breathe free air," thanks in part to the 1772 *Somerset v. Stewart* case, in which the presiding judge, the Lord Chief Justice William Murray, Earl of Mansfield (1705–93), ruled that an enslaved person could successfully sue for their freedom on English soil.[4] Recently, historians have reevaluated the relationship between Lord Mansfield and his biracial great-niece, Dido Elizabeth Belle (1761–1804) – the subject of a 2013 film by Amma Asante – and its possible influence on his decision in the interest of the enslaved. After all, Dido, the daughter of Maria Belle, a slave-ship captive Africans, and Sir John Lindsey (1737–88), Lord Mansfield's nephew and ship captain, could easily have been subject to slavery without such laws to protect her.[5]

The existence of Dido, however, points to a different set of relations that enslaved women carved out for themselves and their children, from Maria Belle, whose daughter – claimed by her father – was raised in the aristocracy, to Sally Hemings (1773–1835) – as Annette Gordon-Reed explores in a previous chapter in this volume – who secured freedom for the children she bore with Thomas Jefferson. The proliferation of a class of mixed-race children – derisively labeled mulattos, quadroons, and octoroons, based on the degree of blackness they possessed – who sometimes obtained free status complicates the position of enslaved women who may have negotiated such freedoms for the children they had with their enslavers. The system of concubinage – mythologized in Creole cities like New Orleans as "plaçage" – had the undesired effect of characterizing enslaved and free women of color as seductive "Jezebels," while abolitionist literature was careful to victimize such women instead, as William Wells Brown (ca. 1814–84) proffers in his 1853 novel *Clotel; or the President's Daughter*, which reimagines one of Sally Hemings's daughters ensnared into slavery, given how she "follows the condition of her mother." This creation of what Frances Smith Foster calls the "ultimate victim"[6] necessitates a more nuanced approach to enslaved women's sexual histories beyond simple victimization and toward an understanding of their agency – limited or otherwise.

Considering the dictates in the nineteenth century of the "cult of true womanhood," which bestowed protection on white womanhood sworn to purity, piety, domesticity, and submissiveness, Black women had to tread carefully in crafting a respectable womanhood for themselves. Hence, Mary Prince (1788–1833), who published the first slave narrative by a Black woman in England in 1831, avoided any explicit discussion of sexual violence or of her own consensual interracial relationship with a white man (Sharpe 2003, 121). The same year, free-born women like Maria W. Stewart (1803–79) in Boston defended Black womanhood by speaking publicly and writing on the subject of Black women's advancement, a precarious venture given her public engagement in the year of the Southampton rebellion led by Nat Turner in Virginia, which culminated in more entrenched laws guarding against slave mobility. Such restrictions eventually led to the formalization of the Underground Railroad moving freedom seekers to northern states and later, to Canada; and a formerly enslaved woman, Harriet Tubman (ca. 1822–1913), who self-emancipated in 1849, would become one of its most famous "conductors."

It is worth noting that during this period, white women who participated in the antislavery movement made parallels between racial slavery and gender oppression. Indeed, it was the sexist exclusion of their right to speak at an antislavery convention in London that led Lucretia Mott (1793–1880) and Elizabeth Cady Stanton (1815–1902) to organize the women's rights convention in Seneca Falls, New York in 1848. What often drove these women's interest in the antislavery movement was the sexual violence that enslaved women suffered. At the 1856 trial of Margaret Garner (1834–58) – immortalized in Toni Morrison's *Beloved* as the freedom-seeking enslaved woman who kills her daughter to prevent her return to slavery – antislavery activist Lucy Stone (1818–93) spoke of the "faded faces of the Negro children" with regard to the mixed-race complexions of Garner's offspring, which to her "tell too plainly to what degradation the female slaves submit. Rather than give her daughter to that life, she killed it" (cited in Taylor 2016, 152).

We never hear Margaret Garner's own words in these public hearings – which Morrison translates as "unspeakable thoughts unspoken" – just as we don't hear the voice of Celia, who was convicted and hanged for killing her enslaver the year before in the *Celia v. Missouri* case, even though she claimed self-defense due to years of sexual abuse. Sojourner Truth (1797–1883) addressed the issue of women's rights and the need for Black women's inclusion in such a movement in a speech to the women's rights convention in Akron, Ohio in 1851, but it was a white feminist, Frances Dana Gage (1808–84), who immortalized her speech as "A'r'n't I a Woman?," rhetorically alluding to the "thirteen children" she had born and seen "sold off to slavery," even though Truth did not have that number of children.[7] And while Truth did endure sexual abuse while enslaved in New York, the earlier recording of her speech does not include such colorful language. This is why Harriet Jacobs (1813–97) – writing as Linda Brent – with her 1861 *Incidents in the Life of a Slave Girl* is significant in addressing from a Black woman's perspective the sexual violence that marked the enslaved girl by the time she reached puberty.

A different generation would experience a new slave narrative as other enslaved women's voices were collected by the Workers Progress Administration (WPA) among the aging formerly enslaved population during the era of the Great Depression. For instance, there was the enslaved Sukie, who nearly killed her enslaver when he tried to rape her. Sukie's story is told by an ex-slave named Fannie Berry, collected among WPA slave narratives in 1937. As Berry described Sukie's resistance to her enslaver, "She tole him no," which led to a fight between the two parties that resulted in Sukie maiming her enslaver when she pushed him into a pot of boiling soap (cited in Perdue, Barden, & Phillips, 49). For her actions, according to Berry, Sukie was sold on the auction block and continued to resist as she vulgarly invited her potential buyers to "see if dey could fine any teef down dere," as she lifted up her dress just as they were inspecting the teeth in her mouth (Ibid.). Sukie was a bold and militant woman, and her resistance seems to have saved other enslaved women, considering that her enslaver stopped perpetrating violence against them.

Other enslaved women would seize the opportunity that emancipation delivered to avoid sexual intimacy, as in the case of emancipated Rose Williams, who decided: "After what I done for de massa ... I's never wants to truck with any man" (cited in Giddings 1984, 74). Rose, who was forced by her enslaver to have children with another slave named Rufus, practiced a form of freedom in her self-determination to remain unpartnered, which might even correlate with the "queer formations of freedom" that Vanessa M. Holden addresses in a previous chapter in this volume. These women's narratives speak bold truths about the vicious forms of racism and sexual violence, at the malevolent intersection of which lies the experience of Black women who resisted.

This legacy of violence continued to haunt Black women even after emancipation, when as Evelyn Brooks Higginbotham argues, they embraced a "politics of respectability" to guard against the most pernicious stereotypes and misogynoir, which shaped the segregationist policies that eventually developed.[8] Indeed, the lynchings spawned from the post-Reconstruction era relied on beliefs of Black hypersexuality – both of Black men and of Black women, the latter often being subjected to both intra- and interracial sexual violence. The racial politics of the sexual hysteria concerning Black men and white women led anti-lynching activist and journalist Ida B. Wells-Barnett (1862–1931) to declare that "nobody believes the threadbare lie" (cited in Giddings 1984, 29) that white supremacists were spreading about Black rapists and innocent white womanhood; she was subsequently banned from the South for exposing the intersections of racism and sexual violence, in which the Black-rapist myth provided cover for the prevalent violence against Black communities – including women and children.

Nonetheless, Ida B. Wells boldly confronted lynch law, urging African Americans to migrate from the South and withhold their economic power while also advocating for self-defense, as she carried a pistol – concealed under her petticoats – determined to "'sell my life as dearly as possible'" (cited in Giddings, 20). She eventually took her anti-lynching fight abroad on a tour of England, financed by Black club women who eventually came together in the wake of the *Plessy v. Ferguson* Supreme Court decision, which legalized segregation, to form the National Association of Colored Women at an 1896 convention in Washington, DC, attended by the likes of Wells, Harriet Tubman, and the association's first president Mary Church Terrell (1863–1954), among others. They organized in the face of intense white supremacy and recognized that they must defend themselves from continuous slander and violence against Black womanhood.

These struggles continued into the twentieth century, and the oppressive links between sexual violence and racism proliferating throughout the Jim Crow South followed African American women north during the Great Migration to urban communities. Specifically, their experience of abuse as domestics in white households set an early precedent for sexual harassment in the workplace. Subsequently, historian Darlene Clark Hine describes the "culture of dissemblance" of Black women during this era, in which they "shielded their inner lives" as survivors of rape, which contributed to a silencing on sexual subjects as well as the politics of respectability shaping the public lives of African American women.[9]

However, other historians, like Kali N. Gross and Talitha L. LeFlouria, explored lives beyond respectability, such as those of incarcerated women, who were much more vulnerable to incidents of sexual violence, in their respective works *Colored Amazons* (2006) and *Chained in Silence* (2015). Meanwhile, Danielle McGuire's *At the Dark End of the Street* re-centers Black women's resistance to sexual violence as the impetus for the civil rights movement, as represented by Rosa Parks when she investigated the brutal gang rape of Recy Taylor, as previously mentioned. Parks's anti-rape activism shaped the Montgomery bus boycotts that she and other women – specifically those in the Women's Political Council of Montgomery, Alabama – organized in 1955, when Parks refused to give up her seat on a segregated bus. Her act of resistance resonated for African American women, who were not only racially discriminated against but were also subject to interracial sexual harassment and abuse when riding public transportation.

It is no wonder, with this intergenerational history of racialized sexual violence, that Black women would be at the forefront of anti-violence movements. During the 1970s and 1980s, Black women writers, as Gillespie explored in the previous chapter, began breaking the silence and dismantling the culture of dissemblance concerning their experiences as sexual assault survivors, specifically within Black communities, which revealed a different dynamic when perpetrators are Black instead of white men. Their literary explorations had set the stage for a larger legal battle that would establish political, cultural, and social standards for how the United States would address sexual harassment, represented in the cases brought by Mechelle Vinson and Anita Hill, as explored in the following.

The legacies of Mechelle Vinson and Anita Hill

The women who organized the 1955 Montgomery bus boycotts not only created a public platform that launched Martin Luther King, Jr. (1929–68) as a civil rights leader; they also inspired behind-the-scenes leaders like Ella Baker (1903–86), who had trained activists like Rosa Parks in grassroots organizing when working in a leadership position at the NAACP. Baker went on to coordinate the Southern Christian Leadership Conference (SCLC), setting the organization's agenda while King served as its figurehead, and later organized young people for the Student Nonviolent Coordinating Committee (SCLC), which drove such actions as voter registration drives and freedom rides. These efforts, shaping the civil rights movement, helped birth the Civil Rights Act of 1964.[10]

Congress specifically enacted Title VII of the Civil Rights Act, which makes it "an unlawful employment practice for an employer … to discriminate against any individual with respect to his compensation, terms, conditions, or privileges of employment, because of such individual's race, color, religion, sex, or national origin."[11] Interestingly, the prohibition against sex discrimination was inserted into the bill at the last minute, specifically because opponents of the Civil Rights Act thought the inclusion of *sex* would derail its chances of passing into law. As a consequence, there is very little legislative history upon which courts could rely in interpreting claims of sex discrimination. Sexual harassment is not specifically mentioned in Title VII, and therefore it is a product of judicial interpretation. The courts have relied upon guidance from the Equal Employment Opportunity Commission (EEOC), which enforces federal civil rights law and provides the national framework for defining and interpreting such laws. Black women file sexual harassment charges at the EEOC at almost three times the rate of white women and are disproportionately represented among women who file such claims.[12] These figures are consistent with findings that women of color are more likely to experience sexual harassment on the job.[13]

Perhaps it should not be surprising, then, that it was the stories of two Black women that awakened the American public to the reality faced by women in the workplace. The case of Mechelle Vinson framed an interpretation of sex discrimination under the 1964 Civil Rights Act that included instances of sexual harassment, while the Anita Hill case animated the popular understanding of what constitutes sexual harassment in the workplace and how prevalent it is for many women. Though their allegations were quite different and their legal significance distinct, Mechelle Vinson and Anita Hill played pivotal roles in promoting a popular understanding of sexual harassment and in expanding the boundaries of anti-discrimination law.

Setting the stage for more than three decades of Supreme Court jurisprudence, Mechelle Vinson's lawsuit against her employer was momentous. For the first time, the Supreme Court, in a unanimous decision, held that sexual harassment was sex discrimination and as such, prohibited by Title VII. The decision continues to define the legal parameters of sexual harassment law today. The case was filed in 1978 and worked its way to the United States Supreme Court, which issued a decision in Vinson's favor in 1986. Vinson was 19 years old and recently separated from her husband when she started working as a teller-trainee at the Capital City Federal Savings Bank (later Meritor Savings Bank) in northeast Washington, DC. Over the course of the next four years, she rose to the position of assistant branch manager, until she was fired for "excessive use" of sick leave. Her supervisor was the branch manager Sidney Taylor, whom Vinson initially regarded as a father figure. During those four years, Vinson alleged she was subject to constant sexual assault and harassment by Taylor, who was also a married church deacon with seven children. The harassment began with an act of rape a few months after she joined the bank. Taylor asked her out for dinner at a restaurant attached to a motel. After dinner, Vinson recounted,

> He said, "I have been better to you, more than your husband." I said, "Well, Mr. Taylor, I appreciate that." And he says, "I don't want appreciation, I want to go to bed with you." I said, "I don't want to go to bed with you." … And he says, "Just like I hired you, I'll fire you, just like I made you, I'll break you, and if you don't do what I say then I'll have you killed." … And that's how it started.

According to Vinson,

> Taylor … made repeated demands upon her for sexual favors, usually at the branch, both during and after business hours; she estimated that over the next several years she had intercourse with him some 40 or 50 times. In addition, respondent testified that Taylor fondled her in front of other employees, followed her into the women's restroom when she went there alone, exposed himself to her, and even forcibly raped her on several occasions. These activities ceased after 1977, respondent stated, when she started going with a steady boyfriend.[14]

These allegations were disputed by Taylor, who testified at trial that he

> never fondled her, never made suggestive remarks to her, never engaged in sexual intercourse with her, and never asked her to do so. He contended instead that respondent made her accusations in response to a business-related dispute … The bank also denied respondent's allegations and asserted that any sexual harassment by Taylor was unknown to the bank and engaged in without its consent or approval.[15]

Without determining whether the allegations were true, the United States District Court for the District of Columbia denied relief, finding that Vinson was not a victim of sexual harassment or sexual discrimination and that

> [i]f [Vinson] and Taylor did engage in an intimate or sexual relationship during the time of [Vinson's] employment with [the bank], that relationship was a voluntary one having nothing to do with her continued employment at [the bank] or her advancement or promotions at that institution.[16]

Vinson appealed the decision to the Court of Appeals, which reversed the decision and remanded it to the District Court. The defendant appealed that decision, making it the first sexual harassment case to reach the Supreme Court. Until then, the lower courts were divided on the question of whether sexual harassment was a form of sex discrimination under Title VII. In a unanimous decision written by William Rehnquist, a conservative justice appointed to the court by Richard Nixon, the Supreme Court held that a claim of hostile environment and sexual harassment was a form of sex discrimination actionable under Title VII. Justice Rehnquist stated that "Without question, when a supervisor sexually harasses a subordinate because of the subordinate's sex, that supervisor 'discriminate[s]' on the basis of sex."[17] The court went further and held that the correct inquiry on issues of sexual harassment was whether sexual advances were *unwelcome*, not whether an employee's participation in them was *voluntary*. In addition, the court decided that the language of Title VII is not limited to "economic" or "tangible" discrimination. Rather, the language of Title VII "evinces a congressional intent 'to strike at the entire spectrum of disparate treatment of men and women'" in employment.[18]

The importance of the decision cannot be overstated. In deciding the case, the Court recognized and acknowledged the harm of a longstanding and common cultural practice that disproportionately affected women's experience in the workplace and deemed it unlawful. Vinson's case was the product of years of feminist advocacy and recast the law of sex discrimination to prohibit behavior previously considered "normal" in the workplace. This decision also radically altered the theory of sex discrimination and provided parameters for determining what type of workplace behavior contravenes antidiscrimination law. It took another five years, however, before sexual harassment gained national importance when Anita Hill testified before the Senate Judiciary Committee in 1991, alleging that then Supreme Court nominee Clarence Thomas had engaged in a series of sexually harassing behavior.

Interestingly, Vinson's and Hill's stories are temporally connected to Thomas's tenure at the EEOC. During the period when Vinson's case was making its way to the Supreme Court, Thomas was the chairman of the EEOC, and Hill was his assistant, so they would both have been aware of Vinson's case. At the time when he was leading the agency responsible for enforcing sexual harassment laws, Thomas was, according to Hill, engaged in exactly the kind of behavior that the EEOC had previously deemed discriminatory. In an odd twist, the Supreme Court's decision in Vinson, written by a conservative justice, went further in recognizing the harms of sexual harassment than Thomas would have as the chair of the EEOC. The 1980 guidelines drafted by the EEOC had already recognized that a particular work *environment* could form the basis of a discrimination claim. But Thomas objected to the guidelines of his own agency, which recognized hostile work environment claims (as opposed to quid pro quo claims).[19] In fact, when Vinson's case reached the Circuit Court, Thomas and a majority of the five EEOC commissioners were more sympathetic to the bank's defense than to Vinson's complaint. But because the court's opinion would have undermined its own work, the EEOC filed an amicus brief that supported the hostile environment theory but argued that Vinson's claim did not fit within it.[20] Others at the EEOC, including Anita Hill, vigorously defended the guidelines and supported Mechelle Vinson's claims.[21]

Anita Hill's testimony at the Congressional hearings did not alter the existing legal standard for sexual harassment, and yet its impact on the popular understanding of sexual harassment in the workplace was enormous. Though her allegations did not include sexual assault, they were otherwise similar to Vinson's in that she alleged an ongoing pattern of unwelcome sexually explicit harassment by her workplace supervisor. Their stories were told in very different venues – Vinson's within the judicial system and Hill's within the political realm. But because her testimony was broadcast to millions around the world, Hill's allegations had a much larger impact on making sexual harassment part of a national – even global – conversation about the treatment of women in the workplace.

Anita Hill and Clarence Thomas, both from poor rural backgrounds, both African American Yale Law School graduates, and both successful in their legal careers, met at the Department of Education in 1981 when Thomas hired Hill to be his special assistant in the department's Office of Civil Rights. Hill was later hired as Thomas's assistant again after he took a job as chairman of the EEOC. Hill would later testify that Thomas had harassed her in both positions. Hill alleged that Thomas repeatedly asked her to go out with him and would talk to her about sex and pornography.[22]

Six years later, during his confirmation hearings, liberals criticized Thomas's record as Chair of the EEOC, arguing that his approach to civil rights mirrored that of the Reagan administration, characterized by a lukewarm embrace of civil rights enforcement and opposition to affirmative action.[23] But it was Anita Hill's allegations against Thomas that garnered international attention and changed the public discussion of women's experience of sexual harassment in the workplace. What is seared in people's memory is the spectacle of a young professional Black woman testifying before an all-white, all-male judiciary committee, her outsider status on full display as she was asked a series of insensitive questions by 14 white men skeptical of her motives and wary of suggestions that what Clarence Thomas had said to her was anything more than typical workplace banter. And yet, her groundbreaking testimony struck a nerve among women whose experiences at work were reflected in Hill's allegations.

The year after Hill's testimony, complaints to the EEOC about sexual harassment increased by 50 percent and led to the "Year of the Woman," in which a record number of women ran for Congress – much like in recent years when the "women's march" in 2017, in the wake of Hillary Clinton's stunning loss of the U.S. presidential election to an outwardly sexist and racist Donald J. Trump, led to more women running for political office and breaking the silence on sexual violence in the #MeToo movement. In 2018, Anita Hill's treatment at the hands of the Senate Judiciary Committee served as a powerful memory during the confirmation hearing of the Supreme Court nominee Brett Kavanaugh, who faced sexual assault allegations by Professor Christine Blasey Ford. Like Thomas, Kavanaugh was ultimately confirmed. But because of the brave and bold actions of women like Mechelle Vinson and Anita Hill, sexual harassment is now understood as a common form of discrimination, and its prohibition is firmly established in civil rights law in the United States.

Conclusion

Sexual coercion has been an entrenched feature of Black women's experience in the United States from chattel slavery to the present day. It was slavery that first defined the legal parameters of access to the bodies of Black women and girls. White supremacy in the form of Jim Crow and northern segregation continued slavery's degradation of Black women and restructured legal impediments to full citizenship, rendering them unprotected against violence and sexual assault.[24] Today, violence against Black women by private and state actors (police, teachers, health care workers, and social workers) remains routine.

From #SayHerName – ignited by Kimberlé Crenshaw – which remembers those Black women and girls murdered and abused by police, who are often forgotten in public discourse on police brutality (including sexual assault), to #MuteRKelly, in support of the Black survivors of R&B singer Robert Kelly (recently documented in dream hampton's *Surviving R. Kelly*) and other perpetrators of intraracial sexual violence, Black women continue to sound the alarm despite their marginalization. Indeed, it was their experiences at the intersection of racism and sexism that ignited the civil rights movement and forced the issue of sex discrimination. Because of their efforts, not only do we have a legal definition of sexual harassment but Title VII in the Civil Rights Act has also extended to LGBTQ rights, as interpreted by the Supreme Court in 2020. Such occurrences have reinforced what the Combahee River Collective has stated, based on the sentiments of civil rights activist Fannie Lou Hamer (1917–77): "When black women are free, everyone else gets free."[24]

Black women as a group and as individuals continue to resist multiple forms of oppression. By bringing to light their mistreatment in the workplace, Vinson and Hill have made some of the most consequential changes to popular understandings and legal definitions of sexual harassment. Situated within a centuries-long history of sexual violence, their silence-breaking, advanced decades before #MeToo, continues to serve as a shining example of and impetus for the contemporary feminist movement.

Notes

1 Oprah Winfrey Cecil B. DeMille Award Acceptance Speech at the Golden Globe Awards (January 7, 2018). Available: www.youtube.com/watch?v=TTyiq-JpM-0&t=1s (emphasis in original).
2 To understand the gendered nature of the Middle Passage, see Sowande' M. Mustakeem, *Slavery at Sea: Terror, Sex, and Sickness in the Passage* (Chicago: University of Illinois Press, 2016), 82–3.
3 Afua Cooper, *The Hanging of Angelique: The Untold Story of Canadian Slavery and the Burning of Old Montreal* (Athens: University of Georgia Press, 2006).
4 William R. Cotter, "The Somerset Case and the Abolition of Slavery in England," *History* 79, no. 255 (1994): 31–56.
5 Kumose Inose, "What Was Remembered and What Was Forgotten in Britain in the Bicentenary of the Abolition of the Slave Trade?" In *Abolitions as a Global Experience*, 50–71, edited by Hideaki Suzuki (Singapore: NUS Press, 2016), 58.
6 Frances Smith Foster, "Ultimate Victims: Black Women in Slave Narratives," *America Culture* 1, no. 4 (1978): 845–54.
7 Nell Painter, *Sojourner Truth: A Life, A Symbol* (New York: W.W. Norton & Co., 1995).
8 Evelyn Brooks Higginbotham, "African American Women's History and the Metalanguage of Race," *Signs* 17, no. 2 (1992): 251–74.
9 Darlene Clark Hine, "Rape and the Inner Lives of Black Women in the Middle West," *Signs* 14, no. 4 (1989): 912–20.
10 Barbara Ransby, *Ella Baker and the Black Freedom Movement: A Radical Democratic Vision* (Chapel Hill: University of North Carolina Press, 2005).
11 42 U.S.C. § 2000e-2(a)(1).
12 An Analysis of Sexual Harassment Charges filed by Working Women at PAGES 5–6.
13 Recent research suggests that the difference in the rates of EEOC filings "reflects the fact that black women are perceived as having relatively little power in workplaces, and are therefore viewed as being less likely to file a complaint." https://onlinelibrary.wiley.com/doi/abs/10.1111/gwao.12394]
14 Meritor Savings Bank v. Vinson, 477 U.S. 57 (1986) at 60.
15 477 U.S. 57 (1986) at 61.
16 Vinson v Taylor 23 FEP Cases at 42.
17 477 U.S. 57 (1986) at 64.
18 Ibid.
19 Gillian Thomas, *Because of Sex: One Law, Ten Cases, and Fifty Years That Changed American Women's Lives at Work* (New York: Picador, 2017), 98.
20 Ibid.
21 Ibid.
22 For a timeline of events, see Nina Totenberg, "A Timeline of Clarence Thomas-Anita Hill Controversy as Kavanaugh to Face Accuser." www.npr.org/2018/09/23/650138049/a-timeline-of-clarence-thomas-anita-hill-controversy-as-kavanaugh-to-face-accuse
23 www.latimes.com/archives/la-xpm-1991-07-03-mn-1550-story.html
24 Combahee River Collective, "Black Feminist Statement" (1977).

Primary source

Meritor Savings Bank v. Vinson, 477 U.S. 57 (1986).

Works cited

Brown, William Wells. *Clotel; or the President's Daughter: A Narrative of Slave Life in the United States*. London: Partridge & Oakey, 1853.
Cooper, Afua. *The Hanging of Angelique: The Untold Story of Canadian Slavery and the Burning of Old Montreal*. Athens: University of Georgia Press, 2006.
Cotter, William R. "The Somerset Case and the Abolition of Slavery in England." *History* 79, no. 255 (1994): 31–56.
Crenshaw, Kimberlé. "Mapping the Margins: Intersectionality, Identity Politics, and Violence against Women of Color." *Stanford Law Review* 43, no. 6 (1993, [1991]): 1241–1299.

Foster, Frances Smith. "Ultimate Victims: Black Women in Slave Narratives." *America Culture* 1, no. 4 (1978): 845–854.

Giddings, Paula. *When and Where I Enter: The Impact of Black Women on Race and Sex in America.* New York: William Morrow & Co., 1984.

Gross, Kali. *Colored Amazons: Crime, Violence, and Black Women in the City of Brotherly Love, 1880–1910.* Durham: Duke University Press, 2006.

Higginbotham, Evelyn Brooks. "African American Women's History and the Metalanguage of Race." *Signs* 17, no. 2 (1992): 251–274.

Hine, Darlene Clark. "Rape and the Inner Lives of Black Women in the Middle West," *Signs* 14, no. 4 (1989): 912–920.

Inose, Kumose. "What Was Remembered and What Was Forgotten in Britain in the Bicentenary of the Abolition of the Slave Trade?" In *Abolitions as a Global Experience,* 50–71, ed. Hideaki Suzuki. Singapore: NUS Press, 2016, 58.

Jacobs, Harriet. *Incidents in the Life of a Slave Girl.* Cambridge: Harvard University Press, 1987, 1861.

LeFlouria, Tabitha L. *Chained in Silence: Black Women and Convict Labor in the New South.* Chapel Hill: University of North Carolina Press, 2015.

McGuire, Danielle. *At the Dark End of the Street: Black Women, Rape, and Resistance – A New History of the Civil Rights History from Rosa Parks to the Rise of Black Power.* New York: Random House, 2010.

Morrison, Toni. *Beloved.* New York: Alfred A. Knopf, 1987.

Mustakeem, Sowande' M. *Slavery at Sea: Terror, Sex, and Sickness in the Middle Passage.* Chicago: University of Illinois Press, 2016.

Painter, Nell. *Sojourner Truth: A Life, a Symbol.* New York: W.W. Norton & Co., 1995.

Perdue, Charles L., Jr., Thomas E. Barden, and Robert K. Phillips, eds. *Weevils in the Wheat: Interviews with Virginia Ex-Slaves.* Charlottesville: University Press of Virginia, 1976.

Ransby, Barbara. *Ella Baker and the Black Freedom Movement: A Radical Democratic Vision.* Chapel Hill: University of North Carolina Press, 2005.

Sharpe, Jenny. *Ghosts of Slavery: A Literary Archaeology of Black Women's Lives.* Minneapolis: University of Minnesota Press, 2003.

Taylor, Nikki M. *Driven Toward Madness: The Fugitive Slave Margaret Garner and Tragedy on the Ohio.* Athens: Ohio University Press, 2016.

Thomas, Gillian. *Because of Sex: One Law, Ten Cases, and Fifty Years That Changed American Women's Lives at Work.* New York: St. Martin's Press, 2016.

35

African women's political leadership

Global lessons for feminism

Gretchen Bauer

Since the political transitions of the late 1980s and early 1990s, women's political leadership – in particular women's presence in political office – has grown markedly across the African continent. Indeed, women activists and their organizations were among those who helped to topple single-party rule and military regimes or bring an end to decades of conflict, leading to political transitions. As recently as 2019, African countries were among world leaders in terms of women's representation in parliament, including 13 African countries among the top 50 countries that have 30 percent women or more, with the tiny East African nation of Rwanda leading the world with 68 percent women in its Chamber of Deputies. Ethiopia, Rwanda, Seychelles, and South Africa are 4 of the 12 countries worldwide that have gender parity cabinets – 50 percent women and 50 percent men as ministers.

Women's political leadership before the transitions of the 1990s

Women's political leadership in Africa is not a new phenomenon. Sheldon (2017, xiii–xv) describes the long history of women leaders and women's leadership across the continent. Many of the following examples have already been explored in previous chapters of this volume. To name a few early women leaders, there were Amina, who ruled a wide swathe of West Africa in the sixteenth century, and Nzinga, who led the resistance against the Portuguese in south-western Africa in the seventeenth century; market women who expanded trade networks and served as intermediaries between Europeans and Africans; and enslaved women who served as soldiers for the king of Dahomey in the seventeenth and eighteenth centuries (Sheldon 2017, xiii–xv). In many places, women's societies existed alongside those for men, providing political and religious leadership. As Sheldon further notes (2017, xiii–xv), the expansion of Islam and Christianity in the nineteenth century offered some leadership opportunities as well as some access to formal education for women, among many other influences on women's lives. Women's political leadership in the twentieth century is better known and better documented; across the continent, women resisted the imposition of colonial rule from the turn of the twentieth century. In the then Gold Coast, Yaa Asantewaa led the last Asante war against the British in 1900, a war known in Ghana as the Yaa Asantewaa War, and she was not the only woman at the time to exert political or religious leadership (Aidoo 1985, Boahen 2000, Brempong 2000). Sheldon (2017, xiii–xv) recounts the examples of women spiritual leaders such as Nyabingi in Uganda and Nehanda in Zimbabwe and the early twentieth-century women who protested the expansion of pass laws to women in South Africa or the imposition of taxes on women in Nigeria – what came to be known as the Women's War in Aba, Nigeria.

Women were also integral to the overthrow of colonialism across the continent, playing important leadership roles in nationalist movements and liberation struggles – from Bibi Titi Mohammed in Tanzania, to Mabel Dove Danquah and Hannah Kudjoe in Ghana, to Funmilayo Ransome Kuti in Nigeria, to the women at the base of nationalist movements who mobilized the masses, as in Guinea, to the women combatants and freedom fighters from exile seeking independence and an end to apartheid in Namibia and South Africa, to mention a very few (Allman 2009, Becker 1995, Denzer 2005, Gadzepo 2005, Geiger 1987, 1996, Hassim 2005, Johnson-Odim 2009, Sackeyfio-Lenoch 2018, Schmidt 2002).

On the whole, however, some scholars argue that – relative to men – women in Africa experienced significant losses in both power and authority under colonialism (Berger and White 1999, Parpart 1988, Staudt 1987):

> For most African women (with the exception of some urban women) the colonial period was characterized by significant losses in both power and authority ... new opportunities eventually appeared for [men], while women's economic and political rights often diminished. Colonial officials ignored potential female candidates for chiefships, scholarships and other benefits. Many female institutions were destroyed.
>
> *(Parpart 1988, 210)*

One may also argue that political independence beginning in the 1960s did not necessarily restore women's rights and institutions. Rather, in many African countries, there was a quick turn to single party or military rule (a return to the authoritarian rule of the colonial period), during which political power was highly centralized in the executive, if not an executive, and constitutions were abandoned, legislatures dissolved, judiciaries ignored, political parties proscribed, and independent organizing outlawed (Bauer 2011, 89).

Elections were seldom held, so no women or men were being elected to political office. But this is not to say that military regimes eschewed the participation of women; on the contrary, when they were not scapegoating and abusing market and other successful women, authoritarian military regimes such as those in Nigeria in the 1980s and 1990s, according to Mama (1998, 4), improvised a banal game of gender politics, which became a key mechanism through which militarism was extended, legitimized, and consolidated. Mama (1995, 41) referred to this as femocracy: an anti-democratic female power structure, which claims to exist for the advancement of ordinary women but is unable to do so because it is dominated by a small clique of women whose authority derives from being married to powerful men ... the small clique of women being primarily First Ladies.[1]

Especially in some settler colonies in southern Africa, armed liberation struggles lasted into the late twentieth century, while in other countries across the continent, enduring civil conflicts eclipsed the early gains of independence (Becker 1995, Hassim 2005, Mashanini 1991, Namhila 1997, Turshen and Twagiramariya 1998). Women were freedom fighters, combatants, victims, survivors, leaders of peace movements, negotiators of peace agreements, and participants in peace and reconstruction processes. In some cases, women in exile had opportunities for education and training that they might otherwise not have had. As later research would show (Hughes and Tripp 2015), the greatest gains in women's political representation in twenty-first-century

Africa would be attained in those countries just emerging from years of conflict. Indeed, many scholars have noted how gender relations may be altered during periods of conflict and war. Conflict and war may help to weaken patriarchal structures and shift gender roles, while post-conflict transitional governments draft new constitutions and establish new laws and institutions, often with input from mobilized national women's movements (Adams 2008, 479, Bauer and Britton 2006, Pankhurst 2002, 127). For Liberia, Fuest (2008, 202) suggested that female gains, not only female losses, could follow from the devastating conflict in that country – though only with the leadership of women's organizations or mobilized women's movements.

Women's political leadership since the transitions of the 1990s

Beginning in the late 1980s and continuing into the 1990s, regime change swept across Africa as people took to the streets to protest years of economic decline, political corruption, and state decay. Women played an important role in the unfolding political transitions, as Tripp pointed out (2001, 142–4): "Like student organizations, labor unions and human rights activists, women's organizations openly opposed corrupt and repressive regimes through public demonstrations and other military actions." Moreover, once change was underway, women and their organiza-tions took advantage of the initial political openings to push for even greater gains. Women consolidated independent women's organizations, demanded women's expanded participation in politics, including through affirmative action policies, and even formed their own political parties in countries as diverse as Zambia, Zimbabwe, Lesotho, and Kenya (Tripp 2001). Women like 2004 Nobel Peace Prize winner Wangari Maathai (2006) initially led civil society or com-munity-based organizations like the Greenbelt Movement, which planted trees across a defor-ested Kenya, and then added mounting political demands, in her case eventually becoming a member of parliament, but not before being beaten and imprisoned by a resistant untransformed state. In a number of countries, once old regimes had been toppled and political transitions were underway, women (thanks to mobilized national women's movements) gained seats at the table and participated in the drafting of new constitutions and electoral laws resulting, in several cases, in the adoption of electoral gender quotas for parliaments and/or affirmative action policies more widely for governments – a trend that has hardly abated well into the twenty-first century as a second wave of quota adoption washes over the continent (Bauer and Britton 2006, Bauer 2016). A brief focus on three African countries reveals some early accomplishments and remain-ing challenges to women's political leadership across the continent in the 2020s and beyond.

Liberia: women's peace movement and first elected woman president

Liberia illustrates the ways in which African women have contributed to ending conflict and securing peace and also to gaining access to political office. In 2011, then president of Liberia, Ellen Johnson Sirleaf, and leader of the Women of Liberia Mass Action for Peace women's non-violent peace movement, Leymah Gbowee, shared the Nobel Peace Prize (along with Yemeni human rights activist Tawakul Karman) for their "non-violent struggle for the safety of women and for women's rights to full participation in peace-building work." More specifically, the prize recognized the contributions that Liberian women had made to ending two decades of intermittent civil conflict and gruesome war (culminating in the second Liberian civil war) and helping to elect Africa's first democratically elected woman president. Women's organizations in Liberia had come together and "raised awareness about the conflict and its effect on civilians, pressured ruling factions to participate in peace talks, advocated for the inclusion of women in peace negotiations and provided support to those displaced by the conflict" (Adams 2008, 481,

Gbowee 2011). Once the war was over and an election was underway, they provided support to the woman candidate, Ellen Johnson Sirleaf, a Harvard-trained economist, among many other accomplishments, who would go on to win the presidency in the second round of voting.

In more than a century of settler or "Americo-Liberian" rule in Liberia, highly educated elite women had occupied leadership roles – in politics, including as cabinet ministers, in academia as university lecturers and even presidents, and in the professions, among others. By contrast, Liberia's early twenty-first-century women's movements were more grassroots in nature and importantly, relied upon Muslim and Christian women joining forces. In her inaugural address as president of Liberia in 2006, Ellen Johnson Sirleaf acknowledged the women of Liberia and their organizations that had mobilized to end the war and had propelled her into power. In her memoir, Johnson Sirleaf (2009, 264) recalled the women of Liberia as her "secret weapon" in the 2005 election.

Unlike in many other post-conflict African countries, however, women in Liberia were not able to secure an electoral gender quota for the national legislature; instead, political parties made vague promises about more women candidates. But using her power as the executive, President Johnson Sirleaf appointed many women to her first cabinet a decade before gender parity cabinets became more common in Africa and the world. She also appointed women as county superintendents, sought to recruit more women into the military and the police, and promoted national programs that supported school girls, market women, and women farmers. An early symbolic act was to change the inscription on the Supreme Court building from "Let Justice Be Done to All Men" to "Let Justice Be Done to All" (Bauer 2011, 100–1). President Johnson Sirleaf served two six-year terms as Liberia's leader, acting on behalf of women in many ways; it is not yet clear how enduring her legacy of gains for women and girls will be.

Rwanda: women's feminist leadership in an authoritarian polity

Across the continent from Liberia, women and their organizations also contributed to securing a post-conflict peace and reconstruction from the mid-1990s onward in Rwanda. Since 2003, Rwanda, site of a horrific genocide in the early 1990s, has led the world in women's representation in a single or lower house of parliament, and since 2008, Rwanda has had more women than men in its Chamber of Deputies. Currently, Rwanda is one of four African countries with a gender parity cabinet. Historically, women had not held significant positions in government in Rwanda; but already in the post-genocide transitional government (1994 to 2003), 10 women were appointed to cabinet posts, and the first post-genocide election in 2003 brought 49 percent women to the Chamber of Deputies (Bauer 2011, 93–4).

Women's organizations had existed in the pre-genocide period in Rwanda and had formed, in part, in order to participate in the political reform process of the early 1990s. Their organization led to women's increased political participation in the post-genocide period (Longman 2006, Issifu 2015). In addition, Rwanda's 2003 constitution created government-wide gender quotas reaching all branches of government (sometimes two quotas, as in the case of parliament) as well as all levels of government (from the cell to the national level). Devlin and Elgie (2008, 251) attributed striking changes in parliamentary culture (in the social climate – greater confidence and greater solidarity among women MPs and a better working relationship between women and men MPs), as well as more prominent cabinet appointments for women, to women's increased presence in parliament. In addition, women MPs suggested to Devlin and Elgie that a gender agenda was "guaranteed" by the presence of more women in government. Furthermore, some Rwandan women MPs expressed a commitment to an international feminism and to seeing their accomplishments replicated in other countries – a potential South–North diffusion of ideas. These accomplishments are a result of constitutional requirements and the agency of political leaders (Devlin and Elgie 2008, 251).

Rwanda's government is becoming increasingly authoritarian – presidential term limits have been abandoned, and no political opposition is tolerated. Many observers insist that the gender parity in government serves as window dressing to the international community and/or as a way of deflecting closer examination and criticism of the never-ending Kagame regime and its dictates. In an optimistic reading, Burnet (2008, 361) suggested some years ago that in the longer term, women's increased presence in government could help to undo authoritarian trends and that even gender initiatives handed down from above and implemented by authoritarian regimes could lead to transformation. She further opined that women's increased representation in even an authoritarian government could lead to their more meaningful participation in a genuine democracy – one day – as a result of such transformations.

Across Africa, those countries with the greatest presence of women in parliament have adopted one or another type of electoral gender quota for parliament and have likely set and met targets for other branches of government as well, as has Rwanda. In the second wave of quota adoption in Africa, countries are implementing stronger legislated (as opposed to voluntary) quotas that may require gender parity (rather than a mere 20 or 30 percent of seats or positions), as Tunisia, Senegal, and Zimbabwe have done in recent years. Those countries with the lowest representations of women in Africa, like Ghana and Nigeria, have no electoral gender quota and use the difficult single member district (SMD) electoral system for elections to parliament, among other challenges.

Ghana: women's ongoing struggles for political office

Ghana is often heralded as one of the most successful emerging democracies on the African continent, with an economy that has been growing steadily since its transition from decades of military rule to multiparty politics in the early 1990s. In Ghana, women made up nearly half of business owners in 2018, according to the Mastercard Foundation;[2] indeed, powerful and wealthy market women from Makola Market in Accra and Central Market in Kumasi, among others, have been objects of scrutiny and abuse as far back as the colonial period, when European administrators sought to undermine the prominent position of women traders (Asare 2018). They helped to fund the Convention People's Party and the struggle for independence and then were violently scapegoated and had their markets burned under the military rule of Flight Lt Jerry Rawlings in the 1980s. And yet despite this economic and political might, women in Ghana lag far behind their peers in many countries across the continent in their representation in government. The Ghana case illustrates some of the remaining challenges for women's political leadership in Africa.

First and foremost, Ghana is like many of the countries in Africa that have fewer women in parliament in that it uses the "woman-unfriendly" SMD electoral system and no electoral gender quota.[3] In a system in which candidates stand in individual constituencies, women candidates are disadvantaged, discouraged, and disincentivized by the exorbitant cost of politics, a debilitating politics of insult, and a national legislature that is the weakest branch of government (Bauer and Darkwah 2019). In general elections, women win in proportion to their candidacies, but there is little evidence that political parties have made recruiting more women candidates a priority. Yet, Ghana's 13 percent women in parliament is still higher than in neighboring Nigeria, the country that ranks lowest in Africa with only 6 percent women in its parliament. Nigeria's post-independence trajectory was similar to Ghana's, with alternating periods of military and civil rule, though Nigeria's military rule extended into the late 1990s, resulting in a delayed political transition.

Civil society activist and author Ayisha Osori (2017) was a candidate in the 2015 party primaries in Nigeria, deciding to stand, among other reasons, because she wanted to see more people who looked like her in government.[4] She has documented well the challenges facing women aspirants for parliament in the country that ranks lowest in Africa – despite its status as the continent's most populous nation and largest economy. She describes the costs of running (the impossibility of running without lots of money), the power and lack of accountability of party leaders and office holders, the need to win the endorsement of First Ladies, the incessant middle of the night meetings and other opportunities to criticize women candidates' morals, the need for constitutional and electoral system changes, the lack of good governance, and more. In Nigeria too, a failure to recognize that the playing field is not level keeps women candidates low in numbers and on the fringes.

In both countries, there might be a higher percentage of women in the executive branch – as cabinet ministers. Indeed, cabinet ministers are appointed rather than elected, and so individual presidents may easily appoint more women to cabinet; they may even construct "gender parity" cabinets! The argument that there are not enough "qualified" women for political office has been thoroughly discredited in Africa, as in the rest of the world. Across the continent, there are "binders full" of potential outstanding women candidates or political appointees, as in the rest of the world. For example, Adams et al. (2016, 158) report that following the 2012 election in Ghana, one non-governmental organization, WILDAF, presented a petition to the newly elected president that included the names of 65 women who could be considered for government posts and called on the parliament appointment committee to reject any list of appointments that did not include 40 percent women – though that did not transpire.

Impacts of women's political leadership: substantive and symbolic representation

In seeking to assess the impact of women's political leadership around the world, scholars have deployed two concepts: the substantive representation of women's interests and the symbolic representation of women's interests. Substantive representation refers to advancing women's interests through the policy making process, whether publicly or behind the scenes; this may be measured, for example, in terms of promoting or accomplishing certain policy agendas or legislative items. Of course, passing laws is only the first step in a long process of implementation and enforcement. Symbolic representation refers to altering gendered ideas about the roles of women and men in politics, raising awareness of what women can achieve, legitimating women as political actors, and encouraging women to become more involved in politics themselves as voters, activists, candidates, and leaders (Franceschet et al. 2012, 15–18). In many ways, symbolic representation effects may be the most transformative, taking place as they do outside national legislatures, and yet in educating people about women's leadership capabilities, they may also help to bring more women into parliaments. Moreover, it is through symbolic representation effects that cultural changes are most likely to occur.

A review of the scholarship on the substantive representation impacts of more women in parliament suggests that many such impacts may be identified (Bauer 2019). For example, Medie (2013) has described how the women's movement in Liberia has been successful in training the police to enforce the new rape law, resulting in a lower rate of withdrawal of cases. She argues that women's groups have been bolstered in doing this by a favorable political context. Across the continent, scholars have shown that in those countries with more women in parliament for longer periods of time – like Rwanda, South Africa, Tanzania, and Uganda – new laws have been passed in the areas of gender-based violence, family law, and land rights that address women's interests (Bauer 2019).

Examples of symbolic representation effects of more women in parliament exist as well. So, for example, Bauer (2016) found in Botswana that early role models – women ministers and women members of parliament – inspired other women in Botswana to believe that they too, like men, could be chiefs – positions that had traditionally never been available to women (except as regents). Burnet (2011, 320–1) found in Rwanda that with the dramatic increases in women's presence in government, women had "won respect" in their families and communities. Burnet (2011, 317–19) observes that quotas had a widespread impact in changing ordinary Rwandans' perceptions of women as political leaders, increasing the political and social agency of women (for example, women speaking out more at meetings), and leading to increased autonomy for women as "economic subjects" and vis-a-vis domestic resources.

Conclusion: African women leading the way

In twenty-first-century Africa, it appears that centuries-old traditions of women's leadership, women's large and varied contributions to independence and liberation, women's participation and leadership at United Nations conferences and other international venues, and women's roles in securing peace and designing post-conflict dispensations, including new constitutions and electoral laws, have paved the way for a new women's political leadership across the continent. In countries as varied as Senegal, Tunisia, and Zimbabwe, gender parity laws for parliament have been adopted, and in Ethiopia, Rwanda, Seychelles, and South Africa, leaders have exercised their agency to appoint gender parity cabinets.

Of course, there are other sides to herstory in Africa. Overall, women and girls still lag behind men and boys in most socioeconomic indicators. Women and girls in rural areas remain particularly disadvantaged. Violence, including sexual abuse, against women and girls, not just in elections but in everyday life and especially in conflict, remains an ongoing physical threat. Patriarchy endures across Africa, as it does across the world, with a new externally generated but internally embraced (Christian and Muslim) religious fundamentalism bringing a suffocating conservatism.

African women's political leadership in the twenty-first century may not always be labeled as feminist, but often it is. Loose coalitions of younger women, especially vocal on social media, like Pepperdem Ministries in Ghana or Feminist Collective in Kenya, or longer-standing publications like *Feminist Africa* in South Africa or the Africa-wide, 30-year-old advocacy organization Femnet, are pushing generations of women and men to embrace the feminist goal of gender equality. They seek to provide platforms for the feminist agenda, to support women's aspirations in politics and decision making, and to work toward ending practices such as child, early, and forced marriage, female genital cutting, persecuting "witches," and more (Prah 2007). Going forward, Africa's women political leaders will be more numerous and effective when working in concert with women activists and their organizations, across political divides, and in more conducive political contexts.

Notes

1 Jibrin (2004) describes this as the First Lady Syndrome as applied to Ghana and Nigeria in particular.
2 https://newsroom.mastercard.com/mea/press-releases/africa-a-world-leader-in-women-business-owners-mastercard-index-of-women-entrepreneurs/
3 The proportional representation (PR) electoral system is considered much more "woman-friendly" – voters vote for the party rather than individual candidates – and it is also more amenable to adding an electoral gender quota – simply add and distribute women candidates on party lists.
4 See also Tamale (1999) for similar stories of standing for parliament in Uganda.

References

Adams, Melinda. "Liberia's Election of Ellen Johnson Sirleaf and Women's Executive Leadership in Africa." *Politics & Gender* 4, no. 3 (2008): xx–xx.

Adams, Melinda, John Scherpereel and Suraj Jacob. "The Representation of Women in African Legislatures and Cabinets: An Examination with Reference to Ghana." *Journal of Women, Politics and Policy* 37 (2016): 145–167.

Aidoo, Agnes A. "Women in the History and Culture of Ghana." *Research Review* 1, no. 1 (1985): 14–51.

Allman, Jean. "The Disappearing of Hannah Kudjoe: Nationalism, Feminism and the Tyrannies of History." *Journal of Women's History* 21 (2009): 13–35.

Asare, Abena Ampofoa. *Truth Without Reconciliation: A Human Rights History of Ghana*. Philadelphia: University of Pennsylvania Press, 2018.

Bauer, Gretchen. "Women in Executives: Sub-Saharan Africa." In *Women in Executive Power: a Global Overview*, edited by Gretchen Bauer and Manon Tremblay, 85–104. New York: Routledge, 2011.

Bauer, Gretchen. "'What is Wrong with a Woman Being Chief?' Women Chiefs and Symbolic and Substantive Representation in Botswana." *Journal of Asian and African Studies* 51, no. 2 (2016): 222–237.

Bauer, Gretchen. "Women in African Parliaments: Progress and Prospects." In *The Palgrave Handbook of Africa Women's Studies*, edited by Olajumoke Yacob-Haliso and Toyin Falola. New York: Palgrave, 2019.

Bauer, Gretchen and Hannah Britton, eds. *Women in African Parliaments*. Boulder: Lynne Rienner Publishers, 2006.

Bauer, Gretchen and Akosua Darkwah. "'Some Money Has to be Going': Discounted Filing Fees to Bring More Women into Parliament in Ghana." In *Gendered Electoral Financing: Money, Power and Representation in Comparative Perspective*, edited by Ragnhild Muriaas, Vibeke Wang and Rainbow Murray, 133–135. New York: Routledge, 2019.

Becker, Heike. *Namibian Women's Movement 1980 to 1992: From Anti-colonial Resistance to Reconstruction*. Bonn: IKO, 1995.

Berger, Iris, Frances White and Cathy Skidmore-Hess, eds. *Women in Sub-Saharan Africa: Restoring Women to History*. Bloomington: University of Indiana Press, 1999.

Boahen, A. Adu. "Yaa Asantewaa in the Yaa Asantewaa War of 1900: Military Leader or Symbolic Head?" *Ghana Studies* 3 (2000): 111–135.

Brempong, Arhin. 2000. "The Role of Nana Yaa Asantewaa in the 1900 Asante War of Resistance." *Ghana Studies* 3 (2000): 97–110.

Burnet, Jennie. "Gender Balance and the Meanings of Women in Government in Post-genocide Rwanda." *African Affairs* 107, no. 428 (2008): 361–368.

Burnet, Jennie. "'Women Have Found Respect': Gender Quotas, Symbolic Representation and Female Empowerment in Rwanda." *Politics & Gender* 7, no. 3 (2011): 303–334.

Denzer, LaRay. "Gender and Decolonization: A Study of Three Women in West African Public Life." In *Readings in Gender in Africa*, edited by Andrea Cornwall, 217–224. London: James Currey, 2005.

Devlin, Claire and Robert Elgie. "The Effect of Increased Women's Representation in Parliament: The Case of Rwanda." *Parliamentary Affairs* 61, no. 2 (2008): 237–254.

Franceschet, Susan, Mona Lena Krook and Jennifer Piscopo. "Conceptualizing the Impact of Quotas." In *The Impact of Gender Quotas*, edited by Susan Franceschet, Mona Lena Krook and Jennifer Piscopo, 3–26. New York: Oxford University Press, 2012.

Fuest, Veronica. "'This is the Time to Get in Front': Changing Roles and Opportunities for Women in Liberia." *African Affairs* 107, no. 427 (2008): 201–224.

Gadzekpo, Audrey. "The Hidden History of Women in Ghanaian Print Culture." In *African Gender Studies: A Reader*, edited by Oyeronke Oyewumi, 279–297. Basingstoke: Palgrave Macmillan, 2005.

Gbowee, Leymah. *Mighty Be Our Powers: How Sisterhood, Prayer and Sex Changed a Nation at War*. New York: Basic Books, 2011.

Geiger, Susan. "Women in Nationalist Struggle: TANU Activists in Dar es Salaam." *The International Journal of African Historical Studies* 20, no.1 (1987): 1–26.

Geiger, Susan. "Tanganyikan Nationalism as 'Women's Work': Life Histories, Collective Biography and Changing Historiography." *Journal of African History* 37 (1996): 465–478.

Hassim, Shireen. *Women's Organizations and Democracy in South Africa: Contesting Authority*. Madison: University of Wisconsin Press, 2005.

Hughes, Melanie and Aili Mari Tripp. "Civil War and Trajectories of Change in Women's Political Representation in Africa, 1985–2010." *Social Forces* 93, no. 4 (2015): 1513–1540.

Issifu, Abdul Karim. "The Role of African Women in Post-Conflict Peace Building: The Case of Rwanda." *Journal of Pan African Studies* 8, no. 9 (2015): 63–78.

Jibrin, Ibrahim. "The First Lady Syndrome and the Marginalisation of Women from Power: Opportunities or Compromises for Gender Equality?" *Feminist Africa* 3 (2004).

Johnson-Odim, Cheryl. "'For Their Freedoms': The Anti-Imperialist and International Feminist Activity of Funmilayo Ransome-Kuti in Nigeria." *Women Studies International Forum* 32, no. 1 (2009): 51–59.

Johnson Sirleaf, Ellen. *This Child Will be Great: Memoir of a Remarkable Life by Africa's First Woman President.* New York: HarperCollins, 2009.

Longman, Timothy. "Rwanda: Achieving Equality or Serving an Authoritarian State." In *Women in African Parliaments*, edited by Gretchen Bauer and Hannah Britton. Boulder: Lynne Rienner Publishers, 2006.

Maathai, Wangari. *Unbowed: A Memoir.* New York: Anchor Books, 2006.

Mama, Amina. "Feminism or Femocracy? State Feminism and Democratisation in Nigeria." *Africa Development* 20 (1995): 37–58.

Mama, Amina. "Khaki in the Family: Gender Discourses and Militarism in Nigeria." *African Studies Review* 41 (1998): 1–18.

Mashinini, Emma. *Strikes Have Followed Me All My Life: A South African Autobiography.* New York: Routledge, 1991.

Medie, Peace. Fighting Gender Based Violence: The Women's Movement and the Enforcement of Rape Law in Liberia. *African Affairs* 112, no. 448 (2013): 377–397.

Namhila, Ellen Ndeshi. *The Price of Freedom.* Windhoek: New Namibia Books, 1997.

Osori, Ayisha. *Love Does Not Win Elections.* Lagos: Narrative Landscape Press, 2017.

Pankhurst, Donna. "Women and Politics in Africa: The Case of Uganda." *Parliamentary Affairs* 55, no. 1 (2002): 119–128.

Parpart, Jane. "Women and the State in Africa." In *The Precarious Balance: State and Society in Africa*, edited by Donald Rothchild and Naomi Chazan. Boulder: Westview Press, 1988.

Prah, Mansah. *Ghana's Feminist Movement: Aspirations, Challenges, Achievements.* Accra: IDEG, 2007.

Sackeyfio-Lenoch, Naaborko. "Women's International Alliances in an Emergent Ghana." *Journal of West African History* 4, no. 1 (2018): 27–56.

Schmidt, Elizabeth. "'Emancipate Your Husbands': Women and Nationalism in Guinea, 1953-1958." In *Women in African Colonial Histories: An Introduction*, edited by Susan Geiger, Nakanyike Musisi and Jean Allman. Bloomington: Indiana University Press, 2002.

Sheldon, Kathleen. *African Women: Early History to the 21ˢᵗ Century.* Bloomington: Indiana University Press, 2017.

Staudt, Kathleen. "Women's Politics, the State and Capitalist Transformation in Africa." In *Studies in Class and Power in Africa*, edited by Irving Markovitz, 193–208. New York: Oxford University Press, 1987.

Tamale, Sylvia. *When Hens Begin to Crow: Gender and Parliamentary Politics in Uganda.* Boulder: Westview Press, 1999.

Tripp, Aili Mari. "The New Political Activism in Africa." *Journal of Democracy* 2 (2001): 144–155.

Turshen, Meredith and Clotilde Twagiramariya, eds. *What Women Do in Wartime: Gender and Conflict in Africa.* Trenton: Zed Books, 1998.

Taylor & Francis eBooks

www.taylorfrancis.com

A single destination for eBooks from Taylor & Francis
with increased functionality and an improved user
experience to meet the needs of our customers.

90,000+ eBooks of award-winning academic content in
Humanities, Social Science, Science, Technology, Engineering,
and Medical written by a global network of editors and authors.

TAYLOR & FRANCIS EBOOKS OFFERS:

A streamlined
experience for
our library
customers

A single point
of discovery
for all of our
eBook content

Improved
search and
discovery of
content at both
book and
chapter level

REQUEST A FREE TRIAL
support@taylorfrancis.com

For Product Safety Concerns and Information please contact our EU
representative GPSR@taylorandfrancis.com
Taylor & Francis Verlag GmbH, Kaufingerstraße 24, 80331 München, Germany